Kazakhstan

WITHDRAWN

the Bradt Travel Guide

Paul Brummell

Updated by
Sophie Ibbotson and Max Lovell-Hoare

edition
2

www.bradtguides.com

Bradt Travel Guides Ltd, UK
The Globe Pequot Press Inc, USA

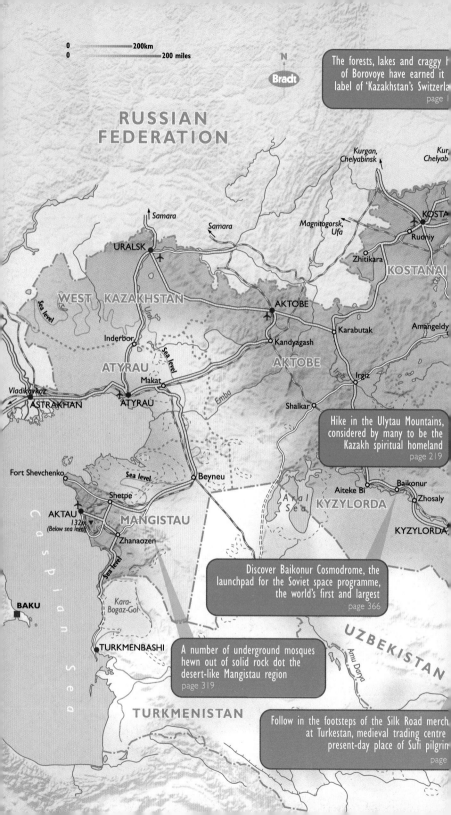

0 200km
0 200 miles

Bradt

N

The forests, lakes and craggy h
of Borovoye have earned it
label of 'Kazakhstan's Switzerla
page 1

RUSSIAN
FEDERATION

Kurgan,
Chelyabinsk

Kur
Chelyab

↑ Samara

Samara

Magnitogorsk,
Ufa

KOSTA

Rudniy

URALSK

Zhitikara

KOSTANAI

Sea level

WEST KAZAKHSTAN

AKTOBE

Karabutak

Amangeldy

Inderbor

Kandyagash

AKTOBE

Sea level

ATYRAU

Makat

Irgiz

Vladikavkaz

Emba

ASTRAKHAN

ATYRAU

Shalkar

Hike in the Ulytau Mountains,
considered by many to be the
Kazakh spiritual homeland
page 219

Fort Shevchenko

Sea level

Beyneu

Aral
Sea

Aiteke Bi

Baikonur

KYZYLORDA

Zhosaly

Shetpe

AKTAU
132m ▼
(Below sea level)

MANGISTAU

Zhanaozen

KYZYLORDA

Caspian Sea

Discover Baikonur Cosmodrome, the
launchpad for the Soviet space programme,
the world's first and largest
page 366

BAKU

Kara-
Bogaz-Gol

UZBEKISTAN

TURKMENBASHI

A number of underground mosques
hewn out of solid rock dot the
desert-like Mangistau region
page 319

Amu Darya

TURKMENISTAN

Follow in the footsteps of the Silk Road merch
at Turkestan, medieval trading centre
present-day place of Sufi pilgrin
page

RUSSIAN FEDERATION

The Kazakh capital Astana is the ultimate boomtown, its modern architecture mushrooming up from the surrounding steppe
page 73

Straddling Kazakhstan, Russia, Mongolia and China, the Altai Mountains are thought by some to be the legendary Buddhist kingdom of Shambala
page 234

Despite its infamy as the site of Soviet nuclear tests, Semey is home to fine Tsarist architecture, and has connections with Dostoevsky
page 239

Marvel at the exquisite terracotta tiling in the Mausoleum of Aisha Bibi
page 196

Spot herds of gazelles in Altyn Emel National Park
page 176

Dare yourself to take on some challenging white-water rafting in the 80km-long Charyn Canyon
page 170

Explore the Aksu Zhabagly National Nature Reserve, home to the white-clawed Tian Shan bear, the Siberian ibex and an astounding number of tulips
page 393

Soak up the atmosphere in Almaty, Kazakhstan's most cosmopolitan city
page 117

Novosibirsk

PETROPAVL   OMSK

Barnaul, Novosibirsk

RTH KAZAKHSTAN

KSHETAU
Schuchinsk

Makinsk

PAVLODAR

Barnaul, Novosibirsk

AKMOLA

Ekibastuz

PAVLODAR

ASTANA

Semey

UST KAMENOGORSK

Temirtau   KARAGANDA

Georgievka

Karkaraly

Kokpekti

KARAGANDA

EAST KAZAKHSTAN

Zaisan

Kyzylzhar

Ayagoz

Taskesken

Tacheng

Zhezkazgan

Moiynty   Balkhash

Usharal

Lake Balkhash

Dzhungar Gate

Saryshagan

Urumqi

Shyganak

TALDYKORGAN

ALMATY

Aisha Bibi

Saryozek

Zharkent

SOUTH KAZAKH-STAN

ZHAMBYL

Chu

Kapchagai

Turkestan

Chu

ALMATY   Kegen

TARAZ   Kulan

Khan Tengri
6995m

BISHKEK

HYMKENT

Tashkent, Samarkand

SHKENT

K Y R G Y Z S T A N

CHINA

arkand

Kazakhstan
Don't
miss...

Astana
The audacious new capital
arising from the steppe
(MEP) page 73

Almaty
Kazakhstan's most cosmopolitan
city, at the foot of the Tian Shan
Mountains (BM/A) page 117

Baikonur Cosmodrome

The launch pad of the Soviet space programme, from where Yuri Gagarin set out on his historic journey in 1961
(PB) page 365

Turkestan

The Timurid Mausoleum of Khodja Ahmed Yassaui is Kazakhstan's most important pilgrimage site
(MEP) page 378

Altai Mountains

The home, some speculate, of the legendary Buddhist kingdom of Shambala
(PF/A) page 234

left & below left The centre of Astana is replete with imposing architecture, including the blue-domed President's Cultural Centre (MN/DT) and Khan Shatyr, the world's largest tent and the most recent addition to Astana's skyline (EL) pages 89 and 97

below The pyramid-shaped Palace of Peace and Harmony, with 'The Cradle' at its apex, decorated with stained glass images of doves representing the peaceful coexistence of Kazakhstan's 130 nationalities (EL) page 100

bottom Outside Astana's main court, the Monument to Justice depicts three wise judges, each representing a different *zhuz* (territory-based tribe) (AD/A) page 93

КАЗЫБЕК БИ   ТӨЛЕ БИ   ӘЙТЕКЕ БИ

above Almaty's remarkable Cathedral of the Holy Ascension is one of the world's tallest wooden buildings, the legacy of a time wen the main building material in this earthquake-wary city was wood (PB) page 147

below Chess players congregate in Panfilov Park, Almaty, for a timed speed version of the game (SS) page 146

above Tamgaly is home to more than 4,000 petroglyphs, most dating back to the Bronze Age (SS) page 164

below The ubiquitous yurt is the traditional dwelling of the nomadic Kazakhs (IP/DT) page 18

AUTHOR

Paul Brummell is a career diplomat who joined the Foreign and Commonwealth Office in 1987. He has served in Islamabad and Rome, and as British Ambassador to Turkmenistan from 2002 to 2005. He was British Ambassador to Kazakhstan, and concurrently non-resident Ambassador to Kyrgyzstan from 2005 to 2009. He was shortlisted for the 1999 Shiva Naipaul Memorial Prize for an article on the San Remo Song Festival. He is a Fellow of the Royal Geographical Society and a member of the Royal Society for Asian Affairs. See page vi for his author story.

UPDATERS

Sophie Ibbotson and **Max Lovell-Hoare** run Maximum Exposure Productions, a media and logistics company that covers the CIS, Iran, Afghanistan and Pakistan. They have lived in central Asia since 2008 and work closely with intergovernmental institutions, NGOs, local governments and private companies to increase exposure of, and investment in, the region. Sophie is a member of the council at the Royal Society for Asian Affairs and is on the editorial board of *Asian Affairs*. Max has lectured to the RSAA and the Royal Asiatic Society, and his photographs of central Asia have been exhibited and published internationally.

UPDATES WEBSITE AND FEEDBACK REQUEST

While every attempt has been made to ensure that details within this guide are as accurate as possible at the time of going to print, Kazakhstan is a fast-changing country. Inflationary pressures are high, which means price information is particularly vulnerable to rapid change. New hotels open, restaurants change styles, regulations are modified, flight and railway timetables are amended. While the information presented in this book was that encountered at the time of research, do be aware that some things are likely to have changed by the time you visit. Any information regarding changes, recommendations regarding further places of interest to include, good restaurants and comfortable hotels, or warnings about places which were not up to scratch, would be gratefully received. They will be invaluable in the preparation of the next edition of the guide. Please send to: Bradt Travel Guides Ltd, IDC House, The Vale, Chalfont St Peter, Bucks SL9 9RZ; 01753 893444; e info@bradtguides.com. Alternatively you can add a review of the book to www.bradtguides.com or Amazon. Periodically our authors post travel updates and reader feedback on the website. Check www.bradtguides.com/guidebook-updates for any news.

PUBLISHER'S FOREWORD   *Adrian Phillips*

Authors of pioneering Bradt guides are so often motivated by the wish to challenge inaccurate Western perceptions of a given country – essentially they are determined to set the record straight. Paul Brummell certainly had his work cut out; when the Borat comedy was released, it presented stereotypes with bells on, and since then the people of Kazakhstan have had little choice but to grin and bear them. Paul's entertaining, intelligent and immaculately written book reveals a very different place. The world's ninth-largest country contains new and sophisticated cityscapes, rich wildlife and a cherished cultural heritage. Its varied spread of travel experiences is sure to surprise and reward the pioneering traveller willing to go in search of the real Kazakhstan.

Second edition published November 2011   First published August 2008

Bradt Travel Guides Ltd, IDC House, The Vale, Chalfont St Peter, Bucks SL9 9RZ, England;
www.bradtguides.com
Published in the USA by The Globe Pequot Press Inc,
PO Box 480, Guilford, Connecticut 06437-0480

ISBN-13: 978 1 84162 369 6
British Library Cataloguing in Publication Data
A catalogue record for this book is available from the British Library

Photographs Alamy: Art Directors & TRIP (AD/A), Pavel Filatov (PF/A), ITPhoto (ITP/A),
Robert Kerr (RK/A), Luxio (L/A), Buddy Mays (BM/A); Paul Brummell (PB); Dreamstime:
Anatoly Butyrin (AB/A), Mikhail Nikolayev (MN/DT), Ilya Postnikov (IP/DT); FLPA: Neil
Bowman (NB/FLPA), Tim Fitzharris/Minden Pictures (TF/MP/FLPA), Christian Hütter/
ImageBroker (CH/IB/FLPA), ImageBroker (IB/FLPA); Getty Images: Vyacheslav Oseledko
(VO/G); Eric Lafforgue (EL); Maximum Exposure Productions (MEP); SuperStock (SS)
Front cover A Kazakh berkutchi at a traditional hunting festival, Nura (VO/G)
Back cover Mausoleum of Rabigha Begum Sultan, (SI); Tian Shan Mountains, Central
Kazakhstan (IB/FLPA)
Title page Wall painting, Astana (SS); Kazakh fabric (L/A); Ile Alatau National Park (IB/FLPA)

Maps David McCutcheon
Colour map Relief map bases by Nick Rowland FRGS

Typeset from the author's disk by Wakewing
Production managed by Jellyfish Print Solutions and manufactured in India

Acknowledgements

For their help with the first edition, many thanks go to everyone at the British Embassy in Astana, Embassy Office in Almaty and Trade and Investment Office in Atyrau for their wonderful support. Thanks to Seamus Bennett at VSO and all at the Ecotourism Information Resource Centre and their local partners for their advice and information on community-based tourism in Kazakhstan. Thanks to Michael Frechetti, Renato Sala, Jean-Marc Deom and Rebecca Beardmore for helping me to discover some of the Bronze and Iron Age sites in Almaty Region. Thanks to all those in and around the travel industry in Kazakhstan who gave me their time, and valuable insights, including, but not restricted to, Folke von Knobloch, Charles van der Leeuw, David Berghof, Kazbek Valiev, Gulgaisha Kassenkhanova, Klara Duisengalieva, Lucy Kelaart and Summer Coish. Thanks to Andrew Page, Mike Welch and Niall Cullens at the Foreign and Commonwealth Office, to Tricia Hayne for helping me get started on this path, and to Hilary Bradt, Donald Greig, Adrian Phillips, Emma Thomson and all at Bradt Travel Guides for their faith in the project. Thanks to His Excellency Erlan Idrissov, Kazakhstan's Ambassador in Washington, and previously London, for his encouragement. Particular thanks go to Tish and Larissa Prouse for being such fine travelling companions around Pavlodar and East Kazakhstan regions, to Catherine Inglehearn for great trips to Malinovka and Karkaraly, to Marona van Heuvel for allowing me to join her research trip to meet a survivor of the ALZHIR camp, to Ronnie Anderson for his help in West Kazakhstan, and above all to Ainur Baimyrza for her considerable and indispensable efforts on the Kazakh language section. And thanks to all those in Kazakhstan who have shared with me a little of the treasures and traditions of their country. The comments presented herein do not necessarily reflect the views of the Foreign and Commonwealth Office.

The updaters of the second edition would like to offer their special thanks to Ben Tavener, Jyldyz Idigeeva and Ainura Temiralieva for deploying their superior language skills and persistently pursuing information in the remotest corners of Kazakhstan.

Contents

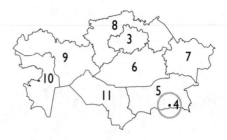

LIST OF MAPS

The writer Christopher Robbins subtitled his 2008 book documenting his travels in Kazakhstan as 'the land that disappeared'. His point here is that Kazakhstan is the ninth-largest country in the world, covering some 1.8% of the land surface of the globe, yet few in the West know anything about the place beyond its name.

My aim in this guide is to provide the pointers to enable the visitor to uncover the diverse and fascinating country which fills this little-known space on the map. The hospitality of the people of Kazakhstan ensured that my travels around the country were fuelled by huge plates of *beshbarmak*, and the efficient domestic aviation network and the slow-but-stately railway system helped most of the distances pass effortlessly, though some journeys were more eventful. One trip, which for me summarised both the challenges and fascinations of tourism in Kazakhstan, was a local package holiday to the Rachmanov Springs sanatorium in the Altai Mountains. Instructed to turn up outside the ice hockey stadium in Ust-Kamenogorsk, I discovered that the tour bus assigned to take us to the mountains was a battered Ural truck of distant Soviet vintage, its passenger cabin daubed with worn paintings of *maral* deer in a vague attempt to conjure a holiday spirit. The truck proved as reliable as it looked, and broke down in a stunningly attractive spot amidst fields of sunflowers, with the waters of the Bukhtarma Reservoir glinting below us. The driver's admission that he possessed not the first idea about vehicle maintenance appeared not to faze my fellow passengers. With the air of a group undertaking an annual holiday ritual, the men started on the business of dismantling the engine, banging various components with a hammer in an eventually successful effort to induce life. The women produced sandwiches and a jar of pickled cucumbers, and a miner from Zyryanovsk opened the first of what appeared to be an inexhaustible supply of vodka bottles. Glasses and plastic beakers were passed round to all the passengers, mine accompanied by the only two words of English I ever heard him speak, though which he was to use frequently during the holiday: 'Little drink?'

Kazakhstan deserves to be a 'land that appears' in the consciousness of the pioneering traveller. It is a good time to visit.

Introduction

The newly independent state of Kazakhstan emerged in 1991 out of the former Soviet Union as the ninth-largest country on the planet. It stretches from the snow-capped peaks of the Tian Shan and Altai mountains in the east, across great expanses of wormwood-scented steppe to the Caspian in the west. It may have been the birthplace of the apple, and the tulip. Yuri Gagarin, the first human into space, started his journey from the Baikonur Cosmodrome in the south of the country. Rich in natural resources, Kazakhstan is a major supplier of oil and of a huge range of minerals. It is fashioning a modern new capital, Astana, whose monuments include a pyramid-shaped Palace of Peace and Harmony and a huge transparent tent which covers a beach, golf course and even gondola-filled canals. Both were designed by British architect Lord Foster. Yet for many people in the English-speaking world the name Kazakhstan is best known through the antics of fictional journalist Borat Sagdiyev, the eponymous star of the film *Borat: Cultural Learnings of America for Make Benefit Glorious Nation of Kazakhstan*, whose character and views have nothing to do with those of the country he ostensibly represents.

For those wanting to know what Kazakhstan is actually like, there has never been a better time to come. Keen to attract more visitors, the Kazakhstani authorities have progressively eased the red tape surrounding visits to the country. While visas are still required, visitors from many countries in western Europe, North America, Australia and New Zealand no longer need letters of invitation (LOIs) to get a one-month single-entry tourist visa. And the previously irksome registration requirements have been eased considerably for short-term visitors, with the process now generally an automatic one. The number of good hotels around the country is increasing fast, and the largest cities now boast a wide range of restaurants and a lively and varied nightlife. Some forays have been made into the provision of community-based tourism, offering the chance to stay with Kazakh families in beautiful mountain and lakeside villages. The varied natural environments of Kazakhstan offer excitements for ornithologists in search of the black lark or sociable lapwing, botanists looking for some of the richest diversity of wild tulips to be found anywhere and fishermen dreaming of a 200lb catfish, with specialist tour operators offering packages based around all of these interests.

Much of Kazakhstan was controlled by a long succession of nomadic peoples. Their legacies include artefacts recovered from places of burial, including the beautiful and intricate suit of the so-called Golden Man, comprising thousands of pieces of gold, uncovered from a burial mound of the Scythian period near Almaty. The northern route of the Silk Road ran through the southern part of the country, nurturing important cities. In one, Turkestan, Kazakhstan's most magnificent building is to be found, the turquoise-domed mausoleum of the Sufist spiritual leader Khodja Ahmed Yassaui. The neighbouring city of Otrar, living on today as no more than an archaeological site, has a somewhat unfortunate claim to historical fame as the place in which the ill-considered actions of the city governor brought the predations of the Mongols of Genghis Khan onto central Asia.

The open spaces of Kazakhstan were the setting for several dark historical episodes during the Soviet period, when leaderships were at times all too inclined to view the country essentially as empty space which could be utilised for some of the less savoury tasks required by the Soviet Union. Political and other prisoners were detained in the numerous GuLag labour camps across the steppes of Kazakhstan. Whole peoples, including Germans, Koreans and Chechens, were deported here during World War II under the orders of Stalin, who wanted to keep away from the front lines groups whose loyalty he questioned. At the Semipalatinsk Test Site, 456 nuclear explosions were carried out between 1949 and 1989 at an appalling cost to the health of the local people. The desiccation of the Aral Sea was no environmental accident, but the result of a deliberate policy to boost the area irrigated for cotton production in central Asia.

Following a difficult economic transition post-independence, Kazakhstan has, since the dawn of the new millennium, experienced an economic boom on the back of high world prices for its oil and minerals. It is an increasingly prosperous and self-confident country. Range Rovers and sushi bars are part of the urban architecture of Almaty and Astana. A multi-ethnic country which straddles two continents, Kazakhstan is an expression of a Eurasian ideal. But ethnic Kazakhs are also proud of their nomadic heritage, although nomadism as a way of life was largely a victim of the collectivisation of the late 1920s. An invitation to a traditional Kazakh meal, which may even be held in a yurt, is not to be missed. When presented, as honoured guest, with a sheep's head for division among those around the table, the music of the dombra playing in the background, and your host solicitously enquiring as to whether you would prefer mare's or camel's milk, the exoticism of this fascinating land makes itself most clear. Kazakhstan offers the visitor a wide and rewarding range of travel experiences. None of them will remind you of Borat.

A NOTE ON NAMES AND SPELLINGS

There is a considerable variation in the spellings of Kazakhstani people and places into English. You will encounter frequently in reading about the country both Altai and Altay, Nazarbaev and Nazarbayev. Some place names have three distinct versions: a Russian name; a Kazakh name which has been Russified, ie: to fit Russian spelling rules; and a non-Russified Kazakh name. In the text I have tended to opt for whichever of the widely used options appears to be easiest for the English reader to handle, rather than attempting a linguistically purist or particularly consistent approach. Thus Karaganda rather than Qaraghandy; Chingistau rather than Shyngghystau; and, for that matter, Kazakhstan rather than Qazaqstan. But Semey rather than Semipalatinsk and Petropavl rather than Petropavlovsk (except in respect of historical references). Similarly, some Kazakh words have been pluralised in the text as in English, by the addition of an '-s', to make the relevant phrase a more straightforward read, although this is not how plurals are formed in Kazakh.

Part One

GENERAL INFORMATION

Location The northern part of central Asia, at the heart of the Eurasian landmass

Neighbouring countries Russia, China, Kyrgyzstan, Uzbekistan, Turkmenistan

Area 2,724,900km^2

Climate Extreme continental

Status Republic

Population Approximately 16 million (2010)

Life expectancy 68.2 years

Capital Astana (population approximately 692,000)

Other main towns Almaty, Karaganda, Shymkent, Pavlodar, Taraz, Ust-Kamenogorsk

Major exports Oil and gas, a wide range of minerals (including copper, lead, zinc, chromium, uranium, gold), steel, wheat

GDP (PPP) Approximately US$193.8 billion (2010); GDP (PPP) per capita approximately US$12,500

Official language Kazakh. Russian also recognised as the 'language of interethnic communication'.

Religion (Sunni) Islam predominates, with a large Russian Orthodox minority

Currency Tenge (T)

Exchange rate £1 = T239; US$1 = T147; €1 = T209 (August 2011)

National airline Air Astana

International telephone code +7

Time UTC (GMT) +5 in the western regions of Atyrau, Mangistau, West Kazakhstan and Aktobe. UTC +6 in the rest of Kazakhstan

Electrical voltage 220AC (50Hz)

Weights and measures Metric

Flag A golden sun in the centre, beneath which flies a golden steppe eagle, against a sky blue background. A golden pattern running down the left-hand side represents artistic forms associated with the Kazakh Khanate. Adopted 1992.

National anthem 'Menin Kazakhstanym' ('My Kazakhstan')

National sports Football, ice hockey, boxing, wrestling, weightlifting, cycling, gymnastics and chess are all popular. Traditional games on horseback, such as *kokpar*, played with a goat's carcass, are being encouraged.

Public holidays 1–2 January (New Year's Day); 7 January (Russian Orthodox Christmas); 8 March (International Women's Day); 22 March (Nauryz spring holiday); 1 May (Kazakhstan People's Unity Day); 9 May (Victory Day); 30 August (Constitution Day); 25 October (Republic Day); 16 December (Independence Day); also the Islamic Festival of Kurban Ait (dates determined by lunar calendar)

Background Information

GEOGRAPHY AND CLIMATE

Kazakhstan is big. Covering an area of more than 2.7 million square kilometres, it is the ninth-largest country in the world, and equivalent in size to the whole of western Europe. It accounts for around 1.8% of the world's land, and also has the distinction of being the world's largest landlocked country. It is bordered in the north by Russia, with whom it shares a land border an astonishing 6,846km long, in the east by China, and in the south by the central Asian republics of Kyrgyzstan, Uzbekistan and Turkmenistan. In the west it abuts onto the Caspian. The population of this huge country is around 16 million, giving Kazakhstan the low population density of fewer than six people per square kilometre. While most of Kazakhstan lies geographically in Asia, that part of the west of the country above the Caspian, lying west of the line of the Ural Mountains, is considered part of Europe, giving strength to Kazakhstani claims that it represents both continents (and hence its presence, for example, in the European football body UEFA).

In the east and southeast of the country are high mountain ranges: the Tian Shan along the borders of Kyrgyzstan and China, and the Dzhungarsky Alatau and Altai ranges further north along the Chinese border. Kazakhstan's highest peak, Khan Tengri in the country's southeastern corner, shades 7,000m. In contrast, in the west, close to the Caspian, lie some of the lowest points on the territory of the former Soviet Union. Kazakhstan's lowest land altitude is the Karagiye Depression in Mangistau Region, at –132m. Many of Kazakhstan's rivers flow northwards and westwards from its high ranges, and their continuations in China and central Asia: the Irtysh, with its tributaries including the Ishim and Tobol, flows north into Russia, to join the Ob and thence to the Arctic Ocean. The Syr Darya feeds the Aral Sea; the Ile runs into Lake Balkhash. Many rivers simply expire in the arid expanses which straddle much of the country. In the west of the country the Ural and Emba rivers flow south, rising in the Ural Mountains in Russia, and disgorging into the Caspian. Kazakhstan also boasts some 48,000 lakes.

Belts of pine and birch forest in the north give way to the world's largest dry steppe region, a vast expanse of open grassland covering more than 800,000km². With gradually declining rainfall and increasing temperatures from north to south, the steppe belt gives way to semi-desert and then to desert.

Far from the moderating influences of the oceans, Kazakhstan has an extreme continental climate. Average January temperatures range between –19°C and –4°C, average July temperatures between 19°C and 26°C. Extremes can reach –40°C and 40°C, respectively. There is a considerable variation between north and south, with summers warmer and winters milder in southwestern parts of Kazakhstan. Rainfall is low across most of the country, from around 400mm in the north to 150mm in the south, meaning that irrigation is usually required to support crop growth. Rainfall levels are higher in the Tian Shan and Altai mountains, reaching 1,500mm in some parts of the latter. High winds are a notable feature of Kazakhstan's wide expanses of steppe and semi-desert.

NATURAL HISTORY AND CONSERVATION

STEPPE AND DESERT Kazakhstan contains a wide variety of habitats, but of these it is the steppe, the vast belt of dry grassland running across the country, which lies at the heart of the Kazakh identity. These areas, too dry for the cultivation of crops, promoted the nomadic husbandry so central to Kazakh culture. The steppe landscapes, with their scent of wormwood and billowing waves of feather grass, are an enduring memory of a journey across Kazakhstan, even if the passage may at the time seem monotonous.

One of the most distinctive mammals of the steppe is the saiga, an antelope distinguished by its distinctive bulbous nose, a humpy, flexible proboscis somewhat reminiscent of that of the tapir. This complex nose serves several important functions for the saiga, including helping to warm up the icy air in the winter and filtering out the dust of the steppe. The saiga is a nomadic species, moving northwards in spring, and back southwards in the autumn, travelling in large migrating herds. It can cover 100km a day. Unfortunately for the saiga, the horns of the males are much valued in traditional Chinese medicine. With rhino horn becoming increasingly difficult to obtain due to growing international protection for the animal, the demand for saiga horn rose quickly. Poaching caused a catastrophic drop in the numbers of saiga, from perhaps two million in 1950 to fewer than 60,000 worldwide today. An epidemic of pasteurellosis also served to wipe out 12,000 of the animals in 2010 alone.

Conservation efforts are fighting back. All hunting of saiga is banned in Kazakhstan, though the enforcement of this across the huge territory of the Kazakh steppe is difficult. And a range of international environmental organisations, including the WWF, Frankfurt Zoological Society and Britain's Royal Society for the Protection of Birds, have joined forces with local partners in the Altyn Dala Conservation Initiative, which has advocated the establishment of the Irgiz Turgai Nature Reserve to protect wild ungulates like the saiga as well as the rare bird species, including the Dalmatian pelican, found among the lakes of the lower Irgiz and Turgai river basins. You can read more about efforts to conserve the saiga at www.saiga-conservation.com.

Other ungulates of the steppe and semi-desert include the central Asian wild ass, known in Kazakhstan as *kulan*, an onager which became locally extinct in Kazakhstan in the 1930s. The species was reintroduced from Turkmenistan at the nature reserves of Barsakelmes and later Altyn Emel. The goitered gazelle, known locally as the *jieran*, takes its name from its enlarged larynx.

Not all of the mammals of the steppe are under threat. Numbers of wolves remain high: indeed it is now believed that Kazakhstan may have up to 90,000 wolves, more even than Canada. The reduction in the saiga population, once a key component of the diet of the wolves of Kazakhstan, has however had the knock-on effect of increased attacks by wolves on livestock and, on occasions, children. Not surprisingly, the wolf is therefore seen as a threat in rural communities in Kazakhstan.

The lakes of the steppes play an important role for many migratory bird species, from Dalmatian pelicans to demoiselle cranes. Lake Tengiz in Akmola Region plays host to a large colony of flamingos, which arrive from the Caspian in the late spring.

With reduction in precipitation and increase in temperatures further south, the steppeland gradually turns to belts of semi-desert and then desert. Kazakhstan's main deserts include the Betpak Dala, north of the Syr Darya; the Kyzyl Kum ('Red Sands'), south of the Syr Darya, running into Uzbekistan; and the dry Ust-Urt Plateau, between the Aral Sea and the Caspian. These desert areas vary greatly in character, including deserts of sand, of stone and of salt flats. The wildlife of Kazakhstan's deserts includes endemic species such as the desert dormouse (*Selevinia betpakdalaensis*) and greater fat-tailed jerboa (*Pygeretmus shitkovi*) as well as the large desert monitor lizards, the caracal, a wildcat mostly found in Mangistau Region, and such bird species as the desert lark, houbara bustard, steppe eagle and saker falcon. Among the plants of the desert areas the bushy saxauls, whose deep network of roots helps to bind the sand, have a particularly important place in the lives of the local people, not least as a source of fuel.

MOUNTAIN, FOREST AND WATER The mountain environments of the Tian Shan and Altai ranges offer further habitats. The wild apple trees of the lower slopes of the Zailysky Alatau are reminders that many researchers consider this area to be the homeland of the apple. Along with apricot, aspen and birch they give way at higher altitudes to species such as the Schrenk spruce. The trees most characteristic of the Altai include birch and cedar. The animals of the mountains include one species which is rare, with a population of between 100 and 200 in Kazakhstan, and seen even more rarely, but which is close to the heart of the Kazakh consciousness. This is the snow leopard, which sports a beautiful whitish-grey coat with numerous blackish rosettes, and a long tail, used for balance in difficult mountain environments. It lives above the treeline in summer, coming down into the forests in winter. Other mammals of the mountain areas include the Tian Shan brown bear, Tian Shan ibex, lynx and wolverine. Across a lowland belt in the far north of Kazakhstan stretch pine and birch forests, and there are more forested granite outcrops, 'islands' in the steppe, forming the popular resort areas of Borovoye, Karkaraly and Bayanaul. The forests are home for such species as the elk and Eurasian lynx.

Kazakhstan is a popular destination for fishing holidays, with visitors seeking such challenges as the huge carp to be caught in the Ile River delta. The country's distinctive icthyofauna includes the *uskuch*, a variety of Siberian *lenok* found only in Lake Markakol in East Kazakhstan. But pride of place among Kazakhstan's fish probably goes to its sturgeon of the Caspian and rivers such as the Ural: from the beluga, one of the largest freshwater fish in the world, to the much smaller sterlet. But the prices commanded by the roe of the sturgeon, a dish better known as caviare, have led to its overexploitation, and the beluga is for example now categorised as an endangered species. Other distinctive fauna of the Caspian includes the Caspian seal, a species known for its prominent spots. Large numbers of seal deaths in recent years have been attributed to a virus related to canine distemper. An intriguing animal of the Ural River basin is the Russian desman, a semi-aquatic mammal related to the mole family, but with webbed hind feet.

ENVIRONMENT AND CONSERVATION During the Soviet period, the lands of Kazakhstan were subjected to a considerable amount of environmentally brutal treatment, in the name of economic development and scientific experimentation. The desiccation of the Aral Sea following the diversion of river waters to irrigate the cotton crops of Uzbekistan and Turkmenistan (see page 358), the ploughing of steppeland to support the cultivation of wheat in the Virgin Lands Campaign initiated in the 1950s, which also had the effect of promoting soil erosion (see page

76), and the decades of nuclear testing carried out at the Semipalatinsk Test Site (see page 252), are three of the best known of these environmentally damaging initiatives. The heavy industries set up in Kazakhstan during the Soviet period have also contributed high levels of carbon dioxide emissions, and high rates of contamination of many of the country's rivers with industrial metals. The pollution of agricultural lands and water systems with heavy applications of pesticides and fertilisers, illegal logging, the poaching of rare species, whether for fur, horn, roe, meat or fun, and negative by-products of Kazakhstan's recent economic growth, such as worsening atmospheric pollution above Almaty resulting from higher levels of car ownership, all add up to a daunting set of challenges.

The establishment of a new Environmental Code in Kazakhstan, the designation of more national parks and other protected areas, and the application of fines against industrial enterprises found to have infringed environmental regulations are all signs of an increasing focus on addressing these challenges. There are many excellent examples too of collaboration between international environmental organisations and local Kazakhstani partners, both governmental and NGOs. The partnership between the Royal Society for the Protection of Birds and the Kazakhstani ornithological NGO ASBK, in projects funded by the UK's Darwin Initiative to help protect the sociable lapwing as well as to map the most important bird areas of Kazakhstan, is a good example. But there is a great deal further to go.

HISTORY

EARLIEST TIMES TO THE SCYTHIANS Sites in the Karatau Mountains in the south of the territory of modern-day Kazakhstan and on the Mangyshlak Peninsula in the west are evidence of human occupation in the Palaeolithic period. By the Neolithic period, when the climate of the area had warmed, many parts of Kazakhstan supported human populations. Kazakhstan has considerable amounts of Bronze Age material, drawn mostly from burials in stone-walled coffins, as well as many petroglyphs of the period. There are sites in eastern and central Kazakhstan linked to the Afanesovo culture, from around 3500–2500BC, and to the later Andronovo culture, which flourished around 2300–1000BC west of the Afanesovo sites, but possibly moving eastwards in the second millennium. Some archaeologists, however, dispute this chronology of eastward migration of the Andronovo culture. The economies of the Bronze Age peoples seem predominantly to have been based around pastoralism, with some mining of deposits of copper ore.

From around 1000BC, during the Iron Age, the territories of modern Kazakhstan were occupied by Scythians, nomadic pastoralists who spoke an eastern Iranian language. The term 'Scythians' was used to refer to a widespread group of peoples, inhabiting an area which included territories of present-day Ukraine north of the Black Sea, east to the Altai. Some historians use the term 'Saka' to refer to Scythian peoples specifically of the eastern part of this range, including those in Kazakhstan, though other sources imply that the terms are interchaeological, Scythian being a Greek word, Saka a Persian one. They were nomadic pastoralists, treasuring the horse both as transport and food. The archaeological evidence of Saka culture is, like that of the Bronze Age, based around petroglyphs and, especially, burials, the latter in large earthen mounds known as *kurgans*. Distinctive Saka items include pointed headgear and striking gold ornamentation, especially stylised animal figures. The costume of the 'Golden Man', unearthed from a *kurgan* outside Almaty (see page 168), contains some 4,000 gold pieces.

Scythians lived in confederated tribes, developing alliances, sometimes forced, with sedentary peoples, to whom they offered military protection and animal produce in return for such goods as cereals.

Other groups similar to the Scythians, speaking eastern Iranian languages, but considered as separate peoples by many historians, included the Sarmatians, whose territories lay in present-day Ukraine, European Russia and eastern Balkans, but stretched eastwards as far as the Caspian, and the Massagetae, who lived east of the Caspian. The latter are well known in Kazakhstan and elsewhere in central Asia primarily through the exploits of their Queen Tomyris, who according to an account from Herodotus was responsible for the defeat of Cyrus the Great, the ruler of the mighty Achaemenid Empire. Classical sources tell us that Cyrus left as a trap a vacated camp, full of wine, a drink to which the Massagetae were not accustomed. A group of Massagatae troops captured the camp, got drunk on the wine, and were overpowered by Cyrus's returning troops. Tomyris's son, Spargapises, was captured, and committed suicide out of shame. The enraged Tomyris challenged Cyrus to fight an honourable battle, and defeated his forces. Cyrus himself was beheaded: it is said that Tomyris dipped the head in a leather bag filled with blood, so that he might have his fill of the blood he had so clearly wanted. Given the ending to this story it is perhaps of concern that there are a number of restaurants in Kazakhstan named after Tomyris.

THE WUSUNS TO THE KHOREZMSHAHS Much of the history of the lands of present-day Kazakhstan involves a complex series of migrations and conquests by nomadic tribes, often of Turkic peoples from the east, establishing large but often loose-knit empires, which eventually decline, a process frequently hastened by infighting, making way for new arrivals. Among the successors to the Scythians were the **Wusuns**, whose home originally lay to the northwest of China. Fleeing to the lands of the Ile River in the 2nd century BC after defeat in their homeland by the Xiongnu (the 'push' factor of tribal movements precipitated by a powerful rival in the original homeland area is another common theme), they established control over their new territory. According to contemporary Chinese accounts, the Wusun were nomads who lived in felt tents and drank mare's milk, suggesting that they had much in common culturally with the Kazakhs of modern times. Evidence for the suggestion that they may have been a Turkic people includes the fact that they evidently shared a similar ancestor myth (an abandoned infant son rescued and suckled by a she-wolf) as the later Ashina clan of the Gokturks.

The Wusun's rivals included the **Kangju**, another nomadic state-like entity, and the Xiongnu, a feared tribal group originating in Mongolia. The Great Wall was originally constructed by the Chinese at least in part to keep the latter out. They too constructed a large steppe empire into the lands of present-day Kazakhstan from the 3rd century BC. One tribe which possibly descended from the Xiongnu was a group whose name evoked terror in 5th-century Europe: the Huns. This group of equestrian nomads was able to carve out a great empire, stretching west from the Ural River into the heart of western Europe, thanks in part to superior weaponry, notably the composite bow. But with Attila's death in AD453 the empire of the Huns commenced its decline.

The Huns were pushed out of the region in the 6th century by an alliance between the Sassanids of Persia and the **Gokturks** ('Blue Turks'), a Turkic group which would become the next major nomadic power of the steppe, securing control of the lucrative Silk Road trade. The leaders of the Gokturk confederation were the Ashina clan, with its centre of power in the Orkhon Valley of present-day Mongolia. This was the first Turkic tribe to use the name 'Turk', a name meaning 'solid' or 'strong', which was later applied more widely to all the groups of the Turkic Kaganate. The first Gokturk Empire split into the Eastern and Western Turkic Kaganates, but was reunited in the late 7th century. The Gokturk Empire was thought to fade following the death in AD734 of a leader bearing the unfortunate, to an English reader, name of Bilge. The leadership of Bilge and his younger brother Kul Tegin are however immortalised in stelae found at the Orkhon River, whose inscriptions are the first known texts in Old Turkic, the earliest attested Turkic landscape. In the atrium of the main building of the Eurasian National University in Astana stands a full-sized replica of the stela in memory of Kul Tegin. More striking still is a modern canvas on the rear wall of the atrium, depicting Kul Tegin flying on a snow leopard. Below him are depicted figures from Kazakhstan's history, with both Ablai Khan and President Nazarbaev riding splendid white chargers. The inference clearly intended is a direct lineage from Gokturks to Kazakhs.

The religion of the Gokturks was Tengriism, focused around the thesis that life is about maintaining a harmony with the world in respect of both the sky deity Tengri and his female counterpart the Earth. Tengriism embodies elements of ancestor worship, animism and shamanism; shamans, for example, have a key role in tackling imbalances caused by the interference of malevolent spirits. The powers of the rulers of the Gokturks were considered to come as a mandate from Tengri. But the Gokturks were also tolerant of other religions, and Buddhism, Zoroastrianism, Nestorian Christianity and Islam were all practised within their empire.

As the Gokturk Empire waned, other nomadic groups took centre stage, including the **Karluks**, a Turkic tribe originating from lands west of the Altai Mountains, who gave their name to the Karluk group of Turkic languages, and the **Turgesh**, whose centre of power lay near modern-day Tashkent. An increasingly important new force was that of the Arabs, pressing northwards into central Asia to propagate the religion of Islam. One engagement which in retrospect was highly significant was the Battle of Talas in AD751, fought out on the Talas River between the external powers of the Chinese of the Tang Dynasty, attempting to extend their influence westwards, and the Arabs moving east, together with various local allies. The defeat of the Chinese kept central Asia out of the orbit of that power, and paved the way for the Islamisation of the region. One side effect of the battle was in the capture by the Arab forces of some Chinese experts in the making of paper, resulting in the acquisition of papermaking skills by the Islamic world, from where they spread to Europe. The propagation of Islam in the region was continued by the **Persian Samanids**, Sunni Muslims powerful in the 9th and 10th centuries, who converted many Turkic groups in the southern parts of present-day Kazakhstan.

Another Turkic dynasty, the **Karakhanids**, whose origins lay around Kashgar, expanded westwards in the 10th century at the expense of the Samanids and Karluks. The Karakhanids were converts to Islam, and the process of Islamisation continued under their rule. The Karakhanids in turn made way for the **Khitans**, a Buddhist people of Mongolian origin, whose westwards move was forced by their defeats in their homeland at the hands of the Jurchens. They established the Kara-Khitay Dynasty in the 12th century, the name 'Khitay' being at the root of the Russian word for China, *Kitay*, as well as the old English word Cathay. The Kara-Khitay were in turn defeated around 1212 by the **Khorezmshahs**, whose control of lands in the southern part of Kazakhstan was to be decidedly short-lived in the face of a new arrival from the east, the **Mongols** of Genghis Khan. Another important grouping was the **Kipchaks**, Turkic pastoralists from the Irtysh Region, who had moved into western Siberia by the 9th century, and then migrated further into the Volga Region, their sprawling steppe territories extending even as far as Moldavia and Wallachia. Kipchaks formed an influential group within the empire of the Khorezmshahs: the mother of the Khorezmshah ruler Mohammed II was a Kipchak, and it was the actions of the Kipchak governor of Otrar, in arresting and then executing merchants of Genghis Khan on spying charges, which unleashed the forces of the Mongols onto the region.

THE MONGOLS TO THE TIMURIDS Having united a series of nomadic tribes as the Mongol Confederation, Temujin was acknowledged by a council of Mongol chiefs in 1206 as their leader, and would henceforth be known as **Genghis Khan**. He set about creating an empire which would become the largest contiguous land empire in the history of the world, vastly larger than those of either Rome or Alexander the Great. Famous for their horse archers, but also skilled in the arts of siege warfare, the Mongol troops were highly disciplined and mobile, wearing relatively little armour. Heading westwards, while still engaged in campaigns in China, Genghis Khan defeated what remained of the Kara-Khitay Dynasty, but appeared to be uncertain about how to deal with the Khorezmshahs, considering them as a possible trading partner. The decision was made for him by the Governor of Otrar's seizure of a Mongol caravan and subsequent execution of its members, an act which brought on the Khorezmshahs their annihilation at the hands of the Mongols between 1219 and 1221. The leader of the Khorezmshahs, Mohammed II, eased the Mongols' task by dividing up his forces between several cities, in part because he feared an internal coup. Mohammed II fled from the disaster befalling his empire: the Mongols eventually tracked him down, reportedly hiding on an island in the Caspian.

On Genghis Khan's death in 1227, an assembly of Mongol chiefs ratified the choice of his third son, Ogedei, as his successor. But the control of the empire was parcelled out between Genghis Khan's sons. Thus, for example, his youngest son Tolui received the homeland areas of northern Mongolia. His second son Chagatai was allocated lands in present-day southeastern Kazakhstan, stretching southwards to encompass much of central Asia, known as the Chagatai Khanate. The most distant lands, to the west, should have gone to his eldest son, Jochi. But he was already dead, and so these areas, which would become known as the Golden Horde, were further divided between two of Jochi's sons, Orda and Batu. To Orda, the elder, went the eastern part of this area, running between Lake Balkhash and the Volga. Known as the White Horde, its capital became the town of Syganak, in present-day Kyzylorda Region. To Batu went the lands stretching west of the Ural River, the Blue Horde, with its capital at Sarai on the lower Volga. Batu continued the Mongols' drive westwards, conquering the Kipchak lands west of the Volga and reaching into central Europe, a drive curtailed eventually by power disputes following Ogedei's death.

While the Mongols have a rather barbarous reputation in the West, and their destruction of many of the cities of the Khorezmshahs and others who resisted them was certainly brutal, their rule was also marked by tolerance towards other religions (Genghis Khan was a shamanist) and a positive attitude towards overland trade. With one power, the Mongols, controlling the Silk Routes, these flourished during their rule. This was, for example, the period of Marco Polo's journey to China.

In the west, the lands of the Golden Horde gradually became increasingly Turkic in character. Under Uzbeg Khan in the early 14th century, Islam was adopted as the state religion. It faced a number of setbacks, not least the Black Death, but in 1378 Tokhtamysh, a descendant of Orda and ruler of the White Horde, also managed to secure control of the Blue Horde, briefly re-establishing the Golden Horde as a dominant force, and invading Lithuania and Poland. But Tokhtamysh was defeated by his one-time ally, a Muslim native of present-day Uzbekistan named Timur, who claimed descent from Genghis Khan and is better known in the west as **Tamerlane**. Becoming the ruler of Samarkand, Timur embarked on an empire-building mission that encompassed the Chagatai Khanate and far beyond, earning a reputation for brutality to equal that of the Mongols of Genghis Khan. Timur is, however, also responsible for Kazakhstan's most beautiful building, the Mausoleum of Khodja Ahmed Yassaui in Turkestan. Following his death in 1405, Timurid rule continued under his son Shah Rukh, who ruled from Herat. But within a few years of the latter's death, the Timurid Empire had crumbled.

THE KAZAKH KHANATE The new regimes to emerge at the beginning of the 15th century included the **Nogai Horde**, established by Edigey, an emir of the White Horde and named after Nogai Khan, a great-grandson of Genghis Khan and noted military leader, who had been killed in battle more than a century previously. Its lands stretched from the Ural River to the Volga, with its capital at Saraichik in present-day Atyrau Region. Further to the southeast, Abulkhair Khan, a descendant of Genghis Khan, began to consolidate Uzbek tribes into an Uzbek Confederation. A successful rebellion against Abulkhair in the 1460s resulted in the establishment by Janibek and Kerei Khan of the Kazakh Khanate. Under Janibek's son Kasym Khan, the Kazakh Khanate in the early 16th century expanded to a considerable size. Kasym Khan also instituted the first Kazakh legal code in 1520. The capital of the Khanate was established at Yassi, today's Turkestan, a centre of spiritual power and authority because of the presence there of the Mausoleum of Khodja Ahmed Yassaui.

During the 16th century the nomadic peoples of the Kazakh Khanate evolved a secondary level of allegiance, into one of three *zhuzes*: territorial-based tribal groupings. The territory of each *zhuz* incorporated both summer and winter pastures. The lands of the Great *Zhuz* lay in the Zhetisu, those of the Middle *Zhuz* to the north, and the territories of the Junior *Zhuz* further west, beyond the Aral Sea. Disputes were settled within each *zhuz* by *bis*, arbiters who were appointed out of respect for their wisdom and wise judgement.

External threats exposed the weaknesses of the decentralised character of the *zhuz*-based structure, as the Kazakh Khanate found itself facing a series of aggressors. The threat from the south was to prove the least severe. In the early 16th century, Abulkhair Khan's grandson Mohammed Shaybani succeeded in unifying Uzbek groups into the Shaybanid Empire, centred on Samarkand. He moved against the Kazakh Khanate, but was defeated by Kasym Khan in 1510. Following his death, his empire was eventually to break up into the Khanates of Kokand, Bukhara and Khiva.

A much greater threat came from the east, where in the early 17th century a confederation of several Oirat tribes from western Mongolia, named the Dzhungars, emerged. Their incursions into the territories of the Kazakh Khanate in the late 17th and early 18th centuries were devastating. At the beginning of the 18th century the Kazakh leader Tauke Khan brought together all three *zhuzes* to combat the threat of the Dzhungars, but Kazakh leadership weakened following Tauke Khan's death in 1715. In 1723 came what Kazakhs refer to as the 'Great Disaster', the loss of the Talas region amidst much bloodshed, as the Dzhungars then moved on to Turkestan. The most able Kazakh leader of the period was Abulkhair Khan of the Junior *Zhuz*, and with the Kazakhs having finally agreed a unified response, he took on the role of army leader, securing key defeats over the Dzhungar forces, such as that at Anrakay in 1729.

Another external power now enters the story. The Russian Empire was expanding rapidly, and Tauke Khan had already made generalised soundings of the Russian authorities, given the Kazakh problems with the Dzhungars. Seeing the potential to extend Russian influence eastwards and south, Peter the Great proposed a treaty of protection. This was not taken up, but in 1731 Abulkhair Khan agreed to a deal which allowed Russia to take on the role of protector of the Junior *Zhuz*. The deal was eventually to cost Abulkhair his life: he was murdered in 1748 by Sultan Barak in protest at his pro-Russian policy. The other two *zhuzes* accepted, at least at first, only a much less formalised relationship with Russia. The Great *Zhuz* was to be the last to come under Russian protection: the predations of the Khanate of Kokand to the south finally brought them into the Russian fold in the 1820s. The Russians were meanwhile moving further into the area. They had set up forts at Uralsk and Atyrau in the early 17th century, and more would follow further east, for example at Semipalatinsk and Ust-Kamenogorsk in the early 18th century.

One Kazakh leader of the 18th century is being promoted in the imagery of post-independence Kazakhstan as a strong and resourceful ruler who helped to secure the unity of the Kazakhs and defend their interests against external threats. He is **Ablai Khan**, whose early life forms the subject matter of the film *Nomad* (see page 174). Born Abulmansur, he was the son of a sultan but during the time of Dzhungar predations he concealed his parentage, presenting himself as a simple shepherd. He became a noted *batyr* of the Middle *Zhuz* in the campaigning against the Dzhungars in the 1720s, and took the name Ablai. When at the end of the 1750s the Chinese defeated the Dzhungars, he kept out of the conflict, but placed himself on good terms with the Chinese when it was settled. He played the Russians off against the Chinese in an adeptly balanced foreign policy which has some echoes in contemporary Kazakhstan, while also working to unify the territories of the Kazakh people. He became khan in 1771 and died ten years later.

TSARIST KAZAKHSTAN The Tsarist presence moved through the 18th and 19th centuries from 'protection' to colonisation, with the stationing of increasing numbers of garrisons, impositions on the Kazakhs, such as charges for crossing rivers, a reduction in the powers and authority accorded to the Kazakh khans, until these were abolished altogether, and the encouragement of settlement by Russian peasantry. The last process accelerated through the 19th century, and again in the first years of the 20th, when the agrarian reforms of Russian prime minister Pyotr Stolypin included further promotion of emigration of peasants to Kazakhstan. By 1917, Russians constituted more than 40% of Kazakhstan's population.

Not surprisingly there was a long series of Kazakh revolts against Tsarist impositions, including the rebellion of Syrym Datov in the late 18th century, and that of Makhambet and Isatay in the west in the late 1830s (see page 330). The ultimately unsuccessful rebellion of Kenesary Kasymov, a descendant of Ablai Khan, in the lands of the Middle *Zhuz*, is celebrated in post-independence Kazakhstan as a national liberation movement, and a statue of Kenesary occupies a prominent riverbank site in Astana.

A major series of uprisings took place across Turkestan in the face of the further burdens introduced on the peoples of central Asia during World War I, especially a Tsarist order of June 1916 on the conscription of non-Slav people for the rear service of the army, to allow trained Russian soldiers to be freed up for front-line service. The most organised revolt was that led by Amangeldy Imanov, who managed to pull together a rebel army as well as to organise the manufacture of primitive weapons. Imanov's rebellion focused on a bid to take the town of Turgai in autumn 1916, but the town held firm, and the rebellion was defeated.

If the immigration of Slavonic peoples into Kazakhstan was then very much a feature of the Tsarist period as well as the Soviet one which followed, so was the use of 'remote' Kazakhstan as a place of exile for dissidents. Prominent 19th-century exiles included the Ukrainian writer Shevchenko on the Mangyshlak Peninsula (see page 340) and the Russian writer Dostoevsky in Semipalatinsk (see page 246).

SOVIET KAZAKHSTAN The Bolshevik Revolution in 1917 took place then against a backdrop of considerable discontent in Kazakhstan against Tsarist colonial rule. Kazakh nationalists of the Alash Orda movement, named after a legendary founder of the Kazakh people, sensed their opportunity, and declared their independence at the 'All Kyrgyz Congress' in December 1917 in Orenburg. An Alash Autonomous Government was established under Alikhan Bokeikhanov, basing itself in Semipalatinsk. This loosely allied with White forces under former polar explorer Alexander Kolchak during the Civil War that followed, and by summer 1918 the war had turned against the Bolsheviks, who retained power only in a few cities in the region, though these included Almaty. But through the campaigns of the Bolsheviks' Southern Army Group under Mikhail Frunze, the tide turned during 1919, and with the White forces on the point of defeat, the Alash negotiated terms with the Bolsheviks. Its leadership, including Bokeikhanov, was almost all to perish in the Stalinist repression of the 1930s.

The Kyrgyz Autonomous Soviet Socialist Republic was established in 1920, its name changing to the Kazakh ASSR in 1925, when the Kyrgyz and Kazakhs were officially differentiated. At that point Orenburg, the original capital, was reincorporated into Russia, and the new capital was named as Kyzylorda, moving to Alma-Ata in 1929 with the arrival of the TurkSib Railway to that city. It became a full Soviet Republic, the Kazakh SSR, only in 1936.

The authorities set about building communism in Kazakhstan. To do the job, in 1925 they appointed as head of the regional Communist Party a notorious hardliner named Filipp Goloshchekin, who as the Military Commissar of the Urals Region had been involved in the murder of Tsar Nicholas II and members of his family in Ekaterinburg in 1918. The wealthier peasants, or *kulaks*, were repressed. In 1928 came the announcement from Moscow of the collectivisation of agriculture, a decision which for Kazakhstan meant mass resettlement into collective farms and the obliteration of the traditional nomadic way of life. The programme resulted in famine and mass starvation. *The Silent Steppe* by Mukhamet Shayakhmetov (see page 411) provides a sobering personal account of the enormous hardships faced by Kazakhs during this period. The Kazakh intellectual elite, including many of the ethnic Kazakh figures who had supported the establishment of Bolshevism, largely fell victim to the Stalinist repression of the late 1930s, accused of Kazakh nationalist or pan-Turkic sympathies.

Kazakhstan faced further trials through the tendency of the Soviet authorities to see these lands as remote and largely uninhabited. Stalin continued the Tsarist tradition of using Kazakhstan as a place of exile, sending Trotsky to Alma-Ata in 1928 in internal exile, before expelling him from the Soviet Union altogether the next year. GuLag labour camps were established across the territory of Kazakhstan, and as World War II began whole ethnic groups whose loyalty to the USSR was questioned by Stalin were deported here, away from front lines where it was feared that they might act as fifth columnists. Volga Germans, Chechens and Koreans were all brought here in large numbers, a process which did much to contribute to the complex ethnic mix of modern Kazakhstan. The establishment of a nuclear test site near Semipalatinsk in 1949 is perhaps the most damning of all the decisions based around this habit of viewing much of Kazakhstan as little more than empty space.

The Soviet authorities also embarked on a programme of industrialisation. They promoted the development of mining and heavy industries based around Kazakhstan's considerable mineral wealth: coal in Karaganda, with an adjacent steel plant at Temirtau, copper in Zhezkazgan, and phosphorous in Taraz. Industries also came to Kazakhstan during World War II, moved away from the front line. In agriculture, the Virgin Lands Campaign of the 1950s turned huge expanses of steppeland into wheat fields, diverting major water sources for irrigation. And all of these developments in industry and agriculture were accompanied by further in-migration, especially of Slavonic groups, to help provide the necessary workforce. At independence, Kazakhstan was the only one of the new republics of central Asia in which the 'titular' ethnic group formed a minority of the population.

In 1960, the post of First Secretary of the Kazakhstan Communist Party went to an ethnic Kazakh, Dinmuhammed Kunaev, a protégé of Leonid Brezhnev who had himself headed up the Kazakhstan Communist Party for a brief period in the mid-1950s at the height of the Virgin Lands Campaign. Kunaev lost the job in 1962, but was re-appointed in 1964, and kept it for the next 22 years. He was perceived locally as a strong protector of Kazakhstan's interests, but when Gorbachev took over as Soviet leader in 1985 he seems to have resolved to address concerns about corruption within the Communist Party in Kazakhstan. Kunaev was persuaded to retire, and on 16 December 1986 his successor was presented as Gennady Kolbin, an ethnic Chuvash with no close connections to Kazakhstan. The response was a gathering of students outside the Central Committee building in Almaty on the morning of 17 December, a few hundred at first though numbers rose during the day. A mixed group of Interior Ministry forces and police were ordered to clear the protestors and events turned violent, with many injuries caused by the snow shovels wielded by the law enforcement forces. Clashes continued through the night and into the next day. Casualty figures remain controversial, but at the very least two students are known to have died.

Kolbin lasted as First Secretary for little more than two years, before the job went to Nursultan Nazarbaev, an ethnic Kazakh, in June 1989. Nazarbaev was initially a strong supporter of the continuation of the Soviet Union, fearing that its constituent republics were so economically interdependent that they would struggle to survive as separate entities but, as it became clear that the USSR was destined not to last, moved to ensure an ordered transition to independence, with himself as head of state. On 1 December 1991, he secured election as president, taking more than 98% of the votes cast. On 16 December, Kazakhstan became the last of the republics of the USSR to proclaim its independence.

GOVERNMENT AND POLITICS

Nursultan Nazarbaev has been the dominant political figure of post-independence Kazakhstan. Born in 1940 near Shamalgan, in the foothills of the Tian Shan to the west of Almaty, he started his career in the blast furnace of the then new steel plant at Temirtau, in Karaganda Region. He joined the Communist Party and rose within it to increasingly senior positions, becoming appointed Chairman of the Council of Ministers in Kazakhstan (roughly equivalent to the Prime Ministership) in 1984, when Kunaev was First Secretary, and then to the First Secretaryship himself five years later.

The newly independent state of Kazakhstan was confronted immediately with major challenges. The break-up of the interdependent structures of the USSR deprived many enterprises of raw materials and markets, and industrial output slumped. Kazakhstan remained dependent on financial decisions made in Moscow until the introduction, amid considerable secrecy, of its own currency, the tenge, in November 1993. Nazarbaev embarked on a course of **economic liberalisation**, accompanied by privatisation, measures to attract foreign investment, and efforts to control the money supply in order to reduce inflationary risks. He has focused much attention on training and development, including through the provision of government-funded scholarships for the brightest young students, and has been bold in 'talent spotting' able administrators, who have often secured senior jobs at a young age. The pensions and banking systems became among the best in the region.

The pace of economic reform has not been marked by equivalent progress towards democratisation, and indeed President Nazarbaev has himself in a number of speeches emphasised that, while he sees democratisation as a goal, economic growth should come first, since without a strong economy democratic development risks in his view being destabilising. This prioritisation is seen clearly in Nazarbaev's relations with parliament in the early 1990s. Nazarbaev became concerned that the parliament elected in 1994 under the first, 1993, Constitution of independent Kazakhstan was acting as an obstacle to the implementation of his economic reform agenda, in taking an overly cautious attitude to such issues as the promotion of foreign investment and land privatisation. A ruling of the Constitutional Court upholding a complaint from an unsuccessful candidate about the conduct of the election gave Nazarbaev the justification he needed to dissolve parliament, and temporarily rule by decree. The new **Assembly of the Peoples of Kazakhstan**, a body intended to represent the interests of the diverse ethnic groups making up the population of the country, proposed the extension of the presidential term of office from 1996 to 2000, in the interests of stability, a proposal which was endorsed by a large margin in a referendum in April 1995.

Nazarbaev also moved to change the Constitution, putting forward a new draft which was again endorsed by a national referendum, in August 1995. The new Constitution was avowedly presidential in style. The president is commander-in-chief of the armed forces, and was given control of many key appointments, including the prime minister, the heads of regional administrations and the chairman of the new Constitutional Council. A bicameral parliament was established. The lower chamber, the Majilis, was elected under a mostly constituency-based system. The upper chamber, the Senate, consisted of representatives from each of the regions of Kazakhstan, plus some presidential appointees. Parliamentary elections under the new rules in December 1995 produced a parliament which was much less fractious, and more supportive of the reform programme. Nazarbaev was reconfirmed as president by large margins in presidential elections in 1999 and 2005, and the snap election in April 2011 awarded him 95.5% of votes.

With Kazakhstan having enjoyed GDP growth rates of more than 10% a year between 2000 and 2005, Nazarbaev increasingly talked of Kazakhstan's readiness for democratisation. The conclusions of a State Commission on Democratisation formed the basis for Constitutional amendments passed in May 2007, which were billed by Nazarbaev as moving Kazakhstan from a presidential system of governance to a presidential/parliamentary one. Both chambers of parliament were increased in size, with a move to a proportional representation system for elections to the Majilis in order to encourage political party development. The prime minister would henceforth be taken from the largest party in parliament. The presidential term of office was reduced from seven years to five. Some judicial and local government reforms were also introduced. The previous bar on the president from also holding membership of a political party was lifted, a change which led to a much closer personal identification between Nazarbaev and the pro-presidential party Nur Otan, which he now headed. Amid some international controversy, the amendments also lifted the two-term limit on holding the presidency in respect of the first president of Kazakhstan (ie: Nazarbaev). In parliamentary elections in August 2007, Nur Otan emerged as the only party represented in the Majilis, since none of the opposition groups was able to reach the 7% threshold.

The main current opposition groupings in Kazakhstan have their origins in the Democratic Choice of Kazakhstan, an organisation founded in 2001 by a number of politicians previously associated with the regime, including Galymzhan Zhakiyanov (a former Governor of Pavlodar), Oraz Zhandosov (a former Central Bank Chairman) and Mukhtar Ablyazov (a former Energy Minister). Their platform was based around calls for further economic and political reform and a countering of corruption among the political elite. The organisation split after a year, with a moderate faction setting up a new party, **Ak Zhol** (White Path), which secured just one seat in the 2004 parliamentary elections, which they did not take up, complaining of widespread electoral malpractice. In 2005, this group split in turn, the new group taking the name True Ak Zhol. A banner coalition of some of these opposition groups, For a Just Kazakhstan, proved the main opposition to President Nazarbaev in the 2005 presidential elections. Their candidate, a one-time Prosecutor General and Majilis chairman named Zharmakhan Tuyakbay, polled 6.6% of the vote. Other opposition forces have weakened since the early independence years: these include the communists and a number of Kazakh nationalist groups (which included a new Alash party, headed by Sabet-Kazy Akatay).

In foreign policy, Nazarbaev has attempted to retain a balanced approach, maintaining friendly relations with his two large neighbours, Russia and China, while avoiding being drawn too heavily into the sphere of influence of any one power, and courting investment and technical advice from the US and EU. The official renouncement of the nuclear weapons with which Kazakhstan found itself at independence earned him much praise internationally, though there is some discussion as to whether Kazakhstan has actually decommissioned all the devices.

Nazarbayev has not cultivated an obvious successor and, after more than 20 years at the helm, any transition of power will be a difficult one. Foreign investors rate the lack of a clear succession plan as the single greatest threat to Kazakhstan's stability and, by extension, to the stability of the whole central Asian region.

ECONOMY

The 1990s were economically extremely difficult for Kazakhstan. The break-up of the USSR led to the loss of the traditional partnerships and markets of Kazakhstan's industries, which had been developed to meet the needs of a command economy, and Kazakhstan experienced a sharp economic contraction in the early part of the decade. The Russian financial crisis of 1998 brought a further blow. Food production also decreased sharply in the early 1990s, following the dissolution of the collective farm system, and there was a decline both in the acreage of arable land and in the number of livestock. Since 2000, however, annual economic growth has averaged 8%, helped by rising world market prices for oil and many of the metals exported by

Kazakhstan. Per capita GDP has increased 12-fold since 1994, the unemployment rate has declined, and Kazakhstan has shown a marked improvement in respect of indices of poverty.

Oil has been an important factor behind Kazakhstan's recent economic success. In 2010, Kazakhstan produced some 80 million tonnes of **crude oil**, and it is on track to produce 150 million tonnes a year by 2015. Three major fields operated by foreign consortia are at the heart of this planned growth. The onshore Tengiz oilfield and Karachaganak gas condensate field are already in production. The offshore Kashagan oilfield is being developed by Italian operators AGIP KCO, at the helm of a large consortium. But this huge field, one of the largest discoveries worldwide in recent decades, represents a tough challenge: it is deep, under high pressure, rich in noxious hydrogen sulphide and lies in shallow waters of the Caspian subject to ice cover for several months of the year. It has already been subject to project delays and cost overruns.

Export routes for the oil include the Caspian Pipeline Consortium (CPC) and Atyrau–Samara pipelines into Russia, the Atasu–Alashankou pipeline, opened in 2006, into China, and plans to feed into the Baku–Tbilisi–Ceyhan pipeline, running from Azerbaijan to Turkey, by tankers plying the Caspian. While still keen to attract foreign know-how, Kazakhstan has become increasingly assertive as regards the negotiation of new oil deals, in demanding a larger role for Kazakhstan's state hydrocarbons company KazMunaiGas as well as in increasingly tough taxation and environmental regimes.

Kazakhstan's natural resource wealth does not stop at oil. Kazakhstanis like to boast that, beneath their soils, almost everything in the periodic table of elements can be found, and the country certainly has a wide range of minerals: gold, silver, copper, lead, chromite, phosphorous, iron ore, beryllium, manganese, titanium, bauxite and many more. It has ambitions to become the world's largest exporter of **uranium**, and also has appreciable reserves of coal. In agriculture, Kazakhstan is a significant exporter of grain.

The Kazakhstan authorities are alive to the risks of a heavy dependence on exports of oil and minerals: for example, those of the so-called 'Dutch disease', where overheating causes the rest of the economy to become uncompetitive. The Central Bank has worked hard to control the money supply, to mitigate the risks of inflation. Kazakhstan established a national oil fund, using a model borrowed from Norway: the idea is that oil receipts will be used in part for currency stabilisation, in part to support activities promoting the diversification of the economy. In the latter regard, the government has identified a series of priority economic clusters they aim to promote, including petrochemicals, textiles and tourism. There are some considerable challenges facing the diversification programme; for example as regards securing a workable future for the large heavy machine building plants, whose activities were often focused on the needs of the Soviet defence industry, which the country has inherited from the Soviet period.

Kazakhstan's recent economic growth has also been marked by a rapid recent expansion in the services and construction sectors, the latter including the many building projects in the new capital of Astana. The heavy external indebtedness of many Kazakhstani banks meant that the impact of the US sub-prime mortgage crisis striking in 2007 was pronounced in Kazakhstan, though advanced planning did enable the government to put aside funds for public works projects during the crisis. Property prices in Almaty and Astana, which had fallen 45% from their peak in 2007, are now climbing again, though high interest rates keep many Kazakhstanis off the property ladder.

The past few years have also seen a large increase in Kazakhstani investments overseas. Kazakhstan is a major investor in both Kyrgyzstan and Georgia, and its companies are increasingly looking further afield. Private equity funds such as the Kazakh Growth Fund, supported by the European Bank, are spearheading this expansion.

President Nazarbaev has set Kazakhstan the task of joining the ranks of the world's 50 most competitive economies. In 2010, Kazakhstan was ranked 72nd, immediately below Bulgaria and above Peru. Economic growth is hampered by a number of factors, including continuing high levels of corruption and the need to reduce bureaucracy.

PEOPLE AND CULTURE

MULTI-ETHNIC KAZAKHSTAN A stroll around central Almaty will give you a clear sense of Kazakhstan's ethnic diversity, as a broad mix of European and Asiatic faces greets you. The most recent census data, from 2009, recorded that ethnic Kazakhs comprised 63.1% of the population, with ethnic Russians comprising 23.7%. Other minority groups are much smaller: Uzbeks were in 2009 the next most numerous, at 2.9% of the population, followed by Ukrainians (2.1%) and Germans (also 2.1%). There are a large number of other groups with smaller but significant populations, including Koreans, Chechens, Uighurs, Tatars and Greeks. The history of Kazakhstan during the Tsarist and Soviet periods as a place in which colonists and dissidents were sent from Slavonic areas, and in the Stalinist period as one to which whole ethnic groups were deported, does much to explain this complex mix. President Nazarbaev makes frequent reference in his speeches to Kazakhstan's qualities as a country in which a diverse range of ethnic groups are able to coexist peacefully, and he has been careful to ensure that the rights of minority ethnic groups are preserved, for example in retaining an official status for the Russian language, as the 'language of interethnic communication'. The Assembly of the Peoples of Kazakhstan, which has branches in all regional capitals in Kazakhstan, was a body set up by Nazarbaev to represent the interests of the different ethnic groups.

But the ethnic composition of the country is changing. The proportion of the population comprising ethnic Kazakhs, for example, stood at around 74% at the turn of the 20th century. By 1989, mainly through the in-migration of settlers and deportees, it had slumped to around 40%. But following the break-up of the Soviet Union, there was a strong out-migration by a number of mainly European groups, perceiving opportunities to be greater in their ethnic homelands. A large proportion of Kazakhstan's ethnic German and Greek populations departed, as well as smaller percentages, but considerable numbers, of Russians and Ukrainians. The overall population of Kazakhstan dropped in the first few years following independence. The numbers of Kazakhs, in contrast, increased. Birth rates among the ethnic Kazakh population are higher than those of the Slavonic groups. The latest figures show a fertility rate for ethnic Russians of just under 1.4, compared with 1.9 for Russian-speaking ethnic Kazakhs, and 2.9 for Kazakh-speaking Kazakhs. The in-migration since independence of *oralmans*, ethnic Kazakhs from outside Kazakhstan, has also contributed to the rise in the ethnic Kazakh population. Thus today, ethnic Kazakhs form a clear majority of the population. The percentage of the population from other parts of central Asia, especially Uzbeks, Kyrgyz and Tajiks, is also rising, with inflows, especially of seasonal and other temporary migrants, related to the better employment opportunities and salaries available in Kazakhstan.

The principal dwelling of the nomadic Kazakhs, the circular, felt-covered yurt is a potent image of Kazakh culture. Few Kazakhs now live in yurts, although they are still used by some pastoralists who move their herds into summer mountain pastures. If you see a yurt in a Kazakh town, or along a roadside, chances are that you have found a café. But the imagery of the yurt remains central to Kazakh ethnic identity, and provides national cultural symbolism deployed by the authorities of independent Kazakhstan. The *shanyrak* is the round frame incorporating a wooden lattice found at the top of the yurt: the structure through which the smoke of the central fire is dispersed. The highest point of the yurt, it provides a symbol of the unity and well-being of the family. The *shanyrak* is passed down from generation to generation, even when other parts of the yurt are replaced. Unlike neighbouring Kyrgyzstan, Kazakhstan did not go so far as to place an image of the *shanyrak* on its national flag, but it is on the State Emblem. The image of a broken *shanyrak* is often used by artists to depict tragedy; for example, in paintings and sculptures commemorating the victims of Stalinist repression or the famine of the early 1930s.

The *shanyrak*, which has to withstand considerable pressures, is made of durable birch wood, while the rest of the wooden frame is made of willow. This consists of dome poles (*uyk*), and a trellis structure which makes up the walls. The latter is divided up into a series of sections, known as *kanat*. The more *kanat* used, the bigger the yurt. Most yurts are between six and eight *kanat*, though much larger ceremonial yurts are possible. The yurt has a two-leaved wooden door called an *esik* or *sykyrlauyk* (the latter word means 'squeaky', as the door was supposed to make a noise to herald arrivals). A series of ropes and ribbons hold everything together, and the yurt is then covered with felt. Ornamented reed mats (*shym shi*) encircle the frame.

Looking from the door, the right-hand side of the yurt was considered the female area, with the householders' bed at the far end and household equipment nearer the door. The left-hand side was the male area, with hunting equipment and saddles close to the door. The space opposite the entrance, known as the *tor*, was an honoured area allotted to guests. The belongings of the family, in decorated chests, and piles of bedding, would also characteristically be placed here. The family would generally sit around the fireplace in the centre of the room: the fire was considered to be the protector of the yurt.

There are strong variations in ethnic composition between regions. Ethnic Russians form the large majority of the population of the North Kazakhstan Region, while around 96% of the population of Kyzylorda Region in the south is ethnically Kazakh.

THE KAZAKHS There are many theories as to the meaning of the word 'Kazakh': that in most common currency suggests that it means 'free'. The complex genesis of the Kazakhs, as descendants of a mix of Turkic tribes, Mongols and to some extent Indo-Iranian groups such as Sarmatians and Scythians, has resulted in a marked diversity of Kazakh physical features. Common attributes include Mongoloid features, relatively fair skin, high cheekbones and a tendency towards black hair.

Most ethnic Kazakhs are members of one of the three *zhuzes* (the name literally means 'hundred'), broad tribal groupings: the Great *Zhuz* predominating in the southeast, including Almaty, the Middle *Zhuz* further north, including Astana, and the Junior *Zhuz* to the west. Within each *zhuz* are a number of tribes, known as *taipa*. Each *taipa* in turn comprises a number of clans, *ru*. It is important for each Kazakh to know their family tree back for seven generations on the male line. President Nazarbaev once described the knowledge of genealogy for the steppe Kazakh as akin to the compass for the sailor: a device which fixes their position. By tradition, marriage between individuals related over seven generations was forbidden. Traditional positions of authority included the *bi*, a wise man appointed to the role of arbiter by virtue of the respect he held in the community, and the *batyr*, or warrior. The heroic deeds of many Kazakh *batyrs* in their fights against their Dzhungar adversaries are commemorated in equestrian statues appearing right across Kazakhstan.

Two groups, considered to represent a steppe nobility, or 'white bone' (in contrast to the 'black bone' of ordinary Kazakhs), lay outside the system of *zhuzes*. The *Tore*, who traditionally bore the title of sultan, traced their lineage back to Genghis Khan himself. The *Khodja* were descendants of Arabian missionaries who had brought Islam to the area, and carried a spiritual authority. A less exalted group outside the *zhuzes* was the *Tolengit*, descendants of Dzhungar captives.

KAZAKH CULTURE While around 40% of the population of Kazakhstan lives in rural areas, this is overwhelmingly in settled, not nomadic, communities, although some pastoralists do still move animals seasonally. Nonetheless, the traditions and artefacts of nomadism lie at the heart of Kazakh culture. The yurt (see box), hunting with eagles, and a dish of *beshbarmak* are invoked frequently in the symbolism of the post-independence state, whether by government sources or advertisements on television. Epic poetry, recounted by *akyns*, and accompanied by *dombra* playing, remains popular, and some young Kazakh pop bands are experimenting with the use of traditional Kazakh instruments and musical styles alongside Western ones. Horsemeat remains a revered part of the Kazakh diet, even if the urban elite has also developed a decided fondness for sushi. Traditional chunky silver jewellery is in vogue among young Kazakhs keen to explore their ethnic identity.

Following independence, there has been an attempt by the authorities to further promote Kazakh cultural traditions, though with some awareness of the need to also balance this with the cultures of the other ethnic groups present in Kazakhstan. Traditional horse-based sports are a good example, where at race tracks across the country you may find, especially on public holidays, performances of some of the games dating back to Kazakh nomadism alongside Western-style horse races. One of the most popular is *kokpar*, whose rules are basically about horsemen grabbing the carcass of a headless goat and scoring a goal with it. The rules of the game have however been modernised: there is even a federation governing the sport. Rather than the scrums of old, there is a marked pitch and four players from each side are on the field at any one time. Unlike *kokpar*, *kyz kuu* ('catch the girl') is regarded more as a piece of fun than serious sport: on the outward leg of this two-horse race, whose participants usually wear traditional Kazakh costumes, boy chases girl, aiming to kiss her if he catches her. On the return journey girl chases boy, her objective being to give him a good thrashing with her horse whip. Another horse-based sport enjoying a revival is *alaman baiga*, a long-distance horse race, which originated with the need of the nomadic Kazakhs to promote endurance in horses. The jockeys are by tradition small boys.

The way in which Kazakh traditions have often been preserved, sometimes revived, but also adapted for changing times (in which they sit alongside practices drawn from other cultures), is seen clearly in contemporary Kazakh weddings. These remain major events, taking place across several days, with a reception given by the family of the bride preceding the wedding proper, whose components include civil registration, possibly a religious ceremony, and a drive around town to the main monuments of the city accompanied by noisy honking of car horns, bottles of sweet Soviet 'champagne' or vodka, and the inevitable video camera. A reception hosted by the groom's family rounds off the proceedings.

A typical wedding of a middle-class urban Kazakh family will include many elements familiar internationally: the bride in a white wedding dress, fireworks, and embarrassing disco dancing from the bride's father. But it will also incorporate a number of modern takes on Kazakh traditions. One of the most important is *betashar*, a ceremony of the revealing of the bride's face to the relatives of the groom, accompanied by gifts from the latter. *Shashu*, the showering of the wedding couple with sweets and coins for prosperity, is another popular element of the wedding. The elaborate traditional procedures associated with matchmaking have largely died out, although parents do frequently retain an influence in the choice of spouse, and the payment of a bride price, *kalym*, is still usual.

LANGUAGE

Kazakh is part of the Kipchak family of Turkic languages, its closest linguistic relatives within that family including Karakalpak and Nogay. It was established in 1989 as the official language of Kazakhstan, a status confirmed under the 1993 Constitution. It has been written in several different alphabets. An Arabic script was traditionally used, although the Tsarist Russian authorities encouraged the use of a Cyrillic alphabet devised by the Kazakh educator Ibrai Altynsarin. This was not widely taken up, however. In the late 1920s the Soviet authorities switched to the use of a Latin-based alphabet, though this in turn was replaced in 1940 by a revised Cyrillic alphabet developed by Sarsen Amanzholov. A Latin script is however used to render Kazakh on some internet-based sources, and is also widely used informally by the Kazakh diaspora in Turkey and Western countries. The government of Kazakhstan did examine the case for moving officially from a Cyrillic- to Latin-based script, following the example of some other countries of the former Soviet Union, but President Nazarbayev decided that as it would cost US$300 million and take between ten and 12 years, it was not a priority.

Russian retains a formal status as the 'language of interethnic communication', and in many ways remains the lingua franca in Kazakhstan as it is spoken by 84% of Kazakhstanis. Kazakh is not widely spoken among the country's ethnic Russian and other Slavonic minorities, and the legacy of the Soviet Union, in which knowledge of the Russian language was an important requirement for career success, has meant that in urban areas in particular many ethnic Kazakhs who were educated in Russian-medium schools, do not have a good knowledge of Kazakh either. But the position of Kazakh is gradually strengthening. The in-migration of ethnic Kazakh *oralmans*, many of whom do not speak Russian, and higher rates of out-migration of ethnic Russian and Slavonic groups, have altered the demographic picture since independence. The government has introduced a number of measures to promote the Kazakh language, for example television and radio stations are required to provide at least 50% of their broadcasting in Kazakh; civil servants who are not ethnic Kazakhs receive a pay bonus if they are able to speak good Kazakh; and the

Constitution provides that the president must be a fluent speaker of the language. There is a strong regional dimension to Kazakh- and Russian-language abilities. In the southern regions of South Kazakhstan and Kyzylorda in particular, the Kazakh language is clearly dominant, and you will hear little Russian spoken. In Petropavl in North Kazakhstan the reverse is true.

President Nazarbaev has urged citizens of Kazakhstan to master three languages: Kazakh, Russian and English. The emphasis placed by the government on encouragement of knowledge of English, as a global language, to bolster the economic competitiveness of Kazakhstan, is demonstrated by its focus on the teaching of English in schools and in the government-funded scholarships provided under its Bolashak programme for study at universities in the United States and United Kingdom. You will find some English spoken in hotels, restaurants and other establishments connected with tourism in the major cities, especially Almaty and Astana. You may however find it difficult to track down an English speaker in small towns or rural areas. Young Kazakhs are often keen to practise their English with foreign visitors.

RELIGION

Kazakhstan's complex ethnic mix does much to explain the country's religious diversity. Ethnic Kazakhs are historically Sunni Muslims of the Hanafi School, and Islam constitutes the largest religious group, but the Russian Orthodox faith is professed by around one-third of the population. Other religions present in Kazakhstan include Roman Catholicism, especially among the ethnic German, Ukrainian and Polish communities. Pope John Paul II visited Kazakhstan in 2001. There are also, *inter alia*, many Protestant and Baptist groups, and a small Jewish community. Under the 1995 Constitution, Kazakhstan is a secular state, and President Nazarbaev pays frequent attention in his speeches to the religious tolerance found in modern Kazakhstan. The presence in the centre of Astana of a mosque, Russian Orthodox church, Catholic church and Jewish synagogue, is frequently cited as an example. A triennial Congress of World and Traditional Religions has been meeting in Astana since 2003, an initiative of President Nazarbaev, to promote interfaith dialogue. There have, however, been some concerns raised internationally about the treatment of certain more proselytising religious groups, both Christian and Muslim, and about the handling of a dispute over the title to the farm and cottages of the Hare Krishna community outside Almaty.

Rates of mosque attendance and observance of the Ramadan fast are relatively low, in part the result of Kazakhstan having lived under more than seven decades of officially atheist communist rule, but these are rising. The brand of Islam practised by the nomadic Kazakhs always incorporated certain pre-Islamic elements, including shrine pilgrimage and worshipping at the graves of ancestors. Sufi mysticism, which appeared to incorporate some traditional practices within Islamic worship, was highly influential, and the mausoleum of the Sufi figure Khodja Ahmed Yassaui at Turkestan is a major place of pilgrimage, as it has been for centuries. The wearing of amulets remains popular, often in 'Islamised' forms; for example, amulets containing verses from the Koran.

There are echoes too in modern Kazakhstan of Tengriism, the traditional religious belief of the early Turkic nomads who occupied Kazakh territory, though more often in a broader cultural than strictly religious sense. Tengriism took its name from that of the deity of the sky, and included an important role for shamans in helping to secure salvation from evil spirits. Mountains, with their appearance as a bridge between earth and heavens, played a particularly important role in Tengriism, and it is no accident that Kazakhstan's highest mountain is named Khan Tengri. Even the in-flight magazine of Air Astana is named *Tengri*.

EDUCATION

Kazakhstan has a mandatory secondary education system and the UN estimates adult literacy in the country to be over 99%, significantly higher than in many parts of Europe. The statistics are roughly equal for males and females.

Education is free up to the age of 18, and students are taught in both Kazakh and Russian. The curriculum is determined by the Ministry of Education, which also issues approved textbooks. From the age of 15, students must remain in education but can decide whether to join a training programme, take a combined vocational and academic course at a lycée or go to college for a general academic education.

There are over 50 universities in Kazakhstan, most of which are in Almaty and Astana. These are a mixture of private and public institutions, both bound by the same state-specified curriculum requirements, and they include a number of international organisations, most notably the Kazakh–American University and the Kazakh–British Technical University. The merit-based Bolashak scholarship programme funds top students to study abroad and covers both their tuition fees and living costs. About 1,800 students are abroad with the programme at any one time, and they are expected to return to work in Kazakhstan for five years on completion of their course.

Private education is increasingly popular in Kazakhstan. This is in part due to under-funding in the state sector, but also because parents have greater disposable income and want to give their children the advantages that well-equipped classrooms, well-qualified and often international staff, and access to other well-connected families confer. The English boarding school Haileybury has already opened campuses in Almaty and Astana, and the American Quality Schools International (QSI) has four branches across the country.

2

Practical Information

WHEN TO VISIT

Kazakhstan's extreme continental climate makes for large seasonal variations, with hot summers and cold winters. The large size of the country makes for big regional variations too. In general, the northern regions are at least a few degrees colder than the south.

Thus winter in northern Kazakhstan means snow cover between November and April, and temperatures regularly below –20°C. In Kyzylorda and Mangistau regions, there is relatively little snow, and winter temperatures which, while still often below zero, are nothing like as extreme. Winter brings with it opportunities for snow-related sports across Kazakhstan, including downhill skiing at Chimbulak and Ak Bulak outside Almaty. Cities in the north build elaborate 'villages' of ice sculptures. On crisp, cold but sunny winter days, Kazakhstan is perhaps at its most beautiful. However, for everyone except winter sports enthusiasts winter is nonetheless deservedly the low season for tourism. The cold weather inevitably restricts movement, and travel schedules are also subject to disruption: for example, flight delays caused by freezing fog or snowstorms. If you do come to Kazakhstan in winter, you will need to prepare your wardrobe carefully for the cold (see *What to take*, page 44).

The Nauryz festival on 22 March announces the arrival of spring, with festive yurts placed in the squares of the main cities. It can, however, still be cold at this time in the north. Late April and May bring a wonderful carpeting of wild flowers to the steppes, and to the slopes of the mountains. The tulips on the slopes of the Tian Shan in May are a particularly fine sight. The trekking season in Kazakhstan starts to develop around mid-May, running to late September, though some high-altitude routes remain closed until June or July. The summer months are in general an excellent time to come to Kazakhstan, and represent the peak of the tourist season. With temperatures in the southern regions frequently reaching well above 30°C in July and August, budget travellers planning to visit at this time should consider trading up to accommodation with air conditioning. It is also worth bearing in mind that the best-known spots can get pretty packed with domestic tourists in August. If you are heading to any resort area at the height of summer whose attractions include water to swim in, it is a particularly good idea to pre-book your accommodation.

Autumn too can be a good time to visit, especially the south, where in the low-lying areas the weather often remains pleasantly warm, albeit with increasingly chilly evenings, into November. Note that Almaty hosts the Kazakhstan International Oil and Gas Exhibition in the first week of October: at this time many mid- and top-range hotels raise their prices, and getting a room at any price can prove difficult.

The regional museums housed in the capitals of every region in Kazakhstan make a fine introduction to the history, nature and economy of the area. But after visiting several of them you start to get the feeling that they have been put together on the basis of a centralised check list. To offer a sense of how similar these museums are to each other, I have devised the game of regional museum bingo. As you tour the museum, make a note when you see any of the following:

- A diorama of a prehistoric scene, featuring little model dinosaurs
- A stuffed wild boar
- A Bronze Age burial
- A portrait of Ablai Khan
- A yurt, or a section of yurt
- A rifle used during the 1916 rebellion led by Amangeldy Imanov
- A list of the Heroes of the Soviet Union from that region
- A Singer sewing machine
- One of the first issue tenge banknotes
- A photograph of President Nazarbaev visiting the region

If you see all ten, shout out 'bingo'. Bonus point if you spot them in the order set out above.

Specialist wildlife and fishing holidays all have their own seasons. For example, as regards fishing, the season for catfishing in the Ile Delta is May–June and September–October. Trout fishing in the Tian Shan is at its best between September and mid-November.

HIGHLIGHTS

Kazakhstan is a vast country. While there are fascinations to be found everywhere, the following are some of the highlights around which, depending on your interests, you may wish to build your trip.

ASTANA Kazakhstan's new capital is a gleaming city of dramatic and inventive architectural compositions rising up out of the central steppe. This place best demonstrates the post-independence achievements and ambitions of Kazakhstan, with its Norman Foster-designed pyramid to peace and harmony, a shark-filled oceanarium thousands of kilometres from the ocean, and the world's biggest tent, a structure complete with indoor waterfalls, an artificial beach and botanic gardens.

ALMATY The largest and most cosmopolitan city in the country, in a beautiful setting at the foot of the Tian Shan Mountains, Almaty has the best range of places to eat and the most vibrant nightlife in Kazakhstan, and it makes an excellent base for exploring the attractions of the wider region.

THE MOUNTAINS Rising from deciduous woodland packed with wild fruit trees, through pine, cedar or spruce forest, to upland meadows and then peaks fringed with glaciers, the mountain ranges on the southern and eastern borders of the country are great environments in which to trek, ride or simply just be. You can be up in the hills in a matter of minutes from the centre of Almaty, and truly beautiful spots such as the Big Almaty Lake are an easy day trip. For mountaineers, Khan Tengri, the beautiful pyramid-shaped peak which marks the highest point in Kazakhstan, offers an irresistible lure. While there are many great places to head for in the mountains, two personal recommendations are the Aksu Zhabagly Nature Reserve in South Kazakhstan (see page 353), where you can stay at some of the best-developed community-based tourism facilities in the country, and the Rachmanov Springs sanatorium (see page 237) high up in the Altai Mountains, where some believe that the legendary Buddhist kingdom of Shambala is to be found.

SITES ALONG THE SILK ROUTE A northern branch of the Silk Route ran for centuries across southern Kazakhstan, with the modern-day towns of Turkestan, Sayram and Taraz all prominent settlements. The architectural legacy of the civilisations which controlled this route includes some of the most beautiful buildings in the region, such as the carved terracotta tilework of the Karakhanid Mausoleum of Aisha Bibi outside Taraz and, above all, the Timurid Mausoleum of Khodja Ahmed Yassaui in Turkestan.

THE INTERIOR OF MANGISTAU REGION As yet receiving very few tourists, this remote area of Kazakhstan offers some stunning desert scenery, with isolated bluffs and white limestone escarpments, underground mosques, necropolises with intricately carved tombs, and the chance to join pilgrims making the long trip to the tomb of prominent Sufi Beket Ata. The regional capital Aktau, on the shores of the Caspian, is an ideal base for trips into the interior.

BAIKONUR Securing the necessary permissions to come here is time-consuming, but the cosmodrome of Baikonur is a fascinating living museum of the history of space exploration, the place from which the first artificial satellite, space dog Laika, Yuri Gagarin and the first space tourist all set off on their historic journeys. A visit here is an expensive but unforgettable one, especially if you can manage to get your trip to coincide with a launch.

THE STEPPE Like love, steppe is all around, at least across vast swathes of Kazakhstan, but it is such a central part of the national identity that you should ensure your programme includes some exposure to this great expanse of grassland, from where you will take memories of the scent of wormwood and circling flights of the steppe eagle. Places to head for include the lakes around Korgalzhyn, with their colony of pink flamingos, the Mausoleum of Abai and Shakarim near Semey, and one of the attractive areas of wooded granite hills, which stand as 'islands' in the steppe. Of these, Borovoye north of Astana is being heavily marketed as a tourist destination. Karkaraly, east of Karaganda, is a quieter alternative.

SUGGESTED ITINERARIES

Many visitors to Kazakhstan have just a few days to spare but, thanks to the concentration of sites in and around Almaty, and the reasonable provision of domestic flights, this shouldn't prevent you from seeing something of the country.

Starting in Almaty, a **weekend** is ample time to visit the city's Panfilov Park and wooden Holy Ascension Cathedral before spending the afternoon getting to know the locals (and doing some all-important souvenir shopping) at Green Bazaar or taking the waters at the Arasan Baths. Spend the evening watching a performance at the Abai Opera and Ballet Theatre before having a nightcap at one of the city's numerous pubs and bars. Rise early the next morning and go to Republic Square and the Independence Monument. Choose between the Central State Museum and the often overlooked Museum of Folk Musical Instruments of Kazakhstan for a strong introduction to Kazakhstan's past and culture. In the late afternoon take the cable car from the city centre to Kok-Tobe, making sure you get your photo taken with The Beatles, and enjoy a drink while you watch the sunset over Almaty.

If you are in Kazakhstan for **a week**, start with a few days in Almaty before heading out into the spectacular Ile Alatau National Park. If it's winter and you're a ski bunny, you'll probably get no further than Chimbulak and Medeu, but hikers should continue a little further to the Aksai Gorge and the unprepossessing village of Ungirtas, which some believe is the hub of the universe. Tamgaly, west of Almaty, is home to the most impressive collection of petroglyphs (ancient rock carvings) in Kazakhstan. There are over 4,000 examples dating from the Bronze Age to the present, and it is well worth spending a full day at this UNESCO World Heritage Site.

Two weeks will allow you to travel further afield without relying on flights. From Almaty travel west to the spectacular Aksu Canyon where the white-water Aksu River has carved 600m-deep channels up to 500m wide through the rock. You can travel by 4x4 or on foot and are guaranteed to see a wide variety of flora and bird life. Shymkent is famous only for its lead smelter and oil refinery, but it makes a convenient stopover point for Sayram, an ancient oasis inhabited by Nestorians and later overrun by Muslim forces and then again by Genghis Khan. Sections of the fortified walls remain, as do several mausoleums and the 15m-high Hisr Paygambar Minaret. Travelling north, stop at the tomb of Islamic mystic Arystan Bab before reaching the more famous site in Turkestan, where Bab's disciple Khodja Ahmed Yassaui is interred. His mausoleum is the finest work of Timurid architecture in Kazakhstan, and the neighbouring tombs and mosques have also been well restored. If you have the time and money to afford a permit, don't miss a trip to Baikonur. Sputnik, Yuri Gagarin and Dennis Tito, the world's first space tourist, all blasted into space from this empty stretch of Kazakh steppe. Modern rocket launches can still be seen from up to 1,000km away. Make your last major stop the remains of the Aral Sea. Aralsk (Aral town) is understandably bleak, but the ships in the desert make a poignant sight, as does the railway station mosaic commemorating local fishermen's efforts to fight famine in 1920s Russia. Return to Almaty from Kyzylorda, the former Kazakh capital with its attractive Russian Orthodox church, making sure you see the 9th-century caravanserai at Sauran before departing.

If you are lucky enough to have **three to four weeks** in Kazakhstan, you will have ample time to explore the country and may even consider trekking over the border to Kyrgyzstan to see the best of the Tian Shan Mountains. Consider hiring a car and, having done a trek in the breathtaking Charyn Canyon east of the city, drive north from Almaty to the 614km-long Lake Balkhash. Wild boar, wolves, pelicans and reed cats (*Felis chaus*) are all present in significant numbers, and the lake's shallow waters are a fisherman's dream. Continuing north, Karaganda provides an insight into more harrowing aspects of Kazakhstan's past: migrants and prisoners slaved here well into the 1950s, forced to exploit the region's mineral wealth. Their stories are told at the Karaganda Regional Historical Museum, and also by the industrial decay that litters the landscape. Break your journey with a few days of indulgence in Astana and marvel at the eccentric architecture of landmarks such as the Palace of Peace and Harmony, the Baiterek observation tower and, of course, Lord Foster's newly completed giant tent (the Khan Shatyr). Providing you are not agoraphobic, you should then work your way west through the central steppe, camping when weather permits to take in some serious stargazing. Keep your eyes peeled for the steppe eagles, marmots and Bactrian camels and head towards Aral, finishing your trip by completing the two-week itinerary in reverse.

TOUR OPERATORS

Given Kazakhstan's huge size, most tour operators in the country itself have a regional rather than nationwide focus. Kazakhstani tour operators are therefore listed in the relevant regional chapters of this guide. The list below covers a range of overseas operators with experience of working in Kazakhstan. An effort has been made to try and include companies covering different areas of specialism, from operators focused on wildlife tours to agencies concentrating on providing visa support and administrative arrangements for business travellers.

UK

Birdquest Two Jays, Kemple End, Stonyhurst, Lancs BB7 9QY; 01254 826317; f 01254 826317; e birders@birdquest.co.uk; www. birdquest.co.uk. Birdwatching specialists, whose 13-day 'Turkestan' programme in late May covers Almaty, the Ile River, Taukum Desert, Tian Shan Mountains, Astana & surrounding steppe areas. Target species include Pallas's sandgrouse & Mongolian finch in Almaty Region; demoiselle crane & black lark in Akmola Region.

Dragoman Overland Camp Green, Debenham, Stowmarket, Suffolk IP14 6LA; 01728 861133; f 01728 861127; e info@dragoman.co.uk; www. dragoman.com. Providing truck-based adventure holidays, they offer Kazakhstan as part of an 11-week 'Russia & Mongolia' overland programme from St Petersburg to Beijing. Destinations covered in Kazakhstan include the ship cemetery near Aralsk, Sauran, Turkestan, the Aksu Zhabagly Nature Reserve, Almaty, & the Tian Shan & Altai mountains.

Explore Worldwide Nelson Hse, 55 Victoria Rd, Farnborough, Hants GU14 7PA; 0845 013 1537; f 01252 391110; e res@explore.co.uk; www.explore.co.uk. This large operator has a couple of tours featuring Kazakhstan. The 'Heart of the Celestial Mountains' tour is a 16-day trek in the Tian Shan Mountains culminating at the foot of Khan Tengri. They also have a Central Asia Overland tour, crossing Kazakhstan on a journey between China & Uzbekistan.

Far Frontiers Ninestone, South Deal, Devon EX20 2PZ; 01837 840640; e info@ farfrontiers.com; www.farfrontiers.com. Tailored

itineraries. Programme suggestions include a 15-day 'highlights of Uzbekistan, Kyrgyzstan & Kazakhstan' tour.

Go Russia Boundary Hse Business Centre, Boston Rd, London W7 2QE; 020 3355 7717; e info@justgorussia.co.uk; www.justgorussia. co.uk. Cultural & sightseeing tours. Standard group trips & tailored holidays. Destinations covered in Kazakhstan can be combined with visits to Kyrgyzstan, Turkmenistan & Uzbekistan.

Greentours Leigh Cottage, Gauledge Lane, Longnor, Buxton, Derbys SK17 0PA; f 01298 83563; e enquiries@greentours. co.uk; www.greentours.co.uk. Natural history specialists. Their Kazakhstan programme includes a 17-day 'Dzhungarian Gate' tour from Ust-Kamenogorsk to Almaty via sites in East Kazakhstan & Almaty regions, a tour of similar length covering sites in the Tian Shan & Karatau mountains, & a spring tour to the Aksu Zhabagly Nature Reserve & Zailysky Alatau, focusing on wild tulips. Some of their tours include botanist Anna Ivaschenko, a renowned expert on the tulips of Kazakhstan.

GW Travel Denzell Hse, Denzell Gardens, Durham Rd, Altrincham WA14 4QF; 0161 928 9410; f 0161 941 6101; e sales@gwtravel.co.uk; www.gwtravel.co.uk. Specialists in luxury train tours, they offer a 21-day trip from Moscow to Beijing, using the *Golden Eagle Trans-Siberian Express* to the Chinese/Kazakh border, & the *Shangri La Express* in China.

KE Adventure Travel 32 Lake Rd, Keswick, Cumbria CA12 5DQ; 017687 73966; f 017687

74693; e info@keadventure.com; www.
keadventure.com. Offers the 'Ultimate Tien Shan'
trekking programme, from the Karkara River along
the South Inylchek Glacier to the South Inylchek
base camp, with a helicopter transfer back. They
also offer a Kazakhstan & Kyrgyzstan mountain-
biking programme, er, saddled with the label
'Mountain Mayhem', which involves biking from
the Turgen Gorge to the Karkara Valley, some helibiking, & then a trip into Kyrgyzstan.

Mountain Kingdoms 20 Long St, Wotton-
under-Edge, Glos GL12 7BT; 01453 844400;
f 01453 844422; e info@mountainkingdoms.
com; www.mountainkingdoms.com. Trekking
specialists, they offer a 19-day 'Celestial
Mountains Trek', which includes a crossing of
the Tian Shan Mountains from Almaty to Lake
Issyk Kul in Kyrgyzstan via the 3,990m Aksu Pass,
trekking along the Karkara River & a helicopter
flight to the South Inylchek Glacier base camp.
They also offer the 'Definitive Cultural Tour of
Central Asia', which isn't that, but is an interesting
19-day programme covering Almaty, Charyn
Canyon, Tamgaly Tas petroglyphs & a helicopter
flight to the base of Khan Tengri, as well as
destinations in Kyrgyzstan & Uzbekistan.

Naturetrek Cheriton Mill, Cheriton, Alresford,
Hants SO24 0NG; 01962 733051; f 01962
736426; e info@naturetrek.co.uk; www.
naturetrek.co.uk. Specialists in wildlife & botany
holidays, they offer a 16-day botany tour to the
Kazakh steppes & Tian Shan Mountains in April,
focusing on wild tulips, as well as a 2-week tour
to explore the alpine flora of the Tian Shan. They
also run birdwatching tours.

Regent Holidays Mezzanine Suite, Froomsgate
Hse, Rupert St, Bristol BS1 2QJ; 0845 277 3317;
f 0117 925 4866; e regent@regent-holidays.
co.uk; www.regent-holidays.co.uk. Offers tailored
programmes. Suggested itineraries include an

11-day 'Classic Kazakhstan' tour, covering Almaty,
Shymkent, Turkestan, Aksu Zhabagly, Taraz &
Astana, which promises an excellent introduction
to the country, as well as a 13-day Kazakhstan &
Kyrgyzstan programme, whose Kazakhstan leg
includes Almaty, the Big Almaty Lake, Tamgaly
Tas petroglyphs & Charyn Canyon.

Scott's Tours 141 Whitfield St, London W1T
5EW; 020 7383 5353; f 020 7383 3709;
e enquiries@scottstours.co.uk; www.scottstours.
co.uk. Specialising in the countries of the former
Soviet Union, they offer visa support, & flight &
accommodation bookings.

Silk Road and Beyond Unit 6, Hurlingham
Business Park, 55 Sulivan Rd, London SW6
3DU; 020 7371 3131; f 020 7751 0710;
e sales@silkroadandbeyond.co.uk; www.
silkroadandbeyond.co.uk. Offers tailor-made
itineraries that focus on culture, as well as
wilderness tours & trekking.

Steppes Travel 51 Castle St, Cirencester, Glos
GL7 1QD; 01285 880980; f 01285 885888; e
enquiry@steppestravel.co.uk; www.steppestravel.
co.uk. Specialises in tailored itineraries.

Sunbird Tours 26B The Market Sq, Potton,
Sandy, Beds SG19 2NP; 01767 262522; f 01767
262916; e sunbird@sunbirdtours.co.uk; www.
sunbirdtours.co.uk. Birdwatching specialists
who offer a 19-day 'Birding the Silk Road' tour,
which covers sites in Almaty Region in search
of such species as Himalayan griffons & Pallas's
sandgrouse, the Taukum Desert, where targets
include greater sand plovers & the Houbara
bustard, the Ile River, Tamgaly Tas petroglyphs,
the Tian Shan Mountains, overnighting in
the interesting setting of the astronomical
observatory, & the steppe lakes around Astana.
These central Asia trips are often led by the
company's managing director, who really is called
Steve Rooke.

USA

Mir Corporation Suite 210, 85 South
Washington St, Seattle, WA 98104; +1 206
624 7289; f +1 206 624 7360; e info@mircorp.
com; www.mircorp.com. Former Soviet Union
specialists, their programme includes a 21-day Silk
Road tour by private train, using the *Shangri La
Express* from Beijing to the Kazakh border, & the
Golden Eagle Trans-Siberian Express thereafter to
Moscow. They can also arrange tailored itineraries.

Red Star Travel Suite 102, 123 Queen Anne Av
North, Seattle, WA 98109; +1 206 522 5995;
f +1 206 522 6295; e travel@travel2russia.
com; www.travel2russia.com. Specialists in
travel to Russia & the former Soviet Union. They
provide visa support, accommodation & transport
bookings, & can arrange interpreters. They also
offer tours, including a 22-day 'Central Asian
Safari' which features Almaty.

Wings Suite 109, 1643 N Alvernon, Tucson, AZ 85712; +1 520 320 9868; f +1 520 320 9373; e wings@wingsbirds.com; www.wingsbirds.

com. Birdwatching specialists. They own the British company Sunbird Tours, & offer Sunbird's Kazakhstan programme (see above).

AUSTRALIA
Russian Passport Lvl 1, 12–14 Glenferrie Rd, Malvern 3144; +61 3 9500 0444; f +61 3 9509 0111; e passport@travelcentre.com. au; www.russia-rail.com. Part of the Passport

Travel agency, they offer tours, including a 22-day Beijing to Moscow programme by a mix of rail & road, as well as tailored itineraries with or without a guide.

CANADA
Bestway Tours Suite 206, 8678 Greenall Av, Burnaby, British Columbia V5J 3M6; +1 604 264 7378; f +1 604 264 7774; e bestway@ bestway.com; www.bestway.com. Offers several programmes incorporating Kazakhstan, including a 17-day tour covering the 5 central Asian republics, & a 21-day trip by private train from Beijing to Moscow, via Almaty. Also tailored itineraries.

Silk Road Tours 300–1497 Marine Drive, West Vancouver, British Columbia V7T 1B8; +1 604 925 3831; f +1 604 925 6269; e Canadian32@ gmail.com; www.silkroadtours.com. Iran specialists, though they also offer tailored programmes to Kazakhstan & the other central Asian republics.

GERMANY
Kasachstanreisen 134 Bizetstrasse, Berlin; +49 30 428 52005; e kasachstanreisen@aol. com; www.kasachstanreisen.de. Kazakhstan specialists, who offer visa support, administrative help for business travellers, & tailor-made itineraries.
Studiosus Reisen Postfach 50 60 09, D-80976 München; +49 89 500 600; f +49 89 500 60100; e tours@studiosus.com; www.studiosus. com. Features Kazakhstan as part of an 11-day

central Asia programme as well as a Silk Road tour from Almaty to Beijing.
Ventus Reisen 8 Krefelder Strasse, 10555 Berlin; +49 30 391 00332, +49 30 398 49641; f +49 30 399 5587; e office@ventus.com; www. ventus.com. Offers a 10-day trip starting & finishing in Almaty, covering the Turgen Gorge & Charyn Canyon as well as Bishkek & Lake Issyk Kul in Kyrgyzstan, & an 18-day Silk Road tour from Almaty to Beijing.

RED TAPE

Although there is still some red tape around, Kazakhstan's visa and registration requirements have eased considerably in recent years, and there has never been an easier time to visit the country. Note that rules change, and you are advised to check the latest position with your travel agent or Kazakhstan Embassy before preparing your application.

VISAS Single-entry tourist and business visas valid for one month can now be obtained without the need for a letter of invitation (LOI) for citizens of the following 45 countries: Australia, Austria, Belgium, Bulgaria, Canada, Croatia, Cyprus, Czech Republic, Denmark, Estonia, Finland, France, Germany, Greece, Hungary, Iceland, Ireland, Israel, Italy, Japan, Latvia, Liechtenstein, Lithuania, Luxembourg, Malaysia, Malta, Monaco, the Netherlands, New Zealand, Norway, Poland, Portugal, Romania, Saudi Arabia, Singapore, Slovakia, Slovenia, South Korea, Spain, the Sultanate of Oman, Sweden, Switzerland, the United Arab Emirates, the United Kingdom and the United States.

You will need to submit your passport, valid at least six months beyond the validity of the requested visa, and with at least one full empty page on which the visa can be affixed, a passport-sized photo, a letter (from yourself, or in the case of a business visa your company) setting out the purpose of your visit, and a completed application form. The last can be downloaded from the websites of Kazakhstani diplomatic missions overseas, or from the central Ministry of Foreign Affairs website (*www.mfa.kz*; look under 'Consular information'). Some Kazakhstani missions require you to apply in person; others will accept postal applications. The Kazakhstan Embassy in London has recently changed its rules and will no longer accept either postal or proxy applications.

If you need a visa valid for longer than one month, a multiple-entry visa, or you are a citizen of a country other than the 45 listed above as eligible for simplified procedures, you will need an LOI in order to secure a tourist or business visa. For tourist visas, LOIs can be obtained from licensed Kazakhstani tour operators, who will charge you a fee for this service. They apply to the Ministry of Foreign Affairs Consular Department, and will be given a registration number when the invitation letter is approved. They will then send you the LOI (the Kazakhstan Embassy in London confirms that they accept faxed copies in respect of both business and tourist visa applications), together with the registration number, and you submit these together with your application. For **business visas**, the procedures are broadly similar: the inviting organisation applies to the Ministry of Foreign Affairs Consular Department, and again gets a registration number. You should submit with your application a copy of this LOI, with the registration number, plus a letter from your company confirming the purpose of your visit to Kazakhstan. To minimise any risk that this might be rejected, it should be signed off by someone senior within the company (ideally at director level). If you are applying to come to Kazakhstan for more than three months, you will additionally need to provide a recent negative AIDS test certificate (it is recommended to check the current rules with the embassy in advance of taking any test).

Citizens of the 45 '**simplified procedure**' countries can theoretically also obtain one-month single-entry visas on their arrival in Kazakhstan if entering via Astana, Almaty, Atyrau, Uralsk and Ust-Kamenogorsk airport. But this can only be done with an LOI which has been submitted to the Ministry of Foreign Affairs Consular Department and given a registration number. If you are obtaining this through a local tour operator, they will send you a copy of the LOI, with the registration number, in advance of travel. You should then go to the visa counter at the airport on arrival. Please note that the registration number is essential: there have been cases in which British citizens, turning up with an 'invitation letter' from their Kazakhstani partner company that has not been properly submitted through the Ministry of Foreign Affairs, have been turned away on arrival in Kazakhstan. Airlines unfamiliar with the visa on arrival option may not want to let you board your flight to Kazakhstan, so ensure you have the correct documentation with you and be prepared to argue.

To get a **transit visa**, which can be of no more than five days' duration, you will need to present to the Kazakhstan diplomatic mission a visa valid for entry to the country to which you are headed after your transit in Kazakhstan, together with an air or rail ticket to that country. This can be obtained on arrival at an airport, but you will need to be persistent with the consular staff.

There is a huge variation in the cost of Kazakhstani visas, depending where you apply. At the time of writing, the fees levied by the Kazakhstan Embassy in London ranged from £15 for a transit visa and £26 for a one-month single-entry tourist visa to £250 for a two-year multiple-entry business visa.

On your arrival in Kazakhstan, you will need to fill out a migration card. These are usually doled out by aircraft cabin crews, but you can otherwise find them in the arrivals hall. It is stamped at the border, as is your passport. Keep the migration card safe with your passport: you will need to hand it in to the border guards on departure and may be fined if you lose it.

One rather awkward visa issue relates to those planning to trek or horseride across the Kazakh/Kyrgyz border, since you will have crossed the border without getting the usual stamp in your passport, which could create problems down the line. Several travel agencies run trips which involve remote border crossings; for example, a trek south from Almaty across the Tian Shan to Lake Issyk Kul, and a range of trekking, riding and cycling itineraries around the Karkara River and the foothills of Khan Tengri. You should take individual advice from the travel agency you are using (and cross-border trekking in these remote areas is certainly not an activity you should be attempting alone), but the general advice seems to be that, if your holiday involves a starting point in Kazakhstan, a remote crossing of the border into Kyrgyzstan, and then return into Kazakhstan by either a remote or road crossing, you should get a double-entry Kazakhstan visa and a single-entry Kyrgyzstan one in advance. These should have the same start date, which will allow you to demonstrate to the Kyrgyzstan authorities that you did not enter into Kyrgyzstan before the commencement of the validity of their visa. Depending on where the remote crossing takes place, travel agencies seem to have a range of approaches to try to get the appropriate visa stamps: for example, by travelling to the road crossing south of Karkara, or getting the Kyrgyzstan stamps at the regional office in Karakol.

There are reports that the governments of Kazakhstan and Kyrgyzstan have agreed a regime to provide for the reciprocal acceptance of tourist visas for travellers whose trips took them no further than the border regions of Almaty and Zhambyl regions in Kazakhstan, and Issyk Kul, Talas and Chuy regions in Kyrgyzstan. However, border officials and local embassy staff do not appear to have been informed of the changes, so tourists with the correct documentation may still be turned back from the border. The reciprocal arrangement does not apply to holders of business visas.

CERTIFIED COPIES Since the Kazakhstani police are entitled to carry out routine identity checks, it is recommended that visitors get certified photocopies of their passport photo and visa pages to take around with them for such occasions, to reduce the risks of theft, arbitrary confiscation or loss of the original passport if carried everywhere. While some diplomatic missions offer this service to its citizens for free (including, at the time of research, the US Embassy in Astana and its office in Almaty), others charge a fee. The police on the street may claim not to regard certified copies as acceptable, but if this situation does occur, visitors should request to be taken to the nearest police station, where the certified copy will be inspected and accepted.

REGISTRATION The previous rather irksome registration requirements have now been smoothed for most short-term visitors. Citizens of the 45 'simplified procedure' countries are usually registered automatically either when their visa is issued or when arriving at any Kazakhstani airport, by rail at the Dostyk border crossing with China, by sea at the ports of Aktau and Bautino, or at certain major land border crossings (according to the Ministry of Foreign Affairs website, at the time of research these were Khorgos, Dostyk, Bakhty, Maikapshagai, Kordai and Kolghat). A second stamp on your migration card indicates that you have been registered. The latest regulations suggest that citizens of all countries may now be registered on arrival at the border.

It is the responsibility of the visitor to check they have received this second stamp and, if not, request before leaving the border that it be added to the visa. Failure to do this will necessitate registering at the OVIR within five days or paying a €100 fine (sometimes negotiable) to be able to leave the country.

If you have not been registered, for example because you arrived into Kazakhstan via a minor land border post, or you are not sure whether you have been registered or not, you should register at the local office of OVIR, the Department of Migration Police, within five days of your arrival. You can either root out the OVIR office yourself, who will register you for free, or do this through a travel agent or many hotels, who will charge you a fee for the service. Registration is valid for three months: if you are staying longer, you will need to contact OVIR. Emigration officials may fine you on departure if you stay in Kazakhstan longer than five days without registering.

RESTRICTED AREAS Some areas of Kazakhstan are designated as restricted areas, requiring an additional permit. The most significant from the perspective of tourists are border zones with China and the Baikonur Cosmodrome. The former include parts of the Altai Mountains (including Rachmanov Springs and Lake Markakol), the Dzhungarsky Alatau (including Lepsinsk and the Kora Valley east of Tekeli) and the area around Khan Tengri. The travel agency organising your accommodation should be able to arrange the permit, but you do need to allow plenty of time. Applying at least one month in advance (or 40 days for Baikonur, where permission also needs to be sought from the Russian authorities), ideally more, is recommended.

CUSTOMS REGULATIONS This is another area where regulations have eased. Unless you are otherwise bringing in goods subject to customs duty, you do not actually need to fill out a customs declaration form (available in the airport arrivals hall) if you have less than US$3,000 of foreign currency with you. It can, however, be a good idea to declare on a customs declaration form any expensive items of computer and photographic equipment etc, especially if they look new, to avoid the risk that you may be asked to pay duty on these items on departure. If for any reason you are bringing in Kazakh tenge, you should also declare this on arrival, as you are not allowed to export on departure more than the amount declared on entry to the country. At the time of research, the various duty-free importation limits for adults included two litres of alcohol and a 'reasonable quantity' of perfume for personal use. The IATA Travel Centre website (*www.iatatravelcentre.com*) is one source of information for enquiries about duty-free rules. Note though that Kazakhstani customs regulations have been subject to quite frequent change, and their official website (*www.customs.kz*), though it does have information in English, is not really geared to the individual traveller with questions about duty-free limits.

There are restrictions on the export of antiquities, artworks, carpets, furs and jewellery. For instance, antiquities cannot be exported without a special permit from the Ministry of Culture and Information. If you do buy an item such as a painting, you should keep the purchase receipt as evidence that it is not an antique. The rules in this area are complex, and you should seek specialist advice before making any serious purchases. If you are bringing such items into Kazakhstan (for example, artworks purchased in one of the neighbouring republics), you should declare these on a customs declaration form to avoid any problems when you take them out on departure.

E EMBASSIES

ABROAD The following is a selective list of Kazakhstan's diplomatic missions overseas. There is a full list of every embassy and consulate on the website of the Kazakhstan Ministry of Foreign Affairs (*www.mfa.kz*; click on 'Ministry', then 'Diplomatic missions abroad').

Austria 23 Felix Mottl Strasse, A-1190 Vienna; +43 1 367 6657; e embassy@kazakhstan.at

Azerbaijan H Aliyeva, District 15, h. 8, 10 Baku; +994 12 465 6247; f +994 12 465 6249; e embassyk@azdata.net

Belgium 30 Av Van Bever, 1180 Brussels; +32 2 374 9562; f +32 2 374 5091; e kazakhstan.embassy@swing.be; www.kazakhstanembassy.be

Canada 56 Hawthorne Av, Ottawa, Ontario K1S 0B1; +1 613 88 3705; f +1 613 788 3702; e kazakhembassy@gmail.com; www.kazembassy.ca

China 9 Dong Liu Jie, San Li Tun, Beijing 100600; +86 10 653 22550; f +86 10 653 26183; e kz@kazembchina.org; www.kazembchina.org; also *Ürümqi Passport and Visa Office:* 31 Kunming Rd, Ürümqi; +86 991 381 5857; f +86 991 382 1203; e pvs_mid@yahoo.cn. There are also consulates-general in Hong Kong & Shanghai.

Czech Republic 12 Ul Romaina Rolanda, 16000 Prague 6; +42 0 233 375643; f +42 0 233 375642; e kzembas@bon.cz; www.kazembassy.cz

France 59 Rue Pierre Charron, 75008 Paris; +33 1 45 61 52 06; f +33 1 45 61 52 01; e office@amb-kazakhstan.fr; www.amb-kazakhstan.fr

Germany 14–17 Nordendstrasse, D-13156 Berlin; +49 30 470 07111; f +49 30 470 07125; e info@botschaft-kz.de; www.botschaft-kasachstan.de; also *Frankfurt Consulate-General:* 17 Beethoven Strasse, 60325 Frankfurt am Main; +49 69 971 46731; f +49 69 971 46818; e info.kaz@genconsul.de. There are also consulates or embassy offices in Bonn, Hanover & Munich.

Hungary 59 Kapy U, Budapest 1025; +36 1 275 1300; f +36 1 275 2092; e kazak@axelero.hu

India 61 Poorvi Marg, Vasant Vihar, New Delhi 110057; +91 11 460 07710; f +91 11 460 07701; e info@kazembassy.in; www.kazind.com

Iran 4 North Hedayat St, corner of Masjed Alley, Darrus, Tehran; +98 21 256 5933; f +98 21 254 6400; e iran@asdc.kz; www.kazembassy-iran.org

Italy 471 Via Cassia, 00189 Rome; +39 06 363 01130; f +39 06 362 92675; e kazakhstan.emb@agora.it; www.embkaz.it

Japan 9–8 Himonya 5-chome, Meguroku, Tokyo 152-0003; +81 3 379 15273; f +81 3 379 15279; e jpdiplomemb@gmail.com; www.embkazjp.org

Kyrgyzstan 95-A Mira Prospekt, Bishkek; +996 312 662101; f +996 312 692094; e embassy.kg@mfa.kz; www.kaz-emb.kg

Lithuania 20A/35 Birutes, 08117 Vilnius-4; +370 5 212 2123; f +370 5 231 3580; e kazemb@iti.lt; www.kazembassy.lt

Mongolia 31/6 Zaisan St, 1 khoroo, Khan-Uul District, 'Twin' town, Ulaanbaatar; +97 611 345408; f +97 611341707; e info@kazembassy.mn

Netherlands 69 Nieuwe Parklaan, 2597 LB The Hague; +31 70 427 2220; f +31 70 365 7600; e kazachstan-consul@planet.nl

Pakistan Hse 11, St 45, F-8/1, Islamabad; +92 51 226 2926; f +92 51 226 2806; e embkaz@comsats.net.pk

Poland 14 Ul Królowej Marysieńki, 02954 Warsaw; +48 22 642 2763; f +48 22 642 3427; e kazdipmis@hot.pl; www.kazakhstan.pl

Russia 3A Chistoprudny Bulvar, 01000 Moscow; +7 495 927 1701; f +7 495 608 1549; e moscow@kazembassy.ru; www.kazembassy.ru; also *St Petersburg Consulate-General:* 15 Vilenskiy, Liter A, St Petersburg; +7 812 335 2546; e kazconspb@mail.ru; www.kazconsulate.spb.ru; *Astrakhan Consulate:* 2B Ulitsa Aquarelnaya, 414056, Astrakhan; +7 8512 610007; f +7 8512 251885; e consulrk@astranet.ru; *Omsk Consulate:* 9 Ulitsa Valikhanova, Omsk; +7 3812 325205; e kzconsul@omskcity.com

Spain C/Sotillo, 10 Parque Conde de Orgaz, 28043 Madrid; +34 91 721 6290; f +34 91 721 9374; e embajada@kazesp.org; www.kazesp.org

Tajikistan 31/1 Husein Zoda, Dushanbe; +992 37 221 8940; f +992 37 251 0108; e dipmiskz7@tajnet.com

Turkey 066450 Kilik Ali Sokak No 6, Or-An Diplomatik Sitesi Cankaya, Ankara; +90 312 491 9100; f +90 312 490 4455; e kazank@kazakhstan.org.tr; www.kazakhstan-embassy.org.tr; also *Istanbul Consulate:* Florya Caddesi, No 62 Senlikkoy, Florya, Istanbul; +90 212

2

662 5347; f +90 212 662 5349; e consulkist@
superonline.com
Turkmenistan Hse 13, 11 Garashsyzlik,
744036 Ashgabat; +993 12 480468; f +993 12
480475; e emb@kaztm.info
Ukraine 26 Melnikova, 01901 Kiev; +380 44
489 1858; f +380 44 483 1198; e post@kazakh.
kiev.ua; www.kazembassy.com.ua
United Kingdom 33 Thurloe St, London
SW7 2SD; 020 7581 4646; f 020 7584
8481; e london@kazembassy.org.uk; www.
kazakhstanembassy.org.uk; also *Aberdeen
Consulate:* 10 North Silver St, Aberdeen AB10 1RL;
01224 611923; f 01224 622465;

e kazcon@btconnect.com. At the time of writing
the Aberdeen Consulate was closed until further
notice.
United States 1401 16th St NW, Washington,
DC 20036; +1 202 232 5488; f +1 202 232
5845; e washington@kazakhembus.com; www.
kazakhembus.com; also *New York Consulate:* 535
Fifth Av, 19 Floor, New York 10017; +1 646 370
6331; f +1 646 370 6334; e kzconsulny@un.int;
www.kazconsulny.org
Uzbekistan 23 Chekhov St, 70015 Tashkent;
+998 71 1390986; f +998 71 1521650;
e info@kazembassy.uz

IN KAZAKHSTAN The situation as regards diplomatic representation in Kazakhstan is in considerable flux, with embassies continuing to make the move between the previous capital, Almaty, and the new one, Astana. Because Almaty remains the largest city in Kazakhstan, and an important business and financial centre, many missions have retained representation here. Thus, as regards the United Kingdom, the embassy itself is now located in Astana, but consular and visa work for Kazakhstan is undertaken at the Embassy Office in Almaty. The following is a selective list of embassies in Kazakhstan at the time of research. There is a full list on the website of the Kazakhstan Ministry of Foreign Affairs (*www.mfa.kz*), though this is not kept continuously up to date.

Australia 174B Furmanov St, 3rd Floor, Almaty;
7272 615160; e ahc.kaz@gmail.com; www.
russia.embassy.gov.au
Azerbaijan B-6 Diplomatic Complex, Astana;
7172 241581; f 7172 241532; e astana@
azembassy.kz; www.azembassy.kz; also *Aktau
Consulate:* 4 Microdistrict, 12 Aktau; 7292 336706
Belgium 3rd Floor, 62 Kosmonavtov St, Chubary
District, Astana; 7172 974485; f 7172 977849;
e embassy.astana@diplobel.fed.be; also *Almaty
Consulate:* 117/86 Kazybek Bi St, Almaty; 727
2606863; e belconsul@nursat.kz
Bulgaria Isker Business Centre, 15 Saryarka St,
Astana; 7172 901515; f 7172 901819;
e astanabulemb@mail.bg
Canada 34 Karasai Batyr St, Almaty; 727 250
1151; f 727 258 2493; e almat@international.
gc.ca; also *Astana Office:* 6 Saryarka St, Astana;
7172 793064
China 28 Kabanbai Batyr St, Astana; 7172
793561; f 7172 793565; also *Almaty Office:* 12
Baitasov St, Almaty; 727 270 0221; f 727 291 9902
Czech Republic 13th Floor, Arman Business
Centre, 6 Saryarka Av, Astana; /f 7172 990142;
e astana@embassy.mzv.cz

France 62 Kosmonavtov St, Chubary District,
Astana; 7172 795100; f 7172 795101; www.
ambafrance-kz.kz; also *Almaty Office:* 173
Furmanov St, Almaty; 727 258 2504; f 727 258
2509; e ambafrance@mail.kz
Germany 62 Kosmonavtov St, Chubary District,
Astana; 7172 791200; f 7172 791213; www.
astana.diplo.de; also *Almaty Office:* 173 Furmanov
St, Almaty; 727 250 6155; f 727 272 0499;
www.almaty.diplo.de
Greece 109 Karaotkel, 2 Microdistrict, Astana;
7172 241266; f 7172 244776; e gremb.ast@
mfa.gr
Hungary 9th Floor, 62 Kosmonavtov St, Astana;
7172 550323; f 7172 550324; e mission.ast@
kum.hu; also *General Consulate in Almaty:* 4
Musabaev St, Almaty; 727 255 1308; f 727 258
1837; e mission.ala@kum.hu
India 5th Floor, Kaskad Business Centre, 6/1
Kabanbai Batyr St, Astana; 7172 925700;
f 7172 925715; e hoc.astana@mea.gov.in; also
Almaty Office: 71 Maulenov St, Almaty; 727 278
4455; f 727 278 4685; e cons.almaty@mea.gov.in
Iran 31–33 Lugansky St, Almaty; 727 292
5055; f 727 254 2754; also *Astana Office:* B-7

Diplomatic Complex, Astana; ✆7172 242511; f 7172 241537; e iranembassy@itte.kz

Italy 2nd Floor, 62 Kosmonavtov St, Chubary District, Astana; ✆7172 243390; f 7172 243686; e ambasciata.astana@esteri.it

Japan 5th Floor, 62 Kosmonavtov St, Chubary District, Astana; ✆7172 977843; f 7172 977842; e kobun@null.kz; www.kz.emb-japan.go.jp/jp; also *Almaty Office:* 3rd Floor, 41 Kazybek Bi St; ✆727 298 0600; f 727 298 0601

Kyrgyzstan B-5 Diplomatic Complex, Astana; ✆7172 242024; f 7172 242412; e kr@mail. online.kz; also *Almaty Consulate-General:* 30A Lugansky St, Almaty; ✆727 264 2212; f 727 264 2211; e gen.consul.kz@mail.ru

Latvia Office 122, 12th Floor, 6/1 Kabanbai Batyr Av, Astana; ✆7172 925317; f 7172 925319; e embassy.kazakhstan@mfa.gov.lv; also *Almaty Consulate:* Room 544, 15 Republic Sq, Almaty; ✆727 267 2508; f 727 250 6549; e consulate. kazakhstan@mfa.gov.lv

Lithuania 15 Iskanderov St, Gorny Gigant, Almaty; ✆727 263 1040; f 727 263 1975; e Amb. kz@urm.lt; www.kz.mfa.lt

Mongolia 1 Musabayev St, Almaty; ✆727 269 3536; f 727 258 1727; e info@mongemb.kz

Netherlands 3rd Floor, 62 Kosmonavtov St, Chubary District, Astana; ✆7172 555450; f 7172 555474; e ast@minbuza.nl; www.netherlands-embassy.kz; also *Almaty Office:* 103 Nauryzbai Batyr St, Almaty; ✆727 250 3773; f 727 266 2415; e alm@minbuza.nl

Pakistan 25 Tulebaev St, Almaty; ✆727 273 3548; f 727 273 1300; e parepalmaty@hotmail. com

Poland 6th Floor, Isker Business Centre, 15 Saryarka St, Astana; ✆7172 901011; f 7172 901012; e joanna.jessa@poland.kz; also *Almaty Office:* 9 Zharkentskaya St, Gorny Gigant, Almaty; ✆727 258 1617; f 727 258 1550; e ambpol@ poland.kz

Romania 97 Pushkin St, Almaty; ✆727 261 5772; f 727 258 8317; e ambro@nursat.kz

Russia 4 Baraev St, Astana; ✆7172 221714; f 7172 332209; e rfekz@yandex.ru; www. rfembassy.kz; *Almaty Consulate-General:* 4 Jandosov St, Almaty; ✆727 274 5087; f 727 274 7168; also *Uralsk Consulate:* 78 Oktyabrskaya St; ✆7112 511626; f 7112 242486

Slovak Republic 5 Karaotkel Microdistrict, Astana; ✆7172 241191; f 7172 242048; e zuastana@post.sk

Spain Apt 25, 47 Kenesary St, Astana; ✆7172 201355; f 7172 200317; e emb.astana@mae.es

Tajikistan 15 Marsovaya St, Astana; ✆/f 7172 240929; e embassy_tajic@mbox.kz; also *Almaty Office:* 16 Sanatornaya St, Baganashyl, Almaty; ✆/f 727 269 7059; e tajemb_almaty@ok.kz

Turkey Office 23, 6/1 Kabanbay Batyr St, Astana; ✆7172 925870; f 7172 925874; e astanaturk@gmail.com; also *Almaty Office:* 29 Tole Bi St, Almaty; ✆727 291 3932; f 727 250 6208; e almatyturk@kaznet.kz

Turkmenistan 8/1 Otyrar St Astana; ✆7172 210882; f 7172 210823; e tm_emb@at.kz; also *Almaty Consulate:* 1st Floor, 76/109 Abai Av, Almaty; ✆/f 727 250 9604

Ukraine 57 Auezov St, Astana; ✆7172 217456; f 7172 326811; e embassy_ua@kepter.kz; also *Almaty Consulate-General:* 208 Tchaikovsky St, Almaty; ✆727 262 7073; f 727 269 4062; e gencon_ua@nursat.kz

United Kingdom 6th Floor, 62 Kosmonavtov St, Chubary District, Astana; ✆7172 556200; f 7172 556211; e britishembassy@mail.online. kz; www.ukinkz.fco.gov.uk; also *Almaty Office:* 9th Floor, Samal Towers, 97 Zholdasbekov St, Almaty; ✆727 250 6191; f 727 250 7962; e AlmatyVisaGeneral@fco.gov.uk

United States Bldg 3, St 23–22, Ak Bulak 4, Astana; ✆7172 702100; f 7172 340890; e info@ usembassy.kz; www.usembassy.kz; also *Almaty Office:* 17th Floor, Samal Towers, 97 Zholdasbekov St, Almaty; ✆727 250 4802; f 727 250 4867; e USAKZ@state.gov

Uzbekistan 36 Baribaev St, Almaty; ✆727 291 7886; f 727 291 1055; e emb-uzbekistan@mail.ru

GETTING THERE AND AWAY

BY AIR The easiest way to get to Kazakhstan from western Europe is by air. Almaty and Astana are the two major international airports and both offer modern terminals (a new passenger terminal recently opened in Almaty). Astana airport is the less busy of the two, and many visitors rate it as providing a smoother passage into the country. From London, there are flights to Almaty on Air Astana and British Midland. Other airlines serving Kazakhstan from Europe include Lufthansa, KLM, Austrian Airlines, Air Baltic and Turkish Airlines. There are flights from Frankfurt, Hanover, Istanbul, Amsterdam (to Almaty only) and Vienna (to Astana only). There are as yet no direct flights to Kazakhstan from North America, so you will need to route through one of the European hubs. For travellers seeking connections from Australia or New Zealand, Air Astana's routes to Bangkok, Delhi, Beijing or Dubai, or Seoul (served by both Air Astana and Asiana) or Etihad's routings via the Middle East are probably the most helpful.

There are also some international services to western parts of Kazakhstan, and it is worth remembering that the flight from Almaty to Atyrau takes around three hours, that from Astana to Atyrau around two-and-a-half, so if you are coming from western Europe, flying direct cuts an appreciable amount off your journey time. Air Astana serves Atyrau from both Amsterdam and Istanbul, and it is possible to fly to Aktau via Baku in Azerbaijan, connecting with either the Scat or Air Azal services to the Kazakhstani city.

Another possible routing from western Europe to Kazakhstan which may be worth investigating is via Russia. There are two potential advantages here. One is that there are flights from Moscow to a range of regional airports in Kazakhstan, with companies such as Transaero, so if your destination is not Astana, Almaty or Atyrau, you may find that a routing through Moscow is more convenient. Another is cost. But there are some potential downsides too. If you are transiting through Moscow, please note that the city's various airports are located some distance from each other: arrival at Sheremetevo airport and departure from Domodedovo in particular requires a lengthy transfer. You will also need to check whether your flight arrangements necessitate getting a Russian transit visa. Given uncertainties about maintenance procedures on some aircraft used for regional flights, if your proposed routing involves an unfamiliar airline you may wish to check whether the carrier is listed among those airlines subject to an operating ban within the European Community. The list is available at www.air-ban.europa.eu.

Connections within central Asia are not extensive, but you can fly from Almaty to Ashgabat, Bishkek, Dushanbe and Tashkent, as well as to Ürümqi in western China, and there are also connections from Astana to Tashkent and Ürümqi. There are services from Almaty, Astana, Atyrau and Aktau to destinations in the south Caucasus.

Contact details of all airlines serving Kazakhstan are set out in the *Getting there and around* sections of the relevant cities in Part Two of this guide. There is no airport tax payable on departure in Kazakhstan.

BY RAIL There is a range of railway connections between Kazakhstan and Russia, and some services to destinations in Ukraine. The most useful service is probably the 'fast' (though this is relative) train which runs every two days between Moscow and Almaty. It is known as Train 8 in the Almaty direction, Train 7 in the Moscow one, or alternatively as *The Kazakhstan*. It takes more than three full days (you depart Moscow in the late evening of day one, arriving in Almaty in the early morning of day five), and offers a choice of *lyux* (two-berth sleepers), *kupe* (four-berth sleepers) or *platzkart* (bunks in an open compartment) accommodation, plus a restaurant car. At the time of writing, the cost of a ticket ranged from T23,700 (around US$160) for a basic *platzkart*, to T75,000 (over US$500) for a *lyux*. From Almaty there are other services to the central Russian cities of Novosibirsk, Sverdlovsk and Novokuznetsk, as well as Simferopol in the Crimea. From Astana you can take a train to Moscow, St Petersburg, Kiev, Sverdlovsk, Omsk and Novokuznetsk. Kazakhstan Temir Zholy, the state railway company, announced that with effect from Christmas Day 2007 it was possible once a week to travel from Astana to Berlin in the same railway carriage. The pros and cons of rail travel in this part of the world are set out in the *Getting around* section of this chapter (see page 48). Locomotion is certainly not fast, and you are advised to check the timetable carefully to ensure you do not choose a particularly somnolent option. The extent to which you enjoy the experience is likely to depend heavily on the fellow passengers you find yourself sharing a compartment with, and the volume of vodka you are happy to share with them.

One routing being billed as a southerly alternative to the Trans-Siberian Railway is the 'Silk Route' to China, from Moscow to Beijing via Almaty and Ürümqi. A number of operators (see *Tour operators*, page 27) run tours along this route using private trains, aimed at the luxury end of the travel market, but you can travel the route on ordinary trains, starting with Train 8 from Moscow to Almaty. From Almaty there is a twice-weekly service, the Zhibek Zholy, to Ürümqi in western China, leaving late in the evening of day one, arriving early in the morning on day three. Since China uses a standard gauge of 1.435m, and Kazakhstan uses the broad gauge of 1.52m found across the former Soviet Union, there is a long wait at the Dostyk border crossing while the bogies are changed. You have a choice of soft class (four-berth sleepers) or hard class (bunks in an open compartment). From Ürümqi there is a daily train to Beijing.

As regards rail services south to Uzbekistan, the main route is that of the Tsarist-era Orenburg–Tashkent railway, which runs through Aktobe and Kyzylorda. There are services on this route to Tashkent from Moscow, Chelyabinsk, Ufa and Kharkov. To join this line from Almaty, change at Arys. There is also a weekly train from Almaty to Nukus in Uzbekistan, and a more westerly railway line into Uzbekistan, which runs into the western region of Karakalpakstan. A twice-weekly service from Saratov to Tashkent uses this line, which passes through Atyrau in western Kazakhstan and Samarkand in Uzbekistan. There are also trains terminating in Bishkek in Kyrgyzstan but, unless for the love of the train, it doesn't make sense to travel by rail from Almaty to Bishkek, since the routing is so circuitous that the journey is much quicker by road.

The general advice applicable to all trains in Kazakhstan, to buy your tickets well in advance, is even more necessary in the case of international trains. The Almaty–Moscow and Almaty–Ürümqi services both have a reputation for booking up quickly.

BY ROAD There are numerous bus services between cities in northern Kazakhstan and various Russian cities. Some examples are given under individual city entries in Part Two of this guide. But before shelling out for that bus ticket from Aktobe to St Petersburg, do bear in mind that long bus journeys, even in the 'luxury' coaches which have started to appear on some routes, can be decidedly cramped and uncomfortable. At least in trains you can walk around. Driver fatigue can also be an issue. There are many crossing points between Kazakhstan and Russia along their lengthy land border: the best advice for those travelling under their own steam at these, and indeed at other land border crossings around Kazakhstan, is to arrive early in the day and be patient. Note that most border crossings are not open at night, although the crossing on the M32 north of Uralsk is a notable exception.

The main road crossing of the border with China is at Khorgos, east of Zharkent in Almaty Region. There is a bus most days from the Sairan bus station in Almaty to Ürümqi. There are also crossings further north, at Bakhty and Maikapshagai in East Kazakhstan, which may be of interest if you are travelling Chinawards from Ust-Kamenogorsk. As regards Kyrgyzstan, the major border crossing is at Kordai, on the upgraded Almaty to Bishkek road. Buses depart for Bishkek from the Sairan bus station in Almaty, and in summer there are also departures for the popular resort area of Lake Issyk Kul. The border crossing at Kordai is usually fairly straightforward, as is the crossing further west between Taraz and Bishkek, served by *marshrutkas*. There is another, summer-only, crossing further east, at the Karkara Valley, which makes for a particularly scenic way to get from Kazakhstan to Karakol and the eastern part of Lake Issyk Kul, though note that there is no public transport beyond Kegen in Kazakhstan, around 30km short of the border.

As regards the border with Uzbekistan, the main road crossing is at Chernyaevka, on the main road between Shymkent and Tashkent. Plenty of public transport heads in this direction from Shymkent. Tashkent is only a few kilometres over the border, which is open 24 hours a day. In the event that Chernyaevka is closed, there is another crossing approximately 40km southwest near Abay that is used predominantly by lorries. There are two decidedly remote road crossings much further west, serving Mangistau Region. One of these runs southeast of Beyneu, alongside the railway, into Karakalpakstan in Uzbekistan. The other runs south of Zhanaozen, along the east coast of the Caspian, into Turkmenistan, taking you to the port of Turkmenbashi. These options require both pre-planning and for you to either have or hire your own transport.

BY SEA There is a ferry every few days across the Caspian from Baku to Aktau, but it doesn't run to a fixed timetable. You may have to wait up to a week for a boat as one will only leave when its cargo deck is full. The crossing usually takes 16–20 hours (though two to three days is not uncommon on older boats or in bad weather) and the price, negotiable at your point of departure, is US$100–120 per person. You will need to bring your own food on board and may be expected to pay extra for a cabin. If you are travelling to Baku, you will require a visa before leaving Kazakhstan as they are not available on arrival.

+ HEALTH   *with Dr Felicity Nicholson*

BEFORE YOU GO You should seek up-to-date advice in good time (at least two months) before your departure from your general practitioner, or a specialised travel clinic such as those in the following list. It is recommended that you are up to date with all your primary courses and boosters including diphtheria, tetanus and polio – now given as the all-in-one vaccine (Revaxis) which lasts for ten years. Hepatitis A vaccine is also recommended and can be given even close to the time of departure. One dose will protect for a year and a booster dose given at least six months later will extend coverage for 25 years. This vaccine may be available on the NHS. Additional immunisations to be considered, depending on how long you will be staying in Kazakhstan and your intended activities and lifestyle, include hepatitis B, rabies and tick-borne encephalitis. Vaccination against typhoid may also be advised for those travelling to more rural areas, particularly where there may be difficulty in ensuring safe food and water supplies.

Hepatitis B is recommended for those working in a medical setting or with children. The vaccine schedule comprises three doses which ideally should be given over a six-month period. If time is short then it can be given at zero, one and two months or for those aged 16 or over using Engerix B it can be given over a minimum of 21 days. Both these more rapid courses need to be boosted after a year.

Rabies is present throughout the country, but is usually easy to avoid unless you are working with animals. A rabies vaccine may also be advisable if you plan to be 24 hours or more from reliable sources of treatment. Like hepatitis B, rabies vaccine comprises three doses and can be given over a minimum of 21 days (see *In Kazakhstan*, below).

Tick-borne encephalitis is a viral infection spread by infected ticks and is more common between April and September. If you intend to go trekking in forested areas during these months, then it would be wise to get immunised. In the Tian Shan Mountains around Almaty, tick-borne encephalitis appears to be a particular risk from April to June. The vaccine is not readily available in the UK, but can be obtained on a named-patient basis from some travel clinics. However, even if you are unable to get the vaccine there are some sensible precautions you can take, as there are for other tick-borne diseases such as Crimean-Congo haemorrhagic fever.

Make sure that you wear a hat, long-sleeved tops and trousers tucked into socks and boots. Use a tick repellent and always check for ticks at the end of the day, not forgetting the head, in particular behind the ears of children. Ticks should ideally be removed as soon as possible, as leaving ticks on the body increases the chance of infection. They should be removed with special tick tweezers that can be bought in good travel shops. Failing that you can use your fingernails by grasping the tick as close to your body as possible and pulling steadily and firmly away at right angles to your skin. The tick will then come away complete as long as you do not jerk or twist. If possible douse the wound with alcohol (any spirit will do) or iodine. Irritants (eg: Olbas oil) or lit cigarettes are to be discouraged since they can cause the ticks to regurgitate and therefore increase the risk of disease. An area of spreading redness around the bite site, or a rash or fever coming on a few days or more after the bite, should stimulate a trip to the doctor. Malaria is not a problem in Kazakhstan.

While pharmacies in Kazakhstan, especially in the main cities, are increasingly well equipped, it would be worth packing one or two basic medicines, such as oral rehydration salts. You should ensure too that your travel insurance covers you for medical expenses, including for possible medical evacuation.

IN KAZAKHSTAN Diarrhoeal diseases and other gastrointestinal infections are fairly common, especially during the summer months. You should ensure that you observe good hygiene practices, such as handwashing, using bottled water, including for cleaning teeth, and avoiding foods which commonly cause problems, such as poorly washed salads, and ice cream and seafood of doubtful provenance. Treat these infections with plenty of fluids, adding oral rehydration salts, and rest. You should consult a doctor as soon as possible if the diarrhoea is accompanied by blood or mucus, or by a high fever, or if it persists for longer than three days. Unpasteurised milk and dairy products should be avoided, not least because diseases such as brucellosis are present in Kazakhstan. It is best to steer clear of freshwater fish in northern Kazakhstan, or at least ensure that it is well cooked, because of the presence of the parasite opisthorchiasis, or cat liver fluke, in the fish of some rivers in this area.

Rabies is present in Kazakhstan, so you should avoid contact with unfamiliar animals. Any animal bite, scratch or a lick over an open wound should be thoroughly cleaned with plenty of soap and water. Apply an antiseptic and seek immediate medical advice as soon as possible as regards post-exposure treatment, whether or not you have had the pre-exposure immunisation. If you have had all three pre-exposure doses of vaccine then you will not need the expensive and often hard-to-come-by rabies immunoglobulin. So if you are going to be away from the main cities it is wise to be vaccinated before you go (see *Before you go*, page 38).

Guard against the risks of snakebite, for example by not turning over stones or exploring crevices in archaeological sites, and avoiding walking after dark in the countryside,

If you are bitten, you are unlikely to have received venom; keeping this fact in mind may help you to stay calm. Many so-called first-aid techniques do more harm than good: cutting into the wound is harmful; tourniquets are dangerous; suction and electrical inactivation devices do not work. The only treatment is antivenom. In case of a bite that you fear may have been from a venomous snake:

- Try to keep calm – it is likely that no venom has been dispensed.
- Prevent movement of the bitten limb by applying a splint.
- Keep the bitten limb BELOW heart height to slow the spread of any venom.
- If you have a crêpe bandage, wrap it around the whole limb (eg: all the way from the toes to the thigh), as tight as you would for a sprained ankle or a muscle pull.

And remember:

- NEVER give aspirin; you may take paracetamol, which is safe.
- NEVER cut or suck the wound.
- DO NOT apply ice packs.
- DO NOT apply potassium permanganate.

Seek medical help promptly by evacuating to the nearest hospital that may have antivenom.

If spending time in Kazakhstan's high mountains, you should take the usual precautions appropriate to this kind of environment. This includes protecting yourself against the effects of the sun, being prepared for sudden changes in the weather (including by taking spare clothing with you), wearing good hiking boots with adequate ankle support, and being alert to the risks of avalanches, especially in the spring. It is also important to be aware of the possibility of altitude sickness: symptoms include headache, nausea and confusion, and these can herald the onset of serious altitude-related illnesses. Descend to a lower altitude if anyone in your group appears to be starting to experience these symptoms.

Take care in winter when walking on icy pavements. You should wear good rubber-soled boots. One of the several available brands of patented spiked or metal-coiled devices worn over shoes can be helpful in particularly slippery conditions, if you don't mind the bemused stares of the locals when you put them on or take them off. One brand called Yaktrax (*www.yaktrax.com*) is particularly popular among the expatriate community.

Sexually transmitted diseases (STDs) are widespread, including syphilis, gonorrhea, chlamydia and hepatitis B and C. Numbers infected with HIV in Kazakhstan have been growing rapidly in recent years and most sufferers are unaware they carry the disease. You should engage only in safe sexual practices.

TRAVEL CLINICS AND HEALTH INFORMATION A full list of current travel clinic websites worldwide is available from the International Society of Travel Medicine on www.istm.org. For journey preparation information, consult www.tripprep.com. Information about various medications may be found on www.emedicine.com.

United Kingdom

Berkeley Travel Clinic 32 Berkeley St, London W1J 8EL (near Green Park tube station); 020 7629 6233

Cambridge Travel Clinic 41 Hills Rd, Cambridge CB2 1NT; 01223 367362; e enquiries@travelclinic.ltd.uk; www.travelclinic.ltd.uk; 10.00–16.00 Mon–Tue & Sat, 12.00–19.00 Wed–Thu, 11.00–18.00 Fri. Clinic also in Ipswich.

Edinburgh Travel Health Clinic 14 East Preston St, Newington, Edinburgh EH8 9QA; 0131 667 1030; www. edinburghtravelhealthclinic.co.uk. Provides inoculations & anti-malarial prophylaxis, & advises on travel-related health risks.

Fleet Street Travel Clinic 29 Fleet St, London EC4Y 1AA; 020 7353 5678; f 020 7353 5500; www.fleetstreetclinic.com; 08.45–20.00 Mon–Thu, 08.45–17.30 Fri. Vaccinations, travel products & latest advice.

Hospital for Tropical Diseases Travel Clinic Mortimer Market Bldg, Capper St (off Tottenham Court Rd), London WC1E 6AU; 020 7388 9600; www.thehtd.org. Offers consultations & advice, & is able to provide all necessary drugs & vaccines for travellers. Runs a healthline (*020 7950 7799*) for country-specific information & health hazards. Also stocks nets, water purification equipment & personal protection measures.

Interhealth Worldwide Partnership Hse, 157 Waterloo Rd, London SE1 8US; 020 7902 9000; e info@interhealth.org.uk; www.interhealth.org. uk. Competitively priced, one-stop travel health service. All profits go to their affiliated company, InterHealth, which provides health care for overseas workers on Christian projects.

Liverpool School of Tropical Medicine Pembroke Pl, Liverpool L3 5QA; 0151 708 9393;

f 0151 705 3223; www.welltravelledclinics.co.uk. Offering advice & inoculations for those working or holidaying abroad.

MASTA (Medical Advisory Service for Travellers Abroad) Moorfield Rd, Yeadon, Leeds, West Yorks LS19 7BN; 0330 100 4207; www.masta-travel-health.com. Provides travel health advice, anti-malarials & vaccinations. There are over 25 MASTA pre-travel clinics in Britain; call or check online for the nearest. Clinics also sell mosquito nets, medical kits, insect protection & travel hygiene products.

NHS travel website www.fitfortravel.scot. nhs.uk. Provides country-by-country advice on immunisations & malaria, plus details of recent developments, & a list of relevant health organisations.

Nomad Travel Store/Clinic 3–4 Wellington Terrace, Turnpike Lane, London N8 0PX; 020 8889 7014; travel-health line (office hours only) 0906 863 3414; e sales@nomadtravel.co.uk; www.nomadtravel.co.uk. Also at 43 Bernard St, London WC1N 1LJ; 020 7833 4114; 52 Grosvenor Gardens, London SW1W 0AG; 020 7823 5823; & in Bishop's Stortford, Bristol, Manchester & Southampton. For health advice, equipment such as mosquito nets & other anti-bug devices, & an excellent range of adventure travel gear.

Trailfinders Travel Clinic 194 Kensington High St, London W8 7RG; 020 7938 3999; www. trailfinders.com/travelessentials/travelclinic.htm; 09.00–17.00 Mon–Wed & Fri, 09.00–18.00 Thu, 10.00–17.15 Sat.

Travelpharm The Travelpharm website, www.travelpharm.com, offers up-to-date guidance on travel-related health & has a range of medications (inc anti-malarials) available through their online pharmacy.

Irish Republic

Tropical Medical Bureau 54 Grafton St, Dublin 2; 1850 487674; e graftonstreet@tmb.ie; www.tmb.ie. A useful website specific to tropical

destinations. Also check website for other bureaux locations throughout Ireland.

USA

Centers for Disease Control 1600 Clifton Rd, Atlanta, GA 30333; 800 232 4636; travellers' health hotline 888 232 6348; e cdcinfo@cdc. gov. www.cdc.gov/travel. The central source of

travel information in the USA. The invaluable *Health Information for International Travel*, published annually, is available from the Division of Quarantine at this address.

Connaught Laboratories Pasteur Merieux Connaught, Route 611, PO Box 187, Swiftwater, PA 18370; 800 822 2463. They will send you a free list of specialist tropical-medicine physicians in your state.

IAMAT (International Association for Medical Assistance to Travelers) 1623 Military Rd, 279,

Niagara Falls, NY 14304-1745; 716 754 4883; e info@iamat.org; www.iamat.org. A non-profit organisation that provides lists of English-speaking doctors abroad.

International Medicine Center 915 Gessner Rd, Suite 525, Houston, TX 77024; 713 550 2000; f 713 973 0805; www.traveldoc.com

Canada
IAMAT Suite 1, 1287 St Clair Av W, Toronto, Ontario M6E 1B8; 416 652 0137; www.iamat. org. Clinic also in Ontario: 519 836 0102

TMVC Suite 314, 1030 W Georgia St, Vancouver, British Columbia V6E 2Y3; 1 888 288 8682; e appointments@tmvc.com; www.tmvc.com. Private clinic with several outlets in Canada.

Australia, New Zealand, Singapore
IAMAT Papanui Rd, Christchurch 5, New Zealand; www.iamat.org

TMVC 1300 65 88 44; www.tmvc.com.au. Clinics in Australia, New Zealand & Singapore, including: *Auckland* Canterbury Arcade, 170 Queen St; 9 373 3531; e auckland@ traveldoctor.co.nz; *Brisbane* 75a, Astor Terrace,

Spring Hill, QLD 4000; 7 3815 6900; e brisbane@traveldoctor.com.au; *Melbourne* 393 Little Bourke St, 2nd Floor, VIC 3000; 3 9935 8100; e melbourne@traveldoctor.com.au; *Sydney* Dymocks Bldg, 7th Floor, 428 George St, NSW 2000; 2 9221 7133; e sydney@traveldoctor. com.au

South Africa and Namibia
SAA-Netcare Travel Clinics Picbel Arcade, 11th Floor, Room 1107, 58 Strand St, Cape Town; 21 419 3172; www.travelclinic.co.za. Clinics throughout South Africa.

TMVC NHC Health Centre, Cnr Beyers Naude & Waugh Northcliff; PO Box 48499, Roosevelt Park, 2129 (postal address); 011 888 7488; www. tmvc.com.au. Consult website for details of other clinics in South Africa & Namibia.

Switzerland
IAMAT 57 Chemin des Voirets, 1212 Grand Lancy, Geneva; www.iamat.org

SAFETY

There is a risk of **pickpocketing**, especially in crowded places such as markets and busy public transport. Ensure that you keep your money and documents somewhere secure. If you are driving, don't leave valuables visible in your parked vehicle: there have been reports of 'smash and grab' thefts.

While the informal **taxi system** in operation throughout the region provides a quick and cost-effective means of getting around town, it does carry with it certain risks, and you should be alert to these if you decide to hail a car, particularly at night. If a car stops for you that you do not particularly like the look of (because it appears to be in poor condition, or the driver seems drunk, or there are two or more men in it), simply wave it away again. The locals do this all the time. There have been serious incidents of violent robbery involving foreigners leaving bars and clubs late in the evening, sometimes somewhat incapacitated by drink, who have taken informal 'taxis' waiting outside the premises. If you are leaving a club or bar late, it is much safer to get the establishment to call an official taxi for you.

The taxi drivers waiting for arriving passengers at Almaty airport are a particularly frequent source of complaints. Often this is simply a matter of overcharging, but there have been more sinister incidents, including drivers taking arriving visitors into the middle of nowhere, and demanding money to return them to the centre of the city. If you need to take a taxi from the airport into the city, book an official one at the desk just before you leave the arrivals hall, or call 255 5333. There have also been reports of people posing at the airport as 'meet and greet' representatives, sent by the passenger's inviting organisation to collect them. In some cases they seem to have been able to get hold of passengers' names, adding to the credibility of the story. They then drive you off somewhere remote and extort money to take you to your destination (similar to the taxi driver scam mentioned above). If you are being met at the airport, establish clearly in advance with your inviting organisation the arrangements, including how the person meeting you will be identified.

Although levels of violent **crime** in Kazakhstan are relatively low, muggings, especially at night, are a concern. The oil boom towns in the west of the country, especially Atyrau, are particularly problematic in this respect. You should avoid walking alone at night, and keep to well-illuminated areas.

There are a few street scams in operation in the larger cities, especially Almaty. One of the most frequent is the 'dropped wallet' scam, which exists in several variants. A wallet is left on the pavement in a prominent position, where the mark walking towards it easily spots it, just as someone else is 'passing by' (or it is the 'passer-by' who spots the wallet, pointing it out to the mark). The objective of the 'passer-by' is to engage the mark in a conversation in which he will propose that they divide up the money. A second person arrives, claiming to be the owner of the wallet, takes it back and alleges that some money has been stolen. He threatens to go to the police, with the objective of extorting money from the mark in order not to do so. Aggressive begging is also becoming an issue in some cities.

The **spiking of drinks** has been reported in clubs and bars in Almaty, where the motive is generally robbery rather than sex, and the targets more often men than women. Keep a close eye on your drink. The effects of alcohol are at the root of many reported violent incidents in Kazakhstan. If a fight breaks out in the bar you are in, pay up quickly and leave.

Cases of extortion of money by police and other law enforcement officers are less common in Kazakhstan than they used to be (though petty corruption on the part of the traffic police remains a considerable problem). Police in Kazakhstan are allowed, perfectly legitimately, to request to see identification documents, and you should co-operate with this. There have, however, been concerns about extortion by people impersonating law enforcement officers: if you have any doubts about the bona fides of the person who has stopped you, you are entitled to ask to see their credentials before producing your passport. If you doubt the legitimacy of the 'officer', or are being asked for a bribe, try to take down their name and badge number, as well as the registration number of any vehicle. Do not get into the back of a police car or go anywhere else that you cannot be seen by passers-by. If in doubt, ask to accompany the officer to the closest police station to resolve any matters (invented or otherwise) there.

You should consult the travel advice issued by your government for the latest security advice before you travel. For the United Kingdom this can be found at www.fco.gov.uk/travel, for the United States at www.travel.state.gov.

ROAD SAFETY Driving standards in Kazakhstan are generally poor. The wide variety of vehicles on the roads, from decrepit Soviet-era makes to large modern 4x4s, makes for traffic travelling at different speeds. Overtaking on the inside, and illegal U-turns, are among many common infringements, and road rage is increasingly an issue on the gridlocked streets of Almaty. The poor state of repair of some roads, with pot-holes and often inadequate or non-existent street lighting, adds to the difficulties. In rural areas, animals and pedestrians wandering into the road present a considerable risk. If you are driving in Kazakhstan, you will need to display care and caution, always wear a seat belt, and never drink and drive (Kazakhstani legislation is in any case strict on this score). Try to avoid driving outside cities after dark as roads are poorly lit and other vehicles may not have working lights.

When on foot, you should avoid the local practice of crossing busy roads by walking out to the centre of the road and waiting for a gap in the oncoming traffic, even if this means taking a detour to cross the road at the next set of traffic lights. Do not expect cars to stop for you, even if you are on a zebra crossing.

FOCUS GROUPS The usual personal safety precautions should be exercised for **women travellers**. You should dress modestly, especially in conservative southern and western Kazakhstan and in rural areas (although this is not a practice always followed by the locals). Particular caution should be taken when hailing taxis; phoning for a cab, or getting the establishment you are in to do this for you, is a safer option.

Unaccompanied women may receive unwanted attention in bars and clubs but this is usually deflected with a few terse words. If the harassment continues, alert the management or leave the premises and find a more pleasant alternative. Try to avoid physical confrontation as alcohol-fuelled violence is not uncommon.

Homosexuality has been legal in Kazakhstan since 1997, but whilst a small **gay scene** has developed in Almaty, same-sex relationships are still often seen to be symptomatic of illness. Visitors are advised against showing open signs of affection in public, especially away from the larger cities. Kazakhstan's largest LGBT website is www.gays.kz; it has information both about the gay community and details of forthcoming events.

Disabled visitors may experience difficulty travelling in Kazakhstan. Public transport is rarely able to carry wheelchairs, few buildings have disabled access, and streets are littered with trip hazards such as broken paving, uncovered manholes and utility pipes. Hotel rooms are often spread over multiple floors without lifts, and assistance from staff is not guaranteed. If you have a disability and are travelling to Kazakhstan, you would be advised to travel with a companion who can help you when the country's infrastructure and customer service fall short.

Travel with **children** is relatively easy given Kazakhstanis' focus on family life. Children are welcomed in restaurants and shops but you may have difficulty manoeuvring pushchairs in and out of buildings and along broken pavements. Nappies, baby food and other similar items are widely available in supermarkets, but you are unlikely to find European brands outside of major cities. Journeys by car and public transport are often long and uncomfortable, which may deter families with younger children from travelling into the interior of the country.

WHAT TO TAKE

You may wish to consider the following, in addition to the usual holiday packing.

- **Plug adaptors** Sockets in Kazakhstan are the twin round pin, continental European type. The voltage is 220V.

- **A torch** Many parts of Kazakhstani cities are poorly lit at night, and pavements may conceal dangers such as uncovered manholes. Power cuts are not uncommon. If you are planning to camp, or use homestays in rural areas, you'll need a torch to navigate to the latrine at night.
- **Mosquito repellent** Kazakhstan may not be a malarial country, but the swarms of mosquitoes you may encounter in summer among its lakes and forests can still damage your enjoyment of your holiday. Make sure you also pack long-sleeved tops (you'll also need these for visiting conservative areas and religious sites).
- **Warm clothing** If you are planning a trip to Kazakhstan in the winter months (which in the north of the country means November to April), you need to treat its cold temperatures with respect, with good warm clothing minimising areas of exposed skin. The locals wrap themselves in fur: fur coats and hats; fur-lined gloves and boots. If this is the path you wish to follow, appropriate fur clothing is probably best purchased on arrival in Kazakhstan. But if you do not want to wear fur clothing, and simply in order to be adequately attired from the moment of your arrival in Kazakhstan, outdoor adventure shops are probably the best source of suitably warm garments. Be aware, however, that many shops, hotels and restaurants are heated to high temperatures in winter months. Therefore, unless you are planning to spend a great deal of time in outdoor pursuits, you may find that items like thermal underwear become counterproductive, as they leave you sweltering when you are inside. The best advice is to take a cue from the locals: dress in several layers, with particularly warm outer garments which get checked in at the cloakroom when you arrive at your restaurant or club.
- **Good footwear** In winter, wear rubber-soled boots. You may also wish to consider the detachable metal spike or coil devices sold in many outdoor adventure stores as protection against the ice. If you are trekking, good hiking boots are essential.
- **Flip-flops** As well as at the beach, you'll need these on visits to public baths, and inside at homestay accommodation (shoes are left at the front door in Kazakhstani homes). They also come in useful on long train journeys.
- If you will be staying in bottom-range accommodation, a **sheet sleeping bag**, of the kind used by youth hostellers, can help save you from unsavoury bedding. A **universal sink plug** is also worth packing, as are wet wipes for those times when the hotel taps run dry.
- Good **suncream**, a **lip salve**, **sunglasses** and a spare set of any **prescription glasses**.
- Small **gift items** related to your home country make ideal presents for hosts.

$ MONEY

Kazakhstan's currency, the tenge, was introduced on 15 November 1993, replacing the rouble (15 November is still commemorated as the 'day of national currency'). The tenge is in theory subdivided into a smaller unit, the tiyn (1 tenge = 100 tiyn), but the latter have not been minted since 1993, their value is negligible, and they are no longer found in general circulation. There are notes to the values of 10,000, 5,000, 2,000, 1,000, 500 and 200 tenge, and coins of 100, 50, 20, five, two and one tenge.

New notes were introduced in 2006. These are much more elaborate affairs than the previous versions, and were designed by a team headed by Mendybai Alin, Senior Designer of the Central Bank. In contrast to the earlier notes, which featured a portrait of scientist Al Farabi, the new notes portray no personalities. Instead, the obverse side of each note features the Baiterek Tower, together with the state flag and national anthem, abstract designs based on petroglyphs, and an open-palmed hand apparently reaching up towards the tower. President Nazarbaev's signature is written across the hand. The reverse side features the outline of the map of Kazakhstan, within which are depicted different sights on different denominations: feather-grass steppe and the building of the Ministry of Transport and Communications on the T200 note; and the presidential palace of Ak Orda and the Charyn Canyon on the T10,000 one. The denomination is written in Kazakh on the obverse side; in Russian on the reverse.

BANKS The banking system in Kazakhstan is well developed. Major Kazakhstani banks include Kazkommertsbank, Bank Turan Alem and Halyk Bank, and there are also a few branches of foreign banks such as HSBC, ABN Amro and Citibank, though these are restricted to the largest cities. Banking hours typically run from around 09.00 to 18.00 Monday to Friday, though opening and closing times vary slightly (the HSBC branch in Almaty is, for example, open from 08.30 to 17.30). Most bank branches also close for lunch, from 13.00 to 14.00. A few are open on Saturdays, usually in the morning.

ATMS ATMs are probably the most straightforward means of getting money. These are moderately easy to find in urban Kazakhstan (the term to use when asking directions to one is *bankomat*), typically inside and outside banks, in shopping centres, the lobbies of modern office complexes and at larger railway stations. They generally accept Visa and MasterCard, as well as all cards displaying a Maestro or Cirrus symbol, though there are some variations between the machines belonging to different banks as regards what cards are acceptable. On inserting your card, you are typically offered a choice of languages, including English. There is normally a T30,000 limit on any individual cash withdrawal, but if you need more money, you can simply take T30,000 out in the first transaction, and then immediately repeat the procedure, subject to the limit on your own card. Do not expect to find ATMs in smaller towns.

CASH US dollars in cash are also good to bring out: they can be converted into tenge at one of the licensed exchange bureaux, found as little kiosks all over the place. Your US dollars should be from notes issued after 2000, and free from tears or blemishes. It is worth asking for a receipt (and retaining those from your ATM transactions), although, unlike some other countries in the region, you are highly unlikely to be asked by anyone to produce your exchange receipts. In Kazakhstan, as everywhere, be alert to the risks of robbery around ATMs and exchange offices. Please note that you are required to pay for purchases in tenge, even though some swankier stores confusingly sometimes display their prices in US dollars, or 'YE' ('units'), another name for dollars also found in Russia. If you are travelling outside the main cities, make sure you have an ample supply of local currency as there is a shortage of ATMs, and local people may be unable to exchange large quantities of dollars.

CREDIT CARDS Credit cards are increasingly accepted in the smarter hotels, restaurants and shops in Kazakhstan's cities. Visa is probably the most widely accepted card. Except at places like the big international hotels, it is unwise to rely on being able to use a credit card: the plaintive apology of the waitress that their credit-card machine is out of order is quite a common sound in Kazakhstan's restaurants. And in small towns and rural areas, as well as cheaper joints in the cities, you are unlikely to be able to use them at all.

TRAVELLERS' CHEQUES Travellers' cheques are potentially useful as emergency back-up funding, for example if an ATM eats your card. Not all banks will change them, but in larger towns you will usually to be able to find one that does. US dollar travellers' cheques are probably best, to avoid the risk that you may be levied additional exchange rate charges.

BUDGETING

On average Kazakhstan is considerably cheaper for the visitor than the countries of western Europe, but is more expensive than more southerly parts of central Asia, such as Kyrgyzstan, a function of its faster economic growth since independence. But averages mean very little, as there is a chasm between the prices of budget and luxury options in Kazakhstan. In many parts of Kazakhstan a rural homestay, on full-board terms, with an NGO providing community-based tourism was available at the time of research for no more than T3,600 (US$30) a night, while a top-range hotel in Almaty or Astana, on a room-only basis, cost upwards of T48,000 (US$400) a night. A cheap meal of *shashlik*, a salad, bread and a beer in a basic café can be had across most of the country for no more than T1,000 (US$8) per person, while a meal in one of the classier Almaty or Astana restaurants could set you back upwards of T12,000 (US$100). There are also strong geographical variations in costs, with Almaty and Astana much more expensive than the rest of the country, and the oil boom towns in the west, particularly Atyrau and Aktau, also pricey.

The fact that most Kazakhstani tour operators work on the basis of providing tailored programmes (you tell them what you want, and they put together an itinerary) does have the advantage of giving the visitor a programme specific to their interests. The downside, however, is that this can work out particularly expensive for single travellers or couples, who end up shelling out for the full cost of the guide and transport. It may be worth considering the small number of operators who do offer scheduled packages, such as Blast for cheap day trips around Almaty, and Asia Discovery for longer tours (see page 123). Or stick to public transport, which is generally cheap. A bus journey between Astana and Kokshetau, a trip of some five hours, for example, costs around T1,000 (US$8).

Prices of basic foodstuffs in an Astana supermarket at the time of research were as follows:

• Oranges (1kg)	T360 (US$3)
• Apples (1kg)	T300–400 (US$2–2.70)
• Mineral water (1l, local brand)	T80 (US$0.54)
• Bread (loaf)	T80 (US$0.54)
• Milk (1l)	T220 (US$1.50)
• Fizzy soda (50cl)	T80 (US$0.54)
• Beer (500ml, bottle, local brand)	T140–240 (US$0.95–1.60)

Astana prices are at the top end of the scale in Kazakhstan, and those in supermarkets are higher than the prices obtainable at the bazaars, especially for fruit and vegetables, so the above list represents the top of the range at the time of research. With inflation figures a little under 8%, however, the cost of a basket of goods is rising rapidly everywhere.

BY AIR Given Kazakhstan's huge size, internal flights are an important means of getting around the country. There is a relatively well-developed domestic network, with flights to every regional capital, as well as to a small number of other large towns, such as Semey and Zhezkazgan. Almaty and Astana are the main hubs of the domestic network, though there are also a few direct connections between other cities. The national carrier is Air Astana, a joint venture between the government of Kazakhstan and BAE Systems, which started out in 2002, and took over as national carrier two years later on the demise of Air Kazakhstan. The airline's rapidly expanding fleet is made up solely of Western aircraft: Airbus A-320 and A-321, Boeing 757 and 767 and Fokker 50.

The most important routes, including the flights between Almaty and Astana and those serving Atyrau and Aktau, use Boeing and Airbus aircraft and offer service standards to match those of western European carriers: travel from Astana to Almaty on a Friday evening, or Almaty to Astana on the last flight on Sunday, and the plane will be filled with senior Kazakhstani officials, heading between work in Astana and second homes in Almaty. Air Astana's flights to smaller regional capitals across northern Kazakhstan are different in character: these are 'social' routes, subsidised by the Kazakhstan government, and for which the ticket price is low. The downside is that they tend to be contracted out to other companies, such as Tulpar Air Service, who use old Soviet aircrafts, typically the Antonov An-24, a 44-seat twin turboprop which first flew in 1960 and which NATO for some reason gave the reporting name 'Coke' – a plastic cupful of which is likely to be about the highlight of the in-flight service you get.

There are other Kazakhstani airlines serving domestic routes. The largest network after Air Astana is that of a Shymkent-based airline named Scat, whose logo is a propeller, a fact which gives you an indication of the type of aircraft you are likely to fly on. Their network is strongest in southern and western parts of Kazakhstan, with flights across the Caspian to various destinations in the south Caucasus, and they also serve several local airports in East Kazakhstan Region. Their prices are somewhat lower than those of Air Astana (at the time of research, an economy-class flight from Shymkent to Almaty with Scat was T14,200, against prices starting at T17,000 with Air Astana). But their fleet is made up mostly of Antonov An-24 turboprops, supplemented with a few real curiosities, including a couple of leased BAC 1-11s, veteran British jet airliners formerly in service with the Romanian airline Tarom. On some local routes within East Kazakhstan Region, they still use the Antonov An-2, a propeller-driven biplane which first flew in 1947, carries up to 12 passengers, and has been given the affectionate nickname Kukuruznik ('maize worker') since it was originally designed predominantly for agricultural use.

The remaining domestic airlines serve just one or two routes. They include Zhetisu Airlines, which operates the route between Taldykorgan and Astana; SemeyAvia, which has flights between Semey and Almaty; and Kokshetau Airlines, which has a route from Almaty to Kokshetau, then on to Petropavl. All use the Yakovlev Yak-40, a veteran three-engined aircraft, entered through a door in the rear of the plane, and nicknamed the 'flying whistle' because of its distinctive humming sound. The Yak-40 has relatively little baggage space, so bear in mind that your baggage allowance on these flights may be lower than usual. Zhetisu Airlines for example allows only 10kg.

Check-in procedures typically start 90 minutes before the scheduled flight time, closing 45 minutes before take-off, though confirm the situation for your specific flight when you book. Snow and fog can cause flight cancellations and lengthy delays, even at Kazakhstan's major airports, so keep this in mind if you are travelling during the winter months.

BY RAIL While not a fast way to travel – taking their long stops at stations into account, Kazakhstan's trains average something like 40km/h – the train is a great way to appreciate the enormity of the country, as you sweep through great expanses of steppe and desert, and offers good opportunities for interacting with the local people, who will be your companions for many hours. It is also worth bearing in mind that train travel is less likely to be disrupted by winter weather menaces such as freezing fog than is domestic air travel.

Services are operated by Kazakhstan's national rail company, Kazakhstan Temir Zholy. There are some local trains, known as *elektrichki*, though these often compete rather poorly time-wise with bus services to the same destinations. But it is the long-distance train which really symbolises rail travel in Kazakhstan. These typically offer up to four classes of accommodation, though not all are available on all trains. A *lyux* compartment converts into two beds; a *kupe* into a four-bunk compartment. Both of these compartments are lockable. A *platzkart* is a six-bunk open compartment. Some trains also have an *obshy* ('general') compartment, where you don't get a bed at all. *Lyux* and *kupe* compartments offer more comfort and security, though a *platzkart* gives you the opportunity to interact with a wider range of local people. Prices are markedly cheaper than flying. At the time of writing, for example, tariffs on the Almaty to Shymkent route ranged from T2,500 for a place in a *platzkart* to between T6,000 and T7,000 for one in a *lyux*.

Railway carriages typically have a toilet at either end, and there is also a samovar at the end of every carriage, dispensing hot water. The attendant on each carriage sells tea bags, if you haven't brought your own. The attendant also doles out bedding, for which a small charge is payable. The safest place to store your bags is in the containers beneath the seats/lower bunks. Kazakhstani train passengers typically bring industrial quantities of food with them, supplementing their supplies *en route* at stations, where there are invariably plenty of places to buy pies, snacks, fruit and drinks on the platforms. If there is a restaurant car on the train, it will scarcely be used. Your enjoyment of the experience of travelling by train will depend heavily on your fellow passengers. Most travellers report positive experiences of friendly welcomes and hospitable sharing of food, though insistent requests from the fellow occupants of your compartment that you join them in vodka toasts can quickly become wearing. Drunken passengers on trains can also prove a real problem.

There is one notably fast domestic train in Kazakhstan, the overnight Tulpar service between Almaty and Astana, which feels much more like a western European fast train than the typical slow-paced Kazakhstani long-distance trains and which makes only three stops *en route*. The modern Tulpar with its pale blue interior décor nonetheless does not get universally high marks from the Kazakhstani travelling public, as it is rather cramped when compared with the slow and sedate older trains. Instead of samovars at the end of the carriages, there are plastic water coolers. A sign of the times, I suppose. Services on the Tulpar are much more expensive than on other trains, and there is a further supplement if you use it on a weekend or public holiday. Tariffs on the Tulpar at the time of writing ranged from around T11,000 for a *platzkart* place during the week (compared with T4,500 for a *platzkart* on an ordinary Almaty to Astana train) to some T19,500 for a *lyux* at the weekend, not far short of the cost of an economy-class air ticket.

One word of caution regarding train travel in northern Kazakhstan: the railway network, dating from Tsarist and Soviet times, shows no concern for the borders of the independent countries of the former Soviet Union. Between several Kazakhstani regional capitals the railway dips into and then back out of Russian territory. This is the case between Uralsk and Aktobe, Aktobe and Kostanai, and Semey and Ust-Kamenogorsk. You may therefore need a Russian transit visa to take these routes. The rules in this area appear however to be hazy. For example, the Kazakhstan train from Moscow to Almaty enters Kazakhstan and then passes briefly back into Russian territory, before going back into Kazakhstan again. It is a moot point therefore whether you actually need double-entry Russian and Kazakhstani visas to take it. However, at the time of research, most travel agents seemed to be advising that single-entry visas for each country were sufficient, though you should check this point when you book.

Kazakhstani long-distance trains get booked up: you should therefore aim to buy your ticket well in advance of travel. Buying through a travel agency will cost you more in agent's commission, but will save you the strains of a disorderly queue and often abrupt, harassed service at the railway station booking office.

BY ROAD Intercity buses tend to be both a little faster and cheaper than the train. The fare for the 13-hour trip from Almaty to Shymkent was for example around T2,200 at the time of research. The quality of buses serving intercity routes in Kazakhstan is gradually improving, but there are still a fair few clapped-out examples around. In general, buses make a reasonable option for trips of up to a few hours between adjacent cities, but the train is a more comfortable option for really long-distance travel.

Also plying the roads between Kazakhstani cities, and generally also leaving from outside the bus station, are minivans, or *marshrutkas*. Unlike buses, these generally do not operate to a fixed timetable, but leave when the van is full, or when the driver is bored of waiting. These tend to be faster than the buses, but journeys can at times be quite alarming, with the drivers, in a hurry to maximise the number of trips they make, racing faster than the condition of the road or van often warrants. Another, slightly more expensive, option is a shared taxi. These are considered to have four seats, and again depart when the taxi is full. You should specify that you only want one seat, as drivers will probably assume that foreigners want to hire the whole car. The front seat is the one to aim for if you get the choice (you won't, unless you're the first customer, in which case you'll then have to wait for three more clients before the taxi is ready to depart). Again, be warned that some drivers have a reckless approach to the road. You should check before you agree on the car that seat belts are fitted, and working. Finally, hiring the whole taxi is an option worth considering, for example if you're getting bored waiting for other passengers to turn up, or you want to go to the kind of destination not usually served (for example an archaeological site, for which you'll need to negotiate a price carefully, stipulating how long the driver will be expected to wait at the site, and that he will bring you back). Hiring a full taxi costs four times the fare for one person on a standard intercity route.

If driving your own vehicle, be sure to take plenty of water, food and fuel, as rest stops are infrequent and the intermittent petrol stations, particularly in the west of Kazakhstan, do run dry. The sight of a fellow motorist hitching by the side of the road with a plastic jerry can in hand is unnervingly frequent, and there is no pretence at a breakdown service. At the time of writing, the M32 between Uralsk and Shymkent, and the main road between Shymkent and Almaty, were both undergoing major reconstruction work. Although once completed the new roads will significantly reduce driving times in the south and the west of Kazakhstan, in the meantime drivers should anticipate delays, diversions and long stretches of off-road driving. A snow shovel in winter is useful and can be bought in the bazaars.

URBAN TRANSPORT Regional capitals and other large towns in Kazakhstan are generally served by reasonably efficient urban public transport networks, comprising some combination of buses, minibuses, trolleybuses and trams. Fares are very cheap: typically T30–40. In Almaty you can expect to pay T25 for a tram ride and T50 for the bus. The vehicles in service are often decidedly elderly. Note though that services generally cease running well before midnight. These are supplemented by a well-developed unofficial taxi system. Hail a car simply by standing by the side of the road and making an up-and-down motion with an outstretched, downward-pointing arm. Agree destination and price before you get in, taking the opportunity to size up the driver (see *Safety*, page 42, for advice regarding the use of unofficial taxis, which always carries some element of risk). Typical fares at the time of research ranged from around T300 for a trip within the city centre of one of the smaller regional capitals to perhaps double that for an equivalent trip in Astana or Almaty. All the main towns in Kazakhstan also have official taxis which can be telephoned. The relevant city entries in this guide give a selection of phone numbers. Phoning for a taxi is more expensive than hailing a car on the street, though it has important safety benefits and is particularly recommended at night.

 ## ACCOMMODATION

During the recent years of rapid economic growth in Kazakhstan, the picture as regards hotel accommodation has transformed. In Almaty, Astana and the oil boom towns of the west, smart four- and five-star hotels run by international chains cater to the upper end of the business travel market. Elsewhere, once shoddy Soviet hotels have been refurbished, and new mid-range ones built, offering air conditioning, satellite television and reliable supplies of hot water, though often in rather bland buildings (frequently faced with silver-coloured metallic-look tiles, for some reason). The sharp rise in the wealth of better-off Kazakhstanis has helped to fuel a mushrooming growth in smarter accommodation in resort areas, from lakeside hotels around Borovoye to chalet-style mountain retreats in the Zailysky Alatau.

For the most part, the effect of this uplift in Kazakhstan's accommodation stock has been positive. Few will mourn the passing of the days when the only hotel options in some cities were unrenovated Soviet-era crumbling firetraps. But a downside is the increasing paucity of options for the budget traveller. Almaty in particular presents a real challenge for visitors looking for budget options, as once relatively cheap hotels like the Alma-Ata have been smartened up, and their prices cranked up to match. The 'retiring rooms' at most of the major railway stations are one standby, though it would simply get too depressing to use these for more than the occasional night. Overnight train journeys themselves offer a good deal for the budget traveller, as you get a night's 'accommodation' thrown in with your transport. And at the time of writing there was still to be found in most regional capitals at least one survivor from the hotel styles of the Soviet Union, with a *dizhurnaya* on every floor, clunking lifts and stucco-covered lobbies. The great merit of these places is that they invariably offer a wide range of prices, with at least some budget-end rooms with worn-out parquet floors and tiny wooden beds. It is to be hoped that the programmes of renovation under way in many of the hotels of this type do not eliminate altogether their stocks of budget rooms. On a more positive note, there are a few examples of new hotels specifically aiming to provide clean, cheap and wholesome accommodation for the budget traveller: the Baiterek Sapar Motel in Shymkent is one.

Kazakhstan lags behind some of its neighbours in the region as regards the provision of good-value accommodation specifically aimed at foreign tourists, with attention paid to highlighting the culture and traditions of the country. One notable exception though is a network of ecotourism options, focused on the Ecotourism Information Resource Centre in Almaty (see page 123). The establishment of this network has benefited from the support of international organisations such as Voluntary Service Overseas and the Eurasia Foundation, as well as corporate donors such as ExxonMobil. It is based around homestays in some of the most attractive rural communities across Kazakhstan, on a full-board basis. The groups co-ordinating the project on the ground can usually put together local tours, cultural programmes and sometimes activities such as horseriding. The programme provides a fascinating and relatively low-cost way to experience country life in Kazakhstan. Details of the individual homestays are flagged up in the relevant sections of this guide.

The cost of accommodation is highest in Almaty, where you will have to pay upwards of US$150 a night for a decidedly ordinary room with en suite in a modest hotel. A similar hotel room in one of the non-oil boom regional capitals would set you back perhaps US$70. A room in one of the top-range international hotels in Almaty is upwards of US$400 a night. Hotel prices in Astana are not far behind, and Atyrau is also expensive. Bear in mind too that the prices of the business-class hotels in Almaty are jacked up further for the Kazakhstan International Oil and Gas Exhibition in the first week of October, when rooms are at a premium. On the other hand, full-board accommodation in one of the community-based ecotourism options, or in a down-at-heel but enjoyable sanatorium or Soviet-style holiday complex in an attractive lakeside environment in northern Kazakhstan, can be had for less than US$45 a night

One irritant is the reservation fee, normally equating to at least 20% of the cost of the first night's accommodation, charged by some hotels. Mid-range places in the northern regions of Kazakhstan seem to be particularly prone to levying such a fee. If you just turn up on spec, you don't pay. The latter can, however, occasionally prove a hazardous strategy, as I found out when turning up in Semey on 7 July 2007 without a reserved room, to find that every hotel in town seemed to be fully booked up with wedding parties, who had decided that the lucky-sounding date of 7/7/07 represented the perfect time to get married. If you arrive at your hotel late in the evening, and plan to leave early the next day, it may be worth enquiring about a half-day rate, sometimes offered for stays of less than 12 hours. This doesn't always work, but there's no harm in asking.

✖ EATING AND DRINKING

FOOD Kazakh cuisine is heavily based on the nomadic past of the Kazakh people. It is dominated by meat (especially mutton and horse) and various milk products, many of which have no direct English translation. The techniques of preparation emerged out of the importance of ensuring food preservation: thus there are many dishes based around smoked meat and soured milk. Meat is an important part of the Kazakh diet, and there are numerous jokes about the legendary capacity of Kazakhs for consuming huge quantities of the stuff (the punch lines tend to be of a 'right, where's the main course?' nature). An invitation to a Kazakh feast provides a great opportunity to try many of the classic dishes of Kazakh cuisine together with the rituals which accompany their apportionment, though most dishes are also available in Kazakh or generic central Asian restaurants.

A Kazakh feast tends to be referred to as a *dastarkhan*, actually the name of the low table around which Kazakhs traditionally sat, on the floor or propped up against cushions, to eat their meals. In rural areas, this form of dining is still common; in larger towns, chairs and tables have taken over, at least among wealthier Kazakh families. On arrival, you will find the table already laden with things to eat, typically fruits, nuts and a range of salad dishes. Tea is served into handle-less cups called *pialas*, and will be constantly refilled throughout the meal, even as vodka toasts are called for, and other drinks, such as *kumiss*, a drink of fermented mare's milk, are also passed round. Appetisers are brought out, focused heavily on sliced meats. Pride of place here goes to various sliced sausages made from horse meat of varying degrees of fattiness: among the most important varieties are *kazy*, *karta* and *shuzhuk*. There may also be a range of pastries on offer, such as a meat-filled variety, *samsa*, found throughout the region. *Kurt*, little balls of dried curd,

is a salty snack which has the effect of draining all moisture from your mouth. At some point during the meal a dish of *kuirdak* will be served. This is made from the internal organs of a sheep or other freshly slaughtered animal: these are cut into small pieces, together with lumps of fat from the animal, cooked in oil, and served with onion and pepper.

The focus of the meal, and the signature dish of Kazakh cuisine, is *beshbarmak*. The name means, literally, 'five fingers', a reference to the traditional way of eating the stuff and not, fortunately, to its ingredients. It is generally served in a large dish, placed in the centre of the table. It involves large lumps of horse meat or mutton, boiled on the bone, which are scattered across a bed of flat layers of pasta which has been boiled up in broth. Onion cut into rings, garlic and a scattering of parsley and fennel, completes the dish. The broth, *sorpa*, is served up separately, in pialas.

Before the *beshbarmak* is doled out, one tradition which is often incorporated into such a feast, particularly if there is a distinguished guest to be honoured, is the presentation to that guest of a boiled sheep's head, or *koy bas*. Since a foreign visitor may well count as the 'distinguished guest', be aware that this could be coming your way. The ritual here is that the guest is given a knife, and cuts off pieces from the head, apportioning them to the others around the table. This is traditionally done by identifying pieces appropriate to individual recipients: thus young people often receive a piece of ear, so they may listen well to their elders. You needn't worry too much about getting this symbolism right; if you can cut small pieces of meat from the head and apportion them, starting with the eldest person around the table and continuing in approximate age order, you will be considered to have discharged your distinguished guest function well. The lumps of meat on the *beshbarmak* itself are also distributed on the basis of various traditional customs. Thus elderly or honoured guests tend to be given meat from around the hip, while it is never done to offer brains to children, for fear that they may become weak-willed, or a knee bone to an unmarried woman, lest she be left on the shelf (given the elbow?). *Ak nan*, a type of bread flavoured with onion, is often eaten with *beshbarmak*.

Sweet dishes served after the *beshbarmak* (though they may have been sitting on the table throughout the meal) include *irimshik*, which is not actually itself particularly sweet: it's a dry yellowish/orange dish, made of soured cow's or sheep's milk which has been boiled and dried. It is however an ingredient of the classic Kazakh sweet, *zhent*, which also contains millet, sugar, raisins and butter and has a rather powdery consistency. *Baursaki*, small, spherical, fried doughnuts, have an important place in Kazakhstani culture, and feature in many forms of commemorative and celebratory meals. Fruit will also be served at this time. Do expect the unexpected in a Kazakh feast: the *kuirdak* is for example occasionally served right at the end of the meal, after the sweets.

The multi-ethnic character of Kazakhstan and the centuries of trading and interactions along the Silk Routes mean that the cuisine of modern Kazakhstan incorporates a large number of influences alongside those drawn from the nomadic Kazakhs. You will find here some of the dishes popular throughout the region, such as *plov*, a rice-based dish served with lumps of meat, and pieces of carrot and onion. In Kazakhstan it is sometimes made in a sweet form, with the addition of dried raisins and apricots. *Manty* are also popular. These are dumplings, filled with spiced lamb or beef, sometimes with chopped pumpkin added, and cooked on a steamer. A range of noodle dishes are brought from Uighur cuisine, while *shashlik*, skewered lumps of various barbecued meats, cooked over hot coals and served with raw onion, is a south Caucasus speciality popular across the region. Korean-style spicy vegetable salads are also found on many menus. Kazakhstan's large ethnic Russian community has ensured the presence of numerous classic Russian dishes, including salads such as the chopped vegetable in mayonnaise confection described on menus here as *olivye* but known in western Europe as Russian salad, the ravioli-like *pelmeni*, sweet and savoury pancakes, or *blini*, and soups such as *borscht*.

Fuelled by the increasing wealth and aspirations of many Kazakhstanis, a whole range of newer arrivals from around the globe has supplemented these longer-established dishes. Thus, as the *Where to eat* sections under individual towns make clear, it is possible in the larger cities to find Italian, Mexican or French restaurants. Sushi is currently all the rage among the Kazakhstani elite. Note that in Kazakhstani restaurants side dishes such as vegetables do not usually come automatically with your main dish, and have to be ordered separately. A 10% service charge is typically added. Tipping beyond this is not expected. Many restaurants in Kazakhstan offer a business lunch: this will usually be a set meal or a buffet. These tend to be good value, and are usually served promptly, though they are often fairly unexciting.

Restaurants are usually open every day, typically from noon until the last diner has finished up in the evening, though some close for an hour or two mid-afternoon.

DRINK The drink most closely associated with the traditional Kazakh diet is *kumiss*, prepared from fermented mare's milk, and believed by Kazakhs to have numerous health-giving properties, from the stabilisation of the nervous system to the treatment of tuberculosis. In parts of the south and west of the country, including Kyzylorda and Mangistau regions, it is supplanted by *shubat*, prepared from fermented camel's milk, whose advocates ascribe it an equally impressive range of curative properties, recommending it for the treatment of tuberculosis, diabetes and stomach ulcers. Both *kumiss* and *shubat* have a slight fizzy quality and a sour flavour, and are definitely acquired tastes. A foreign delegation greeted on arrival into Kazakhstan by their Kazakh hosts may well be confronted with a girl in traditional dress holding out bowls of *kumiss* and *shubat*, accompanied with *baursaki*.

Another important drink for Kazakhs is tea. Green tea is popular, especially in the south of the country, but 'black' tea, in other words the standard tea of the English-speaking world, is more prevalent. Ethnic Russians drink this black, sometimes with lemon, but, unusually for the region, Kazakhs traditionally drink their tea with milk. Do not be surprised if your host fills your tea cup only half full: it is an invitation for you to continue speaking. Once your cup is filled, you know it is time to leave. Coffee tends to be hit-and-miss, though there is an increasing range of coffee places in Almaty offering the cappuccinos and lattes you get back home.

Although some Kazakhstanis refrain from alcohol on religious grounds, the legacy of Tsarist and then Soviet rule has brought with it a tradition of vodka drinking. There are numerous local brands, from expensive varieties such as Snow Queen, which boasts that it has been distilled five times, to cheap and rather unpleasant products. You should avoid the cheapest offerings, particularly from outlets such as kiosks. Kazakhstan also produces a broad range of drinkable if rather sweet brandy, known locally as *konyak*. There are plenty of reasonable Kazakhstani beers: brands to look out for include Tian Shan, Shymkent and Karaganda. In swankier bars and restaurants in Astana and Almaty local beers and spirits do not however always feature on the menu, as they have been elbowed out by imported products. Belgian beers such as Hoegaarden are currently particularly in vogue.

PUBLIC HOLIDAYS AND FESTIVALS

Kazakhstan currently celebrates the following public holidays:

1–2 January	New Year
7 January	Russian Orthodox Christmas
8 March	International Women's Day
22 March	Nauryz
1 May	Day of Unity of the People of Kazakhstan
9 May	Victory Day
30 August	Constitution Day
25 October	Republic Day
16 December	Independence Day

The Islamic festival of Kurban Ait, whose dates are determined by the lunar calendar and which therefore vary from year to year, is also a public holiday.

The most interesting public holiday from the perspective of visitors to Kazakhstan is Nauryz, a festival with deep-seated roots, held throughout the region on or close to the vernal equinox, which commemorates the arrival of spring. 'Nauryz' is itself translated as 'new day' in languages related to Farsi, and it is traditionally the occasion for a 'spring clean' of the home. Debts are supposed to be paid in time for Nauryz, and quarrels resolved. Regarded by the Soviet authorities as an anachronism, it was restored as a public holiday in 1988. The numerous traditions involving Nauryz involve the preparation of a milky-coloured thick soup named *nauryz-kozhe*. This is made differently in different parts of Kazakhstan, but the essential requirement is that it must use seven ingredients: for example, sour milk, water, meat, salt, butter, flour and millet. By tradition it should be consumed on the day in seven different homes. Other Kazakh specialities, such as the sweet dish *zhent*, are also frequently served at Nauryz.

The Nauryz festival is traditionally the occasion for competitions of different kinds, including games on horseback, such as *kokpar, kyz kuu* and *alaman baiga* (see page 18), wrestling competitions and *aityses*, poetry duels between dombra-strumming akyns. Modern-day Nauryz competitions sometimes include such variants as the making of the largest *baursak*, or doughnut, and an award for the best-presented yurt. The act of swinging on a large swing, an *altybakan*, is also associated with Nauryz. At the end of the day you should fill all your vessels at home with spring water, grain or milk to ensure that your prosperity does not desert you. At Nauryz, yurts are set up at the central squares of many Kazakh cities, with competitions and performances of traditional songs and dances held in the squares. It is also worth asking about any programmes of traditional Kazakh horse games, which may be held at the town race track.

The two religious holidays, Russian Orthodox Christmas and Kurban Ait, were formally declared public holidays in 2006: it is characteristic of the determination President Nazarbaev has shown to display even-handedness between the main religious and ethnic minority groups in Kazakhstan that he simultaneously awarded public-holiday status to one Christian festival and one Islamic one. Kurban Ait is the festival known in some other parts of the Islamic world as Eid al-Adha, commemorating the willingness of Ibrahim to sacrifice his son when commanded to do so by Allah. Families who have the money to do so should on this day sacrifice an animal, giving a large proportion of the meat to poor families, and using the rest for a holiday meal.

Three of the public holidays mark important events in the calendar of post-independent Kazakhstan. Republic Day commemorates the adoption on 25 October 1990 of the declaration of state sovereignty by the supreme representative body of the Kazakhstan Soviet Socialist Republic, Independence Day the adoption by the Kazakhstan parliament on 16 December 1991 of the law establishing independence (16 December also marks the anniversary of the 1986 Zheltoksan demonstrations in Almaty), and Constitution Day the adoption of the 1995 Constitution on 30 August that year. There are few specific activities of touristic interest associated with these days, though they may be marked by concerts and possibly firework displays in the main squares of the largest cities.

Other holidays are survivals from the Soviet period. Victory Day celebrates the defeat of Nazism in 1945, and recognises the sacrifices of those who helped secure it. Commemorations centre on wreath layings at war memorials, but in larger cities may be more elaborate, even including battle re-enactments. International Women's Day, a popular holiday throughout the former Soviet Union, is the occasion for giving presents to, and generally feting, women. New Year's Day is a kind of national sleep-in, following the all-night partying on New Year's Eve. The 1 May was in the Soviet period the International Workers' Solidarity Day. Kazakhstan has kept the date but changed the purpose: as the Day of Unity of the People of Kazakhstan it is now a celebration of the ethnic diversity of the country.

Note that, where a holiday falls close to a weekend, the Kazakhstan government often re-jigs the weekend completely, to create a three-day break. Thus if a public holiday falls on a Thursday, it is likely that the government will announce Friday as a day off too, but declare the following Sunday, in compensation, as a working day. Those planning business meetings should note that such announcements have in the past sometimes been made only a few days in advance.

 SHOPPING

In Kazakhstan's cities you should experience few difficulties as regards food and general shopping. Supermarkets such as the somewhat unfortunately named Gros chain and the more upmarket and expensive Ramstor generally open seven days a week, stay open until late into the evening and are typically well stocked. It is worth bearing in mind too that the delicatessen counters of supermarkets can be a cheap place to put together a picnic lunch: they will usually heat up dishes such as *plov* or meat pies for you, and they offer a broad selection of salads. Some small stores and kiosks selling drinks, cigarettes and basic groceries are open 24 hours, though at night you might have to rap on the kiosk window to get the sleeping sales assistant to wake up and serve you. Bazaars offer the cheapest shopping, though note that they typically close quite early, especially during the winter months, when you might find stallholders packing up by 17.00. Specialist shops also typically close early in the evenings, and may be closed or operate shorter hours on Sundays and sometimes Saturdays.

Kazakhstan is not the best country for souvenir shopping. The attractiveness and price of the handicrafts on offer tend to compare relatively unfavourably with those to be found in central Asian neighbours such as Kyrgyzstan and Uzbekistan. Moreover, several of the most typical Kazakh souvenirs don't always appeal to Western visitors. The *kamchy*, for example, is a leather horse whip, an item hung by many Kazakhs in their homes, as a symbol of the protection of the house. But the decoration borne by the *kamchy* frequently includes a deer's hoof nailed to the side. Still if you did feel like leaving Kazakhstan with one of these items, you would be in the company of US astronaut Peggy Whitson, who was gifted one by the Russian Federal Space Agency before her launch from Baikonur in October 2007 to become the first female commander of the International Space Station. The amused Western press speculated as to whether it was intended that she would use it to keep her team in check.

Other souvenir versions of traditional items of the Kazakh nomads include the torsuk, a leather vessel used for carrying *kumiss*, which in its souvenir incarnation often has 'Kazakhstan' written on the front, lest you forget its provenance. If you are invited as a guest of honour to a Kazakh dinner, you may be presented with a lavishly embroidered cloak, a *chapan*, together with matching hat and belt. The *tubiteika*, an embroidered skullcap, can make an interesting small gift. Souvenir shops across Kazakhstan also tend to offer a broad range of felt items. Slippers and waistcoats can make for good purchases; the smiley felt camels and felt yurt trinket boxes are perhaps a matter of taste. Dolls in Kazakh costume, and Kazakh musical instruments, from *dombras* and *kobyzes* to smaller instruments such as clay whistles, known as *syrnais*, are also available. Before investing in any antiquities or expensive carpets or artworks you should check the position regarding any export restrictions in respect of the item concerned (see page 32).

Other items which can make a good souvenir include a bottle of Kazakh vodka or brandy. Some bottles feature steppe eagles and other suitably Kazakh-looking designs. The souvenir collection of Kazakh music, *Musical Kazakhstan*, issued by the Kazakh Cinema Distribution company, with one DVD and two CDs in a presentation pack, makes a nice gift, although the selection is firmly a middle-of-the-road offering. The best place to look for it is probably the music store Meloman, which has branches in all the main cities. This is also the store to get your Kazakh films and pop music.

ARTS AND ENTERTAINMENT

MUSIC Music played a hugely important role for the nomadic Kazakhs. With no written literary tradition, the work of poets, who would customarily accompany their renditions with music provided by a two-stringed guitar, the *dombra*, was an important means of the transmission of historical and cultural information. *Akyns* were improvising poets/musicians whose talent was best demonstrated at the *aitys*, a contest between *akyns*, like a kind of musical debate, in which *akyns* gave alternating performances, responding to each other through the medium of improvised verses, accompanied by the music of the *dombra*. The *zhirau* was a reciter of epic stories, and often held a key political position as a close adviser of the khan. The later *zhirshy* was also a performer of epic works, a task which required a prodigious memory in addition to sound musical skills: the text of the epic *Batyr Koblandy* ran to around 6,500 lines. An individual short piece of music is a *kui*, an instrumentalist a *kuishy*.

Music featured in all important life events of the Kazakhs: declarations of love were for example customarily made in song. The *akyn* was a key figure in ceremonies such as weddings, whose musical moments included the wedding song *zhar-zhar*, performed between the friends of the bride and groom.

Apart from the dombra, important traditional Kazakh instruments include the kobyz, played with a bow, whose origins are associated with the possibly legendary figure of Korkut Ata (see page 368), and an instrument closely associated with shamanism, as its sounds were considered to offer protection against death and to be able to drive out evil spirits. Because of these associations, the *kobyz* was an instrument discouraged by the Soviet authorities, though it has now returned to prominence. The *sybyzgy* is a long flute; the *shan kobyz*, known elsewhere as a Jew's harp, is a metallic reed instrument placed between the teeth, the mouth serving as a natural resonator. The *zhetigen* is an instrument with seven strings strung across sheeps' vertebrae. A particularly sad story attaches to its origins – it is said that an old man created each string of horse hair to mark the death during a particularly long and fierce winter of each of his seven children; by the end of the winter all were dead, and the *zhetigen* was complete. There is also a huge range of percussion instruments. The *syrnai* is an ocarina, or clay whistle. The *tuyuktas* is like the props used by radio sound engineers to make the sound of horse's hooves, except that in the case of the *tuyuktas* this is done by banging two real horse's hooves together.

The compositions of a range of Kazakh musicians of the 19th and early 20th centuries, among them Kurmangazy, Zhambyl Zhabaev and the songs of writer Abai Kunanbaev, remain widely known today. In the Soviet period, musical ensembles were created using traditional instruments but were modelled on Western orchestras. Some of the instruments were modernised too, such that the strings of the *dombra* are now typically made of nylon rather than the traditional gut. The creation in 1980 of the Otrar Sazy ensemble by Nurgisa Tlendiev was in part a reaction against what many Kazakhs viewed as the excessive Europeanisation of Kazakh music, by focusing on traditional techniques.

The arrival of the Russians brought Western classical music to Kazakhstan, and there have been many notable Kazakhstani classical musicians. Most of the best known internationally have however moved outside Kazakhstan. These include violinist Marat Bisengaliev (*www.maratbisengaliev.com*), who is based in the United Kingdom. He participated in the inaugural performance at the Royal Albert Hall in 2006 of *Tlep*, a composition by the Welsh composer Karl Jenkins, based around the life of Kazakh *kobyz* player Tlep Aspantaiuly, an ancestor of businessman Sapar Iskakov, who commissioned the piece. The composition used traditional Kazakh instruments alongside more familiar ones. Also currently based in Britain are soprano Elena Kelessidi, born in Kazakhstan of ethnic Greek parentage, who made her debut at the Royal Opera House in 1996 as Violetta in *La Traviata*, and the Kazakhstan-born sisters of piano trio the Bekova Trio (*www.bekovatrio.com*).

Middle-of-the-road popular music of the kind known throughout the former Soviet Union as estrada attracted large audiences in Kazakhstan from the 1960s: noted Kazakh singers in this genre included Rosa Baglanova and Rosa Rimbaeva, the latter still belting out her numbers to middle-aged audiences across the country. As regards the contemporary popular music scene the most famous Kazakhstani band internationally is now based in Moscow, and is regarded by many as more a Russian band than a Kazakhstani one. A'Studio (*www.astudio.ru*) started out as the backing group for Rosa Rimbaeva in the early 1980s, before setting up in 1987 as Almata, then Almata Studio. They were talent spotted by Russian singer Alla Pugacheva, and dropped the link to Almaty in their name. Now fronted by the young Georgian vocalist Katy Topuria, their dance music even saw them graze the UK charts in 2006, with the single 'SOS'.

Several bands offer interesting attempts to fuse Kazakh traditional music with rock or pop. Ulytau (*www.ulytau.ru*) describe themselves as 'Kazakh ethno-rock', and combine *dombra*, violin and electric guitar in exuberant instrumental offerings – well worth checking out. Urker (*www.urker.kz*; their website features an English-language version) are a pop group established in 1993, fusing Kazakh styles and instruments with Western ones. *Dombra* player Asylbek Ensepov brings the instrument into new contexts, as with his rendition of the theme from *Pulp Fiction*.

A number of new faces have emerged through the television talent show *Super Star KZ*, a kind of local version of *Pop Idol*. Pop groups All Davai, Rahat-lukum, A'Studio, Metis, FM and Tekilla have a wide following, and there is a predictably long list of girl bands around: Dauys-International seem to be about the best of the bunch. Male vocalist Batyr is Batyrkhan Shukenov, formerly with A'Studio. One of my favourite Kazakhstani groups is the melodic and mellow pop duo Musicola (*www.musicola.ru*). Stores of the Meloman chain should be able to offer the latest CD offerings of most of the above.

LITERATURE The development of Kazakh literature is closely allied to that of its music, as an oral tradition focused on the tales and epic poetry of the *akyns* and *zhiraus*. The epics were often based around the heroic exploits of Kazakh warriors, *batyrs*, the stories invoking the spiritual interventions of the saints, ancestors and forces of nature in a blending of religious traditions, and normally also featuring a remarkable horse of great speed and strength belonging to the hero as well as the assistance of a beautiful woman. Epic love stories, such as *Kyz-Zhibek*, were also

2

popular. Individual works start to be known from the 18th century, including some of those of Bukhar Zhirau, an adviser to Ablai Khan. In the 19th century, works of poets such as Makhambet Utemisov expressed concern about the increasing Russian control over the region.

The leading Kazakh literary figure of the 19th century, and regarded by many as the founder of modern Kazakh literature as a written rather than simply oral form of communication, was Abai Kunanbaev. His works drew from the oral tradition of the steppe, from Islamic authors such as Navoi and from Russian literature, in which he was immersed through his friendship with exiled Russian intellectuals in Semipalatinsk. He wrote poetry and songs, especially lyrics about love, translated Russian poetry into Kazakh and set down an ethical code, through a series of short essays, or Words.

A whole generation of Kazakh writers in the early 20th century was put to death in the Stalinist repression of the 1930s, for fear that its leading figures were too close to nationalist or pan-Turkic sentiments. Shakarim Kudaiberdiev, Saken Seifullin, Ilyas Zhansugurov and Beimbet Mailin were among those killed. One of the few prominent Kazakh writers to be spared was Mukhtar Auezov, whose writings did much to promote the work of Abai, as well as to provide a wider picture of Kazakh traditions. Significant writers of the later Soviet period include Ilyas Esenberlin, whose *The Nomads* is an immensely detailed account of the history of the Kazakh khanates, and poet Olzhas Suleimenov, who wrote in Russian and later became a prominent anti-nuclear-testing campaigner at the helm of the Nevada–Semipalatinsk movement. Suleimenov's 1975 book *AZ i YA*, its title combining the Kazakh and Russian words for 'I' to make the sound 'Asia', was his most controversial literary work, condemned by the Moscow establishment for its glorification of what they regarded as the feudal nomadic culture. It took an intervention from the then First Secretary of the Communist Party of Kazakhstan, Dinmuhammed Kunaev, to save Suleimenov's career.

A small number of Kazakh writers have come to the fore more recently, though little of their work has been translated. Among them the best known are perhaps Ilia Odegov, author of *Zvuk, s kotorim vstaet solnse* and *Bez dvuh odin*, and Ramil Aitkaliev, the writer of *Pesnia 81*.

See *Appendix 3, Further reading*, page 411, for more information on literature from Kazakhstan.

CINEMA The film industry in Kazakhstan has its origins in the production of documentaries in Almaty in the 1930s. The first Kazakh feature film, *Amangeldy* (1939), about the leader of the 1916 revolution Amangeldy Imanov, was however the work of Lenfilm in Leningrad. Filmmaking in Kazakhstan was given a boost by the dislocations caused by World War II, as the main Soviet studios, Mosfilm and Lenfilm, were both evacuated to Almaty in 1941, where they were combined with the Almaty Film Studio to produce the Central United Film Studio, which ran until 1944. Much of the great Soviet director Sergei Eisenstein's two-part epic *Ivan the Terrible* was filmed in Kazakhstan.

In the **post-war Soviet period**, the major figure of Kazakhstan's film industry was director Shaken Aimanov, in whose honour the Kazfilm studios were renamed in 1984. Notable films of this period include a number of historical epics, such as the tragic love story *Kyz-Zhibek* (1970), and a trio of action films involving a secret agent, played by Asanali Ashimov, who uses all manner of derring-do to defeat the enemies of communism. The first in the trilogy, *The End of the Ataman* (1970), was set in 1921 and was directed by Aimanov. The second, *Trans-Siberian*

Express (1977), directed by Eldor Urazbaev and set in 1927, featured a complicated plot involving the defeat of counter-revolutionaries planning to kill a Japanese businessman on a train bound for Moscow, on which our hero was masquerading as a cabaret manager. The third in the trilogy, *Manchurian Version* (1989), was set in 1945 Manchuria. The films, with their central hero played by a Kazakh actor, were, as well as entertainment, part of the efforts of the Soviet establishment to demonstrate that the Kazakh people fully supported communism.

With perestroika in the Soviet Union of the late 1980s emerged a **new wave** of young Kazakhstani filmmakers, ready to challenge the cinematic establishment. A shot in the arm was provided, quite literally, by *The Needle* (1989), the first film directed by Rashid Nugmanov, who cast as his central figure Viktor Tsoi, front-man of the rock group Kino and already a hero to disaffected Soviet youth. Kino also contributed to the soundtrack. Tsoi's character returns to Alma-Ata to collect money he is owed, only to find out that his former girlfriend has become a drug addict. He decides to fight against the drug pushers and it all ends badly. Nugmanov's *The Wild East* (1993), loosely based on Kurosawa's *Seven Samurai*, involves a group of dwarves, runaways from the circus, who bring in the magnificent seven to protect them from the predations of motorbike-riding Mongolian hoodlums. (No, I'm not making this up.) Nugmanov moved to Paris in 1993, where he has been associated with Kazakhstani political opposition groups.

Other filmmakers of post-independence Kazakhstan to have achieved success at international festivals include Satybaldy Narimbetov. His *Biography of a Young Accordion Player* (1994) is a tale of a small boy growing up in a Kazakh village during World War II. *Leila's Prayer* (2002) focuses on a girl from a village close to the Semipalatinsk nuclear test site, whose mother, father and aunt all die of unexplained diseases and whose prayer is that her baby son should live to old age. Darezhan Omirbaev's *Killer* (1998), a Kazakh–French co-production, is a tragic tale highlighting the economic difficulties faced by Kazakhstanis in the 1990s. A young Almaty driver causes a minor motor accident when taking his wife and newborn baby back home from the hospital. Unable to pay for the damage, he gets sucked into crime. Amir Karakulov has garnered critical praise for a number of films, including *Homewrecker* (1991), a tale of two brothers in love with the same girl. Again, it all ends badly. A newer arrival on the scene is Rustem Abdrashev. His directorial debut was *Renaissance Island* (2004), a tale of the first love of an aspiring poet set against the historical backdrop of the desiccation of the Aral Sea.

One problem is that very few of these films have been widely seen by audiences in Kazakhstan. Domestic distributors have preferred to rely on a diet of dubbed Hollywood blockbusters and big-budget Russian movies, with the result that post-independence Kazakhstani cinema has developed something of a reputation as being more likely to be found in Western art houses and international competitions than on screens in Kazakhstan. One occasion which does offer the opportunity to see a range of Kazakhstani films is the annual Eurasia International Film Festival, held in Almaty in September. This also attracts a few international stars: guests have included Catherine Deneuve and Steven Seagal. Details of the festival are on www.eurasiaiff.kz.

The big-budget Kazakhstan film has however now arrived. *Nomad* (see page 174), with its international crew and cast, was an officially supported attempt to bring a film based on the exploits of Kazakh warriors of the 18th century onto international screens. *Racketeer* (2007), directed by Akhan Sataev, about a young Almaty boxer in the tough economic climate of the 1990s, was billed as the first purely commercially oriented film made in post-independence Kazakhstan, and proved a considerable box-office draw. One Kazakh director, though now based in

Russia, Timur Bekmambetov, has also had success internationally in commercial cinema projects, particularly with the Russian fantasy features *Night Watch* (2004) and *Day Watch* (2006). Bekmambetov now seems to have his sights set on Hollywood, and his film *Wanted* (2008) starred James McAvoy, Morgan Freeman and Angelina Jolie. Sadly it was not the great success that its star-studded line-up might suggest.

Foreign directors to have set films in Kazakhstan include Volker Schloendorff, whose *Ulzhan* treks the passage across the country of a weary Frenchman, heading for the holy mountain of Khan Tengri. The rural schoolteacher Ulzhan becomes his protector.

Cinemas in Kazakhstan range from draughty Soviet survivals to modern multiplex complexes. Ticket prices are lower than those in western Europe or North America, but there is little shown in English. Films originally made in English are almost invariably dubbed, not subtitled.

THEATRE Theatre arrived in Kazakhstan with the Russians. The first performance of a Kazakh play is generally believed to have been the premiere of Mukhtar Auezov's *Enlik-Kebek*, performed in 1917 in a specially adapted yurt near Semipalatinsk. The first Kazakh drama theatre was established in Kyzylorda, then the capital, in the 1920s. The evacuation to Kazakhstan of some of the brightest lights of Soviet theatre during World War II also served to promote the development of theatre in Kazakhstan.

Wartime evacuation stimulated the development of ballet too, with the legendary Soviet ballerina Galina Ulanova one of those to dance on the stages of Almaty during the war period. Kazakhstan remains an important training ground for ballet stars who have progressed onto the world stage, among them Altynai Asylmuratova, a former leading ballerina with the Kirov Ballet. Opera also arrived with the Russians. Operas based around Kazakh legends and traditions were developed from the 1930s, including those penned by Evgeny Brusilovsky, born in Rostov on Don but who settled in Almaty in 1933. His operas include *Abai* and *Kyz-Zhibek*.

For the visitor, the opera and ballet on offer at the Abai Opera and Ballet Theatre in Almaty and Baiseitova Opera and Ballet Theatre in Astana are among the best bargains the country has to offer: good-quality performances at a fraction of the price you would pay in western Europe or North America. The repertoires are mostly Russian and western European classics, but they sometimes show Kazakh operas and ballets too. Most large cities have both a Kazakh and a Russian drama theatre, sometimes sharing the same premises, but you'll of course need to have the relevant language to appreciate the performance. Experimental theatre is also on offer in Almaty through companies like Art i Shock, whose provocative *Back in the USSR*, about girls growing up under communism, was performed in London at the Riverside Studios.

PHOTOGRAPHY

Memory cards, film and other camera accessories are not widely available outside Astana and Almaty, so carry ample supplies with you for your trip. You might also want to consider packing a lens cloth, lens cleaner and a can of compressed air as the dust gets absolutely everywhere, particularly when out on the steppe, and can ruin your shots if it gets on the lens or the chip.

Kazakh police and other government officials are not keen on being photographed, so keep your camera down when they are present and be prepared to delete any recent shots at their request. Bridges, government buildings, railway stations, airports and sensitive areas (such as the Polygon and around Baikonur) are not considered suitable photographic subjects, and your equipment may be confiscated if you are taking photos of these too indiscreetly.

Members of the public, particularly children, are generally keen to have their photograph taken, though it is still polite to ask first. You may occasionally be asked for payment, but this is not required unless it has been arranged in advance. If you have a digital camera, be sure to show your subject their image on the screen and, if you volunteer to send them a copy, remember to do so on your return home as it avoids disappointment.

❱ MEDIA AND COMMUNICATIONS

MEDIA There is a more developed private media in Kazakhstan than in other parts of central Asia, though there is a concentration of holdings around a few groups within the political and business elite. The Russian-language *Kazakhstanskaya Pravda* and Kazakh-language *Yegemen Qazaqstan* newspapers are state owned, and provide exhaustive positive coverage of government business. Privately owned papers broadly supportive of the authorities include *Ekspress K, Liter* and *Novoye Pokoleniye*. A wide range of views is available among Kazakhstan's print media, and there are papers supportive of political opposition groups, such as *Svoboda Slova*, though these can be difficult to find outside Almaty. There have, however, been international concerns expressed regarding various apparent forms of harassment of some opposition media outlets and, more recently, fatal attacks on journalists. Many newspapers are weeklies, often released on Thursdays. National television and radio channels are all broadly supportive of the government. Kazakhstan and Kazakhstan Radio are the state-run television and radio stations respectively. Television and radio channels are required to transmit at least 50% of their content in the Kazakh language, and there are also limits on the amount of foreign programming which can be shown.

There are few local newspapers in English. The Almaty-based *Kazakhstan Monitor* and *Almaty Herald*, both weeklies offering a few local news articles coupled with syndicated international general-interest stories, and the Bishkek-based *Times of Central Asia* (*www.timesca.com*), which offers a weekly digest of regional news, are the main options, though are not always easy to find. The satellite channel Caspionet offers an English-language news programme, alternating with Kazakh and Russian editions of the same programme, though its content tends to be dull, and is delivered by bored-sounding announcers. Internet-based news services offer a better range of English news. The website of Kazinform, the national information agency (*www.inform.kz*), is an up-to-date source of information from a government perspective. The online news agency Gazeta.kz (*www.gazeta.kz*) also has good English-language coverage.

If you are coming to Kazakhstan to live, you or your company might wish to consider one of the subscription-based news services. An English-language service is offered by Interfax Kazakhstan (℅ *727 250 1390;* e *almaty@interfax.kz; www. interfax.kz*). At the premium end of the range, you can set up a service tailored by country or topic with Bbc Monitoring (℅ *0118 948 6289;* f *0118 948 6331; www. monitor.bbc.co.uk*).

COMMUNICATIONS
Telephone To telephone into Kazakhstan, you need to dial the relevant international access code from the country from which you are calling (eg: 00

from the United Kingdom, 011 from the United States) followed by 7 (Kazakhstan's country code), then the relevant city code (given at the start of each of the city entries through this guide), then the number.

Calling out from Kazakhstan, you need first to dial Kazakhstan's international access code, which is 8, followed by a pause until you hear the tone, then 10, and thereafter the relevant country code (eg: 44 for the United Kingdom), city code and number. If you are calling another number within Kazakhstan, you need to dial 8 (the trunk code) before the number to make long-distance calls and for calls to a mobile telephone. If you are calling within the same administrative region (oblast), replace the first three digits of the town code with a 2.

Mobile-phone coverage tends to be good in and around urban areas, and networks are slowly being expanded to include more remote rural and mountain areas. The main service providers are Kcell, Beeline, Activ and K-Mobile. There

FOOTBALL IN KAZAKHSTAN

The British press was not greatly enthused by the qualifying group in which the England football team found itself for the 2010 World Cup. The main focus of press attention following the 2007 draw was the presence of Croatia, the team which had only a few days previously ended England's hopes of reaching the European finals in 2008. But the presence of Kazakhstan in the group did not cheer the sports writers either, except in the sense of providing an excuse for a joke or two about Borat. Their major concern appeared less to do with the quality of the Kazakhstan team than with the sheer distance involved in getting there, as they bemoaned England's 'hellish travel schedule'. FIFA currently ranks Kazakhstan as 137th in the world.

But according to some accounts, it was travellers from England, in this case merchants visiting Semipalatinsk during the Tsarist period, who brought football to Kazakhstan in the first place. Pavlodar soon followed Semipalatinsk in setting up teams. Club sides from Kazakhstan competed in Soviet football from the 1930s, with Kairat Almaty making the semi-finals of the Soviet Cup in 1963. Post-independence, a Kazakhstan Football Association was set up, and accepted into the Asian Football Confederation. As a country with territory in Europe as well as Asia, Kazakhstan unusually switched regional federations, joining UEFA in 2002. Its teams have to date had little success in European club competitions, though the national side notched up an impressive home win against Serbia in the Euro 2008 qualifiers.

The domestic game is now managed by the Football Federation of Kazakhstan. I was intrigued to note that their website (*www.kff.kz*) includes a 'beach football' page. Mind you, this was blank at the time of writing. There is a 12-member Premier League, with matches played from March to early November. Fixtures are generally at weekends, with afternoon kick-offs in spring and autumn, and evening ones during the heat of summer. Corruption has been a concern, and the Federation took the step of disqualifying one club, Ekibastuzets, from the 2008 season following charges of match fixing in the previous one. Many of the main clubs trace their histories back well into the Soviet period, though they have often undergone bewilderingly frequent changes of name. The Shymkent team founded as Dinamo Shymkent in 1949 has, for example, been known successively as Yenbek, Metallurg, Meliorator, Zhiger and Dostyk, and is now FC Ordabasy.

are roaming agreements in place with most of the international mobile-phone companies. Phones on the street are operated by cards, which can be purchased from many kiosks. After inserting the card, the number of units remaining will be displayed. You can then dial your number. When you are connected, press the button with the 'lips' symbol to speak. You can also make calls from many offices of the state communications company, Kazakhtelecom: pay at the counter, then wait to be summoned to a booth to make your call. The convenience of making that call home straight from your hotel room will come with a hefty charge. There are various phonecards available, sold from the mobile-phone shops and kiosks which seem to be taking over Kazakhstan's cities, and these offer cheaper-rate international and long-distance calls. The various mobile-phone shops will also sell you a SIM card: well worth considering if you will be in Kazakhstan for some time.

Internet Kazakhtelecom is the main internet service provider. Internet access in Kazakhstan tends to be relatively expensive, though the government has acknowledged the need to address the high costs and often low quality of what is available. There are numerous internet cafés in the main cities but little or no coverage elsewhere. A small but growing number of cafés and hotels in Almaty and Astana offer Wi-Fi: this is sometimes (but not always) free.

Post KazPost is the national postal service. Its website (*www.kazpost.kz*) offers interesting background on the philatelic products on sale at larger branches, including commemorative stamps and first-day covers. If you need to send anything valuable, urgent or important, one of the major international courier companies would be a better bet. **DHL** (*www.dhl.kz*; their website has an English-language version) has offices in most regional capitals, usually open between Monday and Friday. FedEx is represented in Kazakhstan by the Almaty-based company **Emex** (℃ 727 250 3566; e *sales@emex.kz*). You should, however, be aware that the service provided out of Kazakhstan even by international courier companies tends not to be particularly fast in comparison with some parts of the world, a function of the relatively limited range of flight connections.

BUSINESS

The government of post-independence Kazakhstan has been keen to promote foreign investment and, given the country's natural resource wealth, a great deal has been forthcoming. With several years of economic growth running at or close to 10% per annum, after the difficult years of the 1990s, Kazakhstan became more confident, and the terms on offer to new foreign investors, especially in the oil and gas sector, were increasingly tough. Kazakhstan was however one of the first to be hit by the global economic crisis in 2008 due to its reliance on the banking sector and the oil industry. This led to a decline in economic growth from 8.5% in 2007 to just 1.2% in 2009, before rebounding unexpectedly to 7% in 2010.

Outward investments of Kazakhstani companies have become an important part of the overall business picture, and Kazakhstani companies are increasingly prominent on the London Stock Exchange, where several major businesses have raised money through Initial Public Offerings (IPOs). In 2005, copper company Kazakhmys, in what was the first primary London listing by a company from the former Soviet Union, entered straight into the FTSE 100, knocking brewers Whitbread out of the list in the process.

Current priorities of the Kazakhstan government include the development of Almaty as a regional financial centre, and the diversification of the economy away from overdependence on oil and gas. The authorities are also keen to promote the development of local Kazakhstani content, which includes awarding more sub-contracts to Kazakhstani companies in large oil and gas operations, encouragement to foreign companies to focus on the training and development of local workers, and the localisation of some jobs formerly held by expatriates (restrictions on the numbers of work permits issued are used to achieve the last). The focus on local content has been a spur to the establishment of limited liability partnerships (LLPs) or joint-stock companies (JSCs) in Kazakhstan, rather than on foreign firms simply setting up representative offices to promote their interests in the country.

Doing business in Kazakhstan requires careful research. Company structures, business relationships, professional qualifications and the value given to contracts may not be consistent with those found in the West, so you will need to spend time identifying where clan, familial and political ties will influence your business model and choice of in-country partners and staff. If you are looking to set up a business you will need to find a 'roof' – a well-connected, politically and commercially astute patron who is paid a fee to share your commercial outlook and protect your financial interests in the country.

The bureaucracy can be considerable, and you will need to be clear as regards such issues as licences, customs and taxation, as well as how, and when, you will get paid. Accounting can be extremely 'creative' so be prepared to pay for a full audit by a reputable international firm before investing. The request for bribes is commonplace, both in the private and public sectors, and you should attempt to formalise these into fees, complete with invoice, wherever possible so that all parties know what is expected. Get to know the true cost of everything involved before you commit to any financial arrangement. Invoice padding is a particularly common occurrence.

There is more information for British exporters at www.uktradeinvest.gov.uk. A number of law practices in Almaty are experienced in guiding foreign companies through the options involved in setting up in Kazakhstan. It is advised that contracts be written under English or Swiss law and the place of arbitration be specified from the outset. The major international accounting firms have offices in Almaty, and a few have branches in Astana and Atyrau. International banks are well represented in Kazakhstan and, although the interest rates they offer may be lower than the local competition, they have greater long-term stability and transparency, and a wider range of financial products on offer.

It is important to have researched the market thoroughly before meeting potential Kazakhstani clients. In a fast-growing emerging market, Kazakhstanis in senior positions, especially procurement directors, are inundated by would-be suppliers of goods and services. You need to have put in the research to be able to demonstrate why your product is needed by the company, you should have promotional materials available in Russian, and you need to have investigated the quality standards used by the company (the old Soviet GOST standards are still in widespread use in many industries, though not everywhere) and be able to certify that your product meets them. Personal contact is vital, but only when you have done your research. Business is status-orientated, so establish in advance who you will be dealing with, their relative position, age and motivations. Initial business meetings tend to be quite formal, though, as a business relationship develops, you may typically be invited for an evening of Kazakh hospitality around a *dastarkhan* (see page 53), as it helps all parties get to know one another better.

The commercial landscape of Kazakhstan is littered with the remnants of Western businesses that had identified potential in the country but failed to take into account local realities. Research and the ability to harness those realities is the key to success.

Several companies organise trade fairs in Kazakhstan. Most of the largest exhibitions are run by ITECA (*www.iteca.kz*; their website gives dates and further information), the central Asian part of the ITE Group. These include KITF (travel and tourism; Almaty in April); KAZBUILD (building and construction; Almaty in September) and KIOGE (oil and gas; Almaty in October). Other exhibition organisers include TNT (*www.tntexpo.com*) and Kazexpo (*www.kazexpo.kz*).

BUYING PROPERTY

Foreign citizens, other than permanent residents of Kazakhstan, are not allowed to own property in the country. However, companies and other legal entities, whether they are based in Kazakhstan or not, may acquire property, and this is the most common legal way of circumventing the property ownership restriction.

CULTURAL ETIQUETTE

Hospitality towards guests is an important part of Kazakh culture. If you are invited to a Kazakh home, you should take a small gift for your hosts. A souvenir item, like a picture book, from your home country is ideal, but if you have brought nothing suitable with you a gift such as a bouquet of flowers (get an odd number) is fine. Note that an invitation to go to someone's house for 'a cup of tea' invariably means something more substantial: often a full meal. If you are invited out for a restaurant meal, your host will be expecting to pay, and may take offence if you offer to contribute to the costs. On entering a home in Kazakhstan (true for an ethnic Russian family as well as a Kazakh one, and for a yurt as well as a flat) you should remove your shoes at the door. There is usually a mixture of assorted slippers and flip-flops available to wear around the house. You should not shake hands across a doorway or step on the threshold of a yurt. You should also be wary of admiring too fulsomely a belonging of your hosts such as an attractive ornament: they may feel bound to present it to you.

Let your host tell you where he would like you to sit around the table or *dastarkhan*. This will often be at the head of the table or, if you are being treated to a Kazakh meal in a traditional yurt, at the back of the yurt, furthest away from the door, since these are the places usually assigned to 'honoured guests'. Don't try to challenge this decision. There will be far more food than you could possibly eat, and you are not expected to finish everything. If you have a clean plate your host will simply pile more food onto it. On the other hand, you should try to eat as heartily as you feel able. However much you tuck in, your host will probably express the view that you are only picking at your meal, and urge you to eat more.

The specific etiquette surrounding the presentation to the honoured guest of a sheep's head, or *koy bas*, is discussed on page 54. One other area steeped in conventions is the practice of toasts. Not all Kazakhs drink alcohol, and it is not served at every function, but the legacy of Tsarist Russia and the Soviet Union has implanted in Kazakhstan the tradition of toasts, most frequently with vodka, though sometimes brandy, whisky or wine. There is a strong risk that you will come under pressure to drink more than you are comfortable with. The key rules of surviving a lengthy series of toasts include ensuring that you drink plenty of water

2

The name 'Kazakhstan' is best known to many in western Europe and North America through the activities of journalist Borat Sagdiyev. But Mr Sagdiyev is a fictional character, portrayed by British comedian Sacha Baron Cohen. In his 'Guides to Britain' and 'Guides to USA', shown on Cohen's *Da Ali G Show*, and in the hit movie *Borat: Cultural Learnings of America for Make Benefit Glorious Nation of Kazakhstan*, the character displays wildly offensive views, including anti-Semitism and reactionary attitudes towards women's rights, in a bid to get his unsuspecting interviewees to expose their prejudices on camera. He engages too in unacceptable public behaviour, whether inviting a prostitute to meet him at a dinner party to which he has been invited, disrupting a convention of mortgage brokers with a naked brawl with his producer, or endeavouring to abduct actress Pamela Anderson in his 'marriage sack', all in order to get a reaction from those around him. The fact that 'Kazakhstan' was chosen as the home country of this comic creation probably largely just reflects the consideration that few people in Britain or the USA knew very much about the country, thus allowing Sacha Baron Cohen to ascribe to his comic creation any views and traits that he wanted.

But Kazakhstan is a real country, not a fictional one, and there was understandable concern in the country that it was being portrayed as a land of reactionary views which had nothing to do with the history and attitudes of the real Kazakhstan. The country's Ministry of Foreign Affairs took exception to Borat's portrayal of their country at the MTV Europe Music Awards in Lisbon in November 2005, and the internet domain name www.borat.kz was suspended. The movie does not seem to have been formally banned in Kazakhstan, but it wasn't distributed.

But when President Nazarbaev visited London in November 2006, he took a notably conciliatory line towards the character in his comments to the British press, and the Kazakhstan authorities have recognised that negative publicity can have positive results. Kazakhstan's Minister for Tourism and Sport acknowledged that the *Borat* movie had boosted foreign tourism to Kazakhstan.

The Kazakhstanis are now getting their revenge, as director Erkin Rakishev has produced his own sequel, *My Brother Borat*, which will be released internationally in 2011. The sequel sees an American journalist travelling around the country with Borat's mentally ill brother Bilo (kept in a cage in the original film), having discovered him in a psychiatric ward with Osama Bin Laden and George Bush.

and fruit juice, and keep eating between toasts; that you try to get whoever is filling your glass between toasts to add just a little each time by horizontal hand signals or the Russian phrase *chyt chyt* ('just a little'); and above all to recognise that you don't have to drain your glass at every toast, however much some of the people around the table will be encouraging you to. As a rule, the first toast, your own toast, a toast made 'to the ladies' (during which the men around the table all stand), and the last toast should be downed in one (though beware of fake 'final toasts' which prove to be anything but); for all the others a small sip is fine. Your host or a designated toastmaster, if appointed, will usually make clear when you are expected to give your toast. This needn't be anything elaborate (though it can be, if you are feeling inspired): the main thing is to remember to offer warm thanks to your hosts for their hospitality.

At the end of the meal, thanks are given by the act of bringing the hands together in front of the face, then moving them down in an action symbolising a washing gesture. This is the signal for everyone to get up from the table. You shouldn't continue to pick at food after this point.

In general, a positive attitude to Kazakhstan and an interest in its culture and traditions will be much appreciated.

TRAVELLING POSITIVELY

When asking Kazakhstani friends what was the best advice they thought I could give to foreign visitors to ensure they gave something back to the country they were visiting, one recommendation kept coming up. It was that visitors to Kazakhstan should get to know the country and its people and that, on returning home, they should then explain to their friends and work colleagues what this country, too little known in the West, was really like. They should explain that it was a very different place from other countries whose names end with '-stan'. They should explain about its beauty, and achievements. And they should explain that it had nothing at all to do with the image of 'Kazakhstan' peddled by Borat.

A thoroughly worthwhile initiative named 'Stuff Your Rucksack' has been set up by television presenter Kate Humble. The website (*www.stuffyourrucksack.com*) lists organisations around the world looking for modest help (an orphanage in need of children's toys, perhaps): the idea is that travellers will consult the website before their trip, make contact with a listed organisation where they are going, and stuff their rucksack with a few items requested by the group. The charity gets what it needs, and the traveller gets to interact with local people in a context far removed from the usual tourist experience.

If you plan to visit Shymkent during your travels in Kazakhstan, one dedicated group which welcomes visitors is Crossroads Central Asia (*7A Chekov St, Shymkent;* (7252) 546284; e *admin@crossroads.kz; www.crossroads.kz*). Crossroads assists charities and welfare institutions across central Asia and in Afghanistan by providing not money but quality donated goods. They welcome donations of items such as children's clothes, toys, stationery, shoes, camping and sporting equipment.

Part Two

THE GUIDE

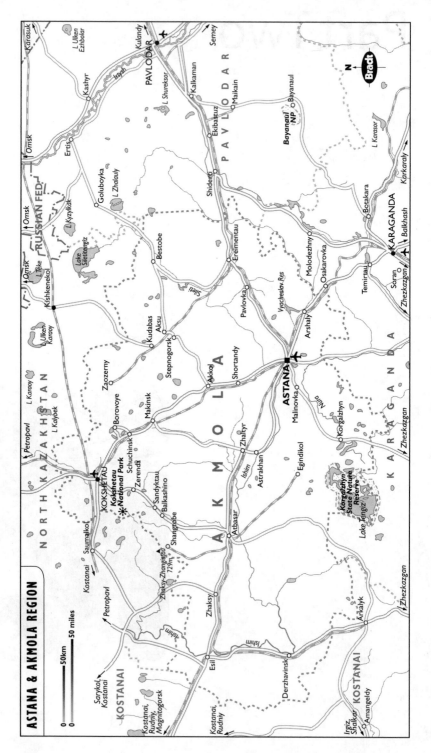

ASTANA & AKMOLA REGION

0 ⊢——⊣ 50km
0 ⊢——⊣ 50 miles

3

Astana and Akmola Region

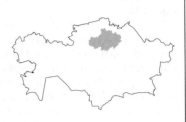

Astana is an urban expression of Kazakhstan's post-independence achievements, a statement of an increasingly wealthy and confident country. The city is rich with the symbols of the post-independence regime: a tower based around the imagery of the Kazakh 'tree of life', a pyramid to celebrate peace and inter-religious harmony and, in a nod to the nomadic history of the Kazakhs combined with a modern consumerism, a giant transparent tent which shelters a shopping and entertainment complex from the extremes of this steppe climate. The politicians and officials working in the city, which has been Kazakhstan's capital only since 1997, are housed in apartment complexes of increasing architectural audacity: shimmering to represent the northern lights, or aping one of the Stalinist-era 'Seven Sisters' skyscrapers in Moscow. To get a clear sense of Kazakhstan's aspirations, you should come here. Akmola Region, surrounding the capital, also has a number of worthwhile places to visit. Top of the list are the lakes and forested hills of Borovoye, 'Kazakhstan's Switzerland' as the tour agencies bill it, and the steppe lakes around Korgalzhyn, home to the world's most northerly colony of pink flamingos and a paradise for birdwatchers.

ASTANA   *Telephone code: 7172*

The capital of Kazakhstan since 1997, Astana has grown at a staggering rate. With a population of little more than 300,000 when it inherited the mantle of national capital from Almaty, it grew to beyond half a million in just a few years. Plans that Astana would top one million people by 2030 have been revised forwards. President Nazarbaev wants Astana not just to grow, but also to be special, a sparkling symbol of independent Kazakhstan. World-renowned architects have been enlisted to help build the city: its general plan designed by Japanese architect Kisho Kurokawa, some of its most eye-catching buildings by Norman Foster. The rise in the cost of borrowing precipitated by the US sub-prime mortgage crisis in 2007 slowed the building boom, but the skyline of Astana remains dominated by cranes as the new capital continues to take shape on the steppe.

HISTORY Kazakhstan's archaeologists have devoted much recent attention to establishing a long historical pedigree for Astana, not least to downplay suggestions that the nation's capital may have started its life as a Russian fort. The remains of a settlement, possibly Buzuk, established by Turkic tribes in the 8th or 9th century, have been identified on the outskirts of the modern city. This had been deserted by the 13th century, though the site was used for burials for several more centuries. At the centre of the modern city, on the banks of the River Ishim, a site known as Karaotkel, 'black ford', was long used as a crossing place of the river. And it was here in 1830 that the Tsarist authorities started to construct a fortress, which would be named Akmola.

There are many different interpretations of the origins of the name Akmola, which by one account derives from the Kazakh 'white grave'. Some believe that the name refers to the white-domed Mausoleum of Niyaz Bi, an adviser to Ablai Khan, which reportedly stood near the site. Others suggest that it refers to a limestone hillock, which had some burials at its summit. Another version has it that the name is not to do with death, but milk, arguing that the name comes from Ak Mol, 'white abundance', a reference to the rich dairy products of the area. To add to the confusion, Akmola was probably not the geographical name associated with the eventual site of the fortress at all, but with the place originally chosen for it, more than 30km away, which proved to be too prone to flooding.

The fortress was one of the targets of the ultimately unsuccessful rebellion of Kazakhs led by Kenesary Kasymov in the late 1830s, who called on the Tsarist authorities to take down their fortresses in Kazakh territories. Akmola received town status in 1862, and gradually developed into a trading centre between Russia and central Asia. From 1852 a popular market known as Konstantinov's Fair was held each year at the end of May and the beginning of June. Its site was that of the present-day Congress Hall. Following the arrival of the railway in the late 1920s, Astana developed into an important railway centre, especially with the later extension of the track to bring coal from Karaganda to Russia. The town's population was swelled with the arrival of deportees from the 1930s: Akmola lay close to the ALZHIR labour camp, which housed the wives and children of convicted 'betrayers of the homeland'.

The character of this quiet regional capital changed dramatically in 1954 when Khrushchev launched the **Virgin Lands Campaign**, to develop large swathes of the Kazakhstani steppe for grain production (see box, page 76). Akmola, which already housed an agricultural machinery factory, was one of the centres of the Virgin Lands programme. Some 3.5 million hectares of virgin land was ploughed in the region between 1953 and 1956. In 1961, the town was renamed Tselinograd, 'virgin lands city'. Large numbers of five-storey apartment blocks were built to cope with the rapidly growing population.

Following independence, the city was given back the name Akmola in 1992. In 1994, on the initiative of President Nazarbaev, the Kazakhstan authorities announced that the capital would be relocated from Almaty to Astana. On 10 December 1997, by a presidential decree, Akmola was duly named as the capital of Kazakhstan. In May of the following year the new capital city was renamed Astana, which in Kazakh simply means 'capital'.

The decision to relocate the capital was not universally welcomed, particularly in cosmopolitan Almaty, some of whose citizens still tend to regard Astana as a place of exile in the frozen north. Numerous theories have been advanced as to why Nazarbaev decided to move the capital, almost all of which probably offer part of the explanation. Official accounts tend to stress the centrality of Astana's location, both in respect of the country and of the Eurasian landmass as a whole: the city serves as a bridge, it is argued, between Europe and Asia. The constraints on the further urban expansion of Almaty, hemmed in by the Tian Shan Mountains, and its vulnerability to earthquakes, are also often mentioned. Some academics have favoured geopolitical explanations, citing Almaty's proximity to China, and also apparent concerns in the immediate post-independence years about the direction of focus of parts of northern Kazakhstan, with large ethnic Russian populations and close links with Russia. Bringing the capital closer to the north was perhaps

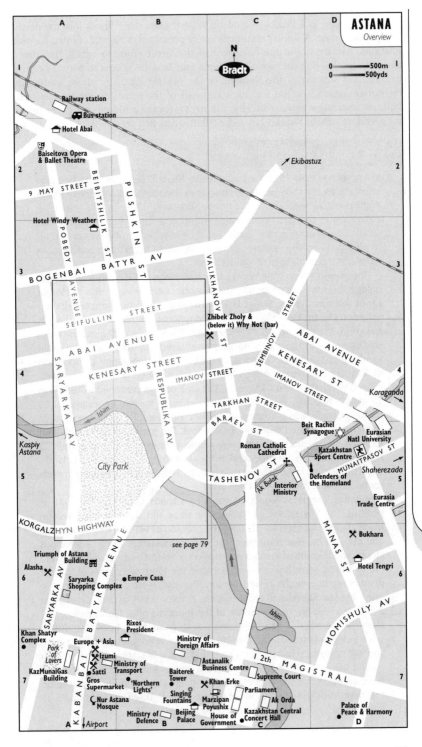

seen, they argue, as a means of binding these regions more firmly into the newly independent state. A similar argument is also presented in respect of intra-Kazakh relations. Almaty sits in the heartland of the Great *Zhuz*, to which Nazarbaev also belongs. Moving the capital to Astana may have been seen in part as helping to build the support of the Kazakhs of the Middle *Zhuz*, in whose traditional territories Astana lies. But I think a key part of the equation was the desire to build an impressive new capital city, a showcase for the achievements of the newly independent state of Kazakhstan and a tribute to its first president.

THE VIRGIN LANDS CAMPAIGN

In a speech in early 1954 the Soviet leader Nikita Khrushchev launched into an attack on the state of Soviet agriculture. He identified a major shortage of grain which, he argued, could not be addressed simply by more intensive cultivation in the traditional grain-producing areas in Russia. Rather, the production of grain in new lands would be required. A plan was drawn up to plough 40 million hectares of virgin steppe in Kazakhstan and western Siberia, and put this to grain production.

The inauguration of the Virgin Lands Campaign in 1954 was marked with great zeal. Hundreds of thousands of people were brought into the Virgin Lands from across the Soviet Union. The first train into Akmola bringing volunteers for the new scheme arrived from Almaty on 2 March 1954; the first train from Moscow arrived three days later. While many of the students and soldiers enlisted to help with the campaign stayed only temporarily, the Virgin Lands Campaign had an important effect on the demographic composition of northern Kazakhstan, greatly boosting the numbers of Slavonic peoples, especially Russians and Ukrainians. The area of land ploughed in 1954 was 19 million hectares, well above the target of 13 million. An additional 14 million hectares was ploughed in the following year. The total crop area in Kazakhstan increased more than three-fold. The harvest of 1956 appeared to vindicate the success of the programme, with more than half of the 125 million tonnes of grain produced in the USSR coming from the new lands. Grain production in Kazakhstan rose from an average of less than four million tonnes a year to more than 14 million.

But the long-term legacy of the Virgin Lands Campaign was not as positive. The low rainfall of the steppe areas and short growing season made these lands far from ideal for the growing of wheat. Deep ploughing, and the year-on-year planting of grain, in combination with the ferocious steppe winds, resulted in major soil erosion problems. Harvest volumes were highly erratic. Some lessons were learnt: in the 1960s techniques of shallow planting were brought in, and perennial grasses were planted in a bid to retain the soil. Kazakhstan today remains a major centre of grain production and indeed export, though some of the more marginal lands, particularly along the southern belt of the area put to grain, have been abandoned since independence. On the drive from Astana to Korgalzhyn, for example, you will pass many former fields reverting to a wild state, punctuated with rusting pieces of abandoned agricultural equipment. It is difficult to avoid the conclusion that the Virgin Lands Campaign should rightly be placed on that depressingly long list of Soviet initiatives undertaken in Kazakhstan with little regard for the environmental consequences.

GETTING THERE AND AROUND

By air Astana's **airport** (✆ *777777, 702999;* f *777050;* e *astanaairport@inbox.kz*) sits some 14km outside the centre. To get there take Kabanbai Batyr Avenue south of town, turning left at the roundabout dominated by a large golden monument. The passenger terminal, designed by the celebrated Japanese architect Kisho Kurokawa, centres on a green dome somewhat resembling the eye of a giant insect. A viewing gallery in the dome (take the lift to the fifth floor) offers a good view of the runway and large expanses of steppe beyond. Operated by Malaysia Airports Holdings, Astana airport is quieter than Almaty, and most travellers report a reasonably smooth experience on arrival and departure. Taxi drivers wait at the airport entrance to pounce on arriving passengers, but it is advisable to organise an official yellow and white cab at the kiosk in the arrivals hall. Expect to pay around T3,300 for a transfer into the town centre. If the kiosk is closed, you can call ✆ 244646 to arrange a cab but note that the receptionist speaks no English.

Airlines The following were the airlines serving Astana at the time of research, though with the city progressively developing as a destination, this list is likely to grow. Where the airline has its own ticket office in town, this is indicated below. The Air Astana office in Astana, as elsewhere in Kazakhstan, doubles as the office of Otrar Travel, the General Service Agent for the airline. Where there is no dedicated airline ticket office, you should be able to book through one of Astana's general travel agencies (see page 78).

✈ **Air Arabia** www.airarabia.com. Flies twice a week to Sharjah on an A-320 Airbus.

✈ **Air Astana** 9 Respublika Av; ✆210764, 591404; f 216742, 591408; e tse.cto@airastana. com; www.airastana.com. The national carrier has an extensive network of domestic routes serving Astana, including 4–8 flights daily to Almaty, 1 daily to each of Atyrau, Kyzylorda, Kostanai, Taraz & Ust-Kamenogorsk, 6 a week to each of Zhezkazgan, Petropavl & Semey, 5 to Pavlodar & 4 to Aktobe & Uralsk. Air Astana's international routes from Astana are currently 5 a week to Moscow (Sheremetevo), Frankfurt (3), Istanbul (2), Dubai (2) & Hanover (1).

✈ **Atyrau Airways** 3 flights weekly to Aktau, 2 to Uralsk & 1 to Atyrau aboard a Tupolev TU-134.

✈ **Austrian Airlines** Hotel Okan Intercontinental, 113 Abai Av; ✆390000; www. aua.com. Airport office: ✆(3172) 777304. 3 flights a week to Vienna on Boeing 737s.

✈ **Lufthansa** Astana airport; ✆777771, 777774, 286493; f 777773; e lufthansaastana@ dlh.de; www.lufthansa.com. For ticketing ✆(727) 3335025. Operates 2 flights a week between Almaty, Astana & Frankfurt.

✈ **Novosibirsk Avia** 1 flight a week to Novosibirsk on an An-24.

✈ **Rossiya** www.rossiya-airlines.com. Formerly known as Pulkovo Airlines, this Russian carrier has 1 flight a week to St Petersburg.

✈ **Scat** www.scat.kz. This Shymkent-based carrier has 1 flight a day to Shymkent, & 6 a week to Aktau via Aktobe.

✈ **Transaero** 7 Druzhba St; ✆/f 317040, 318350; e tse.sale@transaero.kz; www. transaero.ru. Alternative office: 9 Ekilas-Dukenuly St ✆911400. Daily flight to Moscow (Domodedovo) on Boeing 737 aircraft.

✈ **Turkish Airlines** 2nd Floor, Astana airport; ✆777020; f 777883; www.thy.com. Operates 1 flight a week to Istanbul.

✈ **Uzbekistan Airways** Room 17, 31 Saryarka Av; ✆236043; f 328244; e tse@uzairways.com; www.uzairways.com. Uzbekistan's national carrier offers 2 flights a week to Tashkent.

✈ **Zhetisu** Domestic carrier offering a daily flight to Taldykorgan in the cramped confinement of a Soviet-era Yak-40.

By rail Astana's **railway station** [75 A1] (*1 Guitte St;* ✆ *933926, 933917, 380707*) lies at the northern end of town. To get there, head north up Pobedy Avenue, which ends its run at the Baiseitova Opera and Ballet Theatre. From here, Birzhan Sal Street runs northeastwards for a few hundred metres to the curved frontage and glass-sided clock tower of the modern railway station building, with the old building tacked on as a western extension of the new. The station is bright and efficient looking, with signs in English as well as Kazakh and Russian, though the ticket office and enquiry desk staff are the usual mix of mostly brusque and occasionally helpful.

There are at least six trains daily to Almaty, most taking between 19 and 23 hours, though the more expensive sleek-lined Tulpar, which departs from both Almaty and Astana at 19.15, does the trip in a little over 13 hours, making for a convenient overnight journey. This is particularly worth contemplating as an alternative to flying in winter, when air schedules are particularly liable to disruption from fog and snowstorms. Karaganda is served by these trains, and is also the southern terminus of four additional routes, although not all of these run every day. There is also a daily train to Kyzylorda, and one every two days to Zhezkazgan. In a northward direction, a couple of trains run daily to both Kostanai and Petropavl, and two or three a day terminate at Pavlodar. There are also several trains to destinations in Russia and the Ukraine, including Moscow, St Petersburg, Kiev, Omsk and Sverdlovsk, although most of these run no more than every other day.

By road Astana's Saparzhai **bus station** [75 A1] (✆ 381135) lies at the eastern end of the square outside the railway station: the large 'Saparzhai' sign marks out the building. There is a bus roughly every 30 minutes to Karaganda, 12 departures a day to Stepnogorsk, at least seven a day to Semey, seven a day to Korgalzhyn, one to Borovoye, several departures daily to Kokshetau and Petropavl, and more frequent departures to Pavlodar. Long-distance **taxis** tout for business in the square outside the bus station.

By taxi Among the numerous numbers to call for a **taxi** are ✆ 947947, ✆ 370808, ✆ 317020, ✆ 318980, ✆ 283333 and ✆ 244000. Taxi fares are higher than in most parts of Kazakhstan: expect to pay upwards of T500 for a short hailed ride in daytime; perhaps three-times that for a ride booked by telephone in late evening.

TOUR OPERATORS AND AIRLINE OFFICES

Akmolaturist Office 22, Hotel Abai, 33 Respublika Av; ✆/f 330812; e akmtourist@cmgp. online.kz. Organises tailored excursions around Astana, as well as half-day tours to Malinovka & to the Kabanbai Batyr Mausoleum, & full-day or longer tours to Korgalzhyn. The company's office is located inside the Hotel Abai, which it also manages.

Sayat Office 3, 23 Kabanbai Batyr Av; ✆ 555544; f 555544; e sayat777@mail.ru. This large agency, mainly geared towards providing overseas holidays for Kazakhstanis, also organises tailored Astana city tours, programmes to Borovoye, & transport & accommodation bookings.

✈ **Transavia** 44 Beibitshilik St; ✆ 580506; f 580404; www.transavia-travel.kz. Airline tickets.

⌂ **WHERE TO STAY**
Top-range

⌂ **Comfort Hotel** [79 C7] (50 rooms) 60 Kosmonavtov St; ✆ 244444, 245444; f 240524; e info@comforthotel.kz; www.comforthotel.kz. This 2-storey pink-walled building is set behind railings not far from the circus on the left bank. The hotel lives up to its name by providing a

comfortable, if not exactly exciting, option at the bottom end of the top range: rooms have en-suite showers & there is central AC. Discounts are available for long-stay guests, diplomats & UN personnel. $$$$$

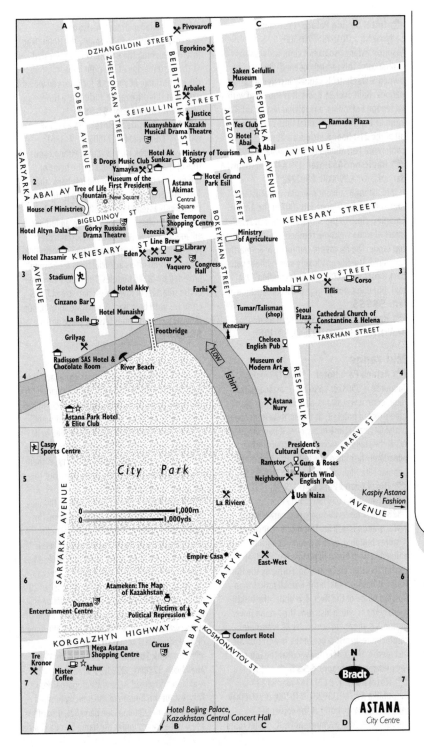

ASTANA
City Centre

🏨 **Hotel Beijing Palace** (151 rooms) 27 Sagynak St; ☎ 701515; 🖷 701500; e soluxe.astana@soluxeint.com; www.soluxe-astana.com. This recently opened, Chinese-owned 5-star hotel is vaguely inspired by a pagoda. Built over 25 floors, it is equipped with a wide range of rooms, a revolving restaurant & a karaoke bar. The Presidential suite encompasses all of the 21st floor & includes a library, conference hall, dining room & sauna. **$$$$$**

🏨 **Radisson SAS Hotel** [79 A4] (181 rooms) 4 Saryarka Av; ☎ 990000; 🖷 992222; e info.astana@radissonsas.com; www.astana.radissonsas.com. Opened in 2007 in the Arman Complex, close to the Saryarka Bridge, this hotel injected some welcome competition into Astana's top range. The rooms are comfortable & smartly furnished. The Queen's luxury suite will set you back a cool US$5,000 a night (excluding 12% tax), but don't worry – the price does include b/fast. **$$$$$**

🏨 **Ramada Plaza** [79 D2] (228 rooms) 47 Abai Av; ☎ 391000, 391040; 🖷 391010;

Mid-range

🏨 **Astana Park Hotel** [79 A4] (28 rooms) 2 Turana St; ☎ 556333; 🖷 556303; e astana-park@rambler.ru; www.astana-park.kz. This low-slung, green-roofed hotel sits at the northwestern corner of the City Park, close to the river. It has centralised AC, & the standard rooms are functionally but adequately furnished. The hotel also houses the popular Elite Nightclub (see page 87). **$$$$**

🏨 **Hotel Grand Park Esil** [79 B2] (132 rooms) 8 Beibitshilik St; ☎ 591901, 591915; 🖷 328818; e reservations@grandparkesil.kz; www.grandparkesil.kz. This nicely renovated 4-storey building, with a columned façade enlivened with horns of plenty, has an ideal central location on Central Sq. Formerly the Hotel Ishim, it has now taken the Kazakh rather than Russian name of the river, & is under the Turkish management which also runs the Astana Tower business & shopping centre. Its AC rooms are comfortable, b/fast & use of the health club are included, & the hotel sits overall at the top end of the mid-range category. **$$$$**

🏨 **Hotel Abai** [79 C2] (157 rooms) 33 Respublika Av; ☎/🖷 330201, 330100; e 330414@mail.ru. This large hotel at the corner of Respublika & Abai avenues shows its Soviet roots

e hotel@ramadaplazaastana.kz; www.ramadaplazaastana.kz. Formerly the Hotel Okan Intercontinental, the Ramada Plaza is located at the eastern edge of the right bank. It offers the comfortable AC rooms & facilities you would expect at this price range, including a fitness centre with indoor pool. **$$$$$**

🏨 **Rixos President Hotel** [75 B7] (168 rooms) 7 Kunaeva St; ☎ 245050; 🖷 243361; e rixosastana@bk.ru; www.rixosastana.com. One of the few hotel options at the heart of the government quarter of the left bank, the Turkish-run Rixos is a grey building lying within the curious assemblage of cottages rented out to foreign embassies known as the 'diplomatic village'. As you walk in, ladies in Kazakh dress press dried fruit & nuts on you. Well, not literally. A large atrium offers artificial trees & birdsong provided by caged budgies. The rooms are some of the smartest in town, with flat-screen TVs & en suites with both bath & separate shower, but slow service sometimes lets the place down. **$$$$$**

in the dizhurnayas on every floor, the chandeliers & heavy tiling in the lobby, & the overloaded lifts. There are airline & railway booking offices in the foyer. The standard rooms have fans but no AC, tired brown-hued décor, & small wooden beds. Framed photographs of Borovoye try to brighten the place up. Like most hotels of this type, there is a large variety of room types & rates, but the prices are no bargain. **$$$**

🏨 **Hotel Akky** [79 A3] (28 rooms) 22 Riskulov St; ☎ 752700; 🖷 324199; e akkuy@inbox.ru. This pink-walled hotel, in a quiet but central right bank location, was one of the first smart hotels built in the new capital city of Astana. While it has since been eclipsed by 5-star arrivals it offers a comfortable place to stay. A reservation fee of 20% of the cost of the first night's accommodation is levied. The 'White Swan' suitably displays a pair of china swans in the foyer. It comes under the wing of the Presidential Administration. **$$$**

🏨 **Hotel Ak Sunkar** [79 B2] (7 rooms) 29 Abai Av; ☎ 328890, 327256; 🖷 327232; e aksunkarkz@mail.ru; www.europa-palace.kz. This restaurant, housed in the Ionic-columned former October Cinema (see page 82), also offers a few hotel rooms under the name Europa Palace.

The standard rooms have no AC & are nothing special, though are at least less expensive than most city-centre options: 'semi-luxe' rooms have AC but are still quite small. **$$$**

⌂ **Hotel Altyn Dala** [79 A3] (140 rooms) 18/1 Bigeldinov St; ↘323311, 327749; ℱ 320978; ℯ altyn_dala@mail.ru. This hotel consists of 2 quite different adjacent buildings. The more expensive rooms are housed in a new 8-storey block at the corner of Bigeldinov & Pionerskaya streets. They offer flat-screen TVs, showers replete with numerous dials & buttons, & a key-card entry system, though AC had not yet been installed at the time of research. The cheaper rooms are to be found in a 2-storey brick building in quiet Pionerskaya St round the side: rooms have AC, parquet floor, & are clean if a little tired-looking. B/fast &, curiously, lunch are included in the room rate. **$$$**

⌂ **Hotel Munaishy** [79 B3] (12 rooms) 14 Irchenko St; ↘325340; ℯ munaishi_hotel@ ok.kz. This hotel has a great riverside location. It lies within the Prestige apartment block, known locally as the 'Kursk', after the stricken Russian submarine, a reference to its long grey form & the conning-tower-like structure on the roof. This building was put up by a state oil enterprise, & while the hotel is now privately run, the 'Oil Worker' does indeed still count many Kazakh oil sector employees amongst its clients. The cream & brown-coloured rooms are boring, but fine, though only the 'luxe' rooms have AC. Altogether one of the best options in this price range. **$$$**

Budget

⌂ **Hotel Astana** [75 A1] (15 rooms) Railway station, 1 Gete St; ↘932897. The Hotel Astana is located inside the railway station building: head for the far western end of the station & go up the pink-walled balustraded staircase. This place is basically the railway station retiring room, upgraded to make it feel more like a hotel than transit accommodation. They offer dbls with small en-suite shower rooms, as well as cheaper dbls with shared toilets & showers. There are also 6-bed dormitory rooms with shared bathrooms on offer, &, at the other end of the scale, 'luxe' rooms with AC & an en-suite bathroom. **$$** without en suite; **$$$** with en suite

⌂ **Hotel Abai** [75 A2] (18 rooms) 3A Birzhan Sal St; ↘933296; ℱ 932985. Housed in a red

⌂ **Hotel Tengri** [75 D6] (128 rooms) 1A Vavilov St; ↘955064, 413841; ℱ 955038; ℯ reservation@tengrihotel.kz; www.tengrihotel. kz. This tall red-brick building offers comfortable carpeted rooms with en suites, though no AC, & friendly staff. Its peripheral location, east of the centre near the apartment blocks of the 3rd Microdistrict, is the main drawback. **$$$**

⌂ **Hotel Windy Weather** [75 A3] (33 rooms) 47/2 Beibitshilik St; ↘315979. The name of this hotel sums up Astana's climate rather well. North of the centre, it has a modern-looking metallic & blue glass exterior, with a cylindrical protuberance at the end housing a spiral staircase. The rooms have AC & are simply furnished, & the standard rooms are small. There is a booking fee of 25% of the 1st night's accommodation. Prices include b/fast. **$$$**

⌂ **Hotel Zhasamir** [79 A3] (21 rooms) 17 Kenesary St; ↘323397, 323097; ℱ 323095; ℯ jasamir@mail.ru; www.jasamir.kz. This is an ugly metallic-tiled building in a central location on Kenesary St. Some of the rooms are a riot of rose: pink walls with pink bedspreads & pink-toned prints of underdressed ladies. There are en-suite showers off every room & a beauty salon next to the foyer. Room rates include b/fast. **$$$**

⌂ **Kaspiy Astana Hotel** (38 rooms) 9 Takha Khuseyna St; ↘224354; ℯ otel_kaspii@mail.ru. A quiet, comfortable & reasonably well-equipped hotel away from the city centre. Room rates include b/fast & there is a small restaurant on site. **$$$**

& silver building 400m in front of the railway station on Birzhan Sal St, in front of a local bazaar, the Abai represents a better deal in the budget range than the Astana at the station. Their basic dbls have shared shower & toilet; a 'semi-luxe' will get you a small en suite. They also have sgl rooms with a shower & toilet shared between 2 rooms. There is no AC. If you take a taxi here, be sure to specify the street, or you will be taken to the better-known Hotel Abai on Respublika Av. **$$**

⌂ **Hotel Saparzhai Astana** [75 A1] (20 rooms) Bus station; ↘381136, 303496. This place, all beige lino & fake wooden panelling, sits on the top floor of the bus station. The entrance is on the northwestern side of the balcony which runs around the main station hall, marked with a small 'hotel' sign in Kazakh & Russian. They have 12 cheap dbls with shared facilities, & a few more expensive rooms with en-suite showers. A

depressing place to stay, but about the cheapest option in town. **$** without en suite; **$$** with en suite.

✗ WHERE TO EAT AND DRINK

The good news is that there is a burgeoning range of restaurants to fuel this growing city, with new arrivals opening up every month. Themed restaurants, often with a somewhat artificial feel, are the flavour of the city, though the menus rarely seem to follow the theme very closely. Sushi, in particular, crops up in the most unlikely settings. The bad news is that there are few appetising choices at the lower end of the price bracket. In summer, beer and *shashlik* places in the central park offer an enjoyable option. Fast-food joints in the main shopping centres are another budget standby.

Right-bank restaurants

✗ **Grilyag** [79 A4] 8 Irchenko St; ✆325222. Formerly the Derby Bar & Grill, a model Big Ben on the riverfront points the way to this restaurant housed in the Arman Complex. The wooden panelling, booths around the walls & TV screens dotted around the place may suggest a pub, but this is really a restaurant offering a mix of European & Japanese dishes: haggis through to pizza & sushi. They offer live music Tue–Sat. $$$$$

✗ **Pivovaroff** [79 B1] 24 Beibitshilik St; ✆328866; e pivovaroff@mail.ru. Descend past an array of agricultural implements to this basement restaurant & microbrewery, which offers a Teutonic-styled experience of a sausage-laden menu washed down with filtered or unfiltered beer brewed on the premises. This being Kazakhstan, they offer a 'steppe sausage', made with horsemeat. The bar stays open until 02.00. $$$$$

✗ **Tiflis** [79 D3] 14 Imanov St; ✆221226. This Georgian restaurant offers a tastefully decorated interior on 2 floors, with stone columns & photographs of Georgian yesteryears on the walls. The entrance is mocked-up to resemble a Tbilisi street-scene, right down to the manhole cover. They offer a good range of Georgian dishes, including a fine selection of *shashlik*, which is presented on little wooden supports, lifting the meat above burning embers. The English menu describes one dish as 'lamb's pluck wrapped in stomach reticulum with spices'. Perhaps it sounds better in Georgian. $$$$$

✗ **Vaquero** [79 B3] 5 Beibitshilik St; ✆390121, 328653. This place brings the flavours of the Americas to Astana, including *fajitas* &

steak Buenos Aires. The décor takes its cue from the Wild West, with murals of horses on the walls & seat covers sewn from denim. The bar stays open until 04.00 at w/ends, but you'll pay T1,200 for a bottle of Stella. $$$$$

✗ **Venezia** [79 B3] 9 Beibitshilik St; ✆753906. Located in the rather unromantic setting of the Sine Tempore Shopping Centre, the Venezia has something of a summer conservatory ambience, with its tables divided by pots of artificial foliage. The Italian menu is however good quality, including an excellent buffet of antipasti. $$$$$

✗ **Zhibek Zholy** [75 B4] 46 Abai Av; ✆216656. This exuberantly decorated place offers an overpowering assemblage of columns, balustrades & general glitz. There is a dancefloor & pink-tinted mural of a central Asian cityscape on a lower level. A balconied area upstairs is divided into a bland Moroccan-themed space & a more interesting Kazakh one, with mock petroglyphs on the walls. There are separate Chinese, European & Kazakh menus, the last offering a good range of *beshbarmak*. $$$$$

✗ **Ak Sunkar** [79 B2] 29 Abai Av; ✆328890, 327256; e akshumkarkz@mail.ru. Still frequently referred to by its former name of Europa Palace, the Ak Sunkar occupies the renovated neo-classical building which once housed the October Cinema. The food is European, there is a bar in the foyer, but the real selling point of this place is the dining room, where tables occupy the balconied rows of the old cinema stalls, which have had their seats taken out. Live music is performed from the stage, where the silver screen once stood. $$$$

✕ Arbalet [79 B1] 16 Beibitshilik St; 324060, 324070. The entrance to this medieval-themed basement restaurant is marked by a large model crossbow on the outside wall. The interior is decorated with weaponry & suits of armour, there are wooden tables & high-backed chairs, & the waitresses wear curious 'medieval wench as dressed by Laura Ashley' outfits. The food comprises a range of central Asian & European dishes, including *shashlik* & a hearty range of sausages. At lunchtime they serve a business lunch (⊕ *12.00–17.00*) & prices are discounted by 30%. $$$$

✕ Eden [79 B3] 24 Kenesary St; 324316. Under renovation at the time of writing but due to re-open by the end of 2011, this smart restaurant is centrally located & slightly less expensive than most of its competition. The Russian-tinged European dishes are pretty good. $$$$

✕ Egorkino [79 B1] 93 Auezov St; 323878, 326137; e egorkino@mail.ru; www.egorkino.kz. This atmospheric Russian restaurant sits just north of the city centre. Inside, Russian knick-knacks, wooden beams, tables & chairs, & waitresses dressed in Russian peasant outfits combine to create a Russian village feel, a theme continued in the summer terrace outside, where the woodcarver has been given free rein. The menu is stuffed with classic Russian dishes, washed down, if you are really in the mood for something traditional, with a glass of honey & horseradish-flavoured *kvass*. There is also a Russian delicatessen on the premises (322490; ⊕ 09.00–22.00 Mon–Fri, 09.00–20.00 Sat–Sun) if your meal put you in the mood for more of this kind of fare. $$$$

✕ Farhi [79 C3] 3 Bokeykhan St; 229523; e farhi@arka.kz; www.arka.kz. This central place is one of the best venues in Astana for Kazakh & other central Asian cuisine. You dine in a circular hall, built to resemble a *yurt*, at tables discreetly divided by wooden lattices. The *beshbarmak* is a good traditional choice here: if you want to show real Kazakh hospitality towards your dining companions they will prepare a sheep's head if you order in advance. In good 'new Kazakh' tradition they also serve sushi. In summer, they have a sister restaurant named **Ali Baba**, decked out like a central Asian village & set around the terrace next door. $$$$

✕ Seoul Plaza [79 C3] 12/2 Respublika Av; 328010; e seoul_plaza@bk.ru. Tucked away behind Respublika Av, the Seoul Plaza houses both a nightclub & a restaurant. The latter is divided up into separate booths done up like oriental houses with little sloping roofs. The menu encompasses Korean, Japanese & European dishes, & the bar is open until 06.00. $$$$

✕ Bukhara [75 D6] Bldg 7, Microdistrict 3; 351932. Marooned among the Soviet apartment blocks of Microdistrict 3, lies this striking stone-walled building guarded by 2 warriors. The interior is decked out in a cluttered central Asian village style, with plastic grapes hanging from the ceiling. The menu includes European & central Asian choices, with Kazakh standards like *beshbarmak*. To get here, you really need to find a taxi driver who knows the place. $$$

✕ Neighbour Café [79 C5] 12 Samal Microdistrict; 223951; ⊕ 10.00–23.00. This basic place sits among the shops on the 1st floor of the Astana Tower development, & is accessed by the stairs in the foyer of Ramstor. It offers a salad buffet, some simple pasta dishes, burgers & kebabs, as well as 'cheery shake', made from 'cheery juice'. They also offer an 'SAS Cocktail', consisting of orange juice, ice cream, milk & honey. So that's how the troops get fit. The food is nothing special, but it's not a bad option for a quick & relatively inexpensive lunch. $$$

✕ Shaherezada 7 Zhumabaev St, 5th Microdistrict; 356857. I'm including this place as representative of a particular class of restaurant in Astana: large central Asian-themed complexes, decorated to resemble medieval Silk Road towns, mostly located in the suburbs & offering a mix of central Asian & international food, loud Russian & Kazakh music, & dancing. They can offer evenings ranging from the hideous to the magical, depending on your mood & the other customers. The Shaherezada is on the eastern side of town, its overpowering décor including walls heavy with painted reliefs, carved wooden doors & strange latticework around the lights. The menu includes Uzbek, European & Korean dishes. $$$

✕ Yamayka [79 B2] 27 Abai Av; 323569. Here's an intriguing prospect: a Jamaican restaurant in the heart of the Kazakhstani steppe. The menu, disappointingly, trawls across a range of international styles, even making room for *beshbarmak*, though only if you bring along 9 friends. They do attempt to conjure the Caribbean with the Jamaica steak ('served with Bob Marley's lovely sauce', confides the menu mysteriously). Eat under straw umbrellas beneath a fluffy cloud-covered sky, with a wave-lapped beach painted on the far wall. $$$

✖ **Samovar** [79 B3] 24 Kenesary St; ☎ 321111; ⏰ 24hrs. A stuffed bear wearing a red tunic greets you at the entrance to this cheerful

Left-bank restaurants

✖ **Europe + Asia** [75 A7] 30A Kabanbai Batyr Av; ☎ 592411. Close to the tower housing the Ministry of Transport and Communications, this restaurant formerly known as Aristocrat strives for elegance, with its dark wood, heavy curtains & waiters in velvet jackets. The phonetic rendering of the French dishes on its English-language menu rather lets it down though, with 'fua-gra' & 'buaybes'. 'Chicken beast on grill' seems somewhat alarming, too. The menu, which also includes a good range of pasta, is ambitious, but service is slow. A Corona will set you back T600. $$$$$

✖ **Khan Erke** [75 B7] 1/14 Kunaeva Sq; ☎ 971247. From street level, you climb a flight of stairs decorated to resemble the walls of a cave, emerging into a large & sumptuous room, its chandeliers & columns aiming to evoke the khan's palace. The menu offers Kazakh, European & Japanese dishes. You may though find this place either completely empty (especially at w/end lunchtimes) or accommodating a noisy celebration. $$$$$

✖ **La Riviere** [79 C5] 2 Kabanbai Batyr Av; ☎ 242260; e la-riviere@mail.ru; www.la-riviere.kz. This secluded restaurant, in the quiet eastern part of City Park, aims to offer its wealthy clientele the experience of dining in a French château ambience in the centre of Kazakhstan. A circular courtyard is centred on a fountain decorated with golden obelisk & classical statues. A grand, balustraded staircase leads to the entrance of the restaurant building, its exterior décor embellished with Ionic columns & rooftop statues. The mainly European dishes are impeccably presented, the gold-tinted interior sumptuous, & the prices predictably high. $$$$$

✖ **Satti** [75 A7] 32 Kabanbai Batyr Av; ☎ 242848; e satti@arka.kz. Built around a central dome supported by pillars sporting vaguely floral

& relatively inexpensive Russian restaurant, liberally decorated, as you might expect, with samovars. They offer a good selection of traditional Russian dishes. This is also the place to come for a pancake b/fast. There is another branch on the left bank near the KazMunaiGas building (*22/2 Kabanbai Batyr Av;* ☎ *974171;* ⏰ *from 12.00*), wood panelled in a bid to resemble the interior of a Russian country cottage. $$

designs, this Kazakh restaurant on the side of the circular space to the east of the KazMunaiGas building is a favoured lunch venue for members of the government. There is live music in the evenings, & in summer open-air dining on the rooftop terrace. Satti offers Kazakh & central Asian dishes, as well as some international choices, like Caesar salad. The small Japanese restaurant next door, **Izumi** (☎ *242723*), is under the same management, & offers good sushi at high prices. The bar is open 24 hrs. $$$$$

✖ **Tre Kronor** [79 A7] 17 Saryarka Av; ☎ 402050. Under the same ownership as Satti & Izumi, the Tre Kronor is a large Swedish-themed restaurant, another of the 'cuisines of the world' places on Saryarka Av. The Tre Kronor is set out on 2 floors, the 2nd a balcony around a large central space, with lounge-style live music on offer from 21.00. Murals on the walls display bucolic paintings, the cow-hide sofas will not be to everyone's taste, & the waitresses sport vaguely Scandinavian outfits. The food is heavy on meat, with a good selection of sausages, & a few Swedish dishes such as a herring salad. There is also a nightclub upstairs (⏰ *from midnight*). $$$$$

✖ **Alasha** [75 A6] 29 Turan Av; ☎ 402121; e astana@alasha.kz; www.alasha.kz. Alasha is built in the style of a monument of the medieval Silk Road, with a blue dome & tiled portal. It has carved wooden pillars, Uzbek ceramics in niches on the walls & live music at 21.00 nightly, but the capacious central hall gives the place a rather barn-like feel. The menu covers Uzbek & Kazakh dishes, Korean salads & a long list of *shashlik*, including that 'barbecue delicacy', testicles. $$$$

✖ **East-West** [79 C6] 2/2 Kabanbai Batyr Av; ☎ 244034. This restaurant ambitiously sets out to offer cuisines from around the world, each presented on 1 of 5 differently coloured menu boards. The interior of the place is parcelled out into zones whose décor & colour schemes broadly match those of the menus. So there is a pale yellow Italian space, decorated with murals

Bars

♀ 8 Drops Music Club   [79 B2] 29 Abai Av; ☏ 467018. Lively karaoke bar with songs in English, Russian & Kazakh. Host encourages competition between the tables. Also another branch at 6/4 Kabanbai Batyr Av.

♀ Boulevard Grill   14 Kunayev St; ☏ 244531. Close to the Baiterek Tower, this bar is built on 2 levels & has large plasma screen TVs. There are 25 varieties of shish kebab on the menu. $$$$

♀ Chelsea English Pub   [79 C4] 7 Respublika Av; ☏ 217727. The wooden booths, Houses of Parliament mural in the foyer & fake red brickwork attempt to offer the feel of Blighty, but the row of hubble-bubble pipes standing on top of the bar in the centre of the room indicate that the clientele is more new Kazakh than Olde England. The international menu includes a range of 'apperetisers', the beer is pricey, & this is surely the only 'Chelsea Pub' in existence which sports Arsenal memorabilia on its walls. $$$$$

♀ Cinzano Bar   [79 A3] 5 Pobedy Av; ☏ 319789. Near the Arman Complex on the right bank, this is the little sister of Almaty's Cinzano Bar, offering a red, black & white colour scheme with swirling rose designs & framed Marilyn prints on the walls, & a menu majoring in sushi, plus a few pasta & European meat dishes. There are plenty of Cinzano-related cocktails, & you can even order a Cinzano-flavoured hookah to a backdrop of lounge music & Fashion TV. $$$$$

♀ Guns and Roses   [79 C3] 11 Samal Microdistrict; ☏ 591809. Unmissable beside the red

of cypresses, a green Kazakh zone & an orange Indian area. With an Indian chef, that cuisine comes particularly recommended. At lunchtime they serve a buffet business lunch to workers from the nearby offices. $$$$

telephone box, this Irish-style pub serves draught beers & ales. Popular location with expats.

♀ Line Brew Bar   [79 B3] 20 Kenesary; ☏ 236373. In this Belgian pub cleverly disguised as a crusader castle, you'll not only find foreign beers but also a surprisingly good BBQ. There is live music & a lively crowd most nights of the week. $$$$$

♀ North Wind English Pub   [79 C5] 12 Samal Microdistrict; ☏ 223346, 223951. With a red telephone box outside the entrance, on the side of the building accommodating the right-bank branch of the Turkish Ramstor supermarket, this English pub features such English fare as the 'original English pan pizza' (tomato, mozzarella, parmesan & oregano, since you asked) among a wide-ranging menu stretching from beef curry to T-bone steak. Arranged around a central bar, the décor aims to capture the English pub atmosphere, but the place is rather sterile, & the prices are distinctly steep. There's live music in the evenings. $$$$$

♀ Why Not   [75 B4] 102 Abai Av; ☏ 210507. Decorated in shades of brown, with mosaic columns, white leather chairs & Fashion TV, this lounge bar sits below the Zhibek Zholy Restaurant (see page 82). Why Not offers international dishes from the Zhibek Zholy menu, lounge music & barmen attempting juggling routines with cocktail shakers. The *tiramisu* arrives with 'tiramisu' written in chocolate sauce across the plate; in case you forgot what you ordered, presumably. $$$$$

Cafés

⌨ Corso   [79 D3] 12 Imanov St; ☏ 537300. Opposite the Cinema City complex, the Corso offers a cosy interior decorated in shades of brown, circular wooden tables with coffee-coloured tablecloths, & a selection of cakes & sandwiches to accompany your tea or coffee. Hookahs & alcohol are also on the menu.

⌨ La Belle   [79 A3] 12 Irchenko St; ☏ 230600; www.labelle.kz; ⊕ 12.00–02.00. This

café, in the shadow of the Arman apartment block, attempts to offer the flavour of the Parisian right bank on that of Astana. Prints of Parisian scenes & mock French-style window boxes decorate the walls: a well-heeled local crowd comes here for coffee & cake during the daytime; brandy & cigars late into the evening. Wi-Fi available.

⌨ Library Café   [79 B3] 61/1 Kenesary St; ☏ 200801. Tuck into American-style coffee &

3

desserts whilst enjoying a wide range of fiction & classic novels. Wi-Fi available.

⊑**Madlen** 12/1 Tauelsyzdyk St; ☏ 689679; www.madlen.kz. Reasonably priced coffee house with a good selection of sandwiches, cakes, pies & Danish pastries. Close to the Baiterek Tower.

⊑**Marzipan Poyushix** [75 C7] Fontanov Sq; ☏ 243714. This brightly decorated café makes a good place to stop off for a coffee or light lunch during a left-bank sightseeing trip. Along with teas & coffees, they offer sandwiches, pizza & a limited range of mains, as well as a long list of cocktails. $$$

⊑**Mister Coffee** [79 A7] 15 Turan Av; ☏ 901033; ⊕ 10.00 onwards. Located near the Mega Mall, this coffee house uses only organically grown Arabica beans. The confectionery is said to be the best in Astana.

⊑**Shambala** [79 C3] 30 Respublika Av; ☏ 333225. Recently expanded café with an Indian flavour. Cuisine is a mix of European & Kazakh, & there is a dance floor with live music. $$$

ENTERTAINMENT A useful English-language listings guide to what's on in Astana is www.edgekazakhstan.com. If you can read Russian, the local monthly listings magazine *Vybiray*, distributed free in several bars and restaurants in the town, offers listings of upcoming cinema and theatre programmes.

Theatres and concert halls The theatre season in Astana runs roughly from early October until late June.

🎭 **Baiseitova National Opera and Ballet Theatre** [75 A2] 10 Eserbilna St; ☏ 392761; e astana_opera@mail.ru; www.astana-anshlag. kz; booking office ⊕ 10.00–19.00. Housed in the former Cultural Palace of Railway Workers near the railway station, this offers a worthwhile repertoire, combining crowd-pleasers from Mozart & Tchaikovsky with less well-known Kazakhstani works. Performances generally start at 19.00 w/days, 18.00 w/ends & ticket prices are T500–1500.

🎭 **Congress Hall** [79 B3] 32 Kenesary St; ☏ 752383, 752200; booking office ⊕ 10.00–20.00. In the centre of the 'old town', at the southern end of Central Sq, this venue showcases middle-of-the-road pop & variety acts. It started out life in the early 1960s as the Palace of Virgin Land Workers, but was renovated in the 1990s. The auditorium seats 1600 people & the Congress Hall is home to an orchestra, 2 dance companies & a circus.

🎭 **Gorky Russian Drama Theatre** [79 B2] 11 Zheltoksan St; ☏ 328223, 324053; f 320570; e gorky_theatre@mail.ru; www.grdt.kz; booking office ⊕ 10.00–19.00 Tue–Sun. Centrally located on the right bank, this serves up a menu of Russian classics. Performances generally start at 18.00, though there may also be a daytime performance of a play focused on a younger audience. Adult tickets are a reasonable T600.

🎭 **Kazakhstan Central Concert Hall** 10/1 Orynbor St; ☏ 705302. Houses a 3,500-seat auditorium for film screenings, & a 2nd auditorium for performing arts including ballet & classical music concerts.

🎭 **Kuanyshbaev Kazakh Musical Drama Theatre** [79 B2] 47A Omarov St; ☏ 323624, 323512; booking office ⊕ 10.00–19.00. Kazakh-language performances. The theatre was established in 1991 by Zhakyp Omarov, after whom the street on which it stands is named.

Outdoors Given the huge annual temperature range of Astana's continental climate, your experience of the city will depend greatly on the time of year you come. In summer, Astana offers a **beach** on the River Ishim (⊕ 08.00–22.00 daily; admission adult/child T100/50). This sits at the north edge of City Park, close to the footbridge across the river. Fresh sand is brought in every spring. The consumption of alcohol is not allowed. Also banned is swimming beyond the buoys or after dark. Pedalos are available for hire.

If you come to Astana in the depths of winter, one attraction not to be missed is the **ice town**. Usually opened just in time for the New Year holiday, this consists of a set of themed structures, constructed out of blocks of ice. These typically include famous buildings of the world, from the Taj Mahal to the Baiterek Tower, or world mythology, featuring an icy Trojan Horse. In the year of mythology, I felt the explanatory map of the structures didn't quite enter into the spirit of fantasy, offering such descriptions as 'fairytale castle type A'. Several of the larger structures always incorporate ice slides: hire a plastic mat (T200) or slide down on a piece of cardboard box to keep (relatively) dry. There will usually be someone dressed up as Dyed Moroz, 'Grandfather Frost', the local equivalent of Santa Claus, who across the former Soviet Union always has a female companion, the Snow Maiden, here wearing a rather unmaidenlike but entirely necessary puffy protective outfit against the cold. Pay a small sum to be photographed with them. The location of the ice town changes from year to year. Recent venues have included the front of the Duman Entertainment Centre and the northwest corner of City Park, opposite the Caspy Sports Centre. It is also interesting to watch the process of construction and transportation of the blocks of ice from the frozen River Ishim during December. This usually takes place along the stretch of river east of the Saryarka Bridge. Other cities across northern Kazakhstan also build ice towns of varying sizes, though that in Astana is probably the best.

Ice skating is a popular winter activity, with outdoor opportunities including the River Ishim itself as well as a rink set out in Central Square. There is also an indoor ice skating rink at the **Kazakhstan Sport Centre** [75 D5] (*9 Munaitpasov St*; \ *353491, 353490*; ⊕ *08.00–22.00 daily*). This multi-sports complex, which also offers a public swimming bath, lies east of the centre close to the Ak Bulak Canal. Another option, also on the eastern side of town, is **Ice Club** (*24 Petrova St*; \ *341906*), close to the Eurasia Trade Centre. It offers both ice skating and ten-pin bowling. Skates are available for hire at all these places. **Cross-country skiing** is also popular, on a track laid out in City Park, or even on the Ishim River itself. In the heart of winter, the Ishim River is even the venue for car rallying: watch them skid on a track usually laid out along the stretch of river between the footbridge and Kabanbai Batyr Bridge.

Nightlife Astana has a developing range of nightclubs. They rarely get going before midnight, and most run until 05.00 or 06.00. One word of warning before sitting yourself down in that comfortable-looking armchair: be aware that a table charge is levied at many clubs. While your food and drinks bill is often deductible from the table charge, the latter can be steep. Astana's plushest club, Chocolate Room, is a prime example. There are few good live music venues in town, though many restaurants (see above) also offer live music in the evenings.

☆ **Azhur** [79 A7] 27 Turan Av; \ 402034; ⊕ midnight onwards. One of the newest clubs in Astana, Azhur is compact but regularly hosts DJs from Russia & Europe. There is a strict dress code & face control.

☆ **Chocolate Room** [79 A4] 2 Saryarka Av; \ 990000, (7015) 500017; e salamlar3020@mail.ru; ⊕ 23.00–05.00 Thu–Sat. Below the Radisson SAS Hotel (the entrance is on the river side of the building), this smart venue is the nightclub favoured by Astana's elite. Dress up to get in, & don't get here before midnight.

☆ **Elite Club** [79 A4] Astana Park Hotel, City Park, 2 Turana Av; \ 556333; e astana-park@ rambler.ru; www.astana-park.kz; ⊕ 19.00–03.00 Tue–Sun. In the Astana Park Hotel, the Elite stands just across the river from the rival attractions of Chocolate. Heavy red & gold décor.

☆ **Fashion** 4 Mailin St; \ 222777; www.fusion.com.kz; ⊕ from 22.00 Fri–Sat. One of the most popular clubs in Astana, Fashion caters to a dedicated under 30s crowd. The club regularly hosts foreign DJs, & organises themed parties & stage shows. Drinks & entry are pricey.

☆ **Seoul Plaza** [79 C4] 16/2 Respublika Av; \ 328010, 328462; e seoul_plaza@bk.ru; ⊕ 22.00–06.00 daily. Centrally located club, just behind Respublika Av.

☆ **Yes Club** [79 C2] 33A Respublika Av; 330214; ⏰ live music from around 22.00–02.00 daily. On the north side of the Hotel Abai, this is an Astana rarity: a venue in which live music is the real focus of proceedings, rather than an accompaniment to dining. Yes Club showcases local bands performing mainly 1980s music. Despite the name, you are unlikely to hear *Tales from Topographic Oceans*. The décor consists mainly of photos of groups performing here; the food is a mix of central Asian & international dishes, including pizza.

SHOPPING Astana is no shopper's paradise, but the range of stores is increasing rapidly with the opening of new shopping malls. The **Mega Astana** Shopping Centre [79 A7] (791851; *www.astana.megacenter.kz*) opened in 2007 opposite the Duman Entertainment Centre on the left bank: it contains a branch of the Turkish Ramstor supermarket chain, amusements for children and a multiplex cinema. Another shopping complex, **Saryarka** [75 A6] (515599; *www.saryarka.kz*), a few hundred metres to the south along Saryarka Avenue, offers a mall with outlets of many big-name Western clothing brands, plus another multiplex cinema (the Mega Astana and Saryarka complexes between them offer 14 screens, all run by the KinoPark group). Further south along Saryarka Avenue, the ambitious **Khan Shatyr** complex [75 A7] (see page 97), offers designer shops and upmarket boutiques, as well as a range of entertainment options. More quotidian left-bank options include a couple of convenient branches of the **Gros** supermarket chain, on the 'Round Square' in front of the KazMunaiGas building [75 A7], and in the **Astanalik Business Centre** at the northeast corner of the square on which the Baiterek Tower stands.

On the right bank, the former Soviet TsUM department store has now been remodelled as the **Sine Tempore** Shopping Centre [79 B2] (753807; ⏰ 10.00–21.00 *daily, supermarket 08.00–22.00 daily*), standing on Central Square in the heart of the city. This offers a collection of boutiques selling an uninspiring range of Western designer names at inflated prices. More usefully, there is also a small supermarket in the complex. There is a centrally located branch of **Ramstor** [79 C5] (*1 Respublika Av;* 223901; ⏰ 09.00–23.00 *daily*), close to the Kabanbai Batyr Bridge over the Ishim, in the shadow of the banana-yellow Astana Tower office block. There is a wider range of outlets at the **Eurasia Trade Centre** [75 D5] (*3 Microdistrict 2A;* ⏰ 10.00–20.00 *daily, closed second Mon of the month*). This ugly hangar-like building contains a large selection of shops as well as a produce market. It is however inconveniently sited in the eastern part of town.

Souvenirs and books The largest dedicated souvenir shop in town is the store named both **Tumar** and **Talisman** [79 C3] (*7 Respublika Av;* 214196; ⏰ 10.00–20.00 *daily*). Not all of the items on offer are to everyone's taste, and I doubt that one or two of them are to anyone's, but this is the place to come for that reminder of your Kazakhstan holiday, whether it be a model yurt made of malachite, a leather *kumiss* holder, a bit of wood sporting petroglyph-style drawings or a stuffed wild boar head. There are also souvenir shops at **Empire Casa** (*11 Kabanbai Batyr Av;* 688800), on the top floor of the Sine Tempore shopping centre and near the main entrance of the Eurasia Trade Centre.

English-language books are difficult to find in Astana. The main international hotels have some, with the bookstore in the lobby of the Rixos President Hotel particularly useful. City maps are quite widely available from local bookstores. The souvenir shop on the ground floor of the Baiterek Tower also sells maps and postcards.

MEDICAL

✚ **International SOS Astana Clinic** [79 B2] 8 Beibitshilik St; 580957, 580935; f 580936; e site@internationalsos.com; ⏰ 09.00–18.00 Mon–Fri, with 24hr emergency cover & its own ambulance. Centrally located in the Hotel Grand Park Esil, this clinic offers English-speaking doctors & the support of the International SOS group. However, it is geared up to corporate clients: others have to pay a hefty 'non-member fee' just to access the service, with consultation & treatment charges on top of this.

✚ **National Research Medical Centre**
42 Ablai Khan Av; ☏ 232926, 233909; ☎ 232927;

⊕ 08.00–17.00 Mon–Fri. The clinic in this modern hospital, also known locally as the 'Fitzpatrick Hospital' after the company which built it, operates on a 'fee for service' basis, though with higher charges for foreigners than Kazakhstanis. The place is well equipped, with 24hr emergency cover, but there are no guarantees you will be seen by English-speaking staff.

WHAT TO SEE
Right bank

President's Cultural Centre [79 C5] (*1 Respublika Av;* ☏ *443233*) At the northern end of the bridge carrying Kabanbai Batyr Avenue across the River Ishim the road passes under a large, 'three-legged' monument. This is named **Ush Naiza** ('Three Spears'), symbolising the unity of the three *zhuzes* within the independent state of Kazakhstan. The next intersection beyond this is dominated by the blue-domed building of the President's Cultural Centre of the Republic of Kazakhstan, the dome standing atop a central drum enlivened with vertical blue panels. Side wings radiate out from this central part of the building. The building houses a **museum** (*1 Baraev St;* ⊕ *10.00–18.00 Tue–Sun, last admission 17.00, closed on the last day of the month; admission free*) boasting 143,000 artefacts and a library with 700,000 items. This is laid out on balconies running around the large central space under the dome. On the ground floor, in the very centre of the building and surrounded by a protective railing, are the symbols of independent Kazakhstan: the flag, State Emblem, a bound copy of the Constitution and the text of the national anthem. Around this centrepiece are other innovations of the independent state: its banknotes, awards and military uniforms. Gifts to President Nazarbaev from world leaders are also on display, as is Nazarbaev's Honorary Citizenship of Astana.

A side room on the ground floor holds a large Kazakh ethnographic display, centred on a yurt. This includes chunky silver jewellery dating from the 18th and 19th centuries, wooden household utensils, hunting equipment, costumes and musical instruments. One floor up is archaeology, which has exhibits on the main sites in Kazakhstan from the Stone Age onwards, including a model of a jewellery-bedecked 'Andronov woman', Turkic *balbals*, ceramics of the 10th to 15th centuries from Otrar, Altyntobe and Taraz, terracotta tiles from the Mausoleum of Aisha Bibi and models of several mausolea, including those of Khodja Ahmed Yassaui and Beket Ata. A side room, just before the *balbals*, is centred on a model of the Golden Man in his suit of treasures. This fine reproduction is the work of Krym Altynbekov, who restored the original Golden Man. The surrounding cases contain silver jewellery, mostly from the private collection of former prime minister Imangali Tasmagambetov. Note the large circular matchmaker's ring: worn over two fingers to symbolise its owner's role in joining two people together.

History is on the next floor up, starting with displays on the Kazakh Khanate, including Ablai Khan's seal and copies of the correspondence between Abulkhair Khan and the Russian empress Anna. The arrival of Tsarist power is depicted by the emblems of the Russian administrative regions, and by the belongings of Russian immigrants. Photo-led displays describe the 1916 uprising, Civil War, collectivisation, Stalinist repression and World War II. A German barometer, stuck at '*Regen oder Wind*', is displayed as a 'spoil of war'. A display on the Virgin Lands

Campaign includes the Order of Lenin given to the Kazakh SSR in 1956 in honour of its fine wheat production figures. An exuberant red-hued display of Soviet awards is followed by sombre items on the Afghan war and the Almaty rioting of December 1986. A mean-looking truncheon illustrates the latter.

The next floor focuses on post-independence Kazakhstan. There are displays about Islam and the Russian Orthodox Church, and then the development of Astana. Fragments of brick found at the Buzuk site are on display. A large mural of a Proton rocket appears to belong to an entirely different exhibition, as the photographs and utensils around it describe the growth of Akmola. Perhaps they couldn't get it off the wall? There is a display of children's clothes produced by the Manshuk Mametova Garment Factory of Tselinograd, their quality hinting at trouble ahead when capitalism struck. A display on the transformation of Akmola into the capital city of Astana includes models of some of the striking new buildings of the capital, among them the National Academy of Music, its façade resembling the curves of a piano. The top floor of the museum houses temporary art exhibitions.

Along Respublika Avenue Respublika Avenue, which runs north from the President's Cultural Centre, provides the central north–south axis of the right bank. Its buildings were refaced in 2007 to provide a smarter and more unitary appearance for one of the most important thoroughfares of the city. Heading northwards along it, you reach on your left after a few hundred metres Astana's **Museum of Modern Art** [79 C4] (*3 Respublika Av;* \ *215433; www.msi-astana.kz;* ☉ *10.00–18.00 Tue–Sat, 10.00–17.00 Sun; admission T200 for foreign citizens*). Its origins lying in a 1979 exhibition in honour of the 25th anniversary of the Virgin Lands Campaign, this hosts a range of temporary exhibitions.

A block further north, take the narrow lane off to the right and this brings you to the **Cathedral Church of Constantine and Helena** [79 D4]. This Russian Orthodox church was built in the 1850s with financial support from the Cossack community of Akmola. It was originally to be named in honour of Saints Peter and Paul, but the Tsarist authorities decided that it should be given the names of Saints Constantine and Helena. It first stood in the Akmola Fortress, but with the growth of the Cossack *stanitsa* and the establishment of another church, to Alexander Nevsky (the latter destroyed during the Soviet period), the Cossacks of the town petitioned for the Constantine and Helena Church to be moved to the *stanitsa*. It was so moved in 1900. Today surrounded by apartment blocks, Soviet and modern, the yellow-walled church has an octagonal tower surmounted by an onion dome, with a smaller octagonal tower, also crowned with an onion dome, above the entrance on the western side of the building.

Around Central Square [79 B2] Three blocks further north, at the corner of Respublika Avenue and Kenesary Street, sits a little corner of town dedicated to the game of chess. There is a large outdoor chess set in the square here, behind which are young trees, identified by accompanying plaques as having been planted by noted chess players, including former world champions Spassky and Karpov. A couple of boxy, canvas-sided sculptures, their designs based on chessboard themes, complete the ensemble.

Turn left along Kenesary Street. One block along, beyond the intersection with Auezov Street, the beige-tiled building on your left is the one-time municipal administration, which now houses the **Ministry of Agriculture** [79 C3]. One of the characteristic recent features of Astana is the shifting of government buildings into more prestigious locations, as new premises are built on the left bank, vacating properties on the right one, which are in turn occupied by government departments 'trading up'. The most striking feature of this building is its embellishment with two curious structures which have the appearance of huge golf balls with spears running through them. The Tsarist-era building opposite, with porthole-like windows in the roof, was the house of the merchant Kubrin. It is now occupied by the Ukrainian Embassy. It is said that a tunnel used to connect it with Kubrin's trade house, to the west. This building, still standing at the corner of Beibitshilik and Kenesary streets, has a four-sided green dome at its corner and now accommodates the Astana supermarket.

Kenesary Street passes across the southern end of Central Square, at the heart of the right bank. The south side of the square is occupied by the Congress Hall concert venue. At the northern end of the square, the tall building faced with a combination of beige tiles and dark glass was the first Astana home of Kazakhstan's parliament, prior to its move to smarter premises on the left bank. Sessions were held in the circular chamber behind the main tower. It is currently occupied by various government bodies, including the **Ministry of Tourism and Sport** [79 B2]. Nearby, on the west side of the square, the lower beige tile and glass-faced building now houses the **city administration** [79 B2].

The statuary in the square involve a three-tiered fountain, on the north side of which is a naked boy in a Kazakh hat standing on the back of a wolf. On the opposite side a girl collects water under the watchful gaze of a leopard. A toy train chugs children around the square, which is also the venue for evening pop concerts on major holidays.

Museum of the First President of Kazakhstan [79 B2] (*11 Beibitshilik St; ☏751214, 751292; www.prezidentsmuseum.kz; ⊕ Tue–Sun for set tours only, starting at 10.30, 12.00, 14.30 & 16.00; admission free*) Take Abai Avenue westwards from the north end of Central Square. On your left is the entrance to the Museum of the First President of Kazakhstan. This is housed in President Nazarbaev's former residence in Astana, a blue-domed building with cream-coloured tiled walls, vacated by the president with the construction of the new Ak Orda building on the left bank. Although described as a 'residence', this is a building in which the president worked, and held official meetings and functions, rather than lived. The building was completed in 1997, serving as the presidential residence until 2004.

The building can only be visited with a guided tour, held every 90 minutes throughout the day. If you are bringing a large group, or are keen to get a guided tour in English, it's best to ring in advance, otherwise just turn up before the set time. The tour may start out either on the third or fourth floor. The fourth is centred on a domed hall, the top of the dome decorated like a *shanyrak* in homage to a Kazakh yurt. This was used for meetings with senior foreign delegations, and regional fora such as the Shanghai Co-operation Organisation. The president's chair, slightly taller than the others round the table, is protected by a red ribbon barrier. This floor also includes displays of gifts presented to President Nazarbaev by foreign leaders, including a leather-bound copy of the epic *Manas* from Kyrgyz interim president Otunbayeva, a wood and gold chess set from the President of Armenia, and a gold and silver horse statue from the President of Tajikistan. There is a range of sporting gifts, too, including a 2006 World Cup match football, a tennis ball autographed by Boris Becker, and the gold-coloured bicycle on which Alexander Vinokourov won the Vuelta a España in 2006.

One floor down are displays about Nazarbaev's life, starting with the 'Atameken Hall', which covers the president's roots and early life. His family tree is displayed, as well as a picture of the warrior Karasai Batyr, a member of his Shaprashty tribe. There are photographs of his childhood in Shamalgan, examination cards showing his high marks, and a diorama depicting the young future president and his father on the pastures of Ush Konyr, looking towards a herd of horses. A video of the boy band MuzArt singing the song 'Ush Konyr', lyrics by Nursultan Nazarbaev, plays continuously. In the next room, which held government meetings, there are displays about Nazarbaev's time as a metalworker, covering his training in Dneprodzerzhinsk in Ukraine, and his work in the blast furnaces at Temirtau. There are also photographs taken during his career in the Communist Party.

The tour then takes you through the outer office and into the office in which President Nazarbaev worked for seven years. A wall map of Kazakhstan lights up to show the oil, gas and mineral resources. Also on the wall is a white felt mat, used during the president's reinauguration ceremony in 2006. This aimed to replicate the tradition in which Kazakh khans were confirmed in office by being raised aloft on white felt. In President Nazarbaev's case, he simply stood on the mat. The Golden Hall beyond has a large oval table around which meetings between the president and foreign delegations were held. Display cases cover such actions as the drafting of the Constitution and the closure of the Semipalatinsk Test Site. Next comes the ornate ceremonial hall, at which, *inter alia*, official awards were given out. Here are displayed the numerous awards Nazarbaev has received from foreign states, as well as the Golden Order of Merit of the International Amateur Boxing Association. In the next room are documents conferring on the president the Honorary Citizenships of Dneprodzerzhinsk and Seoul, as well as the cloaks of the universities to have awarded him honorary degrees. Beyond is a room containing books both given to and written by President Nazarbaev, the latter including foreign translations of works such as *Neither Rightists Nor Leftists*. There is also a collection of Korans, including one taken into space by cosmonaut Talgat Musabaev.

In the next room, centred on another oval table, Kazakhstan's Security Council used to sit. Since the responsibilities of this body are matters of defence and security it is perhaps appropriate that the gifts presented to President Nazarbaev on show in this room are items of weaponry, though I confess to being puzzled by the thought process which goes on in deciding that a 9mm machine gun would make the perfect present.

New Square [79 B2] Immediately to the west of the Museum of the First President of Kazakhstan stands the large rectangle of green known as New Square. This is centred on a fountain named **The Tree of Life** [79 A2]. At the heart of the fountain is a stylised depiction of the *Baiterek*, the tree of life of Kazakh legend. It takes the form of a large ball decorated with swirly floral designs. The interior of the ball is favoured by nesting birds, giving the fountain an additional aural quality as the sound of birdsong rings out. Animal figures, which apparently symbolise the four elements according to Turkic traditions, complete the ensemble, though I'm curious as to how a sheep came to represent fire. The bull representing water appears not to have been doing his job: the fountain is usually dry.

On the west side of the square is the **House of Ministries** [79 A2], completed in 1999. With a metallic-tiled and glass-walled exterior, the most interesting architectural feature of the building is that, in plan, it takes the form of a giant dollar sign. Appropriately enough, it currently houses Kazakhstan's Finance Ministry.

North of Central Square Back at Central Square, take Beibitshilik Street northwards. One block on, outside the pink-walled columned building housing

Astana's court, is the **Monument to Justice** [79 B1], erected in 1998. This statue depicts the seated figures of Kazybek Bi, Tole Bi and Aiteke Bi, the respected wise judges, each representing a different *zhuz*, who in the 18th century promoted the unity of the Kazakh tribes in combating the threat posed by the Dzhungars. An inscription in Kazakh, Russian and English addresses the importance not only of fair judgments, but also of both unity and indeed authority: 'If there is no owner of the fire, your motherland will be enveloped in flames.'

A further block north, turn right onto Seifullin Street. Another block on, at the corner of Seifullin and Auezov streets, stands the attractive single-storey log-walled house built for a 19th-century merchant named Kazantsev. It now houses the recently restored **Saken Seifullin Museum** [79 G1] (*20 Auezov St;* ☏ *60859, 60712;* ☺ *10.00–18.00 Tue–Sun; admission adult/student T100/50*). Seifullin, born in 1894 in the present-day Karaganda Region, was a Kazakh writer and political activist. He studied in Akmola before teacher training in Omsk. His political activities took over from his brief career as a rural teacher, as, back in Akmola, he created the Zhas Kazakh ('Young Kazakh') movement and supported the Bolshevik Revolution. One of his poems written at this time is credited with being the first piece of Soviet literature written in the Kazakh language. He became a member of the Soviet authorities in Akmola, and was arrested when the White forces took control of the town in June 1918. Escaping from captivity, he returned to Akmola via a spell in Aulie-Ata. He edited the newspaper *Enbekshi Kazakh* ('Kazakh Worker'), became Chairman of the Council of People's Commissars of the Kazakh Soviet Socialist Republic, and headed the delegation from Kazakhstan which attended Lenin's funeral in 1924. But like many intellectual ethnic Kazakh politicians, he was considered as suspect for his 'nationalist' views, and fell victim to Stalin's repression. He was shot on 25 February 1938.

The museum authorities insist that you wear canvas slippers over your shoes. These refuse to stay on properly, causing you to shuffle round the exhibits. The first room contains photographs of the moustachioed Seifullin, as well as a large wall carpet portraying the writer and Lake Borovoye. This room takes you to a corridor, with the rest of the museum's collection off it. The first room on the left has photographs of his early life. Then comes a room focusing on the revolutionary and early Soviet periods, with a model of the house in Akmola in which he lived and a large painting portraying his arrest in 1918. There is a photograph of the smart house in Orenburg in which he lived from 1922–25. Photographs of Seifullin from the early 1920s show his moustache varying enormously in length, from clipped-above-the-mouth to twirly and expansive.

The next room offers display cases with items of his clothing, both Western and Eastern in style, a battered suitcase and an umbrella. There is a mock-up of his study across the corridor. The frontispieces of his works are displayed, in both the Arabic and Cyrillic scripts, as well as photographs of his family life. A gold pocket watch was presented to him by the government in 1936 to mark the 20th anniversary of his literary and public activity. Just two years later he was shot as an enemy of the people, an episode covered in the next room, which also includes books written about the (rehabilitated) Seifullin, and a display of items related to the centenary of his birth in 1994, including a postage stamp issued to mark the occasion.

Outside the museum is a **statue of Seifullin**, installed in 1994 as part of the commemorations of the centenary of his birth. It depicts the seated artist in a relaxed mood, his coat slung over the back of his chair.

Continuing east along Seifullin Street, turn right at the next intersection onto Respublika Avenue. One block along, at the intersection with Abai Avenue, stands a bulky statue of the Kazakh poet **Abai** [79 C2], wrapping a cloak around himself as protection against the cold. The monument was installed in 2000, suitably located in front of the Hotel Abai. A somewhat downcast expression on the poet's face suggests that he may have stayed there.

Ak Bulak Canal There are a few sites strung along the Ak Bulak Canal east of the city centre. Get a taxi to drop you at the Manas Street bridge over the canal. On the north side stands Astana's red-brick **Roman Catholic cathedral** [75 C5]. Plaques inside the entrance recall the visit of Pope John Paul II to Kazakhstan in 2001. Across the canal, the brown-hued tower topped with a large Kazakhstan flag houses the **Interior Ministry** [75 C5]. Opposite this is a park focused on the **Defenders of the Homeland Monument** [75 D5]. This attractive structure takes the form of a tapering ribbed column with a circular base adorned with metal spheres. It is topped by ears of wheat, in a reference to Astana's Virgin Lands heritage. A mother reaches forward from the column, proffering a golden metal bowl. An inscription below her concludes that, where there is one motherland, there is one heart and one desire. An eternal flame burning in front of the column is set not in the five-pointed star of Soviet memorials but in a metal base resembling the shield of a Kazakh warrior. There are friezes along two segments of marble-tiled wall behind the monument. One portrays Kazakh warriors battling their Dzhungar foes; the other depicts Kazakhstanis fighting in World War II, their families fretting at home. A line of young conifers immediately to the south of the monument has been planted by visiting heads of state.

The walk eastwards along the canalside from this monument is pleasant in good weather. Across the canal is the pastel blue-painted modern **Beit Rachel Synagogue** [75 D5], with its octagonal domed tower. Ahead stands the **Kazakhstan Sport Centre** [75 D5], whose futuristic design of sloping, metallic tile-faced exterior walls is somewhat undermined by the onset of shabbiness. It is the home of the Bars Astana ice hockey team, which plays in the Russian league. Underneath the flyover beyond, you reach the beige-toned main building of the **Eurasian National University** [75 D5], with its columned façade. The university is named in honour of Lev Gumilev, a Russian historian of Eurasian peoples and son of the poet Anna Akhmatova.

Left bank
City Park This large and welcome area of greenery lies on the south side of the Ishim River, immediately across from the right-bank town centre. A footbridge at the southern end of Zheltoksan Street brings you into the park, and there are also entrances from Saryarka Avenue down its western flank and Kabanbai Batyr Avenue to the east. The park is a popular place to come in summer, with daytime crowds heading to the beach along the riverside, and the watery attractions of the aquapark immediately behind it. There are basic funfair-type attractions, including such old favourites as a room of distorting mirrors, mostly priced around T100–300. On summer evenings, the beer and *shashlik* served up at the cafés in the park make for a good way to round off a day of sightseeing.

One park attraction I would recommend against visiting is the small private **zoo** (m +7 705 302 7313; ⊕ *winter 12.00–18.00 daily, summer 11.00–dusk daily; admission adult/child T500/300*). This is located under a café in the windowless ground floor of the pink-walled building behind the aquapark. Its main focus is reptiles in glass cases, often illustrated with signs proclaiming 'poisonous!' and 'bite kills!' A glass case containing a crocodile warns that 'the crocodile is alive!', and indeed most of the time it is impossible to tell, as the poor creature stands motionless in its glass-sided coffin. A fierce-looking scorpion patrols a glass case with an alarmingly large crack down the front. At the dark far end of the room is the particularly distressing sight of a baboon, a marmot and some macaques in metal cages, the shrill squeals of the baboon echoing around the dungeon-like chamber. A rabbit and some guinea pigs at the entrance attempt to provide a cuddly feeling.

More uplifting is the walk along the riverbank. There are fine promenades along both the right and left banks. In summer you can rent pedalos of varying degrees of antiquity. Standing on the right bank of the river, at the southern end of Bokeykhan Street, though best viewed from City Park looking across the Ishim, is the **Monument to Kenesary** [79 C4]. This large equestrian statue of the Kazakh leader of a 19th-century rebellion against Tsarist rule stands on a mighty plinth. Kenesary is gazing to his right towards the footbridge, as if wondering whether riders on horseback are allowed to use it.

Atameken At the southeastern edge of the City Park, at the corner of Kabanbai Batyr Avenue and the Korgalzhyn Highway, stands the **Monument to the Victims of Political Repression** [79 B6]. It stands on a rounded hillock, symbolising an ancient burial mound. A flight of steps leads up the eastern side of the hill. This is flanked by a wall decorated with symbolic images: a tree withering in a drought-afflicted land, oppressed people with their heads bowed forward, a list of the Stalinist internment camps on Kazakhstan's territory, and metal birds struggling to free themselves from their traps. A tall metal obelisk rises from the top of the mound. An inscription nearby lists the categories of victims commemorated by the monument, from those killed during the establishment of Soviet power, through victims of famine, epidemic, deportation and internment, political prisoners and dissidents, to the victims of the events of December 1986 in Almaty. Across the Korgalzhyn Highway from the monument, the building looking rather like a concrete spaceship is Astana's **circus** [79 B7] (*2/1 Korgalzhyn Highway;* `\` *244059; booking office* ⊕ *10.00–18.00 when there is a circus in town; admission T600–2,500*). Built in 2005, the building seats spectators and is equipped for ice shows as well as traditional circus acts.

Behind the Monument to the Victims of Political Repression, walking back into the park, a path runs past a line of sculptures based on *balbals*. To the right are a couple of mock Iron Age burial mounds. The path brings you to a prodigious number of flags: Kazakhstani flags, flags of Astana, and simply flags made out of colourful material. These, er, flag up the entrance to one of Astana's quirkier sites, **Atameken: The Map of Kazakhstan** [79 B6] (*6 Kabanbai Batyr Av;* `\` *221636;* e *atameken@rambler.ru;* ⊕ *summer 10.00–midnight Tue–Sun, 16.00–midnight Mon; closed in winter; admission T200*). Over a 1.7ha site, Atameken offers a 3D picture of Kazakhstan in miniature, a large map of the country over which are dotted models of the best-known historical monuments, statues and quite a few industrial enterprises.

From the entrance, a large pond stretches ahead of you. It takes a little while to work out that this represents the Caspian, viewed from the south. The pond is full of model flamingos, seals and sturgeon, the last floating on the surface like crocodiles. You enter Kazakhstan through Mangistau Region, where you can walk through a model of the Shakpak Ata underground mosque to arrive in downtown Aktau. Not all of the regions are yet as elaborately presented as Mangistau, with its artificial pink mountains and walk-through canyons, but a visit to Atameken represents a great way to get an overview of the attractions of Kazakhstan: a rocket

3

preparing to be launched from Baikonur, the Khodja Ahmed Yassaui Mausoleum in Turkestan, and Almaty, in its glorious setting beneath the snow-covered peaks of the Tian Shan. A couple of magpies were walking (jay walking?) across Almaty when I visited, looking like strange avian monsters. Each region is illustrated with up to two dozen models, though the model-makers were evidently struggling for inspiration in one or two regions. Kostanai, for example, gets only eight models – and one of those is an asbestos factory. Stylised model buildings representing the different ethnic groups making up the population of Kazakhstan are also scattered around the map. The felt yurts and toy camels arranged on the astroturf surface do admittedly rather give the impression that a child has been playing there.

Right in the centre of this map of Kazakhstan is a two-storey hangar-like building with a corrugated metal roof. The top floor is devoted to a large model of Astana's left bank, running from Khan Shatyr to the Ak Orda. The pyramid-shaped Palace of Peace and Harmony does not quite fit in on its rightful spot, so has been squeezed into a corner. The right bank of Astana is demoted to a ground-level spot, just to the right of the hangar-like building.

Note that if you don't wish to pay the video or photography fees (*T300/200, respectively*) you will be asked to leave your camera at the ticket office.

Duman Entertainment Centre [79 A6] (*4 Kabanbai Batyr Av;* \ *242222;* f *242490;* e *duman@duman.kz; www.duman.kz;* ⊕ *10.00–20.00 Tue–Sun*) At the southwest corner of the City Park, close to the junction of the Korgalzhyn Highway with Saryarka Avenue, sits the Duman Entertainment Centre. Pillars decorated with illuminated fish mark the entrance to this complex, which was opened in 2003. Its main hall is a huge and rather sterile-looking circular space, which has been divided up into four geographical zones representing, respectively, America, Greece, China and Kazakhstan. Each is decorated with models of famous sites from those countries. Thus Kazakhstan offers a model of the Khodja Ahmed Yassaui Mausoleum, the Independence Monument in Almaty and a space rocket about to take off from Baikonur. You are invited to view the space rocket by climbing a few steps to the nearby viewing platform, an act which is essentially pointless. America is represented by a wigwam, totem poles, the Statue of Liberty, a bucking bronco ride and a backdrop of skyscrapers. Greece has some white marble-look classical statuary, and China offers a section of Great Wall. Apart from eating and drinking at the cafés situated in each of these zones, there is not actually a great deal to do.

Of more interest, and the real reason to visit the place, is the **oceanarium** (*admission adult/child T1,000/500*). Follow the model dolphins in. The displays start with aquaria filled with the fish of Kazakhstan, including carp, catfish, and the variety of *lenok* found only at Lake Markakol, as well as a tank of the enchanting, primeval-looking sturgeon. You then head into the Amazon, with a large tank of piranhas, the skull of a cow artistically placed at the bottom. There is a large open tank of cat shark, usually a native of the Indian and Pacific oceans, but these were born here in 2004. I wonder if this makes them the sharks born furthest from the sea in world history. You then walk through a perspex tunnel, around and beneath sharks (including nurse, reef and leopard sharks), groupers and rays. Soft music plays in the background, and the effect is astonishingly soothing. At least, until the sharks appear to head straight towards you.

The aquaria continue with the brightly coloured fish of the coral reefs. There is a tank of sea horses, somehow looking as though they are blessed with an eternal serenity. Then come poisonous sea creatures, such as the stone fish and spotted moray, before there's another perspex tunnel, this one commencing with some colourful reef fish before you get another turn with the sharks. You can buy shells and glass dolphins in the souvenir shop on the way out.

The Duman Centre also offers a **5D Cinema** (*admission adult/child T700/350*) where you can expect to be physically shaken inside a six-seater pod whilst watching a stereoscopic show with 'fantastic real audio'. You'll be pleased to know that those responsible for the clear-up of Chernobyl and other nuclear disasters, and those living in asylums, can enter the complex for free.

Khan Shatyr [75 A7] (*www.khanshatyr.com*) From the Duman Entertainment Centre take Saryarka Avenue southwards. With a line of new restaurants on your right and shopping malls on your left, this area is a new central hub in the growing city. Many of the apartment blocks in Astana display some interesting architectural touches and inspirations. The large clustered skyscraper construction to your left, with little obelisks adorning its roof areas, is one of the most intriguing. Named the **Triumph of Astana** building [75 A6], it appears to draw its inspiration direct from the Stalinist 'Seven Sisters' skyscrapers which are prominent features of the Moscow skyline.

Around 1.5km south of Duman is the 150m-high Khan Shatyr, the world's largest tent. Designed by British architect Lord Foster, this is the latest addition to Astana's already eccentric skyline. Although from the outside the tent appears to be leaning precariously, on the inside you can clearly see the intricate and surprisingly attractive latticework of steel that supports much of the structure's weight. This view is not unlike the inside of a beehive, and the precision with which each glazed panel interconnects with the next is striking. The complex is maintained at 24°C year round and includes a waterpark, indoor canals with gondolas, a mini golf course, a miniature train, designer label boutiques, a cinema and spa, restaurants, apartments and a large central performance space. Entrance to the inside beach is US$60 per day.

Along the Nurzhol Boulevard

Standing in front of Khan Shatyr, look east. The large arch within the KazMunaiGas building frames a view towards the Baiterek Tower and the blue dome of the presidential palace beyond. This axis, the green Nurzhol Boulevard, forms the fulcrum of the administrative centre of the city, a promenade some 2km long past ministries and prestige apartment blocks.

Standing between Saryarka Avenue and the KazMunaiGas building is the **Park of Lovers** [75 A7], laid out in 2005. You are welcomed in by a young, smiling Kazakh couple, the girl wearing a decidedly diaphanous dress, which perhaps explains the boy's smiles. Behind this is a fountain containing a sculpture which appears to consist of a ring of large silver horseshoes. To the south of the park is a complex of cylindrical apartment blocks locally known variously as the 'seven barrels', 'seven batteries' or 'seven beer cans'. The park is currently a fairly desolate place, but will perhaps improve as its young trees grow and the area develops.

Walk eastwards, passing under the large arch at the centre of the **KazMunaiGas** building [75 A7], which helps to give that structure the local nickname of the 'elevator', as it is said to resemble a grain elevator. As well as the offices of the state oil company KazMunaiGas, the building also houses the Ministry of Energy and the state holdings company Samruk. Beyond KazMunaiGas, a ring of buildings continues the architectural composition, forming an urban amphitheatre which is named, with geometrical illogicality, **Round Square**. The main north–south artery, Kabanbai Batyr Avenue, impudently darts across the centre of this, by means of a flyover. Various pieces of statuary have been added to soften the monumentalism of the architecture. Walking down into the square from the KazMunaiGas building you pass a pelican swallowing a fish. On the flyover above you is a statue of a girl striding purposefully against the evidently strong wind. A group of metal horses graze on the side of the square to your left.

Immediately to the east of Round Square, the skyscraper to your left with a slanting roof and curved sides faced with reddish-brown reflective panels houses the **Ministry of Transport and Communications** [75 A7], as well as other government bodies. It has been nicknamed both the 'swordfish', a reference to the spike at the top of the roof, and the 'cigarette lighter', a reference to its overall shape. With unfortunate irony, the cigarette lighter caught fire in 2006, causing considerable damage.

A detour to the right at the next intersection brings you after one block to the **Nur Astana Mosque** [75 A7], an attractive modern construction, with a central golden dome rising to 43m, some 25 smaller domes around it, and flanked by four minarets, each 62m tall and topped with their own small golden domes. The mosque, which can provide space for up to 5,000 worshippers, was funded by the Emir of Qatar.

Back on Nurzhol Boulevard, continue eastwards. The trio of 'wavy' sided, green-glass-faced apartment blocks on your right is named the **Northern Lights** [75 B7], the idea being that its shimmering forms will evoke the aurora borealis among those who behold it. There is a planned development of slender tilting green skyscrapers opposite, to be named Emerald Towers. There are more sculptures along your route, from a dancing Kazakh girl to a camel bearing a *shanyrak*. Some take their inspiration from the images found on petroglyphs, such as a statue of an archer standing astride a curly-horned ibex.

Baiterek Tower [75 B7] (✆ 240835, 240836; f 241588; ◷ *summer 10.00–22.00 daily, winter 10.00–21.00 daily; admission adult/child T500/150*) At the heart of a large square centred on the Nurzhol Boulevard stands a monument which has become a symbol of Astana and indeed of post-independence Kazakhstan, the Baiterek Tower. It takes the form of a tall tower topped with a large golden globe, the latter positioned at a height of 97m in commemoration of Astana's elevation to the status of state capital in 1997. A white metal structure branches out beneath the golden ball, appearing to cradle it. The form of the monument is heavy with symbolism. Plaques in Russian and Kazakh at the entrance explain the background. According, we are told, to an ancient Kazakh legend, on the banks of the World River grew the tree of life, Baiterek. The roots of the tree lay in the subterranean world, its trunk in the earthly one and its crown in the heavens. Each year the sacred bird Samruk laid a golden egg in the crown of this tree, only for it to be consumed by the dragon Aidakhar, which lived at the base of it. This annual routine of egg laying and destruction symbolised the switch between summer and winter, day and night, good and evil.

The entrance to the monument is on its south side. You descend some steps to the subterranean world, which is given a somewhat aquatic theme. There is an aquarium, and a café decorated with an undersea mural. A lift, offering an accompaniment of soft Kazakh music, takes you up into the egg. There is an excellent, albeit gold-tinted, view in all directions: north to the apartment blocks of the right bank, east to the Ak Orda and Palace of Peace and Harmony, and south and west beyond the construction sites of the expanding city to the great expanses of open steppe beyond. Steps take you up to a higher viewing floor, which also offers a model of the left bank buildings.

Ascend a spiral staircase to the highest platform within the golden dome. Here stands a green malachite plinth, on top of which is a disc made of 5kg of solid silver. Resting on this in turn is a triangular-shaped 2kg lump of gold, into which is pressed the handprint of President Nazarbaev. Guides urge visitors to place their hands in that of the president and make a wish. When official delegations visit this place, loud patriotic music starts up when each senior visitor places their hand inside the imprint of that of the president. Next to this plinth is a slanted wooden table topped with half a globe, around which are arranged the signatures of the representatives of 17 religions attending the first Congress of World and Traditional Religions held in Astana, an interfaith dialogue initiative of President Nazarbaev. An inscription in Kazakh and English expresses the hope that Kazakhstan, the land of peace and accord, be blessed.

Another somewhat egg-shaped building, the grey structure on the west side of the square, is part of the national archive. The beige-walled, columned building occupying the north side of the square is home to the **Ministry of Foreign Affairs** [75 B7]. Its partner on the south side of the square, with a small pyramid structure at the centre of its roof, houses the **Ministry of Defence** [75 B7]. Another interesting architectural composition stands just to the east of the Ministry of Foreign Affairs building: a cylindrical structure topped by a communications tower which gives the whole building the appearance of a giant syringe. It houses the Astanalik Business Centre.

On the east side of the square, as Nurzhol Boulevard continues its eastward march, is the fountain composition known as the **Singing Fountains** [75 B7] for the synchronised music and water performances provided during summer evenings, from around 21.00. Around here are scattered some more interesting pieces of sculpture: giant plastic versions of Kazakh jewellery, including chunky rings and bracelets, and canvas-covered elephants, giraffes and camels, which look like giant stuffed toys.

Around the Ak Orda At the east end of Nurzhol Boulevard are two tall conical buildings, faced in a covering of reflective gold. North and south of these a large, curving, wall-like building, which houses various government ministries and agencies, essentially serves to enclose the space to its east, up to the bank of the River Ishim beyond. In this enclosed space lie the seats of legislative, executive and judicial power in Kazakhstan. The wall-like building is punctured by two roads serving the institutions beyond: large tiled arches within the framework of the building make way for the roads. Take either of these, respectively one block north and south of Nurzhol Boulevard. They bring you into a large and rather bleak square. Standing on this your attention is immediately drawn to the huge bay-fronted building on the eastern side of the square, which houses the presidential palace, the **Ak Orda** [75 C7]. This is a sumptuous building, with a blue and gold dome topped with a spire with a sun at its apex, a steppe eagle flying beneath, symbols drawn from the Kazakhstan flag. As you would expect, the building is fenced off and well guarded. It is the president's place of work, not his residence, and also houses the staff of the Presidential Administration.

On the north side of the square, the low white-tiled building, square in plan, houses the **Supreme Court** [75 C7]. In the middle of the entrance staircase to the building, which was opened in 2004, is a statue of the Greek goddess Themis, representing justice, her eyes blindfolded as she holds the balanced scales in front of her. The undulating structure at the south side of the square, under construction at the time of research, will be an entertainment complex, apparently. On the west side of the square stand three skyscrapers, their entrances on a raised courtyard reached by taking a flight of stairs up from the square. The tower to the left of this staircase is the **House of Government** [75 C7], home, *inter alia*, to the prime minister's office. The two towers to the right of the staircase house Kazakhstan's **parliament** [75 C7]. The tower topped with beige domes decorated with green diamonds houses the offices of the Senate, the upper chamber of parliament. The plainer tower behind is home to the offices of the lower chamber, the Majilis.

Palace of Peace and Harmony [75 D7] (*1 Tauelsizdik St;* \ *744744;* f *744745;* ⊕ *10.00–17.00 daily; excursions T650*) In September 2003, Astana hosted the First Congress of World and Traditional Religions. Encouraged by the success of the event, which had been his initiative, President Nazarbaev decided to make it a triennial occasion. He also decided that a permanent home would be constructed for meetings of the Congress, which would be a global centre for religious understanding and the renunciation of violence. In the following year Foster and Partners were brought in as architects, and the building was designed and constructed in the short period of two years, allowing for its opening in September 2006 to host the Second Congress. Taking the form of a pyramid, as a structure with no denominational connotations, the building is named the Palace of Peace and Harmony. The building lies along the axis running through the KazMunaiGas building, Baiterek Tower and Ak Orda, but stands on the opposite side of the Ishim River to the Ak Orda. It is a long walk to get here, and not a particularly pleasant one as it passes through an area of ongoing construction work, and there is not yet much public transport out here, so you are probably best off negotiating with a taxi driver to bring you here and wait for you. The building makes for an impressive sight. On a 15m-high earth-covered mound the 62m pyramid rises up, constructed of a steel frame, its lower levels covered in granite. You enter from the east side of the structure, into the side of the mound. It is compulsory to take a guided tour. The first impression given on entering the pyramid is, like Doctor Who's *Tardis*, one of much greater size inside than out. This is largely explained by the fact that the earth-covered mound is itself part of the structure.

The guided tour will take you first to an exhibition covering the inspirations for and construction of the building, including architectural sketches and displays placing the pyramid among the ranks of the great religious buildings of the world. You are then taken to see the 1,350-seat **opera house** which lies at the bottom of the building, with three rows of curved balconies. Montserrat Caballé performed at the inauguration of the opera house, though it does not yet host regular performances. Light enters the opera house from the atrium above, through triangular glass slivers arranged in a circle to make the form of the sun. You are then taken up a flight of stairs to view a large model of the ambitious future development plans for Astana.

The next destination on the tour is the **Cheops Atrium** (the rooms in the pyramid have mostly been given Egyptian names), a marble-floored central space, rising 40m high. You will also be shown models of the other grand projects in Kazakhstan on which the Turkish construction company, Sembol, is working, including a mooted development to be called Indoor City, which aims to provide exactly that: a complex of apartments, shops, even medical and educational facilities, allowing for life with minimal exposure to the tough Astana winters in a complex in which internal transportation will be provided by boats floating down a canal. A slanted elevator then takes you up the side of the pyramid. The seventh floor holds the **State Museum of Gold and Precious Metals** (\ *489278;* ⊕ *10.00–17.30 Tue–Sun, closed Mon & last Thu of the month*). This has a replica of the costume of the Golden Man, with further display cases containing copies of individual elements from the Golden Man costume. A second hall contains items of Kazakh silver jewellery, as well as hunting implements and items of horse decoration. The guided tours don't always cover this museum, which isn't, frankly, a great tragedy.

The elevator also takes you to the eighth floor, where you are deposited at the base of the **Winter Garden**. A flight of steps winds up the sides of the pyramid past walls lined with plants in a curious 'hanging garden' effect. The steps take you to the **Cradle**, the uppermost space of the pyramid. A circular white conference table runs around the room, the space in the middle dropping down into the atrium adding to its resemblance to a giant Polo mint. The walls of the Cradle are stained glass, the work of British artist Brian Clarke. Beneath a central sun are depicted 130 doves, representing the 130 nationalities living in peace in Kazakhstan. The doves are depicted in a realistic style, only very large, giving them a slightly sinister quality. Looking at them you get a sense of how the Tippi Hedren character must have felt in *The Birds*.

AROUND ASTANA

MAUSOLEUM OF KABANBAI BATYR Take Kabanbai Batyr Avenue southwards from the centre of town. After 11km you reach a roundabout. Go straight ahead, rather than left for the airport, passing after a further 1km the turning to Astana's **hippodrome**, inaugurated in 2007, on your right. After a further 20km, take the turning to the left signposted by a billboard depicting the **Kabanbai Batyr Mausoleum**. The monument, clearly visible ahead at the top of a low ridge, is reached after another 3.5km. Inaugurated in 2000, the red-brick mausoleum is cylindrical in form, with decorative corrugated ribs, rising to a cone which is intended to evoke the form of a warrior's helmet. The tomb inside honours the 18th-century Kazakh warrior Kabanbai Batyr, a hero of the campaigning against the Dzhungars. It takes the form of a stylised *koytas*, whose sides are etched with drawings of the warrior's weaponry.

MALINOVKA Taking the Korgalzhyn road running southwestwards from Astana, the somewhat down-at-heel settlement of Malinovka lies 34km from the capital. Here, between 1937 and 1946, operated one of the most notorious internment camps on Kazakh territory: a camp for the wives of those who had been deemed to have betrayed the USSR. It was named **ALZHIR**: the Russian initials spelling out 'Akmola Camp for the Wives of Betrayers of the Homeland'.

Immediately beyond a checkpoint, a plaque on the left-hand side of the road directs you to a **Museum in Memory of the Victims of Repression** (499455; +7 701 778 2801; alzhir@bk.ru; 10.00–18.00 Tue–Sat; admission adult/child T150/80). Opened by President Nazarbaev in 2007, the building has a conical shape, sheared off at the top. The exhibits occupy two floors, and include a grille on which artificial hands clutch at the bars. A mirror behind the grille gives the impression that the visitor to the museum is incarcerated behind those bars. There is also a mock-up of part of a barrack block at the camp, with its spartan iron bed. There are photographs and personal belongings of the prisoners, and displays related to wider aspects of the history of repression in Kazakhstan, including collectivisation, the extermination of leading Kazakh intellectuals in the Stalinist period, deportations and the suppression of the protests in Almaty in 1986 against the appointment of Gennady Kolbin as First Secretary of the Kazakhstan Communist Party. A sculpture in the central hall of the museum, displaying birds flying around a wire-mesh looped cage, symbolises freedom and captivity.

3

In front of the museum is an 18m-high **Arch of Grief**, its shape and mirrored exterior apparently aiming to evoke a traditional Kazakh female headdress. Behind this are two powerful compositions by sculptor Zhenis Moldabaev. That on the left is entitled *Despair*: a man is slumped in a chair, his countenance suggesting helplessness. On the right is *Hope and Fight*: a female prisoner of ALZHIR dreams of freedom, a book of poetry in her hand. Behind the museum is a wall bearing the names of the thousands of women and children incarcerated in ALZHIR.

Beyond the museum is an older and more basic memorial to those who were imprisoned in the camp: a **memory alley** for the victims of political repression of the 1930s to the 1950s. This runs a few hundred metres to the settlement of Malinovka, lined by rusting metal signs listing the female victims of the regime at ALZHIR and thoughtfully placed benches. At the end of this memory lane is a monument: a red Soviet star torn open by a jagged wound. A slogan in Russian and Kazakh on an adjacent billboard urges us not to forget the tragedies of the past in order not to relive them. Another billboard records the text of presidential decree 3443 of 5 April 1997, establishing 31 May as the day of remembrance of the victims of political repression.

The settlement of Malinovka stands beyond, like a decaying forgotten corner of the Soviet Union. Its crumbling five-storey apartment blocks still bear their communist-era rooftop slogans: 'peace to the world'; 'glory of labour'. Their balconies are decorated with stylised fluffy white clouds. One battered sign records

LIFE IN THE CAMPS

I accompanied a Dutch journalist to a modest flat in the old city of Astana, the home of Anna Nizamutdinova, a diminutive 90-year-old widow who lived with her boisterous cat, Greshka, meaning 'sinner', who nibbled at our toes as she recounted the many tragedies she had faced, and overcome, during her long life. She had lived in Vladivostok with her husband and two small children. In 1938, her husband, who worked for the Soviet secret service, the NKVD, had been denounced as a betrayer of the homeland, according to Anna for no greater reason than that his boss had also been so denounced. She and her husband were imprisoned. Her children were taken to an orphanage, where both died. She and other female prisoners were herded at gunpoint onto railway wagons meant for the transport of animals, and journeyed for 17 days in appalling conditions until they arrived in Kazakhstan. She was interned at the ALZHIR camp for eight years, until 1946.

She described a typical day at camp. Living in great wooden barracks, sleeping 400 women in bunk beds, they were woken at 06.00. Breakfast was always porridge, served with one teaspoon of melted butter which was dribbled into the centre of their meal such that the women used to describe their breakfast as 'porridge with a hole'. There was tea, but never sugar. Lunch and dinner were mostly cabbage and potato. Bread was 'more precious than gold', Anna recalled: adults received a daily ration of 500g, children just 300g. The only meat they ever saw was from the head of a sheep: the rest of the animal was destined for the Red Army forces at the front. Their work, for ten hours each day, was also geared to the support of the war effort. They sewed uniforms, achieving such a good quality that the camp boss once informed them that Stalin, the man who was responsible for their incarceration, had sent his thanks. They also raised crops and livestock for the war effort. At one point they were required to dig a reservoir for animals to water at, and were kept in tents at the site until well past the onset of winter. They were optimistically, 'we believe in the future'. The House of Culture features a mosaic of cosmonauts on its exterior wall, a sign at the entrance promised a discotheque that evening, entrance fee T100.

KORGALZHYN *Telephone code: 71637*

A network of lakes fed by the River Nura, southwest of Astana, Korgalzhyn is a wonderful location for birdwatching, providing a home for the world's most northerly colony of pink flamingos, as well as significant populations of pelicans, demoiselle cranes, and a number of rare species which bring birdwatchers here from western Europe on specialist tours. These include the black lark and the sociable lapwing, the latter the subject of an ongoing scientific collaboration between Britain's Royal Society for the Protection of Birds and a Kazakhstani ornithological NGO named ASBK. Crossed by major migratory bird routes, Korgalzhyn is a summer home to a wide variety of species.

The Korgalzhyn State Nature Reserve, which covers some 2,370km², was first designated in 1968. It is a candidate for designation as a UNESCO World Heritage Site. The lakes in the network become progressively more salty with increasing distance from the ingress of the River Nura, such that the waters of the lakes in the eastern part of the reserve are relatively fresh, while those of the largest lake in the system, Lake Tengiz, in the west, itself covering a surface area of 1,590km², are only

always too cold, shivering in inadequate clothes and beneath meagre blankets. They had no coal or wood: they cut rushes to fuel the ovens in the barrack blocks. Their periods stopped.

Anna's job in the camp was that of cook. She was given a fat old mare in order to be able to deliver lunches to those working in the fields, and lived in fear that the ailing beast might die on her, for which she would receive punishment. She passed a Kazakh village on the way to the fields, where she recalled bartering yeast for *ayran*. Newcomers like herself had good relations with the local Kazakhs: the two communities shared what little they had during the years of adversity. Nor did Anna have any complaints about the conduct of the guards, who she said recognised that the women interred in the camp had committed no crime. True, the camp commander received numerous awards as a result of their efforts, but he was basically a good sort. When one woman, separated from her five children, hanged herself, the commander came round to every barrack block, promising the women that good times would come, and urging them not to lose heart.

On her release from ALZHIR in 1946 she initially found it difficult to find anywhere to live: people were scared of renting out rooms to those who were married to 'betrayers of the homeland'. But eventually she re-established her life. She found out that her husband had been executed; that he was now fully pardoned was a somewhat bitter irony. But her own full pardon resulted in the receipt of compensation money from the authorities in Vladivostok in respect of the goods and property which had been taken from her and her husband. With no family to return to in Vladivostok, Anna began a second life in Akmola, working in a restaurant and marrying a 38-year-old baker. She bore him three children, and was proud of the musical achievements of her grandchildren: one an opera singer, another a pianist.

slightly less salty than those of the Dead Sea. The breeding colonies of flamingos lie mostly on islands in Lake Tengiz.

PRACTICALITIES A visit to Korgalzhyn State Nature Reserve starts with the village of Korgalzhyn, 130km to the southwest of Astana. Several buses a day make the trip here from Astana bus station. You will first need to head to the office of the **nature reserve administration** (*20 Madina St, Korgalzhyn;* \ *21650;* ⊕ *09.30–13.00 & 14.30–17.30 Mon–Fri*) in the village, in order to register and purchase a permit for entry into the reserve. If you are arriving at the weekend, you should phone the previous week during office hours to arrange for an appointment. The reserve itself lies further to the west; the barrier marking the entrance to the reserve is some 38km beyond Korgalzhyn. Another 15km beyond that and you reach the hamlet of **Karazhar**, whose cottages were home to researchers during the Soviet period, on the shores of the freshwater **Lake Sultankeldy,** meaning 'the sultan came'. The lake gets its name from a stopover here by the 19th-century Kazakh rebel leader Kenesary, on his way to Ulytau for his 'coronation'.

While Korgalzhyn is doable as a day trip from Astana, the fact that the best places to see flamingos are in the less accessible western parts of the reserve (the shores of Little Lake Tengiz, to the north of Karazhar, are the easiest to reach of the most likely locations), and the attractiveness of the landscape, encourage an overnight stop. There is a simple green-roofed dacha on the shores of Lake Sultankeldy at Karazhar, with a plaque on the wall testifying to its use by Dinmuhammed Kunaev, then the First Secretary of the Communist Party of Kazakhstan, between 1962 and 1976. Some simple log cabins and a yurt have also been put up here, together with outdoor showers. This basic accommodation can be booked through Akmolaturist in Astana (see page 78), who also organise transport to the reserve and can arrange your permit for you. The other main accommodation option is a homestay in Korgalzhyn village, which can be booked through the **NGO Rodnik** (*Office 5, 20 Madina St, Korgalzhyn;* \ *21043;* e *oorodnik@mail.ru*), which is based at the nature reserve administration building. Rodnik is one of the partners of the Ecotourism Information Resource Centre in Almaty (see page 123), and you can also book through them. Rodnik can also arrange hire of transport, tents and sleeping bags and horses.

Flamingo season at Korgalzhyn runs from around mid-April until September.

KOKSHETAU *Telephone code: 7162*

Founded in 1824 as a Cossack settlement on the southern shore of the Kopa Lake, Kokshetau is the capital of Akmola Region. It is a leafy, laid-back city at the heart of Kazakhstan's wheat belt. Most of the billboards you see when coming into town seem to be advertising the merits of different tractors or combine harvesters. In the centre of town, just in front of the regional historical museum, an inscription on a wall-like monument records a decree of the Presidium of the Supreme Soviet of the USSR from 1958, awarding Kokshetav Oblast the Order of Lenin by virtue of its success in surpassing the yearly plan for bread production. Following independence, the Soviet name for the city, Kokshetav, was altered to the more Kazakh-sounding Kokshetau.

While not a tourist town, Kokshetau is a pleasant enough place for an overnight stay, and a good gateway to the Kokshetau National Park and to Borovoye. Walk around town on an early summer evening and you are likely to see locals holding small leafy branches: these serve as switches for largely futile attempts to ward off the prodigious quantities of mosquitoes.

GETTING THERE AND AROUND The **railway station** (⌕ 292222) sits at the eastern end of the long Abai Street, Kokshetau's central thoroughfare. A tall concrete clock tower guides you to it. Among the trains passing this way are the daily services between Almaty and Petropavl, Kyzylorda and Petropavl, and Karaganda and Kostanai. There are also less frequent trains passing northwards on to various Russian destinations, including Moscow, Sverdlovsk and Omsk, and local electric train services to Erementau (daily) and Astana (Saturday, Sunday, Monday and Tuesday). As you leave the station, you are greeted by a tall column on which stands a statue of a woman holding her arms aloft, hopefully in joy at your arrival.

The **bus station** (⌕ 252404) is across the square in front of the railway station, and to the left. It is a crumbling Soviet building with graffiti-covered wooden seats and small birds flying around in search of crumbs, or the exit. There are departures to Astana (five hours), Petropavl (four hours), Zerenda, four a day to Omsk, and a few to Borovoye (two hours). In the square between the bus and railway stations gather a range of **taxis** and **minibuses** offering to take you to Astana or Petropavl.

It is also possible to fly to Koskhetau. The **airport** is served by Kokshetau Avia, who operate a Yak-40 four times a week on a route running between Almaty and Petropavl, via Kokshetau. In town, numbers to dial for local **taxi** companies include ⌕ 252727, ⌕ 252929 and ⌕ 253737. Buses in town cost T30.

TOUR OPERATOR
Ecos Ecotourism Development Centre 37 Chapaev St; ⌕/f 266460. Run by the enthusiastic Karlygash & Irina, this NGO organises good-value homestays with Kazakhstani families in 3 locations in or close to the Kokshetau National Park: at Imantau & Ayirtau in North Kazakhstan Region (see page 280) & Sandyktau in Akmola Region (see page 109).

⌂ WHERE TO STAY
⌂ **Hotel Dastyr** (6 rooms) 194 Auezov St; ⌕ 253038, 255430; e dastyr_1@mail.ru. The curious metal cupola marks out this place, not far from the central park. Downstairs is a cavernous restaurant of the type likely to be booked out by wedding parties at w/ends. The rooms upstairs are quite nicely furnished, but only the 'luxe' rooms have en suites, the place gets very hot in summer, & the rooms are altogether priced higher than they deserve. **$$**

⌂ **Hotel Dostyk** (70 rooms) 69 Abai St; ⌕ 254445, 233716; f 251747; e Hotel-dostyk@ mail.kz. The 'Friendship Hotel' looks bright & modern from the outside, proudly displaying its 3 stars. Don't be fooled by the facelift though: this is a Soviet-style place with *dizhurnaya* on every floor doling out your b/fast coupons, unreliable water supply & ancient lifts. But it is very central &, with some of the rooms reasonably renovated, there are options here to suit most budgets. **$$**

⌂ **Hotel Kokshetau** 106 Abai St; ⌕ 256427, 256422. A typical 9-storey Soviet-era relic, shabby & with unfriendly administration, but in a very central location on the main square. The receptionist refused to tell me how many rooms the hotel possesses, saying that the information was 'restricted'! There is a bewildering range of prices, depending, for example, whether the room in question has a TV, whether the TV is in colour, & whether it has the cable channels. All rooms have en suites, though the cheapest lack phone, TV & fridge. **$$**

⌂ **Hotel Zhekebatyr** (28 rooms) 184 Auezov St; ⌕ 269635, 269634; f 269637; e zhekebatyr@ mail.ru. This 4-storey building with a pale green & white exterior colour scheme lies at the top of Kokshetau's hotel range. You are welcomed in by door chimes & a remarkably garish, glittery frieze of the Goluboy Zaliv in Borovoye. The corridors are heavily populated by house plants & the rooms are well furnished, all with en suites. Prices include b/fast & VAT, though there is an annoying booking fee set at 25% of the 1st night's accommodation. **$$**

⌂ **Railway Station Retiring Rooms** ⌕ 293393. On the top floor of the railway station building, this place offers very basic rooms, with shared toilets. **$**

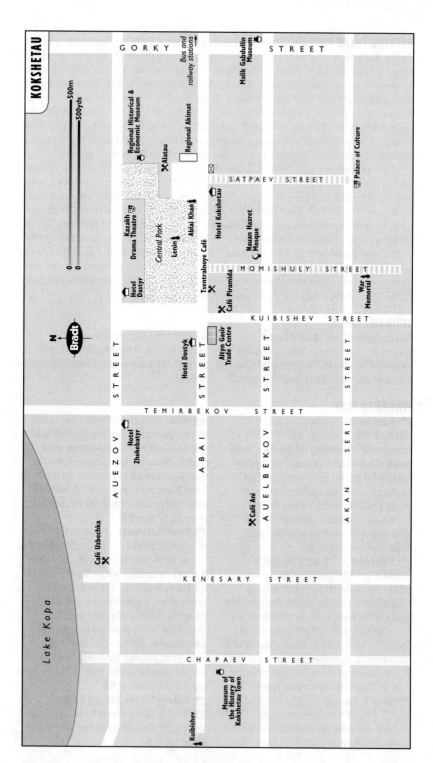

KOKSHETAU

Lake Kopa

N Bradt

0 500m
0 500yds

GORKY STREET

Bus and
railway stations

Malik Gabdullin
Museum

STREET

Regional Historical &
Economic Museum

✕ Alatau

Regional Akimat

Palace of Culture

SATPAEV STREET

Kazakh
Drama Theatre

Central Park

Lenin

Ablai Khan

Hotel Kokshetau

Nauan Hazret
Mosque

Hotel
Dastyr

Tsentralnoye Café

MOMISHULY STREET

✕ Café Piramida

War
Memorial

KUIBISHEV STREET

AUEZOV STREET

ABAI STREET

Hotel Dostyk

Altyn Gasir
Trade Centre

STREET

AUELBEKOV STREET

AKAN SERI STREET

TEMIRBEKOV STREET

Hotel
Zhekebatyr

Café Uzbechka ✕

✕ Café Ani

KENESARY STREET

CHAPAEV STREET

Museum of
the History of
Kokshetau Town

Kuibishev

✗ WHERE TO EAT

✗ **Alatau** 1 Satpaev St; ↘401025. Aquaria & plastic fruit trees decorate this restaurant housed next to the building which once accommodated the Ministry of Nature Protection. The menu is a broad mix of Russian & international dishes, the décor is an uninspiring blue & white pairing, & they offer live music in the evenings. $$$

✗ **Café Piramida** 93A Dzerzhinsky St; ↘255688. This bright & airy place opposite the central shopping centre offers a café downstairs, a restaurant above, & a little glass pyramid stuck on top of the building. The menu offers Italian, European & Russian dishes, the last including a wide choice of pancakes, though the food is nothing special. $$$

✗ **Café Ani** 49 Auelbekov St; ↘266429. Pleasant Armenian restaurant on the western side of town. They have tables outside in summer. The food is good, though the chef gets heavy on the garlic. $$

✗ **Café Uzbechka** 95 Auezov St; ↘264808. This is an attractive Uzbek-themed restaurant, west of the town centre not far from the southern shore of the Kopa lake. There is an outdoor summer café, complete with terrace for dancing, & a colourfully decorated indoor eating area. The waitresses wear brightly patterned Uzbek dress. $$

✗ **Tsentralnoye Café** 86 Abai St; ↘257824. A basic place with wooden tables & benches & a range of pre-prepared dishes on display in a glass cabinet, ready to be heated up. The 'Central Café' is indeed centrally located, opposite the park. $

WHAT TO SEE

Around the central square The main thoroughfare is Abai Street, which scythes west to east through the town, where it ends at the railway station. The town centres on a large and bare square, at the intersection of Abai and Satpaev streets. On the eastern side of this sits the **regional** *akimat*, in a modern cream and brown-toned building. The north side of the square is occupied by a long building with a Corinthian-columned façade, which temporarily housed the Ministry of Nature Protection until a new home was built for the Ministry in Astana. On the west side of the square is a statue of **Ablai Khan**, depicted squatting regally, his right hand on his hip in a display of relaxed strength. Behind the Kazakh ruler rises a very tall stalk of wheat, on the tip of which a bird is flying.

Behind the Ablai Khan statue is a **central park**, which features a few run-down fairground rides, and discos on summer weekend evenings. In the park is also a statue of a defiant-looking **Lenin**, standing next to a simple Soviet monument to the Kazakhstanis killed in the Civil War. From the park, the pedestrianised Momishuly Street runs south. A bust of war hero Talgat Bigdelinov, a pilot who notched up 305 combat missions, shot down seven enemy aircraft and was twice made Hero of the Soviet Union, is followed by a series of polished stones inscribed with the names of the Hero Cities of the Soviet Union. These run for two blocks, ending up at the **war memorial**. A young flag-bearing soldier kneels before an eternal flame. Behind him rises a peculiar silvery sculpture of a star with a point missing. The portraits of local war heroes are presented on the surrounding wall, in alphabetical order, starting with Bigdelinov. One block north of the war memorial, at the corner of Momishuly and Auelbekov streets, is the delightful wooden **Nauan Hazret Mosque**, its octagonal wooden minaret rising to a spire.

From the central square, pedestrianised Satpaev Street runs south a couple of blocks to the ugly modern grey metallic-faced **Palace of Culture**, which also incorporates the Russian Drama Theatre.

Regional Historical and Economic Museum (*35 Kalinin St; ↘ 255792;* ⊕ *09.00–13.00 & 14.00–18.00 Mon–Sat; admission adult/child T60/30*) Immediately to the north of the central square, just beyond the regional *akimat* building, sit

a couple of attractive two-storey Tsarist-era brick buildings, built by a merchant whose wealth lay in the vodka business. One of these is now a university building, the other houses the Regional Historical and Economic Museum. Not one of the more interesting regional museums in Kazakhstan, this offers a display of minerals and semi-precious stones in the foyer, and rooms on the ground floor devoted to palaeontology and to World War II, the latter focused on displays related to local war heroes such as nurse Maria Smirnova-Kykharskaya, whose photos show her resolute and steely eyed, a recipient of the Florence Nightingale Medal.

Upstairs, a geology room features a display on the Vasilkovsky gold mine, a few kilometres out of town, and there is a dull display on flora and fauna. The history room includes items about the Kazakh khanates, including the weaponry of Kazakh fighters and household utensils such as an *astau*, a large wooden tray on which meat would be piled when guests were entertained. It also covers the arrival of Slavonic migrants, with interesting photographs of the early Cossack settlement, and a plan of the town from 1907 showing Kokshetav already laid out in a grid pattern on the southern shore of Lake Kopa. There are also displays on the modern life of the region, covering its local factories, such as an assembly plant for Kamaz lorries, wheat production, and the stars of the local theatres. The last room features temporary exhibitions, usually focusing on one of the various ethnic groups making up the local population. When I visited it was the turn of the Russians: linen, balalaikas, spinning wheels and carved wooden furniture.

Malik Gabdullin Museum (*123 Auelbekov St;* \ *257627;* ☉ *9.00–18.00 daily; admission foreign citizen/adult/child T120/100/30*) At the corner of Auelbekov and Gorky streets, on the eastern side of the town centre, the modern-looking two-storey wooden building houses the Museum of the Hero of the Soviet Union Malik Gabdullin. Opened in 2005 by President Nazarbaev, this is rather an interesting museum to a man who combined wartime bravery with peacetime literary success. A model displays the small two-room building in which Malik Gabdullin was born in 1915, in a village 30km from Kokshetau. When he was made a Hero of the Soviet Union in 1943, the authorities constructed for his family a larger and nicer wooden house adjacent to this, but his pious father donated the wood from this building to efforts to reconstruct the Kokshetau mosque, when the latter was damaged by fire in 1956. While young Malik was studying in Almaty, his mother and nine siblings all died in the famine of the early 1930s. Malik studied at the Abai Teaching University in Almaty, but his dissertation on the Kazakh writer Beimbet Mailin resulted in trouble in the late 1930s, when Mailin fell victim to Stalin's repression, and he was briefly deprived of his Komsomol membership. His research career recovered, and under the tutelage of Auezov he began a work on the Kazakh epic tale *Batyr Koblandy*.

The outbreak of war disrupted Gabdullin's studies, and he joined Panfilov's 316th Rifle Division. Various military items are on display, including Gabdullin's shaving kit. A diorama depicts the action for which Gabdullin received his award of Hero of the Soviet Union: a group of entrenched Russian soldiers managing to fend off attacking German tanks with the use of their hand grenades. A uniform is on display, decorated with his many medals, including the five-pointed star and red ribbon of the Hero of the Soviet Union. When peace came, Gabdullin resumed his studies, finally getting his work on Batyr Koblandy published in 1947. He wrote popular books in both Russian and Kazakh about his wartime experiences, took up politics, becoming a Deputy of the Supreme Soviet of the USSR, and enjoyed a successful academic career, becoming a professor of literature. He died in 1973, at the age of 58. His death mask is on display. His homely looking study is also mocked up, complete with *dombra* on the sofa.

Old town   West of the centre many attractive single-storey log-built houses survive, usually featuring painted wooden shutters. A couple of particularly fine examples, both enjoying official recognition as historical monuments, are the whitewashed wooden cottage at 22 Kenesary Street, at the corner of Abai, with intricate carving at the base of the roof, and the cottage at 33 Dzherzhinskiy Street. The latter sits opposite a small **Museum of the History of Kokshetau Town** (*32 Chapaev St; 265786, 26468;* ⏰ *09.00–13.00 & 14.00–18.00 Mon–Fri; admission for foreign citizens/locals T200/100*), itself housed in a single-storey wooden building.

Abai Street ends on the side of a line of low hills marking the western edge of town. At the end of Kokshetau's main thoroughfare, amidst the wooden bungalows of the old part of town, stands a tall statue of a young, rather studenty-looking **Valerian Kuibishev**, a Bolshevik military commander during the Civil War and key figure behind the first Five-Year Plan, who gave his name to the city of Samara during the Soviet period.

KOKSHETAU NATIONAL PARK

Straddling two regions, Akmola and North Kazakhstan (see page 279), the Kokshetau National Nature Park was designated in 1996 and occupies a large area to the south and west of Kokshetau. While both scenically and touristically rather lower key than the better-known resort area of Borovoye, the park offers some attractive landscapes: undulating hills, punctuated by many lakes, and covered with a mix of steppe and of pine and birch forests. Woodland inhabitants include elk, deer and bears.

ZERENDA   Among the most popular places to head for on the Akmola Region side of the park is the village of Zerenda, founded as a Cossack settlement, 45km to the south of Kokshetau (an hour by bus), which sits on the eastern side of a pleasant lake fringed by birch and pine woods. Several holiday complexes line the far side of the lake from the village. One upmarket place to stay is the **Zeren Holiday Centre** (*(71632) 21306, 22594;* f *(71632) 21815;* e *zeren_zeren@rambler.ru; www.zeren.kz;* **$$$$**). Some 6km from the centre of Zerenda village, the complex features a main hotel block and separate two-bedroom wooden cottages, all kitted out to a high standard. There is a gym, indoor swimming pool and walking trails through the pine forests, plus the opportunity to hire various sporting equipment, including snowmobiles in winter and boats in summer. This does not come cheap, though prices do include meals.

The road from Zerenda village to the Zeren Holiday Centre continues on towards the village of Lobanovo, which lies in North Kazakhstan Region. Some 22km along this road from the Zeren Centre, as the hamlet of **Karsak** appears on the right-hand side of the road, you can make out several *kurgans* across the plains. These take the form of low mounds with large flat stones sticking up above ground level, forming circles on the mounds. They are believed to date from the Andronov period.

SANDYKTAU   A very different accommodation option from the plush Zeren Holiday Centre is to be found in the village of Sandyktau, 45km to the south of Zerenda along the main road from Kokshetau towards Atbasar. Here, the Kokshetau-based NGO Ecos (see page 105) can arrange **homestays (\$)** at one of four houses in the village. All the houses participating in the scheme have indoor toilets and showers, whose installation was funded with support from ExxonMobil, and offer basic but comfortable bedrooms. The accommodation is provided on a full-board basis, with meals cooked by the host family. Most of the participating families in Sandyktau are ethnic Russians. The bus fare to Sandyktau from Kokshetau is T310: take a bus heading to Balkashino or Shantobe. Ecos can also arrange a taxi to ferry you between Kokshetau and Sandyktau, for around T7,500 for the return trip.

A stay in Sandyktau offers an excellent insight into life in a Kazakhstani village, where the noises around you are mostly provided by dogs and chickens, punctuated by the occasional putt-putting of a passing elderly motorbike. While Sandyktau lies outside the territory of the Kokshetau National Park, there are some interesting walking and horseriding possibilities, mostly focused on the Sandyktau Hills which lie between the village and another settlement, **Novoromanovka**, to the southeast. Novoromanovka is an attractive small settlement of Cossack log-walled single-storey buildings with blue and white decorated shutters, and Ecos has plans to develop community-based tourism here too. The hills apparently get their name from the Kazakh word *sunduk*, meaning a box or chest, probably from the box-like form of the range, though one local tale has it that the forces under White Russian commander Aleksandr Kolchak, passing this way and under heavy pressure from Bolshevik troops, buried somewhere in these hills a chest containing valuable treasures. Which, needless to say, has never been found. The hills are covered with pine forest. One of the places to head for is an outcrop of granite, offering excellent views across the forest canopy. Ecos can arrange a guide for T4,500 a day.

The district capital, **Balkashino**, lying 10km to the south of Sandyktau, is little more than a village itself. Its central square is worth a look, with a silver statue of Lenin on one side, a pitched-roofed Orthodox church with a single onion dome on the other.

BOROVOYE

This landscape of lakes, hills, weathered granite outcrops, and pine and birch forests offers some of the most picturesque scenery in northern Kazakhstan, and attracts gushing tourist agency labels such as 'Kazakhstan's Switzerland' and 'the pearl of Kazakhstan'. Named, since 2000, the Burabay National Nature Park, the western boundary of this landscape is formed by the boomerang-shaped Kokshetau Mountains, which run roughly north to south. The 'Blue Mountains' do indeed take on that hue when viewed from afar across the surrounding steppe. Around the foothills of the Kokshetau Mountains lie several lakes, and most of the area's tourist infrastructure lies along the shores of two: Lake Schuche and Lake Borovoye. The Kokshetau Mountains are covered with forests, and the carpet of forest continues across the lower hills lying to their east.

The area already attracts large numbers of domestic tourists and visitors from those parts of Russia abutting the Kazakhstani border, but there are ambitious plans to develop tourism further given Borovoye's location as the natural weekend playground for the growing new capital of Astana. (There are few other obvious tourism options within reasonable distance of the capital.) Since April 2007, the district in which Borovoye is located has been one of only two in Kazakhstan in which gambling establishments have been permitted, as the authorities seek to focus Kazakhstan's casinos out of the cities and into new purpose-built resorts. Given that the distinctive landscape of this region covers a relatively small territory, it must be hoped that these development plans take account of Borovoye's fragile environment. Some new buildings already give rise to concerns on this score.

The local telephone codes are 71636 for the town of Schuchinsk and 71630 for the village of Borovoye, but are repeated in the text below against each phone number given to avoid confusion.

GETTING THERE AND AROUND The gateway to the Borovoye resort area is the district capital, Schuchinsk, an uninspiring small town of 42,000 people close to the southern shores of Lake Schuche. Schuchinsk lies on both the main road and the railway route between Astana and Kokshetau, around 235km north of the Kazakhstani capital and 72km to the southeast of Kokshetau.

Schuchinsk **railway station** (*(71636) 64401*) goes by the name of Borovoye Resort. It is a stop for the daily departures between Almaty and Petropavl, Kyzylorda and Petropavl, and Karaganda and Kostanai. There are also less frequent trains to Pavlodar, as well as Russian destinations including Moscow, Sverdlovsk and Omsk. More local electric train routes include a daily service running between Kokshetau and Erementau. There is also a useful service between Astana and Kokshetau, running four times a week (Saturday–Tuesday), which at the time of research involved an arrival from Astana at 09.40, and a departure for Astana at 19.58. This does make it possible to visit Borovoye as an (albeit long and tiring) day trip by rail from Astana.

The **bus station** (*(71636) 64888*) stands in front of the railway station and to the right. There are departures every few minutes to Kokshetau, 13 a day to Astana, seven a day to Petropavl, two daily to Pavlodar, via Astana, and two daily to Omsk.

From the bus station, the village of Borovoye is around 30km, though the holiday complexes around Lake Schuche are much closer. There are 18 buses a day (running between 06.00 and 18.20) from Schuchinsk bus station to Borovoye (T120), and places in private minibuses available for little more. Since many of the holiday complexes are at out-of-town lakeside sites, a taxi may prove a better bet, and there are usually some outside the bus and railway stations (*or* (*(71636) 32222*). These should cost around T500–1,000, depending on your resort, though the drivers may hold out for more, especially in high season.

TOUR OPERATOR
Leader Travel Agency 33 Ablai Khan St, Schuchinsk; ((71636) 45013; f (71636) 45525; e info@lta.kz; www.lta.kz. This Schuchinsk-based agency specialises in bookings for a wide range of hotels & sanatoria in the Borovoye area.

 WHERE TO STAY Note that prices for most accommodation options in Borovoye rise by around 20%, sometimes more, between June and August.

Around Lake Schuche
Park Hotel Kokshetau (33 rooms) (71636) 41998; f 41999; e kokshetauhotel@mail.ru, www.4star.kz. A ranch-style balconied building on the steeper western side of Lake Schuche, this attractively furnished hotel is at the top of the price range for the area. Only the plastic palm trees in the corridors detract from the tastefulness of the place. Use of the smart health centre is included in the room rate, as is b/fast. Only the most expensive rooms have good lake views, though. Expect most of your fellow guests to be wealthy 'New Kazakhs'. **$$$$$**

Hotel Samal (21 rooms) (71636) 90318, 90228; f (71636) 90203; e info@samal-otel.com; www.samal-otel.com. Located close to the northeastern corner of Lake Schuche, on the other side of the road from the lake, the Samal consists of a group of several modern buildings clustered together, with a further block under construction at the time of research. The rooms are nicely furnished, & there is an indoor pool, but the set meals (inc in the room rate) are nothing special & the lack of a lakeside location is a definite minus. **$$$$**

3

🏠 **Hotel Almaz** (48 rooms) ⋎f (71636) 90225, 90310. At the northeastern corner of Lake Schuche, close to the Zeleniy Bor Sanatorium, the Almaz is a 5-storey building with concrete balconies, set amongst woodland, which gives the impression of having seen better days. Room rates include (uninspiring) FB. **$$**

🏠 **Zeleniy Bor Sanatorium** (280 beds) ☎ (71636) 90245, 90294; f (71636) 90247; e greenwood@mail.kz. This sanatorium retains a strong flavour of the Soviet era, with somewhat tired accommodation blocks enlivened by golden balconies. The place lives up to its name, 'green forest', lying deep in mixed birch & pine woodland, 500m from the road on the northeastern bank of Lake Schuche. A smiley totem pole greets you as you turn off the main road. A path runs down to the lake past cute wooden sculptures of mermaids & crocodiles, & the Zeleniy Bor boasts its own stretch of beach. The food is regimented sanatorium fare, & various baths & massage treatments are available. There is a wide range of rooms; the cheapest sgls are basic, with cot-like wooden beds. Prices rise by around 40% Jun–Aug. **$$**

🏠 **Railway Station Retiring Rooms** (7 rooms) ☎ (71636) 64105. Located on the 3rd floor of the Borovoye Resort railway station, these retiring rooms are basic but clean, & worth considering if you are arriving or departing at an awkward hour. The 'luxe' room has en-suite facilities. **$**

Around Lake Borovoye

🏠 **Okzhetpes Sanatorium** (122 rooms) ☎ (71630) 75101, 72388; f (71630) 71133; e okzhetpes@mail.ru; www.okzhetpes.com. In an idyllic setting amidst birch & pine woods close to the Goluboy Zaliv, the Okzhetpes is a smart option, a Soviet-era sanatorium, always a favoured spot for the local elite, which was renovated by the Italian oil company ENI in 2002 & is now managed by the Presidential Administration. Senior Kazakhstani civil servants come here for conferences & short breaks. The main block is a 7-storey building, in front of which stands a statue of a bare-chested archer, straining to project his arrow to the summit of the adjacent Okzhetpes Hill. Various attached blocks house further accommodation, a fitness centre, sports hall, swimming pool & treatment block. Room rates, which include FB, alter with the season; they are highest Jun–Aug & lowest in Apr, Oct & Nov. **$$$$$**

🏠 **Hotel Gloriya** (12 rooms) 4 Kokshe St, Borovoye village; ⋎f (71630) 72366. This is a 3-storey modern brick building across the road from the nature museum on the eastern side of Borovoye village. Rooms are functional, with parquet floors & en-suite showers, but it's a rather bland option, without the charm of some of the lakeside choices. **$$$**

🏠 **Hotel Nursat** (39 rooms) Borovoye village; ☎ (71630) 71301, 71001; f (71630) 71504; e bereke2030@mail.ru; www.bereke-burabai. com. Offering a somewhat similar deal to its near neighbour, the Gloriya, the Nursat has reasonably furnished rooms with en suites & wooden floors, though no AC. It is rather antiseptic; set on the wrong side of the road from the lake, & in grounds which consist of little more than a car park. The external walls of this red-brick building rise to repeated points, giving it a vaguely fortified aspect. **$$$**

🏠 **Saturn Guest House** (12 rooms) ⋎f (71630) 71899. This pitched-roofed brick building has a plum position on a promontory jutting into the eastern side of Lake Borovoye. It lies about 3km southeast of Borovoye village. Turn off the main road towards the lake immediately to the south of the Hotel Alem, an uninspiring option under the same ownership as the Nursat. The Saturn is sighted after 600m, just beyond a barrier related to the activities of a neighbouring geological research station. The internal brick corridors give the place something of a monastic feel. It has a lakeside gazebo & catamarans for hire, & is altogether a restful option, though short on entertainment. **$$$**

✘ **WHERE TO EAT** With so many of the visitors to Borovoye staying in sanatoria on full-board arrangements, there is not a particularly wide range of good places to eat. The following two choices are close to some of the main tourist destinations on lakes Schuche and Borovoye, respectively, and so make convenient options, but one is nothing special and the other is an eyesore.

✕ Zhumbaktas Restaurant ＼(71630) 72304. An intrusive tinted glass-fronted modern building, belting out pop music across the otherwise idyllic Goluboy Zaliv towards its namesake rock formation; I am loath to publicise this place at all. An equally environmentally unsympathetic hotel has been constructed next door, & is called the Ablai Khan. The smart cream interior is at least more calming. The food claims to blend European & Latin American influences. $$$

✕ Edem Café ＼(71636) 90221. A wooden hut close to the northeastern shores of Lake Schuche, not far from the Hotel Samal, this is basically a beer & *shashlik* place with loud music, a karaoke machine, plastic flowers draped around the windows & a concrete-floored dance area. $$

WHAT TO SEE
From Lake Schuche to Lake Borovoye
Some 18km² in size, **Lake Schuche** is the deepest lake in the area. It sits immediately to the north of the town of Schuchinsk. Its western side abuts onto the forest-covered Kokshetau Mountains. The eastern banks are gentler, with birches and rounded rocks close to the lake shore. It is a popular resort area, with several hotels and sanatoria along its shores, but its attractions are rather more low key than those of the more picturesque Lake Borovoye.

Two main roads run from Schuchinsk to Lake Borovoye. The more interesting is the western option. From Schuchinsk, head northwards, passing the southern shores of Lake Schuche on your left. At 9km from the centre of town, take the left turn at the fork in the road. You are then confronted by a barrier, levying a fee of T218 per person for entry into the Burabay National Nature Park. The road passes through pine forest, Lake Schuche lying unseen off to the left. Some 6km on are a range of accommodation options clustered around the northeastern corner of Lake Schuche, including the Zeleniy Bor Sanatorium and Almaz and Samal hotels (see above).

Some 5km further on, a lay-by on the right-hand side of the road lies at the foot of a flight of steps which leads up to a curious monument: a rain shelter in the form of a concrete mussel (the place is known by locals as the rakushka – 'mussel'). From this monument, walk further up along the ridge, alongside a line of boulders which serves as a natural wall. You soon reach a glade, around which the trees are covered with votive scraps of material. The view from here towards the line of the Kokshetau Mountains to the southwest is excellent; the crests of the hills are said to trace the shape of the face of a sleeping giant warrior. They do indeed seem to take the form of forehead, nose and mouth; at least, if you don't stare too hard.

Another 5km on, and the road passes through a large glade, known as **Ablai Khan's Clearing**. There is a car park on the right, and a couple of souvenir stalls in summer, where you can buy photographs of Lake Borovoye pasted onto bits of birch wood. The glade has been identified as a place in which Ablai Khan, a Kazakh leader of the 18th century, set up camp and marshalled his forces. To the left of the road is a tall, post-independence monument: a tiled spear reaching skyward, with an eagle at its apex. A roundel on the side of the monument depicts Ablai Khan riding a snow leopard. In the field surrounding the monument stand some modern stone *balbals*, like mute lieutenants of the long-departed leader. A path behind the monument leads up into the pine forest at the back of the glade. A few metres in you come across a broad, flat rock, oval in plan, on which three further rocks are perched. This ensemble is known as **Ablai Khan's Throne**. Local practice involves walking round this several times anticlockwise (when I was there an argument broke out between visitors as to whether the correct number of times was seven or ten), before then finding a pine tree which appears to be agreeable, giving it a hug, and making a wish.

The largest of the hills behind the glade is the 947m Mount Kokshe, the highest peak of the Kokshetau Mountains, which also goes by the Russian name of Sinyukha. Both names hint at the bluish tint of the mountains when viewed from a distance. To the right of this are two hills which together look rather like a sleeping hedgehog, one resembling its podgy belly, the other its pointy nose. Ablai Khan's Clearing is also known as the Yasnaya Polyana, or 'Bright Clearing' (Clear Clearing?), since it is said that the sun always shines here, even when the adjacent forest is shrouded in cloud.

The Goluboy Zaliv At 1km beyond Ablai Khan's Clearing, you reach Lake Borovoye, little more than 10km² in surface area, and the heart of the Burabay National Nature Park. The road runs around its most picturesque part, here at the northwest corner of the lake, an inlet known as the Goluboy Zaliv, or Blue Bay. The focus of this is a rocky offshore outcrop, whose form vaguely suggests that of a Sphinx, named **Zhumbaktas**. This faces towards a steep-sided hill of bare granite, known as **Okzhetpes**, lying along the western side of the bay. The juxtaposition of these two striking stone features with the blue waters of the lake makes for a highly photogenic ensemble, and it is one which illustrates many tourist materials related to Kazakhstan.

There are three places around the bay at which you can hire rowing boats in summer, either to take out yourself or with an oarsman who will give you a commentary on the legend surrounding Zhumbaktas, the 'mystery rock', as he rows you around it. The story runs roughly as follows. Ablai Khan returned here after his successful campaigning, with many treasures captured from his foes and these were divided up amongst his lieutenants. But they could not agree on who would take the most prized item of all, a beautiful young Dzhungar girl. The *batyrs* started to fight amongst themselves for the girl. She then decided on a competition which she knew was unwinnable, as a ruse to secure her passage home. She arranged for her handkerchief to be placed at the top of the hill now known as Okzhetpes, and said that she would submit herself to anyone who could shoot the handkerchief with an arrow fired from the base of the hill. All failed, and hence the hill took on the name Okzhetpes, which means, in Kazakh, 'unreachable by arrows'. But finding herself still barred from returning home to her true love, the girl jumped to her death into the lake. The Zhumbaktas stone then rose up out of it as a tribute to her bravery and fidelity.

The 'face' of the Sphinx-like Zhumbaktas rock is said to resemble from certain angles that of a beautiful young woman, with a short pointy nose. From other angles the face changes character, to resemble a hawk-nosed old crone. Zhumbaktas today is disappointingly covered in graffiti, the marks of celebration from the people who had the strength necessary to row or swim the several metres from the shore, or indeed to walk across in winter. The oldest visible defacement is dated 1905. The oarsmen of the Goluboy Zaliv share the apparent fascination of everyone in Borovoye with rocks that look like animals, or household items. There is an elephant on the top of Okzhetpes; a giant left shoe lying on one of the slabs of granite which makes up Zhumbaktas; and, seen from one angle, a flying saucer has landed on Zhumbaktas.

From the north side of the Goluboy Zaliv a path crosses an isthmus, a few hundred metres across at its narrowest point, to the adjacent **Lake Bolshoye Chebachye**. Covering 25km², this is the largest of the lakes at the foot of the Kokshetau Mountains. It is populated by islands and near islands, the latter connected to the mainland by spits of land. From the slopes of the eastern end of the Kokshetau Mountains there are fine views to be had across the two lakes and the isthmus between them.

Borovoye Nature Museum (⏰ *10.00–18.30 Tue–Sun; admission adult/child T200/100*) Some 3km on from the Goluboy Zaliv, another barrier signals the end of the national nature park and the arrival of the village of Borovoye. Taking the main road through this, you reach, on the far side of the village, the Borovoye Nature Museum. Located in a wooden building by the side of the lake on the right-hand side of the road, this provides a good, basic introduction to the ecology of the national park. The displays start with a room devoted to the birds of the forest and steppe. In a tableau of an eagle devouring a rabbit, the taxidermist has somewhat theatrically daubed red paint across the eagle's beak. Upstairs, the tour continues with a room devoted to waterfowl, with a stuffed pelican eating a wooden fish. A room devoted to the wealth of the forests has a large relief map of the park, and cases showcasing the forest insects, mosses, mushrooms and cones. Back on the ground floor, the next room focuses on four-footed animals, with deer, bear, boar and saiga, and a couple of particularly vicious-looking stuffed polecats, devouring a bird. The last are kept inside a glass case, evidently for added safety. The next room looks at nature protection, with a display devoted to some of the endangered species found in the park. The last room looks at minerals, with samples on display and photographs of interesting rock formations.

During the summer months, the museum may also house a temporary **Kunstkamera** (*separate admission charge adult/child T150/100*). Brought up from Almaty to catch the summer tourist market, this rather ghoulish collection of 'rarities and marvels' combines deformed stuffed animals (a double-headed kitten and the like) with pickled displays showing the disastrous effects of smoking, alcoholism and drug abuse on various human organs. All rather unpleasant.

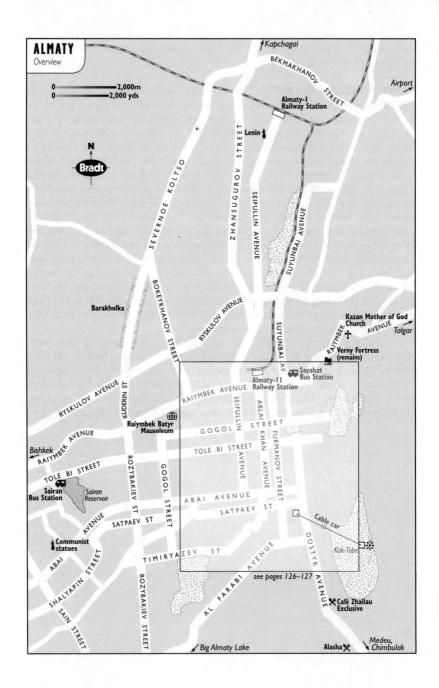

ALMATY
Overview

0 ——————— 2,000m
0 ——————— 2,000 yds

Bradt

N

Kapchagai

BEKMAKHANOV STREET

Airport

Almaty-1 Railway Station

Lenin

SEVERNOE KOLTSO

ZHANSUGUROV STREET

SEIFULLIN AVENUE

SUYUNBAI AVENUE

BOKEYKHANOV STREET

RYSKULOV AVENUE

Barakholka

Kazan Mother of God Church

RAIYMBEK AVENUE

Talgar

Verny Fortress (remains)

RYSKULOV AVENUE

KUDERIN ST

RAIYMBEK AVENUE

Raiymbek Batyr Mausoleum

RAIYMBEK AVENUE

Almaty-11 Railway Station

Sayahat Bus Station

GOGOL STREET

SEIFULLIN AVENUE

ABLAI KHAN AVENUE

FURMANOV STREET

Bishkek

TOLE BI STREET

TOLE BI STREET

ROZYBAKIEV ST

GOGOL STREET

ABAI AVENUE

Sairan Bus Station

Sairan Reservoir

SATPAEV ST

SATPAEV ST

ABAI AVENUE

Cable car

Communist statues

SHALYAPIN STREET

SAIN STREET

ABAI AVENUE

ROZYBAKIEV STREET

TIMIRYAZEV ST

AL FARABI AVENUE

DOSTYK AVENUE

Kok-Tobe

see pages 126–127

Café Zhailau Exclusive

Big Almaty Lake

Alasha

Medeu, Chimbulak

4

Almaty

Telephone code: 727

Almaty may have lost its status as the capital city of Kazakhstan in 1997, but it remains the largest and most cosmopolitan city in the country, and Kazakhstan's financial, cultural and educational hub. Most international flights arrive in Almaty; it has the widest range of hotels, restaurants and bars you will find in Kazakhstan. You will hear more Russian spoken here than Kazakh: Almaty is one of the places in which the broad ethnic diversity of Kazakhstan is most apparent, with expatriates working for the many foreign firms headquartered here adding to the mix.

There is no attractive 'old city': an earthquake in 1887 left just one brick building standing. But there are some interesting museums, attractive parks and intriguing buildings chronicling Almaty's Tsarist, Soviet and post-independence history. A stunning location adds much to Almaty's allure. The city sits at the northern foot of the Zailysky Alatau range, the northernmost line of the mighty Tian Shan Mountains. The peaks, rising above 4,000m and snow-capped for much of the year, offer a beautiful southern backdrop to the city, though the smog which sometimes hangs over the urban area all too frequently has the effect of spiriting the mountains away. The Zailysky Alatau are easily accessible: the starting points for some excellent trekking routes amidst Tian Shan firs and up to mountain passes and glaciers are just a few minutes' drive from the centre of town.

The city itself is built on a slope, with the highest ground to the south, at the foot of the mountains. Across this slope meander several streams – the Bolshaya Almatinka, Malaya Almatinka and Esentai – each fed by snow melt from the mountains. The water from these streams fuels an irrigation system dating from the 19th century, with channels known as *aryks* running alongside the grid-patterned city streets. These provided the water to support lines of poplar trees, which give Almaty a verdant appearance. This is altogether a city which can beguile, whose easy-going charms lure visitors to stay longer than planned.

HISTORY

Semi-nomadic peoples have long lived in the northern foothills of the Zailysky Alatau. The remains of a Sak settlement dated to around the 7th to 3rd century BC has been uncovered beneath part of the modern city. With the development of trade routes under the Karakhanids from the 10th century, urban development in this area was promoted. The settlement of Almatu grew and developed as a station along the Silk Road. The sacking of the place by the Mongols in the 13th century, and subsequent depredations at the hands of the Timurids and Dzhungars, meant that it was not to recover any importance until the arrival of the Russians.

The Tsarist government decided to construct a fort near the site of the old settlement, to protect the area from the ambitions of the Kokand Khanate. The

Almaty HISTORY

4

Zailysky Fort was completed in 1854, but renamed Verny ('Loyal') the next year, presumably as a statement of the desired attitude of the place towards the Tsar. Siberian Cossacks settled in two neighbourhoods, the Bolshaya Almatinskaya Stanitsa and Malaya Almatinskaya Stanitsa, close to the fortress. Both were built in grid patterns and centred on churches. Tatars, many of them from Semipalatinsk, formed a Tatar suburb and occupied themselves with trading. In 1867, Verny became the administrative centre of the new Semirechie Region, part of the Governor-Generalship of Turkestan. A new town was laid out, following the grid pattern of the Bolshaya Almatinskaya Stanitsa, and settled by a new influx of immigrants, mostly peasants from Voronezh.

On 28 May 1887, a **major earthquake** struck, flattening almost all of the brick buildings of the young town. The wooden dwellings of the Bolshaya and Malaya *stanitsas* were rather less badly affected, and thereafter wood for a time became the preferred construction material. The wooden constructions of architect Andrei Pavlovich Zenkov were particularly fine: his Vosnesensky ('Ascension') Cathedral dominated the city skyline when it was built in 1907, and is still one of the tallest wooden constructions in the world. The cathedral, and several other wooden structures built by Zenkov, survived a second severe earthquake, which struck the town on 22 December 1910.

In 1921, the new Soviet authorities renamed the place Alma-Ata ('Father of the Apple'), a Kazakh-language version of the pre-Tsarist name of the town. The capital of the republic was moved here, from Kyzylorda, in 1929. This act, coupled with the opening the following year of the Turkestan–Siberian (TurkSib) Railway, which gave Almaty a rail connection to Moscow, provided a major spur to urban development. World War II also promoted Almaty's importance, as many enterprises, research and cultural organisations were moved here from the more vulnerable western parts of the USSR. **Mass housing construction** came in the 1950s, and accelerated in subsequent decades. Apartment blocks became taller: five storeys, then seven, nine and 12, often constructed using prefabricated concrete panels. In the late 1970s and early 1980s, the First Secretary of the Communist Party of Kazakhstan, Dinmuhammed Kunaev, an ally of Brezhnev, supported a programme of the construction of grand new buildings in an effort to make the city a worthy capital of the Soviet Socialist Republic. The Hotel Kazakhstan and Arasan Baths are among the products of this period.

Following independence, the city's name was altered again, amended in 1993 by the Supreme Council of Kazakhstan from Alma-Ata to Almaty, to reflect more closely the historical name. In 1995, a presidential decree announced that the capital of Kazakhstan would be transferred to Akmola, far to the north. A further decree in 1997 declared Akmola (now Astana) the capital, effective as from 10 December of that year. A parallel decree on the status of Almaty emphasised though that the government intended the former capital to continue to develop, as a financial, business and research centre. Recent government focus has been on developing Almaty as a regional financial centre, to serve the whole of central Asia. The move of the capital to the north did nothing to dent the construction boom in Almaty, though the fallout from the credit squeeze resulting from the US sub-prime mortgage crisis striking in 2007 was been felt in this city as elsewhere. Business centres and modern hotels nonetheless continue to sprout across the urban landscape, and the planned Marriott will top the tallest building in central Asia. Apartment blocks continue to be built, but detached housing is a more important component of the new housing mix than in post-war Soviet times. This includes luxury gated developments in suburbs such as Gorny Gigant, at the foot of the mountains, serving the new Kazakhstani elite, and unplanned developments constructed by new Kazakh migrants from rural areas, such as around the suburb of Shanyrak. Almaty may no longer be Kazakhstan's capital, but it remains by far its most important urban centre and a highlight of any trip to Kazakhstan.

GETTING THERE AND AWAY

BY AIR Almaty airport (`\ 270 3333; *www.almatyairport.com*), the main aviation hub of the country, is modern and reasonably smart and has a new passenger terminal. It has a distinguished place in aviation history, not least as the destination for the world's first supersonic passenger jet, the 'rabbit-eared' Tu-144, which first flew on 31 December 1968, just ahead of Concorde, and ran a passenger route from Moscow to Alma-Ata from 1977–78. Heavy fuel consumption proved its downfall.

The airport sits at the northeastern edge of town, some 12km from the centre. The taxi drivers standing in wait in the arrivals hall, who will try to grab your bag as you pass to secure your custom, are notorious for fleecing arriving foreigners. A much better option is to arrange a taxi at the desk immediately before you leave the baggage hall, which charges approximately T2,500 for a taxi to the town centre. The service is also contactable by telephone on `\ 255 5333. Problems in securing a fairly priced taxi are but one among a rather long list of complaints reported by travellers in respect of various services in and around Almaty airport. Aggressive baggage porters and difficult customs officials on departure have also been reported. And while the waitresses at the airport cafés may sport English-language badges gloriously describing each of them as a 'barmaiden', you should watch carefully both what you are being charged and your change.

If you really want a smooth passage through the airport, and are prepared to pay a premium rate to get it, Almaty travel agencies can arrange the use of the **VIP facilities** for around T22,000. If you have booked this for your arrival, look for the person holding up a board with your name on at the arrivals gate. You will then be taken to the VIP lounge for completion of the immigration procedures. Hand over your baggage identification tag to have your bags collected by a porter, and wait. Unless you have no checked baggage, the use of the VIP facility does not however actually speed up your exit from the airport – the delivery of your bag will be if anything slightly slower than if you had collected it at the carousel yourself – and my advice would be to save your money.

If you are on a budget, it is possible to get from the airport to the city centre by bus or *marshrutka* (minibus). Bus 501 will take you to railway station Almaty-II, bus 540 goes to Dostyk and Kazybek Bi, and bus 572 goes to Green Bazaar.

Airlines The following airlines served Almaty at the time of research.

✈ **Air Arabia** www.airarabia.com. 2 flights a week to Sharjah.

✈ **Air Astana** 4A Zakarpatskaya St; `\ 258 4135; f 259 8701. Airport ticketing office: 2nd Floor, 28 Office, Almaty airport; `\ 270 3327; f 270 3221; e ala.ato@airastana.com. 24hr call centre: `\ 244 4477; f 270 3221; e call.centre@ airastana.com. The national carrier operates an extensive domestic network out of Almaty, including at least 4 & up to 8 flights daily to Astana, between 1 & 3 a day to Aktau, 1 or 2 a day to each of Atyrau, Kyzylorda & Shymkent (with a circuitous twice-weekly flight going to Atyrau via both Kyzylorda & Shymkent), 1 a day to each of Aktobe, Karaganda, Pavlodar & Ust-Kamenogorsk, & 4 flights weekly to Uralsk. It flies internationally to Moscow (2 a day), Dubai (1 a day), Beijing (6 a week), Istanbul (4 a week direct, with 3 more via Atyrau & another 2 via Astana), Bangkok (3 a week), London, Seoul

& Delhi (each 2 a week), & serves Frankfurt (3 a week) & Hanover (1 a week) via Astana, & Amsterdam (4 a week) via Atyrau. It also flies seasonally to Antalya.

✈ **Air Baltic** www.airbaltic.com. This low-cost Latvian carrier offers 2 flights per week to Riga, which serves as the airline's European hub.

✈ **Asiana** Suite 343, Hotel Aksunkar, 2 Mailin St; 257 1166; f 257 1222; www.flyasiana.com. Flies twice a week to Seoul.

✈ **BMI** 43 Dostyk Av; 272 4040; f 272 4747; www.flybmi.com. Codeshare with Astraeus. Offers 3 flights weekly to London & Bishkek.

✈ **China Southern Airlines** www.csair.com. Offers 6 flights a week to Ürümqi on a Boeing 757.

✈ **Kam Air** www.flykamair.com. 1–2 flights a week to Kabul on Afghanistan's first private airline. Occasional routings via Dushanbe.

✈ **KLM** Hotel Otrar, 73 Gogol St; 250 7747; f 250 9183; e almaty@klm.com; www.klm.com. 5 flights a week to Amsterdam.

✈ **Lufthansa** Hotel Rahat, 29/6 Satpaev St; 250 5052; f 250 5062; e lufthansaalmaty@ dlh.de; www.lufthansa.com. 5 flights a week to Frankfurt direct, with another 2 via Astana.

✈ **Rossiya** 65 Furmanov St; 273 2611; f 273 5531; e alatofv@rossiya-airlines.com; www. rossiya-airlines.com. Formerly Pulkovo Airlines, they have 2 flights a week to St Petersburg.

✈ **Scat** www.scat.kz. This Shymkent-based carrier offers 1 flight daily to Kostanai, 4 a week to Petropavl, 2 a week to Aktau, with 2 more via Kyzylorda, 2 a week to each of Aktobe, Semey, Shymkent, Ust-Kamenogorsk & Zhezkazgan, & 1 a week to Atyrau. Internationally, it flies 3 times a week to Dushanbe, twice to Tashkent

BIG APPLES

Almaty has always been associated with the apple. The fruit is entwined with the name of the city: '*alma*', in Kazakh, means 'apple'. The Tian Shan Mountains were one of the homes of the wild apple trees from which our cultivated apples are descended. But one variety of apple is particularly associated with Almaty: the *aport*, a huge, red-skinned apple which became a symbol of the city.

The *aport* was introduced into Almaty in 1865 by a migrant from Voronezh, one Igor Redko. In the soils of Voronezh, the variety had not particularly distinguished itself, but once planted around Almaty, at altitudes between around 900m and 1,200m, the apples burgeoned in size, weighing in at 0.5kg a time. Some scientists argue that this flourishing is an indication that the Almaty area was the original homeland of the *aport*; the apple tree was returning to its roots, as it were. The large red apples of Almaty became one of the prized food products of the Soviet Union, served at many a Kremlin dinner.

You will not however find the giant red *aport* of old in the markets of Almaty today. Poor horticultural practice, the collapse of the collective farms following the break-up of the USSR, and the construction of prestige suburban housing in the 900–1,200m belt formerly given over to the apple orchards have all contributed to its decline. The apples you will find in bazaars and on supermarket shelves are most likely to be imports from China, red and shiny but complete with a bewildering array of nasty chemical residues. Researchers are currently trying to restore the variety, and the horticultural practices needed to sustain it, so Almaty fruit bowls may once again groan beneath the huge red *aport*.

The largest and most cosmopolitan city in the country, its major financial centre and transport hub, yet not the capital city, Almaty has much in common with the other Big Apple. Unlike New York, however, it also has much to do with real big apples.

& twice to Bayan-Ulegey (Mongolia) via Ust-Kamenogorsk.

✈ **SemeyAvia** 5 flights a week to Semey on a Yak-40.

✈ **Sky Georgia** www.skygeorgia.org. Formerly Georgian National Airlines. Flights direct to Tbilisi twice a week.

✈ **Tajik Air** www.tajik-air.com. 3 flights weekly to Dushanbe, & 1 a week to Khudzhant via Korgan Tobe.

✈ **Transaero** 53 Furmanov St; ✆/f 250 2376; e ala.sale@transaero.kz; www.transaero.ru; ⏰ 09.00–21.00. Daily flights to both Sheremetevo & Domodedovo airports in Moscow on Boeing 737s.

✈ **Turkish Airlines** 100G Furmanov St; ✆ 266 5669; f 250 6219; e sales@turkishairlines.kz; www.thy.com. 5 flights a week to Istanbul, with onward connections to destinations in Europe & the USA.

✈ **Turkmenistan Airlines** 79 Timiryazev St; ✆ 253 9700; f 245 5860; www. turkmenistanairlines.com. 2 flights a week to Ashgabat on Turkmenistan's national carrier.

✈ **Ukrainian-Mediterranean Airlines** www.umairlines.com. 1 flight a week to Kiev.

✈ **Uzbekistan Airways** 21V Kunaev St; ✆ 244 6689; f 261 2775; e ala@uzairways.com; www. uzairways.com. Uzbekistan's national carrier offers 1 flight daily to Tashkent.

✈ **Zhezkazgan Avia** 4 flights a week to Zhezkazgan on a Yak-40.

BY RAIL Almaty has two railway stations. The less convenient is **Almaty-I** (✆ 296 3392), which sits around 10km north of the city centre, at the northern end of Seifullin Avenue. The station building has a modern, metallic look; the sense of efficiency inside is however rather dented by the harassed staff at the information counter and the knots of taxi drivers, waiting to pounce on arriving passengers. In the small scrap of park in front of the station is a 1970s statue of early Soviet functionary Alibi Zhankeldin, sporting a greatcoat to keep out the cold.

Fortunately, most (though not all) trains continue on to end their journey at the much more central station of **Almaty-II** [126 C1] (✆ 296 5344, 296 5544), which lies at the north end of Ablai Khan Avenue, at the northern edge of the city centre. The architecture here is one of faded Soviet grandeur, with Corinthian columns and chandeliered ceiling. A notice in the foyer sets out a dauntingly long list of regulations, starting with the observation that deputies of the Kazakhstan parliament are allowed to queue-jump. Left luggage is to be found in a part of the building to the left of the main foyer, described for some reason as 'The International Hall'.

Three trains daily from Almaty terminate at Astana, including the overnight fast train, the Tulpar, which does the journey in around 13 hours (other trains take at least 19). There are also one or more trains daily terminating at Shymkent, Petropavl, Semey, Aktobe, Kostanai, Pavlodar, Karaganda and Zashita (close to Ust-Kamenogorsk). Less frequent departures terminate at Atyrau, Uralsk, Mangyshlak and Zhezkazgan. International departures include a train every two days to Moscow, two a week to Urumchi, two a week to Simferopol (Ukraine), one a week to Nukus (Uzbekistan), and several to destinations in Russia including Novosibirsk, Novokuznetsk and Sverdlovsk. There are also departures to Bishkek, but the route is circuitous, and the journey takes far longer by train than road.

Booking offices for the national railway company are located across the city, including at 50 Timuryazov (✆ 260 4637), 249 Tole Bi (✆ 240 8949) and 59 Dostyk (✆ 291 4982).

BY ROAD There are two main bus stations. The more important is the **Sairan bus station** (64A Utegen Batyr St; ✆ 276 2644, 276 0806; e sairan@arna.kz), also known as the new bus station, which sits some 7km west of the centre along the long Tole Bi Street, immediately beyond the Sairan Reservoir. The latter is a pleasant enough recreation area in summer. The Sairan bus station is a classic piece of Soviet transport architecture: a powerful rectangle of a building with an oversized flat roof. It is the main terminus for long-distance bus routes. Among the many destinations served are some eight buses a day to Taraz, and two or more to each of Shymkent, Balkhash, Karaganda and Ust-Kamenogorsk. Some of these journeys can be pretty arduous: Ust-Kamenogorsk, for example, is a 21-hour trip. Sairan also serves destinations within Almaty Oblast to the north and west of the city, including ten buses a day to Taldykorgan, five to Zharkent, a bus every 20 minutes until 20.00 to Kapchagai, and frequent departures to towns to the west of Almaty such as Uzunagash, Fabrichnoe and Kargaly. There is a popular summer-only service from here to the lakeside resorts of Issyk Kul in Kyrgyzstan, with departures to Balykchy and Cholpan Ata, taking around eight-and-a-half hours to reach the last, with the somewhat curious timetable of departures at five-minute intervals, 22.00–23.10.

The **Sayahat bus station** [126 E1] (*15 Suyunbaya Av;* \ *380 7444*), sometimes referred to as the old bus station, is most useful for local destinations to the east of Almaty, especially Talgar and Esik. The Soviet-era main building stands next to the traffic-clogged junction of Raimbek and Suyunbai avenues, on the northern side of the city centre. The old main building itself is, however, now taken over by clothes stalls and little shops offering services ranging from manicures to dentistry. The frequent buses and minibuses to Talgar and Esik depart from the corner of Suyunbaya Avenue and Tashkentskaya. You pay on board. A place in a minibus to Esik, for example, costs T200. Other destinations are served from a new single-storey terminal building around the back of the old one. There are, for example, 17 departures daily to Taldykorgan and four to Tekeli. Pay for these destinations in advance, at the booking office. **Taxis** offering seats to destinations across Almaty Oblast cluster in front of the old terminal building.

There are however plans to move both bus stations to more peripheral locations in order to ease city-centre traffic congestion.

GETTING AROUND

The grid-patterned road network of central Almaty was designed to support Soviet levels of car ownership far lower than those of oil-rich post-independence Kazakhstan. The result is gridlock of all those new Japanese 4x4s. The clogged roads of Kazakhstan's largest city are its least attractive feature. An underground network was planned in Soviet times; construction continues, although deadlines have repeatedly been revised. Building sites decorated with an 'M' symbol, dotted around the centre of town, are the only visible signs of this future metro network though, as everything has ground to a standstill pending the outcome of a court battle in London. It is also questionable how many residents would use a metro given the fear of seismic activity in the area. But current surface transport options, traffic jams apart, are actually pretty efficient. There is an extensive network of trams, trolleybuses, buses and minibuses, for which the fare is T25 for the tram and T50 for the bus. Pay the conductor on board, either as you get off or when prodded to do so. Attempting to pay with a high-denomination banknote will produce a scowl. Note that buses tend to stop running well before midnight.

Simply sticking out your arm at the side of a busy street will usually cause someone to stop within a couple of minutes. As elsewhere in Kazakhstan, use your discretion as to whether to get in the car, being particularly wary of vehicles with more than one male occupant. The fare for a short daytime journey should be around T400–

500: agree it in advance. There are several bookable taxi services: numbers to ring include ☏ 058 and ☏ 255 5333. Fares are more expensive than simply getting a car to stop, but this is the safer option, and is particularly recommended at night. If at all possible, avoid taxis waiting outside bars and clubs in the late evening: you may well get ripped off, or worse.

TOUR OPERATORS AND AIRLINE OFFICES

Alpina XXI 278-1 Dostyk Av; ☏ 264 0325, 254 1648; e info@alpina.kz; www.alpina.kz. This operator runs alpine chalet-style hotels in several locations in the Zailysky Alatau, as well as the Hotel Alpina Three Stars in Balkhash & a guesthouse at Uzunaral on Lake Balkhash. They provide tailored mountain- & fishing-related programmes, including helicopter excursions, helibiking trips for mountain bikers, mountaineering expeditions & fishing on Lake Balkhash.

Asia Discovery Office 19, 61 Abai Av; ☏ 260 1393; f 250 8108; e info@asia-discovery.kz, asia_discovery@inbox.ru; www.asia-discovery. nursat.kz. This agency was set up in 2000 by the Union of National Nature Parks of Kazakhstan, & many of its tours are focused on the Ile Alatau & Altyn Emel national parks. It offers a range of programmed tours, including an interesting ethnography tour, trekking & horseriding tours to Lake Issyk Kul in Kyrgyzstan, & rafting on the Ile (gentle) & Koksu (not gentle) rivers. They can also put together tailored specialist programmes for ornithologists, botanists, geologists & even entomologists. Also visa support, flight, train & hotel bookings.

Ecotourism Information Resource Centre 71 Zheltoksan St; ☏ 278 0289; f 279 8146; e ecocentre.kz@gmail.com; www.eco-tourism. kz. Organises community-based accommodation among rural communities in several locations across Kazakhstan, including the Aksu Zhabagly Nature Reserve in South Kazakhstan, Katon Karagai in the Altai Mountains & the lakes of Korgalzhyn in Akmola Oblast (further details are in the relevant regional sections of this guide). The centre has been set up with the support of several international donors, including the Eurasia Foundation, USAID, ExxonMobil & the British-based organisation Voluntary Service Overseas. Its homestays offer a fascinating insight into life in rural Kazakhstan, & are thoroughly recommended. Some visitors have, however, reported a drop in the standard of service provided by the centre following the departure of expatriate volunteers.

Indra-Tour 191 Abai Av; ☏ 250 1512, 250 6114; e mail@indratour.net; www.indratour.net/?en. Formerly known as Blast, this budget travel agent offers excursions in & around Almaty, as well as rock climbing, rafting & lake trips. Prices are reasonable.

Jibek Joly 55 Ablai Khan Av; ☏ 232 5640, 232 5889; f 232 6523; e info@jibekjoly.kz, jjoly@ kazmail.asdc.kz; www.jibekjoly.kz. They have a 2nd office at 96 Aytiev St (☏ 243 4442). Agency based at the Hotel Zhetisu, which they manage, offering a range of tourist support services & tailored tours, including options focused on birdwatching, horseriding & history. They also run several accommodation options in Almaty Region, notably a tourist complex at the Kolsai Lakes & a hotel at Baiseit, 130km east of Almaty.

Kan Tengri 10 Kasteyev St; ☏ 291 0880, 291 0200; f 291 2010; e info@kantengri.kz; www. kantengri.kz. Headed by Kazbek Valiev, the first Kazakhstani to reach the summit of Everest & the President of the Kazakhstan Mountaineering Federation, Kan Tengri occupies an important place in mountain-related tourism in Kazakhstan. The company runs the Karkara Camp near the Karkara River in the southeastern part of Almaty Region, from where in summer they organise helicopter transfers to tented base camps at the North Inylchek (Kazakhstan) & South Inylchek (Kyrgyzstan) glaciers, either side of the mighty Khan Tengri peak. They can arrange a 24-day ascent of Khan Tengri, for serious mountaineers, as well as trekking routes around the base camps. They run another base camp, at Bayankol, used for ascents of the 6,400m Mramornaya Stena ('Marble Wall'). In a different vein, they offer fishing programmes in the Ile Delta, focused on catfish of 100lb or more, where tourists are accommodated in a tented camp. They also offer tailored mountain-biking, horseriding & birdwatching programmes.

Karla Makatova m +7 701 755 2086; e kmakatova@yahoo.com. English-speaking independent operator popular with Almaty expatriates. Organises tailored sightseeing & trekking tours around Almaty.

Max Travel Star 137 Zheltoksan St; √f 272 5070, 267 4017; e olga@maxtravel.kz; www. maxtravel.kz. The background to the rather odd name of this agency: Max is the son of the General Director, they found there was already a Max Travel, so added a 'Star'. They offer tailor-made programmes, including short trips in & around Almaty & longer tours around Almaty Region, overnighting in tents.

Stantours m +7 707 118 4619, +49 (3212) 1039960 (Germany); e info@stantours.com; www.stantours.com. Run by German expatriate David Berghof, this agency, which operates without an office, is well attuned to the needs of independent travellers. David Berghof's main passion is Turkmenistan, but Stantours can put together tailored tours across the region.

Tour Asia 359 Radostovtsa St; ☏ 248 2573; f 249 7936; e office@tourasia.kz; www.tourasia. kz. Specialists in outdoor pursuits, they can set up tailored mountaineering, trekking, horseriding & birdwatching programmes, though also services such as visa support, transport bookings & local tours around Almaty. They work with several Spanish tour operators.

✈ Transavia 85 Dostyk Av; ☏ 261 0414; www. transavia-travel.kz. Air ticket agency. They have a second branch at 104 Zheltoksan St (☏ *258 3306*).

Turan-Asia 66/8 Ablai Khan Av; ☏ 273 0371, 273 0596; f 273 5874; e turanasia@belight.net; www.turanasia.kz. They have a second office at 111a Zheltoksan St (☏ *266 3687; e info@ turanasia.kz*). Experienced agency, which offers visa support, hotel & transport bookings, & a wide range of tailored programmes, including the cities of the Silk Route by train or road, the Baikonur Cosmodrome & Almaty city trips. They can also set up birdwatching, horseriding, mountain-biking & trekking itineraries.

WHERE TO STAY

Accommodation rates in Almaty are substantially higher than those of most parts of Kazakhstan. The top-range room rates would not look out of place in some of the pricier European capitals, and the rates for some very ordinary mid-category hotels hit the 'luxury' price-code bracket, which is defined on a Kazakhstan-wide basis. You may be able to negotiate a discount, but not during events such as the Kazakhstan International Oil and Gas Exhibition (KIOGE) during the first week of October, when just finding a room can be a challenge, and several of the more upmarket hotels slap a hefty premium on their usual rates.

TOP-RANGE

⌂ Dostyk Hotel [127 D5] (72 rooms) 36 Kurmangazy St; ☏ 258 2270; e info@dostyk. kz; www.dostyk.kz. Centrally located, newly renovated hotel in a historic building. Rooms are well lit & stylish. The hotel has a luxurious spa, a popular bar, & a choice of international cuisine in the restaurant. The Presidential suite will set you back upwards of T155,000. Airport pick-up is T3,500 one-way, or T4,000 return. **$$$$$**

⌂ Grand Hotel Tien Shan [126 E4] (78 rooms) 115 Bogenbai Batyr St; ☏ 244 9600; f 244 4007; e reservations@ts-hotels.kz; www. ts-hotels.kz. This yellow-walled, Corinthian-columned building in the centre of town offers smartly furnished, centrally AC rooms. The hotel is particularly proud of its 'Bali Spa Centre' in the

basement. Corridors decorated with Balinese stone heads lead off to various massage rooms, saunas & a Turkish bath, & there is a pleasant pool. There is a full range of (steeply priced) massages on offer, including Cleopatra's Massage, billed as the favourite of the Egyptian queen. She appears to have been fond of seaweed. **$$$$$**

⌂ Hotel Ambassador [126 C4] (50 rooms) 121 Zheltoksan St; ☏ 250 8989, 250 8945; f 272 6441; e info@ambassadorhotel. kz; www.ambassadorhotel.kz. Built in 1936, with a bright yellow-painted exterior sporting balustraded balconies & Corinthian columns framing the entrance, the Ambassador has a little more character than most Almaty hotels. The AC bedrooms are pleasantly laid out with antique-style furniture. Popular with Turkish businessmen, the hotel also features the Bodrum Bar in the basement, with a house band belting out Turkish, English & Russian numbers. They offer a free airport pick-up. **$$$$$**

🏠 **Hotel Kazakhstan** [127 E5] (363 rooms) 52 Dostyk Av; 259 0909, 291 9101; f 291 9600, 250 7811, 250 7809; e info@khotel.kz. This 25-storey hotel, topped with what appears to be a golden crown, was built in the late 1970s, & is one of the most distinctive buildings in Almaty. The foyer has been given a recent makeover, which has sadly removed the lights resembling models of molecules & other echoes of the Soviet Union, in favour of golden statues of Kazakh girls bearing baskets of fruit & cups of *kumiss*. **$$$$$**

🏠 **Hotel Rahat** [127 A6] (285 rooms) 29/6 Satpaev St; 250 1234; f 250 8888. Formerly the Hyatt Regency, the Hotel Rahat is under new management but looking somewhat tired. It is a well-established & reasonably efficient business-class hotel, offering all the facilities you would expect in this range though at room rates not for the faint of wallet. A glass roof, whose form is inspired by the Kazakh yurt, covers a large central space onto which 10 balconied floors look out. Glass elevators take you up. **$$$$$**

🏠 **Hotel Tien Shan** [126 E4] (31 rooms) 151 Kunaev St; 272 0866; f 291 9162; e interhotel_tienshan@nursat.kz; www.

MID-RANGE

🏠 **Astana International Hotel** [127 B6] (114 rooms) 113 Baitursynuly St; 250 7050; f 250 1060; e reservation@astana-hotel.com; www.astana-hotel.com. A simply furnished but bright & comfortable hotel, whose balconied rooms offer AC, en-suite showers & Wi-Fi. Not the most attractive of buildings, but this not a bad option at the top of the mid-range bracket. They will arrange free collection from the airport, though there is a charge to take you back. **$$$$**

🏠 **Hotel Grand AiSer** [127 B6] (55 rooms) 1 Pozharsky St; 250 3350; f 292 6133; e info@ grandaiserhotel.kz; www.grandaiserhotel.kz. At the corner of Baitursynuly & Satpaev streets, this is one of several basically mid-range hotels in Almaty which appears to have added a 'Grand' to its name in a bid to justify decidedly full rates. The calligraphic rendition of the hotel's name

tien-shan-kz.narod.ru. Functional 3-star hotel in a good, central, spot, offering bland but comfortable rooms. Watch the charges for additional services though, some of which are well above the average in this category: for example, T4,000 for airport transfers. If you are coming here by taxi, specify the address to the driver, or you'll probably get taken to the nearby Grand Hotel Tien Shan. **$$$$$**

🏠 **Intercontinental Almaty The Ankara in Kazakhstan** [127 C6] (277 rooms) 181 Zheltoksan St; 250 5000; f 258 2100; e info@ interconti-almaty.kz; www.intercontinental.com. Several re-brandings have given the place both a cumbersome name & a somewhat confused personality: it is known by locals variously as The Ankara, The Regent & The Intercontinental. This Turkish-managed place was opened in 1996 in the presence of the presidents of Turkey & Kazakhstan. It serves an international business clientele, with comfortable rooms, fitness centre, sauna, a range of dining options & a good, central location close to Republic Sq. The service has an occasionally galling bonhomie, like the sign on the minibar, which they refer to as the 'refreshment centre', welcoming you 'to the smallest bar in Almaty'. A single complementary orange comes with a sign informing you that it is the 'fruit of the week'. There is jazz music on offer in the Members Bar (evenings except Sun). **$$$$$**

on the top of the building makes it look, at first glance, like 'AiSor', & in truth this angular, blue-glass fronted structure is not Almaty's most attractive. The lobby is cramped, the rooms unremarkable, & previous visitors were sorely disappointed. **$$$$**

🏠 **Hotel Kazzhol** [126 C3] (119 rooms) 127/1 Zhibek Zholy St; 250 8927, 250 8944; f 250 8927; e hotel-kazzhol@arna.kz; www. hotelkazzhol.kz. In a secluded, though potentially hard-to-find, spot in the centre of the residential block between Gogol, Zhibek Zholy, Nauryzbai Batyr & Seifullin, this renovated 3-star hotel is a good option in the price category. All rooms have AC & en suites. Prices include b/fast & VAT. **$$$$**

🏠 **Hotel Otrar** [126 E3] (161 rooms) 73 Gogol St; 250 6848, 250 6830; f 250 6809, 250 6811; e otrar@group.kz; www.group.kz. The Otrar has

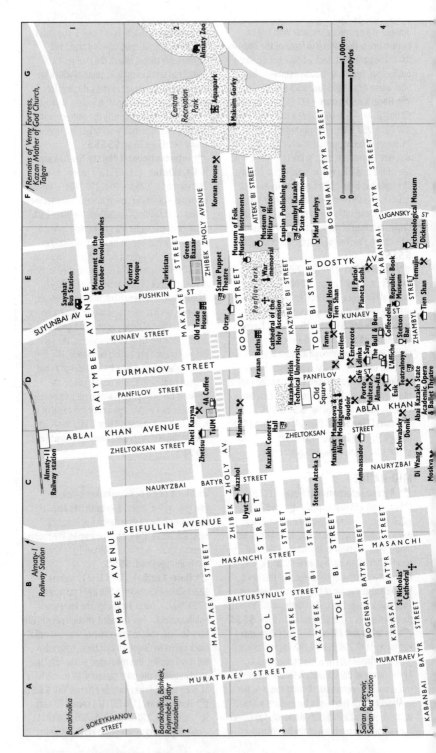

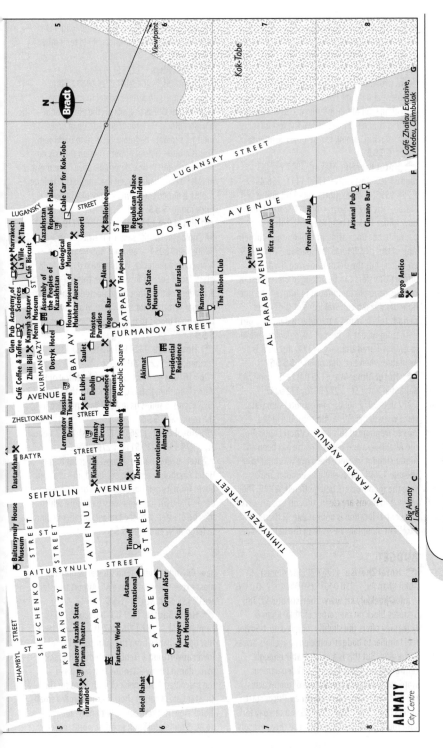

ALMATY
City Centre

Kok-Tobe

LUGANSKY STREET

DOSTYK AVENUE

Cable Car for Kok-Tobe
Kazakhstan Republic Palace
Marrakech
La Ville
Café Biscuit
Thai
Assorti
Bibliotheque
Republican Palace of Schoolchildren

Glen Pub Academy of Sciences
Kanysh Satpaev
Assembly of the Peoples of Kazakhstan
Meml Museum
Geological Museum
Café Coffee & Toffee
Zhili Bili
House Museum of Mukhtar Auezov

SATPAEV Tri Apelsina

Alem
Vogue Bar
Dostyk Hotel
KURMANGAZY ST

Central State Museum
Grand Eurasia
Favor
Al FARABI AVENUE

AV
Saulet
Fhloston Paradise
Ramstor
The Albion Club
Ritz Palace

ABAI AVENUE
FURMANOV STREET

Ex Libris
Dublin
Independence Monument
Republic Square

Premier Alatau

Lermontov Russian Drama Theatre
ZHELTOKSAN STREET

Akimat
Presidential Residence

Arsenal Pub
Cinzano Bar

Almaty Circus
Dawn of Freedom

Borgo Antico

Dastarkhan
BATYR STREET

Kishak
Zheruick

Intercontinental Almaty

AL FARABI AVENUE

Baitursynuly House Museum
SEIFULLIN AVENUE

SHEVCHENKO STREET

BAITURSYNULY STREET

Tinkoff
TIMIRYAZEV STREET

Big Almaty Lake

KURMANGAZY AVENUE

Astana International
Grand AiSer

Fantasy World

SATPAEV STREET

ABAI AVENUE

ZHAMBYL STREET

Princess Turandot
Auezov Kazakh State Drama Theatre

Kasteyev State Arts Museum

Hotel Rahat

Viewpoint

Café Zhailau Exclusive, Medeu, Chimbulak

N

Bradt

Almaty WHERE TO STAY

4

127

an excellent central location overlooking Panfilov Park, though Gogol St is decidedly noisy. All rooms have AC, & most offer a small balcony. The quieter upper floors have been designated as 'business floors' with more expensive rooms (inc the Presidential suite at T120,000) offering benefits such as an hour of free internet access & 2 items of clothing laundered free per day. The restaurant is a domed room, aiming to resemble the interior of a yurt. **$$$$**

🏠 **Hotel Premier Alatau** [127 F7] (53 rooms) 105 Dostyk Av; ✆ 258 1111, 258 4312; f 258 1555; e alatauhotel@mail.ru; www.alatau-hotel.kz. A Soviet-built 9-storey hotel, now under Turkish management, this is a passable but unexciting option on the southern side of the city. Rooms are spacious, with AC & en suites, but the décor is looking tired. Free airport transfers can be arranged on request. A curious concrete monument in front of the hotel honours Kazakh cultural icons of the Soviet period. This features a falconer, a dancer, a girl gathering wheat &, best of all, a *dombra* player in groovy flared trousers. A 12% discount is available when booking online. **$$$$**

🏠 **Hotel Alma-Ata** [126 D4] (255 rooms) 85 Kabanbai Batyr St; ✆ 272 0070, 272 0047; f 272 0080, 272 0060; e info@hotel-alma-ata.com; www.hotel-Alma-Ata.com. The broad curved frontage of this 8-storey hotel opposite the Abai Opera and Ballet Theatre has been an Almaty landmark since the place was built in the late 1960s. If travelling in summer, make sure the room you are being offered has AC. The renovated rooms are clean, though sgls are small. The central location is unbeatable, & there are excellent mountain views from the balconies on

BUDGET

🏠 **Hotel Zhetisu** [126 C2] (187 rooms) 55 Ablai Khan Av; ✆ 250 0407, 250 0444; f 250 0416; e info@jibekjoly.kz; www.zhetysuhotel.kz. This 5-storey block on the corner of Ablai Khan & Makataev offers the slightly rumpled post-Soviet feel familiar to budget-conscious travellers across the region. But this is a comfortable enough central option, close to the TsUM department store, with a wide permutation of rooms across the mid-price & budget categories. Prices start at US$12 for a dormitory bed, & you can pay for your room in multiples of 6hrs. The cheapest sgls

the higher floors, but the place is no longer the budget bargain that travellers of old remember. **$$$–$$$$**

🏠 **Hotel Alem** [127 E5] (9 rooms) 7A Valikhanov St; ✆ 264 3141; f 262 1892. This place, comprising former hostel rooms of the Agricultural University, sits on the 2nd floor of a hostel block. Each room is made up of an AC lounge, separate bedroom & en-suite bathroom. This is a quiet central option, though there is no restaurant, but it would perhaps have been more helpful if they had skipped the minibars & lounge rooms & aimed the Alem at more of a budget price range. **$$$**

🏠 **Hotel Grand Eurasia** [127 E6] (79 rooms) 9A Zholdasbekov St, Samal 1 District; ✆ 380 8080; f 380 8054; e eurasia_hotel@mail.ru; www.eurasiahotel.kz. Within the red marble- & glass-faced Eurasia Trade Centre, this is a clean & modern option, though characterless both as regards its interior & its location among residential blocks to the south of the city centre. **$$$**

🏠 **Hotel Saya** [126 D4] (12 rooms) 135 Furmanov St; ✆ 261 2484, 261 1749, 272 3265; f 261 1610. A comfortable enough central option, with clean though basic rooms. Only the 'semi-luxe' rooms & suites have AC. B/fast included in the room rate. **$$$**

🏠 **Hotel Uyut** [126 C3] (74 beds) 127/1 Gogol St; ✆ 279 5511, 279 5111; f 279 8979; e hotel_uyut@mail.ru. Almost adjacent to the Hotel Kazzhol, & similarly secluded, this is a step down from its neighbour in terms of service & décor. The Uyut has some very basic sgls, which may be of interest to the budget traveller willing to forgo AC & en suites. **$$$**

have en-suite toilet but no shower, & only the most expensive rooms have AC. Airport transfers are US$35 each way. **$–$$$**

🏠 **Hotel Saulet** [127 D5] (40 rooms) 187B Furmanov St; ✆ 267 1175, 267 1977; f 267 1969. Just up Furmanov from the large model Eiffel Tower advertising a French perfume store, this place doesn't draw attention to itself. It's in the balconied 4-storey block with signs for the Zhastar Café, a carpet shop, hairdresser & a small 'hotel' sign. It is run-down, with noisy rooms, no AC & unhelpful staff: in other words, exactly the kind of bottom-end hotel which fills an important niche & is increasingly hard to find in central Almaty. There is a Russian billiard room on the ground floor. **$$**

⌂ Hotel Turkistan [126 E2] (66 rooms) 49 Makataev St; 266 4135; f 266 4136. Close to the Green Bazaar, this is one of the better bottom-range options. Sgls have en-suite toilets but shared showers, & no AC, but the rooms are clean. There is a sauna in the basement charged at T3,500/hr, offering Finnish-style sauna, plunge pool, lounge &, ahem, separate bedroom. **$$**

⌂ Hotel Sairan (13 rooms) Sairan bus station, 64A Utegen Batyr St; 276 7272; f 250 6382. This is a separate building, just identified as 'hotel' in Kazakh & Russian, standing next to the Sairan bus station (see page 121). It is not to be confused with a similarly labelled door in the bus station building itself, which is a grim facility used by bus drivers. Rooms at the Sairan are tired looking, & there is no AC, but they have en-suite showers & this is a convenient option before or after a late-night bus journey. Their standard rooms are grandly labelled 'semi-luxe': don't be fooled. **$**

 WHERE TO EAT AND DRINK

Almaty offers by far the widest range of places to eat of any city in Kazakhstan. Burgeoning consumer confidence and the increasingly varied foreign travels of well-to-do Kazakhstanis have helped to fuel a rapid growth of themed restaurants specialising in a wide range of cuisines. There are numerous places to snack on central Asian staples like *plov* and *samsas*, including food courts in and around the main shopping malls, and food stalls at the markets. Major supermarkets such as those of the Ramstor and Gros chains have delicatessen counters with good-value prepared salads, pies and roast chicken, which can form the basis of a summer picnic. At the other end of the spectrum, the top-range hotels offer good but predictably expensive restaurants.

CENTRAL ASIAN

✗ Esik [126 D4] 133A Panfilov St; 272 2035, 272 2037. Cavernous place on the ground floor of the Hotel Alma-Ata, whose décor is best described as Kazakh kitsch: aquaria filled with pottery vases, gold Scythian-inspired friezes, gold curtains & blue-lit domes in the ceiling designed to resemble *shanyraks*. An obelisk out the front is topped by a golden *arkhar*. The service is eager but confused, with waiters massed at the entrance to welcome you in, & there is often an eclectic floorshow ranging from traditional folk music to belly dancing. The menu has an exhaustive range of Kazakh & regional dishes, with several types of *beshbarmak*, including a sturgeon variety. **$$$$$**

✗ Zheti Kazyna [126 D2] 58A Ablai Khan Av; 273 2587. Elegantly decorated central Asian restaurant entered, despite the address, through an *Arabian Nights*-style doorway on Makataev St, with carved columns, fountains & traditional utensils displayed in backlit niches. The interesting menu offers a medley of Kazakh, Uzbek & Uighur dishes. There are 2 other themed

restaurants in the same building: **Tsi**, in the basement, offers a mixed Chinese/Japanese menu, while the smart but uninspiring **Caramel** upstairs offers a range of Russian & European dishes. The English-language menu for the rather pricey Tsi warns of the Chinese seafood salad that: 'it is not affordable at this moment'. **$$$$**

✗ Zheruiyk [127 C6] 500 Seifullin Av; 263 9828. Similar in style to Esik but with prompter service. Food is good quality & the folk dance performances are lively. Expect to see a diversity of national costumes. **$$$$**

✗ Alasha 20 Ospanov St; 254 0700, 271 5670; www.alasha.kz. South of town, just off the main road to Medeu, this attractively decorated restaurant features a summer courtyard modelled on an Uzbek village, a domed foyer with pastel-toned paintwork, & plates, carpets & musical instruments on the walls inside. The menu covers the main central Asian dishes, but the real reason to head out this far is the evening floorshow (from 21.00), which may include a man dancing with a bowl of *plov* on his head

&, in summer, tightrope walkers across the courtyard. $–$$$$

✖ **Kishlak** [127 C5] 540A Seifullin St; ☏ 261 5601. Pass through the turreted brick gate into a shady courtyard & then into the restaurant proper, where a little wooden bridge over a fish-filled fake stream, trailing plastic vines & Uzbek crockery on the walls all attempt to offer the atmosphere of a central Asian village. Reasonably central location, just to the south of the intersection between Seifullin St & Abai Av. Serves all the central Asian staples, including good *plov*. $$$

✖ **Café Zhailau Exclusive** 302 Dostyk Av; ☏ 254 2072. A collection of yurts & *tapchans*

INTERNATIONAL

✖ **Bibliotheque** [127 E8] 116 Dostyk Av; ☏ 262 6122. This smart European restaurant at the corner of Dostyk & Satpaev welcomes you in with wine-related quotations around the door, concluding with one from Count Dracula confirming that he never touches the stuff. It aims for a relaxed drawing-room atmosphere, with rustic wooden chairs & shelves full of books & trinkets. The French-flavoured menu is tempting, though pricey. $$$$$

✖ **Borgo Antico** [127 E8] 11/6 Iskenderov St, Gorny Gigant; ☏ 293 5151, 263 1970; e captainsaif@hotmail.com; www.borgo-antico.kz/ eng/; ⏲ from 12.00. A pricey Italian restaurant inside an ugly modern metallic-tiled building. The location is inconvenient, in the plush southern suburb of Gorny Gigant, but the Roman menu is enticing. A plastic chef offers the thumbs-up sign at the entrance. The wine list is impressive, though rises to some stellar prices. $$$$$

✖ **Boudoir** [126 D4] 134 Bogenbai Batyr St; ☏ 272 5555; www.boudoir.kz. The black exterior tiles framing porthole-like orange signs immediately announce this as a place with claims to hipness. The waiters wear black, the décor is all cream & brown, the music avowedly lounge, with a DJ in the corner. The board-backed menu promises to 'break boundaries & limits'. Not to mention wallets, as the prices push those you would find in upmarket London restaurants. Also, all the prices end in '-69', in a cheesy attempt to be provocative. The speciality here is live mud crabs, served in various Eastern styles. This is probably the only place in Almaty where the

alongside busy Dostyk Av, at the southern edge of town on the road to Medeu. The largest of the yurts is fitted out with wide-screen TV & an ornate chandelier. A broad range of Kazakh & western Chinese dishes, & *shashlik*. $$

✖ **Café Ldinka** [126 D4] Corner Panfilov & Bogenbai Batyr sts; ☏ 272 1222. This circular café transports you back to the Soviet Union, with its serving hatches fashioned in what once must have been a futuristic design, & stained-glass windows offering scenes of Soviet happiness: a steaming samovar, a laden shopping basket, a modern city. The food is a mix of Russian & central Asian dishes & *shashlik*: unremarkable, but inexpensive for central Almaty. $

shashlik is made from kangaroo meat. There is an interesting cocktail menu, with local apples pressed into play for 'The Big Apple'. $$$$$

✖ **Dastarkhan** [127 C5] 75 Shevchenko St; ☏ 272 5427, 272 1317. A warren of small rooms on 2 floors with wood panelling & eclectic décor: wooden aircraft & circus clowns hang from the ceiling, & statues of Laurel & Hardy welcome you into the restaurant. There is a summer terrace outside. The menu offers Russian, central Asian & European dishes. If you are really hungry, 'Russian roulette' features 5 steaks of different types of meat. At lunchtime, most of the diners come for the buffet business lunch. The scurrying waiters & functional furniture make this more a restaurant for a quick meal than somewhere to linger. $$$$$

✖ **Di Wang** [126 C4] 75 Zhambyl St; ☏ 272 3810, 701 2030 505; www.diwang.kz. Funky Cantonese restaurant, all clean lines & dark woods, with sepia-tinted photographs of Chinese nobles on the walls & an aquarium in the middle of the room full of eccentrically shaped fish. The food covers various oriental styles, including Chinese, Japanese & fusion, though the service is rather more haphazard than the top-range price ought to warrant. Be warned that there is nothing on the wine list below T6,000. There is a lounge bar in the basement with murals of giant water lilies & offering a suitably chic feel. The mirrored walls of the urinals are somewhat disconcerting though. $$$$$

✖ **Fame** [126 D4] 115/105 Bogenbai Batyr St; ☏ 244 9627, 244 9629. Entered round the back of the Grand Hotel Tien Shan, this place has photographs of Cruise, Presley & Bowie in the hallway, & the well-heeled (& perhaps locally famous) folk of Almaty at the tables, eating smartly presented international cuisine to the strains of lounge music in a restaurant decorated in shades of brown. $$$$$

✕ **Favor** [127 E7] 45 Al Farabi Av; ✆ 264 6064, 262 9072. This grill bar serves up everything from steak to *shashlik* & sushi. The décor is stylish, the atmosphere friendly & the staff speak English. $$$$$

✕ **Korean House** [126 F2] 2 Gogol St; ✆ 293 9692. Quiet restaurant with tasty, authentic food & efficient service. Waiters bow to you at the table. A meal for 2 including imported wine comes to approx T20,000. $$$$$

✕ **Porto Malteze** [126 D4] 109 Panfilov St; ✆ 273 2178. Upmarket fish restaurant with probably the best salted fish in Kazakhstan. Staff are helpful but be prepared to point & mime as their English is limited. The fish is priced by weight. $$$$$

✕ **Teatralnoye** [126 D4] 51A Zhambyl St; ✆ 272 8777. This elegant restaurant sits immediately to the west of the Abai Opera and Ballet Theatre, at the back of a small park. The interior is all columns, chandeliers & puffy armchairs, with a frieze of an opera scene on the wall & theatre posters in the foyer. A fine terrace garden is one of the nicest summer options in Almaty; on warm autumn lunchtimes you may eat here to the sound of rehearsals from the opera house. Dishes, served beneath silver salvers, are a French-focused international mix, though the menu occasionally tries to be too grand: *shashlik* is described as *brochettes*. $$$$$

✕ **Thai** [127 E5] 50 Dostyk Av; ✆ 291 0190. A challenger for the title of Almaty's swankiest restaurant, this dragon-strewn place offers 2 menus: 'Thai' for, sensibly enough, Thai food, & 'Zen' for Japanese. Plenty of exotic specialities for those with expansive wallets, including snowfish, kobe beef, & horsemeat in *pandan* leaves, the last sounding like Kazakh/Thai fusion. $$$$$

✕ **La Ville** [127 E5] 18 Shevchenko St; ✆ 291 2497; www.la-ville.kz; ⊕ 10.00–midnight. This airy restaurant just next to the Marrakech offers an enticing French/Italian menu. The 'lamb filet mignon with strawberry sauce' gives a sense of the food on offer. $$$$$

✕ **Entrecote** [126 D4] 132 Bogenbai Batyr St; ✆ 296 4415, 296 4416. A central steakhouse on the corner of Bogenbai Batyr & Furmanov, offering a dark interior, summer terrace, & confused, meat-laden menu. Flavoured vodkas include a horseradish & honey variety. There's another branch close to the central stadium (*46A Abai Av;* ✆ *292 5282, 292 5102*). Competitively priced business lunch options available 12.00–16.00. $$$$

✕ **Ex Libris** [127 D5] Corner Abai Av & Zheltoksan St; ✆ 272 1602; www.exlibris. restoran.kz; ⊕ 12.00–C1.00. The name derives from its location, on the side of the national library. The main room is decorated with gold drapes, but is otherwise rather bland. A 2nd room round the back is laid out in pub style with green leather sofas, heavy red wallpaper & a neglected dartboard. The menu sweeps boldly & formlessly across a variety of cuisines, ranging from *beshbarmak* to spaghetti bolognese. $$$$

✕ **Mamamia** [126 D3] 87 Gogol St; ✆ 273 3873. Bright & central Italian restaurant, with a good range of pizzas, pasta & salad dishes. The waitresses are, confusingly, dressed more in central European than Mediterranean style. The **Ciao Pizza** pizzeria is under the same management & offers a similar deal (*81A Tole Bi St;* ✆ *292 7161*). $$$$

✕ **Marrakech** [127 E5] 18 Shevchenko St; ✆ 291 4082. This is a suitably atmospheric nook-filled Moroccan restaurant, serving up tasty *couscous* & *tajine*, mint tea & hookahs, though the wide-screen TV is something of a distraction, as are the odd numbers in which everything is priced. The sturgeon *tajine* offers a hint of Kazakhstan amongst the flavours of Morocco. $$$$

✕ **Il Patio/Planeta Sushi** [126 E4] 43 Dostyk Av; ✆ 295 2542 (Il Patio), 295 2543 (Planeta Sushi); www.rosinter.ru. These Italian & Japanese restaurants, like animals heading for Noah's Ark, are always found in pairs, in several locations across Almaty as well as other cities around the former Soviet Union. Run by the Russian Rosinter Group, there is perhaps inevitably a chain-restaurant feel about the places, but for all that they are nicely decorated & competitively priced. This branch of Il Patio, for example, has a pizza oven burning enticingly in the corner, a wall map of Italy with 'we're here' somewhat improbably

4

marked over Naples &, true to its name, a patio in front. Its business lunch options include access to an 'all you can eat' salad bar, making them good value for the really hungry. The ladies toilet is indicated by a stiletto shoe, the gents by a pipe, which is presumably confusing for pipe-smoking ladies. The geisha-clad waitresses from Planeta Sushi next door help out in Il Patio on slow sushi days, which adds a surreal touch. The other branches include 1 further south at 202 Dostyk Av (*295 4354 (Il Patio), 295 4353 (Planeta Sushi)*) & 1 in the Ramstor shopping centre (*226 Furmanov St;* 250 0949). $$$$

✕ **Schwabsky Domik** [126 D4] 121 Ablai Khan Av; 261 0514; www.shvabskiy-domik.kz. Huge German-themed restaurant, laid out like a rambling central European village. Even the rubbish bins at the front door have little pitched roofs. The lederhosen-wearing staff wish you a cheery '*Guten Tag*' as you walk in. There is German beer on tap, & glass panels in the floor display the extensive wine cellar below. The long menu is heavy on meat, with the 'big assorted sausages' a monument to carnivorous gluttony. The business lunch is available 12.00–16.00. $$$$

✕ **Assorti** [127 E5] 106G Dostyk Av; 291 8171 (Wasabi Sushi), 291 8166 (Zimny Sad), 291 6200 (Medved), 291 4782 (Pizza Assorti); e assorti@assorti.kz. This 3-storey building with a smart half-columned façade, in a central spot near the corner of Dostyk & Abai, offers a real assortment of places to eat beneath its roof. The **Medved** is a themed Russian restaurant on the ground floor, chaotically decorated with fake vegetables & trailing vines, which offers a good range of Russian standards plus a grill menu. A floor up is the **Zimny Sad** ('Winter Garden'), with pot plants, caged birds & piano music. The menu is decorated with pictures of flowers but is otherwise that of the Medved. The **Wasabi Sushi** on the top floor offers plenty of sushi & sashimi & some tempura dishes. It turns into the **Tornado Nightclub** (🕐 22.00–05.00 Thu–Sat) late in the evening. A separate entrance on the ground floor brings you to **Pizza Assorti**, a small pizza & pasta place with stripped pine furniture & overloud Russian pop music. $$$ Medved, Zimny Sad & Pizza Assorti; $$$$$ grill menu & Wasabi Sushi

✕ **Excellent Restaurant** [126 D4] 103 Furmanov St; 267 0348, 267 0359; 🕐 12.00–

02.00 Mon–Thu, 12.00–04.00 Fri–Sat. Formerly RVS Restaurant, this reasonably priced option serves up an intriguing mix of European, Mexican & Kazakh foods. The menu is in Russian only. The business lunch costs T1,050. $$$

✕ **Fhloston Paradise** [127 D5] 193 Furmanov St; 267 1303. A real curiosity; somewhere between café, bar & restaurant, this place is a tribute to Luc Besson's film *The Fifth Element*. Tuck in to a 'Leeloo' salad, which by rights ought to have orange hair & be wrapped in bandages, washed down, if you can bear it, by a 'Fhloston Paradise' cocktail (Baileys, Malibu & whipped cream). The bar is a riot of coloured lights, & the music is loud & insistent. The food quality is variable. $$$

✕ **Moskva** [126 C4] 120 Nauryzbai Batyr St; 261 8612, 272 4555. Opposite the building of the Kazakhstan Olympic Committee, this over-bright restaurant behind a heavy wooden door is enlivened by mannequins dressed up as prominent figures from Russian history, including Ivan the Terrible & Catherine the Great. There is also a frieze of the Kremlin walls. The menu features a range of Russian dishes as well as some international & Kazakh choices, including *beshbarmak*. $$$

✕ **Princess Turandot** [127 A5] 103 Abai Av; 378 5386, 378 5161; www.turandot.kz. Its entrance, on the western side of the Auezov Kazakh State Drama Theatre, is guarded by a couple of Chinese warriors. This burgundy-walled, Chinese-lanterned place is the nicest of a chain of Princess Turandot restaurants & fast-food joints dotted around the city. This is a modestly priced & popular Chinese restaurant, though the Russian pop music & slow service strike discordant notes. There is another branch further west at 157A Abai Av, at the intersection with Rozybakiev St (*250 0399, 244 2076*) & also at 71 Tole Bi St (*267 7508, 317 1117*). $$$

✕ **Temujin** [126 E4] 63 Dostyk Av; 293 8000. Taking its title from Genghis Khan's real name, Temujin introduces itself with awnings outside the restaurant truly fit for a mighty ruler, with little golden tassels as decoration. There is a Mongol warrior on guard near the bar, shields on the walls & paintings of Genghis Khan's fighting hordes. There is also a 'VIP' room with comfy sofas. Like Genghis Khan himself, the menu ranges across many lands, offering a mix of

Mongolian, Chinese, European & Japanese dishes. The service can be disorganised. $$$

✗ **Tri Apelsina** [127 E6] 170 Valikhanov St; 260 7193. The 'Three Oranges' sits set back from Satpaev St, between the main Furmanov & Dostyk thoroughfares. It promises 'fusion' cookery, which means a menu encompassing Italian, Korean, Russian & Uzbek dishes. They are certainly confident of their abilities here: they boast that their Korean recipes are 'X-files', but will sell them to you for US$500. Even the Russian salad is allegedly prepared according to an 'ancient confidential recipe'. The comedy menu

aside, this is a reasonably priced, central option, with tables outside in summer. $$$

✗ **Zhili Bili** [127 D5] 43 Kurmangazy St; 250 1205, 250 7513. 'Once upon a time' is a Russian restaurant at the corner of Furmanov & Kurmangazy streets, with timbered walls on 2 floors, a fake tree in the middle of the room, decoration provided by furs & rustic kitchen utensils, & waitresses in peasant costumes. The set lunch includes their signature drink of *kvass* with honey. There is a second branch at 2 Dostyk Av (273 7982). $$$

BARS

♀ **Cinzano Bar** [127 F8] 109B Dostyk Av; 253 1345; e cinzanokz@mail.ru. With its signature red & black décor, & walls bedecked with images of Marilyn Monroe, this place, next door to the Arsenal Pub, is a favourite haunt of well-heeled young locals. The food menu offers a mix of sushi & European dishes. The cocktail shots are labelled to shock, charmingly allowing you to choose between 'bitch', 'cox', 'cocaine' & 'sin'. There is a resident DJ, & coming here in red shoes gets you a free Cinzano. $$$$$

♀ **Dublin** [127 D5] 45 Baiseitova St; 272 1475; e Dublin_almaty@mail.kz. This Irish-themed pub occupies part of a Soviet-era apartment block in a quiet side street just below Republic Sq. It proudly displays a 'certificate of authenticity' from the Irish Pub Company of Dublin, acknowledging that the place is genuinely styled on a Dublin city Victorian public house. The document puzzles me: confirmation that the place is a genuine imitation as against, presumably, a fake one? So what does a fake imitation Irish pub look like? A French bistro perhaps? Anyway, the place genuinely offers Guinness, Harp & Kilkenny on tap, & a standard range of pub fare. There are 2 floors, with the curiously named 'Western Hall' upstairs & the 'Central Hall' below. The outdoor terrace is pleasant in warm weather. $$$$$

♀ **The Albion Club** [127 E6] 104 Samal 2; 260 7211. Behind the heavy green door in a modern block close to the Ramstor supermarket lies this pub which draws its inspiration from all things British. The upstairs bar is a tribute to Manchester United, with cup final tickets, Lou Macari picture cards, a signed portrait of Sir Bobby Charlton & waiters in football shirts. The bar downstairs

highlights British pop music, & there is a mural of a giant £10 note in the lobby. The wide-ranging menu identifies each dish with the name of a London Underground station, though it is difficult to work out why Oxford Circus should be garlic bread, or Royal Oak represent Caesar salad. It all rather suggests a non-rhyming version of cockney rhyming slang. So, Neasden & chips then. $$$$

♀ **Arsenal Pub** [127 F8] 109B Dostyk Av; 265 2550. The name may echo that of a certain London football team, but the suit of armour, duelling pistols & crossbows decorating the place suggest that the inspiration was a rather different kind of arsenal. Though they do screen Premiership football matches. The place strives for a bierkeller atmosphere, offers Löwenbräu on tap, & has a menu heavy with *shashlik* & sausages. $$$$

♀ **The Bull and Bear** [126 D4] 83 Kabanbai Batyr St; 272 2462; e b_and_b@ok.kz; ⏲ 12.00–01.00. It is apt that a city with regional financial centre aspirations has a pub named in honour of financial markets. The menu gives a detailed 2-page explanation of the origin of the terms for anyone vaguely interested. The place is a basement bar kitted out in identikit English pub fashion, but the location is convenient for the Abai Opera and Ballet Theatre over the road. The menu runs from bar snacks to grilled trout. $$$$

♀ **Dickens** [126 E4] 45 Dostyk Av; 291 1659. The decidedly discreet vine-covered brick exterior of this place at the corner of Shevchenko St & Dostyk Av conceals a smart but bland interior, with the obligatory red British telephone box. The eclectic menu ranges from lamb curry, through *fajitas* to Thai-style beef, with pizza & burgers also on offer. Most of the draught beers are Belgian. Describing itself as an 'English restaurant & pub', this is one of those places which gives a sense of not having decided which of restaurant or pub it is trying to be. $$$$

♀ **Glen Pub** [126 D5] 44 Shevchenko St; ☏ 261 6393. Its exterior suggesting a stylised rocky mountainscape, this is a somewhat functional pub/restaurant, with an international menu incorporating a few Scottish specialities, including Scotch broth & even haggis. The Highland theme is taken further in the good range of whiskies on offer, & in the kilts & tam-o'-shanters sported by the uncomfortable-looking bar staff. They offer a good-value, albeit unexciting, set lunch. $$$$

♀ **Stetson Azteka** [126 C3] 66 Kazybek Bi St; ☏ 279 3030. Its exterior looking like a rose-walled Mexican village in the shadow of the UN outreach centre, this place, in the cul-de-sac of Tchaikovsky St just to the south of Kazybek Bi, is the North American Indian sister of the cowboy Stetson Bar, with a similar menu. From the entrance, you descend into a world of clay pots, chunky wooden tables, brightly painted columns & waitresses dressed as squaws. They do a good-value business lunch, available 12.30–15.00. $$$$

♀ **Stetson Bar** [126 C4] 128 Furmanov St; ☏ 261 2501, 272 6863; www.stetson.kz. Central bar with a 'way-out-west' theme, its window display features cowboy boots, a lasso, a pistol &, er, a stuffed armadillo. Early diners can get b/ fast here as well as 'hangover' soup. The slightly mysterious menu also features 'piratical halibut' & 'mancnurian chicken'. Is that Manchurian or Mancunian? $$$$

CAFÉS

☕ **L'Affiche** [126 D4] 83 Kabanbai Batyr St; ☏ 272 1092. Trendy café in a central spot close to the opera theatre. The décor is dark wood & dark walls, topped by a ceiling painted in tribute to Gauguin. They offer coffee, cocktails, a few international dishes ranging from pasta to pepper steak, & some rather expensive sandwiches. $$$$$

☕ **Café Biscuit** [127 E5] 18 Shevchenko St; ☏ 291 6692, 293 8284. Everything is brown in this central coffee house: there are biscuit-coloured walls, 1 bearing a frieze featuring a

♀ **Tinkoff** [126 B6] 27A Satpaev St; ☏ 292 4900. Part of a Russian chain, this bow-fronted metallic-finished building on Satpaev St contains a bar & microbrewery, offering both filtered & unfiltered beers & European & Japanese menus. The 'one metre sausage' presents a challenge to the really hungry. They also do a sushi business lunch. Tinkoff likes to promote itself – the bus stop outside has the firm's 'T' logo propping up the roof, & Tinkoff baseball caps are on sale in the foyer. But the terrace bar on the roof is an excellent option on hot summer evenings; gazing across at the mountains from here you may be prepared to forgive this place the excesses of its advertising. $$$$

♀ **Vogue Bar** [127 E6] Corner, Satpaev & Furmanov sts; ☏ 264 1699. Smallish, red-toned bar with a vaguely 'fashion' theme & a wealthy young Kazakh clientele. DJ in residence Fri–Sat. Limited international menu. $$$$

♀ **Mad Murphys** [126 E3] 12 Tole Bi St; ☏ 291 2856, 291 5972; www.irishpub.kz. Guinness & Kilkenny on tap, English-speaking bar staff, Britpop, a dartboard, & Union Jacks hanging from the ceiling, Mad Murphys has long been one of Almaty's expatriate hangouts. Decorated with assorted kitchen utensils & other knick-knacks, the place is a little shabby, but the locals seem to like it that way. The pizzas are named after parts of Ireland, such as the 'Tralee Pepperoni'. And why not inspect a 'Wexford'? The beer garden outside, guarded by a red phone box, is pleasant in summer, & the regular live music is entertaining if a little eclectic. Wi-Fi available. $$$

biscuit-coloured dragon, & your order is brought to you by waitresses in biscuit-coloured uniforms. The magazine-style picture menu shows the wide range of cakes on offer. They also have a few pasta & other savoury dishes, sandwiches & pancakes. $$$$

☕ **4A Coffee** [126 D2] 81 Zhibek Zholy Av; ☏ 271 8237; m 701 757 6614; www.4acoffee. com; ☼ 08.00–21.00. This ochre-walled coffee house, with a wooden bar, menu chalked up on the blackboard behind it, & freshly ground coffee for sale, is run by a US expat & would not look out of place in Seattle. The menu also features a limited range of sandwiches & quiche. It's close to the TsUM department store, just off the pedestrian stretch of Zhibek Zholy Av, perfectly located to provide a break from souvenir shopping. $$$

Café Coffee and Toffee [127 D5] 44 Shevchenko St; 261 7416. With a good central location, close to the corner of Shevchenko & Furmanov streets, in the All Trade building, this is a reasonable option for a coffee or light lunch between sightseeing. Strives for a medieval castle look, with wooden beams & stone pillars. Wi-Fi available. $$$

Coffeedelia [126 D4] 79 Kabanbai Batyr St; 272 6409. A mixed Kazakhstani & expatriate clientele slurp their authentic cappuccinos & dig into lunchtime sandwiches at this Kazakh take on the Western coffee-house experience, with its orange-hued décor, snappy, if trite, logos, & Wi-Fi. There is a rather smoky 'VIP' area with comfy sofas & waiter service; for the rest, it is order as you enter & take a number. The place is very popular & people spill out onto the pavement in summer. $$$

ENTERTAINMENT

There are no listings magazines in English. If you can read Russian, *Time Out Almaty* offers comprehensive listings. The twice-monthly magazine *Vibiray Almaty* offers a less full coverage, but is free; distributed in some cafés and hotels.

THEATRES AND CONCERT HALLS Almaty offers an excellent range of opera, ballet, classical music and theatre, though most plays are in either Russian or Kazakh. Ticket prices are very low by Western standards, and the quality of the performances is frequently high. Performances tend to be held rather early in the evening, typically starting around 18.30. Most theatres close during the summer months.

Abai Kazakh State Academic Opera and Ballet Theatre [126 D4] 110 Kabanbai Batyr St; 272 7934, 272 2042; booking office 10.00–18.00. A classically inspired building, completed in 1941, with a balconied façade supported by powerful square columns. Offers a good repertoire of opera & ballet, mixing Russian & Italian favourites with some Kazakh items. Performances begin at 18.30.

Almaty Circus [127 C5] 50 Abai Av; 394 4903, 394 4911; www.circus.com.kz. Not exactly a theatre, but hosts regular live performances nonetheless. These include lions & bears, as well as human performers. Tickets start at T1,000.

Auezov Kazakh State Drama Theatre [127 A5] 103 Abai Av; 292 3307, 292 7393; booking office 10.00–18.00. A piece of late 1970s Soviet architecture, with marble facing & a seated statue of the writer Auezov out the front. Kazakh-language performances.

Kazakh Concert Hall [126 D3] 83 Ablai Khan Av; 279 1426. Housed in a large reddish-hued building, this place offers classical concerts.

Lermontov Russian Drama Theatre [127 D5] 43 Abai Av; 267 3131, 267 3151;

booking office 10.00–18.00, but 10.00–16.00 on performance days. Russian-language plays.

Republic Palace [127 E5] 56 Dostyk Av; 291 5523. Completed in 1970, this textbook piece of Soviet concert-hall architecture, with a large golden roof jutting out beyond its walls, seats 3,000. Performances here are from a mixed bag of mainly middle-of-the-road crooners & light classical performers from across the region, supplemented by occasional, & often unfashionable, Western acts, plus beauty pageants & assorted glitz.

State Puppet Theatre [126 E2] 63 Pushkin St; 273 6921; booking office 10.00–18.00. Close to Panfilov Park, its performances, often starting at 12.00, are aimed at children but require a knowledge of Russian.

Zhambyl Kazakh State Philharmonia [126 E3] 35 Kaldayakov St; 291 8048; booking office 10.00–18.00. Grey building at the corner of Tole Bi & Kaldayakov streets, entered between large square columns. Classical music. Tickets tend to cost T1,000.

4

AMUSEMENT PARKS

Aquapark [126 G2] Central Park of Recreation; ✆274 6797; ⏰ 10.00–19.00 Tue–Sun, 12.00– 22.00 Mon; admission adult/child (below 1.5m) T2,000/1,500 Mon–Fri, T2,500/1,800 Sat/Sun. You enter this waterslide-filled world in the heart of the Central Park through a gate formed by the tentacles of a sombrero-wearing octopus. The slides themselves have gentle, reassuring names, like 'Kamikaze' & 'Niagara'. It's a cooling option in summer, though not necessarily a quiet one, especially at w/ends.

Fantasy World [127 A5] Abai Av, corner with Musrepov Bd; ⏰ 13.00–midnight Mon–Fri, 12.00–midnight Sat–Sun; admission T1,800, with supplements for some rides. Smallish park close to the Hotel Rahat. The star attraction is an inverted steel roller-coaster called 'Anaconda'. There are also dodgems, described here as 'bamper car'.

BATHS The tradition of public baths is a long-standing one of the cities of the Silk Road. It was reinforced with the arrival of the Russians, who brought with them their own tradition of the taking of steam baths, the *banya*. Public bath houses are found in towns throughout Kazakhstan, where they retain an important social function as well as being a means of keeping clean. But if you visit only one bath house during your time in Kazakhstan it should be the **Arasan Baths** [126 D3] (*Aiteke Bi St;* ✆*272 4018;* ⏰ *08.00–22.00 Tue–Sun; ticket office* ⏰ *07.30–21.00; tickets for a 2hr session T1,500 Tue–Fri, T2,000 Sat–Sun*) in the centre of Almaty, the best known and most impressive in the country. They sit on the west side of Panfilov Park, at the corner of Aiteke Bi Street and Kunaev Street. The association with Kunaev is apt, as the baths, opened in 1982, were one of the buildings at the heart of the plans of the then First Secretary of the Communist Party of Kazakhstan to turn Alma-Ata into a grand modern city.

Within the large green-domed concrete building are Russian, Finnish and Eastern baths. The Russian baths are centred on the *parilka*, or steam room, whose inmates slap themselves with pads of leaves of oak, birch or, for the really masochistic, pine, purchased from stallholders outside the building, amid temperatures which reach nostril-burning levels. Don't be surprised to see some of your fellow steam room inhabitants wearing pointy felt hats: they are said to protect the head from the heat of the room. When the heat gets too much, the plunge pool provides starkly cooling relief. The Eastern baths are less extreme, and involve lying on heated marble slabs. Massages are also available, some of which involve applications of honey, but there is nothing gentle about them. There are separate male and female wings.

The interior of the building is a fine example of early 1980s Soviet architecture at its most exuberant: little metal balls dangling from the ceiling, porthole-like windows, balconies with raffish curves, stained glass and mosaic work. You can buy anything in the lobby you may have forgotten: towel, flip-flops, pointy felt hat …

If you are male and are in Almaty on business, your colleagues may invite you and a selection of young ladies to join them in the baths. If this is not your scene, decline the invitation politely. This form of entertainment is often seen as part of the male bonding that will enrich your relationship, and offering it is one of their obligations as your hosts.

NIGHTLIFE Almaty has a lively nightclub scene; locals go out late to party, and venues tend to be either closed or empty until midnight. The (mainly Russian-language) website www.night.kz is a good source of information on upcoming events, which in summer include full-moon club nights at beach locations around Lake Kapchagai. The nightclub dress code in Kazakhstan tends to be fairly smart (locals dress up to go clubbing). As in Astana, be careful of fees charged to sit round a table at many of the plusher places: they are usually deductible from the bar bill, but can be steep. Lounge bars are also firmly in vogue and venues (contact details can be found in the various restaurants or bars listings above) include Boudoir, Di Wang, Fame, Cinzano Bar and Vogue Bar.

☆ **Bounzzy Club** 103 Furmanov St; 267 0353; www.bounzzy.restoran.kz; music from 21.00 nightly. Jazz club, featuring the house Cappuccino Band.

☆ **Chukotka** 40 Gogol St; 273 3974; www.chukotka.kz; 12.00–01.00 Mon–Fri, 12.00—03.00 Sat. Crowded dance bar near Pafilov Park with a young, well-heeled clientele & live music at the w/ends.

☆ **Copacabana** Mira & Pastera; 279 9568; e cocacabana@mail.ru. Lively Latino bar with regular live music. Popular with young expats. Salsa master classes 19.00–21.00 Wed, Thu & Sun. Free entry on Thu. Book a table at the w/end.

☆ **Da Freak** 40 Gogol St; 273 1337; www.dafreakclub.com; midnight–06.00 Fri–Sat. This nightclub in Panfilov Park is a good place for house & techno music, & sometimes features guest DJs flown in from abroad.

☆ **Dream Club Pool Bar** 114 Panfilov St; 272 6784; f 272 9302; 12.00–01.00 daily. While not perhaps everyone's idea of a wild evening, Russian billiards, a popular local game featuring 15 large white balls & 1 mauve one, is played in halls throughout Kazakhstan, from the opulent to the seedy. If you are minded to unfathom the mysteries of the game, this central spot, while not the cheapest, is a good place to come. It offers more than 20 tables, including a couple for the more familiar Western game of pool, & charges T2,000/hr.

☆ **Euphoria** 29/6 Satpaev St; 226 1808; f 226 1807; 17.00–05.00 Fri–Sat, 20.00–02.00 Wed, Thu, Sun. This cavernous nightclub next to the Hotel Rahat proclaims itself 1 of the trendiest venues in town but customers give it mixed reviews. Its prices (inc for entry & for tables) are steeper than most & be aware of the T146,000 tables in the VIP section.

☆ **Gas** 100 Shevchenko St; 272 7474; 22.00–06.00 Wed–Mon. Metal-covered columns give this place an industrial look. There is a separate club upstairs called, perhaps predictably, Petroleum (same contact details & opening hrs, but separate admission), which caters to an older clientele.

☆ **Soho** 65 Kazybek Bi St; 267 0367; www.soho.kz; music from 21.00. Also a bar & restaurant, this place offers live rock music to a mixed Kazakhstani & expat audience. Both Nazareth & Deep Purple have graced the stage here, though the music is usually provided by the house band. It's worth noting that Soho has something of a reputation as a hangout for prostitutes in search of foreign businessmen.

☆ **Tornado** 106G Dostyk Av; 291 8171, 264 5264; 23.00–05.00 Thu–Sat. During these hours, the red-tinted Wasabi Sushi restaurant on the top floor of Assorti (see page 132) turns into a nightclub. There's a room focused on hookah-smoking next door.

SHOPPING

A pedestrianised strip of Zhibek Zholy Avenue, known to locals as Arbat in mimicry of the more substantial pedestrian thoroughfare in Moscow, is as close as Almaty gets to a central shopping district. The department store **TsUM** [126 D2] (10.00–21.00 Mon–Sat, 10.00–20.00 Sun) is here, at the corner with Ablai Khan Avenue, a crowded emporium divided up into many separate outlets grouped by theme, which has served customers since Soviet days. The mobile-phone counters on the ground floor tend to be engulfed by students trying out the latest ringtones. Further to the east along the Zhibek Zholy pedestrian section is the modern Silk Way City mall, heavy with expensive outlets selling Western designer labels.

Other shopping malls are scattered around town, among them the shopping centre on Furmanov Street, to the south of the Central State Museum, centred on a large branch of the **Ramstor** [127 E6] supermarket chain. Visitors are greeted by a smiling green kangaroo, the symbol of the group. The centre also includes a food court, an indoor skating rink and a cinema. Other central shopping malls include **Promenade** on Abai Avenue, and the **Ritz Palace** [127 F7] on Dostyk Avenue.

GREEN BAZAAR [126 E2] (⊕ *Tue–Sun*) Central Almaty has been gradually losing its traditional markets, victims of burgeoning property prices, hygiene regulations and the preference of the local authorities and wealthy shoppers for modern-looking malls. But the Green Bazaar is one resolute survivor, the most interesting and colourful place in the city to buy produce, and well worth visiting simply as a tourist destination. It sits close to the intersection of Zhibek Zholy Avenue and Pushkin Street, a block north of Panfilov Park.

The centrepiece is a suitably green-walled, square-based, building. Inside, the space is divided by four central pillars, two of which house cafés spread around internal balconies. The café at the southwest pillar offers cheap Uzbek food and a good vantage point for looking down onto the bustle of the bazaar below. In the southern part of the bazaar are the sellers of dried fruit and nuts, mostly Uzbeks and Tajiks, who implore foreign tourists to sample their produce. The dried apricots are particularly good. In the western aisles are lines of pickled vegetables, labelled 'eastern salads', including bright mounds of pickled carrot. Here too are honey and milk products. Meat hangs from metal spikes along the aisles of the northern part of the bazaar: note several aisles devoted to the horse. Chicken and pork are found in the eastern part of the building. One particularly interesting section, often overlooked, is a small cluster of stalls in the southwestern corner of the building, whose stallholders offer herbs and grasses in little plastic sachets, dispensed with detailed advice as to how to prepare curative preparations against all manner of ills. One word of warning: the bazaar authorities get shirty with foreign tourists attempting to take photographs.

The bazaar area continues outside the building, with lines of clothes stalls to its west, mostly offering cheap Chinese goods.

BARAKHOLKA (⊕ *Tue–Sun*) This sprawling collection of markets provides ample evidence that the trading networks of the Silk Routes are alive and well. This is the cheapest place to shop in Almaty, though you should expect row upon row of stalls selling Chinese clothing of indifferent quality. There are, however, more interesting items to be found here, including souvenirs. Bargaining is expected, though this is usually more a matter of knocking a little off the original asking price than the protracted haggling at bazaars in north Africa. To get here, head west along any of the main streets in the centre of town, turning north when you reach Rozybakiev Street. This changes its name to Kuderin Street north of the intersection with Raiymbek Avenue, and changes name again to Severnoe Koltso (the northern ring road) across the intersection with Ryskulov Avenue. Note that Almaty's heavy traffic often gets particularly snarled up approaching Barakholka, especially at weekends, and lengthy jams are possible. A trip here is a great experience for lovers of this kind of market; others are likely to find it a strain.

BOOKS English-language books are hard to find in Almaty, though there are reasonably good selections of maps and titles about the region in the bookstores of the Rahat and Intercontinental hotels, and a few books in English, as well as dictionaries and sometimes maps, at ordinary bookstores around town. Another useful place is the small book corner of the **Caspian Publishing House** [126 E3] (*20¾ Kazybek Bi St;* \ *250 1703;* e *cphalma@hotmail.com;* ⊕ *10.00–18.00 Tue–Sun,* *though call ahead*). Currently located next door to the head office of the Central Asia Tourism Corporation, this place sells the somewhat eclectic mix of titles published by the company.

SOUVENIRS The largest collection of souvenir shops in town is on the top floor of TsUM. There are carpet and handicraft stores in the lobbies of both the Central State Museum and the Kasteyev State Arts Museum. The summit of Kok-Tobe (see page 152) is home to a group of reasonably priced souvenir shops. The larger international hotels, including the Intercontinental and Rahat, also have souvenir shops, though prices are likely to be higher. Look out for announcements about a craft fair held a few times a year in the Republican Palace of Schoolchildren at the corner of Dostyk Avenue and Satpaev Street. This brings together artisans from across the region, and serves as reconfirmation that Uzbekistan and Kyrgyzstan produce a generally rather nicer range of handicrafts than does Kazakhstan. It is also possible to buy Kazakhstani souvenirs direct from the men and women who make them at Sheber Aul south of the city (see page 157). A trip here can be combined with one to the Big Almaty Lake to make for a pleasant day excursion.

TREKKING EQUIPMENT Trekking equipment and winter clothing, including recognisable Western brands, are widely available but many items are seconds or copies imported from China. Reasonable quality items can be found at the **Korgan-Centre Robinson** (*60 Ablai Khan St*; ✆ *232 7640*).

MEDICAL

✚ **International Medical Center (IMC)**
235 Mukanov St; ✆ 268 6161; www.imcalmaty. com; ◷ 09.00–14.00 Mon, 09.00–18.00 Tue, 09.00–13.00 Wed, 09.00–19.00 Thu, 09.00–16.00 Fri, 10.00–14.00 Sat. On the western side of the town centre, at the corner of Mukanov & Kabanbai Batyr, this clinic has English-speaking expatriate GPs on its staff, & relatively low-cost consultations.

✚ **International SOS** 11 Lugansky St; ✆ 258 1911; f 258 1585; www.internationalsos.com; ◷ 09.00–18.00 Mon–Fri, 09.00–12.00 Sat. Part of a large international organisation, which offers English-language consultations & a wide range of medical services, including medical evacuations if necessary. Used by many international

organisations in Almaty but its charges are at the top end of the scale.

✚ **Interteach** 275 Furmanov St; ✆ 320 0200; www.interteach.kz; ◷ 08.00–20.00 Mon–Fri, though will take emergency calls 24hrs. Outpatient centre under the wing of the Kazakh National Corporation of Health & Medical Insurance. Can provide a range of medical services including vaccinations, referrals to local hospitals & medical evacuations. Medical equipment available does not match that of the International SOS clinic, & you may not be seen by medical staff with more than very basic English, but charges are substantially cheaper than International SOS.

WHAT TO SEE

AROUND REPUBLIC SQUARE Republic Square is the heart of administrative power in Almaty. Laid out in the early 1980s, this broad expanse of tarmac doesn't feel particularly square-like most of the time, as the traffic on busy Satpaev Street hurtles across it. This is, however, the place to come on major holidays, when the square is closed off to traffic, and frequently hosts live music and firework displays.

The south side of the square is dominated by the imposing pale grey late Soviet bulk of the former Presidential Palace, now housing the **municipal authorities** [127

D6]. The building was deliberately set back some distance to the south of the square, in order not to obstruct the view of the mountains, and is surrounded by gardens. In front of this building is the red marble-faced **rostrum**, from which military parades passing across the square could be inspected. This part of the square is set to be remodelled, with the construction of a new underground shopping mall.

The focus of the north side of the square is a post-independence addition, the graceful obelisk of the **Independence Monument** [127 D6]. This square-based structure, 18m in height, is topped by a replica of the Golden Man (see page 168), his hat and breastplate shining gold in the sun, standing atop a winged snow leopard. At the base of the obelisk, an inscription commemorates Kazakhstan's declarations of sovereignty on 25 October 1990 and independence on 16 December 1991. In front of this stands an open bronze book, representing the Constitution of Kazakhstan, bearing the hand print of the president. The hand print is worn shiny by the number of hands that have been placed into its grooves. An inscription in several languages tells you to make a wish. The English version reads: 'choose and be in bliss!' In the height of summer the effect is more likely to be: 'choose and burn your hand!' This is one of the favoured places for wedding parties in Almaty to be photographed.

Behind the Independence Monument runs a long screen, featuring a series of bronze panels, depicting proud moments from the history of Kazakhstan. These include the defeat of the Persians by the forces of Queen Tomyris and the defeat of the Dzhungars by those of Ablai Khan. The easternmost screen is centred on the bas-relief of President Nazarbaev, his hand on the Constitution, declaring the independence of Kazakhstan. The people and buildings of Kazakhstan standing behind the president form, in silhouette, a map of the country.

The Independence Monument is framed by two 16-storey Soviet buildings to the north, set at jaunty 45° angle to the square, topped by billboards reading, respectively, 'Kazakhstan' and 'Almaty'. Quiet Baiseitova Street running northwards between these buildings is adorned with fountains.

Republic Square was the scene of one of the most emotive events in the recent history of Kazakhstan. The Soviet authorities had on 16 December 1986 replaced the veteran Dinmuhammed Kunaev as First Secretary of the Communist Party of Kazakhstan by Gennady Kolbin, who had been First Secretary in the Russian region of Ulyanovsk. A crowd massed in the square on the following day, protesting not at the departure of Kunaev but the fact that his replacement was an outsider, a non-Kazakh who had never previously worked in Kazakhstan. The rally was brutally broken up by various law and order agencies, wielding truncheons and metal sappers' spades. There were fatalities and many injuries. A plaque on a wall of a building in the northwest corner of the square commemorates the events of 17 December, which are given a more lavish memorial just to the west, as Zheltoksan Street meets Satpaev. The monument here, named the **Dawn of Freedom** [127 D6], was built in 2006 in honour of those killed and injured 20 years previously. A young lady, with beatific expression, is drawn forward as if preparing for flight. She releases a small golden bird. Behind her trails a banner. To her right, are depictions of scenes from Kazakhstan's troubled history, including a chilling tableau of famine-ravaged faces staring out towards the onlooker. To her left, the banner offers a stylised depiction of the 1986 uprising: riot troops brandishing entrenching tools square up to a stone-throwing crowd. Zheltoksan ('December') Street itself is named from the events of December 1986.

THE CENTRAL STATE MUSEUM [127 E6] (*Mikrorayon Samal 1, Bldg 44; \ 264 5650, 264 2200; ⊙ 09.00–17.00 Wed–Mon; admission adult/child T100/50*) Almaty's

largest, though not necessarily its most enjoyable, museum sits a short walk from Republic Square. Head east along Satpaev Street, and then turn right down Furmanov Street at the first crossroads. The museum is housed in a large blue-domed building constructed in the early 1980s, on the east side of Furmanov Street. It is set back from the road amidst gardens. The museum as an institution dates from the 19th century: it was founded in Orenburg, and moved to Almaty in the 1930s.

The large foyer, beneath the central dome, is enlivened by costumed mannequins depicting various periods in the early history of Kazakhstan, including a model of the Golden Man. There is an uninspiring café downstairs (⊕ *10.00–17.00*), several souvenir shops offering carpets and handicrafts, and frequent temporary exhibits.

The permanent exhibits are arranged in four large halls. **Hall 1**, starting downstairs, offers palaeontology and archaeology. The exhibits are arranged in an orderly historical progression from fragments of dinosaurs to a model of the Timurid Mausoleum of Khodja Ahmed Yassaui. Among the items encountered along this historical route is a Bronze Age burial in a stone-walled coffin. There is a fascinating bronze sacrificial table from the 4th or 3rd century BC, found in Almaty Oblast, which depicts a procession of lions around the rim, while in the centre wild animals and birds are feasting on a dead deer. There is an interesting display of *balbals*, standing stones from the Turkic period around the 7th to 9th centuries. A moustachioed man with rather droopy eyes holds up a glass. Another man holds a bird. The exhibition continues upstairs, with displays focusing on the flourishing of urban life from the 10th century. The development of trade along the Silk Routes is illustrated by the presence of a Japanese bowl and engraved Iranian copper dish. A dramatic diorama depicts the Mongols of Genghis Khan storming the city of Otrar. There is an impressive display of items from Saraichik in Atyrau Oblast, including a 14th-century money box, ink pots and a tall bronze lamp. And finally the Mausoleum of Khodja Ahmed Yassaui, represented by pieces of ceramic tile as well as a model of the building.

Hall 2, located amongst the souvenir shops on the ground floor, focuses on ethnography. This is centred on a yurt, standing in the middle of the hall, replete with colourful rugs on the floor and walls, engraved wooden chests, and a bed with elegantly decorated side panels. Along the walls of the hall run various displays. Hunting techniques are depicted with a mannequin of a falconer. There is a model of a waterwheel, turned by ceramic jugs which would alternately fill and empty. An intriguing display, unfortunately in Kazakh only, sets out to demonstrate the distinct genetic and physiological make-up of the Kazakh people. There is a display of items considered to have protective powers against the evil eye: a black and white-striped rope; the claw of a golden eagle; and the skull of a wolf. There are items used by shamans, such as a *kobyz* customised with the addition of a mirror and feathers. There are displays too of costumes, jewellery, musical instruments, religious items and children's games.

Hall 3, on the top floor, is a mix of items on the multi-ethnic character of Kazakhstan and Soviet-period history. The former involves displays of the costumes, artefacts and traditions of many of the ethnic groups which make up modern Kazakhstan, ranging from the several million-strong Russian community to the Assyrians (of whom there are 540 in Kazakhstan, according to the figures presented here). An interesting display on the Korean community was contributed by the Korean State Ethnographic Museum. The rest of the hall commemorates the heroes of Soviet Kazakhstan. There are presentations on various Heroes of Socialist Labour, before you are taken into the war period, with a list of Kazakhstanis earning the title of Hero of the Soviet Union. A diorama depicts a stalwart Red Army defending a wintry line against advancing German tanks.

Hall 4, on the same floor, focuses on post-independence Kazakhstan. There are displays about the State flag and emblem, currency, awards, hydrocarbons wealth and mineral resources, Kazakhstan's role in space exploration and its sporting successes. President Nazarbaev's books are displayed in various languages. The embroidered cloak used at the presidential inauguration of December 1991 is on display, as is the heavy inauguration belt, complete with dagger. A striking wall carpet depicts the leaders of the central Asian states (Nazarbaev is second from the right), commemorating a meeting of the presidents in Bishkek in 1995.

On the other side of Furmanov Street, almost opposite the museum, the white marble-faced square-based building is the **Presidential Residence**, built by the French construction company Bouygues in 1995.

AROUND THE ACADEMY OF SCIENCES

Tulebaev Street From the Central Museum, take Furmanov Street a block-and-a-half north, turning right at Abai Avenue. The first road on your left is the peaceful, leafy, Tulebaev Street, its presence marked by a seated statue of the dinner-jacketed **Mukan Tulebaev**, looking every inch the classical conductor. The numerous plaques affixed to buildings along this street naming leading writers, scientists and politicians attest that this quiet lane in central Almaty was once a favoured address of the Soviet elite.

The **House Museum of Mukhtar Auezov** [127 E5] (*185 Tulebaev St;* \ *263 7467, 262 9274;* ⊕ *10.00–17.00 Tue–Sat; admission T60*) is a fascinating place to visit even if you know nothing about the work of this important post-war Kazakh writer, for the insight it offers into the living standards of the intellectual elite in the Soviet Union of the 1950s. Auezov (1897–1961) survived the purges of the Kazakh intelligentsia in the late 1930s. His four-volume *The Path of Abai*, completed in 1956, served to build the image of the 19th-century Kazakh writer as well as Auezov's reputation. It gave Auezov great standing in the Soviet Union, as well as internationally.

Auezov himself had a hand in the design of this delightful two-storey house, with apple trees in the back garden and decorated borders around the arched windows. He lived here for a decade, from 1951–61, when ill health forced him to seek medical treatment in Moscow. The downstairs rooms, starting with the columned hall, are designed to impress. His dining table extends to accommodate 30 people. The dinner service is from Germany. Various souvenirs from his trips to India and Japan are on display. The third and fourth volumes of *The Path of Abai* were written in the comfortable-looking study, whose bookcases hold 6,000 tomes. Also downstairs is the pink-walled bedroom of his widowed sister.

The rooms upstairs are more modest. The bedroom of Auezov and his (third) wife Valentina features Chinese ornaments. Their daughter Leila's room is identified by a painting of the girl in a yellow dress. Leila went on to marry Askar Kunaev, the President of the Academy of Sciences and brother of the then First Secretary of the Communist Party of Kazakhstan. The bedroom of their son Irnar, a keen ornithologist, is decorated with stuffed birds. An ugly concrete administrative block around the back of the house contains a permanent exhibition of Auezov's life and work. There are photographs of the young Auezov, a collection of his medals, and a display of the many foreign-language editions of *The Path of Abai*. There is a photograph of President Nazarbaev with Kyrgyz writer Chinghiz Aitmatov opening the exhibition hall in 1997, on the 100th anniversary of Auezov's birth. Aitmatov's presence is a reminder of Auezov's role in popularising the Kyrgyz epic poem *Manas*.

Continuing northwards along Tulebaev Street, take the first road to your right, Kurmangazy Street. The first building on the right was built in the early 1970s to house the Kazakh Society of Friendship and Cultural Relations with Foreign Countries. Its circular conference hall apes the form of a yurt. The place had a brief moment of fame on 21 December 1991 as the venue for the meeting of the Heads of State of former constituent parts of the Soviet Union, who signed the agreement on the establishment of the Commonwealth of Independent States here. The building now houses the **Assembly of the Peoples of Kazakhstan** [127 E5].

Academy of Sciences [127 E5]

A block-and-a-half further east along Kurmangazy Street, you reach the vast orange-hued bulk of the Academy of Sciences building, constructed in the 1950s and apparently accommodating some 89,000m² of floorspace. The main façade looks northwards, onto Shevchenko Street. The powerful central part of the building displays the State Emblem of Kazakhstan in the arched space above the main entrance. There are two side wings, whose reliefs still depict a hammer and sickle within a Soviet star. The wing to the west houses the Central Scientific Library. That to the east is reportedly home to a **Museum of Nature**, which usually, however, seems to be closed.

Immediately opposite the main entrance, across Shevchenko Street, stands a statue of the 19th-century Kazakh traveller, soldier and scientist **Chokan Valikhanov**, his right hand on his chin in a gesture of academic contemplation. The pedestrianised lane heading northwards behind the statue is named in Valikhanov's honour.

There are some pleasing fountains and statues in the gardens around the Academy of Sciences building. Nicest of all is a fountain close to the northeast corner of the building: jets of water sprout up from beneath 12 rather whimsical animal statues. These possibly represent signs of the Chinese New Year, though I'm uncertain as to quite what the winged creature which looks like a cross between a kangaroo and a mouse is supposed to be. Or come to that, the statue which looks like something between a snail and a Clanger out of the old children's television series. Just to the south of this fountain is a statue of **Pushkin**, although the great Russian poet never came close to this part of Kazakhstan.

The Academy of Sciences building houses various institutes and scientific organisations, as well as an eclectic mix of other bodies. The central entrance on the southern side of the building, off Kurmangazy Street, for example provides access to the Kazakhstan Press Club and the Ular Art Gallery. This is also the entrance to take for the **Kanysh Satpaev Memorial Museum** [127 E5] (261 6011; ⊕ 10.00–13.00 & 14.00–17.00 Mon–Fri; admission free). Go to the lift on the right-hand side of the foyer, and press for the sixth floor, labelled 'Winter Garden'. The latter is an enclosed glass-roofed space, full of plants and laid out for seminars. The museum is just beyond it. The staff are not used to visitors; you will probably have to wait a few moments while they get the lights switched on. The exhibits offer a decidedly Soviet-style presentation of the career of the first President of the Kazakhstan Academy of Sciences (see box). The first room describes Satpaev's work at Zhezkazgan, with an interesting collection of press cuttings in which Satpaev attempts to persuade sceptics within the Soviet research community of the size and quality of the copper reserves there. The second room is devoted to Satpaev's later career as a senior member of the Soviet scientific establishment. There is a bust of Satpaev in the centre of this room, opposite a large map of the country indicating the main mineral deposits to be found beneath the soils of Kazakhstan. His (somewhat austere) office is preserved behind glass at the end of the room. There is a third room in the museum, but I have no idea what it contains since the staff couldn't get the lights to work when I visited. They did opine that it wasn't particularly interesting.

Republic Book Museum [126 E4] (*94 Kabanbai Batyr St;* ☏ *272 9155, 262 3821;* ⏰ *09.00–17.00 Mon–Fri; admission T150*) Two blocks north of the Academy of Sciences along Kunaev Street, at the intersection with Kabanbai Batyr Street, stands a pale blue building decorated with tall Corinthian columns and golden panels around the façade depicting grape harvest and wine production, presumably hints of an alcohol-oriented past life. The building now has a more refined and austere role, as home to the Republic Book Museum. The museum offers a good overview of Kazakh literature, though many of the displays are in the Kazakh language only. If the main entrance to the museum is locked, try the offices at the back of the building to find someone to let you in.

The rooms take you from the earliest writings on animal skins through roughly chronological displays devoted to the most famous Kazakhstani authors. Abai is featured heavily, with copies of his works, including musical scores, busts and paintings. A quotation from Abai, displayed prominently in four languages, tells us that he wrote for the young generation, not for fun. Zhambyl also gets star billing, as does the Russian poet Pushkin, in a display commemorating the celebration of 2006 as the year of Pushkin in Kazakhstan and the year of Abai in Russia. A quotation from Abai is used, praising Russian science and culture. There is a display on the authors of the World War II period, featuring books with titles like *Kazakhstan in the Battle for Leningrad*, and on into the post-independence period, with the books written by President Nazarbaev.

ALONG DOSTYK AVENUE

Geological Museum [127 E5] (*85 Dostyk Av;* ☏ *291 6316;* ⏰ *10.00–16.00 Tue–Sat; admission adult/child T100/50*) From the Academy of Sciences building, continue eastwards along Kurmangazy Street for another block-and-a-half, turning right onto busy Dostyk Avenue (which some locals still refer to as Lenin Avenue, its Soviet-period name). Well before the next crossroads you reach the Geological Museum on your right. The most interesting feature of this museum is its subterranean setting. You descend in a slow cage-like lift into a museum space set out like a mineshaft. There is a quote from Satpaev, his head displayed as a golden silhouette, about the importance of geological exploration. You pass a wall map displaying Kazakhstan's abundant mineral reserves: press the button, and uranium lights up. And then you reach the main hall of the museum, dominated by an unexcitingly displayed collection of sparkling mineral samples: amethyst, malachite and tourmaline. There is a display of agates, cut and polished to present what appear to be scenes of spindly trees beneath wintry skies. A large side space, featuring a rocky terrain in front of a wall mural of roaming dinosaurs, is used for talks to school groups.

Continuing southwards along Dostyk Avenue, the next junction, with Abai Avenue, is presided over by a statue of **Abai Kunanbaev**, Kazakhstan's great 19th-century writer, atop a large red stone plinth. Abai, book in hand, looks across at KIMEP University over the road with a somewhat pensive expression, as if worried about the lack of application of today's students. There is a square behind the statue, pleasant in summer, and beyond this the long, low façade of the Republic Palace of Culture (see page 135).

A block further to the south, at the corner of Dostyk and Satpaev, the curious building with the golden-domed observatory roof is the **Republican Palace of Schoolchildren** [127 E6], completed in 1981, where Soviet children would carry out extracurricular study and sporting pursuits. It is worth sticking your head inside to gape at the peculiar friezes, featuring reliefs of huge stylised plants.

Archaeological Museum [126 E4] (*44 Dostyk Av;* ☎ *291 8585;* ⏱ *10.00–17.00 Mon–Fri*) If you turn left to the north along Dostyk Avenue from the junction with Kurmangazy Street, rather than right to the south, you encounter after one block the walrus-moustachioed face of the Ukrainian poet **Shevchenko**, staring out from a large lump of rock, looking down along the street named in his honour. A block further to the north, the Kazakh musician **Zhambyl** sits on a rock next to a waterfall, ready to play his *dombra*, while he too surveys the side street bearing his name.

Behind the statue of Zhambyl stands a rather grim-looking apartment block, housing both the Iskra Cinema and the Archaeological Museum. The exhibits of the latter, housed in one large hall, are much less well displayed than the archaeological section of the Central State Museum, and this is really a museum for enthusiasts and rainy days. Among the items on display are boulders inscribed with petroglyphs, five stone *balbals* with oversized human heads, and four large three-legged bronze cauldrons from Almaty Oblast, the cauldrons dated from the 5th to the 3rd centuries BC. There is a large wall map, which serves broadly to demonstrate that there are archaeological sites all over Kazakhstan. There are various artefacts

KANYSH SATPAEV

The career of Kazakhstan's most famous geologist well illustrates the economic imperative behind scientific work, and the political influence scientific success could bring, during the Soviet period. Satpaev was born into an intellectual family in Bayanaul, Pavlodar Oblast, in 1899, in a village which now bears his name. His elder brother and two cousins died in prison camps in 1937, victims of Stalin's repression. Satpaev studied geology at the Tomsk Technological Institute, graduating in 1926. He was assigned to work at the Zhezkazgan copper deposit, where he concluded that reserves of copper were far larger than the estimates made by earlier British and Soviet studies suggested. His work underpinned a major expansion of mining activity at Zhezkazgan, and earned Satpaev the Order of Lenin in 1940.

During World War II he helped organise the exploitation of manganese deposits at Zhezdy, in central Kazakhstan, following the seizure by the Germans in August 1941 of the main existing field under production. Manganese was an important component in the production of armoured steel, and so the rapid development of new reserves was vital for the Soviet war effort. Manganese ore from Zhezdy was being supplied to the steelworks in Magnitogorsk by as early as July 1942.

In 1942, Satpaev was appointed head of the Presidium of the Kazakh branch of the Soviet Academy of Sciences. He worked to set up a Kazakhstan Academy of Sciences, and was elected its first president in 1946. Infighting within the Kazakhstan academic community briefly caused him to lose the job in the 1950s, but he was re-elected president in 1955 and kept the post until he died. He took on political roles as a people's representative to both the Kazakhstan and USSR supreme soviets. In the days before he died in 1964 he was still talking about the development of the mineral resources of Kazakhstan.

Satpaev's name is given to the Geological Institute, streets, schools and villages across Kazakhstan, a town in Karaganda Oblast, a mountain peak, a gladiolus, a small star in the Taurus constellation, and the mineral 'satpayevite'.

uncovered from Scythian burial mounds in the region and, almost obligatory in archaeological museums in Kazakhstan, a reconstructed Golden Man. There are medieval-period ceramics from Silk Road sites such as Otrar. A display about glassware has descriptions in English, unlike the rest of the museum. It runs from the glass beads found in late Bronze Age burials to 10th- to 13th-century glass bottles and vases found at urban sites, when both Otrar and Taraz were centres of glass manufacture.

Panfilov Park [126 E3] Another five blocks to the north along Dostyk Avenue, you reach the southern entrance to the rectangle of greenery in the heart of the city named in honour of the soldiers of the 316th Rifle Division, a unit formed by Major General Ivan Panfilov in Almaty Region, and in particular of a group of 28 men of Panfilov's division, led by Vasily Klochkov, who became icons of the Soviet Union for their exploits in defending Moscow during a fierce battle in November 1941 at Dubosekovo Station near Volokolamsk. Almost all of the 28 were killed in the engagement, during which they reportedly destroyed many German tanks, and all were awarded the title of Hero of the Soviet Union. The '28 Panfilov soldiers' were probably the men of 4 Company of the 2nd Battalion, 1075th Regiment, 316th Rifle Division, though historians have long debated the accuracy of the Soviet version of the events. What is certainly clear is that the 1075th Regiment suffered huge losses in the engagement. Major General Panfilov himself was among those killed in the defence of Moscow.

A statue of **Panfilov** stands at the Dostyk Avenue entrance to the park, his right arm patriotically against his chest. The tiled wall to the left displays the hammer and sickle of the Soviet period; that to the right bears the steppe eagle and sun of post-independence Kazakhstan. The path leading into the park behind this statue is lined with pink bollards, each honouring one of the Panfilov Heroes.

The focus of the eastern side of the park is a huge **war memorial**, its centrepiece a dramatic sculpture of the Panfilov soldiers, their profiles forming a large map of the USSR. From the centre of this a grenade-wielding Red Army soldier seems to be in the process of jumping out. Below the sculpture is a quotation from Klochkov, to the effect that 'Russia is huge but there is nowhere to retreat since Moscow is behind us'. In front of this sculpture is a long black marble sheet, with an eternal flame, and an inscription to the 601,011 Kazakhstanis killed in the war. On the south side of the war memorial complex, the statue of three haggard, war-weary soldiers is a monument to the Kazakhstanis killed in Afghanistan, a very different iconography from the proud memorial to those killed during the Great Patriotic War.

The war memorial is one of the favoured spots in Almaty for newly-weds to be photographed. Cheap local champagne is drunk, and doves set free into the sky (they return later to be re-caged, and then re-released, in a curious wedding cottage industry). On the northeastern corner of the memorial square, the quaint pitched-roofed wooden house with a central spire was built in 1907 by architect A P Zenkov, and once housed the Officers' League. The building now accommodates the **Museum of Folk Musical Instruments of Kazakhstan** [126 E3] (*24 Zenkov St; 291 6326; 09.00–13.00 & 14.00–17.30 Tue–Sun; admission T200*).

From the ornate entrance hall, you pass through two small rooms to the right. The first shows scenes of dancing and instrument playing depicted on petroglyphs, as a demonstration of the antiquity of folk music in Kazakhstan. The second features paintings of the 20th-century composer/conductors Tulebaev and Zhubanov, and a somewhat lonely accordion. The first main room beyond is devoted to wind and percussion instruments, featuring a wide array of clay whistles, horns, flutes, drums and rattles. The next room is devoted to the *kobyz*, whose horse-hair strings are played with a bow. Variants on the theme are also on display, including the *zhezkobyz*, whose strings are made of metal. Next comes a room mostly dedicated to the two-stringed guitar-like *dombra*. Variants displayed here include the *tumar dombra*, with a triangular body. There is also a seven-stringed *zhetigen*, a distant relative of the harp. The next room features instruments which once belonged to some of the leading lights of Kazakhstan's musical history, including *dombras* formerly owned by Abai, Zhambyl and Makhambet Utemisov. The museum also houses a small auditorium, where performances involving the traditional instruments are sometimes held. The museum guides will also offer you a short burst of any instrument of your choice, at T200 a time. The labelling throughout is rather technical in style, and in Russian and Kazakh only.

The eastern edge of the memorial square is bounded by the wall-like 1970s concrete bulk of the Officers' Palace. Here sits a **Museum of Military History** [126 E3] (◝ 291 0619, 291 2784; ⊕ 09.00–13.00 Mon, Wed–Fri) but it can require the most patient of military campaigns to get to visit it. Ascending the flight of steps up from the square, go to the main entrance of the block on your right-hand side. Take the corridor to the right of the entrance, and climb one floor of stairs to Room 211. You may well need to track someone down (try the floor above) to get the museum unlocked.

If the eastern side of Panfilov Park is dominated by the war memorial, and by adjacent buildings with a military past or flavour, the western side of the park is more spiritual. Its centrepiece is the remarkable **Cathedral of the Holy Ascension** [126 E3], built in 1907 by architect Andrei Zenkov during a period in which the main building material of the earthquake-wary city was wood. The cathedral reaches a height of more than 53m, making it one of the tallest wooden buildings in the world. It withstood the earthquakes of the 20th century, including the major tremor of 1910, and remained in remarkably good shape. The use of brackets rather than nails to join the beams together proved particularly inspired protection against the dangers of earthquakes. It was used as a regional historical museum during the Soviet period, but was restored to the Church following Kazakhstan's independence. The cathedral today is a confection of warm pastel shades. Its dome, covered in coloured lozenges, sits atop an octagonal drum. Four smaller domes guard it. On the western side of the cathedral stands a square-based bell tower which rises to an onion dome by way of a lozenge-covered roof. The interior offers a busy assembly of icons and frescoes, the yellow, blue and red stained glass giving a rather summery quality to the light filtering through.

Running between the Holy Ascension Cathedral and the war memorial is the **Alley of Heads of State**, lined with conifers planted by various visiting presidents.

NORTH OF PANFILOV PARK

Around the Central Mosque [126 E2] Take Pushkin Street due north from Panfilov Park, and then the first left onto Zhibek Zholy Avenue where, at the intersection with Valikhanov Street one block on, lies another of the fine buildings designed in the first years of the 20th century by A P Zenkov. This is the **Old Trade House** [126 E2] of merchant Gabdul Valiev, which now houses a textiles store. The roof is particularly fine, with its carved wooden lintel, complex series of pitches and central square-sided tower.

Back on Pushkin Street, another three blocks north you reach on your right the **Central Mosque** [126 E2], the largest in Almaty. Its main blue dome is a local landmark, the signal to drivers coming in from the airport that they are nearing the town centre. The mosque was completed in 1999 and a plaque near the east door records that it was built on the initiative and with the personal support of President Nazarbaev. It is rectangular in plan. The main dome, which tops a cylindrical drum, lies towards its western end. Small, blue-domed minarets rise from each corner. A taller minaret stands slightly apart from the main body of the minaret at the southeast corner. The overall effect is cool and calming.

One block further north, at the northern end of the tree-lined park running along the centre of Pushkin Street, stands a **Monument to the October Revolutionaries** [126 E1]. Constructed in 1967, for the 50th anniversary of the Revolution, this depicts a mix of European- and Asiatic-featured revolutionaries, proudly protecting their banner. The main threat to it now comes from the traffic pollution around the nearby Sayahat bus station.

Old Verny Some little-visited sights linked with the establishment of the old Tsarist settlement of Verny lie to the northeast of the Sayahat bus station. From the station, head east along Raiymbek Avenue. Turn left after three blocks onto Zhetysuskaya Street, and follow this main road (it's a key road out of Almaty to the towns further east) as it curves gently to the right. You encounter several stalls selling roasted chickens to passing motorists. After about ten minutes' walk, you see a mound beside the road on the right. This is a rather degraded reminder of the **Verny Fortress**, dating from 1854. A Soviet-era concrete sign here offers a short history of the fortress, largely ignoring the Tsarist period in favour of the Civil War one. You are told that units of the Red Guard were formed here in 1918 to consolidate Soviet power in the region, and that writer Dimitry Furmanov led efforts to defeat counter-revolutionary activities here in June 1920.

If you continue along the main road, which changes its name to Tatibekov Street, and then turns right into Khaliullin Street, you pass through an old part of town, still known as Malaya Stanitsa after the Cossack settlement founded here in 1861. This remains a district of attractive old single-storey wooden buildings. From Khaliullin Street, the golden domes of **Kazan Mother of God Church** are visible to the right. Dating from the 19th century, when it stood at the centre of the grid-patterned settlement of Malaya Stanitsa, this is the oldest standing church in Almaty.

Central Recreation Park (291 3719; 10.00–17.00 daily; admission T30) From Panfilov Park, head eastwards along Gogol Street. After six blocks, at the eastern end of the street, you reach the main entrance of the Central Recreation Park, marked by a curved double row of Corinthian columns. Beyond this entrance, an avenue lined by neatly tended flowerbeds leads to a golden **Statue of Maksim Gorky** [126 G3], the writer's right hand on hip in a raffishly artistic pose. The park is still known by Almaty-dwellers as Gorky Park. It is a popular place, especially on warm weekend days. The Rodina Cinema lies down the path to the north of the Gorky statue. Behind this is a large and boisterous amusement park, including an aquapark, for which a separate admission fee is charged. The lake in the northern part of the park is mostly, rather disappointingly, bereft of water. In the southern corner of the park, surrounded by a toy railway, is the Ak Bota Children's Town, featuring attractions aimed at tots. The park can be reached by taking buses 65, 94 and 166, or trolley bus 1 or 12 from the town centre.

At the far eastern end of the park, beyond the amusements, sits **Almaty Zoo** [126 G2] (*www.almatyzoo.nursat.kz;* 09.00–19.00; admission T600). The establishment of the zoo was closely associated with Murzakhan Tolebaev, who identified the site in 1935, and oversaw the stocking of the zoo, which opened in November 1937. Tolebaev was decorated for arranging the successful transportation of species from Moscow to Almaty. But, in a reminder of the harsh and fickle political climate of the late 1930s, Tolebaev, who was close to the Alash movement, was arrested by Stalin's secret police less than a month later, and executed the following year.

In something of a departure from the conservation-focused presentations of most Western zoos, one of the first attractions you reach on entering the zoo is a shooting gallery, where you aim at little model animals. You also get the opportunity to have your photograph taken holding a cockatoo, or with a snake wrapped around your neck. There is a broad range of species from around the world: staff recommended the white lion and the hippos. When I visited, a Siberian tiger prowled his cage impressively. Many of the key Kazakhstani species are represented though not, at the time of writing, a snow leopard. But the zoo has a run-down feel. Cages are rusty, and the pens constraining the bears and wolves seem agonisingly small. The zoo is particularly crowded on Sundays and public holidays.

OLD SQUARE AND AROUND A few blocks to the southwest of Panfilov Park, along a broadened stretch of Tole Bi Street, lies Old Square [126 D3], also sometimes referred to as Astana Square. This is dominated by the columned southern façade of the former House of Government, which accommodated Kazakhstan's parliament until the move of the capital to Astana, and which now houses the **Kazakh–British Technical University** [126 D3]. Each of the columns on the façade is topped by a five-pointed Soviet star sitting between Ionic swirls.

The small park to the south of the square offers a pleasant, rose-scented place to stop in summer. Its centrepiece, once a statue of Lenin, is now a monument to two Kazakh heroines of the Great Patriotic War. **Manshuk Mametova** and **Aliya Moldagulova** both posthumously received the highest military honours of the Soviet Union for their feats of bravery, the only central Asian women to be so honoured. The personality cult surrounding them has, surprisingly perhaps, not been dimmed by independence. The two girls stride purposefully to battle. Aliya, the more petite, glamorous even, her rifle slung over her shoulder, and greatcoated Manshuk, arms pounding to a silent beat. Behind them, three toddlers stand on a globe, releasing birds of peace into the sky. The park also houses two pairs of display boards, chronicling Kazakhstan's post-independence achievements, life in Almaty, and the cultural centres of the various ethnic minority groups represented in the city.

On the north side of the House of Government is another small park, stretching to the broad concrete building currently housing the Kazakhstan Stock Exchange. The path between the two buildings is lined with busts of prominent figures of the Civil War and early Soviet period, patriotism gleaming in every stone eye. An inscription on a stone in the centre of the path promises that a monument to honour the conquerors of the Virgin Lands of Kazakhstan will be constructed here. Unlikely, I think.

AROUND ST NICHOLAS'S CATHEDRAL
St Nicholas's Cathedral [126 B4] From Old Square take Tole Bi Street westwards, turning right after five blocks onto Baitursynuly Street. You will see on your left after a couple of blocks the golden onion domes of St Nicholas's Cathedral. The main tower, square in plan, is topped with five onion domes. A square-based bell tower sits to its west. The interior is covered with pastel-toned murals of biblical scenes. The Nikolsky Bazaar, which used to lie immediately to the north of the cathedral, was demolished in 2006, and nothing remains save for a few street-side stalls.

4

Baitursynuly House Museum [127 B5] (📞 *292 1089;* ⊕ *10.00–18.00 Mon–Fri, 10.00–14.00 Sat; admission T150*) A block south of the cathedral, on Baitursynuly Street, sits a yellow-walled bungalow amid well-tended grounds on the left-hand side of the road. This is the Baitursynuly House Museum. Prison apart, it was the last home of the Kazakh writer Ahmet Baitursynuly, a victim of Stalin's purges in 1938. A bust of Baitursynuly, with distinctive heavy, round-framed spectacles, stands in the garden. As a house museum it is somewhat unusual in that it contains very few original artefacts of Baitursynuly's life: little survived Stalin's terror. Instead, you are offered three rooms of photographs and photocopied documents, well laid out but with descriptions in Kazakh only, chronicling his birth in Turgai, his colleagues in the Alash movement, and his work on the Kazakh-language newspaper *Kazakh*. A room focusing on Baitursyuly's fate is modelled to hint at a prison cell. An official document records his sentence of death by firing squad. A few of the items are a little overdone: the old typewriter standing on a plinth, or the jar of earth brought from Baitursynuly's birthplace. The real pleasure of the place is that the guide showing you round may be Baitursynuly's elderly granddaughter, Ayman Baisalova. In a sad irony, she regrets that she is herself unable to speak much Kazakh, as she was largely brought up by Belarusian relatives.

Kasteyev State Arts Museum [127 A6] (*30A Satpaev St;* 📞 *247 8356, 247 6692;* f *247 8669; www.art.nursat.kz;* ⊕ *10.00–18.00 Tue–Sun, last admission 17.30, closed last day of the month; admission adult/student T250/150*) A few blocks southwest of the Baitursynuly House Museum, at the corner of Satpaev Street and Musrepov Boulevard, just opposite the Hotel Rahat, stands the Kasteyev State Arts Museum. Opened in 1976, this is the most important art museum in Kazakhstan, and was renamed in honour of Kazakh painter Abylkhan Kasteyev in 1984. A statue of Kasteyev, holding a palette and sitting in front of an empty frame, lies in the grounds. A real novelty for Kazakhstan, there is an English-language guide to the museum, sponsored by Texaco (a company more associated with a different type of oils), on sale in the lobby for T500. Unfortunately this is now of only limited value, as many of the exhibits have since been reorganised.

The ground floor of the museum is given over to carpet and handicraft sellers. Up the stairs from the lobby you first reach a hall with a pyramidal roof, often used for temporary exhibitions. On your right is a room dedicated to **Kazakh art of the 1930s and 1940s**. This features a number of canvases praising industrial progress, like Y Zaitsev's *Construction Site in Balkhash by Night* (1935), a scene of busy nocturnal labour. The following year he painted a Balkhash building site by day. L Leontiev's *Kolkhoz Bazaar* (1940) is a lively rural market scene. There are scenes of mines, factories and hard-working labourers, but also softer scenes, such as V Eifert's *On the Beach* (1938), an impressionistic summerscape of sunbathers and beach umbrellas. This room leads on to a gallery, which runs around a central courtyard. Head anticlockwise around this gallery, itself decorated with modern Kazakh painting, tapestry, ceramics and glasswork, to reach the other rooms on this floor.

The first room off the gallery to the right features **Western European art of the 16th to 19th centuries**. This is a decidedly mixed bag of works from various European countries, its origins lying in donations in the 1930s to the Kazakh State Art Gallery from the Hermitage and the Pushkin Museum of Fine Arts in Moscow to help develop a collection in Kazakhstan. One feels that they did not hand over anything that would be really missed in Moscow or St Petersburg.

The next room off the gallery is a larger hall dedicated to **Russian art of the 17th to 20th centuries**. This collection was also formed around items arriving from

Moscow and St Petersburg in the 1930s. It includes icons, and a line of portraits and busts of tsars, including F Shubin's 1771 bust of Catherine the Great, crowned with a laurel wreath. Many of the most prominent Russian artists are represented, albeit often by relatively minor pieces. Ilya Repin's *Portrait of the Editor V Bitner* (1912) depicts its twirly-moustachioed subject, editor of the *Bulletin of Knowledge*, at jovial ease behind a cluttered desk. Karl Brullov's *Portrait of V Samoilov as Hamlet*, from the 1840s, depicts the actor, hands on hips, apparently preparing to deliver a hammed-up performance. Two small canvases by Ilya Shishkin offer highly accurate, almost photographic, renderings of scenes from Russian forests. Vasily Maksimov's *Preparations for an Open Air Holiday* (1869), depicting village girls putting on their finery, was apparently discovered in the 1950s, languishing in a secondhand store in Taraz.

The next room off the gallery is **contemporary art**. E Vorobeva's sequence of photographs titled *A Winter Sublimating Object* (2001) gives a sense of this collection. A block of ice shaped like a teapot is placed on a fire and, er, melts. S Atabekov's *Super Soldier* (2005) depicts a *balbal* carrying a machine gun. Next up is **Kazakh art of the 1960s–80s**. This depicts a period of transition. There are still scenes of Soviet achievement, such as Y Yevseev's *Shymkent Phosphorous Factory* (1969), but a new openness starts to creep in. D Aliev's *Rush Hour* (1981) shows a scrum of people attempting to get onto a packed bus. And the same painter's *Family* (1984) is a delightfully intimate painting of parents feeding their two small children in a messy kitchen. A Akanayev's *The Poem about Immortality* is a full-length portrait of poet and environmental campaigner Olzhas Suleimenov, wearing a white safari suit. Many of the canvases are highly colourful: S Aitbaev's *Happiness* (1966) for example, in which a proud young Kazakh couple look confidently towards the future.

The next room goes back one step in time to **Kazakh art of the 1950s and 1960s**, the period in which an identifiable Kazakh school of painting really developed. A Cherkassy's *Dina and Zhambyl* (1946) portrays musician Dina Nurpeisova playing the *dombra* while, next to her, the elderly poet Zhambyl Zhabaev strains forward, as if in an attempt to hear her notes more clearly. Kazakh traditions are explored in several of the works. K Telzhanov's *Kokpar* (1960) is a large, lively canvas, as riders struggle to secure the goat carcass for which they are competing. A Galinbaeva's *A Cup of Kumiss* (1967) depicts both older and younger generations of Kazakh womanhood enjoying the pleasures of mare's milk. Z H Shardenov's 1960 oil painting of the Cathedral of the Holy Ascension is entitled *Central Museum of Kazakhstan*, reflecting the use to which the building was then put in the atheistic USSR.

Continuing around the gallery, the next room is a long hall devoted to the **decorative and applied art of Kazakhstan**, with a good selection of carpets, felt rugs, saddles, jewellery and decorated wooden utensils, as well as the long colourful strips and tassels with which yurts were decorated. The last room off the gallery is devoted to the **paintings of Abylkhan Kasteyev**. The man who gives his name to the gallery was born in 1904 in Zharkent District, into the family of a poor shepherd. He worked as a labourer in Zharkent and on the construction of the TurkSib Railway, but his talent for art was noticed, and he was able to study at the art studio of Russian artist N Khludov in Almaty, and later in Moscow. He is considered to be one of the founders of modern painting in Kazakhstan. The canvases on display feature a series of portraits of some of the heroes of Kazakhstan. Two depict Amangeldy Imanov, leader of the 1916 uprising, and there are portraits too of Kenesary, Zhambyl, an earnest-looking young Abai, and a contemplative Valikhanov. Other canvases portray the successes of Soviet Kazakhstan. There is a scene of celebration in a *kolkhoz*, with singing and dancing beneath a red flag; the arrival of the TurkSib Railway, with the first train cheered on by local peasants; and the hydro-electric station at Kapchagai.

The art continues upstairs. There are two collections here. **Works of the Soviet period** is basically non-Kazakhstani Soviet art. A Deyneka's *In Crimea* (1956) is a blissfully happy summer scene of holidaymakers munching through ice cream and cake in the sun. This is a far cry from P Nikonov's *Our Days* (1960), a far from blissful canvas of frozen workers riding on top of a lorry. **Oriental art of the 18th to 20th centuries** is a disparate collection of ceramics, tapestries and sculpture from China, Japan, Korea, India and Mongolia. A 19th-century Chinese vase with small boys clambering all over it is particularly charming.

KOK-TOBE 'Green Mountain' overlooks central Almaty from the southeast, a natural viewing platform for the city. Once known as Verigin, the hill was renamed Kok-Tobe in 1972, taking its new name from one found in the diaries of medieval merchants. Some 1,100m above sea level, it is topped by a television tower, a mast 327m high, built in the early 1980s, which has become one of the symbols of the city. The sausage-shaped summit of Kok-Tobe features observation balconies armed with coin-operated binoculars, a children's play area, caged birds, and various places to eat, including a restaurant comprising concrete yurts. There is an apple fountain, with water gushing out from the stalk. Throw a coin into the basin at the base of the apple, to ensure that you are very slightly poorer than when you still possessed that coin. A photo-board of 'guests of Kok-Tobe' near the fountain has pictures of celebrities enjoying the air here: Gérard Depardieu in a funny hat, President Nazarbaev and his wife, Steven Seagal in a tracksuit and Miss Universe wearing her sash.

Suitably close to the apple fountain, given their association with Apple Records, is one of the few statues of **The Beatles** to incorporate all the members of the group. Installed in 2007, it is the work of local sculptor Eduard Kazarian, and was commissioned by a group of local businessmen for whom the music of The Beatles in their youth represented an exciting alternative to the Soviet-sanctioned cultural diet. The mop-headed youths cluster around a park bench, on which John (possibly – the sculpted Fab Four faces all look rather similar) is strumming his guitar. The graffiti inscribed on the park bench include contributions from the commissioning businessmen. The path running alongside the statue now bears the name of Beatles Avenue.

The souvenir shops of Kok-Tobe are not bad: several are run by migrants from the more southerly republics of central Asia and stock handicrafts from Kyrgyzstan and Uzbekistan. There are bird boxes nailed onto most of the trees to encourage the avian fauna. Piped music also echoes out from the trees, drowning out the birdsong.

The best way to reach Kok-Tobe is by **cable car** (*operates every 15mins 11.00–midnight Mon, Wed & Thu, 11.00–01.00 Fri–Sun, 16.00–midnight Tue; T800*) from the city centre. The cable car, which started its operations in 1967, runs for 1,627m. It departs from the south side of the Republican Palace of Culture, at the intersection of Abai and Dostyk avenues, from the yellow-painted building with a 'Kok-Tobe' sign on top. It is also possible to walk or drive up, but this will take you out of the city centre: head south along Dostyk Avenue, turning left along Omarov (formerly Klochkov) Street a couple of blocks south of the Hotel Premier Alatau, and then follow the road up until you reach a barrier. If you are driving, you have to park here. A minibus makes the trip from here to the summit every five minutes (*for information ⟍ 244 7444; buses run 09.00–midnight Mon–Thu, 09.00–01.00 Fri–Sun; T300 one-way*). If you are reasonably fit, the bus is scarcely necessary: the walk back down to the car park is a pleasant 20-minute stroll. There is also a taxi stand at the car park (*call ⟍ 255 5333 if there are no taxis waiting*) if you need transport back to the city centre from here.

SUBURBAN MONUMENTS
Raiymbek Batyr Mausoleum
Along busy Raiymbek Avenue, some 3km west of the intersection with Ablai Khan Avenue, the corrugated stone tent standing on the south side of the road is the Raiymbek Batyr Mausoleum, built in 1981 to honour this 18th-century Kazakh warrior who fought the Dzhungars. It is usually locked, though Raiymbek Batyr's tomb is visible through the grilled door. Visitors sit on benches behind the mausoleum while the custodian recites a prayer. Donations are made and small pieces of bread consumed. This is a favoured port of call for wedding parties. A stone camel, shedding a tear, faces the road in front of the monument.

Lenin statues
Travellers who patrol the cities of the former Soviet Union in search of the remaining examples of the once ubiquitous statues of Lenin can find a couple in Almaty, though only in somewhat out-of-the-way locations. A couple of blocks south of the Almaty-I railway station, some 10km north of the city centre, one such statue sits in a small park at the corner of Seifullin Avenue and Sholokhov Street. This seated Lenin leans forward urgently, as if ready to make a telling political point to the passing pigeons.

The second Lenin statue is to be found behind the Saryarka Cinema, on Altynsarin Avenue, in the western part of the city, a little north of the intersection with Abai Avenue. Ironically, the area in front of the Saryarka Cinema remains today one of the sites most often stipulated by the authorities for the holding of authorised demonstrations. The cinema is set back from Altynsarin Avenue, on its western side. Walk round to the back of the cinema and you will encounter a standing statue of the goatee-bearded **Mikhail Kalinin**, left hand holding the lapel of his jacket and generally looking rather pleased with himself. The tree-lined path beyond leads you to a large, golden statue of Lenin, gesturing boldly with his right hand towards a neighbouring apartment block, his cloak slung across his left shoulder. This is Lenin at his proudest and most defiant, even in the suburban exile in which he has been placed. Next to him stands a comparatively diminutive **Frunze**, using the plinth of his statue as a podium. This revolutionary commander appears somewhat disquieted, perhaps discomfited by the fact that his neighbour is cast in so much grander a scale.

The path to the right of the Lenin statue leads through a gate in the wrought-iron fence into **Fantasy Park**, an amusement park offering mini golf, a full range of fairground rides, and a few cages housing such wildlife as goats and peacocks. Of the several places to eat here, the Kishlak Café, offering up central Asian staples to diners seated around plastic tables on a shaded terrace, is probably the best option. Groups of middle-aged men play chess and cards at tables under the trees and on warm days some fashion paper hats out of newspaper as further protection against the sun. A path to the left leads to the main entrance to the park, a turreted gate on Abai Avenue.

ILE ALATAU NATIONAL PARK
The snow-capped peaks of the Zailysky Alatau range form a glorious southern backdrop to Almaty, and at least one trip into the mountains should be included

4

in even a short visit to the city. Two valleys, those of the Malaya Almatinka and Bolshaya Almatinka rivers, are so easily accessible that they have become a natural adjunct to the urban space: Almaty-dwellers head into them every weekend, to ski, toboggan and ice skate in winter, walk and picnic in summer. This does mean that they are far from undiscovered, though the crowds quickly dissipate away from the roads. As with all trips into mountainous areas of Kazakhstan, a guide, who can be organised through one of the travel agencies listed on page 123, is strongly recommended if you are planning anything more than the most basic stroll. Be aware too of the possibility of rapidly changing weather conditions.

MALAYA ALMATINKA RIVER Dostyk Avenue, running southeastwards out of the centre of the city, turns into Gornaya Street and rises into the hills, following the valley of the little Malaya Almatinka River. This is the most straightforward route into the hills: half an hour's drive from the centre of town and you can already be at the cluster of buildings around the large open-air ice rink that marks the holiday complex of Medeu.

Medeu Medeu, some 16km out of town, is located at an attractive spot in the valley at an altitude of between 1,500m and 1,750m, among a mix of evergreens and birches standing beside the fast-flowing waters of the Malaya Almatinka. The focus of the place is the **ice rink** (⬿ *386 9552; www.medey.kz;* ⊕ *12.00–17.00 & 18.00–23.00 daily; adult/child T800/400*), a stadium of a building, with eight large floodlights, which fills the valley floor. Originally built in 1972 but fully renovated in time for the 2011 Asian Winter Games, it was a major training base for the ice skaters of the USSR, and many speed skating world records were set here. A relief on the outer wall of the building depicts two speed skaters straining for victory. Medeu is still an important centre for the training of winter sports athletes from Kazakhstan and elsewhere in the region, though from around November to April, depending on the weather, the ice rink mainly plays host to somewhat less talented city-dwellers, cautiously circling the rink to a backdrop of Russian pop music. The rink stays open until well into the evening. Skate hire costs T800 and requires a deposit of T5,000 or your driving licence. In summer, you can take to the iceless rink, for the rather less exciting prospect of roller-skating.

The other main attraction at Medeu is the **dam** across the valley, which rises up immediately to the south of the ice rink. Constructed in the 1960s by means of controlled explosions, the dam was built to protect Almaty from potentially devastating stone and mudflows precipitated by a combination of heavy rains and the rapid thawing of snow in the mountains. A mudflow following the course of the Malaya Almatinka Gorge caused havoc in 1921. The dam was called into action on 15 July 1973, when some 4.5 million cubic metres of water and debris, flooding down the gorge, were stopped short here. The dam today offers the challenge of some 830 steps from base to top, though there is at least a little café two-thirds of the way up. Most visitors, including large numbers of wedding parties at weekends, simply drive up and park at the top. The view is excellent: northwards down into Medeu, and southwards to Chimbulak and the highest peaks of the Zailysky Alatau. At weekends, you can even have yourself photographed in the company of a slightly lethargic golden eagle, if that is what takes your fancy.

Medeu is so close to town that there is no need to stay here, but Kazakhstan's hosting of the 2011 Asian Winter Games was the perfect opportunity to update the facilities and open new hotels. The 155 Radisson Blu Hotel (due to open early in 2012) will no doubt become the luxury option. At very much at the other end of the scale is the **Hotel Medeu** (✆ 271 6210; $), which is located on the side of the ice rink, and entered from the rink itself. You may find that most of your fellow guests are professional winter sports athletes from across the region, staying in Medeu to train. Ring ahead, as the hotel is sometimes fully booked with these future sports stars. Breakfast is not included in the price of these basic rooms. It is worth paying an extra T500 to get an (admittedly shabby) en-suite shower and toilet, and a balcony.

The cafés clustered around the ice rink are uninspiring and overpriced. The best place to eat in Medeu is the **Kazakh Aul** (*586 Gornaya St;* ✆ *271 6417;* $$$). This offers an excellent, reasonably priced range of Kazakh and central Asian dishes, from horse *beshbarmak* to *manty*. The 'banquet menu' is a full Kazakh meal, from horsemeat sausage to Eastern sweets. The exoticism of the yurts available here is perhaps dented by the corrugated metal roofing they are housed under. You can also eat at tables on a terrace offering a fine view across the valley to the ice rink. To get here, take the left turn just before the main road from Almaty bends to the right on its final approach to the ice rink, and follow the signs to 'Kazakh Aul'.

Medeu is one of the few places in the Ile Alatau National Park which is easy to reach by public transport. Bus 6, which can be picked up along Dostyk Avenue at stops from the Hotel Kazakhstan southwards, will bring you here. At weekends, it changes its name to 6A, and charges extra for the same trip: T65 instead of the usual T40. Medeu is the end of the line. Taxis and minibuses wait here, ready to take you up to the Chimbulak ski resort.

Chimbulak The road twists more steeply up the gorge south of the dam, reaching after a further 4km the ski resort of Chimbulak, the best-developed winter sports venue in Kazakhstan. The origins of the resort lay in the post-war Soviet desire to develop a centre for downhill skiing, and the first Soviet downhill skiing championships were held here in 1950. The facilities have been considerably expanded over the last few years, and Kazakhstan will likely make a bid to host the Winter Olympics here in 2018. Improvements include the construction of a 4.5km gondola from Medeu to Chimbulak, new chairlifts and an upgrading of the restaurants at the resort.

Around the large car park, at an altitude of 2,260m, are scattered the few buildings of the resort (✆f 259 6867, 267 2541; e *chimbulaksr@mail.ru; www. shymbulak.com*. A sequence of three chairlifts takes you up from here to the Talgar Pass, at 3,163m, and a newer chairlift rises separately to 2,785m, to the head of trails used by snowboarders and expert skiers (⊕ *10.00–17.00*). Full-day and half-day passes are available for T5,000 or T2,500. The ski season runs roughly from November to April, with weekdays considerably quieter than weekends. Equipment hire and instruction are available: instructors at the site include former Olympian Aleksandr Artemenko. Ski hire costs T1,200–4,000 per day and snowboards start at T1,000 for a day.

The **Hotel Chimbulak** (*55 rooms;* ✆ *233 8624, 233 2623;* f *233 8082; chimbulak@ nursat.kz;* $$$–$$$$) at the heart of the resort is a comfortable enough if somewhat tired-looking mid-range place, with en suites in all rooms, though the standard rooms are nothing special, and breakfast is not included in the room rates. The circular building adjacent to the hotel houses a passable restaurant. Room rates increase significantly in January.

Tuyuk-Su Gates From Chimbulak, the road continues up the gorge, though deteriorating to a stony track after about 1km. A further 1km on brings you to the isolated but charming **Hotel Vorota Tuyuk-Su** (*26 rooms;* ✆ *264 0325, 254 1648;*

e *info@alpina.kz; www.alpina.kz;* **$$$**, *with their 'VIP cottages', sleeping up to 8, in the luxury price bracket*). Part of the Alpina XXI organisation, which runs several alpine chalet-style mountain hotels in the Zailysky Alatau, this stylishly furnished place features a number of photographs of President Nazarbaev in mountain gear, a T-shirt depicting the writer Abai visible beneath his open tracksuit. These were taken in 1995 during the president's ascent of the mountain peak named after Abai. The cliffs known here as the Tuyuk-Su Gates are a starting point for guided treks to the higher reaches of the valley, including to the Tuyuk-Su Glacier at its head. Breaches to the seasonal lake formed by melt-water from this glacier pose a major flood risk to Almaty, which the dam at Medeu was built to protect.

BOLSHAYA ALMATINKA RIVER The other heavily used route up into the Zailysky Alatau follows the course of the Bolshaya Almatinka River. Head south at the roundabout on Al Farabi Avenue, where this intersects with Navoi Street. A large monumental gate here marks the entrance to a somewhat bleak arboretum. The road leads southwards along the Alma Arasan Gorge, past elite suburban villas, reaching, after about 5km, a stretch dominated by *shashlik*-focused open-air restaurants, most offering loud music and concrete dance floors. City-dwellers flock here on warm evenings. The quality of the food on offer is not high, but this is not the selling point of the restaurants. The **Karlyagash** (\ *269 1537;* $$$), on the right-hand side of the road, is typical of the bunch. Some 7km from the roundabout the road passes a dam, built in the late 1940s by Japanese prisoners of war. A few hundred metres further on, a barrier across the road marks the entrance to the national park (*T200*).

Sunkar Falcon Centre About 100m beyond the barrier marking the entrance to the national park, on the right-hand side of the road, stands the **Sunkar Falcon Centre** (\ *255 3076;* m *+7 701 736 0827; admission T200*). This place (also known as the Sunkar Raptor Sanctuary) was originally established to protect the saker falcon, whose numbers dropped alarmingly following the break-up of the USSR, with the development of the sale of these birds to the Middle East, where they are highly prized for hunting. It has now expanded to encompass a wide range of birds of prey, including even vultures and lammergeyers, housed in lines of cages set amidst elegantly manicured lawns. Larger birds, such as owls and eagles, stand on wooden posts beneath a corrugated roof, their tethers allowing them only to fly to another post a few metres away. More birds of prey fly more freely in a large fenced enclosure, with a net for a roof. There are also lines of cages occupied by *tazys* and other hunting dogs.

Paying the admission charge allows you to walk around the centre, but it is more instructive to attend one of their bird displays (⊕ *Apr–Nov 17.00 Tue–Sun; US$20*). Several birds are exhibited, usually including falcons, an eagle owl and a white-tailed eagle, with the demonstration encompassing hunting techniques.

Tersbutak Valley Some 300m on from the national park entrance, a turning to the left takes you up a side valley, alongside the stream known as Tersbutak. After 7km along a pot-holed tarmac road you reach the secluded **Kumbel Hotel** (*17 rooms;* \f *237 9226, 237 9227;* e *kumbel@asdc.kz; www.kumbel.com;* **$$$$**). This hotel is laid out in imitation Swiss-chalet style, with the walls covered in a log-effect finish. There are hearty wooden tables and chairs in the dining room and a fireplace in the corner. It has an indoor swimming pool, the bar next to which is called the Shocking Blue Bar, presumably in homage to 1970s Dutch pop groups. The place is in a great setting amidst birch trees, at the foot of steeper hills covered with evergreen forest. A ski lift runs up the hillside behind the hotel, offering a 400m ski run. The hotel can organise horse rental at T3,000 per hour, and quad bikes at a whopping T13,500 an hour. They charge a similarly high T15,000 for airport transfers, and T3,000 for transfers into the centre of Almaty.

The Tersbutak Valley is a starting point for onward hiking to an upland pasture known as Kok-Jailau, which lies between the Bolshaya Almatinka and Malaya Almatinka valleys and, for the experienced, to the double summit of the 3,618m Kumbel Peak.

Tau Dastarkhan On the left-hand side of the road, 1km or so into the national park, lies the restaurant and resort complex of **Tau Dastarkan** (*270 5729, 270 5646, 275 9140; www.tau-dastarkhan.kz; $$$$*). Well-heeled Almaty-dwellers head here in their Toyota 4x4s for summer weekend lunches at one of the selection of themed restaurants. The fast-flowing stream of the Bolshaya Almatinka makes for a very attractive setting, the food is of a high quality and this can be an enjoyable, if somewhat artificial, place to come. The restaurants on offer include the **Gorniy**, decorated like a large hunting lodge, its interior replete with furs, stuffed animals and even hunting rifles. Game is, predictably, heavily featured on the central European-themed menu. The **Avlabar** is Georgian, all heavy wooden furniture and fake vines scaling the pillars holding up the hide-decorated roof. Georgian wine is served in terracotta cups. The **Terem** is Russian, a bright pine chalet. The **Zheruik** offers traditional Kazakh fare, while the **Djazdik** is an open-air restaurant offering Kazakh and international dishes amidst the trees. The complex also includes the rather plush **Tau Spa Centre**, with saltwater swimming pools, the **Tau Disco Nightclub** (⊕ *22.00–05.00 Thu–Sun*), which promises the only foam-filled dance floor in Kazakhstan, and cages housing wolves, deer and geese.

Also within the complex is the well-maintained **Hotel Tau House** (*53 rooms;* *270 5729, 270 5646, 275 9140;* f *275 9141;* e *info@tauhouse.kz; www.tauhouse.kz;* **$$$$$**). The rooms, which have a pleasant pine feel, are located in paired terraced cottages laid out around a central courtyard, with the pricier options featuring leather sofas, wide-screen television and real fires. Airport transfers are available for a steep T15,000. Breakfast is not included in the room rate.

Sheber Aul Some 500m further up the valley the road forks. Straight on lies the Prokhodnaya Gorge and the sanatorium of Alma Arasan. The road to the left, signposted to the 'Kosmostantsiya', continues along the course of the Bolshaya Almatinka River. Looking to your left at this junction you will see, on the high ground on the other side of the stream, a collection of somewhat run-down apartment blocks. This is the village of Kokshoky, originally built by the prisoners of war constructing the nearby dam. It is the rather unpromising-looking home of the artisans' community of Sheber Aul, set up in the late Soviet period by the Culture Ministry of the Kazakhstan Soviet Socialist Republic in a bid to revive traditional Kazakh handicrafts. Some 50 craftspeople and their families live here and produce, from workshops mostly based in their own homes, the souvenirs on sale in places like TsUM in Almaty. The families of Sheber Aul produce silver jewellery, whips, little felt yurts, pointy-toed carpet slippers, mock 18th-century weaponry, leather paintings of Kazakh folk heroes and bottles for holding *kumiss*. The prices quoted here are markedly cheaper than those you will pay in Almaty stores: the objects, though, are no less kitsch.

There have been periodic attempts to set this place up as a more attractive tourist destination, but these have foundered. A visitor centre, established with financial support from one of the oil companies, lies idle, the victim of management disputes among the community.

Around the Big Almaty Lake From the junction outside Kokshoky, take the left-hand turning towards 'Kosmostantsiya'. The quality of the road soon starts to deteriorate, and a 4x4 is advised if you plan to go much further than for a picnic along the lower reaches of the stream. Around 7km from the junction, the road passes the GES-1 hydro-electric station. From here, a large metal water pipe leads straight up the valley to the Big Almaty Lake. The walk alongside and, on flatter stretches, on top of the pipe is a popular excursion. Along the initial, steepest, part of the walk, metal steps run next to the pipe.

The road from this point becomes much steeper. Some 5km further on is a good accommodation option if you plan to overnight in this attractive valley, the **Hotel Alpine Rose** (*12 rooms;* 264 0325, 254 1648; e *info@alpina.kz; www.alpina.kz;* **$$$**). Another place in the Alpina XXI Group, this offers rooms of varying quality in three cottages decorated with a combination of timbers and pink paint (perhaps described on the tin as 'alpine rose'?). The pleasant restaurant is decorated with skis, ice axes and crampons.

After another 4km you reach the **Big Almaty Lake**, nestling in a hollow at 2,500m, surrounded by snow-capped peaks. Frozen for several months, the colour of the lake in the warmer months varies according to the season, but at its best, usually in autumn, it is a lush turquoise, a peacock amongst lakes. The 'big' label comes from the name of the stream on which it sits, the Big Almaty River (Bolshaya Almatinka), not as a commentary on the size of the lake itself, which is a somewhat modest 1.6km by 1km. On a fine day, however, this is one of the most beautiful places in all Kazakhstan. It's a great place for a picnic, though you will be far from alone here on sunny summer weekends. A side track to the left just before you reach the lake is the start of the difficult mountain track to Issyk Kul in Kyrgyzstan.

Continuing along the 'main' road beyond the Big Almaty Lake, you see on your right after a further 1.5km the astronomical observatory known by its Russian-language acronym **GAISH**. This is a real jumble of buildings and equipment, some long disused: satellite dishes, domed observatory buildings, and cosmos-directed metal devices which look just like ray guns out of a stock 1930s Hollywood sci-fi movie. It is possible to spend the night here in the observatory's very basic accommodation block (*276 2167, 221 1144; €15pp for accommodation, plus €15pp FB*). Toilets and showers are shared. Lectures are also offered: phone for details.

The road continues winding upwards another 5.5km to the **Kosmostantsiya**, another jumble of buildings forming a semi-abandoned research facility, in this case of the Lebedev Physics Institute for the Study of Cosmic Rays and the National Ionospheric Institute. The Kosmostantsiya is located at an altitude of 3,300m, at the Jusaly-Kezen Pass.

5

The Southeast

The southeastern corner of Kazakhstan, the area of present-day Almaty Region, is known popularly as the 'seven rivers': Zhetisu in Kazakh, or Semirechie in Russian. The name alludes to the many watercourses running across the region from the mountain ranges of the south and east, draining into Lake Balkhash, which runs along the northern edge of the region like a curving cap.

This is a region of great tourist potential, offering a wide range of day trips from Almaty as well as more substantial expeditions. The Tian Shan Mountains, running along the southern edge of the region along the border with Kyrgyzstan, offer beautiful gorges, lakes and glaciers, as well as archaeological sites in their foothills such as Esik, the place of discovery of the Scythian Golden Man, which has become a symbol of independent Kazakhstan. To their north, the Altyn Emel National Park offers the chance to see herds of goitered gazelle and central Asian wild ass, as well as the musical attractions of the 'singing sand dune'. Further north, in a part of the region less frequented by tourists, you will find the undemonstrative regional capital of Taldykorgan and the little-trekked Dzhungarsky Alatau range. There are impressive petroglyph sites right across the region, the best known being that of Tamgaly, west of Almaty. And the region throws up a good number of quirkier places to visit, including the impressive if artificial set from the film *Nomad* on the Ile River and, at Ungirtas, the Hub of the Universe. It is possible that Taraz, to the east of the Zhambyl Region, is the most ancient of the regional capitals of Kazakhstan, with some fine monuments of the Karakhanid era, including the exquisite Mausoleum of Aisha Bibi.

WEST OF ALMATY

The modern highway to Bishkek runs westwards from Almaty. To the south runs the line of the Zailysky Alatau Mountains, behind them Kyrgyzstan, their height gradually decreasing as you head to the west. To the north begins the expanse of the great steppes of Kazakhstan. This area contains many excellent options for day trips from Almaty or stops to make the journey to Bishkek a more leisurely one.

AKSAI GORGE The Ile Alatau National Park, which runs roughly 120km from west to east, encloses the highest peaks of the Zailysky Alatau range. Much of the area of the park is located to the south (see page 153) and east (see page 166) of Almaty, but there are some attractive areas to explore to the southwest of the city too. These are accessed along a procession of gorges running south to north. The closest to Almaty, and one of the most attractive, is the Aksai Gorge.

To get here, head westwards from Almaty along the road which passes through the village of Kamenka, which has now become in effect a western suburb of the

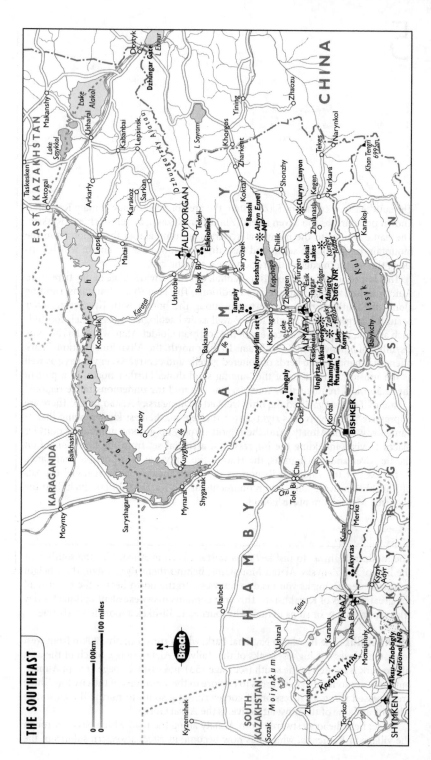

THE SOUTHEAST

N

Bradt

0 — 100km
0 — 100 miles

city. Turn left at the crossroads in Kamenka village, and then right 1km on, to resume the westwards direction. After another 4km you cross the Aksai River. Turn left down the side road immediately beyond the garage on your left, signposted to the 'Hotel Faraon'. After another 2km a barrier marks the entrance to the Ile Alatau National Park (admission T200). The road continues up into the attractive wooded Aksai Gorge, alongside the fast-flowing Aksai River. This is a popular spot for weekend picnickers from the city, and there are a number of picnic sites laid out in the valley, one bearing the sponsorship of Chevron Texaco. There are good hiking opportunities here, including to a small monastery.

The **Bolshoya Almatinka Valley** is also within the Ile Alatau National Park. If you trek 15km along the river you reach the picturesque Bolshoe Almatinskoe lake, which is the starting point of many treks into Kyrgyzstan. The lake itself is 1.6km long, and it remains frozen from November to June, though the water takes on an unusual and attractive turquoise tinge once the melt-water has drained away.

A 40-minute walk west of the lake brings you to the **Tian Shan Astronomical Observatory** (\ 252092; e kurt@tsao.south-capital.kz; admission T500), often still referred to by its Soviet-era acronym GAISH. For more information, see *Chapter 4, page 158*.

USH KONYR Taking the main Bishkek road out of Almaty, the village of **Shamalgan** is signposted to the left around 17km beyond the western outskirts of the city. It is reached after 6km. This village was the childhood home of the future president, Nursultan Nazarbaev. Continue through the village on a rough road twisting up into the mountains. After around 11km you reach a large upland plateau, where herds of horses canter across the undulating ground. This is **Ush Konyr**, the mountain pastures of Nazarbaev's youth, about which the president contributed the lyrics of a song of this title, performed by a Kazakhstani boy band named MuzArt. The edge of the Ush Konyr Plateau is a favoured spot for paragliding: the Central Asia Open Cup has been held here. The road heads across the Ush Konyr Plateau, but you are abruptly stopped after 5km by a sign indicating that the land beyond is private property into which entry is not permitted.

ZHAMBYL MUSEUM AND MAUSOLEUM (⊕ summer 09.00–19.00; winter 09.00–17.00; admission T200) A small village now bearing the name of Zhambyl contains the house where the great Kazakhstani poet and improvising musician Zhambyl Zhabaev (see box, page 162) spent the last years of his life, as well as his mausoleum.

To get here, take the Bishkek road west from Almaty. Turn left onto a road signposted for 'Uzunagash', which sits just beyond a police checkpoint some 45km beyond the edge of the city. After another 6km, you reach a Y-shaped junction in the little town of **Uzunagash**. The left-hand fork takes you straight to a grand equestrian statue of **Karasai Batyr**, a 17th-century warrior, depicted lance aloft and ready for battle. For the Zhambyl Museum though take the right-hand fork. After 11km the road forks again, a sign marked 'Jambyl's Museum' and a relief of the poet direct you to turn left. The village of Zhambyl is reached after a further 2km. Drive through the village, passing a brightly domed modern mosque, to reach the complex housing the Zhambyl Museum and his mausoleum at the end of the road.

You are greeted by a bust of Zhambyl, behind which lies the smart single-storey house in which Zhambyl spent the last years of his life, and which now houses his museum. The building, with an arch over the entrance supported by four square columns, was given to Zhambyl in 1938. The poet lived with members of his family in the rooms to the left of the entrance hall; the rooms to the right were occupied by his literary assistant. The hall is a riot of stucco. Zhambyl's rooms have been preserved: his bedroom and that of his grandchildren; his study, with a wall carpet portraying the leader of the 1916 uprising Amangeldy Imanov; a room for entertaining guests; and most tellingly, his infirmary. Medical staff were always on call. To the right of the hall, the rooms are now laid out with displays about Zhambyl's life and works, though the labelling is only in Kazakh. These displays include extracts from his poetry, gifts from other musicians, and a display about his mentor, Suyunbay Aronov, including a painting of Suyunbay, with shaven head, long white beard and imploring eyes. A modern extension, added in 1996, contains a conference room and more displays, including personal items such as a pair of Zhambyl's glasses, copies of his works, and the awards given to him by the Soviet authorities. A small art gallery contains paintings of the elderly poet sitting

ZHAMBYL

Zhambyl Zhabaev was to become renowned as one of Kazakhstan's great improvising musicians, or *akyns*. In the early 1860s, the young Zhambyl came under the tutelage of a well-known *akyn* named Suyunbay Aronov. Zhambyl developed his skills, and his reputation grew. He knew by heart colossal works such as the Kyrgyz *Epic of Manas*, and composed works of his own, describing the treasures of the Zhetisu region and the exploits of Kazakh heroes such as Utegen Batyr. At a musical competition, an *aitys*, in Verny in 1913, convened in honour of the 300th anniversary of the reign of the Romanov Dynasty, he chose to sing about the corruption of local officials rather than in praise of the Romanovs, and his distaste for the Tsarist rule was also demonstrated by his support for the 1916 uprising, for which he composed works such as *The Black Decree*. He embraced the ideals of the Russian Revolution, and was to become strongly supportive of the Soviet leadership.

In May 1936, he took part in a festival of Kazakh literature and art in Moscow, receiving the award of the Order of the Red Banner of Labour at the end of the month. He made further visits to Moscow, praised the Stalinist leadership in verse, and received more awards. On the outbreak of war, he took up the campaign of the defence of the homeland against Nazism, contributing in September 1941 the poem for which he became best known across the USSR as a whole, *People of Leningrad, My Children*. He died in 1945, at the age of 99.

Most surviving photographs of Zhambyl depict the face of a wizened, white-bearded sage beneath a succession of fur hats. But although he is remembered broadly positively, there is a certain ambivalence about the attitude of many Kazakhstanis towards him, in which the tales of the heroism of Kazakh *batyrs* and poetic encapsulations of the beauty of the landscapes of the Zhetisu are offset by all that praise of Stalin. Some argue that the fact the hagiographic pieces praising the Soviet authorities are written in a good poetic Russian, with no trace of any Kazakh-language original text, suggests that Zhambyl may not actually have been the author of pieces put out in his name towards the end of his long life. This ambivalence is perhaps demonstrated by the fact that Zhambyl's name is still used for that of the region to the west of Almaty Region, but that its capital city, which was also called Zhambyl in Soviet times, has now been reallocated one of its earlier names, Taraz.

smilingly amongst children, or playing his *dombra* on a windswept mountainside. Zhambyl's car, given to the poet in the late 1930s, is still kept in the garage near the house. Zhambyl's house gives a sense of an elderly man being kept alive by the Soviet authorities in order to churn out pro-regime poetry.

From the entrance of the complex, a shady path running to the left of the house, along which have been placed stones bearing inscriptions by or about Zhambyl, takes you to his octagonal turquoise-domed **mausoleum**. There is a simple stone tomb, standing beneath a domed ceiling decorated with tiles bearing elaborate floral motifs. Four arched windows, decorated with golden latticework, let in the light. On the exterior of the building, more floral tiles enliven a curtain of arches running around the walls. Sculptures at the entrance include a big cat, *dombra*, *kopyz* and saddle.

A short path leads from here to the tomb of another musician, **Nurgisa Tlendiev**, who created, in 1980, the Otrar Sazy ensemble, which aimed to use traditional Kazakh instruments and techniques of musicianship in a contemporary context. A statue of the dinner-jacketed Tlendiev shows him standing theatrically, brandishing his *dombra*. A minaret stands behind him, while two swans take flight to his side.

UNGIRTAS A small hill just beyond the unremarkable village of Ungirtas is one of the most intriguing places in Kazakhstan for here, the faithful believe, is the hub of the universe, through which passes a rich stream of cosmic energy.

To get here, head west on the Bishkek road. Some 23km beyond the Uzunagash turning, take the left-hand turning signposted for 'Ungirtas'. You reach Ungirtas village after a further 6km. Taking a right turn in the village, you come to a green hill lying just to the left of the road, after a further 1.5km. The hill is your destination, but your first stop should be the corrugated iron-roofed building on the other side of the road to meet the elderly dervish from Turkestan, Bifatima Dauletova, who uncovered the cosmic secrets of the hill in 1999.

She describes the place, somewhat wordily, as the Aydarli Aydanar Ata Ayman-Sholpan Spiritual Health Centre, a place of the two-way passage of energy between heaven and mother earth, like a cosmic umbilical cord. She explains that humanity is just starting to become mature enough to accept and understand the 'secret knowledge' of reincarnation, knowledge which was traditionally guarded by dragons. This centre is one of the places at which this knowledge can be taught. She and her colleagues are trying to get together the funding to construct a mosque on the site, and a 'Hidden World' Museum of Secret Knowledge. She will show visitors around the simple building. Its walls are covered with her intricate drawings, as well as posters of holy places, such as the Khodja Ahmed Yassaui Mausoleum in Turkestan. Steps lead down to a complex of rock-hewn underground rooms. There is a small mosque, its walls covered with posters of Mecca and, for some reason, one of the Arc de Triomphe. Two other rooms serve as basic overnight accommodation for visitors to the complex. These are decorated with textile screens, covered with drawings by Bifatima, which are said to emit healing energy. In the courtyard outside the building, Bifatima then delivers a benediction to those about to climb the hill. During my visit, this process involved her pouring water over my hands, and then head. She beckoned me to face her, and with a flourish launched a ladleful of water at my face. She asked for my wallet, blew into it, then extracted a note from it, which she folded up. She placed wallet and folded note between my outstretched hands, and then slapped these together, to ensure that I would be wealthy. With slightly sore hands.

On summer weekends the small hill is often packed with visitors. The first port of call on the hillside is marked by two sticks, covered in votive scraps of material, which delimit an energy gate. If one of Bifatima's assistants is around, they will tell you to face the gate, with your hands raised. They note how easy it is to push forward through the air, while pulling back encounters more resistance. Turning around, facing away from the gate, it appears more difficult to push forward, while the air seems to encourage you to pull back. This, they claim, demonstrates the direction of energy flow through the gate. The path continues up and round the hill, passing numerous rocks and cave entrances, all of which are ascribed different healing and energising properties. 'What's this rock good for?' a visitor asks one of Bifatima's assistants. 'Feel it for yourself, and find out.' You are advised to lie back against a vertical stone, and allow its energy to conduct a cleansing process. The instructions from the Spiritual Health Centre get quite precise. A rest of between ten and 20 minutes against the vertical stone is advised (five to ten minutes in winter), with no more than five people leaning against the rock at any one time. In winter, allow a 30-minute break between visitors to allow the energy levels of the rock to re-accumulate.

At the summit of the hill, a standing stone marks the belly button of the world. This is the place through which energy is believed to funnel from cosmos to earth. You are advised to lie on your back around 4m from the stone for a period of between five and seven minutes. Ask for your soul to be cleansed and the energy passing through your body will take from you everything negative, everything hindering you in life, and cast it deep into the ground. A longer exposure here, say the staff of the Spiritual Health Centre, helps combat high blood pressure, asthma, even small tumours.

A smaller reddish-coloured obelisk nearby marks the centre of the energy current moving in the opposite direction, from mother earth to the cosmos. The energy you receive here, like a mother's milk, is said to strengthen and immunise. A stay of ten to 20 minutes here is recommended for those in generally poor health, children and the elderly. But the staff warn that, should you start to feel any unpleasant sensations near either of these energy conduits, you should leave the area immediately.

TAMGALY Situated in a group of hills running north of the line of the Zailysky Alatau, between the Chu and Ile rivers, Tamgaly, from the Kazakh word *tamga*, meaning 'clan sign', is one of the most impressive of the many petroglyph sites in Kazakhstan (see box, opposite). Discovered in the 1950s by the archaeologist Anna Maksimova, it was recognised as a UNESCO World Heritage Site in 2004, and its main petroglyph clusters are now well signposted.

To get here, take the Bishkek road westwards from Almaty. Some 100km to the west of the capital, 6km beyond the village of Targap, take a road heading north, signposted to 'Kopa'. After 25km you cross over the railway at the small settlement of Kopa. Keep heading northwards for another 39km, until a sign to the left pointing to 'Tanbaly' directs you a few hundred metres down a dirt track to the entrance to the site (admission T200). A map at the small car park directs you to five numbered petroglyph clusters, located along both sides of a gentle valley, wherever there are outcrops of flat, exposed rock. Your route around the valley is guided by arrows and 'stop' signs; signs bearing little drawings of snakes alert you to one of the potential hazards of the area.

There are more than 4,000 petroglyphs at Tamgaly. While they cover a long period (modern contributions include a horse's head complete with bridle and even an aeroplane), most of the petroglyphs date from the Bronze Age and early Iron Age. Rock faces are packed with images of deer, some with distinctive branched antlers, bulls, dogs and hunters. Some are very beautiful, such as a petroglyph featuring an embossed cow design inside a larger cow figure which has been pecked out from the rock. Most remarkable of all are the 'sun-headed' figures for which Tamgaly is particularly known. These typically consist of humanoid stick-like figures, with huge round heads. One of these has a certain resemblance to an enormous gooseberry. Another head involves a series of concentric circles around a central 'eye', baubles dangling from the circles. A third head consists of circles of dots. Below this third head is a line of little human figures, like bunting, which appear to be captured in mid-dance.

From the car park, a separate track to the right leads behind a low hillock to some fenced Bronze Age burials. One, for example, features four graves, each lined with large stone slabs, surrounded by an outer ring of stones.

PETROGLYPHS IN KAZAKHSTAN

Petroglyphs are forms of rock art which refer to images created by removing part of the surface of a rock, including by carving, abrasion, pecking and gouging. They are quite different from pictograms, 'cave paintings', which are images drawn or painted onto the rock surface. Kazakhstan offers a huge number of petroglyphs, which are found in many parts of the country, but with a particularly high concentration in the Zhetisu region. Here, petroglyphs are found on a remarkably large number of the potentially suitable surfaces: smooth rock with a metallic patina, close to places then inhabited by humans. The earliest petroglyphs found in Kazakhstan appear to date from the Aeneolithic period, but they reached a particularly high level of development in the Bronze and early Iron ages. Later examples are also found, including carved religious inscriptions and human figures carrying rifles, but the arrival in the medieval period of both paper as a medium of communication, and Islam, with its strictures against the representation of living creatures, led to a sharp decline in the importance of the form.

Petroglyph sites in Kazakhstan are often found close to other archaeological sites, including settlements and burial grounds, whether Bronze Age stone coffins or Iron Age *kurgans*. The petroglyphs of the Bronze Age tend to be pecked out in a relatively realistic style, with thick-bodied figures and a wide choice of subject matter, including many species of animal, as well as humans shown hunting, riding and dancing. From the Middle Bronze Age, these are accompanied by a number of more complex and symbolic designs, such as 'sun-headed' or 'mirror-headed' human figures. Early Iron Age petroglyphs of the Saka period tend to be more stylised two-dimensional images, focusing on a smaller range of subjects, with large numbers of deer and archers on horseback. The style of the petroglyphs often mirrors that of the beautiful Saka golden jewellery: a curly-horned deer with its legs tucked under its body is a typical image of this period. Iron Age petroglyphs of four-legged animals often only depict two of the legs, the others deemed 'hidden' in the two-dimensional image, while Bronze Age petroglyphs tend to show all four.

The petroglyphs of Kazakhstan offer many insights into the world of their creators. Some of the species depicted are no longer to be found in the region, such as cheetahs. Scenes of hunting and dancing offer information about Bronze Age daily life. Scenes depicting sexual relations between men and goats offer perhaps a little too much information.

To the east of Almaty the mountains of the Zailysky Alatau reach their highest points: a long sequence of peaks above 4,600m, with the highest of them the bulky Mount Talgar, which may or may not top 5,000m (its height is variously quoted as 4,973m and 5,017m) but which, either way, is taller than Mont Blanc. The name of the range, which forms part of the Tian Shan system, is a mix of Russian and Kazakh: 'Alatau' in Kazakh refers to the multi-coloured character of the mountains, while the Russian-language prefix 'Zailysky' ('beyond the Ile'), refers to the range lying on the far side, from the perspective of Tsarist Russia, of the Ile River. The area was explored in the 1850s by the Russian geographer Pyotr Semyonov, whose research led him to disprove the theory of one of his teachers, Alexander Humboldt, that the Tian Shan Mountains were volcanic in origin. In 1906, on the 50th anniversary of the first of Semyonov's expeditions to this then little-known area, the Tsar decreed that Semyonov and his descendants had the right to add to their surname the name of the mountain range he had done so much to uncover, and Semyonov became Semyonov-Tianshansky.

The Ile Alatau National Park, established in 1996, covers the northern slopes of the Zailysky Alatau along a 120km stretch from the Shamalgan River west of Almaty to the Turgen River to the east. The crest of the range marks the southern boundary of the park. The areas of the park to the west and south of Almaty are described elsewhere (pages 159 and 153, respectively). The stretch to the east is accessed along roads running southwards along the floors of mountain valleys from a line of small agricultural towns at the foothills of the range: Talgar, Esik and Turgen.

The vegetation belts start with broadleaved forests in the lowland areas, with wild apple trees reminding of the claims of the Tian Shan to be the birthplace of the apple, as well as the apricot, aspen, birch, rowan and hawthorn. With increasing altitude the Schrenk spruce takes centre stage, sometimes accompanied by pine and birch, the trees gradually thinning out to isolated stands of Schrenk spruce, mountain ash and juniper. Among the mammals found in these mountains are deer, wild boar, fox and badger, along with rare species such as the Tian Shan brown bear, central Asian lynx, red wolf, stone marten, and that emblem of Kazakhstan the snow leopard.

TALGAR Some 23km beyond the eastern outskirts of Almaty, the small town of Talgar is the gateway to the **Almaty State Nature Reserve**, administered separately from the Ile Alatau National Park, in which it sits like a cuckoo in the nest. The reserve has a stricter regime than the national park and a permit is required to enter. The history of the reserve dates from 1931, with the designation of part of the basin of the Malaya Almatinka River. The reserve oscillated in size, before being abolished altogether in 1950. It was re-established in 1960, now centred on the Talgar section of the Zailysky Mountains. The reserve covers the stretch between the gorge of the Levy Talgar River to the west and the ridge between the Esik and Turgen rivers to the east. Across more than 70,000ha it covers some of the most dramatic scenery of the Zailysky range, including Mount Talgar itself. Some 30% of the territory of the reserve is covered by glaciers, including the 11km-long Korzhenevsky Glacier, and the Bogatyr Glacier, which stretches close to 10km. These in turn provide the source of the water for the rivers flowing north, whose gorges, including those of the Levy (Left), Sredny (Middle) and Pravy (Right) Talgar rivers, contribute much to the beauty of the reserve.

The nature reserve is a haven for birds, and birdwatchers can expect to see a wide range of species, including Himalayan and Cinereous vultures, three varieties of redstarts, fire-fronted serins and numerous finches. There are also ibisbills, sulphur-bellied warblers and yellow-billed choughs.

To get here, turn right in the town of Talgar along the road signposted to 'Stary Zamok'. A further 2km on your right, stands the building housing the **reserve headquarters** (*727 742 3656, 727 295 6386*), where information about permits can be obtained. There is also a stuffed animal-centred museum here with around 3,000 dusty exhibits. An anti-mudflow dam straddles the valley after another 3km, followed after a further 1.5km by a checkpoint bringing you into the Ile Alatau National Park (admission T200). This is quickly followed by a further checkpoint, marking the entrance to the Almaty State Nature Reserve, where your permit will be checked. Almaty-based travel agencies specialising in trekking and mountaineering (see page 123) should be able to organise permits and a guide for those interested in trekking in the reserve, though an ascent of Mount Talgar is an undertaking for experienced mountaineers only.

Where to stay There are several mountain retreat-type places around Talgar, often catering to wealthier Almaty-dwellers in search of a weekend away from the city smog. At the time of research, the Akbulak Club Resort was under construction and was due to open in stages from 2012 onwards. The resort will include a five-star hotel, a four-star ski lodge, two golf courses and almost 1,800 villas.

Ak Bulak Mountain Resort (63 rooms) Soldatskoye Gorge; ⟍(727) 259 9490, 259 9491; f (727) 259 9492. Lying in an attractive spot at the mouth of the Soldatskoye Gorge, at the foot of the forested uplands, Ak Bulak caters to a wealthy 'new Kazakh' clientele. Built to a vaguely alpine design with a series of pitched roofs, the place offers a wide range of leisure pursuits, with tennis & basketball courts & a football pitch laid out on terraces, an indoor pool, & rental of quad bikes (T10,000/hr). The resort lies at 1,600m. A cable car behind it, followed by a further ascent by chairlift, takes you up to 2,660m & to the start of some 5km of ski & snowboard runs. A ski pass for day visitors costs T6,000; an ascent in the cable car is T1,000, with a further T600 for the chairlift. Airport or city transfers cost T7,000. Liveried porters welcome you into the hotel building, whose rooms & public areas are laid out stylishly, save possibly for the plastic cherry trees in the lobby, though the overall effect is somewhat sterile. The resort lies 13km east of Talgar. Passing the *akimat* building in the centre of Talgar on your right, take the turning to your left, 200m on, marked with a huge sign to 'Ak Bulak'. After a further 1km, turn right onto Sadovaya St, also signposted for Ak Bulak. The road winds gradually upwards. Turn left after a further 8km, & right at the roundabout 1km further on, both clearly signposted, to get to the resort. **$$$$$**

Hotel Stary Zamok (13 rooms) Almaty State Nature Reserve; ⟍(727) 264 0325, 254 1648; e info@alpina.kz; www.alpina.kz. One of several mountain hotels run by the Alpina XXI company, & bookable through their Almaty office, the selling point of this place is its location within the territory of the Almaty State Nature Reserve itself. The requirement to secure a reserve permit seems to be waived if you are staying or eating here: tell the guard at the entrance to the reserve that you are going to the Stary Zamok & he will take a note of your registration number. The hotel is about 700m from the entrance to the reserve, at an altitude of 1,250m. You are not however allowed to leave your car, or to explore the reserve more widely, & in truth the 'Old Castle', a complex of not very old or particularly castle-like buildings, is probably the least attractive of Alpina XXI's mountain retreats. Through its 4-poster beds in the most expensive rooms, paintings of medieval fantasy worlds & copious fireplaces it does at least try to conjure a bygone age, though the 1980s soundtrack served up with the *shashlik* in their timber-beamed restaurant does not help it succeed. **$$$**

ESIK The town of Esik, or Issyk, lies a little more than 40km beyond the eastern outskirts of Almaty. Its recent history dates from 1858, when Cossack settlers established the village of Nadezhdinskaya here, but this was a place of human settlement thousands of years earlier. It was in Esik, from a Saka burial mound of the early Iron Age period, that one of the most important historical treasures ever recovered in Kazakhstan was discovered, the intricate gold suit and headdress belonging to the Golden Man.

The *kurgan* housing the Golden Man no longer exists, the victim of industrial development, but there is a small monument marking its site. From the centre of Esik, take the road heading northwest, which links with the main highway between Chilik and Almaty (a more northerly option than the road passing through Talgar). After some 2.5km, a monument on your left bearing a relief of the Golden Man, in front of an industrial building, marks the spot.

There are however some surviving Saka *kurgans* a short distance away. Continuing along the road, passing on your right buckets of fruit lined up on wooden stands, evidence of the richness of the local fruit growing, you reach after a further 2km a sign, highlighting a track to your left, marked 'Sak's mounds museum'. There are several *kurgans* in the field adjacent to the road, one of which, surrounded by a fence, is quartered by two trenches. Also in the field stands a yurt, containing a small museum of items unearthed from the *kurgans*, including copies of some exquisite pieces of gold Saka jewellery featuring stylised animal designs. The museum is maintained by archaeologist Beken Nurmukhambetov, who lives in an adjacent yurt during the most clement part of the year. He was involved in the original dig which unearthed the Golden Man, and will happily recount his recollections of the unearthing of the Saka figure, as well as his plans for the construction of a museum dedicated to the ancient history of Kazakhstan, in a building modelled on the form of a *kurgan*. The veteran, white-bearded archaeologist wears around his neck a Bronze Age amulet and a mobile phone.

THE GOLDEN MAN

The Golden Man was uncovered in 1969 by a team of archaeologists from the Kazakh Institute of History, Ethnography and Archaeology led by Kemal Akishev, who excavated a large burial mound, or *kurgan*, of the early Iron Age period, in a field just outside Esik. The central burial in the *kurgan* turned out to have been plundered in antiquity, but the archaeologists discovered a second burial in the southern part of the mound which the early grave robbers had missed. Within a tomb constructed of fir logs, a corpse was lying on its back, dressed in a jacket of red-coloured material which was covered with triangular pieces of gold, like a particularly luscious suit of armour. A tall headdress and leather belt bore gold figures of animals, and more gold adorned the figure's boots, sword and dagger. Altogether some 4,000 gold pieces were involved.

The Golden Man has become one of the symbols of post-independence Kazakhstan, replicas are found in museums throughout the country and 'his' image also adorns the Independence Monument in Almaty and the presidential Standard. While many researchers believe the Golden Man to have been a Saka prince, probably around 18 years old, others speculate that the Golden Man may perhaps have been a woman. They argue that other objects found in the tomb are more suggestive of a female than male burial, and that the tall headdress with its lavish decoration and items of jewellery, including earrings and necklace, also suggest a female figure. Among the other notable items found in the tomb was a small silver cup bearing a rare example of an inscription in a Scythian dialect.

Some 600m further along the main road, a *kurgan* on the right-hand side of the road reaches a height of 12m, offering a good view over the burial mounds in the nearby fields.

Lake Esik From the centre of Esik, drive south into the hills alongside the broad and stony floor of the Esik River valley. After 6km you reach a checkpoint marking the entrance to the Ile Alatau National Park. Further south the valley narrows and the views become more beautiful as you climb. After a further 8km, and at a height of 1,760m, Lake Esik comes into view, set against steep conifer-covered slopes. The lake is but a fragment of the size it was before 7 July 1963, when a torrent of melt-water running down the Zharsai River, one of the two main inflows into the lake, destroyed the natural dam and caused much of the lake to be washed away. More than 200 houses further down the valley went with it. The Chairman of the Cabinet of Ministers of the USSR, Kosygin, and First Secretary of the Communist Party of Kazakhstan, Kunaev, were at the lake just before the tragedy struck. The far side of the lake is part of the Almaty State Nature Reserve, to which access is restricted.

As you arrive at the lake, some 300m before the car park on its northern shore, note the face of Lenin painted onto a slab of rock on the right-hand side of the road.

TURGEN At 11km east of Esik, the small town of Turgen was formed in 1868 as Mihailovskoye by Russian settlers. The main attraction here is the beautiful **Turgen Gorge**, within the Ile Alatau National Park. Just before entering the town, turn right towards the mountains. After 5km, you reach the barrier marking the entrance to the national park (admission T200).

After 500m, on your right you reach the **Kieli Bulak Visitor Centre**, though the sign, promising a 'historical, ethnographic and touristic' centre, somewhat oversells the attraction. It features a cutaway artificial *kurgan*, enabling the visitor to enter the log-lined tomb at the heart of the mound. There is also a concrete yurt and a large statue of the Golden Man, featuring a somewhat raffish moustache. He is flanked by a snow leopard on a rock. A couple of hundred metres further down the gorge is the Kieli Bulak spring. A sign in Russian and Kazakh promises eternal youth and beauty, and there are plenty of takers for this kind offer, stopping to fill their bottles with water flowing out of five old metal pipes. The trees above the pool are covered in votive strips. The place is also a favoured spot for wedding parties.

Slightly less than 1km further, on the left-hand side of the road adjacent to the fast-flowing River Turgen, stands the **Turgen Trout Farm**. This place is a popular weekend destination for Almaty-dwellers, and likely to be packed at weekends. The deal here is to hire a fishing rod (T100), which comes with a few pieces of sweetcorn as bait, and stand alongside a rectangular artificial pond, packed with trout. No skill is required: a trout will be hooked within minutes, and anything you catch, you must purchase (T1,400 per kg). You take your catch to the cookhouse in the plastic bag provided, where they will prepare and cook your trout (either fried or as soup: T150 per fish). There is a somewhat grating number of additional charges, including T100 for a plastic plate, T100 to park your car (or T20 per person admission if you arrive by coach) and T300 for one of the nicer tables under the trees at which to eat your fish. But the trout is delicious. You can buy bread, prepared salads and drinks from cafés here to accompany your fish. They also offer horseriding, or a trip in a horse-drawn carriage for the more sedate. The **Royal Fish Hotel**, recently completed, has a modern design which jars in the midst of this beautiful valley.

A further 6km down the valley, on the left of the road, is an accommodation option for urban cowboys, the **Stetson Rancho** (contact details as for Stetson Bar Almaty, see page 134; **$$$$$**). This ranch-style hotel offers horseriding, tennis, a swimming pool, billiards and even a miniature golf course. The restaurant has a chandelier fashioned from a wagon wheel, and there's an 'Apache' bar for those feeling brave. The rooms are nicely furnished: the more expensive ones have a balcony.

The Turgen Gorge holds several impressive waterfalls. One of the most attractive, and easiest to visit, is the **Medvezhy Waterfall** ('Bear Fall'), which has a drop of about 30m. The path up to the waterfall starts some 4km further along the valley from the Stetson Rancho, just beyond a bridge across the Turgen River. The waterfall is a popular place for day trippers from Almaty, and at the starting point for the walk there are picnic tables under the trees, horses for hire, a café and a shop selling Turgen Gold wine as well as soft drinks, snacks and, for some reason, a large number of tins of sardines. The rocky track alongside a side stream is well worn by the many visitors to the waterfall, though is somewhat slippery in places. The waterfall is sited just under 2km from the road.

THE FAR SOUTHEAST

CHARYN CANYON The fast-flowing Charyn River, a tributary of the Ile, forms an attractive canyon some 80km in length during its northward journey from its headwaters in the Tian Shan Mountains across the arid semi-desert east of Almaty. The depth of the canyon reaches as much as 300m where it cuts through the Toraigyr Mountains on its journey. Tour operators bill Charyn as a miniature version of the Grand Canyon. To get here, take the main road east from Almaty, through the small town of Chilik. Around 190km east of Almaty, turn left onto a signposted track. You reach the canyon after a further 9km, and having passed a checkpoint at which a small fee is taken for your entry into the Charyn National Nature Park. From the parking area here, a path heads down into the canyon. Another path, 1km to the north, is steeper but more picturesque. Almaty-based tour operators like Indra-Tour (see page 123) offer lengthy day trips to the canyon; other operators can set up tailored tours, sometimes combining the canyon with the Kolsai Lakes. The Charyn River offers some challenging white-water rafting and canoeing. It is also home to a fish endemic to the region, sporting the rather picturesque name of the naked osman.

The place the tour groups head for in this part of the canyon is a dry side ravine known as the Red Canyon or **Valley of the Castles**. Some 3km long, and up to 100m deep, with a path running along its base, the red sandstone walls of this gorge offer natural sculptures of dramatic form. You will bake here at the height of summer: spring and autumn are ideal times to visit the canyon.

Downstream from this part of the canyon is a remnant of a great forest of **Sogdian ash** which stretched across this area after the last Ice Age. The ribbon of relict forest which has survived is a 25km stretch, sheltered by the canyon. A nature reserve was established here in 1964 to help protect the grove, one of the few large populations of Sogdian ash found anywhere in the world, and this now forms a specially protected area within the Charyn National Park. It is reached via a different road from that for the Valley of the Castles: coming from Almaty turn left on the road towards Shonzhy and Zharkent a few kilometres southeast of the village of Kokpek. Other trees found in the dense patches of forest along the banks of the river include willow, poplar and barberry.

Some scholars believe that the name of the river comes from the Uighur word 'Sharyn', meaning 'ash tree'. Others suggest that it derives from the Turkic root 'Char', which suggests a precipice. The two options are rather fitting, since precipices and ash trees are two of the key components that make Charyn such a fascinating place.

KOLSAI LAKES The Kungey Alatau range is centred on a ridge running east to west, which lies on the border of Kazakhstan and Kyrgyzstan, south and east of the Zailysky Alatau. The most picturesque spot in the Kungey Alatau is a group of three mountain lakes which lie between northern spurs of the range. To get to this place, the Kolsai Lakes, head east from Almaty on the road to Kegen. Just before reaching the Charyn River, turn right on a road passing through the local administrative capital of Zhalanash, and then the village of Saty (the closest place to the lakes served by public transport from Almaty). Beyond Saty, you are charged a park fee to proceed further. Some 295km from Almaty, at a height of some 1,700m above sea level, you reach the lower Kolsai Lake, which is also rather prosaically known as Kolsai 1.

The Almaty-based tour operator Jibek Joly (see page 123) is something of a specialist on the Kolsai Lakes, and has some cottages on offer at the lower lake (**$$$$**). The accommodation available here includes rooms with four beds, doubles with shared facilities and doubles with en suites. It's a highly attractive spot, but with additional charges levied for catering (if you have your own transport, you should bring food with you, as anything sourced locally will be expensive) and even car parking, you pay for the view. Jibek Joly can also organise horseriding, and hire of tents and sleeping bags. Further away from the lake, the village of Saty is one of the new ecotourism options offered by the Ecotourism Information Resource Centre (see page 123), with five homestays available (**$**).

The lakes are in idyllic locations amidst evergreen-covered slopes. The two lower lakes offer fine trout fishing. From Kolsai 1, it is a hike or ride of around 9km to Kolsai 2, the largest and some argue most beautiful of the three, which sits at an altitude of 2,250m. The highest of the lakes, Kolsai 3, is a hard hike of another 6km, and rests at a height of 2,650m. Some travel agencies offer treks from the Kolsai Lakes across the Sarybulak Pass, at 3,270m on the border with Kyrgyzstan, and from there down to Lake Issyk Kul in Kyrgyzstan. The route is the shortest and probably the easiest (though this is relative) of the several trekking routes over the Tian Shan to Issyk Kul.

Another attractive mountain lake on the northern slopes of the Kungey Alatau lies to the east of the Kolsai Lakes. **Lake Kaindy** is notable in particular for the narrow trunks of the spruce trees which rise up from its waters like apparitions. Kaindy is a young lake, formed only in the late 19th century following a landslip, and the submerged trees have not yet decayed. To get here, driving back from the Kolsai Lakes, turn right near the cemetery 1km or so beyond Saty, onto a dirt road requiring a 4x4. You pass a checkpoint, where a park entry fee will be levied, before reaching the lake.

KHAN TENGRI At the far southeastern corner of the country, where the borders of Kazakhstan, Kyrgyzstan and China come together, stands the highest point in Kazakhstan, the mountain named after Tengri, the Turkic god of the heavens. Khan Tengri is a massive marble pyramid, ranking alongside such peaks as the Matterhorn as the most beautiful on earth. At sunset, its marble walls glow red. The north and south streams of the Inylchek Glacier, at more than 60km in length one of the largest in the world outside the polar regions, frame the mountain to the north and south.

The first mountaineer to attempt to climb it was the Austrian explorer Gottfried Merzbacher at the turn of the 20th century. He came to realise that the ascent would require a significant expedition, and left unsuccessful, though did establish the relationships of the various peaks and ranges in the region, as well as giving his name to the intriguing seasonal Lake Merzbacher. The first successful ascent was made by a Ukrainian team led by Mikhail Pogrebetsky in 1931. Khan Tengri was originally thought to be the highest peak in the Tian Shan: it was only in the 1940s, when Peak Pobeda to the south was properly surveyed, that it was discovered that the latter, at 7,439m, rose considerably above Khan Tengri. With its striking pyramidal form, Khan Tengri had just seemed higher than the more solidly proportioned Pobeda.

The height of Khan Tengri itself has been a matter of considerable debate. It was originally determined at 7,193m, a height revised in later surveys to 6,995m. But in sources published within the region its height tends to be given as 7,010m, using the argument that the peak is crowned with a cap of ice, which puts its height above the 7,000m mark. It is one of the qualifying peaks for the Snow Leopard Award, earned by those mountaineers who have climbed all five peaks more than 7,000m in height in the former Soviet Union. Accepting the claim that Khan Tengri does top 7,000m would make it the most northerly peak on earth to reach this height. Otherwise that accolade goes to Peak Pobeda, 16km to the south, which is now officially known as Jengish Chokosu, Kyrgyz for 'Victory Peak'.

Attempting to ascend Khan Tengri is of course for experienced mountaineers only, and requires considerable planning. But even to reach the foothills of the mountain is not straightforward. There are no roads anywhere near the place, and most visitors arrive by helicopter or on a long trek which includes the base of Khan Tengri. The area is also part of a restricted border zone, for which special permission is required. The Almaty-based tour operator Kan Tengri (see page 123) specialises in bringing visitors to the mountain, both mountaineering groups looking to climb it and trekkers with more modest ambitions, and operates much of the infrastructure, including base camps. Tour Asia (see page 124) are also experienced in bringing tours to Khan Tengri.

Most visitors arrive here via the camp at **Karkara** run by Kan Tengri. This is situated some 280km east of Almaty: take the main road east to Kegen, turning south at that village towards the Kyrgyz border. From Karkara a rough track takes you to the camp, which is located amidst meadows close to the Karkara River. Accommodation is in two-person tents or a yurt. There is a separate restaurant/bar block. At the time of research, a stay here cost €30 a day per person, including food. If you are arriving here on an expedition, this will start with the ceremony of raising the national flags of team members at the camp. From Karkara there are trekking options along the Kokzhar River and some good mountain biking, but for most visitors the key to coming here is the transfer by helicopter to one of two Khan Tengri base camps, both operated by the Kan Tengri company. Both tented base camps sit at heights a little above 4,000m. The North Inylchek base camp is on the Kazakh side of the border, close to the North Inylchek Glacier. The South Inylchek base camp is in Kyrgyzstan, and also serves as a base for Peak Pobeda, across the South Inylchek Glacier.

Kan Tengri hires the helicopters, usually Soviet-era Mi-8s, for the summer period (the season for trekking and climbing around the central Tian Shan is a short one, focused on July and August). The flight to the base camps, which takes around 35 minutes, is spectacular. It is not safe if the weather is poor, and bear in mind too the caution expressed in the travel advice notices of some governments about the lack of information on the observance of maintenance procedures on internal flights in the region. At the time of research, Kan Tengri was charging around US$3,500 for a helicopter transfer. These are mostly aimed at groups on organised packages. The helicopters seat 20, and individual travellers may wish to ask the company about the possibility of spare seats on flights, which should be charged at US$200–250 a time. Make sure though that you organise your seat back at the same time!

There is another camp, at **Akkol**, used by some tour operators as an alternative to Karkara. It is closer to Khan Tengri, at an altitude of 2,600m in the Bayankol Valley. To get here you head eastwards from Kegen on the road towards Narynkol, turning off to the south at the village of Tekes. There is tented accommodation as well as beds in hangar-like dormitories. The deal is otherwise similar to Karkara, with helicopter transfers to the North Inylchek and South Inylchek base camps. Note that the Akkol camp is itself in a restricted border zone, for which permission will need to be obtained with the help of the agency organising your trip.

AROUND LAKE KAPCHAGAI

Sitting some 80km to the northeast of Almaty, Lake Kapchagai is actually a large reservoir, 100km long and 22km wide at its widest point, formed by the damming of the Ile River in the late 1960s to provide hydro-electric power and more irrigated land. The construction of the dam has however proved harmful to Lake Balkhash, starving it of some of the Ile River waters so vital to it. Lake Kapchagai offers warm waters and sandy beaches, and has become a favoured summer weekend destination for Almaty-dwellers keen to escape the heat of the city.

KAPCHAGAI AND ITS LAKE Located at the western end of the lake, close to the dam, the town of Kapchagai was established in 1970, accompanying the construction of the hydro-electric power station. It is a town of Soviet-era apartment blocks and green boulevards. A statue of **Lenin** stands in front of the building housing the town administration. Across the square is a statue of **Dinmuhammed Kunaev**, former First Secretary of the Communist Party of Kazakhstan and instrumental in the decisions to build the dam and establish the town. In the rather unkempt park behind this statue is a war memorial, protected by three artillery pieces.

Close to the reservoir within the town stands an **aquapark** (*(72772) 21036;* ⏰ *10.00–20.00 Mon–Fri, 09.00–20.00 Sat–Sun; admission adult/child T1,000/600 Mon–Fri, T1,200/650 Sat–Sun*). It was built to an Italian design in 1994, and features a range of slides and pools as well as a 10m-high water tower. The park becomes very crowded in summer. Further afield, there are numerous beaches around the lake, some of which charge an admission fee. One favoured spot is reached by continuing northwards from Almaty, beyond the turning for Kapchagai town. You descend into the Ile Valley after 4km and, another 2km on, cross over the dam. At the junction 4km further on take the road signposted to Taldykorgan, turning right towards the lake at the large concrete sign, 16km on, marked '*zona otdikha*' – rest zone. The beach here is sandy, and the water warm, but there is very little shade, and the lake here is somewhat dirty. Various forms of craft are available for hire: it is even possible to take to the water astride a large floating banana. While many visitors from Almaty come to Lake Kapchagai as a day trip, there are many holiday cottage options here, some of which are looking down at heel. One of the better choices as a base is **Fiesta ($$)**. This has a good pool, with rooms in a series of cottages around it.

Some smarter, and pricier, resort developments are starting to appear around the lake. One of these is the **Freedom Beach Resort** (*76 rooms & 6 'VIP' cottages;* \ *(72772) 47282; $$$$$*). This is located just off the main road north from Kapchagai, 1km south of the dam. Entered through a Chinese-style gate, the oriental theme is continued with the pagoda roofs on the buildings. They offer balconied hotel rooms, 'VIP' cottages and a pleasant sandy beach shaded by straw umbrellas at the western end of the lake. The Chinese theme continues in the air-conditioned bedrooms, though these are already starting to look a little shabby. Non-guests can use the beach and swimming pool, for a fee. Room rates and most other charges halve outside the peak (June–August) season. It is also possible to rent furnished apartments in the same complex for T3,000–5,000 a night (⬆ *(7057) 685528*).

The town of Kapchagai and the area surrounding it have been targeted for major investment. Under legislation introduced in 2007, Kapchagai is one of only two places in Kazakhstan, along with Schuchinsk/Borovoye, in which casinos and other gambling establishments are now permitted. Proposals for major gambling-focused resort complexes are being drawn up. One proposal envisages the road running between Almaty and Kapchagai as the fulcrum of a ribbon development to be called G4 City. This proposes four new satellite towns: Gate City, the closest to Almaty, will focus on business and commerce; Golden City will be a gambling hub; Growing City, an industrial zone; and finally, along the banks of the lake, Green City, combining residential accommodation with parkland.

NOMAD

The film *Nomad*, based on the exploits of the young Ablai Khan, enjoyed the strong backing of the Kazakhstan authorities and gives a considerable insight into the nation-building motifs of the Kazakhstan government. With a budget reportedly running to US$40 million, a large cast and three credited directors, *Nomad* also served as a statement of the ambitions of the Kazakhstan film industry. It was released in Kazakhstan in 2005, though the launch of an English-language version in the USA did not take place until 2007. The film drew on a wide range of international talent, its directors including the Russian Sergei Bodrov and the Czech New Wave director Ivan Passer. Milos Forman was one of the co-producers.

Somewhat curiously, given the subject matter of the film about the emergence of a strong and confident Kazakhstan, while the main female roles were played by Kazakhstani actresses, most of the male leads went to foreigners. The role of Mansur, the boy who would become the future Ablai Khan, was played by the Mexican actor Kuno Becker. Jay Hernandez, a US actor with Mexican roots, was cast as his friend Erali. And the guiding figure of Oraz, who saved the infant Mansur from the swords of the Dzhungars and then trained him to be a warrior and future leader, was played by the Chinese American actor Jason Scott Lee.

The film starts with the Dzhungar invasions across the lands of the Kazakhs, aided by the failure of the Kazakh tribes to unite. The dream, articulated at the beginning of the film and its central theme, is of a warrior who would one day unite the Kazakhs and drive their enemies out. While praying next to a *balbal* for the Kazakhs to be given their saviour, Oraz hears the cry of a child from the heavens, and knows that the saviour has been born. Dzhungar forces ambush a caravan carrying the sultan's family, killing his wife, but Oraz manages to save the sultan's baby boy, whom he recognises as the future saviour of the Kazakh people. Oraz trains up the boy, Mansur, who is unaware of his true identity, and others of the fittest and finest Kazakh youths, as future warriors. The sultan meets the boy warriors: each introduces himself with his name and tribe except for Mansur, who announces simply that he is a 'Kazakh'. At the sacred tree, Oraz tells the youngsters that to their east lies a large nation, a fire-spitting dragon. To their west is a country like a grizzly bear. The Dzhungars are close by. In this dangerous environment, the only solution for the Kazakhs is unity.

NOMAD FILM SET One of Kazakhstan's more curious attractions is the set of the film *Nomad*, the most lavishly funded Kazakhstani film ever made, which sits in a beautiful setting beneath the steep valley side close to the left bank of the Ile River. To get here, take the main road north from Kapchagai, towards the dam. Turn left across a flyover, signposted to the settlement of Kazakhstan, before you reach it. After 18km you see the first of several unsignposted tracks heading off to the right down into the Ile River canyon. This first track offers the most direct but also one of the steepest descents down the side of the valley to the film set, 4km away, and requires a 4x4 vehicle. There are more gentle options further on, which require you to turn right at the canyon floor and head back eastwards along the track running alongside the bank of the river.

The turrets and mock earthen walls of the film set rise up next to the river as if welcoming the travellers of a Silk Road caravan to a medieval central Asian city. There is a wooden fence round the back with a gate in it. The resident caretaker, who lives next to the set, will let you in for T300. He even issues a receipt. You walk

As Mansur grows to adulthood, the Dzhungar army moves towards Turkestan. They capture Gaukhar, the girl with whom both Mansur and his friend Erali have fallen in love. With the Dzhungars at the gates of the city, they offer its Kazakh defenders the opportunity to decide its fate with a duel. Their toughest warrior, Sharish, played by martial arts expert Mark Dacascos, is pitted against Mansur. The young Kazakh defeats his opponent with a powerful sword swipe passing straight through Sharish's shield. Mansur then learns that the sultan is his father and of his destiny. Mansur becomes Ablai. But he is then captured by the Dzhungars, who have been aided by a traitor in the Kazakh camp. The Dzhungars set Ablai a series of impossible-looking tests to secure his freedom. He dodges arrows with the aid of trick horsemanship, and turns down a marriage proposal from Hocha, the smitten daughter of the Dzhungar khan, played by the Almaty-born ethnic Uighur pop singer Dilnaz Akhmadieva. In his last test, Ablai kills a tough adversary, a warrior whose face is hidden behind a chain-mail mask. But his defeated foe turns out to be his old friend Erali, who submitted to combat with Ablai to allow his friend to fulfil his destiny. Even with the tests surmounted, the Dzhungars have no intention of freeing Ablai, but he escapes from their camp together with Gaukhar on the back of his trusted horse Moonbaby, who the Dzhungars had also taken. They kiss above the Ile River. Ablai and Gaukhar, that is. Not Moonbaby.

The Dzhungars again move against Turkestan. Ablai manages to keep them at bay with the aid of clever tactics involving burning oil, until reinforcements arrive from across the Kazakh lands. The Kazakh tribes have united, and Ablai's destiny has been fulfilled. Ablai spares the life of a small Dzhungar boy, grandson of the Dzhungar khan, who had been nice to him in captivity, and sends the boy back to his grandfather together with a huge globe, which marks out the vast lands of the Kazakhs. A note from Ablai accompanying the globe warns that the native lands of the Kazakhs were bequeathed to them by their ancestors, and anyone attempting to take them will drown in their own blood. The Kazakhs are open to anyone who comes in peace, but will be merciless to their enemies. The film ends with a quotation from President Nazarbaev about the sacred value of Kazakhstan's independence, a gift of our ancestors the nomads.

past a scaffold into a large central square, with a domed bath house, pottery and the minaret of a mosque. The sultan's palace is embellished with turrets and fake tiles. Next to it stands a tree covered with votive scraps of cloth. You can climb up onto the battlements to admire the siege weaponry, ready to launch rocks or boiling oil onto attacking Dzhungar forces, as well as the excellent view across the Ile River. The set is showing inevitable signs of wear and one tower has been vandalised. Fake tiles have fallen off, revealing a wooden frame beneath. But this mock 18th-century city is still a fascinating sight, with its unopenable doors and supporting framework of log-built scaffolding.

TAMGALY TAS This petroglyph site is very different from the confusingly similarly named site of Tamgaly (see page 164), centred not on carvings of the Bronze Age and Iron Age, but on images of Buddha dating from the Dzhungar period.

To get here, take the Kapchagai road from Almaty. Cross over the dam beyond Kapchagai, and after 4km turn left on the road signposted to Bakanas. Take a track to the left after 13km. This starts to descend into the Ile River canyon another 7km on. Turn to the left, signposted to a training ground used by the Ministry of Emergency Situations, and follow the track along the floor of the Ile Valley, the river to your right. A prominent rock outcrop, at the base of which are piled large boulders, is reached after a further couple of kilometres. On these rocks are inscribed the petroglyphs of Tamgaly Tas.

The largest composition features three Buddha images engraved onto a flat stone face, all depicted sitting on lotus flowers, together with inscriptions in the Tibetan script. A further figure, on a boulder to the left, has been identified by researchers as representing the Bodhisattva Nagarjuna. Another Buddha figure is engraved on a separate face, closer to the track alongside the river. There are further inscriptions close to this in Tibetan, Dzhungar and Manchu scripts. Opinions differ as to when the Buddhas were engraved, and by whom, but the most plausible is probably that they were the work of Dzhungars, who converted to Lamaist Buddhism around the 16th century. They may date from around the beginning of the 18th century, when this place was a crossing point of the Ile River. The site was studied in the 1850s by the Kazakh traveller and ethnographer Chokan Valikhanov. It has however suffered at the hands of vandals over the years. Some of the Buddhas have been shot at, and struck with hammers. Modern graffiti has been added to the site, including a portrait of Che Guevara and the information that Dasha and Zhena have visited. With this part of the Ile River valley much used by picnickers, as well as a favoured spot for rock climbers, the need for stronger protection of the site is pressing.

LAKE SORBULAK This small lake, to the northwest of Almaty, is one of the most accessible of Kazakhstan's many excellent birdwatching sites. Take the Bishkek road out of Almaty, turning north on the main Astana road some 30km out of the town centre. Lake Sorbulak is reached after a further 55km, on the right-hand side of the road. Birds frequenting the lake include cranes and pelicans. Signs warn against fishing, swimming and hunting. Not that you would wish to swim here: the lake is a recipient of sewage from Almaty. But the birds seem to like it.

ALTYN EMEL NATIONAL PARK

Established in its present form in 1996, and covering an area of some 460,000ha, the Altyn Emel National Park is one of the largest in Kazakhstan. Its southern boundary is formed by the Ile River and by Lake Kapchagai. The northern boundary of the park is marked by a line of hills, a western spur of the Dzhungar Alatau range, whose name changes from west to east: Degeres, then Altyn Emel, then Koyandytau. It is said that the name 'Altyn Emel', which means 'golden saddle', was given to the hills by Genghis Khan when he passed this way in 1219 and saw them covered with sun-yellowed grass. In the east of the park are two further ranges, Katutau and Aktau. The rest of the park comprises dry plain.

This is one of the best places in Kazakhstan to see herds of wild hoofed mammals. The park boasts a population of some 6,000 goitered gazelle, known as *jieran*. In the 1970s, a small population of central Asian wild ass, or *kulan*, was brought here from the Barsakelmes Nature Reserve, in response to the ecological problems associated with the desiccation of the Aral Sea, which turned Barsakelmes from an island into a peninsula and greatly raised the salinity of the Aral. The wild ass have thrived in Altyn Emel, and now have a population of some 2,000. Much harder to spot are the park's *arkhar*, some 400 in number, which prefer remote upland environments. The park authorities latest projects are the introduction to Altyn Emel of the Przhevalsky horse, using horses brought from Munich Zoo, and the Bukhara deer. The mammals are at their most active, and easiest to spot, early in the morning and late in the afternoon.

The Altyn Emel National Park also boasts some striking archaeological and natural sights, of which the two most important are the Iron Age burial mounds of Besshatyr, and the large *barchan*, or more accurately *barchans*, known as the Singing Sand Dune.

PRACTICALITIES While some national parks in Kazakhstan have taken a cautious approach to tourism, seeing their role as to protect the natural environments from people rather than to attract visitors in, Altyn Emel sees tourism development as one of its central activities. The positive side of this is the provision of relatively good facilities for visitors, including eight tourist cottages scattered across the park, and ease of booking. The park maintains an office in Almaty. The downside is a pretty steep charge to visit the place: foreigners from outside the former Soviet Union are charged T5,800 a day, as against just T800 for Kazakh citizens. This fee is however reduced by 10% for day two, and by 20% for the third and subsequent days, if you are planning a really in-depth visit to the park. Additional fees are levied, reasonably enough, for provision of accommodation, meals, a guide and use of a *banya*, as well as, less logically, for overnight car parking. The guides are mostly park inspectors who can direct you to the sights well enough, but are unable to offer much in the way of explanations about them.

In terms of touristic visits, the park is effectively divided into two separate parts by a specially protected reserve, or *zapovednik*, in the central section, through which tourists are not usually allowed to pass. The village housing the park headquarters, Basshi, is the gateway to the sights of the eastern section of the park, including the Singing Sand Dune, and Aktau and Katutau hills. The western section of the park, containing the Besshatyr burial mounds and Terekty petroglyphs, is best approached direct from Almaty, and you will need to make your payment in advance through the park's Almaty office or a travel agent. The contact details for the park are as follows.

Basshi Office (727) 404 5209; f (727) 237 9144; e altynemel.kadr@mail.ru

Almaty Office Offices 242, 244, Hotel Zhetisu, 55 Ablai Khan Av; f (727) 250 0451; e altynemel-tour@mail.ru; www.altyn-emel.kz

BASSHI From Almaty, take the road to Kapchagai and then towards Taldykorgan, turning off at Saryozek onto the road to Zharkent. Some 60km east of Saryozek, the road enters the territory of the Altyn Emel National Park, winding impressively along the side of a steep valley before crossing a flat plain. The signposted right turn to the park headquarters at Basshi is 22km further on.

Basshi is a small, rural village, in which the park office is well signposted (as 'GNPP Office Altyn Emel'). Visitors are required to come to the park office on arrival, to agree their programme with the park authorities and, unless this has been done already in Almaty, to pay up. There is a small **museum** in the park office, behind a carved wooden door featuring reliefs of the local wildlife. The museum has dioramas of the main sights and landscapes of the park, including the Besshatyr burial mounds, a rock face decorated with petroglyphs, the Aktau and Katutau hills and the Singing Sand Dune. Around the back of the park office stands the **Hotel Altyn Emel** (5 rooms; $), one of the more substantial of the accommodation options run by the park authorities. This is a two-storey building in pleasant gardens, with two single beds in each room and shared indoor facilities. Meals are provided for an additional fee, arranged at the time of booking.

AKTAU AND KATUTAU HILLS The dry, brown-coloured **Katutau Hills** sit 40km southeast of Basshi. Your park guide will direct you along the track which skirts around the southern side of the range, and then along a side route into the hills. The main attraction here is the weathered and pitted outcrops of volcanic rock. The guides propose photographs of visitors inserting an arm or leg into one of the holes formed by erosion. These silent hills are a good place to spot *arkhars*.

From the Katutau Hills, return to the main track, and turn left, continuing your eastward route south of the line of the hills. After 7km turn left (signposted) for Aktau at the fork. Its white hills are now visible behind the browns of Katutau. You reach the southern edge of the **Aktau Hills** after a further 16km. The 'White Mountains', whose strata rise upwards towards the south, are actually a range of colours: there is a large central band of white, but a layer of deep red beneath, dominant at the southern end of the range, and more orange-toned hues above. The combination of colours is striking, and beautiful. The park authorities have set up a picnic area here, and have plans to install an open-air palaeontological museum.

There is a longer, more southerly route from Basshi to the Katutau Hills, taking in a detour to see an old willow tree. From Basshi head south on the tarmac road, which peters out after 16km at the hamlet of Araltobe. Continue southwards on a track passing across the semi-desert plain, reaching after 13km Kosbastau, a collection of buildings which were home to geologists in the Soviet period. In the garden of the park inspector here, behind a wooden fence, stands the gnarled tree, said by the park authorities to be 700 years old, its low, twisted branches propped up by wooden posts. Returning by the same route, turn right where the track divides at the top of the slope above the village. The Katutau Hills are 20km further on.

THE SINGING SAND DUNE From Basshi, head south on the tarmac road towards Araltobe, turning right onto a track across the plain after 5km. A further 2km on you reach the park inspection post of **Shigan**: there is a barrier across the track here, to ensure that all those visiting the Singing Sand Dune have paid their park fees. The **Shigan Guest House** (3 rooms; $) is here. After a further 29km you reach another park inspector's residence, at Minbulak. This translates as 'a thousand springs'; the many water sources across the plain are marked by the clumps of trees dotted around them. The track forks here: take the left turn, signposted in English to 'singing djun'. The track takes you south between the large massif of Ulken Kalkan on your left and the smaller Kishi Kalkan on your right.

After 10km, near the point at which the two hills come close to meeting, is a grove. Here a rough stone path leads to a flight of steps. Walk down these to enter a small clearing, ringed with reeds, in which a rough picnic table and chairs have been fashioned out of willow wood. The spring here has been named in honour of the Kazakh ethnographer **Chokhan Valikhanov**, who stopped at this place on his return from Kashgaria.

After a further 1km you reach the northern end of the **Singing Sand Dune**. Two barchan dunes, reaching a height of 120m and a total length of more than 2km, sit in the funnel of flat land bounded by the Ile River in the south, Ulken Kalkan in the east and Kishi Kalkan in the west. The dunes reach their highest elevation at the southern end; a track runs down the eastern side to enable you to get a good view. But despite the attractiveness of the dunes, and their striking location amidst dry mountains and saxaul-dotted semi-desert plain, visitors mainly come here to listen to the dunes rather than just to see them. The Singing Sand Dune is celebrated in the tourist brochures of Kazakhstani travel companies for emitting a loud humming noise, often likened to that of an aircraft engine. The generation of the noise is related to the movement of the sand: scientists continue to debate whether the movement of air between the sand grains or friction between the grains, possibly linked to the generation of opposite electrical charges, causing repulsion of the grains, is the primary cause of the sound. Local legends offer a different interpretation: that the noise is the groaning of the slumbering evil spirit Shaitan, or perhaps the moans of Genghis Khan and his army, buried beneath the sand.

You may however find that on your visit to the Singing Sand Dune, rather than the humming of the sand, all you get to hear is one of the reasons given by the park guide for an absence of noise: sand too wet; not enough wind; wind in the wrong direction. It is sometimes possible to encourage the vocal talents of the dune by running quickly down the side: the southern slopes of the dune are said to be best for noise generation. Climbing up to the top of the dune is not as easy as it looks though, but the walk is good exercise for the calf muscles.

One worthwhile stop on the way back, 1km or so before Minbulak, is a group of three standing stones known as **Oshak Tas**. These lie to the left of the main track, just to the north of the slopes of the Kishi Kalkan. The standing stones form the eastern side of a small pit, with large stones lying on the other sides. The form is strongly reminiscent of the assemblages of the standing stones at Besshatyr (see page 180). One legend linked with this place is that the standing stones propped up a huge cooking pot, or *kazan*, beneath which a fire was lit, and from which Genghis Khan provided food for his army.

THE TEREKTY PETROGLYPHS AND BESSHATYR The western part of the Altyn Emel National Park is approached from the main road between Kapchagai and Saryozek, turning off at Shengeldi, and then heading eastwards along a heavily pot-holed tarmac road which reaches the western boundary of the park after 36km. Trips into this part of the park should be arranged and paid for in advance through the park's Almaty office (see page 177), and your park guide will be at the post at the park entrance to meet you.

Terekty From the park boundary, a track heads eastwards, running close to the north bank of Lake Kapchagai. After 8km, take another track signposted to 'Tanbaly Tas', in the direction of the range of hills to the north. After a couple of kilometres this passes through a field of small *kurgans*. The track then heads into the Terekty Canyon, which contains the outcrops of flat, dark rock with a metallic sheen which in Kazakhstan so often provide the canvas for petroglyphs. **Terekty** does not disappoint. An outcrop on the right-hand side of the track, pushing forward from the valley side, around 3km north of the *kurgans*, is rich in petroglyphs. There is another cluster 600m further north, on a large face of dark metallic-sheened rock to the left of the track.

The petroglyphs at Terekty include many figures of ibex, with pronounced horns and usually drawn in two dimensions, with only two legs visible. Drawings of mammals with particularly curly horns may represent *arkhars*. Especially distinctive are the deer with multi-branched antlers; some indeed have such tall antlers with so many branches that they appear to be wearing Christmas trees. These may be depictions of Siberian deer, no longer found in these hills. There are a large number of human figures on horseback, often archers. There are also human figures depicted riding camels. There is a circular symbol with rays emanating from it and three dots inside the circle. Is this an early depiction of sunspots?

Kyzylauz Back on the main, eastward-running track, you reach after a further couple of kilometres another track heading northwards into the hills. This heads into a canyon named **Kyzylauz**, the rock at its entrance a reddish hue which gives the place its name. 'Look after nature!' is written in decidedly unnatural-looking white-painted stones placed on the hillside close to the entrance to the canyon. A silver-coloured statue of an eagle guards the canyon mouth. Some 1,500m into the canyon, the track ends at an idyllic spot, a grove of trees around a spring. The nicest, and priciest, of the park's accommodation options is here, the **Kyzylauz Guest House** (4 rooms; **$$$**). Housed in an attractive wooden building, this place has a dining room decorated with stuffed heads of saiga, goitered gazelle and mountain goat. There is also a *banya* with outdoor plunge pool. The rooms are decidedly basic for the price though, with cot-like beds. You can also sleep in the yurt outside, though this has been furnished with five single beds, each with a bedside table which, while adding a certain Western level of comfort, rather defeats the yurt-stay experience. The guesthouse features a 'presidential room', with a large double bed and smart furnishings for which the charge, at the time of research, was US$200 a night, making it perhaps the most expensive hotel room in Kazakhstan with no en-suite facilities.

Back on the eastward-running main track, there is another accommodation option a few kilometres further east. This is the **Zhantogay Guest House** (2 rooms; **$**), next to a park inspector's residence, in a fine location on the northern bank of Lake Kapchagai.

Besshatyr Some 14km east of Zhantogay, take the signposted track to the north for the **Besshatyr** *kurgans*. These are clearly visible beneath the line of hills to their north, and you reach the largest of them after another 4km. There are 31 of these Scythian burial mounds of the Iron Age, in an area some 2km long and 1km wide. Most are covered with dark-coloured fist-sized stones, but some have a finer covering. Besshatyr is an atmospheric place, with an excellent view down the slope to the spot where the Ile River becomes Lake Kapchagai. The largest of the *kurgans* is 17m high, with a diameter of 104m. Its burial vault was walled with logs of Tian Shan spruce. There is a wide range in the size of the *kurgans*: the smallest are less than 1m in height with a diameter of around 6m. The largest *kurgans* are probably the resting places of tribal leaders, while the smallest ones are perhaps the graves of ordinary warriors who distinguished themselves in battle. Many of the *kurgans* were excavated in the late 1950s, their contents including human bones, as well as those of horses, sheep and goats, weaponry, including daggers and arrowheads, felt mats and earthenware pots.

Around the largest of the *kurgans* is a ring of small stones, and then further out a circle of standing stones. There is a second ring of standing stones in some places. The walled enclosures of stones around the northwest side of this *kurgan* were probably, however, the work of shepherds, making pens for their livestock from easily available walling material. The standing stones are often grouped in distinctive clusters: a closely packed line of three stones, the largest in the centre, like a line of pointed incisor teeth, faces the *kurgan*. In front of these are large stones lying on the ground, which form a ring with the standing stones within which a fire may have been lit. To the northeast of the largest *kurgan* a line of seven clusters of standing stones, running from north to south, appears to be divorced from adherence to any one of the *kurgans*.

The main west-to-east track continues eastwards to Minbulak, 25km away. But the section of the national park east of Besshatyr is a specially protected *zapovednik* area, and tourists are not normally allowed to continue this way. Therefore to get to sights such as the Singing Sand Dune (see above) a considerable amount of back-tracking is required, as well as a detour via Basshi.

ZHARKENT *Telephone code: 72831*

The town of Zharkent, the capital of an agricultural district focused on the production of corn, is the last major Kazakhstani settlement before the Khorgos border crossing with China. Established in 1882 close to the Russian Empire's border with China, on an ancient trading route, it was renamed Panfilov in 1942 in honour of Major General Ivan Panfilov, the commander of the 316th Rifle Division and a hero of the defence of Moscow. It is laid out in a grid pattern, with the main thoroughfare, Zhibek Zholy Street, a line of trees and flowers decorating its central reservation, bisecting the town from west to east.

WHERE TO STAY

🏠 **Hotel Atlantic** (5 rooms) 81A Pushkin St; ☏ 52655. This large detached 2-storey white building houses a restaurant on the ground floor, offering a mix of European & Chinese dishes & often given over to large functions ($$), a pub in the basement, described as the Sim Sim Club, & 5 hotel rooms upstairs. These are fine as long as your stay doesn't coincide with a noisy wedding party in the restaurant. Room rates include b/fast & are the same price for dbl & sgl occupancy. **$$**

🏠 **Hotel Zharkent** (8 rooms) 5 Kobikova St; no phone. A combination of pleasantly presented sgl & dbl en-suite rooms with attached bathrooms. B/fast not included in the price. **$$**

🏠 **Hotel Zhibek Zholy** (25 rooms) Molodyozhny village; ☏ 36165, 36166. Zharkent's nicest accommodation option, though only really practical if you have your own transport, sits in the farming settlement of Molodyozhny, 7km out

of town. With arches over its balconied windows, it's a Soviet-era construction which has been renovated. Only the more expensive rooms have AC. Molodyozhny village was formerly named Golovatsky in honour of the much-decorated former head of the collective farm here. With a powerful boss, the farm was able to secure the kind of facilities not available to most Soviet *kolkhozes*. The village square, on which the Hotel Zhibek Zholy stands, is a fine example of late Soviet design. The buildings around it include a House of Culture with tapering walls & a curious sculptural ensemble above the door featuring 2 large white balls & a cone. Nikolay Golovatsky had befriended Konstantin Chernenko, Gorbachev's predecessor as General Secretary of the Communist Party of the Soviet Union, when the two served together as border guards in this region in the 1930s. In his later career Chernenko stayed in this hotel during a visit to his friend's *kolkhoz*: his room was the present-day suite 216 if you are minded to follow in the footsteps of a Soviet leader. There is a bust of the round-faced Golovatsky in the unkempt park next to the square. **$$**

✗ **WHERE TO EAT** The Hotel Atlantic (see above) is another dining option.

✗ **Asil Gasir** Corner Yuldashev & Litfullin sts; ⎷54741. A pink-walled, pink-curtained restaurant, with display cabinets full of kitsch (glittery frog, statuette of a wedding couple, toy pig) & waiters in sparkly gold waistcoats, this place may not win awards for tasteful décor, but its food, a mix of European, central Asian & Chinese dishes, is fine. The *guiry-say*, a spicy meat dish serving 2, is recommended. $$

WHAT TO SEE

Zharkent Mosque The town of Zharkent only has one sight of note but it is a striking one, a Tsarist-era mosque whose design is an exuberant medley of central Asian, Russian and, especially, Chinese influences. In 1887, the leaders of the Muslim community of the young town decided to raise the funds to construct a mosque. The main sponsor and chief organiser of the project was a merchant named Valiakhun Yuldashev. He engaged a Chinese chief architect named Hon Pik. A popular local tale runs that Hon Pik had produced a dazzling building in China. The jealous patrons of that structure resolved on its completion to have him executed, so that he would be unable to repeat his triumph. Hon Pik learnt about their plan and fled, a commission from distant Zharkent coming as the ideal answer to his problems. Zharkent folk will tell you that the glorious structure that he built in China has not survived, and thus that their mosque has no equal. The mosque was completed in 1892. It survived a major earthquake, as well as neglect in the early Soviet period, when it was used as a store. It was restored in the 1970s and turned into the Zharkent Mosque Architectural and Historical Museum, the Soviet authorities choosing to highlight its architectural worth rather than religious function. It remains officially a museum to this day.

The mosque is entered through a powerful arched gate in the central Asian style. It is painted white, and attractively decorated with engraved half-columns, Arabic-language inscriptions and floral designs. On your right as you pass through the gate is a portrait of Yuldashev, swathed in furs and sporting his medals. On reaching the courtyard beyond, look back at the gate through which you have just passed to get an excellent impression of the mix of architectural styles used in the construction of the complex. The gate is topped by a minaret in the form of a delightful two-storied pagoda. On either side are brick cupolas of a more central Asian inspiration. The windows below have a Russian feel.

The main mosque building across the courtyard clearly shows off its Chinese influences. It is surrounded by a line of red-painted wooden columns which support the protruding green roof, turned up at the corners. The beams running beneath the roof are brightly decorated with floral patterns. The wooden interior, spacious enough to hold 1,000 worshippers, is equally impressive. Wooden columns support a decorated, latticed balcony. The *minbar* at the far end of the room has a strongly Chinese feel, and is surrounded by Chinese-style lanterns. The *mihrab* behind it, a scalloped niche with a door in the back, in contrast draws more heavily from central Asiatic traditions. The walls surrounding it are decorated with beautiful geometrical and floral designs. Beams on the wooden ceiling above are striped, like the skin of a tiger. The building was constructed without the use of nails.

Aulieagash Close to the village of Aulieagash, near Zharkent, is a tree said to be possessed of sacred properties. Heading on the main road westwards from Zharkent, towards Almaty, turn right after 16km at the village of Koktal. A further 10km on you reach Aulieagash. Turn right in the village onto a metalled road, crossing a fast-flowing stream. After a couple of kilometres, just beyond the village, take the 200m rough track on your left which leads to a couple of single-storey white-walled buildings. Below these is a metal gate onto which have been tied many coloured handkerchiefs. A crazy-paved path leads through a patch of woodland to an ancient elm tree, its huge trunk said to be the circumference of six pairs of outstretched arms. Its dead lower branches trail down to the ground. A path circles the tree; the faithful follow this and then embrace the tree. Some even sleep beside it. There is a small hollow at the top of one of its roots in which water collects. A spoon has been placed here, allowing visitors to scoop out and then drink the water. It's as brown and gritty as you would expect. Locals claim that the other trees in the wood all lean towards this great tree, in deference to it. Many of the trees do indeed seem to be inclining in its direction.

TALDYKORGAN *Telephone code: 7282*

In 1868, on the site of the winter pasture of Tal-Korgan, west of the Dzhungarsky Alatau Mountains, the settlement of Gavrilovka was established. With its Kazakh name restored, this provincial town was given an economic boost in 2001, when it was named as the capital of the Almaty Region. But it remains a quiet place, a leafy, grid-patterned town laid out on the left bank of the Karatal River. While not a tourist destination in its own right, Taldykorgan serves as a gateway to the beautiful and little-explored mountains of the Dzhungarsky Alatau as well as to the north of the region and routes into East Kazakhstan.

GETTING THERE AND AROUND Taldykorgan's **airport** is 14km northeast of town across the Karatal River. Zhetisu Airlines offers a daily two-hour flight to Astana in a hot and cramped Yak-40. The **railway station** sits a few blocks south of the centre, at the southern end of Shevchenko Street. The sleepy Taldykorgan station lies at the end of a branch line. The adjacent **bus station** (\ *243222*) is potentially more useful. There are frequent departures for Tekeli (one hour) and Almaty (six hours) and a couple a day to Ust-Kamenogorsk. Long-distance **taxis** wait outside the railway station and along Shevchenko Street in front of it. They charge around T1,800 for a seat to Almaty; T7,500 if you want to hire the whole taxi.

Buses within town cost T30. Bus number 7 will take you into the centre from the railway station.

WHERE TO STAY

Hotel Olimpiyets (8 rooms) Tolebaev St; \ 390693. This is a pleasantly presented hotel in a purpose-built building with a garden. Secure parking is available on site & there is a small café. **$$$**

Hotel Taldykorgan (32 rooms) 128/130 Akin Sara St; \ 242372. This centrally located 5-storey pink-painted building has recently been renovated. Prices have increased as a result. **$$$**

Hotel Irat (20 rooms) 7 Garishker Microdistrict; \ 250939. Inconveniently located on the western side of town, close to the university stadium, the Irat is a modern hotel with a blue roof. Activity from the billiard hall next door can mean a noisy night, & the restaurant comprises some depressing cell-like rooms in the basement. **$$**

Hotel Meruert (28 rooms) 119 Zhabaev St; \ 246754, 245689. The 'Pearl' is actually an

5

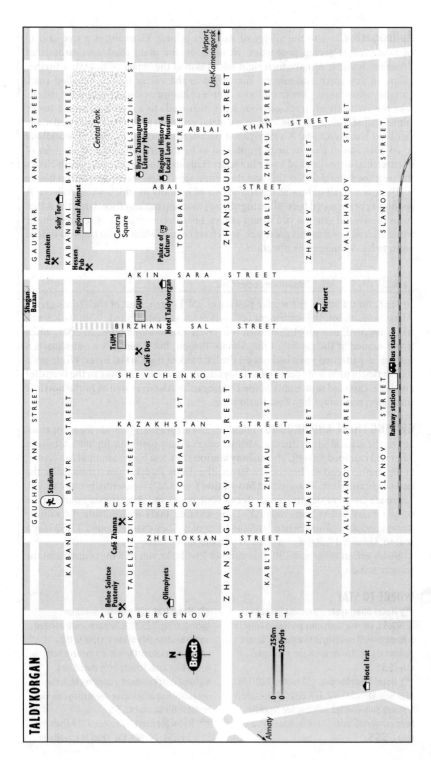

TALDYKORGAN

Central Park

Ilyas Zhansugurov
Literary Museum

Regional History &
Local Lore Museum

Suly Tor

Regional Akimat

Atameken ✗

Central
Square

Hessen
Pub ✗

Palace of
Culture

Shagan-
Bazaar

GUM

Hotel Taldykorgan

Meruert

TsUM

Café Dos ✗

Bus station

Railway station

Stadium

Café Zhanna ✗

Beloe Solntse ✗
Pustelny

Olimpiyets

N

Bradt

0   250m
0   250yds

Almaty

Hotel Irat

Streets labelled on map: GAUKHAR ANA STREET · BATYR STREET · TAUELSIZDIK ST · ABLAI KHAN STREET · KABANBAI BATYR STREET · ZHANSUGUROV STREET · KABLIS ZHIRAU STREET · ZHABAEV STREET · VALIKHANOV STREET · SLANOV STREET · ABAI STREET · TOLEBAEV STREET · AKIN SARA STREET · BIRZHAN SAL STREET · SHEVCHENKO STREET · KAZAKHSTAN STREET · RUSTEMBEKOV STREET · ZHELTOKSAN STREET · ALDABERGENOV STREET

Airport,
Ust-Kamengorsk

ugly brick complex with an oversized & tasteless glass extension, close to the bus station. Rooms have AC, but are unexciting. B/fast is not included in the room rate, & is only available if ordered in advance. The complex also includes a restaurant, fitness centre, nightclub, bowling alley & an outdoor restaurant, where you dine in bamboo huts around a central terrace. **$$**

🏠 **Hotel Suly Tor** (10 rooms) 48A Kabanbai Batyr St; ☎ 273067; f 272228; e sulutorhotel@ mail.ru. The rather ugly exterior makes this a building which would look more at home on an industrial estate, though the yurt outside the entrance has a softening influence. Rooms have AC, b/fast is included in the rates, & the hotel is modern & central, making this a good option. **$$**

✗ **WHERE TO EAT** Scattered around the centre of Taldykorgan are a number of *kumisskhanas*, cafés based inside yurts, whose speciality is serving up bowls of mare's milk, *kumiss*. The following are more substantial eateries.

✗ **Atameken** 54 Kabanbai Batyr St; ☎ 247468, 210034. This nicely restored neo-classical building at the corner of Akin Sara & Kabanbai Batyr streets, the one-time home of the Rodina Cinema, now houses a range of eating & entertainment options. There is a restaurant with an international menu offering a particular focus on Spanish & Turkish dishes, a bar in the foyer with bar stools shaped like cocktails, a cinema, a nightclub (⊕ 23.00–03.00 daily; admission Mon–Fri T300, Sat–Sun men T700, women T500), & an outdoor café in the neighbouring pavilion, offering *shashlik* & assorted mains. **$$**

✗ **Beloe Solntse Pusteniy** 118 Tauelsizdik St; ☎ 221546. This large place, whose unwieldy name is that of a cult Soviet film of 1969, a favoured cinematic choice of cosmonauts preparing for launch, sits west of the centre, & the somewhat uninspiring international menu does nothing to recommend the journey. But the setting is nice: a central Asian fantasy with blue-tiled half-minarets. There is a summer courtyard, as well as a sports bar, the latter decorated with football posters. **$$**

✗ **Café Dos** 85A Tauelsizdik St; ☎ 243035. This place is built to resemble a medieval castle, with a couple of brick turrets facing the street & litter bins shaped like shields. The theme continues inside, with weaponry decorating the walls. There are wooden beams across the ceiling & wooden tables. The food, Russian & international dishes, is nothing special. **$$**

✗ **Café Zhanna** 96 Tauelsizdik St; m +7 701 779 0269. West of the town centre along Tauelsizdik, this blandly decorated place offers a fair range of international & central Asian dishes. You can for example choose between Uighur-style & Turkmen-style *pelmeni*. There is an outside terrace, for summer dining beneath awnings. **$$**

✗ **Hessen Pub** 147 Akin Sara St; ☎ 273826. This place is decked out as a somewhat gloomy bierkeller, & the main entertainment is provided by numerous TV screens. Filtered & unfiltered Hessen Beer (brewed on site) is on offer, & the menu includes Russian, Italian, Mexican & pub dishes, including a rather peculiar collection of 'cheeseburgers', not all of which contain cheese. **$$**

SHOPPING The main street, Tauelsizdik, which in Soviet times bore the name of Lenin, runs east–west through the town. Close to the intersection with Birzhan Sal Street two rival shopping centres, known by their rhyming acronyms of **TsUM** and **GUM**, glare across at each other. The stretch of Birzhan Sal Street to the north of this intersection is pedestrianised. The **Shagan Bazaar** sits a block further north, at the intersection of Birzhan Sal and Gaukhar Ana streets. The trading activity spills out beyond the bazaar along both of these streets in the form of chaotic trade centres and street-front stalls.

WHAT TO SEE

Central square The large expanse of the central square, straddling Tauelsizdik Street, fills much of the block between Akin Sara and Abai streets. The modern fountain in the centre of the square has seven columns of varying heights, representing the seven rivers from which the Zhetisu region takes its name. There is a rather more attractive fountain in the southwestern corner of the square, with four rams supporting a large decorated bowl. The northern side of the square is flanked by a modern glass-fronted building housing the **regional administration**. The southern side is occupied by the **Palace of Culture**, named in honour of poet Ilyas Zhansugurov.

Ilyas Zhansugurov Literary Museum (*59 Tauelsizdik St; \ 270656; ⊕ 09.00– 13.00 & 14.00–18.00 Mon–Fri, 09.00–12.00 Sat; admission T70*) A few metres away, at the corner of Tauelsizdik and Abai streets, sits the Ilyas Zhansugurov Literary Museum. The museum, housed in a merchant's house dating from 1907, an elegant green and white-painted wooden building in front of the Zhetisu Economic Institute, chronicles the life and work of the poet Zhansugurov, who was born in Almaty Region. It was opened in 1984 to commemorate the 90th anniversary of the poet's birth. There is a photograph of Dinmuhammed Kunaev, then First Secretary of the Kazakhstan Communist Party, attending the inauguration, accompanied by Nursultan Nazarbaev. The museum's central corridor is focused on a bust of Zhansugurov at the far wall, set against a backdrop of a sunset across which the silhouettes of birds fly.

The displays chronicle Zhansugurov's childhood, with a model of his wooden-walled school, known as Mamaniya since it was run by three brothers named Mamanov. His early career as a teacher is described, followed by his study of journalism in Moscow. On his return he worked on a Kazakh-language newspaper in Kyzylorda. His somewhat hectic personal life is also covered. Zhansugurov divorced his first wife. His second died in childbirth. He met his third wife in Kyzylorda, but parted from her in favour of the fourth, Fatima. His poetry is described, including *Kulager*, a paean to Kazakh nomadism, and there are copies of the books he wrote for children. He translated Pushkin and Lermontov into Kazakh. A photograph shows him meeting Maksim Gorky during a visit to Moscow in 1934. A painting of Zhansugurov shows the poet swathed in white furs. His desk, typewriter and battered old coat are also on display.

While working in Almaty he was arrested in 1937 as an enemy of the people. In February 1938, he was executed. There are copies of the bureaucratic paperwork related to his arrest and execution. There are copies too of letters written by his wife Fatima in a desperate search for information about her husband. She was only informed in 1957 of his fate. Following Zhansugurov's rehabilitation, his life and work were once again celebrated, and there are displays about the commemoration of various anniversaries of his birth as well as photographs of the capital of the district in which he was born, northeast of Taldykorgan, which now bears the name of Zhansugurov.

Regional Museum of History and Local Lore (*245 Abai St; \ 243058; ⊕ 09.00–13.00 & 14.00–18.00 daily; admission T50*) Just to the south, along Abai Street, sits the Regional History and Local Lore Museum. The displays here kick off with natural history, with stuffed animals populating dioramas of desert, mountain and riverbank scenes, the last featuring a fox enjoying a duck dinner. There is a large wall map of the Altyn Emel National Park, and a display of local rocks and minerals, some fashioned into necklaces and vases. Maps chronicle the expeditionary journeys through the region in the 1850s of Pyotr Semyonov-Tianshansky and Chokan Valikhanov.

History follows, with displays of Bronze and Iron Age implements, photographs of the Tamgaly petroglyphs, a model of the Golden Man and a selection of stone *balbals.* There is a display on the Kazakh khanates and a map of the Great Silk Road, focused on routes passing through the territory of present-day Kazakhstan. The displays continue upstairs with instruments which once belonged to prominent local musicians, a model of the barrel-vaulted tomb of ethnographer Chokan Valikhanov, and household objects of Russian migrants. Coverage of the Soviet period includes the work of industrial enterprises in the region, including miniature models of some ghastly-looking armchairs and a coffee table, the products of the Taldykorgan furniture factory. The achievements of the region's war heroes, including members of Major General Panfilov's 316th Rifle Division, labour heroes and noted artists are all chronicled, as is the work of Dinmuhammed Kunaev, the long-serving First Secretary of the Communist Party of Kazakhstan. There is coverage too of the 1916 uprising, collectivisation and the victims of Stalinist repression. There is a sobering display of the events of 1986 in Almaty, featuring the biographies of three young people killed during or in the aftermath of the unrest. The displays conclude with the post-independence era, featuring a display of books written by President Nazarbaev and a selection of products from the region's factories: ice cream, facial scrub, wine and car batteries.

Central Park One block further east along Tauelsizdik Street, at the northern end of Ablai Khan Street, sits the main entrance to the **Central Park**. Walk between the fake castle gates to a down-at-heel fantasyland, with fairground attractions, open-air cafés and a couple of white yurts housing *kumisskhanas*. To the right of the path leading north from the entrance is a square-sided monument, topped by a small pyramid, honouring K L Maystryuk, commander of a Red Army cavalry regiment set up here during the Civil War, who was killed in fighting around Khiva in 1921.

THE DZHUNGARSKY ALATAU MOUNTAINS

East of Taldykorgan, the Dzhungarsky Alatau Mountains rise up to heights of more than 4,000m, their highest peak, at 4,622m, straddling the Chinese border. They offer some of the most beautiful scenery in Kazakhstan, with glaciers, spruce forests and fast-flowing streams. The mountains are home to the Tian Shan brown bear, and are far less frequented by tourists than the Zailysky Alatau. The problem though is that their proximity to China classifies most of the range as a border zone for which an additional permit is needed. Obtaining the latter, even with the help of a local travel agency, is a time-consuming procedure.

TEKELI Some 40km southeast of Taldykorgan, the former mining town of Tekeli is the starting point for many routes into the Dzhungarsky Alatau. A permit is not needed to come to Tekeli itself, but you are not allowed much further into the hills to the east without one. Tekeli sits at the foot of the mountains, at the confluence of three streams: the Kora, Shizhe and Tekeli. Together these unite to form the Karatal River, the second in importance of the 'Seven Rivers' after the Ile, which flows through Taldykorgan and thence northwards into Lake Balkhash.

Tekeli was formed around a lead-zinc mine, which started its operation in 1942, but whose reserves had waned by the mid-1990s to such an extent that the business collapsed in 1996. The large KazZinc enterprise took it on a year later, but was unable to make it profitable, and the mine is now closed, though metals are still being extracted from the tailings. A silver-coloured statue of **Lenin** stands at the entrance to the complex, on the edge of town, with another Lenin statue close to the turning for the mine from the main road. Attempts to revive the economy of the town include the decision to locate the Kazakhstan campus of the University of Central Asia here, which brings together Kazakhstan, Kyrgyzstan and Tajikistan in a project funded by the Aga Khan and focused on promoting the socio-economic development of mountain communities in central Asia through education and research.

Tekeli enjoys a fine setting, in a tree-covered valley beside a fast-flowing river, but the evidence of its industrial woes is all too clear from the decrepit and in some cases abandoned Soviet apartment blocks. The tour company **Stek** (*1A Auezov St;* m *+7 705 650 7808;* e *sttek@mail.ru*), based in the town, specialises in organising trips into the Dzhungarsky Alatau. You will need to make contact several weeks in advance of your planned date of travel, to allow for processing of the application for the necessary permit.

The Kora Valley One interesting site, situated just out of Tekeli in an upland meadow, is a large rock on which is engraved a drawing of a pagoda-like **Buddhist temple**. An inscription in Sanskrit lies immediately above the engraving, which probably dates from the 18th century. The site was described in 1898 by a professor of Tomsk University named Larionov. Water accumulates in a cavity at the top of the rock. The locals say that this water is possessed of magical, healing properties, never freezing in winter and never drying up in summer. I visited the site with a group of academics from Taldykorgan: though Muslims they lit a fire and recited three times a Buddhist incantation as this, they had heard, offered the prospect that wishes would be granted.

The rock is located in the lower reaches of the Kora Valley. Head out of Tekeli on the poor road running up the valley on its northern side, turning left a couple of kilometres after leaving the town, just before an abandoned-looking factory with a watchtower. After 1km along a rough track, you pass a farm on your right. The rock is a couple of hundred metres beyond this, on the left of the track.

The **Burkhan-Bulak Waterfall**, whose 90m drop makes it the highest in the region, is located 55km from Tekeli in the Kora Valley, which offers superb scenery. Stek Tours (see above) can organise trips here involving a mix of travelling by vehicle and either hiking or horseriding.

ESHKIOLMES AND THE KOKSU RIVER The Eshkiolmes petroglyph site, located along a line of hills to the north of the Koksu River, a western spur of the Dzhungarsky Alatau range, is one of the most extensive in Kazakhstan, containing some 10,000 figures. To reach it, head for the village of Lenino, which lies a few kilometres to the east of the Taldykorgan–Almaty highway, reached from a turn-off 26km south of Taldykorgan. A couple of kilometres beyond the village is a bridge across the Koksu River. Take this, turning right onto a dirt track on the other side of the bridge. The track runs between the river and the hills. After 11km you reach a burial site known as **Kuygan**, which includes both Bronze Age burials and Iron Age *kurgans*. The petroglyphs of **Eshkiolmes** lie in the hills immediately behind this site, spread over several kilometres to both west and east.

The Eshkiolmes Hills are cut by several waterless valleys, providing sheltered sites in winter which perhaps explain the naming of Eshkiolmes – 'goat does not die'. Petroglyphs are found on most of the suitable exposed dark rock surfaces. There are many petroglyphs of both the Bronze Age and Iron Age periods, with stylistic animal engravings of the Saka period particularly well represented, such as deer with pronounced curly horns, their legs tucked neatly under their bodies. There are also many petroglyphs involving images of hunters, archers and chariots. Many of the representations are very small, and some of the sites are rather hard to find or to reach, but the challenge in some ways adds to the appeal of Eshkiolmes, offering a greater sense of achievement than that provided by following the well-marked route at Tamgaly (see page 164).

At the Eshkiolmes site, the Koksu River forms a broad and fertile plain. Following the river back a few kilometres towards its headwaters you reach a more dramatic landscape as the river leaves its canyon. At this point petroglyphs of both the Bronze and Iron ages can also be found on a large rocky outcrop above the fast-flowing river.

LEPSINSK Located on the northern flanks of the Dzhungarsky Alatau range, the remote village of Lepsinsk is of interest as an established community-based tourism location in Kazakhstan, set up with the support of local NGO Uigentas-Agro. There are three homestays available in the village, providing basic accommodation on a full-board basis (**$**), bookable through the Ecotourism Information Resource Centre in Almaty (see page 123). The local co-ordinator is Sabir Mikhalev (\ *(72547) 62055;* e *tic_info@inbox.ru*). The village is in a highly attractive setting, but the project here does not get the visitor numbers it deserves. This is partly because it is located in a restricted border area, which necessitates time-consuming procedures to get a permit, and also because it is a long haul to get here from Almaty. A few buses a day take around 11 hours to make the journey to Kabanbai, from where you can pre-arrange via the Ecotourism Information Resource Centre for a taxi to meet you and take you to Lepsinsk. This should cost around T2,500. There are two buses a day between Kabanbai and Lepsinsk, though these only run on Sunday, Monday, Wednesday and Friday.

The flower-rich meadows around Lepsinsk help explain why this area produces some of Kazakhstan's best honey, and walking or riding to local honey farms are among the pursuits available here. For the more active, there is a demanding trek or ride (July–September only) following the Lepsi River through mixed forests to Zhasilkul, the 'Green Lake'. It is a round trip of around three days.

TARAZ *Telephone code: 7262*

The capital of Zhambyl Region, lying to the east of Almaty Region, Taraz is a city of more than 300,000 people lying on the Talas River. It staked a claim in 2002 to the title of the oldest regional capital in Kazakhstan by commemorating its 2,000th anniversary. This largely rests on the argument that the city can be traced back to the fortress established in the Talas Valley by Zhizhi Shanyu, in concert with the Kangui Union, in the 1st century BC. This formed the basis of the state known as the Western Xiongnu. Zhizhi lost the fortress to invading Hans at the Battle of Zhizhi in 36BC. He also lost his head, which was sent off to the victors. The first clear record of a city at this modern site comes in AD568, when travellers started to describe a Silk Road trading city named Talas. The city came under the control of the Turgesh, a Turkic tribal confederation, and then in the 8th century was ruled by the Karluks, by which time the city seems to have been known as Taraz. The Persian Samanids took control of the Talas Valley in the 9th century, introducing Islam to Taraz.

The Karakhanids arrived at the end of the 10th century, and it was under the Karakhanids in the 11th and 12th centuries that Taraz attained its greatest importance. Several beautiful monuments whose restored features can be seen today in Taraz and its environs date from this period, and the city also boasted a system of underground clay water pipes, an aqueduct and a mint. The power of the Karakhanids weakened in the 12th century, and the city fell to the Khorezmshah Mohammed II in 1210. The rule of the Khorezmshahs lasted only a decade, as Taraz was razed by the Mongols in 1220. Taraz appears to have been renamed as Yany under the Mongols, but progressively lost its significance, and by the establishment of control by the Kazakh Khanate in the 16th century seems to have been a small agricultural settlement.

Under the new rulers of the Talas Valley in the 19th century, the Khanate of Kokand, a fortress was built on the site of the ancient city of Taraz, around which a new town began to grow. This started out with the name of Namangan-i Kochek, since many of the new arrivals to the town came from Namangan in the Ferghana Valley. In 1856, it was renamed Aulie-Ata, 'holy father', honouring the respected Karakhanid ruler whose mausoleum lay in the town. The Russians, under General Mikhail Chernyaev, took the town in 1864. It became an *uyezd* capital three years later. In 1936, the name of the town changed again, to Mirzoyan, in honour of Levon Mirzoyan, the ethnic Armenian who headed the Kazakh Communist Party apparatus from 1933 to 1938. Mirzoyan was executed in that year, a victim of Stalin's repression, which meant that the name of the town was hardly likely to stay as it was. Sure enough, in 1938 it was changed again to Zhambyl, honouring the Kazakh poet Zhambyl Zhabaev (see page 162). Which means that, if I have the reckoning right, and discounting minor variations in spelling (Zhambyl was for example usually spelt in the more Russianised form Dzhambul during the Soviet period), the city has existed under eight different names. In 1997, the longest-lasting historical name, Taraz, was restored to the city.

During the Soviet period, Zhambyl developed into an important centre for the processing of phosphorous, based around rich sources of phosphates in the Karatau Mountains to the southwest, whose mines at one stage accounted for 60% of the Soviet production of phosphorous. Factories producing yellow phosphorous and phosphate fertilisers became important elements of the city's economy but, like many heavy industries across the Soviet Union, they struggled following its break-up. Taraz today offers only a few reminders of its long history but these include some memorable sights, including the stunning Karakhanid Mausoleum of Aisha Bibi outside the town, and one of Kazakhstan's best regional museums. It makes for an excellent stopover of a day or two on routes between the attractions of Almaty Region and those of South Kazakhstan.

GETTING THERE AND AROUND Taraz **airport** (✎ 316126), named Aulie-Ata, lies to the west of the town. Heading out of town on the road towards Shymkent, turn left for the airport just to the west of the gate over the road welcoming you into the city. Air Astana operates a daily Taraz to Astana flight.

Taraz is on the main railway line between Almaty and Shymkent. The **railway station** (✎ 363115) is in the southern part of town, close to the southern end of Komratov Street. The **bus station** is a crumbling Soviet-era building on the northeastern edge of town, on the south side of the Almaty road. There are frequent departures to Shymkent, by *marshrutka*, and departures by both bus and *marshrutka* to Almaty. There are a few daily departures to Bishkek. The *marshrutkas* leave when they are full, rather than work to a specific timetable. This is also a place to pick up taxis serving destinations outside the city. One number to call for **taxis** in town is ✎ 434400. Trolleybus route number 8 runs along Tole Bi Avenue, the main east–west thoroughfare through the centre of town.

TOUR OPERATORS AND AIRLINE OFFICES
✈ **Otrar Travel** 129 Abai Av; ✎ 456656; f 435567; e dmb@otrar.kz; ⊕ 09.00–18.00 — Mon–Fri, 09.00–14.00 Sat. General Service Agent for Air Astana.

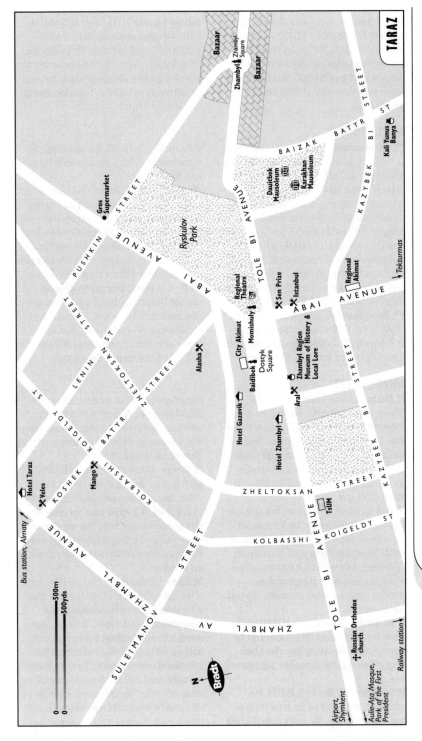

TARAZ

Taraz Travel Business Centre, Zhambyl Hotel, 42 Tole Bi Av; 455968; f 451750; e hotel-zhambyl@nursat.kz. This agency based in the Zhambyl Hotel offers half-day tours of the monuments of ancient Taraz, which includes the out-of-town Mausoleum of Aisha Bibi, & of the site of Akyrtas.

Zolotoy Karavan 111A Dulaty St; 459774; f 346294; e karavan@tarazinfo.kz; www.goldkaravan.narod.ru. The 'Golden Caravan' can set up historical tours of Taraz & surrounding sites as well as itineraries focusing more on the area's natural beauty, to the Aksu Zhabagly Reserve or the Moinkum Desert.

🏠 WHERE TO STAY

🏠 **Hotel Gazovik** (20 rooms) 7A/1 Suleimanov St; 433233, 452042; f 433991; e gazovik_hotel@nursat.kz. The 'Gas Worker', centrally located close to the main Dostyk Sq, offers the best of the rather limited range of hotel accommodation available in Taraz. It is owned by the state enterprise KazTransGas, which is developing the Amangeldy natural gas field in the central part of Zhambyl Region. All rooms have AC & en-suite bathrooms. The standard rooms are plain, but fine. Book a 'luxe' & you get a free plate of dried fruit & 1hr use of the sauna. **$$$$**

🏠 **Hotel Zhambyl** (73 rooms) 42 Tole Bi Av; 454551; f 451750; e hotel-zhambyl@nursat.kz. This venerable-looking renovated 1960s hotel is centrally located, immediately to the west

of Dostyk Sq. It has no lift. The more expensive rooms have AC. B/fast is not included in the room rate. **$$$**

🏠 **Hotel Taraz** (117 rooms) 75A Zhambyl Av; 433811, 433491. Inconveniently sited north of the town centre, the Taraz is a 5-storey Soviet-era building, its exterior painted gaudily in blue & red. The interior is replete with sugary Soviet friezes showing Kazakh girls swinging serenely while their beaus court them with the sound of the *dombra*. The frieze on the 4th floor updates the scene, with two bikini-clad girls on a towel, listening to their transistor radio. The hotel has long & dingy corridors & a wide range of rooms, from AC 'luxe' & 'semi-luxe' to beds in unrefurbished rooms on offer for T1,500. **$** unrenovated; **$$** renovated

✕ WHERE TO EAT

✕ **Alasha** 1A Koshek Batyr St; 436710. Offering a range of Kazakh, Uighur & European dishes, this place is decorated in vaguely Eastern style, & is targeted at large functions. There is a pleasant summer garden outside, with wooden tables & chairs sheltering beneath umbrellas & a concrete dance floor. Beer & *shashlik* is the standard fare here. **$$**

✕ **Aral** 61 Tole Bi Av; no phone. This basic café opposite the Hotel Zhambyl has a mosaic of a storm-tossed ship on its outside wall & anchors astride the adjacent lamp posts. Those seeking a safe refuge here will find an outdoor summer terrace, & a basic range of regional dishes, including *shashlik*, washed down with Karaganda beer on tap. **$$**

✕ **Istanbul** 117A Abai Av; 452529. This simply furnished Turkish café is located not far from the central Dostyk Sq. They offer a basic range of Turkish dishes & excellent pomegranate juice. **$$**

✕ **Sen-Prize** 117 Abai Av; 453726. This centrally located restaurant sits at the corner of Abai & Tole Bi avenues. The food is a mix of Turkish

& assorted international dishes, including pizzas. Dine either in the café room, with metal tables advertising Turkish beer & posters of female pop stars, the more sedate restaurant room, or at tables along the pavement outside. **$$**

✕ **Mango** 67 Koshek Batyr St; 436594. The prices here are cheap & Mango attracts a young crowd. The courtyard is protected by crenellated walls & there are 2 indoor areas, the cosier one with orange-coloured seats. They offer a good range of salads & a Russian/international menu. The mango salad contains several sorts of fruit – but no mango. **$**

✕ **Veles** 128 Koshek Batyr St; 433376. North of the centre, close to the Hotel Taraz, the décor at the Veles is somewhere between central European nobility & farmyard. There are 2 dining rooms, both with fireplaces & deer-head hunting trophies. The larger of the 2 also boasts a fine collection of ceramic chickens. There is a summer courtyard round the back, & an international menu with dishes like 'Texas meat': when I asked what made it Texassy, the reply was that it had tomato ketchup on it. It is at least inexpensive. **$**

SHOPPING Taraz has a sprawling and interesting **bazaar**, which runs along Tole Bi Avenue east of the town centre. The hub of it is **Zhambyl Square**, a busy roundabout centred on a statue of the poet, his right arm outstretched in an evident attempt to direct the traffic. The square is a terminus for several local buses. There is a branch of the **Gros** supermarket chain (⊕ *09.00–23.00*) at the northeastern edge of the town centre, at the corner of Abai Avenue and Pushkin Street. The old Soviet department store, **TsUM**, remodelled for the capitalist age, is on Tole Bi Avenue, 500m west of the Hotel Zhambyl.

WHAT TO SEE

Dostyk Square They do like pink in Taraz. The administrative buildings surrounding the central Dostyk Square, which was named, of course, Lenin Square in the Soviet period, are all painted in a confection of pink and white. The centre of the square is now occupied by an equestrian statue of a local warrior hero named **Baidibek**, who gazes across at the pinkness of the Kazaktelecom office opposite. The **city** *akimat* sits behind the statue, discreet Soviet stars still crowning the half-columns that embellish its façade.

The square is the favoured place for locals to come and stroll on a warm summer evening. The stretch of Tole Bi Avenue passing across the square is closed to traffic by the authorities, but navigation can still be hazardous, as you negotiate past tots in toy cars, teens on roller skates (available for hire at T200 an hour) and a train whose carriages are model swans. A Russian-language music channel, blared out from a large screen in the centre of the square, provides the musical accompaniment. The most brightly illuminated part of the square on summer evenings consists of a line of fluffy sofas, each set in front of huge toy animals or love hearts, beneath illuminated 'Taraz' signs. How about a remarkably kitsch photographic souvenir of your visit?

Zhambyl Region Museum of History and Local Lore (↘ *432585, 433865;* ⊕ *09.00–13.00 & 14.00–18.00 Mon–Sat, closed on the 30th of each month; admission adult/child T150/50*) On the southern side of Dostyk Square, next to the regional marriage registry office, stands the Zhambyl Region Museum of History and Local Lore. This excellent museum was given a facelift for the Taraz 2,000th anniversary celebrations. Displays start with nature and the usual stuffed animal-populated dioramas to illustrate the ecosystems of the region. A stuffed saiga sticks its head into a desert tableau, much to the annoyance of an eagle, flapping its wings furiously at the thought of being upstaged.

Upstairs the displays continue with archaeology. A first room runs from the Stone Age, with a female Bronze Age burial in the centre of the room, and some Scythian artefacts, including a helmet and some delicate animal figures. The next room covers the Karakhanid period, offering a diorama of urban life and some fine ceramic faces with clown-like expressions. Another flight of stairs brings you up to a display on the Kazakh Khanate, illustrated with quotations from President Nazarbaev about the importance for Kazakhs of knowing their ancestors to seven generations. Genealogy for the steppe Kazakh was, says Nazarbaev, like a compass for the sailor. The next room covers the capture of the city by Chernyaev in 1864, and the subsequent arrival of Russian immigrants. There are Dungan and Uzbek household items on show, as well as those of Russian migrants. Kazakh ethnography in the next room includes a life-sized diorama of a nomadic camp, with a woman boiling up the family dinner in front of a yurt. Then comes a room covering the establishment of Soviet power in the region, the arrival of the TurkSib Railway and the repression of the 1930s. Next are displays relating to World War II, with a golden bust of local war hero Bauirzhan Momishuly, one of the commanders of the Panfilov Division who fought bravely in the defence of Moscow. Back downstairs are displays highlighting the ethnic diversity of modern Kazakhstan, and the artistic and sporting figures linked with Taraz.

The real pride of the museum lies in the courtyard at the back, a glass-walled yurt-like building. Inside are two floors of *balbals*, the best collection of these fascinating Turkic stone anthropomorphic figures assembled in Kazakhstan. The *balbals* always faced westwards, but were not associated with places of burial. The sculptures displayed here were found across the southern part of the region, and are helpfully exhibited next to photographs of the sites on which they stood. This collected group of quizzical stone faces makes for an almost disconcerting sight. Also here is a replica of the Golden Man found at Esik, unusually displayed lying horizontally as at burial. There are also copies of gold Scythian jewellery.

In another building, abutting the courtyard, are displays related to the history of Taraz. A somewhat fanciful mural portrays the coronation of Zhizhi Shanyu, back in the 1st century BC, and here depicted as the founder of the town. The procedure being adopted in this portrayal is that used much later for the Kazak khans: the lifting of the new ruler aloft on a white felt carpet. The growth of the city as a trading centre on the Silk Routes is chronicled, and there are ceramic jugs and ossuaries, the latter ghoulishly decorated with little human heads on their lids. A frieze depicts Taraz as a powerful city in the Karakhanid period. There are green glazed ceramics on display which would not look out of place in the catalogue of a modern pottery, but which are several centuries old. And there are fragments of delightful ornamental brickwork from the Mausoleum of Aisha Bibi. A final panel shows modern Taraz.

Another building behind the main museum block houses the Art Museum of L V Brummer, displaying the works of Leonard Brummer, an artist born in Ukraine in 1889 to a German father and French mother. He was deported to the Pavlodar Region of Kazakhstan in 1941, and then moved to Taraz in 1955. He died in 1971 and bequeathed his paintings to the city. They are mostly landscapes of the various places he lived and worked. A 1961 painting of April in Zhambyl depicts a ferociously rutted muddy urban street.

Karakhan and Dauitbek mausolea

At the eastern end of Dostyk Square a resolute-looking statue of war hero **Bauirzhan Momishuly** stands in front of the **regional theatre**. The latter building houses both the Kazakh Drama Theatre (✎ 457989, 457970) and Russian Drama Theatre, the latter entered round the side.

A couple of blocks further east, along Tole Bi Avenue, a yellow and blue arch spanning a side road off to the right points the way to the Karakhan and Dauitbek mausolea. The entrance to the park containing the two buildings is on your left, a short way down this road. You walk along a path between rose bushes to the heavily restored **Karakhan Mausoleum**. Rebuilt at the start of the 20th century, this dates from the 11th or 12th century. The mausoleum is believed to be that of a Karakhanid ruler, the subject of many local legends. Some accounts name the ruler as Shakhmakhmud, the betrothed of the beautiful young Aisha Bibi (see page 196). Unlike his doomed love, Shakhmakhmud lived to a considerable age, spending much of his time in prayer and the pursuit of spiritual goals. He received the name of Aulie-Ata, 'holy father', and it was in his honour that the city took that name in the 19th century. He is today also popularly referred to as Karakhan Bab. The mausoleum is square in plan, with a domed roof. It has a tall portal on its south side, with a large niche within which stands a carved wooden door. Inside, niches in each wall frame latticed windows. The cloth-covered tomb lies in the centre of the building.

The path continues to the more modestly sized **Dauitbek Mausoleum**, honouring a local Mongol governor of less than glowing reputation, who died in 1267. The building is more popularly known locally as the Shamansur Mausoleum. Heavily reconstructed in the 19th century, the mausoleum has a plain exterior, and is again entered beneath a portal on the south side of the building. It is however usually kept locked.

The complex is a popular place for wedding parties, whose visits here tend to be a curious mix of the religious and the secular. A typical pattern involves prayers being said in the Karakhan Mausoleum, followed by the bride and groom waltzing through the surrounding woodland to the choreography of the director of the wedding video.

Kali Yunus Banya From the entrance to the park containing the Karakhan and Dauitbek mausolea, continue southwards onto a rough track where the paved road ends, keeping the fenced park on your left. This track joins Baizak Batyr Street. Turn right onto the latter, and after a couple of blocks you reach on your right the Tsarist-era brick-built municipal bath house known as the **Kali Yunus Banya**. Named after a wealthy merchant, the building is topped with 11 brick domes of varying sizes. You can get up onto the roof by way of a metal staircase at the back of the building. At the time of research, the interior was being readied to become a Museum of Ancient Taraz, with freshly painted murals on the walls of the domed chambers of the building depicting medieval life in Taraz and other towns of the area, including Sauran and Kulan.

West of Dostyk Square Taking Tole Bi Avenue westwards from Dostyk Square, you pass on your left after 1km a Russian Orthodox church, and then, a further 500m on, the **Aulie-Ata Mosque**, completed in 2007. Providing space for 1,200 worshippers, the mosque has a simple pale blue interior beneath a large central dome.

Another 1km further west lies the **Park of the First President of the Republic of Kazakhstan**. Inaugurated during a visit of President Nazarbaev to Taraz in 2007, the park stands opposite the public housing development of the Astana Microdistrict. The park is entered through a curved arcade of nine columns. There is a dynamic statue of 17th-century Kazakh warrior Koshek Batyr, a member of the Shaprashty tribe to which President Nazarbaev also belongs. He holds his hand out in front of him, as if commanding the Dzhungars to stop.

Tekturmas The Mausoleum of Tekturmas dates originally from the 13th century but has been heavily restored. It is stunningly located on a promontory overlooking the Talas River, just beyond the southeastern edge of town. To get here, take Abai Avenue southwards from the city centre, turning left onto Paluan Sholak Street where Abai Avenue runs into the railway line. Turn right under the underpass beneath the railway, onto Zhibek Zholy Street, and then left onto Zhangildin Street after another 500m. Follow the road across the Talas River, turning right 100m further on. The road takes you between undulating hills to Tekturmas, 600m on.

A crazy-paved path, with a low wall on either side, takes you onto the promontory. You reach first a tall brick structure, square in plan, with tall sides with open arches, and topped by a dome. The cloth-covered tomb inside is that of 18th-century Kazakh warrior Mambet Batyr. The path continues a few metres further to the Mausoleum of Tekturmas, which stands at the end of the promontory. It is a brick building with a metal-covered dome. There is a tomb inside. Its occupant, considered to be a pious, spiritual ruler, is identified in some accounts as Sultan

Mahmud Khan. There is an excellent view from behind the mausoleum across the Talas River to the green cityscape of Taraz stretching beyond. On your return, just beyond the Mambet Batyr Mausoleum, it is worth passing through the brick gate on your right, and taking the flight of steps down the side of a hill. These lead to a blocked entrance into the hillside. It is claimed that underground passages run for 120km. This spot is locally believed to project a strong spiritual aura: the remnants of fires next to the blocked entrance are evidence of prayers said here.

AROUND TARAZ

MAUSOLEUM OF AISHA BIBI The beautiful Karakhanid Mausoleum of Aisha Bibi is one place you should definitely see as part of any visit to Zhambyl Region. It sits in the village of the same name, west of Taraz. To get here, take the main road out of Taraz towards Shymkent. Aisha Bibi village lies 8km beyond the western gateway to the city. Within the village, take the signposted left turn to the mausoleum, turning left again (also signposted) where the road forks. The mausoleum is about 500m from the main road. It sits in a fenced compound amidst grounds filled with red rose bushes, making this a delightful spot in season.

The **Mausoleum of Aisha Bibi**, the larger of the two Karakhanid buildings in the compound, is a heavily restored square-based building, originally dating from the 11th or 12th century, with a conical roof. The external decoration is stunning: every spare piece of wall is covered with carved terracotta in a wide range of geometric designs. It is the only monument in central Asia fully covered with carved terracotta tilework. The main entrance is on the eastern side of the building, set in a niche. Niches on the other three walls enclose latticed wooden windows. There is a cloth-covered tomb inside.

Aisha Bibi is the subject of a popular legend in Kazakhstan. While there are numerous variations of the story, it runs broadly as follows. Aisha, of a well-to-do 11th-century family and a descendant of the Prophet, was brought up by her stepfather, Zangi-Ata. The Governor of Taraz, Shakhmakhmud, fell in love with her, and asked for her hand in marriage. This was rejected by Zangi-Ata, since Shakhmakhmud did not have Aisha's distinguished lineage. Aisha defied her stepfather and rode for Taraz to be united with the man she loved, but just short of the city she was bitten by a snake and died. The distraught Shakhmakhmud, who is also known as Karakhan Bab, built this beautiful mausoleum at her place of death. Shakhmakhmud never married, and became a wise and benevolent ruler, receiving the informal title of 'holy father', Aulie-Ata. Since the monument is associated with the eternal qualities of love, and because it is a beautiful place surrounded by red roses, it is a popular spot for wedding couples to come and be photographed.

To the right stands another attractive building, the **Mausoleum of Babazhi Khatun**. This is a 12th-century structure which has also been heavily restored. It has a distinctive 'corrugated' conical dome, with 16 sharp-edged ridges radiating out from the top, looking rather like a hat made in a school origami class. The external walls are plainer than those of the Aisha Bibi Mausoleum, though an Arabic inscription runs across the top of the eastern façade, above the arched entrance. There is no tomb inside the building. Babazhi Khatun is popularly believed to be the friend or nanny of Aisha Bibi, who faithfully tended the latter's mausoleum after her death, and was buried nearby.

AKYRTAS One of the most mysterious medieval sites in Kazakhstan, Akyrtas lies some 45km from Taraz. To get here, take the main road from Taraz towards Almaty.

Around 33km beyond the eastern edge of town, a signposted right turn around 2km west of the village of Aksholak directs you towards Akyrtas. A track then takes you under the railway line and towards the hills to the south. Turn left after around 4km, where the track forks, reaching Akyrtas another 3km on.

The site of Akyrtas is rectangular in plan, covering an area of some 4ha. Its walls are constructed of large red sandstone blocks, which must have been hugely difficult to bring here from their hillside quarry, several hundred metres away. A trench dug alongside the outer wall around the circular tower marking the northwest corner of the structure reveals that the walls rise to a height of more than 4m, most of that below the current level of the ground. The structure contains many rooms, around a central courtyard. One of a number of strange features about the complex is that it was built far from any natural source of water, necessitating a complicated system of water provision. Archaeologists now date the site to no earlier than the middle of the 8th century.

There is no academic agreement as to the nature of the structure at Akyrtas. Some believe that the site represents the ruins of the settlement of Kasribas. Other researchers believe that it was a palace, or a caravanserai. The Russian academic Vasily Bartold thought that it may have been a Nestorian monastery, drawing attention to a carving of a fish, a Christian symbol, on one stone block. The site seems to have been abandoned in an unfinished condition and archaeologists have uncovered no evidence of human habitation. There are indeed some in Kazakhstan who believe that this mysterious structure, with its huge cube-shaped building blocks, was the work not of humans but aliens. The site is claimed by some to possess great powers, and you may find as you walk round the site some of your fellow visitors hugging its stones, or standing motionless in hollows, absorbing its cosmic energies.

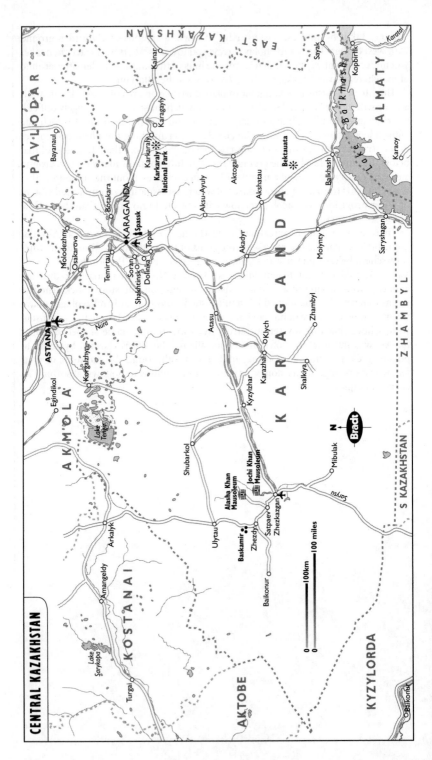

CENTRAL KAZAKHSTAN

6

Central Kazakhstan

Kazakhs call it the Sary Arka, the yellow steppe. It is a huge expanse of undulating grassland, covering the central belt of this vast country: green and verdant in spring, turning yellowish-brown with the drying heat of the summer sun. Karaganda Region is the largest in Kazakhstan. Its environment of steppelands punctuated by industrial cities founded on the coal, copper and steel industries is not of immediate touristic allure, but Karaganda is one of the regions which best give a sense of the emergence of modern Kazakhstan. One of the roots of the multi-ethnic character of the country lies in the Stalinist labour camps found across the region, whose inmates in turn helped to establish the great industrial plants which provided key materials for the Soviet economy. The post-war leaders of Kazakhstan started their careers in these heavy industries: Dinmuhammed Kunaev in an open-cast copper mine north of Balkhash; Nursultan Nazarbaev in the steel plant at Temirtau. The regional capital, Karaganda, offers a good base and has interesting Soviet-era buildings and monuments, and a fair range of hotels and restaurants. The main places to head for as regards the natural environment are a series of granite massifs, forming islands in the steppe. The pine-covered slopes of Karkaraly are a great place to spend a few days of gentle walking, and Ulytau, a land of myths and legends, whose many mausolea include one ascribed to Jochi, son of Genghis Khan, combines historical interest with beautiful scenery.

KARAGANDA   *Telephone code: 7212*

The city of Karaganda, the fourth largest of Kazakhstan with a population close to half a million, takes its name from a shrub, the caragana. Also known as the Siberian peashrub, this offers a springtime bloom of yellow flowers. The name 'Karaganda' is often used in a jocular way in other parts of the former Soviet Union, to refer to the 'middle of nowhere'. And certainly this city, in the heart of the immense steppelands, does have an isolated feel. The presence of a large urban area in this spot is due to the presence of one valuable resource: coal. An apocryphal story has it that the city was founded after a group of nomadic Kazakhs threw rocks on their campfire to extinguish it. One of the rocks burst into flame, and the coal reserves of Karaganda were discovered.

Coal was mined here from the 1850s, but did not develop into a major industry until the 1930s, when the Soviet authorities decided to use the coal reserves of Karaganda to fuel the industries of the Urals. The accomplishment of this task was achieved with the efforts of convict labour, and Karaganda became notorious for its high concentration of labour camps, many grouped in a large area to the southwest of the city known as KarLag (Karagandinsky Lager). Among those sent to the camps here were many thousands of ethnic Germans, deported from the Volga Region as Stalin fretted that they would act as fifth columnists in the war with Nazi Germany. Karaganda retained a large ethnic German population throughout the post-war Soviet period, though many emigrated to Germany following Kazakhstan's independence. The Chechens of the north Caucasus were another ethnic group deemed suspect by Stalin and deported here *en masse*. Akhmad Kadyrov, the former Chechen separatist leader who became President of the Chechen Republic from 2000 until his assassination at a World War II victory parade in 2004, was born in Karaganda.

Karaganda was formally named a city in 1934, and became regional capital two years later. The occupation of the Donbass coalfields by the German forces during World War II further strengthened its importance, as factories supplying coal-mining machinery were relocated here. The city underwent a difficult time in the immediate post-independence period, and the mining industry is working at far less than its peak Soviet levels. Most of the working mines are now run by the Mittal company, providing coal for its steel plant at nearby Temirtau. It remains a dangerous industry, with major accidents in both 2006 and 2008. But there is a new economic optimism in Karaganda, reflected in the modern new stores along the main Bukhar Zhirau Avenue. A sign written along the roadside as you come into Karaganda from the north describes the place as the political and economic buttress of Kazakhstan, and at the heart of Karaganda's self-image is a strong sense that their miners have been central in constructing the post-independence success of Kazakhstan. This includes a political sense as well as an economic one: in the summer of 1989 the miners of Karaganda joined the strike action initiated by their colleagues in the Russian Kuzbass, which was to play an important role in hastening the demise of Soviet power. While the smokestacks in view as you enter the city do not offer an immediately enticing prospect, Karaganda is a pleasant city in which to spend a couple of nights.

It is a very spread-out city with several centres. The 'old town' centres on the original miners' dwellings. The 'new town' to the south was developed on Karaganda's elevation to cityhood in 1934 as the administrative centre, and it is here that the places of interest to the tourist lie.

GETTING THERE AND AROUND The **airport** is 24km out of town. Air Astana operates a daily flight to Almaty, using either a Boeing 737 or smaller Fokker 50 aircraft. The flight time is an hour and ten minutes in the Boeing, double that in the Fokker. There is also one Air Astana flight a week to Frankfurt, and one to Hanover, both stopping *en route* at Kostanai, a testament to the large ethnic German minorities of Karaganda and Kostanai. Transaero operates two flights a week to Moscow; Domodedovo Airlines adds a third.

The **railway station** (433636) is quite centrally located, on the city-centre side of the bridge taking the main Bukhar Zhirau Avenue across the railway tracks. It features a fine Soviet relief along the base of the vaulted ceiling of the main hall. Farmers, factory workers and blast furnace workers carry out their jobs, while eager students watch them, busily taking notes. And so the next generation of Soviet labour was trained. Reliefs in the adjacent 'waiting hall of passengers with children' extol women: as gymnasts, ballerinas, athletes, able mothers and doting grannies. Karaganda is a stop on routes passing north from Almaty to Astana, Petropavl, Kostanai and Pavlodar, as well as the daily train from Kyzylorda to Petropavl. A daily train from Almaty also terminates here. There is a daily connection to Balkhash, and a train on even-numbered dates to Zhezkazgan. There is a train from Karaganda to Moscow, running every two days, and options to other Russian cities, including Omsk, Novokuznetsk and Sverdlovsk. The tariff of charges in the railway station toilet, incidentally, includes a T15 fee to wash your feet in the sink.

The **bus station** (↖ 431818) sits next door, a less distinguished building with overpowering tiled murals on its interior walls: patriotic scenes collide with geometric designs. There is roughly one bus an hour to Astana, one a day to Almaty, one daily to Ust-Kamenogorsk, five a day to Zhezkazgan, five to Karkaraly, three to Balkhash and six to Pavlodar. Tickets to local destinations are sold from a separate ticket office, around the back of the bus station. There are departures every few minutes for Temirtau and the mining town of Shakhtinsk. The local buses depart from the stands in front of this ticket office.

Drivers operating private **minibuses** and **taxis** congregate in the open space in front of the railway and bus stations, calling out their destination: 'Astana' predominates. They depart when full or when the driver gets bored of waiting.

TOUR OPERATORS AND AIRLINE OFFICES

✈ **Konkord** 66A Bukhar Zhirau Av; ↖425010, 911400; f 425010; e transaero@concord.kz, kgf. airport@transaero.kz; www.konkord.kz

✈ **Otrar Travel** 31 Beibitshilik Av; ↖566991; f 300687; e kgf@otrar.kz; www.otrar.kz. General Service Agent for Air Astana.

✈ **Transavia** 24 Erubaev St; ↖426002; f 435596; e transavia_kgd@transavia-travel. kz; www.transavia-travel.kz. Another office at 27 Bukharzirau St; ↖410797; f 426368. Local representative for Domodedovo Airlines. Bookings for airline & railway tickets.

WHERE TO STAY
Top-range and mid-range

⌂ **Hotel Cosmonaut** (46 rooms) 162A Krivoguza St; ↖438555; f 438565; e info@ hotelcosmonaut.kz; www.hotelcosmonaut.kz. A 4-star & reasonably central option, although the site, across the park from the city centre, can feel isolated. The Cosmonaut has a good indoor pool & fitness centre. Its nightclub promises karaoke nights. Internet access is available in the business centre. **$$$$**

⌂ **Hotel Dostar Alem** (40 rooms) 28 Stroiteley Av; ↖400400; f 740202; e dostar-alem@mail.ru; www.dostar-alem.kz. One of the nicest hotels in town, with comfortable rooms, all with en suites, & an airy feel, though the décor of the Hotel 'Between Friends' certainly suggests a liking for the colour orange. The hotel is part of a larger entertainment complex which also includes the Boomer Bowling Club. The main drawback of the place is its rather peripheral location, southeast of the centre. **$$$$**

⌂ **Hotel Chayka** (44 rooms) 11 Michurin St; ↖415332; f 415326; e info@chayka.kz. This must be a strong candidate for the world title of 'hotel named Seagull situated furthest from the sea'. This was the prestige Soviet-era hotel in Karaganda. The main building, dating from the early 1980s, features a circular golden-coloured ornamentation on the roof which looks rather like a kitsch spaceship attempting to land. You stay either in this building or in 2 neighbouring outbuildings. The 2nd of these, 'Block 2', where some of the hotel's more expensive rooms are located, is a piece of local history in itself. In this attractive 2-storey building, older than the rest of the hotel, a generation of cosmonauts rested following their landings back to earth. Plaques on the external walls chronicle the many cosmonauts to have stayed here, among them Valentina Tereshkova, the world's first female cosmonaut, in June 1963. In the foyer of this building is proudly displayed a 1987 Diploma of the Federation of Cosmonauts of the USSR, awarded on the 25th anniversary of the first recuperation stay by cosmonauts at the Chayka Hotel, to the administrators & staff of the hotel for their support of the Soviet space programme. The rooms have been renovated, & are fine, & the hotel is nicely located in a quiet spot adjacent to the main park. The main downside with the Chayka is its policy of charging a booking fee of 50% of the cost of the 1st night's accommodation. **$$$**

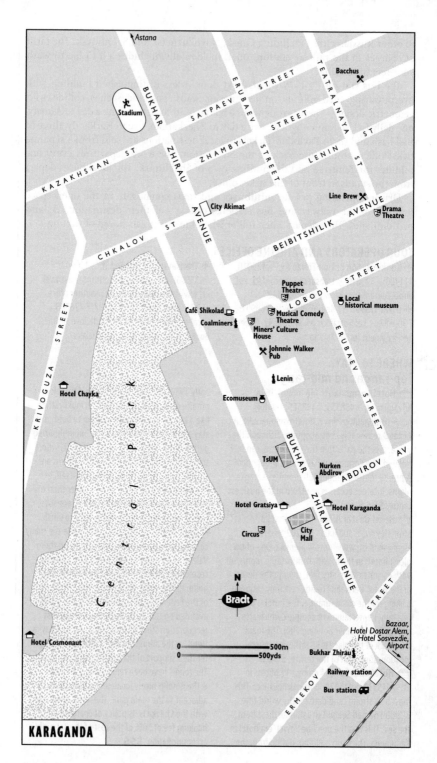

Astana

BUKHAR ZHIRAU ST

SATPAEV STREET

ERUBAEV STREET

TEATRALNAYA ST

Bacchus ✕

Stadium 🏃

KAZAKHSTAN ST

ZHAMBYL STREET

ERUBAEV STREET

LENIN ST

City Akimat ⌂

BEIBITSHILIK AVENUE

Line Brew ✕

Drama Theatre 🎭

CHKALOV ST

BUKHAR ZHIRAU AVENUE

LOBODY STREET

Puppet Theatre 🎭

Local historical museum 🏛

Café Shikolad 💻
Coalminers 👤

Musical Comedy Theatre 🎭

Miners' Culture House

ERUBAEV STREET

KRIVOGUZA STREET

Johnnie Walker ✕ Pub

Hotel Chayka ⌂

Lenin 👤

Ecomuseum ♨

BUKHAR ZHIRAU AVENUE

TsUM ▱

Nurken Abdirov 👤

ABDIROV AV

C e n t r a l   P a r k

Hotel Gratsiya ⌂

Hotel Karaganda ⌂

Circus 🎭

City Mall

N

Bradt

Hotel Cosmonaut ⌂

0 ———— 500m
0 ———— 500yds

Bazaar,
Hotel Dostar Alem,
Hotel Sosvezdie,
Airport

Bukhar Zhirau 👤

Railway station ▱

ERMEKOV STREET

Bus station 🚌

KARAGANDA

Budget

 Hotel Karaganda (42 rooms) 66 Bukhar Zhirau Av; 425005, 425204; f 425060; e altinbatyr1@mail.ru. The deceptively grand, square-columned entrance on Bukhar Zhirau Av hides a run-down hotel. They offer a wide variety of room permutations: the cheapest lack en suites or much at all in the way of comfort. The location is however very central. **$$**

 Hotel Gratsiya (72 beds) 57A Bukhar Zhirau Av; 412459; f 412443; e hotel-gracia@mail.ru. A 5-storey blue-walled building near the circus, the Gratsiya is one of those somewhat faded places found across the former Soviet Union with corridors featuring a strip of worn red carpet lying on top of aged parquet flooring. Only 'semi-luxe' rooms & suites have en-suite facilities, & there is no AC. Rent of a teapot will cost you an additional T50/hr. The Gratsiya is one of several hotels in Karaganda to charge a reservation fee equal to 50% of the cost of the 1st night's accommodation. **$; $$** 'semi-luxe'

 Hotel Sosvezdie (25 rooms) 34 Stroiteley Av; 400630; f 400629; e hotel@sozvezdie. karaganda.kz; www.sozvezdie.karaganda. kz. The 'Constellation' is an 8-storey building, inconveniently located, like the nearby Dostar Alem, to the southeast of the city centre, & illuminated at night by twinkling stars on its external walls. It offers a wide range of options, from basic sgls without en suites to huge 'VIP' rooms, offering vast open spaces & in some cases shocking pink bedrooms. Only the 'VIP' rooms have AC; 'semi-luxe' & above have en suites. **$** 'semi-luxe'; **$$** 'luxe'

 Railway Station Retiring Rooms Very basic & low privacy but clean accommodation is available on the floor above the main concourse at the railway station. The accommodation is separated into male & 'mother & child' rooms, with dbls, trpls, quads & dormitory accommodation available. **$**

✗ WHERE TO EAT

✗ **Line Brew** 24 Beibitshilik Av; 501026, 501223. Part of a chain gradually gaining ground across Kazakhstan, this place offers a vaguely central European medieval décor, with drawbridge at the entrance, stone walls & timbered roofs. The stained-glass windows are a copy of the abbey symbol found on bottles of Leffe beer, & the long list of bottled Belgian beers is one of the main selling points of the place. The other is *shashlik*, cooked in front of you at a BBQ wildly over-embellished with utensils of yesteryear beneath a tiled rooflet. The rest of the menu offers a mishmash of international dishes. The wine list is expensive. **$$$$**

✗ **Bacchus** 42 Zhambyl St; 560822. Music is the focus of this restaurant, whose walls are decorated with large photos of McCartney, Zappa, Dylan & Armstrong. Instruments hang from the ceiling & there's often live music in the evenings. This is also one of those restaurants displaying numerous framed photos of staff & clientele doing crazy things, mostly involving blindfolds, shots of vodka & silly hats, none of which is in evidence when you visit. A 2nd dining hall eschews the music theme in favour of a rather over-fussy formal look. Their speciality is, apparently, cheesecake. **$$$**

♀ **Johnnie Walker Pub** 36 Bukhar Zhirau Av; 411908; f 410287. There are waiters in kilts, tartan lampshades, Scottish flags hanging from the ceiling & haggis on the menu. Johnnie Walker whisky is, appropriately, available in several permutations, including Red & Blue label, though the menu is bereft of malt whisky. The food is decent pub fare, with a nod or 2 to Scotland. There is also a sushi bar, Sakura, in a separate room on the same premises. Don't be surprised to see waitresses in kimonos scuttling across the Scottish pub on their way to the shared kitchen. **$$$**

Cafés

 Café Shikolad 33 Bukhar Zhirau Av; 424768. This small subterranean café close to the coal-miners' statue, with a punning name & youthful clientele, provides a good spot for a mid-sightseeing coffee & cake.

SHOPPING The central stretch of Bukhar Zhirau Avenue running northwestwards from the railway station is the main shopping street in Karaganda. A series of modern shopping malls cluster around the renovated **TsUM** (*53 Bukhar Zhirau Av;* ⊕ *10.00–21.00 daily*), the one-time Soviet department store which now houses a collection of boutiques. The **City Mall** (⊕ *10.00–22.00 daily*), a block to the south of here, houses a Ramstor supermarket. The main **bazaar** is located in a rather bleak spot, to the southeast of the railway bridge along Bukhar Zhirau Avenue.

WHAT TO SEE

Bukhar Zhirau Avenue A walk northwards along Bukhar Zhirau Avenue from the railway station gives a good feel of the city centre, and takes in some interesting monuments. There is a statue of **Bukhar Zhirau** himself, wearing the traditional Kazakh cloak and tall hat, in the park in front of the railway station, as if welcoming new arrivals to the city. Bukhar Zhirau was a poet and adviser to Ablai Khan, the 18th-century khan of the Middle Horde who achieved military successes against the Dzhungars and who strove to create a strong, independent Kazakh state.

A couple of blocks further to the northwest along Bukhar Zhirau Avenue, just beyond the Hotel Karaganda, is a monument to a very different local hero. **Nurken Abdirov** was a young pilot of World War II, posthumously awarded the title of Hero of the Soviet Union when his plane was damaged by enemy fire above Stalingrad in 1943. Rather than attempt to save their own lives, he and gunner Alexandr Komissarov steered the stricken plane to crash into a German column. The drama-packed statue depicts Abdirov, expression defiant, gripping the steering wheel of his plane as one might a bucking bronco.

A block further on, past the line of modern new shopping malls, and a large video screen flashing out adverts, the cityscape reverts to a more Soviet feel. In front of the building housing the headquarters of Mittal Steel's coal operation stands a statue of **Lenin**, greatcoated against the cold, his hand resting on the stone plinth as if in mid-oration. The Soviet theme continues across Bukhar Zhirau Avenue, in the mirror-image buildings housing the regional trades' union office and the geology department. Built in the 1960s, these feature mosaic friezes of industrial workers and geologists. Outside the geology department building stand a couple of large rocks from deposits in the region: one of iron ore, the other of greenish copper porphyry ore.

On the ground floor of the geological department building, unmarked from the street, is the **Ecomuseum** (*47 Bukhar Zhirau Av;* ✆ *413344;* e *ecomuseum@ ecomuseum.kz, ecomuseum@mail.ru; www.ecomuseum.kz;* ⊕ *09.00–18.00 Mon–Fri; admission T100*). Turn right down the corridor from the entrance. Housed in a single hall, with the displays around the walls, this museum is focused mainly on educating local schoolchildren about the importance of protecting the environment. The busy, child-friendly, displays look at mining, industry, nuclear power and military test sites. There is a moving display on the legacy of the nuclear testing carried out during the Soviet period around Semipalatinsk, and another area, mocked up to resemble the control deck of a spaceship, focusing on the debris dropped during launches from the Baikonur site. Ask the staff to lift up the hatch in the floor to reveal large mangled pieces of space junk. The museum is an altogether highly worthwhile initiative, with committed staff.

Continuing northwards along Bukhar Zhirau Avenue, after a further block you reach a statue of two **coal miners**, which has become something of a symbol of Karaganda. The two proud men raise a huge block of coal high above their heads like weightlifters. The path behind this statue takes you to the main entrance of Karaganda's large and attractive **central park**. Facing the statue across Bukhar Zhirau Avenue is the **Miners' Culture House**, built by Japanese prisoners of war to a neo-classical design. Its façade is topped by seven statues, ranging from miner, through soldier and agricultural worker to musician.

Local historical museum (*38 Erubaeva St;* \ *563121, 301136;* e *museum.kz@ mail.ru;* ⊕ *09.00–18.00 daily; admission adult/child T200/100*) Take Lobody Street running around the back of the Miners' Cultural House. This is something of a cultural district of Karaganda: you pass a **musical comedy theatre** on your right and a small **puppet theatre** on your left. At the next intersection, with Erubaev Street, stands the local historical museum, set back from the road. This is one of the better regional museums, with a good number of displays in English, as well as Kazakh and Russian. The first room is devoted to the post-independence achievements of Kazakhstan. Then comes the natural environment. One display here focuses on the 458km Irtysh–Karaganda Canal named after Satpaev, constructed at the beginning of the 1970s to bring additional water supplies to the industries of Karaganda. The next room explores the region's wildlife through the usual array of stuffed animals. The ducks are for some reason translated into English as 'woofs'. A display of the work of the Phytochemistry Institute in Karaganda features a photograph rather charmingly labelled, in English, 'demonstration of foreign scientist'. Another display describes the disintegration of a Proton rocket, fired from the Baikonur launch site, on 5 July 1999. Fragments were scattered across the region. There is a photograph of the rocket's twisted engine, surrounded by worried-looking officials.

Next comes early history, with a model of the Golden Man taking centre stage. There is a Bronze Age burial and a model of a *kurgan* from the early Iron Age. The next room continues the chronology. There is a fragment of turquoise tilework from the 13th-century Mausoleum of Jochi Khan in the Ulytau Mountains, and wall maps depict the Golden Horde and the formation of the Kazakh Khanate. There are displays on the fighting between Kazakhs and Dzhungars. A diorama depicts the ruins of a Kazakh village after the Dzhungars have left. There are photographs of the ceremony of oath-taking of the Kazakhs of the Middle Horde to the Russian Empire. The Tsarist-era resettlement of Slavonic peoples to the area is illustrated by a mock-up of a home of one of the resettled families, with log walls, an icon in the corner, a samovar on the table and large quantities of linen. A copy of a document dating back to 1895 from the Governor of Poltava announces the resettlement of 50 peasant families to Kazakhstan. A display on the lives of the early coal miners includes some appallingly bleak photographs of life below ground, as well as photographs of Honorary Miners, proudly showing off their numerous medals. There is also an ethnographic section, with displays of jewellery and embroidered costumes.

The displays continue upstairs. The next room focuses on the Kazakh nationalist movements of the early part of the 20th century and on the rebellion of 1916, a painting of whose leader, Amangeldy Imanov, dominates the room. Next comes a somewhat dull room, full of photographs of the past stars of the region's theatres, and then a room chronicling the development of coal mining in the region. There is a display about the works of the geologists, such as Aleksandr Gapeev, who explored the area's coal reserves. The establishment of the Kazstroyugol organisation in 1929 heralded a major uplift in efforts to develop the coalfields. Awards given to those involved in the effort are on display, and there are photographs of workers at the Stakhanov Mine No 20, taking its name from a legendarily productive miner.

The next room provides an uneasy combination of displays about the GuLag labour camps with ones about World War II, the latter focusing on local heroes of the military campaign. The GuLag displays include a map showing the huge expanse covered by the administrative area of the Karaganda camp complex known

6

as KarLag. A stark relief at the end of the room depicts those incarcerated at KarLag toiling in shifting rocks, and then laying down to die. The war heroes whose exploits are described in the adjoining displays include Nurken Abdirov, whose mother is rather intrusively photographed gazing at a photo of her son, and Honorary Miner Bekbosin Sikhimbaev, who came out of retirement to go back down the mines in order to dig for victory.

The museum displays continue into the post-war Soviet period. A photo shows the miners of Karaganda holding aloft the billionth tonne of coal extracted. With further abrupt changes of tone, a display on noted local literary figures abuts one on the young men of the region killed in Afghanistan. There is a display on nuclear tests held around Semipalatinsk, and one on the sports stars of Karaganda Region. The next room focuses on space, with a reverential display about Kazakhstan's first cosmonaut, Tokhtar Aubakirov, who hails from Karaganda Region. The tubes of food consumed by the cosmonauts, looking just like toothpaste tubes, are on display. The Soviet space authorities did not go in for alluring presentation: the tubes are labelled, baldly, 'fruit dessert' or 'coffee with milk'. The following room covers post-independence Karaganda, with displays about the industrial enterprises of the region. 'Made in Karaganda' food products are exhibited, including bread, ice cream and chocolate squirrels. The last room focuses on President Nazarbaev, with photographs of the young future president working at the Temirtau steel plant and, as the First Secretary of the Kazakhstan Communist Party, speaking with striking miners in 1989. He is also shown back at the Temirtau blast furnace in 2000, testing the quality of the molten metal.

TEMIRTAU *Telephone code: 7213*

An industrial town of 200,000 people some 40km to the north of Karaganda, Temirtau is the centre of the steel industry in Kazakhstan. Lying on the bank of the Nura River, Temirtau started its life as Zhaur, a settlement founded by a group of settlers from Samara. Zhaur was renamed Samarkand a few years later, and the damming of the Nura River to create the Samarkand Reservoir in the 1930s provided a stimulus to industrial development. A steel industry emerged here during World War II, and Samarkand was renamed Temirtau ('Iron Mountain') in 1945.

The development of large-scale steel production, however, had to await the construction in the 1950s of the Karaganda Steel Mill (Karmet). This huge project required the marshalling of construction brigades from as far afield as Bulgaria. The conditions faced by those building the plant were dreadful, and led to riots in the town at the end of July 1959. Several of the rioters were killed as the Soviet authorities restored order. The first blast furnace went into operation in 1960. Among the early blast furnace workers in the new plant was a young Nursultan Nazarbaev, the future President of Kazakhstan. Billboards around town display photographs of the president, in the uniform of a blast furnace worker, reliving his early work experiences during return visits to Temirtau.

As newly independent Kazakhstan sought out foreign investors to help revive its heavy industries, with their elderly Soviet equipment, the Karaganda Steel Mill moved into foreign hands in 1995 as ISPAT Karmet, now known as Mittal Steel Temirtau. The Mittal logo is omnipresent in the town. Iron ore is brought from the company's mines in Kostanai Region, coal from the mines around Karaganda. The Temirtau plant, one of the largest single-site integrated steel plants anywhere in the world, carries out a long sequence of operations, including coke making, the production of iron in blast furnaces, steel manufacture, hot rolling and galvanising.

Temirtau presents a forbidding landscape to those approaching the town, of smokestacks belching emissions into trails visible several kilometres away. It has some tough social problems too, including the highest levels of HIV infection found in Kazakhstan, and rampant alcoholism. But while in no sense a tourist centre, it is easy to visit from Karaganda, and a few hours here give a good insight both into the pride felt by many Kazakhstanis in the contribution made by their major industrial facilities to the development of their country, and the huge challenge involved in attempting to modernise them.

PRACTICALITIES It is easy enough to get to Temirtau on one of the frequent buses from Karaganda, so there is no real need to overnight here. If you do decide to stay, however, there is a comfortable option on the eastern side of town, close to the entrance to the steel plant. The **Hotel Steel** (*86 rooms; 4 Respublika Av;* f *913601;* **$$$$**) is run by Mittal Steel, and mainly accommodates visitors to their plant. Temirtau is pretty spread out, but a tram service, also operated by Mittal Steel, will get you around town for just T10 a ride.

WHAT TO SEE The long, snaking, Respublika Avenue, formerly known as Lenina, links the old town centre at the western edge of the current settlement to the steel plant on the eastern side of town. Old town and new are separated by the Samarkand Reservoir.

The old town The buildings of this rather charming, if run-down, part of town were in part put up by Japanese prisoners of war in the late 1940s. The centre of the old town is an attractive square, at the corner of Respublika Avenue and Panfilova Street. The **Youth Theatre**, dating from the 1950s, is a rather grand building, with a double row of columns in front of the entrance and round motifs on the façade depicting metalworkers, miners and agricultural workers. The theatre started out life as the Cultural Palace of Metalworkers, before a spell as the German Drama Theatre. The park around the back is gradually reverting to the wild.

Across Respublika Avenue, the square continues as a quiet garden in which a monument to **Lenin** still stands. Behind this is the derelict one-time Palace of Power Engineers, fronted by faded Corinthian columns and a couple of broken statues. The old town is considered a somewhat rough area, to be avoided after dark.

The new town On Respublika Avenue, towards the eastern end of town, sits the main town **park**. Inside this lies Temirtau's most unexpected sight, a **Winter Garden** (⊕ *12.00–19.00; admission T80*). This hangar-like greenhouse was put up in the early 1990s, and a jolly jungle painting over the entrance features smiley panthers and snakes. Inside, the place is filled with palms, banana trees, hibiscus and oleander. There are caged parrots, rabbits and squirrels. Some of the plants have plaques recording that they were planted by some of the leading lights of Kazakhstan: President Nazarbaev's wife and eldest daughter, a former Health Minister, Cosmonaut Tokhtar Aubakirov. Wedding parties come here to be photographed amidst the tropical foliage.

Further west along Respublika Avenue, at the intersection with Metallurgov Avenue, is a **Monument to the Metalworkers**, a metal-faced obelisk beneath which two metalworkers stand. The figure on the right, sampling the molten metal with a ladle, bears a certain resemblance to the young Nazarbaev. Behind the monument, to the right, the concrete building of the Karaganda Musical Comedy Theatre is decorated with the metal heads of miners, metalworkers, cosmonauts and some representing uninterpretable occupations.

The network of Stalinist-era labour camps known as KarLag stretched out over a huge area to the south and west of Karaganda. A museum at Dolinka and monuments at Spassk offer some sense of the appalling conditions faced by the thousands of people incarcerated there.

DOLINKA A somewhat depressed-looking village 36km southwest of Karaganda, where the local shop sells vodka at T40 a shot, Dolinka's claim to historical fame is as the administrative centre of the KarLag labour camp network. To get here, head out of Karaganda towards the mining town of Shakhtinsk and take the next turning on your left after passing a brightly painted sign on your right welcoming you to Novodolinsk village. This brings you into Dolinka. In a mark of continuity with its sad past, there's still a prison here.

Ask in the village to be directed to the **Museum for the Victims of Political Repression** (*(72156) 58222;* m *+7 701 419 2138;* ⊕ *09.00–18.00 Mon–Sat; admission adult/student T50/30).* Housed in one of the wings of a single-storey cream-coloured building, which also accommodates a clinic, this offers a small but well-displayed collection of items relating to the KarLag system. The building itself was a local hospital while the labour camp system was in force. A stone statue of Lenin, clad in winter jacket, stands outside. The number of people incarcerated in the KarLag network reached 65,673 in 1949, spread across camps occupying a large territory. A wall painting, the work of a KarLag artist, depicts Lenin giving orders. Stalin, dutifully searching out a location on a map behind him, is among the lieutenants pictured with him. There is an iron hospital bed on display, complete with chunk of wooden floor underneath and a wooden side cupboard. The museum also displays objects produced by prisoners at local factories, including bricks and ceramic jugs. Personal items on display, including embroidery, a mirror, and a selection of books from the KarLag library, have the perhaps inadvertent effect of seeming to humanise the camps, though one wonders what was going through the mind of prisoners reading the biography of Stalin in the library. Many of those deported here were ethnic Germans, and the items on display include a photograph of the Krieger family as well as a framed inscription reading 'Der Herr ist Mein Hirte'.

Near the museum, the two-storey building beyond the trees with four blue-painted columns along the façade and bricked-up windows was the main administrative building of the KarLag. Locals will tell you that inmates of the camps were tortured in its basement. You can also enter the **camp** (admission adult/student T70/50, T500 for a video or camera permit) itself, though there is little to see, all interesting artefacts having been moved to the museum.

SPASSK At the side of the main road between Karaganda and Balkhash, 36km south of the regional capital, are a moving group of monuments to the many nationalities who died in the KarLag camps, erected by their respective governments. The first monument, in the form of a broken *shanyrak*, is dedicated to 'the victims of repression who found the eternal peace in Kazakh soil'. There then follow monuments to the victims of political repression and prisoners of war who died here from France, Kyrgyzstan, Ukraine, Italy, Germany, Armenia, Lithuania, Finland, Romania, Poland, Hungary, Japan, Belarus and Russia. Black crosses, grouped in threes, lie atop the otherwise unmarked graves adjacent to these.

Spassk was one of the most notorious of the KarLag camps. The monuments lie on the eastern side of the main road, clearly visible from it, opposite a turning marked with a sign to 'Spassk 0.1'.

One of the most scenically beautiful areas of Karaganda Region, Karkaraly, known in Russian as Karkaralinsk, features a range of pine-covered hills, rising to a highest point of 1,403m, emerging from the surrounding steppes. Wind-sculpted rocks and birch-fringed lakes add to the scenic diversity of one of several places to claim the label of 'Kazakhstan's Switzerland'. Some 220km to the east of Karaganda, Karkaraly is a relaxing place to spend a few days, its natural beauty coupled with a small district capital packing a surprisingly rich history are the main draws.

PRACTICALITIES Unlike one of the other pretenders to the 'Kazakhstani Switzerland' crown, Borovoye, Karkaraly boasts little current tourist development. Several Soviet-era sanatoria and pioneer camps, most of which have seen better days, nestle in the hills here. Some are derelict.

One place which has undergone a certain amount of renovation work, and is the best accommodation choice out of the sanatoria options, is the **Shakhtyor House of Rest** (*104 rooms;* \ *31643, 31842;* f *31643;* **$$**). The 'Miner' is run by the Mittal Steel coal department, and the main focus of the place is in providing rest breaks to coal miners from Karaganda. It offers a range of accommodation at various levels of renovation, on a full-board basis. The Shakhtyor is 10km further on from Karkaraly, and is signposted from the town. It occupies a delightful site on the banks of Lake Pashino, hugged by rocky crags. The complex centres on the two-storey building housing the canteen, or 'dining-holl' as the English-language labelling has it, which offers exactly the kind of regimented, cutlet-heavy fare you would expect at these prices. A sports centre, which includes a pool, is a recent addition. There is also a 'downhill ski complex' a couple of kilometres away. This comprises a chairlift and a decidedly modest-scaled ski run. There is a daily excursion by bus from the Shakhtyor to the ski complex in season (bus adult/child T50/25; chairlift T80/30). Occasional excursions are also arranged to Karkaraly town and to the nature museum. One downside of the Shakhtyor is, however, the piped radio music which echoes around the grounds, drowning out the birdsong.

An entirely different accommodation option is offered by the **NGO Karkaraly Ecocentre** (*25 Abai St;* \ *31387;* **$**). Zulfiya Myrsamakova, the co-ordinator, offers three local homestays on a full-board basis. You can also book through the Ecotourism Information Resource Centre in Almaty (see page 123).

There is one bus a day from Karaganda direct to the Shakhtyor House of Rest, rather more between Karaganda and Karkaraly town.

WHAT TO SEE

Karkaraly town The district capital is a pleasant small town of 11,000 people, at the foot of the hills. Many of the houses are single-storey whitewashed cottages with blue window frames. The main street is named after Tokhtar Aubakirov, Kazakhstan's first cosmonaut. The rare step of naming the road after a living personality gives an indication of the reverence in which the name of the district's most famous recent alumnus is held.

A fort was established here in 1824, and Karkaraly developed as a Cossack settlement. In 1868, it became the capital of a Tsarist district, or *uyezd*, forming part of Semipalatinsk Region. The place served out most of the 20th century as something of a farming-focused backwater; its Tsarist buildings today act as reminders of a 19th-century relative heyday when this was an important trading centre, the nearby Koyandinsk fairs attracting far-flung custom.

Kunanbay Mosque One of the most striking buildings of the town is the wooden Kunanbay Mosque, whose square tower topped with a blue-painted spire is visible from a considerable distance. The interior of the mosque includes a beautifully carved wooden *mihrab*, and a *minbar* brightly painted in geometrical designs. The mosque was completed in 1851. Its construction was financed by Kunanbay, the father of Kazakhstan's greatest writer, Abai Kunanbaev, who was a governor, or Aga Sultan, of Karkaraly from 1849–53. The mosque was put to various uses during the Soviet period: pioneer meetings and trade union gatherings were held here, and it also acted as a library before being restored following Kazakhstan's independence.

Karkaraly District Historical Museum (\ *32788;* ⊕ *09.00–18.00 Mon–Sat; admission adult/child T50/25*) A single-storey white-painted building with blue window frames in the centre of the town, the headquarters of the *uyezd* administration in Tsarist times, now houses the District Historical Museum. The first room offers an account of the district's archaeological treasures, the second covers the Kazakh khanates. There are displays on two local leading lights of 18th-century campaigning against the Dzhungars: warrior hero Senkibay Batyr, and Kazybek Bi, judge of the Middle *Zhuz*. The next room combines ethnographic exhibits, including half a yurt, with 19th-century history, featuring photographs of the Koyandinsk fair in action and models of the Kunanbay Mosque and of a wooden house still standing in the town, in which Kunanbay's son, the great writer Abai, once dwelt. The next room covers the Soviet period, combining in close juxtaposition photographs of the victims of the repression of the 1930s with those of Heroes of the Soviet Union nominated for their wartime exploits. The next room covers the post-independence period and is painted a patriotic pale blue. There is a display about Tokhtar Aubakirov, whose 60th birthday, in 2006, is honoured by a photograph of the uniformed cosmonaut appearing to rise up out of a lake. Following a small room focusing on nature is a hall devoted to local art. This includes a couple of models of possible future statues of Madi Bapiuly, a local poet and singer, killed in 1921, who is regarded as a latter-day Robin Hood figure.

A single-storey brick Tsarist-era building across the road from the museum, now housing the district library, was the house of a merchant named **Ryazantsev**. The Russian ethnographer Grigoriy Potanin stayed here on a visit to Karkaraly in 1913.

Around the back of the museum stands Karkaraly's very own **Baiterek Tower**, a smaller-scale version of the one in Astana (see page 98). It was put up in 2004 to celebrate the 180th birthday of the town. Pictures running along the wall behind the monument display the famous names associated with the district, from Kazybek Bi to Tokhtar Aubakirov.

Karkaraly National Park The establishment in 1884 of the Karkaralinsk Forest Reserve marked the start of the protection of these pine-covered granite hills. At Komissarovka, an isolated lakeside spot south of Karkaraly, the wooden forest warden's house, completed in 1913, still stands, offering an attractive vision of pitched roofs and painted window frames against a mountain backdrop. Several administrative changes later, the Karkaraly State National Nature Park was set up in 1998. A favoured site during the Soviet period for industrial workers and young pioneers to get in touch with nature, the Karkaraly Hills hosted the Soviet orienteering championships in 1986.

One of the most popular walking trails through the hills runs north from the Shakhtyor House of Rest to **Lake Shaytankol**. The 'Devil's Lake', nestled amidst an upland terrain of pines and rocky crags, is said to have received its downbeat name from the frequency of the occasions in which locals on hunting trips lost their way home in its vicinity. They concluded that the malevolence of the devil was at work.

One of many legends surrounding the place is a Kazakh tale of doomed love. The story runs that a wealthy man, Tleuberdy, had a beautiful 16-year-old daughter, Sulyshash. She had eyes only for a horse-herder named Altay, but Tleuberdy would never permit his daughter to marry such an impoverished suitor. So Altay and Sulyshash secretly left their village, together with Altay's friend Kaysar. They travelled across great expanses of steppe, eventually finding refuge in the Karkaraly Mountains. They reached Shaytankol Lake. Altay and Kaysar left Sulyshash in a cave by the side of the lake, and went hunting. Kaysar fell to his death from a cliff face while attempting to chase an *arkhar*. In the meantime, the vengeful Tleuberdy had set fire to the forest, to flush out the young lovers. Overcome by smoke, Sulyshash ran out of the cave, and straight into the path of a ferocious tiger. She flung herself into the lake to save herself from this beast. An echo of her words of farewell reached Altay, who rushed back to the lake. But he was too late: only Sulyshash's velvet skullcap remained, bobbing around on the dark waters. Distraught, Altay plunged his dagger into his heart.

A path continues northeastwards from Lake Shaytankol, to another mountain lake, **Basseyn**. This small lake resembles a large stone bath. A path from here leads down into Karkaraly town, past the buildings of the old sanatorium of Sosnoviy Bor. From Sosnoviy Bor another track runs northeastwards to strike habitation at the site of a small stream named Tasbulak. One building here is particularly distinctive: a pitched-roofed wooden building, which houses a **nature museum** (☉ *09.00–19.00 Tue–Sun; admission adult/child T100/50, plus T50 to visit the animal enclosure*). Entering the building, you come face to face with a stuffed *arkhar*. To the right lies a room with stuffed animals of the steppe and forest on display. Beyond is a room focused on ornithology: stuffed birds greet you from all sides. To the left of the entrance is a room devoted to the geography of the park, dominated by a large relief model of the Karkaraly Mountains. Beyond is a botany room, mostly comprising display cases filled with dried flowers. The red triangles indicate species listed in the Red Book, a mark of rarity. Head up the wooden stairs from the entrance to a small second-floor room which combines display cases full of carefully pinned insects with one featuring decorated wooden kitchen utensils.

Outside, your extra T50 payment allows you to walk between two metal fences to a wooden viewing platform. From here you can look across a muddy pen populated by wild boar. There are also a couple of bears, housed in distressingly small cages.

The nature museum is visible from the main road between Karaganda and Karkaraly. It lies 4km north of Karkaraly; take the side turning, in the direction of the mountains, signposted to 'Tasbulak'.

ZHEZKAZGAN   *Telephone code: 7102*

Located in the isolated western steppes of Karaganda Region, the city of Zhezkazgan owes its existence to one mineral: copper. The name 'Zhezkazgan' means, in Kazakh, 'place where copper is extracted'. The mining of copper in this area has a history dating back thousands of years, but Western attention to the mineral wealth of the place was drawn by the journal notes made in 1771 by Captain Nikolai Richkov. The copper reserves were registered to an industrialist named Ushakov in 1847 but serious efforts to extract them awaited the arrival of British investors, in the shape of the Spassky Copper Mine Ltd, registered in 1904. The British scheme involved the mining of copper ore at reserves to the northwest of what is now Zhezkazgan, the mining of coal from deposits around Baikonur (the place from which the modern-day space complex, hundreds of kilometres away, gets its name), further to the west, and the construction of a concentrator, and eventually smelter, at Karsakpay, around 100km from Zhezkazgan, which lay between the two deposits. The arrival of the Bolsheviks put an end to British activity in the region, though the Karsakpay smelter was eventually completed in 1928.

The Soviet-era development of Zhezkazgan owes much to the work of the Kazakhstani geologist Kanysh Satpaev (see page 145), who argued strongly that the estimates of the Zhezkazgan copper reserves on which the British geologists had been working, as well as those favoured by many leading lights of the geological establishment in Moscow, seriously underestimated the true wealth of the place. Satpaev's arguments won the day, and the Soviet authorities decided in 1931 to set about the construction of a major industrial complex here. The use of detention camp labour was a key feature in building the new industrial complex – as it was in the development of the coal mines of Karaganda – and Zhezkazgan was host to a number of labour camps of the StepLag network. One of these, the Kengir camp, located close to the modern-day industrial zone of Zhezkazgan, was the scene of a prisoner rebellion in 1954, forcibly quashed by the authorities (see box, page 214). A few buildings of the Kengir camp still stand near the copper smelter, though they are difficult to make out amongst the detritus of industrial development.

Zhezkazgan received town status in 1954. The completion of the establishment of an integrated copper production facility here, from mines to copper cathode, was achieved with the opening of a copper smelter in the town in 1971. (The copper concentrate had previously been smelted at the former small smelter at Karsakpay, and the larger but distant one at Balkhash.) Two years later, Zhezkazgan added the status of regional capital, though lost it again in the administrative reforms of 1997. The Zhezkazgan copper complex is now part of the copper company Kazakhmys. The operation involves the mining of copper ore at both open pit and underground mines around the satellite town of Satpaev, 18km northwest of Zhezkazgan. Most of this is then brought by railway wagon to the concentrator at Zhezkazgan, where it is processed into a copper concentrate which is piped to the nearby smelter, which produces the copper cathode. Another factory, adjacent to the smelter, produces copper rod from the cathodes. Kazakhmys employs more than 30,000 people at the Zhezkazgan complex, and its logo is everywhere in town.

Zhezkazgan is well off the usual tourist routes, but serves as a good base for exploring the historically rich Ulytau Mountains. Fringed to the north by the Kengir Reservoir, constructed by damming the Kengir River to meet the needs of the copper complex for water, the town's setting is rather attractive. Industrial chimneys apart, that is.

GETTING THERE AND AROUND Zhezkazgan's **airport** is 10km to the south of town. Air Astana operate six flights a week here from Astana. This is one of the 'social flights': uneconomic routes operated at cheap rates (around T13,500 for a single) with government support. At the time of research, the route was contracted out to Tulpar Avia Service, operating Soviet-era An-24 turboprops. They did though have the Air Astana in-flight magazine in the seat pockets. There are also four flights a week to Almaty on a Yak-40 operated by local company Zhezkazgan Avia, and another two to Almaty with the Shymkent-based airline Scat.

The **bus station** is at the southern edge of town, a couple of kilometres to the south of the central Metallurgov Square, down Satpaev Street and over the railway bridge. There are a couple of departures daily to the village of Ulytau. The **railway**

station sits close by. Zhezkazgan is currently the end of a rail spur from Karaganda, though there are plans to continue the railway line westwards from here as part of efforts to encourage Kazakhstan's development as a trade transit route between Europe and China. There are trains every two days to Karaganda and to Astana, and two a week to Almaty.

There is an efficient urban **bus** network, with tickets at T25. There are also plenty of **taxis** around; among the numerous numbers to call are ☏767999, ☏761313 and ☏733447.

🏠 **WHERE TO STAY** All the main hotels in Zhezkazgan are run by Kazakhmys, and are mainly geared to accommodating employees of the company and visiting businesspeople in the copper industry. They do however offer a good range of places to stay.

🏠 **Hotel Baikonur** (12 rooms) Yesenberlin St; ☏711744, 711745; f 711677. The best hotel in town, the Baikonur is an attractive 3-storey stone-walled building set on a promontory above the Kengir Reservoir. Steps lead down from the front of the hotel to a lakeside gazebo. The hotel once served as a place of recuperation for Soviet cosmonauts whose space adventures ended with a landing in the steppes around Zhezkazgan. To get here head 1 block north from Alash Sq along the main Beibitshilik Av, turn right at the traffic lights, & follow the road until it bends sharply to the right. At this point take the side road to the left fringed by nicely tended hedges, which takes you straight to the hotel. **$$$$**

🏠 **Hotel Business Centre** (24 rooms) 3A Jeskozgan St; ☏735900, 736122; f 733409. A less plush version of the Baikonur, also located on the banks of the Kengir River but further to the west. There are minerals on display in the lobby, in case any visitors need reminding about the source of Zhezkazgan's wealth. **$$**

🏠 **Hotel Metallurg** (28 rooms) 19 Timiryazev St; ☏723403, 741338; f 723401. The most basic & also most central of the hotels run by Kazakhmys, the 'Metal Worker' is nothing special, but rooms do all have en-suite shower & AC. **$$**

🏠 **Sport and Fitness Complex Hotel** (31 rooms) 34A Nezavisimosti Av, Satpaev; ☏(71063) 25572, (71063) 74566; f (71063) 74566. Located in the centre of the satellite town of Satpaev, the dorm beds here for T660 may be worth considering if you're travelling on a really tight budget, though there is not much to do in Satpaev. The hotel is part of a modern leisure complex, constructed by Kazakhmys & known by its Russian-language acronym SOK. The whole place makes for an incongruous sight, set amongst the drab 5-storey Soviet apartment blocks of Satpaev. Aside from the hotel, a blue-roofed bungalow, there is a large ice-hockey stadium, home to the Kazakhmys team, young pretenders who are challenging the Torpedo team of Ust-Kamenogorsk for the title of Kazakhstan's finest. The larger of 2 tented structures accommodates an astroturf football pitch; the smaller houses a 50m swimming pool (admission T100). Be sure to call ahead before pitching up at the hotel, as it's really geared for visiting ice hockey & football teams, & if there's a game in town they might not have space for you. **$$**

🍴 **WHERE TO EAT** Zhezkazgan offers plenty of places to eat, but no stand-out options. The restaurants in the Baikonur and Business Centre hotels are probably the most upmarket choices. The following are all central, if nothing special.

🍴 **Baursak** 6 Seifullin Av; ☏724741. This innovative place offers a haven for travellers with children, but is to be avoided for those without. It is a child-focused restaurant with large play area inside, & bouncy castle outside the entrance.

Close to the junction of Seifullin & Beibitshilik – just follow the yelping noise. **$$**

🍴 **Malibu Café** 22 Beibitshilik Av; ☏724003. A picture of a tropical island above the entrance lures you towards the door. Once past it, you

THE KENGIR UPRISING

The death of Stalin in 1953 and the subsequent execution of his hated security chief, Beria, raised hopes among the inmates of the labour camps across the Soviet Union that the camps would be abolished or, at the very least, reformed. Prisoners became increasingly confident in their relations with the camp authorities, resulting in numerous incidents of insubordination of various kinds. In Kengir, the resentment of the prisoners was fuelled by a series of episodes, including the murders of prisoners by guards. The uprising here was also made possible by an alliance between the ordinary criminals and the political prisoners, groups which the GuLag system tried to pit against each other as a means of facilitating overall control.

On the evening of 16 May 1954 the uprising started when a group of the ordinary criminals broke from the men's camp into the service yard, where the food was stored. Some 13 detainees were shot dead by guards in the process. The authorities pretended to give in to the prisoners' demands, an act which allowed them to repair the barrier between camp and service yard while the mollified prisoners were out at work. The prisoners responded by rising up again, this time securing control of the whole camp. They were to keep it for 40 days. During this time, an entirely new structure of camp social relations developed. With the men's and women's camps now linked, male and female prisoners could meet properly. There were improvised weddings, small businesses were established, including a café serving up ersatz coffee, and religious groups were allowed to practise.

A former Red Army colonel named Kuznetzov was chosen as the leader of the prisoners. He set to work putting together a propaganda effort which aimed to portray the prisoners as pro-Soviet, railing against a regime of the camp authorities which took its cue from the discredited Beria. They used hot-air balloons with slogans written on them, leaflet-depositing kites and carrier pigeons in an effort to get their messages out to the settlements beyond the camp. There were a series of negotiations with the authorities, in which the prisoners put forward a set of relatively modest demands, including the punishment of guards responsible for the murder of prisoners, and an end to the barrier between the men's and women's camps. But it increasingly became clear to the prisoners that the authorities were preparing to counter-attack.

On 25 June, snipers shot the prisoners' sentries, the prelude to the storming of the perimeter fence by Soviet forces which included T-34 tanks, as well as dogs and perhaps around 1,700 troops. The Kengir uprising was quickly and brutally brought to an end. Figures for the numbers killed vary widely, from the 37 reported in the Soviet archives to estimates of several hundred from survivors of the camp. Another six of the prisoners' leaders were executed. Kuznetzov was spared execution, probably because he denounced many of his erstwhile colleagues in his confession.

On the day after the defeat of the Kengir uprising, those prisoners who were not moved to other camps were given the task of rebuilding the damaged walls of the Kengir camp. In the slightly longer run though, the Kengir uprising helped hasten the demise of the GuLag system.

encounter a painting of a scantily clad flame-haired girl having just freed herself from her chains. The restaurant inside is a dark & decidedly ordinary place. $$

✗ **Café Aigerim** 20 Beibitshilik Av; ☎723148. The cramped premises, sweltering in summer, don't encourage you to linger, but this is a cheap & central spot for lunch. Pizza costs T300. $

WHAT TO SEE

Metallurgov Square The older part of this young town is centred on Metallurgov ('Metalworkers') Square, a pleasant, leafy place to sit and people-watch. The square, appropriately, features a statue of the geologist **Satpaev**, the man seeming to emerge from the large lump of stone from which he has been sculpted. He cradles a small piece of ore in his left hand. Facing this statue, on the south side of the square, is the columned façade of the **Kazakh Drama Theatre**, once the Cultural Palace of Metalworkers.

The east side of Metallurgov Square is filled by the offices of Kazakhmys: the older yellow-walled building on the square, and two modern glass-walled buildings behind it into which the company has expanded. The central door of the yellow-walled building is the entrance to the **Kazakhmys Museum** (☎ 744383; ⊕ 09.00–12.00 & 13.00–18.00 Mon–Fri; admission adult/child T60/30), which provides a good overview of the history of copper extraction in the region. The first hall features displays emphasising the antiquity of the Ulytau Mountains, the fossil wealth of the area and then, getting down to business, the rich mineral resources found beneath the local soils. Particularly striking are the greenish, branched, almost coral-like lumps of naturally occurring copper. There is a seated statue of Satpaev, surrounded by mineral samples, beneath a map of the mineral resources of the area drawn up by the great geologist. Bronze Age finds demonstrate the antiquity of copper mining in the area, and there is a display of gemstones. Three mannequins are dressed up as historical figures with passing connections to the area: Al Farabi, a rather kindly looking Genghis Khan, and Timur, known in the west as Tamerlane. Close to the last is a copy of the inscription made on a stone in the Ulytau Mountains by Timur in 1391 during his campaign against Tokhtamysh, the last Khan of the White Horde. The original is in St Petersburg. Timur asks those reading the inscription to remember him with a prayer.

The next room focuses on the more recent development of the copper industry. There are photographs relating to the British mining activities in the early years of the 20th century. A display on Satpaev features the desk at which he worked at Karsakpay. The development of the infrastructure of the copper industry is chronicled, with a copper cathode on display, on which has been scrawled 'homeland, receive Zhezkazgan copper'. This dates from the opening of the Zhezkazgan smelter on 23 February 1971. Models give you a sense of the various mines and plants, and their relationships to each other.

Seifullin Avenue and Alash Square From Metallurgov Square, Beibitshilik Avenue, still known to everyone by its Soviet name of Mir, heads northwards. After two blocks you reach the intersection with Seifullin Avenue. Turning right brings you face to face with a Soviet-era monument to the first builders of the city of Zhezkazgan. A copper worker holds up a lump of, presumably, copper, its shape hinting at the Soviet star, while a woman next to him holds up her hand. Behind this stands the Russian Orthodox church, built in 2001 with funding from Kazakhmys, and further back, close to the banks of the reservoir, a rusting and somewhat graffiti-strewn reminder of the Soviet past. A rocket blasts off cosmoswards while a MiG plane circles it, both anchored to the ground by their metal vapour trails. Beneath this monument, on the shores of the reservoir, is what passes in Zhezkazgan for a **beach**. A sign here reads that 'swimming while in a drunken condition is categorically forbidden'.

The much longer stretch of Seifullin Avenue to the west of Beibitshilik has a pleasant piece of park running down its middle, dotted with woodcarvings of gnomes, warriors and the like. Seifullin Avenue was formerly known as the Avenue of Cosmonauts and at its western end, close to the intersection with Nekrasov Street, are further reminders of Zhezkazgan's links with the Soviet space programme. There is a monument to the **cosmonauts**, a ball of interlocking stars, projected skywards. Immediately to the west of this, flanking a rectangular fountain, are lines of pines, each planted by a cosmonaut whose spacecraft landed in the steppes around Zhezkazgan, commemorating their safe return to earth. Plaques in front of a few of the pines identify the planter. There is a frieze of a saluting Yuri Gagarin on the side of one of the apartment blocks overlooking this place. Across Nekrasov Street from here, and looking back down Seifullin Avenue, stands, reasonably enough, a statue of the writer **Seifullin**, a victim of Stalinist repression in the 1930s.

Continuing north along Beibitshilik Avenue beyond the junction with Seifullin Avenue, after a further block you reach the concrete-covered pedestrian space of Alash Square. This is centred on a statue of **Ablai Khan**, where Lenin once stood. The three symbols on the base of the statue, resembling a horseshoe, a doorway and two crossed arrows, represent, respectively, the Great, Middle and Junior *zhuzes*. Their inclusion reflects Ablai Khan's role in uniting the Kazakh people against external foes. At the back of the square is the ten-storey *akimat* building, its size a legacy of the days when Zhezkazgan had the status of regional capital. To the right of the *akimat* is the main building of Zhezkazgan University.

The Zhezkazgan Historical and Archaeological Museum (*22 Alasha Khan Av;* \ *737753;* f *737204;* ☉ *09.00–18.00 Tue–Sun; admission T200 for foreign citizens*) The broad Alasha Khan Avenue heads westwards away from Alash Square. Take this as far as the intersection with Nekrasov Street. Here, on your right, stands the Zhezkazgan Historical and Archaeological Museum. The first room offers palaeontology and minerals, with a diorama of geologists at work. Head down a corridor off this, lined with stuffed animal-filled dioramas illustrating the steppe and waterside ecosystems. The next room features early history. There are Stone Age implements, supplemented by a diorama depicting cave-dwellers. A Bronze Age burial, Scythian-era golden ornaments and a display of *balbals* take the timeline forward. In the centre of the room are models of the many mausolea found in the area, including that of Jochi Khan and that said to be the mausoleum of Alasha Khan, legendary founder of the Kazakh people. The room also includes some ethnographic displays.

Upstairs, you are greeted by a model of the post-independence monument to Kazakhstan's unity, which has been constructed near the village of Ulytau (see page 217). Around this are displays about the Kazakh khans, with a bust of Ablai Khan on show. A diorama depicts Kenesary in mid-campaign. The next room describes life in the area in the first half of the 20th century. A photograph reveals the shockingly bad working conditions of the miners in the Baikonur coal mines. A diorama portrays celebrations of the arrival of the first tractor; another more chillingly illustrates the effects of famine. There is a display on those incarcerated in the StepLag network; another on the local heroes of the Great Patriotic War. The following room focuses on copper extraction and the building of the town of

above left The tranquil shores of Lake Borovoye are becoming increasingly popular as the weekend playground for the capital, Astana (EL) page 110

above The Zhalanash 'ship cemetery' provides a stark illustration of the desiccation of the Aral Sea (PB) page 341

left Chimbulak, at the heart of Ile Alatau National Park, is Kazakhstan's best developed ski resort (MEP) page 155

below The steppeland around Almaty has long been home to semi-nomadic people, including sheep-herding horsemen (IB/FLPA) page 117

above   An old Soviet-style bus stop at Aralsk, once the main port on the Kazakhstan shores of the Aral Sea (AP/A) page 353

below   The Tian Shan mountain range spans the border of Kazakhstan and China, and offers excellent trekking and climbing (IB/FLPA) page 5

above left Semey is home to a graveyard of Communist-era statues, having been moved from their more prominent pre-independence place in the city (ITP/A) page 246

left A Russian Orthodox church in Pavlodar: the Orthodox faith is professed by around one-third of Kazakhs (AB/DT) page 257

below The large Lenin-era commemorative mosaic in Aralsk's railway station depicts this once-dynamic town's contribution when famine struck Russia (MEP) page 356

above Pavlodar's colossal Mashhur Zhusup Mosque has been likened to a shuttlecock, Darth Vader's helmet and a computer game villain (ZA/W) page 265

right Many new buildings are in evidence in Atyrau, the urban hub of Kazakhstan's burgeoning oil industry, including the city's Imangali Mosque (RK/A) page 331

above Horse races take place across the country to celebrate public holidays, as here at Atyrau (RK/A) page 319

left Modern Kazakh cuisine incorporates influences from all over Central Asia, including naan bread, *manty* (steamed dumplings) and *samsa* (meat-filled pastries) (MEP) page 54

below Shymkent's vast bazaar provides an echo of the city's past as a caravanserai on the Silk Route (SI) page 386

above Members of the Kazakh Children's Orchestra: traditional Kazakh instruments include the *dombra*, a two-stringed guitar, and the *kobyz*, played with a bow (AT/A) page 58

right Displays of traditional folk dancing and music form part of the celebrations at Nauryz to mark the arrival of spring (KE) page 56

below Children in a village near Atyrau celebrate the May Day by dressing in costumes representing the different regions (RK/A) page 55

The traditional Kazakh practice of hunting with eagles is seen as symbolic of the country post-independence (SS) page 19

Zhezkazgan. A photograph of Satpaev shows the geologist holding a piece of rock delicately in his hands as one might nurse a glass of good wine. There is a display on the archaeologist Margulan, who excavated sites around the Ulytau Mountains. A presentation on the space programme features photographs of the cosmonauts who landed in the surrounding steppes.

ULYTAU

Ulytau, the 'Great Mountains', rise up from the surrounding steppe some 130km to the northwest of Zhezkazgan. This ancient granite massif is not particularly high: its highest peak, bearing the name White Mosque, reaches a height of 1,131m. But this range, located at the geographical centre of Kazakhstan, has a place at the heart of the development of the Kazakh people. The mountains of Ulytau and the steppes that surround them are full of historical monuments: petroglyphs, barrows adorned with curious stone 'moustaches', and numerous mausolea. It is difficult to separate out the facts from the legends surrounding the area. On the peaks of the mountains here, they say, are buried Tokhtamysh, the great rival of Timur, and Edigey, the Emir of the White Horde who, as an ally of Timur, killed Tokhtamysh in 1406. Mausolea are ascribed to Alasha Khan, the legendary founder of the Kazakh people, and Jochi, son of Genghis Khan. The Kazakh tribes came together close to the Ulytau Mountains to inflict, in 1727, a crucial defeat on the invading Dzhungars at Bulanty to the southwest. It is said that many Kazakh khans were crowned here, a ceremony which involved being raised aloft on a white felt rug. Well-to-do Kazakhs come to these mountains to spend time in an environment considered to be particularly favoured for its cosmic energy, and to eat mutton from local sheep, its taste highly regarded because the local ovine diet is so strong in highly aromatic wormwood. It is no surprise that a Kazakh band aiming to create a sound fusing rock music with the strains of traditional Kazakh instruments should choose Ulytau as its name.

While there are plans to encourage tourism development in the area, there is as yet very little in the way of tourist infrastructure. A couple of buses a day make the journey from Zhezkazgan to the village of Ulytau, but to get to most of the historical sights you'll either need your own transport, or to come to a deal with a taxi driver in Zhezkazgan.

WHAT TO SEE

From Zhezkazgan to Ulytau The road from Zhezkazgan passes through the mining town of Satpaev after 18km. The ventilation towers of the mines create an odd steppe-Manhattan landscape to the northwest of the latter town. A village in the heart of these mines is, confusingly, also called Zhezkazgan. After another 40km you skirt the small settlement of Zhezdy, where during World War II extraction of the local manganese deposits, identified by Satpaev, was commenced in record time after the Germans seized control of what had been the USSR's only production field of manganese, a key component in the production process for armoured metal. Another 19km further on, a track to the left, just before you reach the hamlet of Taldysay, takes you to the archaeological site of **Baskamir**, just a few metres from the road. The plan of a central square-based fortress is marked out by a modern earth wall reconstruction. The remnants of a stone external wall are visible around this. The base of a stone watchtower is visible at the top of the low hill across the road from here: at the sound of the alarm, the inhabitants of the tented settlement around this place would have sought protection within the walls. The settlement appears to have flourished between around the 8th and 12th centuries, when this land was known as Desht-i-Kipchak, 'land of the Kipchaks', divided among the great Kipchak tribal unions. The fortified settlement of Baskamir lay on a northward-bound trade route.

Some 44km further north along the road to Ulytau, at the base of a hill named Ayir Tau, stands a modern **monument to Kazakhstan's unity**, at the site where it is believed that in 1723 the Kazakh *zhuzes* united against their common foe, the Dzhungars. The monument is an imposing one. Four curving buttresses, their form perhaps suggesting bows, come together to create a circular *shanyrak*, above which a spear heads heavenwards. There is a sphere at the centre of the composition. The four buttresses hint at the cardinal points; a reminder that this place has a claim to being the geographical centre of Kazakhstan as well as a historical one.

Ulytau village *(Telephone code: 71035)* The district centre, another 10km further on, is the sleepy village of Ulytau, set in an attractive spot at the foot of the mountains. The administrative heart of the village is a square centred on a statue of two local writers, Bulkishev and Imanzhanov. The *akimat* is on the right-hand side of the square. At the back of the square is the **Ulytau Museum** (*14B Bulkisheva St;* \ *21342;* f *21448; www.ulytau.kz;* ⊕ *09.00–18.00 Mon–Fri; admission free*). The labelling here is all in Kazakh, and there is a somewhat ramshackle quality to some of the displays. In the foyer stands a golden bust of Akin Tayzhan, a jolly-looking accordionist who was killed in 1937, a victim of Stalin's repression. There is a room devoted to Satpaev, featuring a decidedly amateurish statue of the chuckling scientist holding a geological hammer. Photographs of a visit made by Satpaev to the United Kingdom in March 1947, as part of a delegation of the Supreme Soviet of the USSR, show him receiving a souvenir from the Mayor of Sheffield and visiting the Bodleian Library. A nature room offers stuffed animals, including a particularly bad-tempered-looking wolf, arranged in alcoves, and a relief model of the mountains.

Upstairs, there are photographs of local Bronze Age sites and some of the many mausolea populating the surrounding steppe. One room includes an odd mix of Stone Age artefacts, a display about the archaeological work at Baskamir, and some rusting agricultural implements. In the corridor, a chair on which President Nazarbaev sat during a visit to Ulytau is carefully preserved in a glass case. The wolf pelt on the ground below it is a mark of Kazakh leadership. Another room includes a model of the mausoleum of Genghis Khan's son Jochi, a diorama of the inauguration of a new Kazakh khan outside the Mausoleum of Alasha Khan, and another depicting Erden Sandibauly, a 19th-century governor, standing watchfully on the steppe, his horse by his side. Erden is another figure whose mausoleum lies in the area. A last room is dominated by a yurt, with many furs hanging up inside it.

Just outside the village of Ulytau are some good examples of a curious ancient monument known as **'moustachioed'** *kurgans*, whose purpose continues to provoke disagreement amongst archaeologists. Take the main road out of the village heading away from Zhezkazgan, and turn right onto an unmetalled track after 1km or so, just past the sign marking, in the other direction, arrival into the village of Ulytau. A couple of kilometres or so further on, look for piles of stones, indicating *kurgans*, in the wormwood-scented steppe to the left of the track. One of these in particular demonstrates clearly the 'moustachioed' form: two lines of curving stones running out from the *kurgan* enclose a large space to the east of it. At the end of each line of curving stones, furthest from the *kurgan*, is a standing stone. Scientists continue to debate whether these structures are a kind of early astronomical observatory, a ritual complex, an elaborate burial structure, or some combination of all of these.

Mausolea of Alasha Khan and Jochi Khan From Satpaev, take the road running due north in the direction of the village of Malshybay. After 61km, and just short of Malshybay, you see on the left of the road a red-brick mausoleum of the 11th or 12th century. This is ascribed to **Alasha Khan**, the legendary founder of the Kazakh people. A plaque outside the mausoleum displays the tribal signs (*tamga*) of the three *zhuzes* and 24 tribes assigned to them. By tradition, Alasha Khan was the source of all. The mausoleum has been heavily restored, but is a fascinating building. It has a tall portal, with a graceful arch enclosing the entrance doorway. The external walls feature geometric designs of interlocking bricks. The interior is octagonal in plan, with arched niches. A circular brick dome rises to a central aperture. Go to the niche at the inside corner of the building to the left of the door and look up. You will see bricks imprinted with the stamp of a wolf's footprint, a symbol of the then Turkic leaders. From this niche a stairway leads to a narrow internal corridor. Walking around this has the effect of circling the tomb, a ritual said to act, for the faithful, as a cure for various ills. Further steps at the end of this corridor lead up to the roof, from where there is a fine view across the surrounding steppe.

From the Mausoleum of Alasha Khan, head back towards Satpaev for 1km, before turning left onto a steppe track. Head towards a tightly packed clump of trees in the distance, which marks the underground water source from where the drinking water for the town of Zhezkazgan is pumped. A 4x4 is necessary for this route, as there is a brook to be forded, part of the Kengir River system, after a further 23km. Before reaching the brook you will see on higher ground to the left of the track, but the other side of the river from it, a curious stone mausoleum with a 'pitched-roofed' form. This is the **Dombaul Mausoleum**, probably dating from the 9th or 10th century, popularly said to be the mausoleum of a *kobyz*-playing contemporary of the legendary musician Korkut Ata.

A further 2km on from the brook you reach the **Mausoleum of Jochi Khan**, a heavily restored brick building with a turquoise dome, the latter sitting atop a base of 16 points. Like the Mausoleum of Alasha Khan, an arched niche surrounds the entrance doorway. The interior is plain, with a simple brick cupola. The large brick grave is said to be that of Jochi, the narrower one next to it that of his wife. Jochi was the eldest son of Genghis Khan, though carried with him throughout his life the stigma of possible illegitimacy. Genghis Khan's wife, Borte, had been abducted by the Merkit tribe, and gave birth soon after her recovery by Genghis Khan. Jochi was entrusted the westernmost part of Genghis Khan's empire, but a rift developed between Jochi and his father, especially after Genghis Khan chose his third son, Ogedei, over him as his successor. Jochi predeceased his father, as a result of a hunting accident. A Kazakh legend has it that none of Genghis Khan's courtiers had the nerve to tell their leader that his son was dead. Eventually a noted musician transmitted the sad news in a song so beautiful that Genghis Khan's wrath could not fall upon the messenger who had delivered the news.

To get to the Mausoleum of Jochi Khan straight from Zhezkazgan, head out of town through the industrial complex, turn left and you will pass the power station on your right and then the Kengir Reservoir on your left. At 3km out of town, bear right at the fork in the road. Continue along the metalled but somewhat pot-holed road for 22km until you reach the hamlet of Korganbeg, known in Soviet times as Promishlenny. Turn right immediately opposite the hamlet, onto a track which forks after a further 18km. Turn left, and you will reach the Jochi Khan Mausoleum after a few hundred metres. Straight on lies the Dombaul Mausoleum, another 4km away.

The crescent-shaped Lake Balkhash runs for 600km across the northern edge of Almaty Region, like a beret. It varies in width from just 5km to around 70km, and is shallow, with an average depth of less than 6m. A peculiarity of the lake is that it is saline in its deeper eastern section, but fresh water in the shallower western one. The main inflow into the lake, from the Ile River, disgorges fresh water into the western part of the lake. The eastern part, partially enclosed from the west by the Uzunaral Peninsula, lacks this supply of fresh water. The lake has no outflow, and is frozen from around November to March. Environmentalists fear that Lake Balkhash is at risk from similar processes of desiccation to those that have blighted the Aral Sea. The construction of the Kapchagai Dam in the 1960s, and associated development of irrigation agriculture, reduced inflows into the lake from the Ile, and there are concerns that industrial and agricultural development in China's Xinjiang Region, where the headwaters of the Ile lie, will result in enhanced offtakes.

The largest settlement on the shores of the lake, the town of Balkhash (*Telephone code: 71036*), lies in Karaganda Region on its north shore. It is an industrial centre, focused on the processing of copper ore. The plumes discharging from its tall chimneys can be seen from tens of kilometres away, and pass directly over the town when the wind direction is unfavourable. But since Balkhash lies at the mid-point of the 1,200km road journey between Almaty and Astana, it is the obvious place to overnight if you are making this trip by car. As you drive towards the town from Almaty around the north shore of the lake, a trip which involves disappointingly few lakeside panoramas as the road remains for the most part a few kilometres from the shore, you will pass numerous roadside stalls selling smoked fish. Some hang up a cardboard silhouette of a fish to confirm what is on offer.

The development of Balkhash dates to 1928, when a geological expedition from Leningrad led by Mikhail Rusakov determined that there was a major deposit of copper ore at Kounrad, 12km to the north of the present-day town. A decision was taken to develop Balkhash as a copper-processing centre, and construction teams arrived from across the Soviet Union. Balkhash received its urban status in 1937, and a year later the first copper was produced. Dinmuhammed Kunaev, the future First Secretary of the Communist Party of Kazakhstan, started his working career at the Kounrad mine in 1936. The mine, which is a huge open-cast pit, the copper concentrator, smelting and refining operation at Balkhash, and further plants on the site involved in the refining of zinc and precious metals, all now belong to the copper company Kazakhmys.

Balkhash weathered great economic difficulties following the break-up of the USSR, and continues to grapple with a range of environmental and social problems arising from its aged Soviet-era plant and the town's isolation (Karaganda, almost 400km away, is its nearest large neighbour). Along the lakeside promenade, the splinters of broken vodka bottles crunch underfoot. But it makes for a reasonable enough overnight stop.

GETTING THERE AND AROUND The **bus station** (✆ *42751*) is centrally located, opposite the main **bazaar** on Agibai Batyr Street. There are only a small number of departures, with the main long-distance destinations served being Almaty, Astana and Karaganda. The **railway station** is at the northeastern edge of town, at the northern end of Yazov Street. Balkhash however lies on a branch line, and is not served by the main Almaty to Karaganda trains. One daily train makes the trip here from Karaganda. The **airport** is not currently used by scheduled flights, though there are plans to develop a service. There is a central rail and air ticket booking office at 20 Lenin Street (📞 48365; ⏰ 09.00–19.00 daily). **Taxis** are plentiful and to pre-book, call 📞 41045 or 📞 41046.

🏠 WHERE TO STAY

🏠 **Hotel Alpina Three Stars** (17 rooms) 10 Baiseitova St; 📞 46133, 46064; 📠 46155; ✉ hotel_alpina@mail.ru. This is probably the nicest accommodation option in Balkhash, though the competition is not fierce. It is run by the Alpina group, better known for its mountain lodges in Almaty Oblast, though the absence of a lift here does force the guest into doing some climbing. The permanent claim it makes on its rating by including this into the name of the hotel is probably a wise precaution. Its restaurant, not bad, is decorated to resemble a Classical temple, with statues in niches around the walls, which are painted a lurid green. Elsewhere, pink is the favoured colour. The hotel now opens onto Valikhanov St, where it lies set back from the road, adjacent to the city *akimat*. The old entrance on Baiseitova St is now occupied by a billiard & bowling centre, under the same management. Not all rooms have AC, an important consideration in summer. It levies an annoying booking fee for the first night. **$$**

🏠 **Hotel Kazakhmys Corporation** (29 rooms) 31 Karamende Bi St; 📞 40748, 40583; 📠 43021. A 3-storey brick building, in front of the wild & neglected Stroiteley (Builders') Park. The hotel is aimed principally at meeting the needs of visiting members of Kazakhmys's staff & no English is spoken. Only the 'luxe' rooms have AC, & none of the rooms are anything special, though all do have en suites. B/fast is not included in the room rate. **$$**

🏠 **Hotel Balkhash** (36 rooms) 29 Bokeikhanov St; 📞 43830; 📠 44533. A bright yellow 4-storey building at the western end of Karamende Bi St, at the corner with Bokeikhanov, this is a run-down option which bakes in summer. Rooms have en suites, but no AC. B/fast is not included. **$**

🏠 **Hotel Filial 36, Enbek Karaganda** (5 rooms) 14 Bokeikhanov St; 📞 44666. Stuck onto the end of a 5-floor apartment block in a rough part of town near the stadium, this small hotel is as unenticing as its name suggests. It offers basic rooms without AC or en suites. They are, however, cheap. **$**

✕ WHERE TO EAT

✕ **Dostar** Baiseitova St; no phone. On the western side of the unkempt park behind the House of Culture of Metalworkers, the Dostar Restaurant sits upstairs in a block that also houses the Dostar supermarket. It is decorated in the style of a grotto, with a dance floor at 1 end of the room & booths which would have looked fashionable in a provincial British cocktail lounge in the 1960s. The large menu includes a vast range of salads & 'Balkhash-style fish', the latter involving smothering a pike-perch with a topping of cheese, mixed vegetables & mayonnaise. There is an outside terrace in summer. **$$**

✕ **Pyramid Club** 26 Lenin St; 📞 42524. This green building offers an outdoor terrace, across which wafts the smell of *shashlik*. Inside is a billiard hall. **$$**

WHAT TO SEE

Town centre The apex of the town runs along Valikhanov Street, where the **city** *akimat* is located, running downhill towards the lake. At the top of the street is the large and somewhat sterile **Tauelsizdik ('Independence') Square**, remodelled in 2007 as the centrepiece of the town's 70th birthday commemorations. A large equestrian statue of the local 19th-century warrior **Agibai Batyr**, who fought with Kenesary, now stands in the centre. The former occupant of that prized position, a sculpture based around a *shanyrak* design, has now been shifted across the road. The square is framed with four gazebo-like pavilions, sheltering benches.

At the lakeside end of Valikhanov Street stands the **House of Culture of Metalworkers**, a theatre fronted by a line of Corinthian columns, built in 1952. The frieze above this features a column of marchers, headed by a metalworker, followed

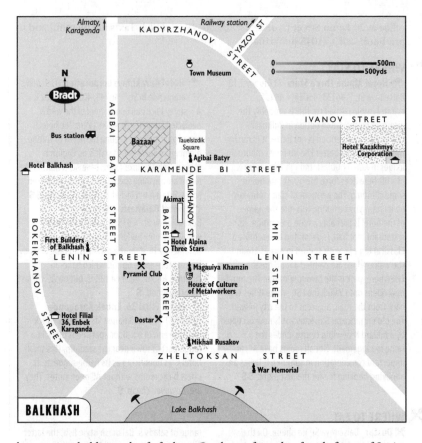

BALKHASH

Map labels:
Almaty, Karaganda
Railway station
KADYRZHANOV STREET
STYAZOV ST
Town Museum
0 — 500m
0 — 500yds
N
Bradt
IVANOV STREET
Bus station
AGIBAI BATYR STREET
Bazaar
Tauelsizdik Square
Hotel Kazakhmys Corporation
Hotel Balkhash
Agibai Batyr
KARAMENDE BI STREET
BOKEIKHANOV STREET
Akimat
VALIKHANOV ST
BAISEITOVA ST
MIR STREET
First Builders of Balkhash
Hotel Alpina Three Stars
LENIN STREET
LENIN STREET
Pyramid Club
Magauiya Khamzin
House of Culture of Metalworkers
Hotel Filial 36, Enbek Karaganda
Dostar
Mikhail Rusakov
ZHELTOKSAN STREET
War Memorial
Lake Balkhash

by a woman holding a sheaf of wheat. On the roof stands a female figure of Soviet piety, releasing a bird. She holds a shield decorated with hammer and sickle and ears of wheat. Flanking the building are silver-coloured statues of metalworker and miner. The interior is opulent. There is also a museum devoted to the history of the copper-processing factory, Balkhashsvetmet. The **Museum of the History of Balkhashsvetmet Production** (✆ 40531; ⊕ 09.00–12.00 & 13.00–17.00; *admission free*) occupies a single room on the ground floor. It covers the history of copper extraction in Balkhash from Rusakov's expedition to the acquisition of the plant by Kazakhmys. There are displays devoted to the individual plants within the complex, and pictures of those who were awarded the title Hero of Socialist Labour through their efforts here. In front of the House of Culture of Metalworkers stands a post-independence statue of local musician **Magauiya Khamzin**, in whose honour the House of Culture has now been renamed. He is depicted in dapper suit beneath a traditional Kazakh cloak, holding his *dombra*.

Just east of here along the broad Lenin Street is a blue-painted building housing part of the local university. The mosaic on its western end wall proclaims 'Glory to Soviet builders!' It pictures a young man with a theodolite and young woman with a trowel. The polluting emissions of the factory smokestacks are treated in the mosaic as symbols of pride; the plumes of smoke are pictured fluttering like banners.

A couple of blocks to the west of the House of Culture of Metalworkers along Lenin Street, to the side of a run-down park, is a monument to the **First Builders**

of Balkhash. A man plunges a spade into the ground with a muscular arm. Next to him is a frieze depicting toiling construction and metalworkers.

The apartment blocks in the centre of town, especially along Valikhanov and Lenin streets, offer some interesting examples of Soviet architecture of the 1940s and 1950s. On the north side of Lenin Street, for example, is a line of attractive blocks with long arches across which balconies are hung and with colonnades beneath the roof. A large inscription gives the date of construction as 1941 and records that this is the House of Skilled Workers of the Copper Factory.

Lakeside The turquoise waters of Lake Balkhash form an attractive southern boundary to the town. Behind the House of Culture of Metalworkers an unkempt stretch of park runs down to the lake. Along the main path within the park, looking out towards the lake, is a statue of the bearded geologist **Mikhail Rusakov**, holding a rolled-up document – his survey of the Kounrad deposit, presumably. Across the road from this statue is a **T-34 tank**, mounted on a pedestal. A plaque records that the tank marks the valiant feats of labour of the people of Balkhash in World War II, in particular in producing the molybdenum required for the production of tank armour. Their exploits, we are told, rank alongside those of the Soviet troops.

Balkhash town sits on a bay named Bertis. In summer the rather dirty lakeside **beaches** are packed until late into the evening by local residents escaping the stifling heat of their apartments. Swimmers paddle around clumps of reeds which lie just offshore. There are some pleasant, though basic, lakeside summer cafés and a small funfair. The promenade at the back of the beaches runs eastwards to a **war memorial**. Steps lead up to a boxy tiled concrete structure, centred on a now extinguished eternal flame.

Balkhash Town Museum (⊕ *09.00–18.00 Tue–Sun; admission T25*) This is not the easiest place to find. It sits in an unmarked windowless brick building amidst the blocks of apartments which make up the Shashybaya Microdistrict immediately to the north of Tauelsizdik Square. Follow Mira Street northwards until it turns into Kadirzhanov Street. Look out for the Cinema Centre on your left. The museum lies behind this.

The displays kick off with descriptions of the leading figures of the area, including Dinmuhammed Kunaev. There is a photograph of the house in which the future First Secretary lived in Kounrad village. This is followed by displays pertaining to the natural world, stuffed animal-populated dioramas of three local environments: the south bank of Balkhash Lake, the steppe north of the town and the granite rocks of Bektauata. A side room is devoted to early history, with a selection of 7th-century *balbals*, some petroglyphs together with modern artworks inspired by them, and a diorama showing Bronze Age metalworkers in action. There is also a reconstruction of a Bronze Age burial in a coffin walled by flat stones. Back in the main hall the displays continue with a family tree of the Middle *Zhuz*, indicating its numerous sub-tribes, and items relating to the Kazakh khanates. There are also musical instruments on display, and features on local musicians such as Shashubay Koshkarbaev, who died in 1952. Photographs show him as a cheerful, white-bearded accordion player. His accordion and Soviet awards are on display.

Next comes ethnography, with a life-size Kazakh village scene including a blacksmith's forge, a yurt, and the lady of the house doing some spinning outside. Then to the birth of Balkhash, with a mock-up of the study of Mikhail Rusakov, and a model of the huge, terraced, open-cast Kounrad mine. There are samples of copper from the Balkhash plant, and the awards given to those who helped develop the local copper industry. A moving display highlights some of those associated with the copper factory who fell foul of Stalin's repression in the 1930s. There are also some hard-to-comprehend models and flowcharts of the factories which make up the Balkhash complex.

FROM BALKHASH TO KARAGANDA

The main road north from Almaty to Astana scythes for almost 400km through largely unpopulated steppe between Balkhash and Karaganda. It is one of the journeys which gives a real sense of the enormity of Kazakhstan, and of its low population density. There are a couple of worthwhile stops *en route*.

BEKTAUATA A group of granite hills, the largest reaching a height of 1,242m, rise from the surrounding steppe like an apparition, visible from many kilometres away. Bektauata offers a natural environment very different from that of the steppe. Juniper grows on the sides of the otherwise bare hills. Clumps of aspen are found at their base. Around the hills are also to be found undulating plateaux of granite, sometimes covered in mosses. It is not surprising that this massif, so unlike all that surrounds it, should be endowed with a spiritual quality by local people. Many graves have been sited at the foot of the hills. One of the most substantial is a grey-brick domed mausoleum, dedicated to musician Shashubay Koshkarbaev, whose tombstone stands immediately behind it.

Bektauata is reached by taking a signposted turning to the right, some 63km north of Balkhash on the Karaganda road. The hills are 12km on, along the red-hued side road. There are several children's summer camps at the base of the hills, mostly owned by factories in Balkhash. One place for adults to stay is the **Sary Arka Rest House** (**$**). Turn left after travelling 8km from the main road, the Sary Arka Rest House lies another 4km on. It sits in a pleasant spot, in the shadow of a hill known as 'Three Teeth'. The accommodation, in small cottages, is very basic though.

AKSU-AYULY Lying on the main road some 250km north of Balkhash, 130km south of Karaganda, the village of Aksu-Ayuly is of touristic interest mainly because a nearby farm offers a homestay opportunity which allows the visitor to learn something of the traditional Kazakh practice of hunting with eagles.

The farm is run by Tileukabyl Esembekuly (e *tleu.e@rambler.ru; www.kusbegi. kz*), one of a small number of dedicated enthusiasts across Kazakhstan dedicated to rediscovering the techniques of hunting with eagles largely lost during the Soviet period. His family also runs the small **Kafe Burkit**, which lies on the east side of the main road, at the northern end of the village next to a petrol station. Photos on the walls of the café show hunters in action, and there is a stuffed eagle behind the bar, protecting the vodka. If you book ahead, Tileukabyl will arrange for you to be met at the café and escorted to the farm, which is difficult to find without a guide. From the café, you head north along the main road for 1.5km, turning off to the right onto the northernmost of two rough roads leading off at this point, opposite another petrol station. After 11km you reach the hamlet of Aktobe. Take the track which runs down into the valley floor beyond this, roughly following a line of telegraph poles to reach the farm a further 11km on.

Tileukabyl can accommodate up to ten guests in basic, twin-bedded rooms (**$$$$**). The rates include full board and an immersion into the history of hunting with eagles in Kazakhstan. If you would like to be involved in any hunting, and to go horseriding, you should agree this in advance.

7

The East

East Kazakhstan offers a great deal for the tourist. The Altai Mountains in the northeast of the region are stunning and unspoilt, a land of cedar woods, villages of log-walled houses established by communities of Old Believers, *maral* deer and radon springs, a place where, according to followers of the spiritualist Nicholas Roerich, the legendary Buddhist kingdom of Shambala may be found. The regional capital, Ust-Kamenogorsk, is a likeable and unpretentious place. Semipalatinsk is one of Kazakhstan's most historically interesting cities, the place of exile of the Russian writer Dostoevsky and strongly associated with two of the most important Kazakh literary figures, Abai and Auezov. The name Semipalatinsk does however carry the stigma of the four decades of nuclear testing conducted in the steppe to the south and west of the city in the infamous 'Polygon'. The renaming of the city as Semey is intended to symbolise a fresh start. With large lakes (and the world's fifth-largest reservoir) rich in fish, fields emblazoned with sunflowers and swaying feather-grass steppe, East Kazakhstan may not be the first port of call for most visitors to Kazakhstan, but it is a high point in the tours of many of those who do make it here.

UST-KAMENOGORSK (OSKEMEN) *Telephone code: 7232*

The capital of East Kazakhstan Region, Ust-Kamenogorsk is an industrial city attractively sited at the confluence of the Irtysh and Ulba rivers. Known in Kazakh as Oskemen, the origins of the town are linked to a military expedition headed by Major Ivan Likharev, who established a fortress here in 1720. Russia under Peter the Great was keen to secure its eastern borders, develop its trade routes further east and explore the mineral wealth of the Altai. The progressive advancement along the Irtysh River, with the establishment of a line of fortresses along its course, was a part of this strategy. The Russian-language name Ust-Kamenogorsk refers to the fact that the two rivers flow out of their rocky valleys just upstream of the town, running into a broad fluvial plain.

The original wooden fortress burnt down in 1765. Its replacement was a grander affair, surrounded by an earth bank and moat, traces of which can still be seen in the part of town known as the Strelka, the tongue of land between the two rivers. A Cossack settlement developed alongside the fortress, receiving town status in 1804, and then in 1868 becoming the administrative capital of an *uyezd* within Semipalatinsk Region. At the turn of the 20th century, Ust-Kamenogorsk remained a town predominantly of single-storey wooden buildings, its economy focused on agricultural processing, and on serving the developing mining, especially gold mining, concerns in the region. In 1939, East Kazakhstan Region, with its capital at Semipalatinsk, was divided into the three regions of Semipalatinsk, Pavlodar and East Kazakhstan. Ust-Kamenogorsk became the capital of the last.

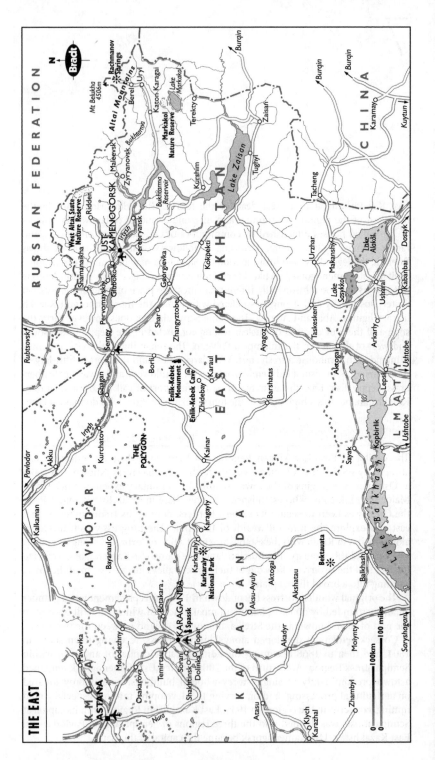

THE EAST

In the period following World War II the city developed into a major centre of non-ferrous metallurgy, based on the ores mined in the surrounding region. A zinc plant came into operation in 1947, and a lead plant soon followed. The Ulba Metallurgical Plant, commissioned in the late 1940s, produced fuel for nuclear power plants. A titanium and magnesium plant was opened in 1965. While many of these factories struggled following the demise of the Soviet Union, Kazakhstan's independence also led to the establishment of a mint in Ust-Kamenogorsk in 1992, producing coins and awards for the new state. Ust-Kamenogorsk became the capital of a much enlarged region in 1997, when Semipalatinsk Region was merged into it. The city had now turned the tables on its once more influential neighbour, Semipalatinsk.

With a skyscape of industrial chimneys on the outskirts of the city, clanking trams ferrying its workers through the streets, and monuments to the achievements of Ust-Kamenogorsk's metalworkers still prominent, this remains a city focused on industrial production, not tourism. But the old centre of town, around Kirov Park, is attractive, as is its riverside setting, and the city overall has a workmanlike charm. As a gateway to the East Kazakhstan Region, and particularly to the scenic beauty of the Altai Mountains to the east, it performs its role well.

GETTING THERE AND AROUND Ust-Kamenogorsk **airport** (✆ *543484*) sits at the northwest edge of the city, off Bazhov Street, some 12km from the centre. Buses 2, 12 and 39 all take you there from the centre. Air Astana offers a daily flight from both Almaty and Astana. Scat also has two flights a week to Almaty, and offers several flights to small airports within East Kazakhstan Region, including four a week to Semey and Ayagoz, two to Zaisan, two to Katon Karagai and two to Kurchum. Note that the Katon Karagai and Kurchum flights use elderly An-2 biplanes. Scat also has two flights a week to Bayan Ulgey (Mongolia). The Russian airline S7 flies weekly to Moscow Domodedovo.

As regards travel within Kazakhstan, the **railway** service to Ust-Kamenogorsk is not particularly helpful. The town is located on a branch line, with departures eastwards to Ridder and to Zyryanovsk, and westwards into Russia. The latter line does then connect with the main northward-bound line from Semipalatinsk, and there are somewhat circuitous services to Almaty and Astana, but you may run into problems on this route if you do not have a Russian visa, since the line passes through Russian territory. If you are really minded to travel from Ust-Kamenogorsk to Almaty by train, it is actually quicker to travel by road the 140km southwest to Zhangiztobe, which lies on the southbound line from Semipalatinsk, and catch the train there, cutting out the long detour into Russia. If it ever materialises, the planned opening of a direct rail link from Almaty to Ust-Kamenogorsk should alter this picture for the better.

The main railway station, Zashita, is in the northwestern suburbs, at the western terminus of the number 3 tram route. The more central Ust-Kamenogorsk station is smaller and less useful. It sits on Mizi Street, at the northern edge of the town centre. The central terminus of the city's four tram lines is also here, as is one of Ust-Kamenogorsk's two **bus stations**. This station (✆ *269394*) serves destinations within East Kazakhstan Region, with several departures daily to Semey, Ridder and Zyryanovsk. The main long-distance bus station is also centrally sited, along Abai Avenue, on the right bank of the River Ulba close to the Palace of Sport. It has at least one bus daily to Almaty, Astana, Karaganda and Pavlodar, has two departures daily to Katon Karagai in the Altai Mountains, and also serves several destinations in Russia, including Omsk, Tomsk and Novosibirsk. Long-distance taxis tout for custom in front of the station.

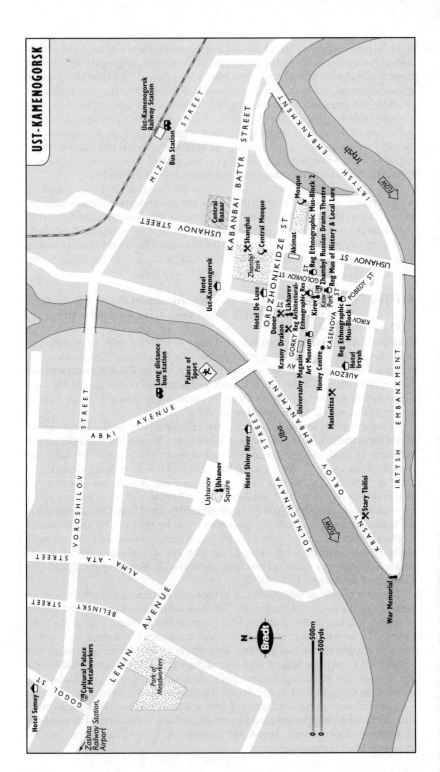

UST-KAMENOGORSK

Ust-Kamenogorsk Railway Station

Bus Station

MIZI STREET

Central Bazaar

KABANBAI BATYR STREET

USHANOV STREET

Zhambyl Park

Shanghai ✗

Central Mosque

Mosque

Hotel Ust-Kamenogorsk

ORDZHONIKIDZE ST

Akimat

Reg Ethnographic Mus–Block 2

Zhambyl Russian Drama Theatre

Hotel De Luxe

Donets ST

Krasny Drakon ✗

Likharev

Reg Architectural–

GORKY ST

Ethnographic Res

Universalny Magazin

Art Museum

Honey Centre

GOLOVKOV ST

Kirov

Kirov Park

Reg Mus of History & Local Lore

POBEDY ST

USHANOV ST

KASENOVA ST

Reg Ethnographic Mus–Block 1

Hotel Irtysh

AUEZOV ST

Maslenitsa ✗

KIROV ST

Long distance bus station

Palace of Sport

ABAI AVENUE

Hotel Shiny River

Ulba

SOLNECHNAYA STREET

EMBANKMENT

ORLOV

FLOW

KRASNY

Stary Tbilisi ✗

IRTYSH EMBANKMENT

War Memorial

VOROSHILOV STREET

ALMA-ATA STREET

BELINSKY STREET

Ushanov Square

Ushanov

Hotel Semey

GOGOL ST

Cultural Palace of Metalworkers

Zashita Railway Station, Airport

LENIN AVENUE

Park of Metalworkers

N

Bradt

0   500m
0   500yds

Irtysh

FLOW

IRTYSH EMBANKMENT

The urban transport network is efficient. The four **tram** routes link the town centre with the northern and western parts of the city. From their central terminus on Mizi Street, all four pass the central bazaar and Zhambyl Park, before crossing the Ulba River and heading north along Abai Avenue. Trams 2 and 3 then head west along Voroshilov Street. Trams 1 and 4 continue further north along Abai. There are numerous bus routes. Numbers to call for local **taxis** include ☎ 523000, ☎ 075 and ☎ 076.

TOUR OPERATORS AND AIRLINE OFFICES

Avia Star Agency 123 Kasenova St; ☎ 252850; f 254740; e aviastaragency@mail.ru. Services include airline tickets, hotel reservations & visa support.

Ecosystem 14/1 Auezov Av; ☎ 571106, 479877; e undp_ukg@ukg.kz; www.altai-es. kz. Both a tourist organisation & campaigning ecological group, Ecosystem can set up a range of adventure- & science-focused programmes across the region, including rafting, horseriding & tours for ornithologists, geologists & botanists. They also offer a 6-day tour into the 'Polygon', site of decades of nuclear testing, suggesting that interested visitors equip themselves with their own radiation monitoring equipment.

Emerald Altay 160 Kabanbai Batyr St; ☎ 243026, 243402 e iz_altay@mail.ru; www. altay.kz. The 'Emerald Altai' runs the Ayuda holiday centre on the shores of the Bukhtarma Reservoir (see page 235), as well as a couple of complexes close to the village of Gornaya Ulbinka, in a forested upland area only around

20km outside Ust-Kamenogorsk, in the direction of Zyryanovsk. The Altai Alps is a winter sports centre, with a 750m ski lift feeding several ski runs; the Izumrudny Health Complex offers a range of treatments, including the Altai speciality of baths infused with the extract from the antlers of *maral* deer.

✈ **Otrar Travel** 4 Ordzhonikidze St; ☎ 576676, 575353; f 243233; e ukk@otrar.kz. General Service Agent for Air Astana.

Rachmanov Springs 2A Voroshilov St; ☎ 763744; f 475719; www.altaytravel.ru. This firm runs the Rachmanov Springs sanatorium, idyllically sited high in the Altai Mountains (see page 234). Their Ust-Kamenogorsk office arranges bookings & transfers to the resort, either on the basis of standard 8-, 16- or 24-day treatment packages or (more expensive) tailored individual transfers. They can also advise about obtaining restricted border zone permits.

WHERE TO STAY

🏠 **Hotel Shiny River** (72 rooms) 8/1 Solnechnaya St; ☎ 766525; f 271418; e reservation@shinyriverhotel.kz; www. shinyriverhotel.kz. This central hotel close to the Ulba River is the smartest in town, with comfortable AC rooms, a sports bar & a sauna. **$$$$**

🏠 **Hotel De Luxe** (5 rooms) 62 Kirov St; ☎ 248802; f 263623; e de_luxe_kirova@mail.ru. This central hotel has just 5 rooms (3 standard, 2 'deluxe') in a building given over partly to offices, but they are reasonably furnished, with AC & small en-suite shower rooms. **$$$**

🏠 **Hotel Semey** (21 rooms) 30 Gogol St; ☎ 522051; f 427276; e semey05@mail.ru. The hotel that seems somewhat confused as to its city is a blue-painted 2-storey building not far from the Cultural House of Metalworkers. Rooms

are reasonably furnished, with AC in all but the cheapest sgls, & this is a good, if not particularly central, option. **$$$**

🏠 **Hotel Irtysh** (87 rooms) 22 Auezov Av; ☎/f 250985. This ugly, centrally located, 10-storey block offers a large range of prices & categories, though the room renovations in various shades of brown do nothing to hide the Soviet legacy of this place. The b/fasts involve a plate of what appears to be leftovers: a slice of pizza, perhaps, or cold beef & macaroni. **$$**

🏠 **Hotel Ust-Kamenogorsk** (16 rooms) 158 Kabanbai Batyr St; ☎ 261801, 261912; f 261603; e hotel-oskemen@yandex.kz; www.hotel-oskemen.kz. This large, central, pink-walled block is a Soviet-style hotel down to its worn wooden floorboards. As usual in this kind of hotel, it offers a wide range of qualities, sizes & prices of rooms.

Only the more expensive, renovated rooms have AC. The en-suite baths are tiny. B/fast is not included in the room rate, & this is altogether not the best deal in town. **$$**

✖ WHERE TO EAT

✖ **Krasny Drakon** 47 Ordzhonikidze St; ✆ 260310, 248765. The 'Red Dragon' is a rather functional building which lies behind impressive oriental gates decorated, reasonably, with red dragons. These actually lie on Gorky St, not far from the central Kirov Park. Another red dragon is coiled around a pillar, ready to strike as you enter. The menu includes a good range of Korean standards, including *bulgogi* & *kimchi*, as well as European & Kazakh dishes. **$$$**

✖ **Shanghai** 59A Ushanov St; ✆ 261173, 264567; e marilynclub@mail.ru; www.marilynclub.kz. Close to the building of the Friendship House of the Assembly of Peoples of East Kazakhstan, this restaurant, offering a mix of European, Japanese & Chinese dishes, also makes a bid to unite different cultures. Walk into the restaurant across a little wooden bridge from the bamboo-walled cloakroom. A message to guests on the front of the menu welcomes diners aboard the yacht *Britannia* as it journeys to 'magnificent & mysterious Shanghai'. The menu ranges from frogs' legs to chop suey via *borscht*. A Mexican menu is available in the summer. **$$$**

✖ **Stary Tbilisi** 117A Krasny Orlov Embankment; ✆ 256392; ⏱ 11.00–01.00. Located on the left bank of the Ulba, close to the confluence with the Irtysh, this Georgian restaurant offers trellises covered with plastic vines, & an intriguing menu, with a good range of Georgian dishes & wines. There are also salads named 'kind wife' & 'angry husband', both of which contain squid, & the tempting 'chicken breasts filled with love'. **$$$**

✖ **Doner** 49 Kirov St; ✆ 240535, 268704. This central fast-food joint has tables outside, a children's play area within, Turkish kebabs, ice cream & brightly coloured cakes. **$$**

✖ **Maslenitsa** 117A Kasenova St; ✆ 250900, 570250. A centrally located barn-like place with a timbered ceiling, this is a Russian restaurant offering a good range of *blini*, salads & basic mains. You pay in advance at the counter, take a number & your seat, & wait – & wait. While the food is good as regards quality & price, this place has taken the 'fast' out of fast food. Maslenitsa is the Russian-themed wing of the **Pizza Blues** chain of pizzerias, which has a network of branches across town. These include branches at 5 Abai Av (✆ 221693), 1 Lenin Av (✆ 271101) & 64 Ushanov St (✆ 252366). **$$**

SHOPPING The **central bazaar** (*142 Kabanbai Batyr St;* ⏱ *Tue–Sun*) sits in the northern part of the centre, at the corner of Ushanov and Kabanbai Batyr streets. There are several shopping centres around it. Right in the town centre, the **Universalny Magazin** on Gorky Street is a shopping centre occupying a worn-looking Soviet building whose exterior decoration appears to comprise groupings of oversized rifle sights.

Altai honey is a good souvenir to pick up here. One central place which specialises in the product is the **Honey Centre** (*56/1 Kasenova St;* ✆ *285121;* e *aitas_bee2@ mail.ru;* ⏱ *09.00–13.00 & 14.00–18.00 Mon–Sat*). They offer a wide range of honey, including some packed in presentation jars.

WHAT TO SEE

Around Kirov Park The small rectangle of park still known as **Kirov Park** (⏱ *winter 07.00–19.00; summer 07.00–21.00*) sits at the centre of Ust-Kamenogorsk's old town, surrounded by metal railings. There is a statue of **Kirov** here, uniformed and proud, raising his open-fingered right hand as if performing a conjuring trick. A plaque nearby identifies the site of the Pokrovsky Cathedral, built in 1888 but demolished during the Stalinist period in 1936. Which means that it survived two years longer than Kirov. The park also contains a number of golden statues, illustrating themes from fairy tales.

Regional Museum of History and Local Lore (*40 Kasenova St;* ✎ *254970, 254933;* ⊕ *09.00–17.00 Wed–Mon; admission adult/child T100/60*) Within the park, its presence signalled by a collection of cannons and some *balbals*, is the Regional Museum of History and Local Lore. Downstairs, there are displays on the nature of East Kazakhstan Region, with stuffed animal-laden dioramas, including a mountain scene featuring *arkhars* and marmot, a riverbank populated by wild boar, and a woodland tableau with a particularly fierce-looking wolverine, evidently grumpy after having been roused by bears blundering through the woods. A rather gory diorama shows a stuffed wolf preparing to stuff on a stuffed roe deer. There is a large stuffed Siberian deer, or *maral*, one of the prides of the Altai, in the centre of the room. There are collections of eggs, pickled reptiles and dead birds. Most of the maps on display, showing off the region's climate, water resources and soils, were still at the time of research based around the region's 1997 boundaries, before the incorporation of the area around Semey. And indeed the museum more generally gives little indication of having yet embraced its wider region. Also on display is a collection of marketable furs, including wolverine, fox, wolf, squirrel, muskrat and Siberian mole.

Upstairs, the displays continue with archaeology, including descriptions of the excavations of Scythian *kurgans* in the region. There is an account of the expedition led by Sergei Chernikov at Chilikty, in Zaisan District, in 1960, with copies of some of the beautiful gold jewellery, in the form of animals such as deer, uncovered from the barrows. A model of one of the Chilikty *kurgans* is also on display. There is also coverage of the *kurgans* at Berel in the Altai Mountains (see page 237). A recreation of a Bronze Age burial uncovered near the village of Zevakino includes a skeleton surrounded by various possessions: jewellery, weaponry, stirrups. An archaeological map of the region shows the wealth of petroglyphs, *kurgans* and stone sculptures to be found across East Kazakhstan. An ethnographic display, centred on a part of the room decked out to resemble a yurt, includes costumes, saddles and household items.

Another room is dedicated to the history of Ust-Kamenogorsk, with an odd collection of items in the centre of the room: an anchor from a riverboat, a model of the Pokrovsky Cathedral and a Singer sewing machine. There is a pastel drawing of Major Likharev, founder of the town, long of hair and narrow of moustache. There are photographs of the working of gold-bearing sands and of the bee-keeping industry at the start of the 20th century. A bee-keeper's hat is on display, as are some school exercise books from the 19th century, with painstakingly executed geometrical drawings. The history of the ferry companies on the Irtysh, whose operations provided a vital transport artery, is chronicled. There is a gramophone, samovars and wall clocks, relics of life in Tsarist Ust-Kamenogorsk. A side room covers World War II, with patriotic posters, descriptions of the exploits of those from the region awarded the title Hero of the Soviet Union, and a boy's-own diorama of a snow-covered battle scene during the fighting for Stalingrad.

The displays continue downstairs with coverage of the post-independence period, including products from the region. There is also a small room devoted to local artists and writers, such as Efim Permitin, who set up the hunting journal *Altai Hunter* in 1923. He is photographed out hunting, a couple of dead birds dangling from his bag. There is a copy of one of his books on display, titled *Love*. Not for birds, presumably. There is also a display on local writer and naturalist Boris Sherbakov, featuring envelopes addressed to him from various international environmental organisations.

Regional Ethnographic Museum The Regional Ethnographic Museum is spread across several locations within and around Kirov Park. At the southwest corner of the park, where Kirov and Kasenova streets meet, stands **Block 1** (*29 Golovkov St;* \ *268529;* ⊕ *10.00–17.00 daily*). Housed in a single-storey Tsarist building dating from 1901, which originally housed a girls' school, this section of the museum focuses on non-Kazakh ethnic groups represented in East Kazakhstan. A Kazakh yurt and Russian wooden hut are pictured above the door. It was closed for refurbishment at the time of writing, but the displays are likely to showcase the costumes, personal and religious items of the many non-Kazakh ethnic groups in the region, including Russians, Germans, Ukrainians and Koreans.

At the opposite corner of the park, at the junction of Gorky and Golovkov streets, is **Block 2** (*59 Gorky St;* \ *263159, 268297;* ⊕ *10.00–17.00 daily; admission adult/child T80/35*). This pink-walled single-storey building was constructed in 1914 as the house and shop of a merchant named Kozhevnikov. It houses displays focused on the traditions of the Kazakh ethnic group. The large first room contains a yurt, six *kanat* (sections) in size. There are also displays of hunting techniques, featuring a stuffed eagle and falcon, weapons, saddles and blacksmiths' tools. The next room has wooden utensils and a display of clothing: coins and buttons sewn onto children's clothes were considered good protection against the evil eye. Kazakh jewellery is displayed; invariably silver, as this was believed to have powers of purification. By tradition Kazakh women were not supposed to prepare food unless they were wearing silver jewellery. A display of musical instruments includes a *kobyz* used by a shaman, with a small mirror in its bowl. The importance of regional trade is illustrated with samovars, porcelain, Chinese silks and a Singer sewing machine. There is a display on religion, including a tiny Koran and a piece of candle from Mecca. Kazakh games are illustrated, including a wooden indented board for the game of *togyzkumalak*. There are also sheep's vertebrae, used in the children's game *asyk*.

In the northern part of the park, close to Block 2, is the open-air section of the museum, the **Regional Architectural-Ethnographic Reserve** (⊕ *summer only 10.00–17.00 daily; admission T50*). This fenced area includes Kazakh dwellings, including a yurt, the winter home of a wealthy Kazakh, and a yurt-shaped stone building, used as a store. There is also a lane of Russian wooden houses, moved here from other locations in the town, including the nicely decorated house of a Cossack *ataman*, and the house in which Pavel Bazhov, author of *The Malachite Casket*, a collection of fairy tales from the Urals, lived from 1919–20.

West of Kirov Park

Taking Tokhtarov Street west from the park, you soon reach on your right the charming two-storey Tsarist-era brick building housing the **East Kazakhstan Art Museum** (*56 Tokhtarov St;* \ *261981;* ⊕ *09.00–18.00 Sun–Fri; summer Mon–Fri; admission T50*). It houses temporary exhibitions, which often fail to inspire: when I visited, it was home to a selection of landscapes by local artists.

A block to the north, at the corner of Kirov and Gorky streets close to the northwestern corner of the park, stands a 1990 monument to the founders of Ust-Kamenogorsk. It portrays a raffish-looking **Major Likharev** in a tricorn hat, his right hand jauntily on his hip, sailing forth in his undersized boat, with jets from the fountain below providing the 'river'.

East of Kirov Park

On the eastern side of the park, along Golovkov Street, there is a fine red-brick Tsarist building housing the **Zhambyl Russian Drama Theatre**

(47 Tokhtarov St; ☏ 452601; booking office ⏰ 12.00–15.00 & 16.00–18.00 Wed–Sun). It was built in 1902 as the House of the People.

Head north one block along Golovkov Street and then turn right onto Gorky Street to reach the large square still known by most local residents as Lenin Square. The building of the **regional administration** fills its western side, but the statue of Lenin which used to stand in front of it was removed in 2002. The pleasant, well-tended square runs eastwards to a modern **mosque**, standing close to the bank of the meandering Irtysh. With a turquoise dome, the mosque is flanked by two tall minarets, rising to slender silver cones. At the centre of the park is a fountain, with sculptures based on the animals of the Chinese New Year.

Around Zhambyl Park

The northwestern corner of Lenin Square abuts the southeastern one of **Zhambyl Park**, surrounded by railings topped by stylised hammers and sickles. In summer you can sup at the open-air Café Medved ('Bear Café'), watching real bears at play in the small **zoo** (⏰ *10.00–17.00; admission adult/child T40/20*).

On the eastern side of the park, along Ushanov Street, is the Tsarist-era **Central Mosque**, a simple single-storey whitewashed brick building with a blue central dome atop a circular drum. Next to this is a two-storey red-brick building, with arched windows highlighted in white. It was built in 1912 as a boys' elementary school, and now serves as the House of Friendship of the Assembly of the Peoples of East Kazakhstan.

Strelka

The spit of land at the confluence of the Irtysh and Ulba rivers is a district known as Strelka. It was the site of the original fortress of Ust-Kamenogorsk. Right at the confluence is a **war memorial**. An eternal flame burns from a Red Army star at the base of a tall column. An inscription records that 51,000 citizens of East Kazakhstan died on the fields of battle during World War II.

Right bank of the Ulba

From the old town, cross the broad and muddy River Ulba by the bridge at the end of Abai Avenue. On reaching the right bank of the Ulba you are confronted with the **Palace of Sport** on your right. This is the home of the KazZinc Torpedo ice hockey team, the best known in Kazakhstan. Ust-Kamenogorsk has developed something of a reputation for nurturing ice hockey stars, several of whom have gone on to careers in the North American NHL, among them Nik Antropov of the Toronto Maple Leafs, Konstantin Pushkarev with the Dallas Stars, and Evgeni Nabokov with the San Jose Sharks.

To your left, Lenin Avenue starts its long westward march, taking you after one block to the busy **Ushanov Square**, centred on a 1973 statue of **Yakov Ushanov**, a young local Bolshevik leader immediately following the Russian Revolution, who was arrested when anti-Bolshevik forces took back control of Ust-Kamenogorsk during the Civil War, and was killed in 1918.

Five blocks further west along Lenin Avenue, you reach on your right the **Cultural Palace of Metalworkers** (*68 Lenin Av*), set back from the street by a quiet square. The façade has 12 Corinthian columns, supporting a Soviet statue of Ust-Kamenogorsk metalworkers in action, stoking fires and testing samples. The place is still used for concerts. It is well worth taking a peek into the main body of the theatre. A frieze on the ceiling depicts Soviet achievement in industry, agriculture and the arts, and the side walls are decorated with Soviet tapestries: the one on the left portrays Lenin rallying the Bolsheviks.

The Altai Mountains straddle four countries: Russia, Kazakhstan, Mongolia and China. That segment falling within Kazakhstan, in the far northeast of the country, gives Kazakhstan some of its most delightful landscapes. Deciduous forests at low altitude, with birch and aspen, rise to mountain taiga, with cedar, pine, silver fir, larch and birch all prominent. Above around 1,800m the forest gives way to mountain meadows, and then to tundra. The highest point, the twin-headed peak of Mount Belukha on the border between Russia and Kazakhstan, reaches 4,506m. The forests, which experience high rainfall, are rich in mushrooms and berries. Mammals found here include bear, *maral* deer, red wolf, elk and sable. There are many charming villages in the area, of log-walled cottages with corrugated metal roofs. Logs for winter heating are piled high outside.

There is a strong spiritual dimension to the Altai Mountains. Old Believers, who separated from the hierarchy of the Russian Orthodox Church in the mid 17th century in protest at the reforms of Patriarch Nikon, found refuge in the remote valleys of the Altai. The graves in local Muslim cemeteries are distinctive: with five- or six-sided wooden pyramidal frames, a little picket fence around the base of the pyramid and a crescent moon at the apex. The size and striking form of Mount Belukha, whose peaks are often shrouded in cloud, have attracted many faiths. Shamans consider the mountain to hold particular significance: its double-headed peak suggests a certain femininity of form which made the mountain for them the female counterpart to Khan Tengri, the home of the male god of the heavens. The spiritual teacher Nicholas Roerich, who spent time in the area with his family during his four-year Asian Expedition in the 1920s, was gripped by the place. Perhaps here might be found the legendary Buddhist kingdom of Shambala, always believed to have been hidden somewhere in central Asia, beyond the peaks of the Himalayas. Followers of Roerich's Agni Yoga make pilgrimages to Mount Belukha.

The pop group Three Dog Night once sang about the virtues of the rain of Shambala in washing away troubles and pain, and certainly the Altai Mountains in Kazakhstan receive plenty of rain. One positive result of this is the abundance of mushrooms and berries to be found in the forests. After rains the locals take to the woods with plastic buckets. Another object of local harvest is the antlers of young *maral* deer. The antlers are a source of pantocrine, believed by adherents to enhance strength and sexual potency, and by some even to ward off the ageing process. The industry, which originated in the area in the 18th century with the Old Believers, involves organised stag farms. The antlers are removed from the young deer and boiled, forming a pantocrine-enriched broth. Several stag farms and sanatoria in the area offer visitors the opportunity of a rejuvenating bath in pantocrine-rich waters. If bathing in antler-infused water is your bag, some of the Ust-Kamenogorsk travel agencies listed on page 229 can help set this up. The season for pantocrine treatments is a short one running roughly from the beginning of June to mid-July.

Some of the most scenically beautiful easternmost parts of Kazakhstan's section of the Altai Mountains, including both Rachmanov Springs and Lake Markakol, unfortunately lie in what is considered to be a sensitive border zone with China, for which a special permit is needed. If you are organising your trip through one of the travel agencies specialising in the area, such as Rachmanov Springs (see page 229), they can help you through the bureaucracy, but you should allow several weeks for the permit application to be processed.

RIDDER AND THE WEST ALTAI Northeast of Ust-Kamenogorsk the land rises towards the peaks of the western part of the beautiful Altai Mountains, marking the border with Russia. Close to the border, the 56,000ha West Altai State Nature Reserve was established in 1991, primarily to preserve the distinctive mountain taiga forest of the area. The gateway to this beautiful and unspoilt scenery is a down-at-heel mining town named Ridder (*Telephone code: 72336*). In 1786, a British engineer named Philip Ridder discovered rich deposits of polymetallic ores here, and mining started in 1791. Earning town status in 1934, Ridder was renamed Leninogorsk in 1941. Its old name was restored in 2002. Ridder today remains a mining and metals-processing centre. The main employer, KazZinc, operates mines, a concentration plant producing zinc, lead, copper and gold concentrate, and a zinc refinery in and around the town. 'We love you Ridder' proclaims a banner strung over the road into town, sponsored by KazZinc.

In the town's central square stands a monument commemorating the 2002 renaming of the town back to Ridder. On a plinth stands a lump of ore. A plaque offers a drawing of Philip Ridder's face above a crossed pick and shovel. Behind the monument is a cultural palace, with hammer and sickle motifs on top of its Corinthian columns. On the opposite side of the square stands a war memorial.

Getting there and around There are frequent **buses** and occasional **trains** from Ust-Kamenogorsk to Ridder, whose small railway station is close to the centre of town. Numbers to call for local **taxis** in Ridder include ⬩25777, ⬩52777 and ⬩24130.

Where to stay

⌂ **Hotel Tourist** (15 rooms) House 24A, 4th Microdistrict; m +7 705 461 4607. This pink-painted building, inconveniently located outside the centre amongst apartment blocks, offers clean if uninspiring 4-bed rooms, without AC. **$$**

⌂ **Eco-tourism Guesthouse** 1 Gagarin St; ⬩24081. NGO Bars offers homestays, as well as beautifully maintained wooden chalets in the woods that sleep up to 8 people in twin beds. Some chalets have saunas, & it is also possible to stay in a yurt. The NGO operates in 2 villages near Ridder: Ermolaevka (40km from Ridder) & Poperechnoe (20km from the town). Book via the Eco-tourism Resource Centre in Almaty (see page 123). **$**

⌂ **Hotel Ridder** (8 rooms) House 22, 4th Microdistrict; ⬩55135. Basic accommodation in a small hotel in 1 of the apartment blocks on the edge of town. Rooms have en suites, but few comforts. **$**

THE ROAD TO KATON KARAGAI The higher-altitude eastern part of Kazakhstan's segment of the Altai Mountains is remote even by Kazakhstani standards. The main route into the area is the road eastwards from Ust-Kamenogorsk to the small town of Katon Karagai. It is a scenic drive, passing in summer amongst fields yellow with sunflowers.

Bukhtarma Reservoir Formed by damming the Irtysh River to the east of Ust-Kamenogorsk, the long Z-shaped Bukhtarma Reservoir, constructed in the 1960s, has a total length of around 600km, and a surface area of 5,490km², making it the fifth-largest reservoir in the world by surface area. A multi-purpose reservoir, it supports a power plant of 675MW, has a storage capacity of 49.8km³, and accounts for a quarter of Kazakhstan's total freshwater fish production. Sturgeon, sterlet and carp are among the species found here. The local authorities are trying to promote the development of fishing tourism, particularly around Lake Zaisan, a large freshwater lake in the eastern part of the region, fed by the waters of the Black Irtysh from China, and in turn feeding into the main Irtysh. Lake Zaisan found itself incorporated into the Bukhtarma Reservoir, as the southeasternmost component of that body of water, its level rising some 6m in the process.

For the citizens of Ust-Kamenogorsk, the construction of the Bukhtarma Reservoir meant the possibility of lakeside beach resorts within reach of the city. There are several holiday bases, most of which are open only during the summer season, offering sand and a range of watersports. One typical option is the **Ayuda Holiday Base ($)**, bookable through the Emerald Altay agency in Ust-Kamenogorsk (see page 229). Operating between 1 June and 30 August, it offers wooden or brick-built corrugated-iron roofed cottages, sleeping between two and nine people. The accommodation is basic, and can normally only be booked on a ten-day package basis, though a stay here offers an interesting insight into how Kazakhstani citizens like to spend their summer holidays. Expect vodka and *shashlik* to feature heavily. Watersports on offer include waterskiing, windsurfing, and taking to the reservoir aboard a giant banana. Ayuda sits on the southern shore of the reservoir, close to its western end. The main route here by road involves heading southeast from Ust-Kamenogorsk on the road towards Samarskoe, and turning left after 100km for the village of Manat. Ayuda is about another 50km from the turning. A shorter route by road is to head east from Ust-Kamenogorsk on the road towards Serebryansk and Katon Karagai, parking your car at the Sadko holiday camp on the north bank of the reservoir (T650). The *Ayuda* ferry makes a trip to Sadko (adult/child T300/150). If you are coming by train, get off at Oktyabrsky on the line between Ust-Kamenogorsk and Zyryanovsk, from where the *Ayuda* ferry will collect you (adult/child T350/175). Check the ferry times when you book and be warned that the train from Ust-Kamenogorsk inconveniently brings you to Oktyabrsky in the early hours of the morning.

The main road to Katon Karagai from Ust-Kamenogorsk runs along the north bank of the Bukhtarma Reservoir. Stallholders along the side of the road offer smoked fish for sale. As you approach the reservoir from Ust-Kamenogorsk you may also see people by the roadside selling maggots (cardboard signs promise *chervi*), an indication of the popularity of leisure fishing at the reservoir. The road encounters a northward-pointing inlet of the reservoir at the Vasilevskaya Crossing, across which a ferry ploughs every couple of hours (T750 for a large car).

Zyryanovsk Sitting to the north of the Bukhtarma Reservoir in the foothills of the Altai, Zyryanovsk is another mining town established in the late 18th century. It is the terminus of the eastbound railway from Ust-Kamenogorsk, and is also served by reasonably frequent buses from Ust-Kamenogorsk, so you may find yourself pitching up here *en route* to the most attractive parts of the Altai to the east, though the shortest road route, using the ferry at the Vasilevskaya Crossing, bypasses the town to the south. As at Ridder, KazZinc is the main employer, operating mines and a concentration plant producing lead, zinc, copper and gold concentrate. Alfred Kokh, the Russian politician and former controversial Chairman of the Russian State Property Committee, was born here.

Despite its industrial character, Zyryanovsk is a relatively green town, with many evergreen and birch trees. A statue of **Lenin** still dominates the main square, with the administrative offices of KazZinc behind it. If you need to overnight here, your best bet is probably the nearby **Central Hotel** (*20 rooms; 22 Sovetskaya St;* \(*72335*) *63999;* **$$**). This offers a wide range of room standards, with air conditioning in the pricier 'luxe' rooms.

Katon Karagai The small town of Katon Karagai is the administrative centre of the remote eastern part of the Kazakhstan segment of the Altai Mountains. The designation of the Katon Karagai National Park, applauded by WWF International as a 'gift to the earth', a globally significant conservation action, gives some welcome additional protection to the area. Katon Karagai is a settlement of single-storey timber cottages supplemented by a few decrepit-looking apartment blocks. It lies in a broad valley, watched over to the south by peaks which retain patches of snow even in summer. There is a charming bazaar of wooden stalls. A couple of the larger shops in the bazaar are ornate wooden constructions with pitched roofs, though the wares on offer tend to be Chinese tracksuits rather than local handicrafts. One good local item on sale in the bazaar is honey, sold in one litre plastic water bottles.

The Ecotourism Information Resource Centre in Almaty (see page 123) offers homestays with local families in several villages in the area (**$**), including Uryl and Berel within the national park, on a full-board basis. A restricted zone permit may be required to stay at some of these, so check with the Centre. The airline Scat flies twice a week to Katon Karagai from Ust-Kamenogorsk, on an Antonov An-2 biplane.

AROUND RACHMANOV SPRINGS From Katon Karagai the road continues eastwards through the attractive Bukhtarma Valley to the village of Uryl, 60km to the east. At this point the road condition deteriorates, as the route heads northwards to Berel, 18km away.

Berel The name of Berel is best known for the Scythian burial ground near the village; four parallel lines of stone-covered *kurgans* of varying sizes, reflecting the differing social standings of their occupants, run roughly in a northwest to southeast direction. Permafrost conditions in the burial chambers have meant the survival of textiles and utensils made from organic materials, as well as human and animal remains, making the site one of considerable archaeological importance. Excavations in the late 1990s uncovered a burial of a man and woman, apparently members of the ruling elite, next to whom were found the well-preserved remains of 13 sacrificed horses, complete with ornamented harnesses, saddles and even headdresses.

The milky-white waters of the Belaya Berel River offer further evidence, according to some, of the maternal qualities of Mount Belukha from whose southern flanks the river flows. The Belaya Berel is a strikingly attractive river, its fast-flowing course offering an underdeveloped potential for white-water rafting. It joins with the Bukhtarma just outside Berel village.

Rachmanov Springs From Berel the track winds alongside the course of the Belaya Berel River, northwards and upwards for 31km, to the sanatorium of Rakhmanov Springs, located at a height of 1,760m in an idyllic landscape dubbed by local tour operators as 'Kazakhstan's Switzerland'. The sanatorium lies close to the northwest shore of the **Big Rachmanov Lake**, a body of water 2.6km long, sandwiched between forested slopes, its waters clear and cold, never reaching temperatures higher than around 12°C. But at the northwestern shore is a warm radon-rich spring, whose curative properties have been exploited since the 18th century. One story surrounding the discovery of this place runs roughly as follows. A hunter named Rachmanov shot a deer close to the lake. The deer tumbled into the waters of the lake, which proved so reinvigorating that the wounded deer, to the astonishment of the hunter, was able to bound off into the woods to its safety.

Rachmanov Springs was a well-known sanatorium in the Soviet period, when it fell under the control of the Zyryanovsk Lead Enterprise. At its heyday, customers flew into Katon Karagai, from where they were brought up to the sanatorium by helicopter. It is now managed by the Ust-Kamenogorsk-based tour operator Rachmanov Springs (see page 229), who have modernised some of the accommodation, though a stay here is still a sanatorium experience as it would have been recognised in Soviet times. The accommodation is based around wooden chalets with shared facilities, in both renovated and slightly cheaper unrenovated chalets (**$$**). Four meals are provided each day, stodgy Russian fare washed down by strong tea. Medical treatments are carried out in Treatment Block Number 3, the name a legacy of the Soviet period when the sanatorium was larger, as there now is only one treatment block. The focus of the treatments is the radon-rich waters. You are assessed by a doctor at the start of your stay, and typically prescribed a daily bath in the warm pool strewn with rocks, coupled with a mix of radon-rich showers, massage and the consumption of herbal teas. The medical staff attempt at somewhat offputting length to dispel 'radon-phobia', assuring clients that the level of radon in the waters is not sufficient to cause any harm through controlled immersion. They claim considerable benefits for disorders of the skin, nervous system and spine.

Stays here are based around a standard programme of one week, and the Rachmanov Springs company organises weekly transfers from Ust-Kamenogorsk in UAZ minibuses or, if you are really unfortunate, a battered Ural lorry converted to an approximate impression of a bus. I landed the latter: the journey took 14 hours, including two enforced stops during which customers of the resort joined the driver in dismantling and then rebuilding the engine. If you have your own transport, you can visit for shorter periods.

Boardwalks of weather-beaten planks link the buildings in the resort. The scent of cedar, carpets of wild meadow flowers, and scurrying chipmunks and squirrels combine to make this an idyllic spot. There are some good walks from the resort. A pass up on the hills behind it offers an excellent view of Mount Belukha, provided the cloud that often shrouds that mountain has lifted. If you walk down from Rachmanov Springs on the road towards Berel, take the path on your right running beside a picnic hut just before the track crosses a small wooden bridge, 3km from the resort. The path brings you to an attractive waterfall. There is another in the hills alongside the Big Rachmanov Lake: hire a rowing boat from the resort to get to it. But you may find that your fellow guests spend much of their spare time in the woods, collecting mushrooms. I worry on their behalf: 'What if you pick an inedible one?' 'All mushrooms are edible. If you're unlucky, you may pick one that you only get to eat once.'

Lake Yazevoe

Taking the road back from Rachmanov Springs towards Berel, you pass across a small wooden bridge after 6km. On the sanatorium side of this, on the left-hand side of the road, is a small wooden chapel with a metal-covered spire. On a good day, there is a fine view of Mount Belukha from this spot.

Further back towards Berel a track to the right, signposted 'Belaya Berel Trail', crosses the Belaya Berel River and then passes through the hamlet of Kariayrik, at the far end of which is a barrier where you need to pay a fee to enter the territory of the Katon Karagai National Park (T206). Continue northwards along the track. A sign on the right-hand side points out the location of the **Yazevoe Waterfall**, a series of ten cascades covering a total length of 200m. The trees along the short path to the waterfall are covered with votive strips of cloth. Further on you reach **Lake Yazevoe**, which sits at an altitude of 1,685m. It is another picturesque mountain lake, 3km in length, offering excellent views towards Mount Belukha when the weather is right. The track continues northwards, eastwards and upwards to **Kokkol**, an abandoned wolfram and molybdenum mine and concentration plant.

LAKE MARKAKOL Another beautiful spot in the Kazakhstan Altai is Lake Markakol, 38km long and 19km wide, standing at an altitude of more than 1,400m and close enough to the Chinese border that a border zone permit is required. It forms the focus of the Markakol Nature Reserve, established in 1976. The surrounding slopes are forested with larch and silver fir, which host brown bear, elk, fox, lynx and *maral*. But the lake's icthyofauna gets particular attention, as Lake Markakol is the only known home to a fish locally called the *uskuch*, a variety of the Siberian *lenok*, a trout. Part of the lake is a protected habitat for the *uskuch* and the arctic grayling, a species of the salmon family.

Lake Markakol is not the easiest place to reach. The only road worthy of the name, and then only just, involves a circuitous southern routing through the village of Terekty. When the weather is dry, and with a 4x4 and an experienced driver who knows the route well, there is a more direct route connecting Lake Markakol with the road to the north between Katon Karagai and Rachmanov Springs. But this route, known as the 'Austrian Road' because it was constructed by Austrian prisoners of war in World War I, is a white-knuckle ride of a journey.

SEMEY (SEMIPALATINSK) *Telephone code: 7222*

The name of Semipalatinsk has internationally become closely identified with the Semipalatinsk Test Site, the location for 456 nuclear explosions between 1949 and 1989 (see page 252). The city has indeed suffered deeply from the health effects of the nuclear tests, both from fallout from tests conducted in the atmosphere and exposure of residents of the city working at the test site. When President Nazarbaev formally renamed the city, using its Kazakh name Semey, one of the reasons given for the switch was that the name Semipalatinsk had negative connotations which might put off potential foreign investors. Yet Semey/Semipalatinsk is also one of Kazakhstan's most historically interesting cities, with some fine Tsarist buildings, a close association with the Kazakh poet Abai, and it was the place of exile of the Russian writer Dostoevsky. There are good museums in the city honouring both Abai and Dostoevsky. While parts of the Semipalatinsk Test Site itself are still not safe to visit, these lie well away from Semey, which offers a rewarding stop on a Kazakhstan tour.

The origins of the city date to Peter the Great's desire to see a line of fortresses along the Irtysh River to help defend the southern parts of the Russian Empire against the predations of the Dzhungars, as well as to develop trade routes and the exploitation of gold deposits. In 1717, one of several expeditions to the area was set up under Colonel Stupin. A detachment of this expedition led by Vasily Cheredov established the fortress of Semipalatinsk on the right bank of the Irtysh in 1718. It received its name, 'seven halls', from the seven buildings of a ruined Buddhist monastery nearby.

The location of the fortress was changed several times because of the flooding of the Irtysh, and it was moved to its present site, 18km from the original location at a place on the river considered less prone to flooding, in 1778. It received town status, as the administrative capital of Semipalatinsk *Uyezd*, in 1782. By this stage it was developing as a trading centre, its original military role having become less important with the removal of the threat from the Dzhungars. A customs office was opened at the fortress in 1748. The town grew throughout the 19th century, with a Cossack settlement to the north of the fortress, a Tartar one to its south. Fairs were held in the town. In 1880, the first steamer ploughed between Semipalatinsk and Tyumen. The present-day coat of arms of the city depicts a camel, symbolising Semipalatinsk's historical importance on the trading routes.

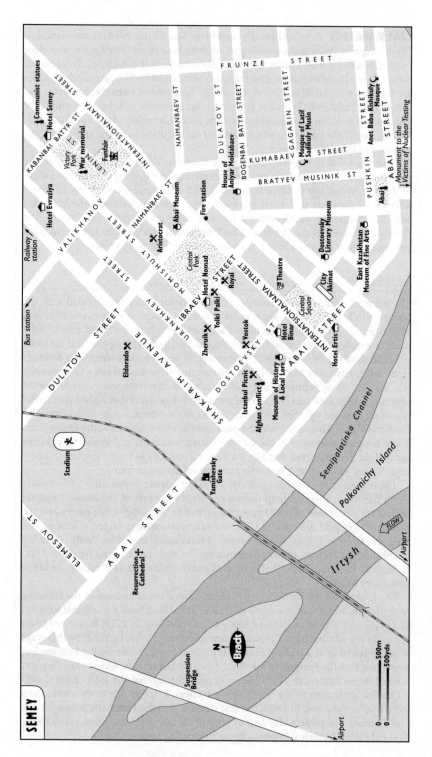

SEMEY

FRUNZE STREET

DULATOV ST

NAIMANBAEV ST

BOGENBAI BATYR Street

GAGARIN STREET

KUMABAEV STREET

BRATYEV MUSINIK ST

PUSHKIN STREET

ABAI STREET

Anet Baba Kishikuly Mosque

Mosque of Latif Sadikuly Musin

House of Aniyar Moldabaev

Monument to the Victims of Nuclear Testing

Abai

Communist statues

Hotel Semey

KABANBAI BATYR ST

LENIN STREET

INTERNATSIONALNAYA

Victory Park

War memorial

Funfair

VICTORY ST

ST

Fire station

NAIMANBAEV ST

Abai Museum

Hotel Evraziya

VALIKHANOV STREET

NAIMANBAEV STREET

Aristocrat

MOMISHULY STREET

Railway station

Central Park

Hotel Nomad

Royal

STREET

Dostoevsky Literary Museum

East Kazakhstan Museum of Fine Arts

Theatre

City Akimat

INTERNATSIONALNAYA STREET

Central Square

Bus station

STREET

DULATOV STREET

URANKHAEV STREET

SHAKARIM AVENUE

Eldorado

Zheruik

Yolki Palki

Vostok

DOSTOEVSKY STREET

ABAI STREET

Hotel Binar

ST

Hotel Ertis

Istanbul Picnic

Afghan Conflict

Museum of History & Local Lore

Stadium

Yamishevsky Gate

ELEMESOV ST

ABAI STREET

Resurrection Cathedral

Sempalatinka Channel

Polkovnichy Island

FLOW

Airport

Irtysh

N

Bradt

0   500m
0   500yds

Suspension Bridge

Airport

Airport

Semipalatinsk, which was briefly renamed Alash Kala, became the capital of the short-lived Alash Autonomous Government headed by Alikhan Bokeikhanov, which lasted from 1917–20. The Alash Government initially formed part of a disparate group of White forces lined up against the Bolsheviks, but later sought an alliance with the Bolsheviks as the Civil War turned in favour of the latter. The Alash Autonomous Government ceased to exist in August 1920, when the Kyrgyz Autonomous Soviet Socialist Republic was established.

Semey has weathered economic hardships in the post-independence period. Its Soviet industrial base was focused on light industry and food processing. The city's industries were particularly noted for the provision of clothing and canned meat for the Soviet army. These did not well equip Semey for the arrival of a market economy. The loss of its status as a regional capital following the administrative reforms of 1997, when Semipalatinsk Region was merged into East Kazakhstan, provided a further blow. A sense of decline has affected even its football team. Semey has claims to be the birthplace of football in Kazakhstan, and its club Yelimay Semipalatinsk was three times Kazakhstan champion in the 1990s. But the club, now called FC Semey, currently languishes in the First (that is, Second) Division. But the construction, with Japanese support, of a suspension bridge across the Irtysh, with pylons 90m in height, provides a symbol of optimism for the renewed growth of the city.

GETTING THERE AND AROUND The **airport** (☏ 340244; e info@semey.avia.kz), whose proud title of Semey International Airport is just about justified by a weekly flight to Moscow on the Russian airline S7, is around 13km from the city centre. Take the road south towards Karaul and Zhidebay, passing a MiG aircraft displayed on a concrete stick as you leave the city. Turn left (signposted for the airport) at a roundabout lying incongruously amongst empty steppe. Bus route 33 in theory connects the airport and town, but only runs a couple of times a day, and is not well co-ordinated with the flight times. The airport building clearly displays its Soviet origins and offers few facilities. There are five flights a week to Almaty on a cramped Yak-40 aircraft operated by the local airline SemeyAvia. Scat also has two flights a week to Almaty and four to Ust-Kamenogorsk, two of which take a circuitous route via Ayagoz. Air Astana flies six times a week between Semey and Astana, on an An-24.

The **railway station** is in the northern part of the city, at the northern end of the busy Shakarim Avenue. It is the northern terminus of a daily train to Almaty, and also lies on the route between Almaty and Zashita (Ust-Kamenogorsk) as well as destinations in Russia. There are less frequent departures to Pavlodar and Astana. The **bus station** is closer in, at the northwest edge of the city centre close to the main bazaar. Buses within the town cost T25.

TOUR OPERATOR AND AIRLINE OFFICE
✈ **Avia Agency** Office 49, 128 Naimanbaev St; ☏ 560818; f 560262; e danaavia_plx@mail. ru; ⏰ 09.00–19.00. General Service Agent for Air Astana.

⌂ WHERE TO STAY
⌂ **Hotel Nomad** (37 rooms) 149 Ibraev St; ☏ 520444; f 569440; e info@hotelnomad. kz; www.hotelnomad.kz. This smart hotel overlooking the Central Park is the plushest in town. It is an 8-storey brick building which looks like it has been transplanted from a wealthy Parisian street. Its foyer is full of wall clocks, each telling a different time. The rooms are neatly furnished in shades of cream, with decidedly firm beds. The restaurant features a self-playing piano & a b/fast buffet comprising mainly cake. **$$$$**

🏠 **Hotel Evraziya** (4 rooms) 69 Urankhaev St; ☎ 569391. This 3-storey pink-walled building, which housed a casino before the government's 2007 legislation closing them, sits on a pedestrian stretch of Urankhaev St. Its 4 rooms have AC & are nicely refurbished. **$$$**

🏠 **Hotel Binar** (21 rooms) 6 Lenin St; ☎ 523639, 523934; f 561558; e binar2006@ yandex.ru. This 2-storey Tsarist-era building with pastel green walls is right in the centre of town: its AC rooms are a good, convenient option, though some of those on the ground floor suffer from damp. The housekeepers also for some reason hide the bed pillows in wardrobes or chests of drawers. The walls of some rooms here sparkle with embedded mineral flakes, making for a somewhat kitsch décor. There is a wide range of room standards & prices on offer, & 8 different b/fast permutations to choose from. They charge an advance booking fee of 30% of the cost of the first night. **$$**

🏠 **Hotel Ertis** 97 Abai St; ☎ 566477, 566460; f 566462. The hotel occupies the upper floors of a really ugly 11-storey red-brick building on the south side of the Central Square, close to the city administration. The 'luxe' rooms apart, beds are small & en suites basic, & there is no AC, but some of the rooms offer the compensation of great views down to the Irtysh River flowing behind the hotel. **$** unrenovated; **$$** 'semi-luxe'

🏠 **Hotel Semey** (80 rooms) 26 Kabanbai Batyr St; ☎ 563604, 563605; f 561809; e semey@ semstar.com; www.semey.semstar.com. This 5-storey brick building sits at the north end of Park Pobedy: a Soviet-era hotel with the characteristic long, rather dim, corridors & wide range of room types. Only the most expensive 'luxe' rooms have AC. For travellers on a tight budget, there are some really basic rooms with shared facilities. **$** without en suite; **$$** with en suite

✖ WHERE TO EAT

✖ **Aristocrat** 25A Lenin St; ☎ 567435; ⏱ 11.00–01.00. This is a pink confection near the Abai Museum with pitched roofs & a cut-out figure of an aristocrat tipping his top hat in your direction from the top of the building. The rather plush interior is decorated in green & gold. In summer all action takes place on the terrace, where you eat beneath red awnings enlivened with flashing lights. There is live music & live crayfish in the fountain, though the life expectancy of the latter depends on how many diners are in a shellfish mood. Among the *shashliks* on offer is sterlet, the fish beloved of the Tsarist Russian imperial court. **$$$**

✖ **Eldorado** 9 Shakarim Av; ☎ 525842, 569650. The Eldorado is a single-storey brick- & pink-walled complex set back from the main Shakarim Av. It houses a supermarket & pub as well as one of Semey's smartest restaurants, a somewhat bland place, with beige walls decorated with paintings of orangey sunsets, a beige piano & green marble columns. The food is a mix of Kazakh & European dishes. There are tables outside in the summer. **$$**

✖ **Istanbul Picnic** 3 Momishuly St; ☎ 565200. This Turkish place, half a step up from a fast-food joint, serves kebabs, *plov*, pizzas & *pide* within a functional blue-walled interior. No alcohol is served. **$$**

✖ **Royal** 145A Ibraev St; ☎ 524885. This is a smart but unexciting place, enlivened with an aquarium stocked with multi-coloured fish & a fireplace at the end of the room. The international menu has some interesting combinations, such as mutton with asparagus & pork with banana. **$$**

✖ **Vostok** Corner Momishuly & Dostoevsky sts; ☎ 561677. This large & basic place features Uighur cuisine, Karaganda beer on tap, 2 floors & often live music. Outside in summer you can eat in a garden with roses, a fountain decorated with battered concrete dolphins & little wooden pavilions for more discreet dining. At w/ends it can get pretty lively, as diners take to the dance floor. **$$**

✖ **Yolki Palki** 147 Ibraev St; ☎ 525747. Its name a Russian expression meaning something like 'crikey!', this basement place offers wooden tables & benches, a beamed ceiling, & decoration featuring furs, balalaikas & stuffed animals. It's under the same ownership, the Burzhuy Restaurant Group, as the nearby Royal Restaurant. The menu offers a mix of Russian & international dishes. **$$**

✖ **Zheruik** 11 Momishuly St; ☎ 523659; ⏱ 08.30 (for b/fast)–midnight. This cheap city-centre canteen has a clean-looking interior with columns covered by pink & green mosaic work. **$**

WHAT TO SEE

West of the Central Square The large rectangular space which forms Semey's Central Square has an energetic line of fountains down the middle and a circular plinth aching for a statue to be installed. The undistinguished five-storey concrete building housing the **city administration** runs along the eastern side of the square.

Semipalatinsk Museum of History and Local Lore (*90 Abai St;* ⟍ *522119;* ⊕ *09.00–17.00 Mon–Sat, closed the last Fri of the month; admission T100*) A block west of the Central Square, along Abai Street, stands the Semipalatinsk Museum of History and Local Lore. It is housed in the single-storey white-walled late 19th-century building which in Tsarist times accommodated the Governor of Semipalatinsk Region. Its grounds, which are home to cannons and an old tractor, are entered through a charming gate. The museum is one of the oldest in Kazakhstan, dating from 1883, when its collections were put together by a group of political exiles in the city, many having been sent here because of their associations with the Narodnaya Volya revolutionary movement. Evgeny Mikhaelis was the main founder of the museum: among those friends on whom he drew for help was the great Kazakh writer Abai Kunanbaev. The museum was moved into its current building in the late 1970s.

There is a map of East Kazakhstan Region in the foyer, together with books written by President Nazarbaev and a Kazakhstan flag and State arms. The first room looks at prehistory, with little dioramas depicting dinosaur-populated eras, fragments of dinosaur eggs found around Lake Zaisan, and large mammoth teeth. There is also a map depicting the location of mineral resources across the territory of the old Semipalatinsk Region. A large diorama populated with stuffed animals runs down the side of the next hall, natural history, running from a mountain landscape with bear, *arkhar* and snow leopard, through a desert scene to a steppe landscape with an eagle flying overhead, ending in an ancient pine forest, with elk, badger and several owls amongst the trees. There is a duck-filled watery diorama opposite. The next room offers a quick canter through the history of the area, from Stone Age implements through chain mail armour to the establishment of Semipalatinsk. There is a model of the original wooden fortress, a wooden tower at each corner and a church in the centre, and the large lock, weighing 8kg, from the Yamishevsky Gate into the city. There are also some Kazakh ethnographic items on display.

Next comes a room focusing on the development of Semipalatinsk as a trading centre. A map shows the large size of Semipalatinsk Region in 1854, when it embraced Karkaraly, Pavlodar and Ust-Kamenogorsk. There are displays of traded items like large Chinese vases and a Russian coffee maker, the household goods of immigrant peasants from other corners of the Russian Empire, and photographs of early paddle steamers ploughing the Irtysh. There is also a mocked-up drawing room of a wealthy family of the town in the early 20th century. In the next room is a selection of items found in a Kazakh yurt, together with more photographs of old Semipalatinsk. The works of Abai Kunanbaev are on display, as are photographs of his friends, including museum founder Evgeny Mikhaelis.

The next room, decorated in reddish tones, offers displays related to World War II as well as the history of nuclear testing at the Semipalatinsk Test Site. There are cut-through diagrams showing the set-up of nuclear tests carried out in both horizontal tunnels and vertical boreholes, photographs of Lake Chagan, the 'Atomic Lake', and a display about the anti-nuclear movement, with photographs of rallies, and a plastic bag with the logo of the Nevada-Semipalatinsk movement. There are also disturbing photographs of local residents with gruesome deformities. A copy of President Nazarbaev's 1991 decree announcing the closure of the nuclear test site is also on display. The final room combines temporary exhibitions with displays relating to prominent local figures.

West along Abai Street Taking Abai Street northwestwards from the Museum of History and Local Lore, you pass on your left after one block the grand Doric-columned, yellow-walled façade of the Semey Academy of Medicine. Opposite stands a **monument** to those killed in Afghanistan in the 1980s. A young man kneels in front of his grieving mother. The names of those killed are inscribed on the wall behind.

Three blocks further on along Abai Street, in a somewhat desolate location close to an underpass, is the restored **Yamishevsky Gate**, the only one of the gates into the Tsarist fortress of Semipalatinsk to have survived. It is a pleasant, whitewashed structure, guarded by a couple of 18th-century cannons, though unfortunately seems to be used as the neighbourhood public conveniences. A short stretch of cobbled street runs artistically through it. Beyond the underpass, a further three blocks on, stands the pastel green-shaded **Resurrection Cathedral**. Built between 1857 and 1860, this is centred on an octagonal tower on which stands a blue roof topped with an onion dome. On the western side of the building is a graceful bell tower, with an octagonal tower standing atop a square one, all topped by another onion dome. Another four blocks along Abai brings you to the northern approach to the modern **suspension bridge** across the Irtysh River, its 90m-tall pylons serving as symbols of the aspirations of the city to regain its standing as a leading trade centre.

North of the Central Square A couple of blocks to the north of the Central Square, with its main entrances on the interrupted Lenin Street, is Semey's **Central Park**, centred on a dry fountain and mostly comprising unkempt woodland. It does offer a couple of basic cafés though, which are pleasant in summer. Immediately beyond the park, at the corner of Lenin and Dulatov streets, stands the museum complex devoted to the poet Abai.

Abai Museum (*12 Lenin St;* ☏ *522422;* ⊕ *10.00–12.30 & 14.00–17.00 Wed–Sun, closed the last day of each month; admission adult/student T125/75*) Semey is closely associated with the poet and philosopher Abai Kunanbaev, revered today as the most important Kazakh literary figure, who was born in the hills of Chingistau south of the city (see page 250). It is therefore fitting that right in the centre of town stands the large complex of the Abai Museum. The complex consists of several buildings. It was organised in 1995 to mark the 150th anniversary of the poet's birth. The main entrance is in the stylish Tsarist-era building, with half-columns around the windows, on Lenin Street. Behind this is a green-domed concrete building. Further along stands a wooden mosque, with an octagonal minaret in its centre, and the wooden building of the *madrasa* of Ahmet Riza, at which Abai studied from 1855–59. The *madrasa* was moved to its current site as part of the anniversary works. A seated statue of Abai, with empty sockets for eyes, gazes unseeingly towards the *madrasa* building.

On entering the museum you climb the stairs towards a statue of Abai, in a serene white colour, against a tapestry backdrop. The exhibition halls begin to the left. The first displays a wall map of the places associated with Abai, and his family tree. A tapestry by Shami Kozhakhanov, one of several created in 1995 as part of the anniversary celebrations, depicts Abai as a horse, being pursued by a wolf, representing reactionary forces pitted against him, while swans in flight represent his creative works. The next room contains photographs of 19th-century

Semipalatinsk, as well as a copy of a pencil portrait of Abai drawn in 1887 by Lobanovsky, a Russian friend of the poet. Also on display are the writing desk, bookcase and mirror from Aniyar Moldabaev's house in Semipalatinsk, used by Abai when he stayed there.

Moving into the concrete building constructed in 1995 as an extension to the museum, you next reach an art gallery. This includes paintings and drawings of the poet, and of some of the places linked with him and his works, such as the Mausoleum of Zere and Ulzhan, Abai's grandmother and mother. The museum holds 11 paintings by the noted Kazakh artist Abylkhan Kasteyev. One of these depicts Abai as a learned-looking boy, squatting in front of an open exercise book. Another shows an adult Abai writing poetry. Next comes a room full of late 19th-century furniture.

Heading into the heart of the new block, a room to the right highlights the life of the nomadic Kazakhs, with a yurt, lavishly floored with felt rugs and containing a four-poster bed with nicely decorated base, set in a steppe diorama against a painted backdrop of a Kazakh family and their horses. There are also items of clothing and jewellery on display. Opposite is an interesting room which sets out to illustrate the three sources of inspiration for Abai's work. The first is Kazakh culture and oral literary tradition, represented by a tapestry behind a bust of the poet, on which are depicted *balbals*, *dombra* and *kobyz*. A frieze illustrates the second source, Eastern literature, with portraits of central Asian and other Eastern literary figures, such as Al Farabi and Navoi. The third source of inspiration, Russian and Western literature, is illustrated by another frieze depicting writers such as Pushkin, Dostoevsky and Lermontov, as well as western European literary greats such as Byron.

A circular room under the dome once housed an audio-visual display, which no longer functions. Rooms on either side of this offer little of interest beyond friezes and comfy sofas. Up the stairs are a couple of rooms showcasing Abai's works. One highlights his poetry and his best-known maxims: most set out in Kazakh only, though a few Russian-language versions are included. The other room focuses on Abai's translations of the works of other poets, including Pushkin, Lermontov and (through Lermontov's Russian-language versions) Goethe and Byron. There is also a display on Abai's songs. Back downstairs is a room of items associated with the celebrations of the 150th anniversary of the poet's birth, including carpets bearing his portrait, vases and a huge 'memory book'.

The displays then continue downstairs back in the Tsarist-era building. A long room has a display of the works of Shakarim Kudaiberdiev, Abai's nephew, who followed in the footsteps of his uncle as a poet and philosopher, but who fell victim to the Stalinist regime in 1931. There are briefer displays highlighting the literary works of other relatives and pupils of Abai. Then come items related to the writer Mukhtar Auezov, also a native of the region, who did much to popularise the work of Abai. A large Kozhakhanov tapestry at the end of the room, entitled *Consonance*, features a balding Auezov sitting attentively at the feet of an ethereal Abai. The last room looks at Abai's legacy, with medals associated with various anniversary commemorations of his birth, a frieze of the Abai and Shakarim Mausoleum at Zhidebay and a model of the museum complex.

Fire station At the corner of Internatsionalnaya and Dulatov streets, opposite the southern edge of the Abai museum complex, stands an intriguing red-brick building with a tall tower, giving it the whiff of an old lighthouse, topped with a red Soviet star. It is a fire station. On the side wall is a memorial to firefighters killed during World War II as well as those killed across Kazakhstan while carrying out their duties since then. An action-packed frieze shows firefighters in the midst of a raging inferno.

Head two blocks east along Dulatov Street, turning south onto Bratyev Musinik Street where Dulatov Street curves. After one block you reach on your right, at the corner with Bogenbai Batyr Street, the former house of **Aniyar Moldabaev**, a relative and pupil of Abai. The two-storey building, which has a brick ground floor and wooden first floor, now houses a small museum devoted to the writer Mukhtar Auezov.

Around Victory Park Continuing north along Lenin Street from the Abai Museum, you reach after a couple of blocks the southern end of **Victory Park** (Park Pobedy), studded by monuments to World War II. A T-34 tank was placed here on a concrete pedestal in 1995, as part of the 50th anniversary celebrations of the end of the war, demonstrating that the practice of putting items of weaponry on plinths did not stop with the end of the Soviet Union. Immediately to the north of this is Heroes Alley, with each of the local Heroes of the Soviet Union commemorated by a pink stone monument. Just beyond this is the main composition of the square, featuring a tall **obelisk** topped by a victorious rider, an adjacent eternal flame and a powerful statue of a falling soldier, straining to keep his machine gun held up. Across a pedestrianised stretch of Lenin Street on the eastern side of Victory Park is a small **funfair**.

The large concrete bulk of the Hotel Semey stands at the northern end of Victory Park. There is an intriguing collection of **communist statues** behind it, set out in a double line as an open-air gallery. Take Lenin Street (appropriately) northwards beyond the intersection with Kabanbai Batyr Street, and you will see the statues in parkland on your left. The ensemble is dominated by a huge statue of Lenin, which once stood at the heart of the Central Square. In front of this are two lines of busts and smaller statues of communist notables, each standing on round concrete plinths. I made the overall tally ten Lenins, three identical-looking busts of Kirov, a Marx and a Frunze. The statues have had a somewhat itinerant life following the fall of the Soviet Union. They were originally assembled close to the Irtysh River, not far from the Central Square, but were moved to make way for a construction project there.

East of the Central Square

Dostoevsky Literary Museum (*118 Dostoevsky St;* `\` *524976;* e *muz-dost@ rambler.ru;* ⊕ *09.00–18.00 Mon–Sat; admission T100*) The streets to the east of the Central Square are an old part of town, with single-storey wooden Tsarist houses, crumbling Soviet apartment blocks and brightly hued modern structures forming an often chaotic jumble. One block behind the city *akimat* building stands the Dostoevsky Literary Museum. The museum is centred on the modest log-walled building in which the great Russian writer Dostoevsky lived in exile from 1857–59 (see box, page 248). A plaque on the outside wall records that he met here with the scholars Chokan Valikhanov and Pyotr Semyonov-Tianshansky. Dostoevsky's house is dwarfed by the large concrete extension added in the 1970s, with a large relief of Dostoevsky's face on the outside wall.

A plaque in the foyer records the 1971 decision of the Council of Ministers of the Kazakh Soviet Socialist Republic to open the museum. The main display is upstairs in the modern extension. There are exhibits related to the writer's early career in St Petersburg. In the centre of the room, the period of his imprisonment in Omsk is illustrated by a striking space walled off by a composition featuring 400 wooden faces, entitled *The House of the Dead* and inspired by Dostoevsky's semi-autobiographical account of prison life. There are sinister-looking drawings by the artist A Korsakova, used to illustrate Dostoevsky's *The House of the Dead*, and leg irons, weighing 4kg, of the type Dostoevsky had to wear throughout his time in Omsk.

Dostoevsky's exile in Semipalatinsk is illustrated by a relief plan of the grid-patterned town and with contemporary photographs of the town and of his friends, including Baron Wrangel, Pyotr Semyonov-Tianshansky and Maria Isaeva. There is an 1859 photograph of Dostoevsky and Chokan Valikhanov together, used as the inspiration for the statue of the two intellectuals outside the museum. There are also illustrations by Korsakova used for the novellas *Uncle's Dream* and *The Friend of the Family*, on which Dostoevsky worked in Semipalatinsk. Haunting, wide-eyed, accusing faces are drawn in a smudgy style. Dostoevsky's later life and career are also covered, with family photographs and displays on his major novels, the latter illustrated with more drawings by Korsakova. There are also Kazakh-language translations of Dostoevsky's works on display. The room is decorated with a swirly 1970s Soviet frieze of Dostoevsky and his works.

The interior of the apartment in which Dostoevsky and his new bride lived from 1857–59 has been recreated from the memoirs of a Semipalatinsk resident named Z Sytina. There is a dining room, with samovar and tea set ready for guests. Samples of the writer's handwriting are displayed in his study. The ground floor of the Soviet extension houses temporary exhibitions, such as displays of work by local schoolchildren.

Next to the Dostoevsky Literary Museum is a statue of the seated Russian writer with Kazakh scholar Chokan Valikhanov. The inspiration for the statue is the 1859 photograph of the two together, of which you can see a copy in the museum, but a comparison of the two is instructive, particularly in respect of Valikhanov. The dashing and resolute figure of the statue seems a long way from the face which stares out from the photograph. Dostoevsky, in contrast, is balding throughout.

A few blocks east of the Dostoevsky Literary Museum, amidst the grid pattern of small streets in this old part of town, stands the pastel-green-shaded Tsarist-era **Mosque of Latif Sadikuly Musin**. A cylindrical minaret rises to a green cone at the eastern end of the building. There is a large flattish dome behind it, standing on a low circular drum.

East Kazakhstan Museum of Fine Arts (Nevzorov Fine Arts Museum) (108

Pushkin St; ✎ 522007; f 523184; e muznevz@yandex.ru; ⊕ 10.00–17.30 Tue–Sat; admission T100) Heading east along Abai Street from the Central Square, you reach on your left after three blocks the imposing Ionic-columned façade of the grand grey-painted building which houses the Nevzorov Fine Arts Museum. The museum has an interesting history. Opened in 1985, and finding itself sorely in need of artworks, the museum made overtures to a Moscow-based art collector named Yuli Nevzorov, who had considerably expanded the collection of Russian art which had built up in his family over two generations. In the late 1980s, Nevzorov and his family agreed to present the museum with more than 500 works of Russian, Soviet and western European art. In 1991, the museum was renamed in honour of the Nevzorov family in recognition of this gift. The oldest part of the building dates from the 1870s, when it was built for a local merchant named Fyodor Stepanov.

A portrait of Yuli Nevzorov hangs in the foyer of the museum. There is also a shop here, with a good range of local painting and jewellery on sale. The collection is extensive, and as you tour the many rooms you may start to wish uncharitably that Nevzorov had been a little less generous. The best place to start, to give an approximately chronological tour, is room 14 on the top floor, which houses icons and some 18th- and 19th-century Russian painting. A portrait by Vasily Tropinin from the 1840s, *Old Woman Cutting her Fingernails*, is an unusual and tender depiction of the artist's wife. The next room contains a couple of classical woodland fantasies by Karl Brullov, including a depiction of Diana being seized by a lustful satyr while Endymion sleeps. There is more 19th-century Russian painting in the next two rooms, including some fine landscapes, such as Ivan Shishkin's *Winter in a Forest* from 1890, a chilly black and white scene. The next two rooms cover the end of the 19th and early 20th centuries, with canvases such as a 1928 still life of *Vegetables and Woodcocks* by Pyotr Konchalovsky, grandfather of the noted Russian filmmakers Andrei Konchalovsky and Nikita Mikhailov. Most of the items in the next room, graphics, were gifts to the fledgling museum in Semipalatinsk from the Pushkin Museum in Moscow, including a work by Rembrandt of *The Descent from the Cross*.

The next room is devoted to western European painting, a mixed bag which includes a large canvas of a Norwegian fjord by 19th-century English artist Henry Enfield. Ukrainian art is showcased in the following room, including a couple of pleasing rural paintings by Mikola Pimonenko. *Laundress* (1909) depicts a bare-footed girl in a red dress doing the laundry, while an 1896 canvas portrays the man of the house returning home clearly the worse for wear: his wife stands ready to greet him, a stick concealed behind her. There is art from the late Soviet period in the next room, including Alexander Sitnikov's *The Concert* from 1984, its canvas burning a fierce red, a painting dedicated to Shostakovich.

The exhibitions continue downstairs, where the focus is on the art of Kazakhstan. Dulat Aliev's *Bazaar* from 1985 portrays a frosty-looking winter market scene. Note the pair of drunks in the bottom right corner of the canvas. V Kolmakov's

DOSTOEVSKY IN SEMEY

Born in 1821, Fyodor Dostoevsky was already a well-known literary figure in St Petersburg, thanks to the success of his first novel, *Poor Folk*, when he began in 1847 to attend the weekly discussion meetings hosted by Butasevich-Petrashevsky. The Petrashevsky Circle espoused utopian socialist viewpoints. With 1848 a year of revolution across Europe, Tsar Nicholas I was anxious to clamp down hard on such talk, and in April 1849 members of the group were arrested. Dostoevsky was considered to be one of the most serious offenders, as he had read out Belinsky's banned *Letter to Gogol* at a gathering, and was found to be in possession of two prohibited utopian socialist books. He was therefore one of the members of the group sentenced to death by firing squad. In December 1849, he and his colleagues were taken onto an icy St Petersburg square to be shot. And nothing happened. It transpired that Tsar Nicholas I, who liked a jape, had ordered a mock execution. Dostoevsky's punishment was actually to spend four years in the prison labour camp at Omsk in Siberia. His relief at not having been shot was soon tempered by the grim reality of prison life.

On his release in 1854 he was required to serve in the Siberian Regiment, and in March that year he was registered as a private in the First Siberian Company of the Seventh Line Battalion in Semipalatinsk. Dostoevsky was to spend five years in the city. He started out by living in the barracks, then moved to a room in a decrepit windowless log cabin, full of cockroaches. His position in Semipalatinsk was greatly improved by his friendship with Baron Wrangel, the young public prosecutor who had read *Poor Folk* and sought out the exiled writer. Dostoevsky spent part of 1855 with Wrangel in a *dacha* named Kazakh Garden. Through Wrangel, Dostoevsky was able to meet the members of the local intellectual community, including explorer Pyotr Semyonov-Tianshansky. Dostoevsky had already met

Semipalatinsk street scene from 1912 shows the Alexander Nevsky Church, which was destroyed in the Soviet period, as well as the artist's workshop, the name 'Kolmakov' emblazoned across a large billboard, allowing for no mistaking the identity of the painter. Also downstairs are temporary exhibitions, and the works of local schoolchildren line the corridor.

East along Abai Street There is a scrap of park to the east of the Nevzorov Fine Arts Museum, along Abai Street. Here stands a solid-looking statue of **Abai**, the poet holding his right hand to his chest. Three blocks further east along Abai Street stands the **Anet Baba Kishikuly Mosque**, which dates from the late 1850s. Its entrance, on the eastern side of the building, is topped by a small green dome. Minarets, irregular octagons in plan, stand either side of the entrance. The main body of the mosque is roofed by a flattish green dome.

Monument to the Victims of Nuclear Testing Turning right off Abai Street opposite the Abai monument, you cross a bridge over the Semipalatinka Channel to reach the park-covered Polkovnichy Island, which with its open-air summer cafés serves as a retreat from the city on warm weekends. At 1km from the turning off Abai, a track to the left leads to the striking Monument to the Victims of Nuclear Testing. The work of architect Shota Valikhanov, the monument, which was inaugurated in 2001, is also named *Stronger than Death*.

Kazakh scholar Chokan Valikhanov in Omsk, following his release from prison, and renewed his acquaintance in Semipalatinsk. He urged Valikhanov to serve his homeland by 'enlightened intercession' with Russia.

Dostoevsky also fell in love in Semipalatinsk. The object of his affections was attractive, blonde-haired Maria Dmitrievna Isaeva, the long-suffering wife of an alcoholic local customs officer, Alexander Isaev. Maria Isaeva appears to have been both manipulative and rather neurotic, and Wrangel came to the conclusion that Maria felt sorry for Dostoevsky but did not really love him. Disaster for Dostoevsky came in May 1855 when Isaev, whose drinking had lost him his job in Semipalatinsk, moved to Kuznetsk. The writer was separated from his beloved Maria. Isaev died soon afterwards. Through the lobbying efforts of Wrangel, Dostoevsky secured a commission, giving him hope that he would be able to marry the woman with whom he had fallen so deeply in love. But a rival appeared for Maria's affections: a young Kuznetsk schoolteacher named Nikolai Vergunov. Dostoevsky made a risky visit to Kuznetsk, and persuaded Maria to marry him. They were wed in that town in February 1857: in a strange touch, his rival Vergunov was a witness at the wedding.

Back in Semipalatinsk, the couple rented an apartment in the house of the postmaster, Liapukhin, the building around which the museum is based. But married life does not seem to have been a happy one for Dostoevsky or his new bride. The writer's epilepsy made an unwelcome appearance on his honeymoon: a bad omen of further torments to come. Exile for Dostoevsky ended in 1859, when he was able to live first in Tver and then St Petersburg. Maria however remained unhappy and became increasingly sick, dying of tuberculosis in 1864. Dostoevsky was later to find domestic happiness with Anna Snitkina, the young stenographer he had hired to cope with the merciless deadlines imposed on him by his mounting financial problems.

The monument is a 25m wall in the shape of a large tombstone, standing on a 6m-high mound. Into the tombstone is cut a space in the shape of a nuclear mushroom cloud. At the base of this is a white marble sculpture of a woman, trying to protect her baby from the explosion by covering it with her outstretched arms. To the right of the monument stands a black marble wall on which is etched a map of Kazakhstan. This is an unfinished composition which was intended to portray the sites across Kazakhstan associated with high levels of nuclear radiation. To the left of the monument is another small mound on which stands a tree covered with votive offerings. The *Stronger than Death* monument is a moving composition in a tranquil setting.

CHINGISTAU

In the hills of Chingistau, south of Semey, lie places associated with the lives of the great Kazakh writers Abai, Shakarim and Auezov. Chingistau is an attractive, sparsely populated area, offering excellent possibilities for a literary-focused day tour to some of the sites linked to the three men.

From Semey, head south out of town on the road to the airport and Karaul. Some 11km out of town, you reach a roundabout, with a turning to the left for the airport. Instead of taking this turning, continue straight on towards Karaul. The road quality immediately deteriorates, with an increase in the number of pot-holes.

BORLI Some 78km south of the roundabout, a left turn to the small and rather windswept village of Borli is marked with a concrete sign to the Auezov House Museum. Borli is 3km away. Next to a car park at the front of the village stands the whitewashed single-storey building housing the **Mukhtar Auezov House Museum** (admission adult/child T60/30). It is in theory open daily, though you may well need to ask around the village to find someone to open it up. Mukhtar Auezov was born in Borli in 1897, into a nomadic family. He was known for his plays, such as *Enlik-Kebek*, a Romeo and Juliet-like tale of doomed love between a boy and girl belonging to two tribes, as well as for his works *Abai* and *The Path of Abai*, about the life and writings of Abai Kunanbaev.

The bust of Auezov greets you as you enter the museum. Exhibits include photographs of his school life in Semipalatinsk. There is a photograph of the line-up of the Semipalatinsk football team, Yarish, with Auezov, one of the first Kazakhs to play football, as a defender. Future geologist Kanysh Satpaev was in the same team, which was clearly characterised by strong intellectual firepower. I hope their footballing skills matched. (Although, if they were the first team in Kazakhstan, one does rather wonder who it was they actually played. Perhaps that's why they went for intellectuals.) Also here is a model of the twin yurt in which *Enlik-Kebek* was first performed in the nearby wintering settlement of Aigerim in 1917. A relief map of the area depicts the various locations associated with Abai and Auezov. There are photographs of Auezov at work and of his family life (he was married three times). One rather chilling snap shows Auezov among other leading supporters of the Kazakh Alash movement: of the seven faces in the photograph, Auezov was one of only two to survive the Stalinist repression of the 1930s.

The displays chronicle a writer who became an increasingly prominent member of the Soviet intellectual elite. There is a model of the rather grand house in Almaty in which he lived as a successful writer, and which houses another museum to him (see page 142). There are photographs of Auezov travelling the world – standing in front of the Grand Canyon as part of a 1960 delegation of Soviet writers, and being photographed before the Taj Mahal – and a souvenir fish-shaped ashtray he brought back from India is on display. There are photographs too of the performances of his plays. One room is devoted to Auezov's return visits to his homeland; a grand figure returning to the land which nurtured him. There is a photograph of a local elder giving a white camel to his grandson on the occasion of his 80th birthday commemorations in 1977. Another room is a traditional Kazakh larder, or *toshala*: a windowless room with thick stone walls. In the centre are four tree trunks with stumpy branches on which meat would be hung.

Near the museum stands a cream-coloured domed mausoleum surrounded by a low fence. This is the **Mausoleum of Omarkhan and Nurzhamal**, Auezov's parents. The present mausoleum was built in 1995 as part of the commemorations associated with the 150th anniversary of Abai's birth.

ON THE TRAIL OF ENLIK AND KEBEK From Borli, back on the road south towards Karaul, you pass on the right-hand side of the road after a further 38km the **Enlik-Kebek Monument**. Standing at the summit of a low hill, this is a tiled obelisk, beneath which lies a cenotaph. The railings around the monument are covered in votive strips of material. The story of Enlik and Kebek, popularised by Auezov's play, is about the terrible consequences of the conflict between different Kazakh tribes, and therefore a plea for the unity of the Kazakhs. Enlik and Kebek were deeply in love but they lived in a period in the 18th century of deep tribal divisions, and Enlik came from the Matai tribe while Kebek was from the Tobykty. They were forbidden by their elders from being together. Unable to accept this stricture, they fled to the Chingistau Hills, where they hid out in a cave. A child was born. But they were discovered, and caught. The penalties were savage. Enlik and Kibek were drawn and quartered, and their child thrown to his death into a canyon.

The cave in which Enlik and Kebek are reputed to have lived can also be visited. Another 25km south on the main road, take the right-hand turning signposted to 'Enlik-Kebek'. This brings you onto a rough track through the hills, ending 7km on at a large graffiti-covered red rock, a place known as Uitas, or 'house-stone'. Around the back of the rock is a shallow cave, on whose walls is a rather touching painting of Enlik cradling her child, while Kebek stands guard at the entrance, though all of this has been smothered by graffiti.

ZHIDEBAY The village of Zhidebay is closely associated with the life of the Kazakh writer Abai Kunanbaev, and houses the huge modern mausoleum of Abai and his nephew, Shakarim Kudaiberdiev. To get here, continue south along the road towards Karaul. Some 23km south of the turning for the cave of Enlik and Kibek, there is a signposted right turn to Zhidebay, which lies 10km down this side road. The twin white towers of the Abai and Shakarim mausoleum complex are visible across the steppe from tens of kilometres away.

Abai House Museum (**↖** *(72252) 91811;* ⊕ *10.00–18.00 Wed–Sun; admission adult/child T80/40)* The road ends at a car park, at the back of which stands the Abai House Museum. Abai was born in 1845 at a spring called Kaskabulak, not far from Borli. The single-storey house at Zhidebay, which now accommodates the museum, was passed on the death of Abai's father Kunanbay to the poet's much-loved younger brother Ospan. But Ospan died young, in 1892, at which point, in accordance with Kazakh tradition, Abai and his family moved into the house, taking Ospan's widow Erkezhan under their wing. Abai wintered in this house for the rest of his life.

There is a large stone bust of Abai in the garden. The poet's carriage is preserved in a glass case in the stables. Inside the museum, Abai's family tree is set out in the foyer. The kitchen contains samovars and wooden utensils, including a large wooden bowl for serving *kumiss*. A sitting room follows, and then Abai's study, in which is exhibited a beautifully decorated bed which belonged to his wife Dilda, as well as the poet's *dombra*. Two games are displayed here, a chess set and the board for the Kazakh game *togyzkumalak*, illustrating the role of both local and external cultures in Abai's life. In the room occupied by Erkezhan are elegant bone-decorated wooden chests. A display in the corridor contains personal items belonging to Abai, such as his pocket watch. There is also a larder room, or *toshala*, similar to that in the Auezov museum in Borli. Meat could also be cured in this room, for which the hole in the roof would be closed. Also in this room is a fierce-looking metal trap targeted at wolves.

At the side of a car park outside the museum is a stone circle on which stands a small pyramid. This is the **Monument to the Geographical Centre of Eurasia**, which appears rather conveniently to have been determined to lie almost at the door of the former home of Kazakhstan's greatest writer.

Mausoleum of Abai and Shakarim To the right of the Abai House Museum, standing 1km or so away, is the huge Mausoleum of Abai and Shakarim. The complex was inaugurated in 1995, in the presence of President Nazarbaev, on the occasion of the 150th anniversary of Abai's birth. Two tall white towers, with

THE 'POLYGON'

The Soviet Union's project to produce an atomic bomb started in a low-key way in 1943, with physicist Igor Kurchatov being appointed as scientific director. But espionage information about the US project, and the bombings of Hiroshima and Nagasaki in 1945, pushed the issue centre-stage. The Soviet Union's objective was to produce a working weapon on the US design as quickly as it could. Lavrenti Beria, Stalin's feared former security chief, was appointed administrative director to drive the project. In 1947, Beria selected an area of the Kazakh steppe to the south and west of Semipalatinsk to be the test site for the project, callously and inaccurately describing the area as uninhabited. On 29 August 1949, in the presence of Beria, the first bomb, 'First Lightning', was detonated from a tower in the Experimental Field of the Semipalatinsk Test Site. Closely resembling the US 'Fat Man' bomb, it had a yield of 22 kilotons. It was nicknamed 'Joe One' by the Americans, in a reference to Stalin.

Until the last test was carried out in 1989, the Semipalatinsk Test Site, also known somewhat geometrically as the 'Polygon', was the host to 456 nuclear explosions, with a cumulative power output some 2,500 times the Hiroshima bomb. Some 116 of these were atmospheric tests, conducted at the Experimental Field. When such atmospheric tests were banned by the Partial Test Ban Treaty of 1963, the focus of the testing moved to sites further south within the 'Polygon', particularly in a network of tunnels in the Degelen Mountains, and boreholes in the Balapan Complex. There were 340 of these underground tests. One of the most infamous of the later explosions was the Chagan test of 15 January 1965, part of a Soviet programme to explore peaceful uses for nuclear explosions. Conducted on the dry bed of the Chagan River, the explosion formed a crater which aimed to dam the river during its peak springtime flow. The result was the formation of Lake Chagan, better known as the Atomic Lake.

ribbed sides, stand on top of a building in the form of a broad three-platformed ziggurat, the three levels representing the ascension from the subterranean to the heavenly. Its base is a rectangle, some 200m long and 65m wide. Just outside the main entrance to the building is a white-walled mosque, oval in plan with four conical domes. The mosque is a simple but stylish building. Its interior, illuminated from the tops of the four domes, is dominated by a large central column, producing the overall effect of a building divided into a series of cells.

At the entrance of the mausoleum complex is a font-like structure filled with earth from the land of Abai and Shakarim. Pass through a corridor to a small amphitheatre, where recitals of Abai's work are sometimes given. Climb up the steps here to reach the pebble-covered roof of the building, from which are entered the two tall mausolea. These, standing close to each end of the platform, are tall white towers, tapering from wide bases. The slightly taller of the two towers, rising to almost 38m, is the mausoleum of Abai. Its interior features a domed ceiling covered with ornate geometric designs. Next to the tomb of Abai is a smaller one, that of his beloved younger brother Ospan. The interior of the mausoleum of Shakarim, Abai's nephew and a victim of Stalinist repression, is also domed, this time decorated with blue designs resembling droplets of water, or tears. The tomb of Shakarim's younger brother is also here.

Between the Abai and Shakarim Mausoleum and the Abai House Museum stands the much smaller **Mausoleum of Zere and Ulzhan**. Zere was Abai's paternal grandmother; Ulzhan was his mother. Their mausoleum is an interesting design, with stone walls radiating out from a central space.

The results of the nuclear testing for the people of the area included high rates of cancers and a host of other medical problems, as well as many cases of physical deformity. The radiation effects of the nuclear testing were monitored in the Soviet period by institutions with titles deliberately designed to mislead, such as the Brucellosis Dispensary No 4, whose work had nothing to do with brucellosis. The concerns of local people about the test site found shape in the Nevada-Semipalatinsk anti-nuclear movement, headed up by Kazakh poet Olzhas Suleimenov, which was established in February 1989. It held numerous peace marches, meetings and conferences. As the old Soviet order collapsed, the movement carried the day, and no further tests were held after that year. On 29 August 1991, Nazarbaev signed a decree closing the Semipalatinsk Test Site.

The boreholes and tunnels have been sealed with the help of US support through the Co-operative Threat Reduction Programme, but the legacies of four decades of nuclear testing will be harder to erase. Large swathes of land within the 18,000km^2 of the 'Polygon' are still contaminated, and the health effects of the testing, both physical and psychological, are still with the local people. There have also been many stories about the looting of contaminated copper cable inside the tunnels: there is a ready market, despite the risks. And the Semipalatinsk 'Polygon' was not the only nuclear test site in Kazakhstan. At Azgir, in Atyrau Region, 17 underground nuclear explosions were conducted between 1966 and 1979 to develop technologies to create large underground cavities. This found practical application at the Lira site in West Kazakhstan in 1983–84, when deep underground explosions were used to establish storage facilities for gas condensate. The dangerous legacy of the Soviet Union's nuclear testing thus still remains very much with Kazakhstan.

Back on the main road, the largest village in the area, **Karaul**, is another 14km to the south beyond the turning off to Zhidebay. Predictably enough, there is a statue of Abai in its central square. There are a couple of uninspiring cafés here, but if the weather is fine you would be much better off bringing a picnic with you from Semey and eating it in the scenic Chingistau Hills.

KURCHATOV

Some 140km west of Semey, Kurchatov served as the headquarters for the programme of nuclear testing carried out between 1949 and 1989 at the Semipalatinsk Test Site, which lay to the south and west of the town (see box, page 252). In the Soviet period this was a closed town, known only by its postal code, though was later given the name Kurchatov in honour of the first scientific director of the Soviet atomic bomb project. Employing in its heyday some 40,000 people, its population has now fallen to around 10,000. Today, the town houses various research institutes of the National Nuclear Centre of Kazakhstan, established in 1992 on the basis of the infrastructure of the Semipalatinsk Test Site. Some new facilities are being built in the town, including a nuclear 'technopark', but for the most part Kurchatov has a semi-derelict appearance, with its occupied buildings standing amongst abandoned two- and three-storey 1950s blocks from which wild dogs howl at night. Some of these buildings were once grand affairs, with columns topped with five-pointed stars separating glassless windows. One derelict building still has the word 'hotel' written above the space where a door once stood.

PRACTICALITIES There are no longer restrictions in place on visiting Kurchatov. The checkpoints which used to stand outside the town have been dismantled. It may be possible to overnight here, by arrangement with the **National Nuclear Centre** (*6 Tauelsizdik St;* \ *(72251) 23333;* f *(72251) 73858;* e *nnc@nnc.kz; www.nnc.kz*). The Centre and the various research institutes under its banner run small hotels in the town, which are primarily intended for official visitors, but they may be willing to put up tourists. These include a building known as the **Cottage** (12 rooms; **$$**), standing behind balustraded railings to the right of the *akimat* building in the centre of town. This is a boxy two-storey building, put up in the 1970s to accommodate a planned visit from the then Soviet Defence Minister, Marshal Ustinov, which never materialised. The hotel offers the combination of spacious rooms, parquet flooring and worn carpets you would expect of faded accommodation originally built for the Soviet elite. Three **buses** a day make the trip from Semey to Kurchatov. **Trains** also stop here, though the station, just outside the town, is called not Kurchatov but Degelen, a legacy perhaps of the Soviet secrecy surrounding the location of the place.

Should you visit the 'Polygon'? Some East Kazakhstan tour operators, such as Ecosystem in Ust-Kamenogorsk (see page 229), offer visits to the former Semipalatinsk Test Site, and the National Nuclear Centre advises that many places within the 'Polygon' are safe to visit, though others are not. The Karaganda-based NGO Ecomuseum (see page 204) has produced a useful map of the 'Polygon', showing areas in which radiation levels are particularly high. Logically enough, the places at which the tests took place tend to fall into the latter category, and with some sources concluding that visits to the nuclear test sites should not be made without specialist equipment and an expert guide, this book takes you no further than Kurchatov.

WHAT TO SEE The town centres on a square, at the end of Kurchatov Street, dominated by a large statue of the shaggy-bearded **Igor Kurchatov**. The scientist was famous for his unruly beard, which grew long initially because of his promise not to cut it until the atomic bomb programme was shown to be a success. Behind the statue, the building with the Ionic-columned façade once housed the headquarters of the Semipalatinsk Test Site administration, and now accommodates the town *akimat*. To the right stands the head office of the National Nuclear Centre: a two-storey building with a balustraded balcony above the entrance. A plaque records that Igor Kurchatov lived and worked in the building from 1949–55.

The Cottage accommodation mentioned above stands between the National Nuclear Centre and *akimat* buildings, in the corner of the square. Behind it, in the same balustraded enclosure, is another accommodation unit, a green-walled building belonging to the Institute of Geophysical Research. Just beyond this is a two-storey cottage behind railings. This is the building constructed for **Lavrenti Beria**, who was to use it for a grand total of three nights. In a glorious piece of irony, Beria's cottage has now been converted to accommodate a Russian Orthodox church.

Heading away from the central square along Kurchatov Street, you reach on your right the two-storey green-walled building housing the **Institute of Radiation Safety and Ecology** (*(72251) 23413; www.irse-rk.kz*). A bust of Kurchatov stands outside the building, bearing a quotation expressing Kurchatov's pride in his work. On the second floor of the building is a **museum** (*(72251) 23413;* ⊕ *09.00–18.00 Mon–Fri*). This is not strictly open to the public, but the staff say they are happy to welcome visitors with an interest in the subject matter who call in advance. Some of the labelling is in English as well as Russian.

A bust of Kurchatov welcomes you into the museum. The displays start to the right, with a gruesome series of pickled animal parts in jars, showing the results of exposure to the nuclear testing. The labels describe such outcomes as 'dog bladder wall haemorrhage', 'second and third degree burns of pig skin' and 'dog liver failure'. There is a map of the 'Polygon', and descriptions of some of the leading scientists of the atomic bomb project, including Yuli Khariton and future dissident Andrei Sakharov. There is a chilling model of the Experimental Field, at which the atmospheric tests were carried out, laid out for a bomb to be detonated from a tower. Arranged around the tower, in segments rather like slices of cake, are areas set out with tanks, aircraft, buildings and, distressingly, tethered animals, to measure the effects of the blast on the military hardware, civilian infrastructure and animal life. Lines of concrete instrumentation buildings also fanned out from the tower.

There is a cut-through model of one of the tunnels in the Degelen Mountains. A large lump of granite, taken from the epicentre of the first underground explosion at Degelen in 1961, is kept in a perspex box. Lift the box to see how the explosion has transformed the heavy granite into the lightest of rocks, something like pumice. A weirdly warped casing pipe, like a piece of abstract sculpture, is a legacy of a test at the Balapan Complex in 1972, and there is a cut-through model of one of the boreholes at Balapan. There is also plenty of equipment on display, including instrumentation panels, cameras and dosimeters. A small side room is devoted to Kurchatov, with photographs of the wildly bearded scientist and copies of his handwriting. The first person to sign the visitors' book kept here, when the museum opened in 1972, was Yuli Khariton.

If the town of Kurchatov has a semi-derelict appearance, on the drive back towards Semey you pass on your left a town which has been totally abandoned. **Chagan** was another former closed town, the site of an airbase used for large bombers.

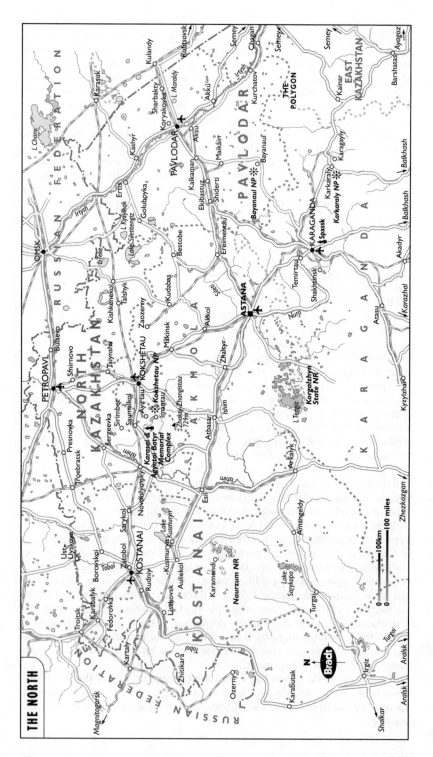

8

The North

The three most northerly regions of Pavlodar, North Kazakhstan and Kostanai feel much more part of Siberia than central Asia. Along with Akmola Region to the south, they were part of the heartland of the Virgin Lands Campaign of the 1950s to grow wheat across the Kazakhstani steppe, and remain important wheat-producing areas today. They are also lands of birch woods, of numerous lakes, and of rivers flowing northwards to join the Ob and then the Arctic Ocean. Ethnic Russians form a large percentage of the population, especially in North Kazakhstan Region. There is a European feel to many of the settlements, notably the small villages of log-walled houses with attractively decorated wooden shutters. The centres of the three regional capitals are enlivened by red-brick Tsarist buildings. Pavlodar, on the broad River Irtysh, Petropavl with its associations with Ablai Khan, and Kostanai with its pedestrianised centre, all make for pleasant places to spend a couple of days. Areas of natural beauty include the pine-covered weathered slopes of Bayanaul, one of the upland 'islands' in the Kazakhstani steppe, the mixed pine and birch forests and lakes of the Kokshetau National Park, and the Naurzum Nature Reserve, home to the Schrenk's tulip and to the most southerly lowland pine forest in Kazakhstan.

PAVLODAR *Telephone code: 7182*

Attractively sited on the right bank of the broad River Irtysh, Pavlodar is an industrial city which preserves some fine Tsarist-era buildings. It originated as the Russian military outpost of Koryakovsk, established in 1720 with a garrison of 48 people, taking its name from the nearby Lake Koryakovsk, from which salt was extracted. As the 18th century progressed, Koryakovsk became less military in character, and increasingly focused on the salt trade. In 1838, it was reorganised as the Koryakovsk *stanitsa*, its development promoted by its location on the bank of the navigable Irtysh. Its merchants lobbied with increasing fervour for the award of town status, and their persistence was rewarded in 1861 by the granting of such a status to the settlement, which would be renamed Pavlodar in honour of the newly born Grand Duke Pavel Alexandrovich, the eighth child of Tsar Alexander II by his first wife. Grand Duke Pavel, who was to become a general in the Russian army, had a difficult life. Widowed young, he then married a commoner, causing his estrangement from the Russian court and years of exile in France. He was eventually reconciled with the court, his wife granted a royal title, but was imprisoned in St Petersburg by the Bolsheviks in 1918 and executed the following year.

Pavlodar became an *uyezd* administrative centre in 1868, and as the 19th century came to a close an increasing number of smart brick buildings joined the log-walled structures of the town. The large-scale growth that led to Pavlodar becoming a major urban centre had to wait until the 1950s, when Pavlodar Region was selected to play

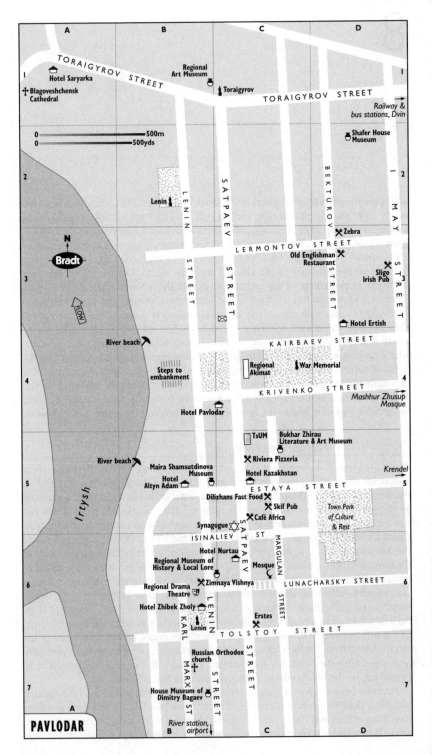

PAVLODAR

a key role in the Virgin Lands Campaign. The Soviet authorities also earmarked Pavlodar and its region for industrial development. Construction teams and specialists were brought here from across the Soviet Union. The extensive coal deposits around Ekibastuz were to be used as the basis for a major power-generation programme. A series of new industrial enterprises were established in Pavlodar. The first alumina was produced at the Pavlodar aluminium factory in 1964. The first 'Kazakhstan' tractor rolled off the production line at the Pavlodar Tractor Factory in 1968. An oil refinery started production a decade later, processing oil from Russian Siberia. The Pavlodar Chemical Plant was established, a dual-purpose facility intended to produce both chemicals for civilian uses and, secretly, chemical weapons agents. The first nine-storey apartment block was built in Pavlodar in the late 1970s, and soon became the housing standard for the population of the town, which grew rapidly beyond 300,000. Independence brought industrial and population decline, though new investors have been brought in, and the city has an increasingly confident air

GETTING THERE AND AROUND The **airport** (570546) is 14km southeast of town. Air Astana operates a daily flight from Almaty, and flies five times a week to Astana. The **railway station** (372144) is a modern building with a dark interior, northeast of the town centre. Two trains from Almaty terminate here: one a daily train, the other running every two days. There is also a daily train to Astana. Other trains stopping here include one every four days between Karaganda and Novokuznetsk (Russia) and one every two days between Astana and Ridder, and there are options to various destinations in Russia and Ukraine, including Moscow, Sverdlovsk, Kiev and Novosibirsk.

The main **bus station** (544664) stands on the western side of the square in front of the railway station. It is a distinctive building of red-tinted glass, entered beneath a large red letter 'A'. There are departures roughly every 30 minutes to Ekibastuz, several daily to Bayanaul, Karaganda, Astana and Semey, and a few to Russian destinations, including Omsk and Novosibirsk. Confusingly, there is another bus station, run by Pavlodarvoksalservis (373568), with its ticket office in the same building as the railway station. This mainly serves destinations in Russia.

The River Irtysh was long an important transport artery for Pavlodar, and there is still a **river station** (320303), although river trips are now taken as pleasure cruises rather than as a serious means of transportation. They offer motorboat trips of roughly one hour's duration along the river (approx every 2hrs 11.00–00.30; adult/child T300–400/150–200), with evening departures made to the strains of loud pop music. There are also longer, roughly two-hour, trips on a restaurant boat (T800).

Numbers to call for local **taxis** include 320606, 320003 and 555050.

TOUR OPERATOR AND AIRLINE OFFICE

✈ **Otrar Travel** 59 Toraigyrov St; 534594; f 320091; e pwq@otrar.kz. General Service Agent for Air Astana.

WHERE TO STAY
Note that most of the hotels listed below charge a reservation fee equal to 25% of the first night's room rate.

🏠 **Hotel Ertish** [258 D3] (92 rooms) 79 Bekturov St; 770977; f 770877; e info@ertishhotel.kz; www.ertishhotel.kz. The finest hotel in town, though somewhat fully priced for provincial Pavlodar, the Ertish offers well-furnished AC rooms in a centrally located 8-floor building. In summer the rooftop Terrace Steak House offers an attractive open panorama across the city (meals $$$), though the astroturf flooring & the non-availability of many of the drinks on their menu dent the appeal. $$$$$

🏠 **Hotel Nurtau** [258 C6] (23 rooms) 168 Satpaev St; \/f 320885. With its metallic-finished exterior, & airy, AC rooms decorated in shades of cream, the Nurtau is one of those hotels which is comfortable enough, but leaves no lasting impression. The modern design jars amidst the Tsarist buildings of the old town. $$$$

🏠 **Hotel Altyn Adam** [258 B5] (6 rooms) 30 Estaya St; \ 324433. The 3-storey 'Golden Man' hotel features golden-coloured brickwork & a quiet central location close to the river, albeit immediately over the road from a car wash. The foyer is decorated with mock petroglyphs, & the AC rooms are nicely furnished, making this small hotel not a bad option if you can forgive the publicity photograph on the front of their brochure, which shows the place surrounded by tall snow-dusted evergreens which do not actually exist. B/fast is included in the room rate. $$$

🏠 **Hotel Pavlodar** [258 C4] (30 rooms) 23 Krivenko St; \ 322300, 395501; f 323853. Centrally located, close to the regional administration, the Hotel Pavlodar advertises itself from afar, with a large green sign that runs around the top of the 11-storey building of which it occupies 3 floors. The rooms are spacious & have AC, though the wallpaper & furnishings are tired, & they are decorated with some odd artworks, like a painting of a pink-haired lady playing the flute in an evidently strong breeze.

The wait for the building's single lift can be considerable. $$$

🏠 **Hotel Saryarka** [258 A1] (150 rooms) 1 Toraigyrov St; \ 561901, 561824. This concrete monster with curved façades close to the Blagoveshchensk Cathedral at the northwestern corner of the centre was partially renovated at the time of research. The beds are small & showers grim, & only 'luxe' rooms have AC, but the renovated rooms are better than the unpromising exterior would lead you to expect. $$ unrenovated dbls; $$$ unrenovated dbls

🏠 **Hotel Kazakhstan** [258 C5] (31 rooms) 71 Satpaev St; \ 320520, 320508; f 320533. This yellow-walled 4-storey hotel in the centre of town offers reasonable-value renovated rooms with en suites & AC, though some are suffering from damp. $$

🏠 **Hotel Zhibek Zholy** [258 B6] (7 rooms) 170 Lenin St; \ 337541. Centrally located in a 2-storey red-brick building, once the grand home of a merchant named Balandin, the Zhibek Zholy is a decidedly basic place, stiflingly hot in summer, located above the potentially noisy **Sulu Tau Restaurant**. The latter has recently undergone a change of name, from 'Beautiful Wood' to 'Beautiful Hill', which makes rather little sense for a restaurant located opposite a wooded park, with not a hill in site. The standard rooms have shared facilities, & there is no AC, but with the room rates including dinner as well as b/fast this is potentially a useful option for travellers on a shoestring budget. Payment is by cash only. $

✗ WHERE TO EAT

✗ **Erstes** [258 C6] 109 Satpaev St; \ 329968; e erstes@pavlodar.kz. Erstes offers cheap beer, brewed on the premises, in a large cream-coloured hall focused on a stage, with live music after 21.00. The wide-ranging menu includes Erstes sausages to accompany your beer, as well as sushi. President Nazarbaev officially opened the place in 2003; the tankard he drank from at this occasion is on display alongside those of the Erstes regulars. $$$

🍺 **Krendel** 115 Abai St; \ 301465; e Krendel_PV@mail.ru; www.krendel.kz. A Pavlodar institution, their store downstairs offers a great range of cakes, pastries & donuts, while upstairs is a large coffee house, tastefully decorated in shades of red & brown, with canvas

murals of coffee beans covering the ceiling. The menu is newspaper style, with items on the history of the espresso as well as descriptions of the food on offer. The latter is international, & particularly strong on pastries. The bill is brought to you in a coffee pot. Wi-Fi access is available. Altogether one of the best cafés in Kazakhstan. There is another branch at 25 Ploshad Pobedy St (\ 503565). $$$

✗ **Riviera Pizzeria** [258 C5] 65 Satpaev St; \ 390690, 390691. This is a narrow corridor of a restaurant, with walls, seats & waitresses all dressed in various shades of brown. Canvas portraits of European cities decorate the walls. They have a good range of pizzas, & a selection of international mains. $$$

✗ Skif Pub [258 C5] 118 Margulan St; 323528. Next door to Dilizhans Fast Food & run by the same people, the walls of the 'Scythian' are covered with petroglyphs & paintings of ancient armies, & adorned with clubs, daggers & shields. The standard menu offers a range of pasta, burgers & pizzas, including a Scythian pizza involving sardines, sprats, eggs, onion & cheese. I hadn't realised the Scythians were big sardine eaters. There is also a theme menu, which changes every few weeks, focusing on the cuisine of a different part of the world. The waitresses' outfits change to match. $$$

✗ Sligo Irish Pub [258 D3] 20 1 May St; 555878. Proudly announcing its antiquity ('established 2006'), this burgundy-walled pub juts incongruously from a 9-storey Soviet apartment block near the corner of 1 May & Lermontov streets. There are stained-glass shamrocks over the booths, comfy armchairs & photographs of old Dublin. This is one of those places with a collection of banknotes pinned up on the shelves behind the bar. You can't help feeling the till would be more efficient. The international menu includes Irish stew & Aunt Sally's pancakes (Aunt Sally being evidently a fish lover). $$$

✗ Zebra Restaurant [258 D3] 150/4 Lomova St; 573305; ⊕ 11.00–01.00. Lively restaurant with an extensive menu of east Asian foods, including Vietnamese noodle dishes & sushi. A good-value business lunch is available from 12.00–13.00. There is live music daily from 18.00. $$$

✗ Zimnaya Vishnya [258 B6] 160 Lenin St; 324925. The 'Winter Cherry' is housed in a red-brick building near the Chekov Drama Theatre at the heart of the Tsarist merchants' town. The interior is unexpectedly modern, with a clean-looking white & cherry-coloured décor. The menu offers a mixture of Russian & international standards, they also serve b/fast &, unusually for Kazakhstan, there is a no smoking rule in place from 10.00–15.00. $$$

✗ Café Africa [258 C5] 75 Satpaev St; 324511. This place offers ochre-coloured walls decorated with skins, masks & spears, & there are plenty of dishes hinting at African cuisine. The food when it arrives tends, however, to be more quotidian Russian/European fare, albeit with quite a frequent appearance of pineapple. $$

✗ Dilizhans Fast Food [258 C5] 118 Margulan St; 321273. The 'Stagecoach' features a large map of the road between Pavlodar & Astana hung across the ceiling, with on the walls a selection of the road signs you may, or in some cases probably won't (hot-air ballooning?), encounter *en route*. This central fast-food joint offers pizzas, burgers, omelettes & a few basic meat dishes, served up on plastic plates. $$

✗ Dvin 2 Puteyskiy Gorodok; 533777. This Armenian restaurant is well out of the centre, in the northern part of town beyond the railway track, but the good food & pleasant summer garden, with booths under birch trees & a central line of fountains, may make the taxi journey worthwhile. 'Dvin', their signature dish, is a chunk of nicely spiced lamb. $$

✗ Old Englishman Restaurant [258 D3] 44 Lermontov St; 770677; ⊕ 11.00–02.00. Proclaiming to serve 'World Nations cuisine', the menu is broad but not terribly exciting. Dishes are predominantly bland but the live music on Fri & Sat nights livens up the atmosphere. There is Wi-Fi available. $$

SHOPPING The central department store, TsUM [258 C5] (⊕ *10.00–19.00 Mon–Sat, 10.00–18.00 Sun*), is a blue glass-walled building on Satpaev Street, half a block south of the regional administration.

WHAT TO SEE

Around Satpaev Street Broad and busy Satpaev Street, which runs north–south through the centre of town, is Pavlodar's main thoroughfare, though it is lined with some undistinguished Soviet-era concrete blocks. At the northern end of the street, where it runs into Toraigyrov Street, stands a statue, erected in 2000, of the Kazakh poet **Sultanmakhmut Toraigyrov**, a native of the region. He is depicted standing next to a tree offering the flimsiest of shade. Toraigyrov died in 1920 at the age of just 27; he gives his name to a university and library in the city. In the ugly curved apartment block behind the statue is the **Pavlodar Regional Art Museum** [258

B1] (*44/1 Toraigyrov St;* \ *535811;* ⏰ *09.00–18.00 Tue–Sun; admission adult/student T100/50*). It is given over to temporary exhibitions, mostly of modern local works.

Two long blocks to the south you pass the **post office** on your right, beneath a concrete clock tower: a local landmark, just not a very attractive one. A little further on, across the junction with Kairbaev Street, stands a long, grey, four-storey building on your left housing the **regional administration** [258 C4]. Behind this building is a birch-filled park in which stands a **war memorial** [258 C4], its three concrete needles tapering skywards. In front of the regional administration is another stretch of park, in which fountains play, running to a monumental flight of steps leading down to the promenade along the Irtysh River embankment.

Back on Satpaev Street, head a block further south, turning left onto Estaya Street, and then left again onto Margulan Street. On your right, incongruously sited immediately beyond an ugly Soviet-period apartment block, is a beautiful single-storey wooden building of the Tsarist era, with ornate decoration covering all available exterior surface space and a decorative railing around the roof. The building was pressed into action by the Bolsheviks. A plaque records that the Revolutionary Committee of the Pavlodar *Uyezd* was based here in 1919–20. Another announces that Terenty Deribas, revolutionary and member of the Cheka secret service organisation, the head of the Revolutionary Committee of Pavlodar City, worked in the building between April and August 1920. A silhouette depicts an earnest, bespectacled revolutionary in peaked cap and a beard evidently inspired by Lenin. The building now houses the **Bukhar Zhirau Museum of Literature and Art** [258 C5] (*97 Margulan St;* \ *320124;* ⏰ *09.00–18.00 Mon–Sat; admission T40*). This offers somewhat dry displays, with descriptions in Russian and Kazakh, about the main literary figures from the region. Bukhar Zhirau, poet and adviser to Ablai Khan in the 18th century, who was born in the Bayanaul area, is featured prominently, as is another native of Bayanaul District, the historian and poet Mashhur Zhusup Kopeev, who died in 1931 at the age of 73. The lavish modern mosque in Pavlodar is named in his honour. The 'Museum of Literature and Art' sign on the ground floor of the neighbouring apartment block refers to the offices of the museum administration rather than anything to be visited.

Continuing southwards along Satpaev Street, there is a **synagogue** [258 C5] on your right at the next intersection with Isinaliev Street. Turn left down the latter, and after two blocks you arrive at the entrance to the **Town Park of Culture and Rest** [258 D5]. Just inside the entrance is a stone erected in 1991 to mark those buried in the old city cemetery. Just like the plot from a horror movie, the grounds of the cemetery have now been turned into a place of amusement, with a big wheel, some basic cafés, and pop music wafting around the trees. There is also a monument of revolutionaries pictured in winter gear of fur hats, overcoats and tall boots, honouring those who fell during the establishment of Soviet power in Pavlodar.

A further block to the south on Satpaev Street, at the corner with Lunacharsky Street, you reach on your left a graceful **mosque** [258 C6] sited within a railed enclosure. The octagonal turquoise cone which tops the minaret is a local landmark: the body of the mosque behind it is topped by a flattish turquoise dome. The interior has been sumptuously renovated, with beautiful golden calligraphic designs against a turquoise background, to particularly stunning effect around the *mihrab*. The graceful arched windows and doorways and luxuriant chandeliers complete the effect. The mosque was built in 1905, commissioned by a Tatar named Ramazanov. The main entrance is on Margulan Street, which runs parallel to Satpaev Street to the east.

Along Lenin Street Lenin Street runs parallel to Satpaev Street, one block to the west. The northern end of the street is dominated by unattractive nine-storey Soviet apartment buildings. A rather scruffy **park** on the right is however worth a look, as it serves as a repository for Soviet statuary. There is a tank on a plinth at the entrance, and then within the park a large statue of **Lenin**, clad in a greatcoat, and a concrete panel adorned with the resolute profiles of Lenin, Marx and Engels.

More than a kilometre to the south, on the eastern side of Lenin Street, beyond the gleaming offices of the Nur Otan political party, the single-storey log-built cottage with decorated green and white shutters is home to the **Maira Shamsutdinova Museum** [258 B5] (*135 Lenin St;* ⚲ *327111;* ◷ *09.00–13.00 & 14.00–18.00 Mon–Fri; admission T100*). It honours a popular Kazakh singer, composer and accordion player, who died in 1927 at the age of just 37. I actually had considerable problems getting into the place, as the caretaker on duty insisted that it wasn't worth seeing, and tried to direct me to the regional museum down the road. In truth, he had a point, as this isn't the most interesting museum in town. Maira Shamsutdinova did not actually live in the house, which was built at the turn of the 20th century by the same merchant, Ramazanov, who commissioned the mosque on Margulan Street. The house in which she lived, which lay nearby, no longer exists and the plaque which once graced it is on display in the museum. The guide, as if in explanation for the location of the museum, stressed to me that the Ramazanov house did however frequently play host to local musicians. Other exhibits include one of Maira's teacups, displayed perhaps over-reverentially behind a clear plastic case, set on a plinth. There are several accordions on display, as well as other Kazakh musical instruments, and an iron bed, surrounded by a luscious red curtain, which Maira apparently used when staying with relatives living in the Altai region.

Many of Pavlodar's nicest brick-built Tsarist-era houses are situated along the next stretch of Lenin Street. Some of the buildings sport fine decorated brickwork beneath their roofs and around their windows. At the junction with Lunacharsky Street stands the **Pavlodar Regional Drama Theatre** [258 B6] (⚲ *323363, 323794; www.teatrpavlodar.ru; ticket office* ◷ *12.00–19.00 Tue–Sun*). This is a good place to watch classical Russian dramas. There is a statue of a seated **Chekhov**, staring blankly behind stone spectacles, in the courtyard in front of the theatre.

Pavlodar Region Museum of History and Local Lore [258 B6] (*147 Lenin St;* ⚲ *325924;* ◷ *10.00–18.00 Tue–Sun; admission T300 for foreign citizens*) Just to the north of the theatre, on the opposite side of the road, the Pavlodar regional museum is housed in a pair of adjacent Tsarist-era buildings; a two-storey structure which once housed the post and telegraph office, and a showier single-storey building from 1899 which accommodated the trade centre of a merchant named Derov. The museum is named in honour of Grigory Potanin, a traveller, ethnographer and campaigner for greater autonomy for Siberia.

The first hall is dominated strikingly by the large skeletons of a mammoth and of a giant deer (*Megaceros giganteus*), another extinct species also known as the Irish elk and characterised by the huge spread of its antlers. A smaller skeleton at the back of the hall is that of a hipparion, an extinct three-toed forerunner of the horse. Many of the finds on display come from a site known as the Gusiny Perelyot ('Goose Migration'), on the steep right bank of the Irtysh in the northwestern outskirts of Pavlodar. The hipparion, for example, was unearthed in 1929. A model shows palaeontologists at work there, excavating the face of the cliff. Two rooms of natural history follow, with dioramas depicting characteristic landscapes of the region. A room focusing on early history has a display on the work of Petr Dravert, a meteorite expert who researched the hills around Bayanaul in the 1920s, discovering near Lake Zhasybay some primitive ochre figures, drawn on the walls of a cave which is now named in his honour. Another display describes the work of archaeologist Alkei Margulan, who was born in Bayanaul District.

The next room has displays on the Turkic period and the Kazakh khanates, with a large and rather bloody modern canvas depicting local *batyrs* Olzhabay and Zhasybay battling against the Dzhungar invaders. Kazakh ethnography is covered with a well-appointed yurt and displays of jewellery, costumes and musical instruments. A small room showcasing some of the many ethnic groups represented in the region is followed by one on the arrival of the Russians, with a life-sized model of a Russian family in their wooden hut, photographs of Tsarist Pavlodar and a display on salt collecting from the lakes of the region. Items on the establishment of Soviet power and the tribulations of the Stalinist period give way to a World War II display, with an artillery piece in the centre of the hall.

The next room looks at the industrial development of the region, with photographs of the arrival of trainloads of agricultural workers in 1954, at the onset of the Virgin Lands Campaign, and of the tented settlements in which they initially lived. A display highlights the importance of the coal reserves at Ekibastuz in providing fuel for the many large power stations of the area, and of the high voltage power lines which take the resulting electricity onwards to market. There are displays too on the sporting and artistic stars of the region, with a golden bust of film director and actor Shaken Aimanov, the most important figure in the cinema of Kazakhstan in the post-war Soviet period.

South of the regional museum To the south of the Chekov Theatre is a small square park populated by birch trees, centred on a weathered silver-coloured statue of **Lenin** [258 B6]. There is also a monument here to the victims of the Chernobyl disaster. Along Tolstoy Street, running along the southern boundary of this park, a row of roadside stallholders sell notably gaudy wreaths, with clumps of artificial flowers shrouded in green tinsel. These stalls continue to the left along Karl Marx Street, which intersects Tolstoy Street. A little way down Karl Marx Street is located, with a certain irony, a **Russian Orthodox church** [258 B7]. This has a plain, rather battered, exterior, with two metal octagonal towers above a white-walled brick building. The barrel-vaulted interior has a painting of Christ with the Apostles on the ceiling. This part of town is a district of many old single-storey log-walled cottages.

A couple of blocks further south along Lenin Street beyond the intersection with Tolstoy Street is the **House Museum of Dimitry Bagaev** [258 B7] (*200 Lenin St; 321210; ⏱ 09.00–13.00 & 14.00–18.00 Mon–Fri; admission T100*). Housed in a delightful green-painted wooden cottage, this chronicles the life and work of a prominent photographer and local historian, born in 1884, who lived in the house from 1906 until his death in 1958. His bust is outside, portraying a moustachioed, somewhat stern-looking figure. The two main rooms of the museum display a few items of furniture, including a desk on which stands a picture of the elderly Bagaev, surrounded by his photographs, peering out at the camera over round-framed glasses. The walls are sometimes given over to temporary exhibitions of contemporary photographers, which somewhat distract from the period feel of the place. If Bagaev's photos are not on display, the museum staff will show you an album of his works, which offer a fascinating glimpse into the region in the early

20th century. Two small barefooted boys in a 'red yurt' gaze up at a portrait of Lenin. Salt collectors labour with heavy spades. The most interesting room is a conservatory, constructed by Bagaev for use as his studio. The painted screens used as backdrops to his posed portraits cover the walls: a plush terrace, and a snowy track passing through woodland. Some of his portraits are on display, with subjects leaning self-consciously against a prop obelisk.

Irtysh River embankment One of the most pleasant places in the city in summer, there is a **river beach** here, popular in hot weather. The embankment also provides for a pleasant walk along one of three paths running at different heights. Head south to the river station, or north to the **Blagoveshchensk Cathedral** [258 A1]. The latter is a red-brick building with an octagonal tower topped by a green dome, from which rises a golden onion dome atop a further circular tower, with lower towers bearing smaller onion domes in attendance around it. Completed in 1999, with financial backing from Pavlodar's main industrial enterprises, it features nine bells, ranging in weight from 4kg to 1,024kg. The main entrance lies beneath the bell tower on the western side of the building. The interior has an unfinished appearance, its walls undecorated above the iconostasis. The interior of the green-domed octagonal chapel standing to the northwest of the cathedral is, in contrast, colourfully decorated with wall paintings: locals come to the chapel with plastic bottles in order to stock up on blessed water flowing from a golden cross in the central font.

Shafer House Museum [258 D2] (*19 Bekturov St;* \ *552613;* e *museum_shafer@ mail.kz;* ⊕ *09.00–13.00 & 14.00–18.00 Mon–Fri*) This is not really a museum as such, but rather the remarkable record collection of Pavlodar musicologist Naum Shafer. It is round the back of an apartment block, set back from Bekturov Street in the northeastern part of the town centre. A large part of his apartment has been turned into a library of some 27,000 records, plus many thousands of books. Professor Shafer himself may be on hand to show you some of the gems of his collection: shellac 78 rpm discs which he plays on a wind-up gramophone, replacing the needle every time. I was treated to a rendition of 'Neapolitan Nights' by the London Novelty Orchestra. Professor Shafer, himself a composer under the pseudonym Nami Gitin, is an authority on the Soviet composer Isaak Dunayevsky, who specialised in 'light' operettas and film music. He has released an album of Dunayevsky's collaborations with the writer Mikhail Bulgakov. This is a place for enthusiasts; just don't expect any heavy metal. There is a small concert hall next door, in which Shafer plays records from his collection every Friday at 18.00 (admission free) to an audience of Pavlodar music lovers.

Mashhur Zhusup Mosque Darth Vader's helmet; one of the ghosts from the old PacMan game; a shuttlecock. Many attempts have been made to describe the remarkable design of Pavlodar's large modern mosque. A green dome stands atop a ridged cone. Four tall octagonal minarets surround it. The prayer hall is circular and capacious, with a carved wooden *mihrab*. A large chandelier hangs down from the dome. Light enters through latticed windows. The complex is named in honour of Mashhur Zhusup Kopeev, a prominent local poet and historian of the late 19th and early 20th centuries. It includes a *madrasa* and library. The building is impressive, though is already starting to look somewhat the worse for wear, with some of the green panels lost from one of the minarets, and rust setting in. It is surrounded by birch trees.

The mosque is located on the eastern edge of the town centre. To get here, head east several blocks along Krivenko Street, which runs off Satpaev Street just south of the building housing the regional administration.

AROUND PAVLODAR

The scenery around Pavlodar is a mostly flat landscape of large wheat fields, punctuated by attractive villages and many small lakes. Medicinal properties are attributed to the muds and waters of a number of the latter.

MOYILDY AND LAKE KORYAKOVKA Heading northeast out of Pavlodar on the road towards the villages of Koryakovka and Rozovka, turn left after around 12km, signposted for Moyildy. You pass through a battered and rusty gate into the grounds of the **Moyildy Sanatorium** (*(7182) 356562; (7182) 356533;* **$**). The treatments at this place, well known in the Soviet period, are focused on the apparently health-giving properties of the mud taken from the lake around the back. The buildings are unattractive five- and six-storey concrete blocks, with long corridors with a hospital feel, despite attempts to give them a more homely feel with cages of budgies. The accommodation is basic, and includes four set canteen meals a day and a course of treatment. If you fancy experiencing a sanatorium life little changed in outline from the Soviet period, you will first need to obtain the required medical approval. This can be organised in Pavlodar at the **Asko Clinic** (*20/1 1st of May St; 300303*). While this is a restful spot, there is not a great deal to do, and given that the minimum stay is usually two weeks (though you may be able to negotiate something shorter) you may find that your time here starts to drag.

Continuing northeastwards beyond the turning to Moyildy, you reach after a further 3km a signposted right turn to Koryakovka. Take this, and immediately beyond the turning take the track to the left, which takes you through **Koryakovka** village to the bank of a small lake, remarkable because of its bright pink colour, especially when the sunlight strikes it. The water is fringed by a shoreline of salt, and you may see salt collectors at work here.

LAKE MARALDY Taking the main eastern road out of Pavlodar towards Sharbakty and the Russian border, after around 55km you reach the village of Maraldy. Take the rough track to the right in the village. After around 8km you reach a large circular saltwater lake with a vaguely pinkish hue. This is Lake Maraldy. The muds of the lake are considered to have healing properties, and on summer weekends bathers from Pavlodar come here to smother themselves in it, and then to sunbathe with their whole-body mud packs. Some visitors return home with buckets of the stuff. There is a small, greenish-hued, freshwater lake around 1km behind the main lake. You may see mud-caked visitors getting into their cars and driving to the freshwater lake, using its waters for rinsing the mud and salt off. The place can get packed in high summer, resulting in litter-strewn shorelines.

EKIBASTUZ *(Telephone code: 7187)* This industrial town of 140,000 people, lying about 140km to the southwest of Pavlodar, is an important coal-mining centre, responsible for some two-thirds of Kazakhstan's coal production and the generation of more than half of its electricity. While not a place of obvious tourist attractions, the role of Ekibastuz in helping to fuel the industrial development of Kazakhstan, coupled with historical and engineering interest ranging from the internment in a labour camp here of writer Alexandr Solzhenitsyn to the site of the world's tallest chimney, make this a worthwhile break on the road between Pavlodar and Astana.

Stories about the origin of the curious name of the town, which means 'two heads of salt' in Kazakh, are linked to the **coal reserves** from which Ekibastuz owes its existence. One variant of several similar tales records that a shepherd, cooking his evening meal, noticed that the black stones on which he had propped his cooking pot had caught alight. Realising that these stones were of value, he carefully marked the site by placing two large lumps of salt from a nearby lake on top of each other. The prospector Kosim Pshenbaev is credited with the discovery of the Ekibastuz coal reserves in the 1860s. A Pavlodar merchant named Artemy Derov sought to develop the field commercially, and a settlement was established near Lake Ekibastuz in 1898. The further development of the field in Tsarist times is linked to a British entrepreneur named Leslie Urquhart. He planned to create an integrated metallurgical complex involving the coal reserves of Ekibastuz and lead and zinc mines at Ridder. The Ekibastuz operation was held by the Kirgiz Coal Mining Company, which in turn was owned by the Irtysh Corporation, of which Urquhart was chairman. In addition to the coal mines, he developed a lead refining plant and zinc smelter at Ekibastuz. But the arrival of Soviet power disrupted these plans, and led Urquhart to years of fruitless attempts to secure compensation for the properties nationalised by the Soviet authorities.

The full-scale development of the coal reserves of Ekibastuz did not take place until after World War II. The large-scale open-cast mining of coal began in 1954, and three years later Ekibastuz was given town status. Its economy is today based around three huge open-cast pits, Bogatyr, Severny and Vostochny, but the viewing platforms over these terraced craters are not accessible to casual visitors. The power stations fuelled by the coal from Ekibastuz include two close to the town, catchily titled Ekibastuz GRES-1 and Ekibastuz GRES-2. The latter, more than 25km to the north of the town, claims the distinction of the tallest chimney in the world, at almost 420m. Ekibastuz is linked to other world records. A power line from here, constructed in the late Soviet period, holds the record for the power line designed for the highest transmission voltage. And Marat Zhilanbaev, a local marathon runner with a passion for deserts, has set a range of records in a solitary, and sandy, career, including clocking up 226 marathons in one 365-day period in 1990–91, and running 1,700km across the Sahara in 24 days in 1993.

The story of Ekibastuz was also linked with incarceration, as GuLag labour was used during the initial phases of its post-war development. The writer **Alexandr Solzhenitsyn** was sent to the new camp for political prisoners here in 1950 to serve the last three years of the eight-year sentence he had received in 1945, following the interception of letters implicitly critical of Stalin. Solzhenitsyn's experiences as a bricklayer and labourer in the Ekibastuz camp were to form the basis for *One Day in the Life of Ivan Denisovich*. Another Ekibastuz exile was Georgy Malenkov, a Soviet politician who briefly succeeded Stalin following the latter's death in 1953: Khrushchev quickly replaced him as First Secretary of the Communist Party, but Malenkov lasted another two years in what was essentially the post of Prime Minister. But Malenkov's star was on the wane, a process accelerated by his association with a failed attempt to oust Khrushchev in 1957, and in 1961 he was expelled from the Communist Party and sentenced to internal exile. Like many before him, his place of exile was Kazakhstan, where he worked as director of the thermal power station in Ekibastuz.

Practicalities The centre of Ekibastuz lies around 10km south of the main road between Pavlodar and Astana. Lenin Street, which runs north–south through the town, is the main thoroughfare. The **railway station** (✆ 226615) lies at the northern end of this street, 3km north of the centre. The **bus station** (✆ 342034) is a pink-walled building on the eastern side of Lenin Street, some 500m to its south.

The five-storey **Hotel Ekibastuz** (*72 rooms; 44/20 Lenin St;* ✆ *344102, 345454;* **$$**) is right in the centre of town, at the corner of Lenin and Auezov streets. Its simply furnished rooms have en suites, though only 'semi-luxe' rooms and above have air conditioning. There is not a particularly stimulating choice as regards places to eat in the town, but **Patio Pizza** (*37 Lenin St;* ✆ *341450;* **$$**), just opposite the Hotel Ekibastuz, is fine. It offers pizza, as you would expect, as part of a long international menu.

What to see A good overview of the development of the town is given in the **Ekibastuz History and Local Lore Museum** (*34 Gornyakov St;* ✆ *349692;* ⏱ *09.00–18.00 Mon–Sat; admission T20*). This is housed in a two-storey whitewashed building with 'museum' written on the outside, in Russian, in large red letters. It sits on Gornyakov Street, which intersects with Lenin Street. From the Hotel Ekibastuz, take Lenin Street to the north, turning left after one long block. The museum will come into view on your right.

The museum kicks off with rooms devoted to archaeology and ethnography. Then comes a diorama of a cramped mine shaft of the Tsarist period. Unlike the modern development of the Ekibastuz coal reserves, based around large open-cast pits, the early mines were underground. The next two rooms describe the Tsarist-era development of the reserves. There is a bust of Kosim Pshenbaev, and photographs of the activity of Leslie Urquhart's Kirgiz Coal Mining Company. The next room is devoted to World War II, with photographs of local veterans. It is followed by a display on the labour camp, in operation from 1948 until 1954, in which Solzhenitsyn was incarcerated. There is a copy of *The GuLag Archipelago* on display. The next room looks at the post-war development of Ekibastuz, with a model of the Bogatyr open-cast pit and photographs of the GRES-1 and GRES-2 coal-fired power stations. Displays on the sporting and cultural life of the town in the next two rooms include the T-shirt of long-distance desert runner Marat Zhilanbaev, proclaiming 'I was in the Guinness World of Records', together with a pair of his, understandably dusty, running shoes.

Heading east along Gornyakov Street, crossing over Lenin Street and then following Gornyakov Street to its end, a block away, you reach a large statue of **Lenin**. Behind this, the pink- and lilac-walled building with a façade enlivened by square-based columns is the former Miners' House of Culture, now known as the **Akky Club** and given over to various uninspiring eateries and a hairdresser's salon.

Taking Lenin Street northwards, some 500m north of the intersection with Gornyakov Street stands, on your right, a silver-coloured statue of bearded prospector **Kosim Pshenbaev**, looking proud following the discovery of the Ekibastuz reserves.

BAYANAUL

Situated roughly 200km southwest of Pavlodar, between that city and Karaganda, Bayanaul is one of several small ranges of ancient hills which stand like islands in the Kazakh steppe, offering attractive landscapes of weathered rock outcrops, pine woods and glistening lakes. It was designated a national nature park in 1985. The picturesque Lake Zhasybay, at the heart of the park, is a popular destination for domestic tourism.

BAYANAUL VILLAGE (*Telephone code: 71840*) Arriving on the road from Pavlodar, you will pass, some 12km before reaching the village of Bayanaul, a spring known as **Aulie Bulak**, whose waters are held by some to have healing properties. It sits to the right of the road, the water gushing from a concrete pipe. The surrounding bushes are covered by votive strips of cloth. A *shashlik* stall often plies its trade here catering to those for whom the waters don't sate all appetites.

The village is the administrative capital of the district and is a spread-out settlement of single-storey dwellings, close to a lake. Patches of weathered rock give the place an almost lunar feel. The inhabitants of Bayanaul are proud of the large number of prominent Kazakhs to have been born on their territory, and there is a veritable gallery of statues of the district's famous sons on show in the centre of the village, around the Palace of Culture named after Sultanmakhmut Toraigyrov. This building has a façade decorated with lively mosaics of village celebrations: dancing; eating around a *dastarkhan*; games on horseback. A seated statue of the poet Toraigyrov is in front. Those grouped around him include a pious Bukhar Zhirau, poet and adviser to Ablai Khan, the geologist Kanysh Satpaev and the archaeologist and ethnographer Alkei Margulan. Over the road, next to the blue-domed Musa Mirza Mosque, is a statue of the poet and historian Mashhur Zhusup Kopeev. On a wall of the nearby building housing the district administration is a map of Bayanaul District, showing the places of birth of all these notable locals.

The village also houses a museum devoted to one of them. A pink-walled building, sited, appropriately enough, on Satpaev Street, accommodates the **Kanysh Satpaev Memorial Museum** (*38 Satpaev St;* \ *91344;* ⊕ *09.00–13.00 & 14.00–18.00 Mon–Fri; admission adult/child T50/20*). There is a bust of the noted Kazakh geologist out the front, behind which stands a large metal map of Kazakhstan, highlighting its mineral wealth.

LAKE ZHASYBAY If coming from Pavlodar, turn right onto an asphalted road before reaching Bayanaul village, passing the outskirts of the village on your left. After 5km you reach a checkpoint marking the entrance to **Bayanaul National Nature Park** (admission T357). The road then takes you up into the hills of Bayanaul amidst pine and birch woodland. You reach a crest beyond which the road then hairpins down towards Lake Zhasybay, around 7km from the checkpoint. During the descent towards the lake you pass on your left, atop a low hill, a bust of the 18th-century Kazakh warrior **Zhasybay Batyr**, after whom the lake is named.

Zhasybay is an attractive freshwater lake, with a couple of sandy beaches around which are grouped a series of holiday centres. Some of these, stretched along the longer of the beaches, at the eastern end of the lake, are owned by the main industrial enterprises of Pavlodar Region and are really intended as rest centres for their staff. Others are privately run centres for the general tourist. The small village of Zhasybay, close to the smaller of the beaches, is a rather scruffy place, especially in summer when it seems to consist mainly of cafés serving beer and *shashlik*, and kiosks flogging drink and crisps for visitors heading down to the beach. There is a return bus service to Ekibastuz and to Pavlodar, departing from the centre of the village.

Zhasybay serves as the main base for exploring the rest of the national park. Bayanaul is known for its intriguingly shaped rock formations, especially a large, precariously pitched rock known as **Kempirtas**, which appears from some angles to resemble a witch's head, with a knobbly nose. There are other pleasant freshwater lakes, such as Toraigyr, with much less visitor pressure than Lake Zhasybay experiences. There are petroglyphs close to Lake Zhasybay, and medieval burials, protected by fenced enclosures, on the outskirts of Zhasybay village itself. There is fine walking around the wooded hills. You may even get to see an *arkhar*.

🏠 **Where to stay** The various options around Lake Zhasybay are mostly either steeply priced or very run-down, occasionally even both, and although the room rates in some places include full board, the food is rarely particularly appetising. Come out of season, and you will find most places shut.

🏠 **Samal Holiday Base** (19 'luxe' rooms, plus dormitories) m +7 701 265 6198. Perched on a rocky lakeside outcrop close to Zhasybay village, this place features both pricey & not particularly luxurious 'luxe' rooms, though with en suites, & cheap dormitory beds. The room rates are on an FB basis. **$$$$**

🏠 **Sultan Holiday House** (250 beds) ☏ (71840) 92065. This place, which was formerly called the 'Builder', offers 2 balconied buildings, plus a range of detached wooden cottages with little porches out the front, the whole complex sitting tidily behind a pink concrete wall topped by a decorative balustrade. It offers a wide range of accommodation, including cheapish beds in shared rooms without facilities, but the separate rooms are decidedly expensive, especially as showers & in some cases toilets are shared. The main buildings feature bright interior paintwork

& a rather hostel-like feel. Sultan Holiday House is located in Zhasybay village, but has no lake frontage. **$$$$**

🏠 **Kabdulov House** (6 rooms) m +7 701 531 7029. This is a 2-storey building close to the beach at the eastern end of the lake, away from Zhasybay village, with no sign to identify it as a hotel. Privately run by the Kabdulov family, its rooms are spacious, with reasonable en suites, & most have AC, though the rates are on the high side. **$$$**

🏠 **Beryozovaya Rosha** (58 rooms) ☏ (71840) 92271. This is a scruffy, pebbledashed concrete block, owned by Maikain Gold, whose operation you pass on the road from Pavlodar. It is all rather run-down, with cot-like beds, & there is no AC, but it is cheap, & nicely sited in birch woods close to the Kabdulov House. **$**

PETROPAVL *Telephone code: 7152*

The most northerly of Kazakhstan's regional capitals, Petropavl, also frequently referred to by its more Russified name of Petropavlovsk, has the strong feel of a Siberian town. It lies just some 60km from the Russian border, and ethnic Russians form the bulk of the population. It was founded in 1752 as a Tsarist military fortress named after St Peter (Paul was added later) at a place known as Kyzylzhar on the right bank of the Ishim River. Ablai Khan, the leader of the Middle *Zhuz*, gave his approval for the establishment of the fortress in part because he wanted the Tsarist authorities to establish a market at the site, and indeed Petropavlovsk quickly developed into an important trading centre between Russian merchants and the Kazakhs of the Middle *Zhuz*, as well as more widely with central Asia and western China.

The arrival of the Trans-Siberian Railway in 1896 gave a further impetus to the development of the town, and Petropavlovsk was to become an important railway junction. As the 20th century dawned there was a large increase in the arrival of landless peasantry from across the Russian Empire. Food-processing and leather-working industries developed, joined during World War II by some 20 enterprises evacuated here from more vulnerable parts of the western USSR. In the post-war period, Petropavlovsk was developed by the Soviet authorities as a centre for heavy machine building, focused on the military sector, with four factories producing weaponry such as the missiles and mobile launchers of the SS-21, code-named 'Scarab' in the West. Following independence, these factories in particular have struggled, shorn of their State orders, and have attempted to refocus their work on

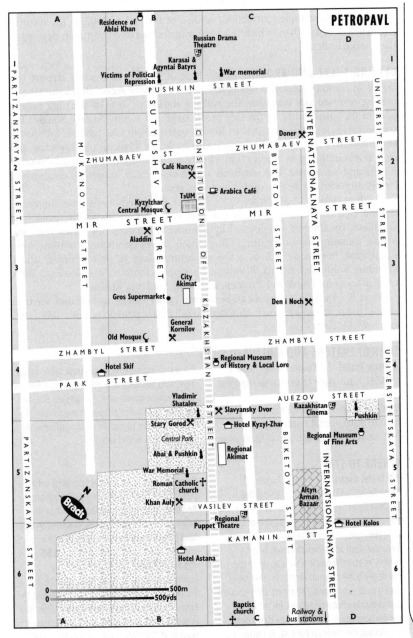

PETROPAVL

- Residence of Ablai Khan
- Russian Drama Theatre
- Karasai & Agyntai Batyrs
- Victims of Political Repression
- War memorial
- PARTIZANSKAYA STREET
- PUSHKIN STREET
- SUTYUSHEV ST
- MUKANOV STREET
- ZHUMABAEV STREET
- CONSTITUTION OF KAZAKHSTAN STREET
- UNIVERSITETSKAYA STREET
- Doner
- ZHUMABAEV STREET
- INTERNATSIONALNAYA STREET
- Café Nancy
- TsUM
- Arabica Café
- BUKETOV STREET
- Kyzylzhar Central Mosque
- MIR STREET
- MIR STREET
- Aladdin
- STREET
- City Akimat
- Gros Supermarket
- Den i Noch
- General Kornilov
- Old Mosque
- ZHAMBYL STREET
- ZHAMBYL STREET
- Hotel Skif
- PARK STREET
- Regional Museum of History & Local Lore
- Vladimir Shatalov
- Slavyansky Dvor
- AUEZOV STREET
- Kazakhstan Cinema
- Pushkin
- Stary Gorod
- Hotel Kyzyl-Zhar
- Central Park
- Regional Museum of Fine Arts
- Abai & Pushkin
- Regional Akimat
- War Memorial
- Roman Catholic church
- Khan Auly
- VASILEV STREET
- Altyn Arman Bazaar
- INTERNATSIONALNAYA STREET
- Regional Puppet Theatre
- KAMANIN STREET
- Hotel Kolos
- PARTIZANSKAYA STREET
- Hotel Astana
- N
- Bradt
- 0   500m
- 0   500yds
- Baptist church
- Railway & bus stations

producing equipment for the oil and gas and railways sectors. They shed workers and this resulted in considerable unemployment in the 1990s, from which the town is now recovering thanks to Kazakhstan's overall economic growth. Petropavl today makes for a pleasant stop, with charming red-brick Tsarist buildings along its pedestrianised central thoroughfare, now named Constitution of Kazakhstan Street. One of these buildings houses the smart and informative regional museum.

The North PETROPAVL

8

271

The town's newest tourist attraction, readied at the end of 2007, is the restored Residence of Ablai Khan, which has been transformed into a museum devoted to the Kazakh leader.

GETTING THERE AND AROUND At the time of writing, Petropavl's **airport** was closed to commercial flights, though this is a relatively recent development and may be reversed at a later date. The **railway station** (383434) is at the eastern edge of the town centre, at the side of the large and scruffy Auezov Square. The station serves many destinations in Russia: westwards to Chelyabinsk, Sverdlovsk and Moscow; eastwards to Krasnoyarsk, Irkutsk and Vladivostok. There are also daily trains initiating in Petropavl to Almaty and Kyzylorda, both passing through Astana and Karaganda. The red-brick Tsarist-era railway station building stands, largely forgotten, to the side of the modern station.

The **bus station** (*1 Medvedev St;* 330369) also stands on Auezov Square. It bears a sign confirming that Petropavlovsk is a town of friendship, peace and goodness. The interior is enlivened by a mosaic frieze depicting buses, taxis and people standing around chatting. The station serves destinations within North Kazakhstan Region as well as a few departures daily to places further afield, including Kokshetau, Astana, Borovoye, Karaganda, Pavlodar and Kostanai. There are also buses for Omsk and Tyumen, across the border in Russia.

There is an efficient network of buses and rather elderly trolleybuses for trips around town, at T30 a journey. Numbers to call for local **taxis** include 055, 007 and 471212.

TOUR OPERATORS AND AIRLINE OFFICES

✈ **Otrar Travel** 115 Zhumabaev St; 490187; f 320091; e ppk@otrar.kz. General Service Agent for Air Astana.
Vladiger Tour 132 Parkovaya St; 428010, 428009; e alex@northkazakhstan.com; www. northkazakhstan.com. Now part of Kazakhstan

Reisen, this company can organise tailor-made itineraries to sights in North Kazakhstan Region & also runs a guesthouse, Serebriyany Bor, in the forests outside Petropavl, aimed mainly at groups of up to 10 people wishing to book the place out as a w/end retreat.

🏠 WHERE TO STAY

🏠 **Hotel Astana** [272 B6] (13 rooms) 1 Kamanin St; 461060, 463030. A secluded 3-storey hotel belonging to the local administration, & located just a couple of blocks from the regional *akimat*, the Astana does not advertise itself at all from the road. Resting behind its metal fence, it retains an air of the privileged hotel accommodation for the Soviet elite it once constituted. The rooms are renovated & reasonably comfortable, save for the orange net curtains which fail to keep the dawn light out. All but the cheapest have AC, & a gym, billiard room & sauna are available for an extra charge. **$$$**
🏠 **Hotel Skif** [272 A4] (23 rooms) 118 Park St; f 468807, 461065; e skif@ae.kz. The 'Scythian' is probably the pick of the hotels in Petropavl, though the competition, it should be said, is not

fierce. The restaurant is nicely decorated, with paintings on the walls inspired by petroglyphs. And there are more petroglyph designs on rocks in the garden. The hotel itself is, however, an ugly brick block. Rooms here are en suites, though no AC, & the rate includes both b/fast & dinner. **$$$**
🏠 **Hotel Kolos** [272 D6] (9 rooms) 82 Internatsionalnaya St; 336900. Housed in a 2-storey pink-walled building near the bazaar, the Kolos offers a few basic rooms with en suites, lino floors & orange net curtains (clearly a Petropavl speciality). The higher-priced rooms have more space & a fridge. B/fast is not included: indeed there is no catering available. **$$**
🏠 **Hotel Kyzyl-Zhar** [272 C5] (114 rooms) 54 Constitution of Kazakhstan St; 461184, 461208; f 490243. A typical large Soviet-era concrete pile in the centre of town, offering a

wide range of rooms & prices. The lifts clank, the *dizhurnayas* on each floor sit behind what look like school desks, pencilling in the names of each occupant of their rooms on a board, & white tiles displaying reliefs of stars overpower the foyer. A statue of a young lady standing in front of a mosaic wall into which is etched a hammer & sickle guards the entrance. The corridors are long & drab, the floors are worn parquet, but the rooms are clean & reasonably priced. **$** unrenovated; **$$** renovated

🛏 Railway Station Retiring Rooms
\ 380944. Basic but clean accommodation in dormitory rooms packed with beds. There are also sgl rooms, & even a 'luxe' – which, unlike the rest, has en-suite facilities. There are 2 separate rest rooms: the one up the stairs at the eastern end of the station doesn't take children; the one at the western end is more family oriented. There is a T20 discount if you are in possession of a valid railway ticket. **$**

✗ WHERE TO EAT

✗ Stary Gorod [272 B5] 41 Constitution of Kazakhstan St; \ 365803, 362672. Entered around the side of the large building with a columned façade at the edge of the central park, the Stary Gorod does not exactly go out of its way to attract custom: you may have to buzz to get in.

It is a smartly but blandly decorated place, with paintings of Parisian street scenes on the walls & waitresses sporting central European-styled outfits. The globetrotting menu skips between Russian, European & central Asian dishes. The **Park City Nightclub** (🕐 *22.00–05.00 Wed–*

TWO SONS OF PETROPAVL

Among the well-known natives of Petropavl are two very different figures. Vladimir Tretchikoff was born here in 1913. The youngest of eight children, his wealthy family fled the city at the time of the Russian Revolution, heading to the Chinese city of Harbin. Tretchikoff developed as an artist, working as a newspaper cartoonist in Shanghai and running an art school in Singapore, spent much of World War II in a Japanese prison camp, and moved after the end of the war to South Africa, where he lived until his death in 2006. His fame rests on reproduction prints of his works, which sold in huge quantities, though they were dismissed by many critics as 'kitsch'. Many of his prints featured oriental subjects: the most famous of all was *The Chinese Girl*, often popularly referred to as *The Green Lady*, a beauty with distinctive bluish-toned skin who became a feature of many 1960s living rooms.

Alexander Vinokourov was born in a village just south of Petropavlovsk in 1973. Trained in Almaty, Vinokourov was to become Kazakhstan's best known and most successful cyclist. He secured fifth place in the 2005 Tour de France as a member of the T-Mobile team headed by Jan Ullrich. For the 2006 Tour de France, Vinokourov moved to a team sponsored by the insurance company Liberty Seguros, which he would be heading. But some members of the team, though not Vinokourov, were implicated in doping allegations, and Liberty Seguros dropped its sponsorship. The Kazakhstani Cycling Federation, headed by then Prime Minister Daniyal Akhmetov, helped to gather together financial support from Kazakhstani companies, and Team Astana was born. Unable to compete in the 2006 Tour de France because the team lacked the minimum six riders, Vinokourov, at the helm of Team Astana, did however secure victory in the last Grand Tour of the 2006 season the Vuelta a España. But if the 2006 season ended in fairy-tale fashion, 2007 was marked by Vinokourov's departure from the Tour de France following a reported positive test for a homologous blood transfusion.

Sun; admission T500) is housed in the same building. $$$$

✕ Café Nancy [272 B2] 9 Constitution of Kazakhstan St; no phone. This place advertises itself strikingly, with a huge model of a cocktail, complete with straw & slice of lemon, perched on its domed roof. Once inside though Café Nancy fails to live up to its promise, with rather sombre décor & an uninspiring Russian/international menu. It does, however, offer chairs with remarkably high backs. $$$

✕ Den i Noch [272 D3] 43 Internatsionalnaya St; 360733. The dark blue décor with jagged yellow fissures is striking, if not exactly mellow, but the Russian-tinged European menu is nothing special. $$$

✕ Khan Auly [272 B5] 29A Vasilev St; 363101. This Uzbek-themed restaurant has brightly coloured ceramics on the walls & Uzbek handicrafts in the niches. There is a fake bridge in the middle of the restaurant & some quiet, cushion-laden corners. An outdoor terrace is pleasant in summer. The menu features a good range of both Uzbek & Kazakh dishes. $$$

✕ Slavyansky Dvor [272 C4] 52 Constitution of Kazakhstan St; no phone. Housed in an attractive single-storey red-brick Tsarist-era building, this place is tastefully furnished, with wooden tables & chairs & period engravings on the bare interior walls. The engravings don't however depict anywhere in Kazakhstan: possibly Poland, thought the waitress. The menu is unusually short, with a selection of fish-stuffed olives as appetisers, though the food is good. $$$

✕ Aladdin [272 B3] 75 Mir St; 462323. Housed on 2 floors, of which the upstairs hall is the nicer, this place attracts a youthful clientele. There are carpets on the walls, a mural depicting a clichéd central Asian village street, & fake vines across the ceiling. The menu offers Kazakh, Russian & European dishes, & *shashlik*. $$

✕ Doner [272 C2] 27 Internatsionalnaya St; 460996; ⏰ until 22.00. The name of this place gives you a good idea of the menu, although the portraits of Tom & Jerry on the restaurant sign are potentially misleading. This is a Turkish fast-food joint, offering a range of kebabs, as well as salads & pizzas. The bright yellow walls are decorated with some Turkish ceramics. Fine for a quick bite. $$

✕ General Kornilov [272 B4] 164 Zhambyl St; 365413. Housed in an attractive single-storey Tsarist-era brick building, with carved wooden pillars holding up the porch, this smart though inexpensive restaurant features a beamed ceiling, a long menu with a vaguely Russian feel, waitresses in period costume, & a painting of General Lavr Kornilov above the entrance. In the foyer, a plaque in Russian chronicles the life of the remarkable general. Kornilov, who had a Cossack father & Kazakh mother, became commander-in-chief of the Russian army during Kerensky's Provisional Government in 1917, was accused by Kerensky of leading a coup attempt against him, & ended up as one of the anti-Bolshevik leaders in the Civil War, in which he was killed in 1918. It's an interesting sign of the way political figures have been re-evaluated following the collapse of the USSR that Kornilov now gets a restaurant named after him. $$

Cafés

☕ Arabica Café [272 C2] 18A Constitution of Kazakhstan St; 465732. This coffee house offers a dark & smoky room, glass-topped tables & lounge music. There is a wide range of teas & coffees on the menu, including cappuccinos flavoured with coconut, banana, caramel & almond, fruit teas & special blends.

SHOPPING TsUM [272 B2] (*13 Constitution of Kazakhstan St*), at the corner of Constitution of Kazakhstan Street and Mir Street, has a 24-hour supermarket on the ground floor, with a range of other shops above. There is a branch of the **Gros** supermarket chain on Sutyushev Street [272 B3], just behind the city *akimat*. The **Altyn Arman Bazaar** [272 D5] (⏰ *08.00–17.00*) is central, sitting between Buketov and Internatsionalnaya streets. It is centred on a large yellow-walled building, with stalls spilling out around it.

WHAT TO SEE
Along Constitution of Kazakhstan Street
Many of Petropavl's oldest buildings and most interesting sights are strung along Constitution of Kazakhstan Street, a pedestrian thoroughfare which runs through the centre of town from southeast to northwest. Locals claim that, at more than 3km, it is longer than Moscow's famous pedestrian street, Arbat. It is referred to henceforth as Constitution Street, for brevity.

Around the regional **akimat** *building* Constitution Street's beginnings, at the southeastern edge of the town centre, are unimpressive. It heads off, almost apologetically, from a scruffy road junction. At the corner with Osipenko Street stands a **Baptist church** [272 C6], occupying a three-storey brick building dating from the Tsarist era, a church spire just visible behind. Walking along Constitution Street, after four short blocks, take a detour to the right along Vasilev Street. The ugly pebbledashed building on your right is the **Regional Puppet Theatre** [272 C5], which serves up a menu of Russian fairy tales, *Winnie the Pooh* and the occasional Kazakh folk story.

Back on Constitution Street, you pass on your left a **Roman Catholic church** [272 B5], dating from the early 20th century, with a façade of sweeping curves, rather Italianate in feel. The interior of this heavily restored building is modern. Immediately beyond is a **war memorial** [272 B5], preceded by two tiled columns on which are inscribed the names of the region's Heroes of the Soviet Union, in Russian and Kazakh. A tree-lined path leads up to the war memorial itself, a tall, four-sided obelisk which appears to be constructed of metal pipes. A wooded park spreads out behind.

The large seven-storey bulk of the **regional** *akimat* building [272 C5], just beyond on the right, its façade punctuated by air conditioners serving just a few of its offices (senior management, perhaps?), stands opposite a modern statue of **Abai and Pushkin**, celebrating the joint year of the two poets commemorated in 2006. Each places his hand against a tree standing between them. The monument is surrounded by a semi-circular arcade, to give it greater gravitas. One block further on, at the entrance to the **Central Park** [272 B5], stands a decidedly battered bust of **Vladimir Shatalov**, a cosmonaut born in Petropavlovsk and twice Hero of the Soviet Union, who flew on three missions of the Soyuz programme. The first was in 1969 with Soyuz 4, whose docking with Soyuz 5 represented the first successful docking of two manned spacecraft.

North Kazakhstan Regional Museum of History and Local Lore [272 C4]
(*48 Constitution of Kazakhstan St;* ✆ *468478;* ◷ *10.00–18.00 Tue–Sun; admission T180*) A block further to the northwest, the whole of the north side of Constitution Street between the junctions with Park and Zhambyl streets is filled with a line of attractive red-brick merchant houses of the Tsarist period. In two of these adjacent properties is accommodated the smartly restored North Kazakhstan Regional Museum of History and Local Lore. The lobby of the museum features, self-referentially, a model of the building in which you are standing, with a wall map of North Kazakhstan Region behind it. The displays start with natural history. A palaeontology room includes mammoth tusks and bison horns, arranged in front of paintings of the animals they once formed part of. A corridor follows, walled with seasonal dioramas populated by stuffed animals. A snowy winter scene depicts lynx eating hare. Summer sees a large elk standing in front of a painted expanse of feather-grass steppe. In autumn a hedgehog burrows amongst the fallen leaves.

North Kazakhstan Region claims 3,000 lakes, and there is, predictably enough, a good range of stuffed waterfowl on show.

Archaeology comes next, with a room devoted to the Stone Age featuring a range of implements. The next room showcases the **Botai culture** of the Eneolithic period, between around 3600BC and 2300BC. This is named after the Botai site, in the southwestern part of North Kazakhstan Region close to the Iman-Burluk River, a tributary of the Ishim. Archaeologists from the Carnegie Museum of Natural History have been collaborating with those of the North Kazakhstan State University for several years in unlocking the secrets of the Botai culture: here, some researchers argue, may have been the place of first domestication of the horse. While this is the subject of continuing academic debate, it is clear that the lives of the Botai people were entwined very closely with horses. They ate horsemeat, drank *kumiss*, made their clothes from the skins of horses, and fashioned tools from horse bones. They may have been among the first peoples to ride horses. There is a model of the Botai settlement, showing the distinctive dwellings of two circular earth-walled rooms, linked by a short corridor, their roofs formed by hides placed across branches, and then covered in turf. The exhibits in this room and the next, covering Bronze Age artefacts, are well presented, with photographs demonstrating how the various tools might originally have been used.

A room devoted to the early Iron Age contains the skeleton of a warrior unearthed in 1972 from a *kurgan* near Pokrovka, southwest of Petropavl. There is a reconstructed head on display, sculpted using the characteristics of the very skull lying in the case. The resultant head has a rather disapproving expression. The next room displays two Turkic-era *balbals*, one male, the other female, artistically placed in front of a painted sunset across a field of grazing horses. Then comes **Kazakh ethnography**, with a yurt standing in front of a mural depicting an encampment of nomads of the Middle *Zhuz*. There is a bloodthirsty painting of the Kazakh victory against the Dzhungars at Anrakay in 1729, and a display of weaponry. More peaceful life is illustrated by a pair of early 20th-century shoes embellished with silver ornamentation, a saddle covered in semi-precious stones, jewellery and a selection of costumes. One late 19th-century Kazakh female costume contains elements of decoration typical of Ukrainian dress, demonstrating a degree of cultural mixing as Slavonic peoples arrived into the area from across the Russian Empire. A copy of the sumptuously embroidered costume of 18th-century Kazakh leader Ablai Khan is on display, as is a reverential modern painting depicting him as a young man squatting beside a friendly snow leopard. The final room downstairs has models of Petropavl's new mosque and Russian Orthodox church, opened symbolically on the same day in 2005.

Upstairs stands a display highlighting the warmth of relations between Kazakhstan and Russia, with photographs of meetings between Nazarbaev and both Yeltsin and Putin. Then follow rooms describing the history of the region from the 18th century, with a model of the wooden fortress of St Peter which became the embryonic town of Petropavlovsk. The construction in 1768 of a church honouring both Saints Peter and Paul heralded the change of name. There are interesting **photographs of old Petropavlovsk**, showing the development of a merchant quarter of smart brick buildings in the upper part of town, which now forms the town centre. The earlier development of the town had been focused on the bottom of the hill, closer to the Ishim River to the west. The lives of the shopkeepers of Petropavlovsk are highlighted in mock-ups of a photo studio and of a shop, with samovars and tins of chocolates for sale. There's a fierce-looking metal door to protect those samovars and chocolates. There is a selection of furniture which might have belonged to a well-to-do merchant, including a piano with a couple of candlesticks to illuminate the keyboard.

The displays in the next room have a red background, signifying **the arrival of Bolshevism**. They chronicle the Civil War, hard fought in northern Kazakhstan, the consolidation of Soviet power and the years of Stalinist repression. There is a display about the writer and poet Magzhan Zhumabaev, considered one of the founders of modern Kazakh literature, who was executed in 1938. The next room focuses on World War II, with exhibits about the 314th Infantry Division, established in the town, and its commanders, including General Afanasii Shemenkov, Hero of the Soviet Union. The home front is also depicted, with an interesting publicity photo of a horse-drawn cart laden with provisions, and bearing a banner proclaiming that everything is for the front, and for victory over the enemy. Post-war displays highlight the Virgin Lands Campaign, in which North Kazakhstan Region was to play a leading role. A map highlights the 19 new *Sovkhoz* farms established in two years of the campaign, mostly in the southern part of the region. The region was awarded the Order of Lenin in 1966 for its record production of grain, meat and milk. The establishment of Petropavlovsk's heavy machine-building plants is outlined, and there is a training spacesuit belonging to Alexander Viktorenko, one of two cosmonauts produced by the region.

The **independence of Kazakhstan** is marked by a change of background colour to turquoise. Key moments in Kazakhstan's independence are described, and there are photographs of Nazarbaev meeting world leaders. The last room focuses on North Kazakhstan Region in the post-independence period, with photographs of new housing, hospital facilities and religious buildings. There are pictures of local celebrities, including cyclist Alexander Vinokourov, and photographs of President Nazarbaev's visits to the region.

On the outside wall of the museum is a plaque, installed in 2005, bearing a relief portraying **Dostoevsky and Valikhanov**. The Russian writer and Kazakh ethnographer are accompanied by a quote from Mukhtar Auezov, to the extent that the friendship between the two men is an excellent testimony of the historical friendship between the Kazakh and Russian peoples. This is one of several examples around Petropavl of attempts to highlight the strength of ties between Russia and Kazakhstan.

***Towards the two* batyrs** A block further northwest, Constitution Street opens out to form a square, the pale-walled four-storey building holding the regional council, or *maslikhat*, to the right, looking across to the ugly building, once a hostel, which accommodates the **city** *akimat* [272 B3].

Six blocks further to the northwest, Constitution Street ends in rather more impressive fashion than it began, at the blue-glass building of the **Russian Drama Theatre** [272 B1]. The square in front of this is dominated by a monument which, following its installation in 1999, has become one of the symbols of Petropavl: the **statue of Karasai and Agyntai** *batyrs* [272 B1]. This commemorates the two Kazakh warriors of different tribes who fought together against the Dzhungars in the 17th century, and who are buried together in the southern part of North Kazakhstan Region (see page 280). The monument provides a symbol of strength through unity. The two warriors, their chests puffed out, stand side by side, their sinewy forearms horizontal as they hold up their lances. With their other arms they jointly hold a shield in front of them like a badge.

To the right of this statue rests a faded monument from another political era, a large concrete **war memorial** [272 C1] honouring the people of North Kazakhstan

Region killed in World War II. Four differently coloured triangular panels, like large sails, converge on an eternal flame which, however, has been extinguished. To the left of the monument to the two *batyrs*, in a stretch of park, stands an abstract **monument to the Victims of Political Repression** [272 B1]: a pyramid, spikes protruding from its sides, stands beneath a triangular lattice tower.

Along Sutyushev Street One block west of Constitution Street, and running parallel to it, is Sutyushev Street, named after a local revolutionary leader killed by White forces during the Civil War. Though not as attractive as Constitution Street, it does offer several worthwhile sights.

Old and new mosques At the corner of Sutyushev and Zhambyl streets stands an attractive **old mosque** [272 B4] with an octagonal brick minaret. The main body of the mosque is painted a pastel green, its windows framed by semi-columns linked by arches. Four blocks to the northwest along Sutyushev Street is the large modern **Kyzylzhar Central Mosque** [272 B2]. A brick building, star-shaped in plan, it has a blue central dome flanked by two tall minarets. The pastel-shaded interior is attractive, with fine mosaic work around the *mihrab*. Financed with support from Saudi Arabia, the mosque was opened on 27 November 2005. In a symbolic move, a new Russian Orthodox place of worship, the Church of the Lord's Ascension, was opened on the same day. This church sits on the edge of town, in the 19th Microdistrict.

Ablai Khan's Residence [272 B1] Another six blocks further to the northwest along Sutyushev Street, just as this commences its drop down to the lower town alongside the River Ishim, stands the Residence of Ablai Khan. The smart, two-storey building, with a central exterior staircase leading to the main entrance, dates from 1829. It long served as a military hospital, and was derelict and collapsing when the local authorities decided to restore it. Its significance lies in the fact that it occupies the site of a wooden building, financed by the Russian authorities under a decree of Catherine the Great, to serve as a residence for Ablai Khan, the Middle *Zhuz* leader soon to be recognised as ruler of all the Kazakhs. Following the establishment of a Russian fortress here in 1752, it had soon become clear that the presence of the Kazakh leader was necessary to help resolve the many squabbles arising between Russians and Kazakhs. Ablai Khan's periodic presence in the developing town was therefore important to the Russian authorities, and so they arranged somewhere for him to live.

A large equestrian statue of Ablai Khan has been placed in the courtyard in front of the residence. To the left has been constructed a wooden *banya*. The building itself has been laid out as a museum to Ablai Khan, whose bust greets the visitor in the entrance hall. To the left, a room focuses on Ablai Khan's early life. There is a frieze depicting Tole Bi offering a blessing to the young man. There is a large model in the centre of the room of the Khodja Ahmed Yassaui Mausoleum in Turkestan, his hometown, and the place of his burial. A map depicts the Dzhungar incursions into Kazakhstan; the resultant years of dire hardship in the 1720s are depicted with trauma-wracked engravings. Another frieze shows Ablai's epic duel with the Dzhungar warrior Sharish. There are descriptions of other Kazakh *batyrs* of the period, and displays of weaponry and hunting equipment. Off this hall, two rooms have been walled with logs, providing a mock-up of Ablai Khan's bedroom and living room in his original wooden house.

To the right of the entrance hall, the displays concentrate on Ablai Khan as leader of the Kazakh people, starting with a painting of him being held aloft on a white felt carpet in 1771 on his election as Khan of all the Kazakhs. There are copies of his correspondence with the Russian authorities, including Catherine the Great's decree on the construction of the wooden house. Another display chronicles Ablai Khan's overtures to China, following the Chinese defeat of the Dzhungars, with documents describing the visits of his emissaries to Peking. The juxtaposition of these serves as a nice demonstration of the deep historical roots of contemporary Kazakhstan's approach of maintaining balance in its foreign policy. There is also a large diorama depicting one of Ablai Khan's battles against the Dzhungars, which chronologically really belongs in the other room, and a painting of the lively market in Petropavlovsk in the 18th century. There are also photographs of the decrepit state of the building before restoration. An adjacent room, again walled with logs, reconstructs the throne room of Ablai Khan's wooden house, where he would have received his official guests.

North Kazakhstan Regional Museum of Fine Arts [272 D5] (*83 314th Infantry Division St; \ 335646; ⊕ 10.00–20.00 daily; admission T100*) The Soviet-era concrete bulk of the **Kazakhstan Cinema** [272 D4] stands at the corner of Internatsionalnaya and Auezov streets. Behind this is a park centred on a rather worn bust of **Pushkin**. At the back of the park stands a delightful log-walled building, a merchant's house dating from 1908. The rear part of the building is two-storey, with a barrel-vaulted roof decorated in green and white lozenges. The front is single-storey, with a conical dome, also lozenge covered, over the entrance. The wooden window frames are stylishly decorated. The building served as a children's home and later a school in the Soviet period, and now houses the North Kazakhstan Regional Museum of Fine Arts. In the first room is a selection of 19th-century Russian icons. Some of these feature a metal cover, called an *oklad*, with holes through which the heads of figures on the underlying painting shine through. A booklet on display shows the icons before and after their often extensive restoration.

The rest of the museum is focused on 20th-century Kazakh painting, exhibited in a rough chronological order through a series of rooms. The first of these, covering the period up to 1950, has a strong coverage of the works of Abylkhan Kasteyev, perhaps the most noted Kazakh painter, including a portrait of the *akyn* Suyunbay, mentor of Zhambyl, his *dombra* resting on the wall behind him, and a scene of threshing at the *kolkhoz*. Coverage of the 1950s and 1960s includes a 1957 portrait by Olga Kuzhelenko of the noted Kazakh singer Roza Baglanova, who offers a grimace-like smile to the viewer as she stands in front of her piano. There are also several paint-heavy works by Zhanatay Shardenov, an artist born in Akmola Region, depicting landscapes through splodges of colour or, in the case of *March Snow in Medeo*, through bleakness-depicting dark tones. Works from the later Soviet period include a large canvas entitled *Hope*, portraying a meeting between Abulkhair Khan and representatives of imperial Russia, a vivid portrait of Kurmangazy, showing the *akyn*, lean and bony, in front of a tattered and broken yurt, and a wonderful 1987 canvas entitled *Hostel*, featuring 16 balconies, the evidently hot residents all out on them, sitting, singing, smoking and stretching.

KOKSHETAU NATIONAL PARK

Established in 1996, the Kokshetau National Nature Park straddles the Akmola and North Kazakhstan regions. That part of the park falling within Akmola Region has been described in Chapter 3 (see page 104), but many of the most attractive landscapes and interesting sites sit in the North Kazakhstan section of the park. The park offers fine scenery of lakes, low hills, rocky outcrops, pine and birch forests, and expanses of steppe. Locals talk animatedly about the range of mushrooms and berries to be found in the forests, and the wildlife includes elk, lynx and polecat.

PRACTICALITIES The North Kazakhstan part of the national park can be reached much more easily from Kokshetau than from Petropavl. The Kokshetau-based NGO Ecos (see page 105) has set up community-based ecotourism projects in two villages in the area: Ayirtau, where they have five homestays, and Imantau, where they have three. The homestays (**$**) offer clean but basic accommodation, with meals cooked by the host family and shared (though indoor) bathroom and toilet. Ecos can arrange taxis to take you to the villages and return you to Kokshetau, and there are a few buses a day from Kokshetau to Imantau.

Both Imantau and Ayirtau are attractively sited close to lakes. In the case of Ayirtau this is the 17km-long, crescent-shaped, Lake Shalkar. Located a couple of kilometres outside the village, and requiring a special park admission fee of T300 per day (though they may charge more for foreigners), this is fringed by birch woodland and supports large populations of hungry mosquitoes in summer. There are a couple of holiday bases on its shores. The closest to Ayirtau is the **Arman Holiday Base** (✆ *(7152) 465215;* **$**), approached by turning left onto a rough track at the checkpoint at which the park admission fee is taken. Arman is 3km further on, right on the lake shore. It is a run-down and basic place, a series of cottages with pitched roofs of corrugated iron, though it is cheap. One curiosity here is a reconstruction of one of the buildings of the Eneolithic Botai culture (see page 276), the work of a local archaeologist named Viktor Zaibert. This consists of two circular, earth-walled rooms with domed roofs fashioned from earth-covered interlocking logs and central fireplaces. A short corridor links the two rooms. From outside, the structure looks rather like two large anthills with a wall running between them. The reconstruction was undertaken as part of a projected open-air museum which has not, as yet, materialised. The Botai site itself is west of here, to the west of the district capital, Saumalkol.

MEMORIAL COMPLEX TO KARASAI AND AGYNTAI *BATYR* Saumalkol, the main settlement in the area, is 22km northwest of Ayirtau. From Saumalkol head southwest on the road towards Ruzaevka, turning left after 3km onto a road signposted to the Karasai and Agyntai Batyr Memorial Complex. Turn right, again signposted to the complex, after a further 13km. The monument itself, two cones on the crest of a low hill, is visible from afar and guides you the final 11km towards it.

The Karasai and Agyntai Batyr Memorial Complex, opened in 1999, honours the two Kazakh warriors of the 17th century who fought together against the Dzhungars for several decades. The focus on these figures in post-independence Kazakhstan, including this lavish memorial complex and a monument in Petropavl (see page 277), is based around the idea of Kazakhs of different tribes working together in pursuit of a greater common goal. Karasai *Batyr* was born in present-day Almaty Region, from the Shaprashty tribe of the Great *Zhuz*. President Nazarbaev belongs to the same tribe, which is perhaps a further factor underpinning Karasai *Batyr's* current popularity. Agyntai Batyr was from the north of the country, a member of the Argyn tribe of the Middle *Zhuz*. Their many joint exploits in battles against the Dzhungars included involvement in the Kazakh victory at the Battle of Orbulak in 1643, and helping to free the Kazakh khan, Salqam Zhangir, from captivity. Karasai *Batyr* died in 1671, at the age of 73, and was reportedly buried here in the Kulshinbay Hills of North Kazakhstan. Agyntai *Batyr* died a year later, and was buried next to his friend.

The form of the monument is striking: two cones of brown brick, 16m in height, vaguely resembling oasthouses or giant termite mounds, stand side by side. In front of them is a slightly smaller building, also circular-based and with a roof shaped like an upside-down ice-cream cone. This is a mosque, its position between the two mausolea symbolically uniting them in prayer. Three tall metal spears fan out in front of each of the two mausolea. Within the mausolea, the two graves – that of Agyntai in the building on the left, Karasai on the right – are marked by a *kulpytas* and *koytas*, engraved with images of their weaponry and the symbols of their tribes. Piles of rocks around the back of the monument symbolise the graves of family members of the *batyrs*. A plaque records that the memorial complex was built under the initiative of President Nazarbaev. The caretaker tends to leave around 18.00, locking up the complex for the night.

SIRIMBET This small village north of Saumalkol is associated with the childhood of noted Kazakh traveller and ethnographer Chokan Valikhanov (see box). To get here from Saumalkol, head north, through pine and birch woodlands, towards the village of Svetloe. After 24km take a signposted right turn to Sirimbet, reaching the village after a further 5km.

A smart single-storey log-walled building in the village houses the **Sirimbet Historical and Ethnographic Museum named after Chokan Valikhanov**. This was opened in 1985 to mark the 150th anniversary of Valikhanov's birth. It occupies a building constructed in 1929, which previously housed a school. You may notice a street of old-looking wooden houses on the way to the museum, which appear to be rather better quality than the buildings in the rest of the village. I was told by local villagers that these 'old' buildings were actually constructed in 1985, along the route visiting VIPs would be taking for the opening of the museum, to make the village seem tidier and more attractive to these senior people.

The foyer houses a carpet produced by the Almaty textile factory, depicting Valikhanov, and a painting of Ablai Khan. A room to the left illustrates Valikhanov's youth, with some of his own fine drawings, including one of the Sirimbet estate which was to prove invaluable to researchers attempting to rebuild it. There is a photograph of Valikhanov at the Omsk Cadet School, 12 years old and already looking poised, and a display about his friendship with Dostoevsky. The next room contains notes and drawings made by Valikhanov as part of his research, including drawings of the Tamgaly Tas petroglyphs. A wall map displays some of his travels, including his journey to Kashgar. The next display, opposite the entrance foyer, is a yurt, with beyond that a room devoted to World War II, with a frieze on the far wall depicting young men with machine guns and riding horses, their wives collecting wheat and raising the children. The last room chronicles the history of the village, which became a grain-producing *Sovkhoz* farm in the early 1960s. There is a display about the work of another noted Valikhanov, Shota, who was born in Sirimbet in 1932. He became an architect responsible for a number of the notable monuments of post-independence Kazakhstan, including the State arms, the Independence Monument in Almaty, the monument to Kenesary in Astana and that to the victims of nuclear testing in Semey. The museum concludes with photographs of some of the institutions across Kazakhstan which bear the name of Chokan Valikhanov.

Sirimbet's other Valikhanov-related sight is the reconstructed **estate of Aiganim**, Chokan Valikhanov's grandmother. It lies outside the village, off the road back towards Saumalkol, and is clearly visible from it. Aiganim, the younger wife of Vali Khan, was not yet 40 when her husband died in 1821. She was well educated,

A polymath who died of tuberculosis short of his 30th birthday, an ethnographer, traveller, geographer, army officer and even spy, Valikhanov has become a revered figure in post-independence Kazakhstan, both as a Kazakh of outstanding intellectual achievement and for the attention he paid to chronicling the culture and traditions of the Kazakh people. There are streets and monuments to Valikhanov across Kazakhstan. When the Central Asian Geographical Society, based in Almaty, announced that they were planning an expedition to sail around the world, it was no surprise that they chose *Chokan Valikhanov* as the name of their yacht.

Valikhanov was born in 1835 in present-day Kostanai Region into a prominent family. His grandfather, Vali Khan, was a grandson of the Kazakh ruler Ablai Khan. He was sent in 1847 to study at the Omsk Cadet School, as his father had done, and served thereafter as an officer in the Russian army, including as adjutant to the governor-general. This work involved travels around Kazakhstan, which he combined with scientific and ethnographic activity. He befriended Dostoevsky during the latter's exile in Semipalatinsk and sought out other intellectuals. He took part in expeditions to Lake Alakol, the Tian Shan and Lake Issyk Kul, and in 1857 was accepted into the Russian Geographical Society, with a recommendation from Pyotr Semyonov-Tianshansky. His research works included studies of Kazakh culture, shamanism and nomadism, he translated part of the great Kyrgyz epic poem *Manas* into Russian, and set down the lyrical Kazakh epic *Kozy-Korpesh and Bayan-Sulu*.

There was another side to the travels of many adventurous military officers and scientists of the Great Game period, both British and Russian, and some of Valikhanov's expeditions also had an intelligence-gathering dimension. It was clearly an advantage for the Russian authorities to be able to turn to members of a Russified central Asian elite for covert missions, their Asiatic appearance and knowledge of the language and culture of the region made them ideal choices. Valikhanov's expedition to Kashgaria in 1858–59, for example, resulted in learned work published in the journal of the Russian Geographical Society, but was also about obtaining political intelligence on a region in which Russia was strongly interested. But he seems to have become frustrated at Russia's colonial ambitions, and devoted himself increasingly to his scientific works. He died in 1865 near Altyn Emel in present-day Almaty Region.

and in widowhood became an influential local figure. She also encouraged young Chokan's academic curiosity during his stays at Sirimbet, which included his holidays from the Omsk Cadet School. The estate was built for Aiganim by a decree of Tsar Alexander I in 1824 and by the order of the then Governor-General of western Siberia, Kaptsevich. The estate, of wooden buildings, included a school, mosque, guesthouse and mill. It was destroyed during the Soviet period, but has been reconstructed on the basis of drawings and descriptions and was opened as an open-air museum in 1994.

The estate comprises several log-walled buildings around a central courtyard, all within a fenced enclosure. The main building includes a smart guest room, with decorated wooden columns, and a range of furnishings linked to the family, including a beautifully decorated box, the work of a brother of Valikhanov who was a talented craftsman. The other wooden buildings are a mosque, whose tower dominates the ensemble, a *banya*, a school building and a store containing a display of household and agricultural implements.

KOSTANAI   *Telephone code: 7142*

Kostanai Region, the westernmost of the three regions forming Kazakhstan's bulbous northern 'cap', is an important centre of wheat production, as well as of a number of key mineral resources, especially iron ore, asbestos and bauxite. Its regional capital, Kostanai, is a pleasant provincial city on the banks of the River Tobol. Kostanai owes its existence to Tsarist-era regional administration. The Tsarist authorities decided that the administration of the Nikolaevsk District, which was being handled from Troitsk, on the territory of present-day Russia, required the establishment of a new urban settlement. In 1870, surveyors chose a site at Urdabai on the banks of the Tobol. But a commission led by the Military Governor of Turgai Region, one Major General Konstantinovich, visiting the place in 1879, decided that the Urdabai site was quite inappropriate for a town and alighted on a new location nearby, at a place called Kustanai. The first settlers arrived from Orenburg in the summer of that year.

In 1893, the settlement was given urban status, and the name of Novonikolaevsk. The latter did not however stick, partly because of the confusing proliferation of towns sharing the name of the new Tsar, and it reverted to Kustanai in 1895. The fertile steppe soils around the town were an attraction for settlers from land-poor parts of the Tsarist Empire, and by 1911 Kustanai already had a population of more than 25,000. Kostanai today retains many attractive red-brick buildings from the Tsarist period. The evacuation of factories to Kostanai during World War II, and the city's post-war role as one of the hubs of the Virgin Lands Campaign, further promoted its development. After weathering the difficult post-independence years, the city displays much renewed development, exemplified by the pedestrianised centre, vibrant on warm summer evenings.

GETTING THERE AND AROUND Kostanai **airport** (✆ *280800*), just beyond the western edge of the city, is served by a daily Air Astana flight from Astana. Scat operates a daily flight from Almaty. There are also several connections between Kostanai and airports in Germany, a measure of the strength of the city's ethnic German minority. These include weekly direct connections on Air Astana with both Frankfurt and Hanover. There are also a further three indirect connections to Frankfurt, and one to Hanover, linking with Air Astana's routes out of Astana.

The **railway station** (✆ *900222*) sits at the northwestern edge of the city centre, at the end of the main Al Farabi Avenue. Reconstructed in 2001, the station offers daily services to both Almaty and Karaganda, as well as a more local daily service to Arkalyk in the southern part of the region. A few trains also run to destinations in Russia, including St Petersburg and Moscow. The statue standing outside the railway station depicts the Kazakh writer Beimbet Mailin, a victim of Stalinist repression. The **bus station** (✆ *255050*) is somewhat inconveniently sited at the southern edge of town, just off Abai Avenue.

There are numerous **taxis**: numbers to call include ✆ 901111, ✆ 543210, ✆ 531111 and ✆ 540001. Among the most useful of the intra-urban bus routes are bus 20, which runs between the bus station and the airport; bus 3, which connects the railway and bus stations, running along both Al Farabi and Abai avenues; and bus 23, which also connects the railway and bus stations, but does so via Baimagambetov Street.

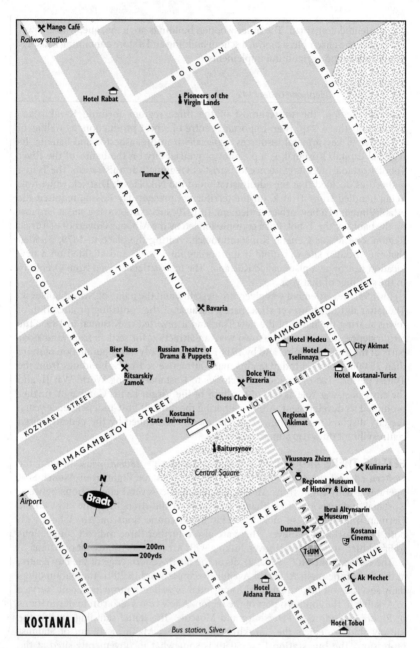

KOSTANAI

Bus station, Silver

WHERE TO STAY

🏠 **Hotel Tobol** (7 rooms) 64 5th April St; 544360, 533060; f 542333. Located in a quiet cul-de-sac on the southeastern side of the city centre, the Tobol is fronted by a restaurant decked out in a garish metallic grey & red colour

scheme. The rooms, all with AC, are smartly furnished, though the prices are somewhat high for Kostanai. **$$$$**

🏠 **Hotel Aidana Plaza** (6 rooms) 53 Tolstoy St; 548686; f 549550. A block away from the central department store, TsUM, this place offers 6 spacious rooms above a former casino: at the time of research there seemed to be vague plans to convert the latter into a restaurant. The building itself is a decidedly ugly modern block, but the rooms themselves are reasonably furnished, with AC & en-suite bathrooms. **$$$**

🏠 **Hotel Medeu** (32 rooms) 166A Baimagambetov St; 📞 545845; f 545945; e medeo@mail.kz; www.medeuhotel.kz. Centrally located, the Medeu is a long cream-coloured block, whose interior combines cream-walled corridors with cream-coloured floor tiles. While among the most upmarket of Kostanai's hotels, it is decidedly bland. No lift. **$$$**

🏠 **Hotel Kostanai-Turist** (60 rooms) 72 Baitursynov St; 📞 545484, 541252; f 540324; e kontur@mail.kz; www.turist.itcom.kz. This externally shabby-looking 6-storey concrete block opened its doors as a hotel in 1974 & retains an unmistakably Soviet feel, with long corridors guarded by *dizhurnayas*. But the rooms themselves have been modernised, & offer cable TV & en-suite showers, & the hotel is centrally located. **$$**

🏠 **Hotel Rabat** (17 rooms) 149 Taran St; 📞 542793; f 543282. A few blocks from the railway station, the Rabat occupies 2 very different buildings: a 2-storey renovated red-brick building out front, & a modern metallic-finished grey & red structure behind it. The 'luxe' rooms are spacious, though furnished in aspirational 1970s style, with radios built into the bed headboards & gold toilet seat covers. All rooms have AC & en suites. **$$**

🏠 **Hotel Tselinnaya** (96 rooms) 95 Baitursynov St; 📞 544366; f 545960; e celinnaya@mail.ru; www.celinnaya.kz. The 'Virgin Lands' Hotel is centrally located on leafy, pedestrianised Baitursynov St, opposite the Hotel Kostanai-Turist. The whole place is decorated in cream & brown tones, presumably in homage to the wheat on which Kostanai's prosperity is based. The rooms are comfortable enough, though nothing special. The *dizhurnayas* here sit behind glass booths. If you stay here for more than 1 night, you get a small discount on the room rate for the 2nd & subsequent nights. **$$**

✕ WHERE TO EAT

✕ **Bavaria** 90 Al Farabi Av; 📞 547705. This central place offers wooden tables separated by latticed partitions, a large menu with the accent on meaty Teutonic dishes, & wide-screen TV offering a diet of music channels. But the main attraction is the unfiltered beer brewed on the premises, apparently to a German recipe. **$$$**

✕ **Ritsarskiy Zamok** 75 Kozybaev St; 📞 508888. 2 knights in armour with lances guard the entrance to the 'Knight's Castle'. Beyond lies a spiral staircase adorned with sumptuous oil paintings, leading into a large refectory, with more armour & plenty of carved wood, including a top table with carved lions for legs & chairs with improbably tall backs. A separate 'VIP room' has 1 wall devoted to a large doll collection. The descriptions on the English-language menu are somewhat unrestrained: how about 'Noble Salmon from the Duke of Lamuel'? Though I did rather like the helpful suggestion that their pastries 'are nice with a mug of beer or some other drink if you want'. **$$$**

✕ **Bier Haus** 75 Kozybaev St; 📞 508864. Next door to the Ritsarskiy Zamok & under the same management, this pub/eatery draws from an eclectic range of influences. There is a turreted wooden bar, beer steins in a glass case, a model of a red British telephone box in the middle of the room & waitresses in frilly tartan skirts. *Shashlik* is served up from a *mangal* in the corner behind a fake stone wall. A model of a bouffant-haired dandy about town sits silently at one of the tables, a freshly prepared meal & glass of wine set out in front of him. **$$**

✕ **Dolce Vita Pizzeria** 72 Al Farabi Av; 📞 543353. This compact & busy central pizzeria offers a broad-based menu, with plenty of pizzas & pasta dishes. This is a good place to stop for lunch whilst touring the central sights. **$$**

✕ **Duman** 67 Al Farabi Av; 📞 546416. A 2-storey restaurant situated at the heart of the pedestrianised section of Al Farabi Av, opposite the TsUM department store. The top floor offers a fine opportunity for people-watching from its broad glass windows. The 'VIP room', also upstairs, is the only part of the restaurant not assailed by pop music. There is also a Russian billiard room upstairs. The food, cheaper than the somewhat formal table settings might suggest, ranges across genres in a scatter-gun way, from *shashlik* to paella. $$

✗ **Mango Café** 138 Al Farabi Av; ☎ 534775. Close to the railway station end of Al Farabi Av, this place offers a functional street-side café, with a comfier restaurant room behind it. The waitresses wear yellow T-shirts, & most sport dyed blonde hair to match them. The menu offers a backdrop of tropical scenes, though the dishes themselves are a quotidian selection of Russian & international staples. $$

✗ **Silver** Michurin Rd; ☎ 267255. In a pleasant spot amongst birch woodland, across the Tobol River from the city, the Silver is a sports club focused on clay-pigeon shooting. The restaurant on site is a barn-like room with wooden log walls. The evening entertainers share the stage with a stuffed wolf, & other victims of the hunt are displayed around the walls including, in a monumental example of poor taste, 3 stuffed marmots behind the bar, 1 carrying a bottle of wine, the others holding glasses. There are also wooden cabins for outdoor dining, & a deer pen near the car park. $$

✗ **Tumar** 133 Taran St; ☎ 533623, 548613. Occupying an impressive-looking 3-storey building opposite the Palace of Sport, with vaguely Kazakh designs adorning its façade, the Tumar offers a menu that encompasses central Asian, Russian & European dishes. The waitresses wear Kazakh skullcaps, but the interior décor sticks to the cream colouring with which much of Kostanai seems to have been afflicted. There's a terrace in front of the building, protected by a large awning. $$

✗ **Vkusnaya Zhizn** 60 Al Farabi Av; ☎ 547843. The 'Tasty Life' is housed in an attractive 2-storey Tsarist-era building next to the regional museum. The downstairs restaurant is decked out in Japanese style, next to which is a simpler bar area in a room with a vaulted ceiling. Upstairs, the interior designers have clearly been given free rein, & have produced a gold-tinted space in Greco-Persian style. The food doesn't really square with the ornate décor: a range of Russian & international staples at low prices. $$

✗ **Kulinaria** 122 Altynsarin St; ⊕ 09.00–20.00 daily, though with interesting logic, closes for lunch from 14.00–15.00. This scruffy canteen is for those looking for experiences straight out of the Soviet Union, from the samovar in the corner to the wooden abacus used to calculate the bill to the dinner ladies in tall blue hats. Equally true to form, the food is cheap & not very good. $

WHAT TO SEE

Along Al Farabi Avenue The main axis of the city is Al Farabi Avenue, which runs in a northwest to southeast line through the centre of town.

Around Central Square At the corner of Al Farabi Avenue and Baimagambetov Street, the attractive terracotta-walled building with Ionic columns decorating the façade is the **Russian Theatre of Drama and Puppets** (*191 Baimagambetov St;* ☎ *397988;* ⊕ *Wed–Sun, performances start at 18.00 Wed–Fri, 17.00 Sat–Sun*). The theatre traces its origins back to 1922. One block further south along Al Farabi Avenue, at the corner with Baitursynov Street, the Tsarist-era brick building houses a school of arts. Opposite this is the town **chess club**, run by the city education department, which sits beneath the clock tower in the same building as the Dolce Vita Pizzeria. The club is named after Anatoliy Ufimtsev, a local amateur chess player who has the distinction of authoring a chess move: the Ufimtsev Defence.

Al Farabi Avenue is pedestrianised for the next four blocks, save for the crossing with busy Altynsarin Street. Just beyond the corner with Baitursynov Street stands the **regional administration** building, a modernised affair proudly showing off a tall, broad, blue-glass façade. Opposite this stands **Central Square**, a pleasant patch of greenery. The columned façade of the **Kostanai State University** stands facing the western side of this, flanked by billboards bearing quotations from President Nazarbaev in Russian and Kazakh: 'I believe in our youth!' Opposite, a broad path scythes through the green square. On the left of this is a statue of **Ahmet Baitursynov**, in whose honour the university is named. The writer is seated, quill pen in hand, ready to be inspired. There is also a pond here, whose inhabitants include swans and a pelican, and there's a small fairground.

Regional Museum of History and Local Lore (*115 Altynsarin St;* ☎ *501023;* ⏰ *10.00–17.00 Tue–Sun; admission adult/child T30/15*) Another block further south, at the corner of Al Farabi Avenue and Altynsarin Street, stands the Regional Museum of History and Local Lore. Housed in an attractive pale green-painted two-storey building built in Tsarist times by a local merchant, and later serving as a department store, this is an interesting museum, although the labelling is in Kazakh and Russian only.

The first room, looking at regional history from the Stone Age, includes a really curious stone squatting figure, hunched and careworn, known as the **Tobol Thinker.** Found on the bank of the River Tobol, it is believed to date to the Bronze Age. There are displays on the fighting against the Dzhungars, Kenesary's revolt, and the 1916 uprising led by Amangeldy Imanov, focused on the Turgai steppe which lies in the remote southern part of present-day Kostanai Region. There are various swords and rifles from the uprising on display, and the score of the *Amangeldy* overture. The next room focuses on the arrival of Slavonic peoples into the region, with a mock-up of a log house built by immigrants of the late 19th and early 20th centuries: there's an icon in the corner, a spinning wheel, and an accordion and balalaika for jolly moments. The displays include some stiffly posed photographs of merchant families, and ladies' costumes as worn by Russians, Ukrainians and Belarusians.

The displays continue upstairs with a room about the **founding of Kostanai**. A 1902 plan shows a grid-patterned town laid out on the north bank of the Tobol River. There are early photographs, including of a broad and muddy-looking Bolshaya ('Big') Street, the present-day Al Farabi Avenue, at the end of the 19th century. There is the mock-up of the drawing room of a merchant's house at the start of the 20th century, with the family's prized crockery carefully displayed in a glass cupboard. There are also displays on the victims of the repression of the 1930s, on the region's literary figures and sports stars, and on Kazakhstan's space programme, Kostanai Region providing one of the expanses of Kazakh steppe onto which returning cosmonauts are prone to land. US astronaut Michael Coats contributes a signed photograph addressed to the Kostanai Historical Museum: 'with appreciation'.

To the left is a room on natural history, whose stuffed animal-filled dioramas include wetland, birch woodland, pine woodland and steppe, the last featuring marmots standing quizzically on their hind legs, hedgehogs snuffling around, and a steppe eagle eating something. A description of the Naurzym State Reserve includes a set of badges and stickers from the international 'Day of the Crane' celebrations, focused on efforts to help save this remarkable bird. And, in common with almost every museum in Kazakhstan, there is a stuffed wild boar. There are displays, too, on the region's minerals wealth, with photographs of the huge, terraced, open-cast pits of the Zhitikara asbestos deposit and Sokolov-Sarbai iron-ore deposit.

Opposite the nature hall is a room focused on World War II, with a mock-up of a wartime living room, with a map in which red and black flags sketch out the front line. There are photographs both of those on the front and of those toiling in the fields and factories to support them. The next room majors on the economic achievements of the region. A display records the award of the Order of Lenin to Kostanai Oblast in 1966 for its successes in agricultural production: it repeated the feat in 1970. A plastic case contains the spools of blue thread which represent the first output of the Kostanai worsted cloth factory lumbered with the name of

'23rd Session of the Communist Party of the Soviet Union'. The rather grim clothes and shoes produced in local factories in the 1970s are on display, and there is a description of the Virgin Lands programme, with photographs of Kunaev, First Secretary of the Kazakh Communist Party, inspecting the wheat fields in the 1970s. Back downstairs are a couple of rooms dedicated to art with paintings and sculptures of horses.

Ibrai Altynsarin Museum (*118A Altynsarin St;* \ *545817, 530364;* ◔ *09.00–17.00 Mon–Sat, closed the last Fri of the month; admission T40*) A further block southwards along Al Farabi Avenue lies an octagonal pavilion with a domed metal roof, housing the Ibrai Altynsarin Museum. Altynsarin, who was born in 1841 in present-day Kostanai Region, was a Kazakh educator, whose varied accomplishments included the establishment of many Kazakh–Russian schools, the use of Western-style educational techniques, and the introduction of a Cyrillic alphabet for written Kazakh. The museum was established in 1991, to mark the 150th anniversary of his birth. The museum building stands close to the site of one of the schools founded by Altynsarin, now occupied by a boarding school for gifted children bearing the name of the educator. A bust of the somewhat wild-haired Alytnsarin is nearby.

The ground floor of the domed pavilion offers displays on Altynsarin's life and work. They trace his life from early childhood with his grandfather, his father having died young, through schooling in Orenburg, to his work as an inspector of schools in the former Turgai Region. There is a model on display of the first Kazakh–Russian school he established, in the settlement of Turgai in 1864. Among the educational establishments he set up were the first schools for Kazakh girls. A bust of Altynsarin on display shows him holding up a book bearing the 42 letters of his Kazakh Cyrillic alphabet. Textbooks written by Altynsarin are also on display. The museum is rather light on personal items, but one of the only two photographs of the educator known to exist is an interesting item, which shows Altynsarin in front of his home. A yurt is pitched in the garden. Apparently he welcomed European guests in his home, Kazakh ones in the yurt, an arrangement, as with his career, which demonstrated his determination to take the positive from both the Russian and Kazakh worlds. He died in 1889, aged just 47.

Upstairs, the displays in the gallery are devoted to poetess Mariam Khakimzhanova, related to Ibray Altynsarin (she was a great-granddaughter of Altynsarin's grandfather, if that makes any sense). Her life spanned most of the 20th century. Her membership card of the Union of Writers of the USSR was signed off by Maksim Gorky. Her work included a poem in honour of Manshuk Mametova, a Kazakh woman posthumously awarded the title of Hero of the Soviet Union for her wartime bravery. A photograph shows Khakimzhanova with Mametova's mother. Museum guides will play a recording of Khakimzhanova reciting her Kazakh-language poetry. Objects on display include a briefcase, given to Khakimzhanova by Nazarbaev. A book she was reading is eerily left open at the page she had reached on her death in 1995.

Around Ak Mechet Continuing southeast along Al Farabi Avenue, the **Kostanai Cinema** offers a Soviet-era frieze now partially obscured by modern advertising billboards in, quite literally, a sign of the changing times.

At the next intersection, of Al Farabi and Abai avenues, stands the delightful Tsarist-era **Ak Mechet**, the 'White Mosque', though its walls today are painted pale blue. The building is distinguished by its three octagonal towers of differing sizes, the tallest of the three a minaret, each topped by a dark blue conical 'hat'. It was built in 1893 with the support of wealthy local merchants such as Abduvaly Yaushev. During the Soviet period it served, variously, as a workers' club, an evacuation point for citizens of Leningrad and a concert hall, and was restored as a mosque in 1991.

Monument to the Pioneers of the Virgin Lands Northwest of the city centre, along Taran Street, close to the intersection with Borodin Street, stands an impressive monument to the pioneers of the Virgin Lands programme. Three young pioneers scatter grain across a furrowed earth. Behind, a wavy relief depicts healthily growing wheat. The reverse side of the relief depicts the back-breaking work of these pioneers to secure the harvest.

A plaque, dated 1997, at the side of the large open concrete space in front of the monument tells you that the Square of the Pioneers of the Virgin Lands also bears the title Sri Chinmoy Peace Square, having joined the 'international oneness family' of more than 1,000 peace monuments across the globe, taking their name from philosopher Sri Chinmoy. This particular monument to peace was adorned with numerous fag ends and pieces of broken bottle when I visited.

ALONG THE TOBOL

Southwest from Kostanai, upstream along the broad Tobol River, lies the industrial heart of Kostanai Region, centred on huge reserves of iron ore, supplemented by deposits of other minerals, such as asbestos and bauxite.

RUDNIY (*Telephone code: 71431*) Some 46km to the southwest of Kostanai, with a population of around 120,000, the town of Rudniy is founded on iron ore. The huge Sarbai deposit here was apparently discovered in 1949, when a pilot with a geological expedition working nearby noticed unusual movements of the plane's compass when he flew over the area. The pilot reported the fact, geologists were sent to Sarbai, and the iron-ore reserves were found. A Soviet decree of 1954 authorised the construction of a mining and smelting complex. Today, the Sokolov-Sarbai Mining Industrial Association (SSGPO) dominates the economy of the town, operating the vast open-cast Sokolov and Sarbai pits and the processing facilities for the production of iron ore in both loose and pellet form for steel plants in Kazakhstan, Russia and China.

The town, spread out along the main road, Lenin Street, is dominated by Soviet-era apartment blocks, and offers little to detain the tourist.

Where to stay and eat Should you wish to stay overnight in Rudniy, the **Hotel Gornyak** (*57 rooms; 24 Lenin St;* ✆ *27970;* **$$**), at the corner of the main square and Lenin Street, is a reasonably comfortable option. The place to head for food and entertainment is the remarkably plush **Miners' Cultural Palace** (*1 Mir St;* ✆ *28608*), which sits at the back of the main square, around which are also assembled the administrative building of the SSGPO and the more modest building of the town *akimat*. The Miners' Cultural Palace houses a range of places to eat, including the Kitaysky Dvorik (✆ *27167*), an ebulliently laid-out Chinese restaurant, the Opera Plaza, aiming for an aristocratic European feel, and the Limpopo, a child-focused café decorated with cartoon jungle animals which also boasts a purpose-built pizza oven. A Soviet-era frieze on one of the interior walls of the building is worth a look: note how the Soviet flag has been replaced by the Kazakhstani one. The complex also offers billiards, ten-pin bowling, a cinema and a nightclub (⊕ *22.00–03.00 Thu, 22.00–05.00 Fri, Sat; admission T600*).

LISAKOVSK (*Telephone code 71433*) Continuing further southwestwards along the road running alongside the Tobol River, you reach Lisakovsk, another town which owes its existence to the post-war discovery of iron-ore deposits. The village of Lisakovka, a small settlement of Tsarist-era migrants from Ukraine, became the nucleus of industrial Lisakovsk, which received its urban status in 1971 and now numbers some 40,000 inhabitants. The town, like many industrial centres in Kazakhstan, experienced some tough years following Kazakhstan's independence, here made more acute because the local iron ore has a high phosphorous content and proved difficult to market. But the securing of Special Economic Zone status, in a bid to diversify the economic base of the town, allowed it to weather the economic crises of the 1990s.

While Lisakovsk may be a young town, human settlement in the area dates back to prehistoric times. Emma Usmanova, an archaeologist from Karaganda State University, has been leading expeditions here since 1985 focusing on Bronze Age burial mounds of the Andronov culture lying outside the town, close to the Tobol River. The finds of these expeditions are nicely displayed in the rather good **Museum of the History and Culture of the Upper Tobol River** (⟍ *34490;* ⊕ *09.00– 17.00 Mon–Fri, 10.00–16.00 Sat*). The first room of the museum is a showcase of the Usmanova expeditions, including a reconstructed female burial, reconstructed heads of Bronze Age men based on the evidence of their skulls, jewellery and ceramics. In the centre of the room is a burnt wooden post, found in a large rectangular pit in the centre of a burial mound, which Usmanova believes was an idol. The next room is focused on the short history of the modern town of Lisakovsk, with samples of the iron ore and bauxite on which the town's development was founded. The Birmingham Torch Award, carefully placed in a niche, was presented to former Akim Albert Rau by the Alabama city in recognition of the imaginative efforts of the town to combat the economic difficulties of the early 1990s. Next comes a room displaying the cultures of the various ethnic groups which make up the population of Lisakovsk. Note the display of fine German wedding garlands. A room devoted to local artworks is followed by a windowless chamber in which are placed some of the museum's most precious works, including gold jewellery of the Andronov culture, silver Kazakh jewellery and, incongruously, some African items brought back by Usmanova from trips there.

The **Baden-Baden Restaurant** (*House 29, 2nd Microdistrict;* ⟍ *39750;* $$) is a reasonable central choice for lunch. Close to the fruit and vegetable market, it sits amidst pleasant grounds of birch trees. The Teutonic theme is strongest upstairs, where you can sit at wooden tables admiring the wild boar head on the wall. There is billiards in the 'green room' and a bar downstairs.

NAURZUM NATURE RESERVE

The Naurzum Nature Reserve, located in the centre of Kostanai Region, some 200km south of Kostanai city itself, was first established in 1931 and now covers more than 190,000ha. It is split into three separate tracts, Naurzum, Tersek and Sipsin, protecting a range of different ecosystems. The Naurzum pine forest, the most southerly found in the flatlands of Kazakhstan, is a fire-maintained ecosystem formed on the wind-blown sands which collected here following the retreat of the glaciers. The patches of pine forest, and other forested areas comprising a mix of birch and aspen, form islands surrounded by open steppe. The area also contains many shallow lakes of varying degrees of salinity, which provide important staging areas for migratory species such as the Siberian crane. The steppe itself is notably rich here, with the Schrenk's tulip, named after a researcher of the St Petersburg Botanical Gardens who made expeditions to northern Kazakhstan in the 1840s, making its appearance in May. Later in the spring, the sight of waving white feather grass coupled with the rich scent of wormwood make a stirring combination.

The reserve is an attractive destination for ornithologists. The rich populations of birds of prey include, for example, four species of eagle: imperial eagle, white-tailed eagle, steppe eagle and golden eagle. Among the other uncommon bird species found at the reserve are demoiselle crane, sociable lapwing, black-winged pratincole and Dalmatian pelican. Mammals include roe deer and elk. The reserve has not always had a smooth ride: during the Soviet period it had to weather a spell of pine planting for timber. But its importance is now more adequately recognised, with a nomination for inclusion into the UNESCO World Heritage list.

The **reserve office** is located in the district capital, the village of Karamendi. To get here take the road south from Kostanai towards Arkalyk, passing through Auliekol (from where the road quality deteriorates), and take the signposted turn westwards to Karamendi, 34km from the turning. There is a small museum at the reserve office, with a single room containing stuffed versions of many of the best-known creatures found in the reserve. The reserve staff are, however, more focused on scientific researchers than tourists, and there is no real tourist infrastructure or smooth system in place for the granting of permits to visit the reserve itself, though the latter can be secured with some persuasiveness and patience.

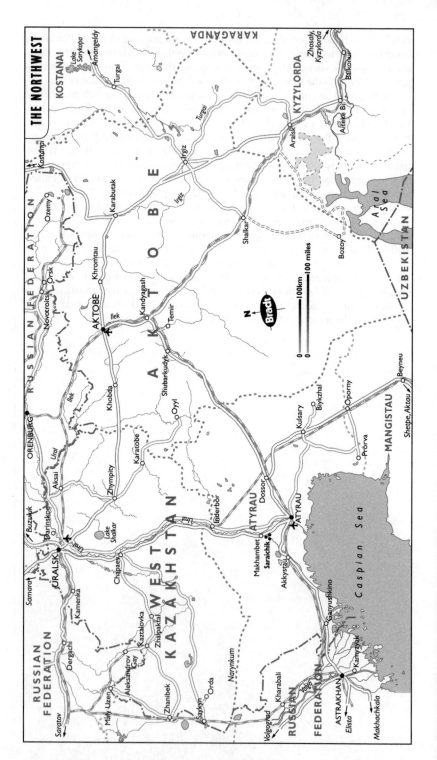

THE NORTHWEST

9

The Northwest

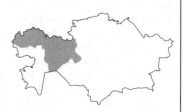

The regions of Aktobe and West Kazakhstan, in the northwest of the country, are well off the usual tourist trail. They are characterised by rolling steppeland, with semi-desert landscapes in the more southerly parts of Aktobe Region, the only region in the country to stretch between the borders of Russia and Uzbekistan. There are significant oil reserves in Aktobe Region, and a major oil and gas condensate field at Karachaganak in West Kazakhstan. Hydrocarbons wealth brings a steady flow of expatriates to both regional capitals, along with the hotel infrastructure to cater for them. Uralsk, the capital of West Kazakhstan Region, has some fine Tsarist architecture and an interesting history, including as one of the centres of the 18th-century Pugachev Rebellion and the only city in Kazakhstan to be visited by the Russian poet Pushkin. Aktobe has no major sights of interest, but is a pleasant enough place for a short visit. Coincidentally, both cities offer museums and monuments to local female heroes of World War II.

AKTOBE *Telephone code: 7132*

The capital of Aktobe Region, Aktobe is a city of more than 300,000 people. Like the surrounding region, it is not a major tourist destination, but there are some quirky attractions here, including sites linked with female sniper Aliya Moldagulova, around whom there is something of a personality cult, and a charmingly down-at-heel planetarium.

Aktobe city has its origins in a Russian military fort, built in 1869 on the left bank of the River Ilek close to the route of caravans passing between Orenburg and Kazalinsk. The name Aktobe, 'white hill', refers to a geographical feature close to the original fort: the modern city seems bereft of obvious hills of any colour. The settlement around the fort steadily grew, through the arrival of migrants from across Tsarist Russia, and the place was designated an *uyezd* capital in 1891, with the Russified name of Aktyubinsk. The development of the town was given a further impulse in 1901, with the arrival of the Tashkent to Orenburg railway. The city of Aktyubinsk was named capital of its region in 1932, and in 1999 was given back its Kazakh name of Aktobe. The modern city is an important regional transport hub. There are two quite separate centres: an 'old town' to the east, focused on the railway station, and a 'new town' further west, with shops and administrative buildings spread out along Abulkhair Khan Avenue.

GETTING THERE AND AROUND The **airport** (✆ *595037*) sits at the southern edge of the city. Air Astana offers four flights a week to Astana, on Fokker 50 turboprops, and a daily flight between Almaty and Aktobe on a Boeing 757 or Airbus. There is also one Air Astana weekly connection between Aktobe and

Frankfurt, though on a less than convenient routing, via Astana. Scat flies six times a week to Aktau, with onward connections to Baku, Mineralnye Vody, Tbilisi or Yerevan depending on the day, and four times a week to Atyrau, with onward connections to Baku. Scat also offer six flights a week to Astana and two a week to both Almaty and Moscow.

The **railway station** [285 F4] (☏ 211777) is at the heart of the old town. Aktobe lies on the route of the Orenburg–Tashkent railway, and trains stopping here include the services from Moscow to Almaty, Tashkent and Bishkek. There are one or two trains daily starting in Aktobe for Almaty, and daily services to Uralsk, Mangyshlak and Atyrau. There is a train every two days to Astana. Aktobe is also served by infrequent services between Tashkent and Ufa, Chelyabinsk and Kharkov. Long-distance taxis are to be found in the square outside the railway station.

There are two **bus stations**. The modern Ekspress bus station [295 C2] (*9zh 312th Infantry Division Av;* ☏ 550226; f 541678) sits on the edge of town, to the north of Aliya Moldagulova Avenue: heading eastwards along that thoroughfare, turn left after crossing over the railway bridge. This is a long-distance station, mostly focused on destinations in Russia, offering reasonably comfortable buses, often boasting television (a mixed blessing) and an on-board toilet. There are two departures daily to Orenburg, two to Orsk and one to Samara, and less frequent departures to Kazan, Ekaterinburg, Moscow, Krasnodar and, for those who really like long bus journeys, St Petersburg. There are also three departures weekly to Kostanai.

The Sapar bus station [295 E2] (*4 312th Infantry Division Av;* ☏ 212661) is further east along the same road. This is a battered, Soviet-era building, with a picture of a winged bus above the ticket counters. It serves various destinations within Aktobe Region of no strong touristic interest, together with some departures to closer destinations in Russia, including five departures daily to Orsk and two to Orenburg. There is also one bus every other day to Astana.

Numbers to call for local **taxis** include ☏ 005 and ☏ 550005.

✈ TOUR OPERATOR AND AIRLINE OFFICE

✈ **Otrar Travel** 67A Abulkhair Khan Av; ☏ 562559; f 550588; e akx@otrar.kz. Other office: Microdistrict 12; ☏ 950180; f 950155. General Service Agent for Air Astana.

 WHERE TO STAY

🏠 **Hotel Albion** [295 F4] (14 rooms) 13 Aiteke Bi St; ☏/f 210018, 211603; e albion_hotel@ mail.ru. Part of the Best Eastern Group, this is the smartest place to stay in town, with colour-coded rooms. The 'white luxe' rooms have a beige colour scheme; the tones in the larger & more expensive 'red luxe' rooms are darker. All have large en suites. There is a small English-style pub next to the restaurant, which offers live music & a dancefloor. If the bland exterior is indeed inspired by Britain, then the model is the kind of hotel found close to motorways. The decidedly steep rates for provincial Aktobe are pitched at the oil business market. B/fast & use of the gym & pool are included in the room rate. **$$$$$**

🏠 **Hotel Amsterdam** [295 C3] (50 rooms) 50A Gaziza Zhubanova St; ☏ 524000, 524001,

524002; e reservation@amsterdamhotel.kz; www.amsterdamhotel.kz. At the eastern end of the new town, the self-proclaimed 5-star Amsterdam offers large AC rooms, extravagant, well-maintained décor & helpful, English-speaking staff. The hotel restaurant has an international menu nudging towards French cuisine, with even snails & frogs' legs on offer. Use of the hotel's sauna & jacuzzi is free for those staying in the most expensive rooms. **$$$$**

🏠 **Hotel Asia** [295 B2] (21 rooms) 138A Eset Batyr St; ☏ 567028, 550690; e aziaaktobe@ yandex.ru. This quiet hotel, set back from Eset Batyr St in the new town, & approached by a rather bumpy track, is not a bad choice at the top of the mid-price category, with spacious, AC rooms & b/fast included in the rate. **$$$**

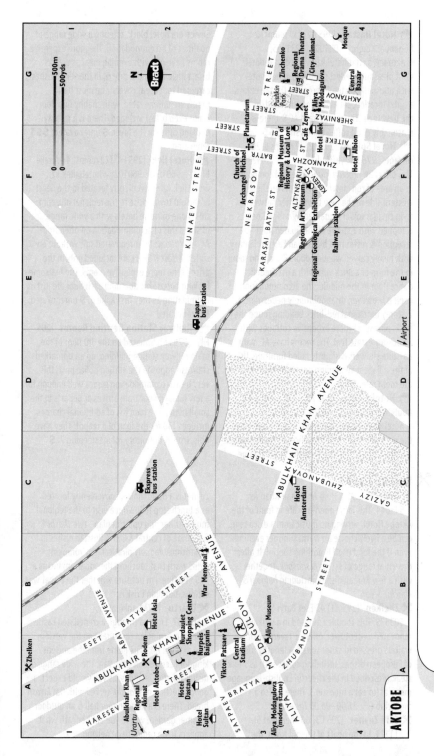

🏠 **Hotel Dastan** [295 A2] (19 rooms) 2 Bogenbai Knight; ☎ 901000; f 231255; e aktobe@dastanhotel.kz; www.dastanhotel.kz. A pleasantly redecorated mid-range hotel with unusually tasteful décor, the Dastan enjoys a quiet location, set away from the road, in the new town. The rooms have AC & there is a reasonably good coffee bar on site. **$$$**

🏠 **Hotel Sultan** [295 A2] (9 rooms & 20 cottages) 276 Bratya Zhubanovy St; ☎ 543239. This offers an *Arabian Nights*-themed compound in an area of run-down apartments on the western side of the new town. Enter between twin circular towers, guarded by winged beasts & topped with a statue of the Golden Man. The reception & restaurant block is an Eastern fantasy, with heavy carved wooden doors & a dining room in the form of a brick yurt with a psychedelic dance floor in the middle. The accommodation itself is, however, disappointingly pedestrian: a 2-storey functional red-brick building round the back, plus some more expensive cottages with a housing-estate feel. The rooms have AC, with en-suite showers & slightly faded furniture. Use of the adjacent swimming pool is not included in the room rate. **$$$**

🏠 **Hotel Aktobe** [295 A2] (250 rooms) 44 Abulkhair Khan Av; ☎ 562829; f 567772; e hotel@aktobe.kz. In a good central location in the new town, close to the offices of the regional administration, the Aktobe is the familiar large

Soviet-era hotel block, offering a wide range of qualities of accommodation. The more expensive rooms have AC, with evening meal as well as b/fast included in the rate &, in the very plushest, carpeted toilet seat covers. The most basic rooms are unrenovated, with shabby lino floors & not even b/fast included. There is a railway booking office in the foyer. **$** unrenovated; **$$$** renovated

🏠 **Hotel Ilek** [295 F4] (72 rooms) 44 Aiteke Bi St; ☎ 960101; f 960102; e hotel@ilek.kz; www.ilek.kz. Conveniently located in the heart of the old town, close to the regional museum, this is one of those hotels with a wide range of standards of accommodation on offer, from AC 'luxe' rooms to unrenovated sgls without en suites. B/fast & Wi-Fi are included only in the price of the more expensive rooms. The fearsome-looking *babushkas* guarding each floor are just as intimidating as they first appear. **$** unrenovated; **$$** renovated

🏠 **Railway Station Retiring Rooms** [295 F4] ☎ 975111. Situated on the 3rd floor of the main railway station building, up an unmarked staircase opposite the station police post, this very basic accommodation serves well enough for a few hours if your train arrives or departs in the small hours. The long list of additional charges includes T30 for the loan of a teapot. They have dbls, trpls & dormitory rooms sleeping 7. **$**

✗ WHERE TO EAT

✗ **Rodem** [295 A2] 44 Abulkhair Khan Av; ☎ 543644. This large open-air café in front of the Aktobe Hotel, serving up music from a disco tent, can be a lively choice on warm summer evenings even if the food itself is nothing special. It offers the usual range of salads & *shashlik*, together with a few Korean dishes, including *bulgogi* & *kimchi*. **$$$**

✗ **Zhelken** [295 A1] 45 Eset Batyr St; ☎ 503575. This complex, housed in a striking renovated water tower, offers a 'tavern' with waiters dressed in sailor suits & a lengthy menu of European dishes, including curios such as shark steak (described in the cheerful English-language menu as 'to eat a monster'). There is also a nightclub (🕐 21.00–06.00 Thu–Sun). **$$$**

✗ **Café Zeynet** [295 C3] 66 Sherniyaz St; ☎ 211111. In the heart of the old town, the

Zeynet is a basic choice, conveniently located as a lunch stop following a visit to the regional museum, serving up Armenian-style *shashlik* & a range of central Asian & Russian dishes in a maritime, vaguely piratical, environment. Signs warn that touching the aquarium incurs a T50,000 fine. I'm not sure whether the threat was serious, but didn't risk it. **$$**

✗ **Urartu** 139A Sankibai Av; ☎ 567707. Entered through a crenellated castle gate, this Armenian restaurant on the western side of town takes its name from the ancient kingdom centred on Lake Van. The wide range of dishes on offer includes, as you would expect, a good selection of *shashlik* served with flat *lavash* bread. There is a large indoor hall & an outdoor summer garden, where you eat beneath what appears to be camouflage netting. **$$**

WHAT TO SEE

Old town The older centre of town, north of the railway station, is relatively more low slung than the new, a district of quiet, tree-lined avenues. From the station, take the green and leafy Kereev Street, which heads off from behind a bust of one General Kereev at the far side of the taxi-filled square. On your left you come to the rather dry collection of rock and mineral samples housed in the **Regional Geological Exhibition** [295 F4] (*7 Kereev St;* \ *215966;* ⊕ *14.00–17.30 Mon–Fri; admission free*). One door further along in the same block is a similarly unexciting **Regional Art Museum** [295 F3] (*7 Kereev St;* \ *968907*). The field gun in the square at the end of the street honours the exploits of the Aktobe citizens who served in the 312th Infantry Division and 101st Brigade. The 312th Infantry Division, established in Aktobe in 1941, was disbanded following the heavy losses suffered during the defence of Moscow. Soldiers from Aktobe fought their way as far as Austria in its successor unit, the 53rd Infantry Division.

Regional Museum of History and Local Lore [295 F3] (*14 Altynsarin St;* \ *211367;* f *211368;* ⊕ *09.00–13.00 & 14.00–18.00 Wed–Mon; admission T50*) Turn right onto Altynsarin Street, and after a block-and-a-half, on your left is a pleasant, two-storey, Tsarist-era building, with four Corinthian columns and a balustraded balcony enlivening the façade. This houses the Regional Museum of History and Local Lore. The first room, natural history, features displays on two meteorite craters in the territory of Aktobe Region. The larger of these, Zhamanshin, an unpromising name which means roughly 'bad place' in Kazakh, is a crater more than 5km in diameter and some 700m deep. There is also a display on the Aidarlyash Creek, approximately 50km east of Aktobe, where an exposed geological section was recognised in 1996 by the International Union of Geological Sciences as the global stratotype section and point for the Permian system. There is a model of a hornless rhinoceros, which apparently inhabited the earth around 40 million years ago and was the largest land-dwelling mammal ever known. The first skeleton of this animal to be uncovered was unearthed in 1912 near Lake Shalkarteniz in the southeastern part of the region.

Further displays highlight the mineral wealth of the region, including the development of oil reserves from the early 1930s and the development of the chromite deposit near the village of Donskoye, now the town of Khromtau, from 1937. Much of Kazakhstan boasts an extreme continental climate, but the extremes in Aktobe Region are sharper than most, with winter temperatures dropping to –48°C, and summer ones reaching +43°C. There is a photo of the golf ball-sized hailstones which fell in 1974. The Turgai Nature Reserve, established in 1968, is illustrated with a diorama filled with stuffed waterbirds. The reserve, covering 348,000ha in the eastern part of the region, includes a network of lakes formed at the confluence of several steppe rivers. The lakes attract large populations of migratory birds in spring and autumn. Other dioramas showcase the wildlife of the desert, riverbank, semi-desert and steppe. And alongside all the stuffed animals there is a foam-stuffed armchair in the middle of the room.

The other room on the ground floor is devoted to archaeology and ethnography. Items on display include Stone Age implements, attractive necklaces from the Sarmat period and a line of stone figures of a range of ages. There are photographs of beautiful carved *kulpytases* from necropoli across the region and a model of the 14th-century Abat-Baitak Mausoleum, to the southwest of Aktobe. Ethnographic displays include the interior of a segment of yurt, jewellery, saddles, and mannequins in Kazakh costume.

The displays continue upstairs. Some of the prodigious number of museum staff may well be switching on the lights as you go to illuminate your ascent. The next room, its inscriptions in the Kazakh language only, focuses on Kazakh heroes linked with the region, such as Abulkhair Khan and Eset Batyr. The next room is about the Tsarist period, the viewpoint of the museum authorities evident from the very first exhibit in the room: an illustration of a claw reaching out to seize Kazakhstan. There are displays on the founding and history of Aktobe, and a description of the work of the pioneer educator Ibrai Altynsarin (see page 288). The displays continue into the pre-war Soviet period, with items on the Civil War, collectivisation, the Alash movement and Stalinist repression. A room devoted to World War II includes descriptions of the local Heroes of the Soviet Union, most prominently female sniper Aliya Moldagulova, whose rather unhappy-looking bust stands at the end of the room. The displays also highlight the efforts of those working behind the line in the factories of Aktobe. The other bust in the room honours a figure very different from Aliya Moldagulova: a bearded farmer named Chaganak Bersiev, whose scythe and Order of Lenin award are on display.

Next comes a room focused on the post-war Soviet period. One side of the room is devoted to the space programme, with a bust of Aktobe-born cosmonaut Viktor Patsaev, killed on the Soyuz 11 mission. Patsaev's posthumous award of Hero of the Soviet Union is on display, as is a model of a scientific research vessel named after him. The other side of the room focuses on the works of local scientific and cultural figures from the Soviet period. The last room highlights the post-independence period. There are displays highlighting the ethnic diversity of the region, and photographs of the schools, hospitals and industries of Aktobe, including a display of local biscuits. The large engraved wooden chairs on which President Nazarbaev and his wife were seated during a visit to Aktobe in 1995 are on display, as is a selection of Nazarbaev's written work.

Around the Planetarium [295 F3] Turning right out of the regional historical museum, turn right again onto Aiteke Bi Street. After two blocks turn left onto Nekrasov Street. You will soon see on your right the **Church of Archangel Michael** [295 F3], a single-storey brick-built Tsarist building, with a domeless interior covered in icons and paintings of Bible scenes. The bell tower is a separate rusty metal construction, rather resembling a military watchtower – only with bells.

Around the back of the church is a real Aktobe curiosity, a **planetarium** [295 F3] (*50A Zhankozha Batyr St;* `211322;` ⊕ *09.00–13.00 & 13.30–17.30 Mon–Fri, 11.00– 15.00 Sun; admission T80, lecture T600*). A white-walled single-storey building with a 10m dome, it was opened in 1967 and mostly caters to local school groups. The enthusiastic director is wont to waive the lecture fee for the few foreign visitors who make it here, and offer a quick tour through the Aktobe night sky for free.

The eastern side of the old town Turning left out of the regional historical museum, and left again onto Sherniyaz Street, you reach the small **Pushkin Park** [295 G3], with a few children's attractions and an open-air *shashlik* place. As you would expect, there is a bust of the Russian poet here, along with a few other pieces of statuary. A battered obelisk, losing its marble-tiled facing, topped by a five-pointed Soviet star, is a monument to those on the Bolshevik side killed during the Civil War. There is a bust too of bony-faced Soviet farmer Chaganak Bersiev.

Across the park, over Akhtanov Street, is a blue arch bearing words of welcome in Kazakh, flanked by Soviet sculptures of a husband holding a small child, crushing what appears to be a broken swastika underfoot, while his wife on the other side of the arch carries a basket brimming with grapes. The path beyond the arch leads up to a **monument to V Zinchenko** [295 G3], the first head of the Aktobe Bolshevik Council. In the gardens next to this monument is the slope-roofed entrance to a one-time nuclear fallout shelter.

To the right sits the **Aktobe Regional Drama Theatre** [295 G3] (*52 Akhtanov St; \ 210377, 221412*), named in honour of writer Takhaui Akhtanov. The square beyond houses the bulky building accommodating the city administration. A pedestrianised stretch of Koblandin Street off to the right is presided over by a bust of Hero of the Soviet Union **Aliya Moldagulova**. This is the Soviet portrayal of the young female sniper: noble, unsmiling, wearing a field cap and sporting her Hero of the Soviet Union medal. It contrasts interestingly with the image offered by post-independence portrayals of the young heroine (see page 301).

A couple of blocks to the east of the *akimat* [295 G3], on the edge of the old town, stands a heavily restored Tsarist-era **mosque** [295 G4]. It has an almost church-like exterior, with octagonal spire atop a red-brick body. The fine interior features two friezes depicting rather more oriental-looking mosques.

South of the city administration, at the southern end of Akhtanov Street, lies the **central bazaar** [295 G4] (⊕ *08.00–19.00*), entered through an arch decorated with wheatsheaves.

New town The centre of Aktobe's new town, west of the old, is strung out along Abulkhair Khan Avenue, a broad road with a line of neatly trimmed trees running down the middle.

Along Abulkhair Khan Avenue The regional *akimat* [295 A2] is housed in a large cream-coloured building set back from Abulkhair Khan Avenue. An equestrian statue of **Abulkhair Khan** [295 A2] stands in front, commemorating the leader of the Junior *Zhuz* in the early 18th century, who led successful campaigns against the Dzhungar incursions, though took an oath of allegiance to the Russian crown in 1731 in a bid to secure Russian support against the Dzhungars. Abulkhair Khan here raises his right arm aloft, palm forward, as if ordering the traffic to stop. A statue of Lenin occupied the spot in the Soviet period.

Heading southeastwards from here along Abulkhair Khan Avenue, you reach on your right a curiously counterpoised ensemble: a modern **mosque** [295 A2], with a tall octagonal brick minaret, stands immediately behind the **Nurdaulet shopping centre** [295 A2], whose exterior décor carries on the mosque's white, blue and turquoise paint scheme. In the gardens immediately south of here sits a statue of the *akyn* **Nurpeis Baiganin** [295 A2], depicted squatting, strumming his *dombra* in the midst of an evidently cheerful song. A rough contemporary of Zhambyl, Baiganin, who died in 1945, was also given many awards by the Soviet authorities for his artistic endeavour. The side walls of a number of the apartment blocks along this stretch of the road are decorated with rousing Soviet scenes.

Further along Abulkhair Khan Avenue, just before reaching the central stadium on your right, is a bust on a red marble obelisk depicting the balding but valiant head of **Viktor Patsaev** [295 B3], a native of Aktyubinsk whose rather unfortunate place in history comes as a member of the second crew to be killed during a space mission. Patsaev had been part of the back-up crew for the 1971 Soyuz 11 mission, a team which replaced the prime crew when a member of the latter was suspected of having contracted tuberculosis. Soyuz 11 made the first successful docking of the world's first space station, Salyut 1, and Patsaev and his fellow crew members remained on board for 22 days, setting new space endurance records. On return to earth however, when the recovery team reached the Soyuz 11 capsule they found that the crew had suffocated to death, a disaster traced to a leaking breathing ventilation valve. Bruises on one of Patsaev's hands suggested a desperate but futile attempt to shut off the valve. Patsaev and his colleagues were promptly named Heroes of the Soviet Union, their ashes buried in the Kremlin Wall, near those of Yuri Gagarin.

Aliya Moldagulova Avenue Immediately south of the **central stadium** [295 B3], Aliya Moldagulova Avenue crosses Abulkhair Khan Avenue. Turn right here, reaching on your right, on the side of an apartment block, the bright orange letters announcing the **Aliya Museum** [295 A3] (*47 Aliya Moldagulova Av;* ⟍ *521598;* ⊕ *10.00–13.00 & 14.00–18.00 Tue–Sun, closed last day of each month; admission T25*). The museum is devoted to the life and early death of the female sniper and Hero of the Soviet Union Aliya Moldagulova (see below).

The museum is based around a long hall, focused on a silver bust of the uniformed and frowning Aliya at the far end. Near the entrance is a painting of our heroine, together with a rather formally worded document awarding a positive assessment to the Memorial Museum of the Hero of the Soviet Union Aliya Moldagulova, opened in Aktyubinsk on 22 April 1985. The museum displays photographs and artefacts illustrating her life. There is a group photograph of a boyish-looking Aliya with other young pioneers, all holding bunches of wheat. A diorama shows Aliya leading the Russian troops across a snowy landscape in an assault on the German

ALIYA AND MANSHUK: KAZAKH HEROINES OF THE SOVIET UNION

Two young Kazakh women, killed in action during World War II and each awarded posthumously the title of Hero of the Soviet Union, became greatly popular figures of the Soviet ideological machine. Their popularity has survived the break-up of the Soviet Union and continues into post-independence Kazakhstan, its focus now changed to emphasise their Kazakh identities.

Aliya Moldagulova became one of the most successful examples of a remarkable band of some 2,000 Soviet women, trained as female snipers. The Soviet authorities found that women often made particularly successful snipers: the Ukrainian Lyudmila Pavlichenko was credited with the deaths of more than 300 German soldiers. Only around one in four of the female snipers of the Soviet Union survived the war.

Aliya was born on 15 June 1925 in the village of Bulak, in Aktobe Region. Her mother was shot dead in 1931 in the years of famine by a guard patrolling potato fields, and her father, Nurmukhambet Sarkulov, was a victim of Stalinist repression. She went to live with her uncle, Aubakir Moldagulov, and took her mother's surname, Moldagulova. Aubakir was a railwayman, and Aliya moved with him, heading to Moscow in 1935 when Aubakir was accepted into the Moscow Military Transportation Academy. This was then relocated to Leningrad. The family's apartment there was small, and Aliya ended up in a children's home. Following the outbreak of war, the academy was moved to Tashkent, but Aliya opted to remain in the Leningrad children's home. She served as a rooftop lookout during the blockade and, according to the Soviet version of her life, shared her meagre food rations with a weak girl from the home named Katya.

Seeking to become a pilot, Aliya was enrolled into the Aviation Technical School in Rybinsk in 1942, but was then switched to the Women's Sniper Training School trenches. The museum also features Aliya tapestries, her Hero of the Soviet Union certificate and a bag containing earth from her grave. There is a model of a ship bearing her name and a photograph of the Kazakh singer Roza Rimbaeva wearing a Red Army field cap while performing her hit song 'Aliya'. Across the road from the museum stands a market named the Aliya Bazaar.

A block further westwards along Aliya Moldagulova Avenue, at the corner with Bratya Zhubanovy Street, stands a modern statue of **Aliya Moldagulova** [295 A3]. This provides a fine example of how the iconography of the Soviet period has been adapted to the changing tastes and requirements of post-independence Kazakhstan. Unlike the Soviet statue of her in the old town (see page 299), Aliya is portrayed not as obedient soldier but as liberated young woman, almost a sex symbol. She is still in uniform, but her skirt stops above the knee and the field cap is gone. There is no Hero of the Soviet Union medal pinned to her chest. She is almost smiling. A frieze running behind the statue illustrates her Kazakhness, tracing the history of Kazakhstan from the khanates through the Tsarist period to the engineering projects of the Soviet one. Aliya is depicted leading her colleagues forward into battle. Then there is a scene depicting the post-independence period: a sapling is watered in front of different generations of Kazakhs and the monuments of newly independent Kazakhstan. Wedding couples come here to be photographed and to lay flowers at Aliya's feet.

Taking Aliya Moldagulova Avenue eastwards from the intersection with Abulkhair Khan Avenue, you reach on your left, just beyond the junction with Eset

near Moscow in December of that year, after having repeatedly volunteered for active duty. A good pupil, but weakened physically by the effects of the blockade, she was given the chance to stay at the school as an instructor but refused, wanting to serve on the front lines. She arrived on the northwestern front in August 1943, notching her first two 'kills' on her second day. Her eventual tally was to reach 91 German soldiers killed. In January 1944, with the Red Army now on the offensive, her unit was ordered to capture a section of railway near the station of Nasva and the nearby village of Kazachika. During the fighting she reportedly put a machine gun out of action with a hand grenade, and rallied the troops around her with her cries of 'forward for the motherland!' She died in battle on 14 January 1944.

Manshuk Mametova was from West Kazakhstan Region. A student at the Medical Institute in Almaty, she became not a sniper but a machine gunner, another position for which women were frequently put into action. Serving with the 21st Rifle Division, she died on 15 October 1943 in the fighting for the town of Nevel in Pskov Region in the present-day Russian Federation. She remained with her machine gun to allow the members of her detachment to retreat. She became the first Soviet Asian woman to receive the award of Hero of the Soviet Union. The graves of both Aliya and Manshuk lie in Pskov Region.

The stories of Aliya and Manshuk are still told with pride and reverence, but the museums devoted to their lives now offer, in post-independence Kazakhstan, a slight change of emphasis in retelling their life stories. Aliya, we are told, liked to read the poetry of Zhambyl and to sing Kazakh songs. And her cry of 'forward for the motherland!' was made, emphasises the museum guide, in the Kazakh language.

Batyr Street, a rather striking **war memorial** [295 B2]. Into a tall needle of stone is carved a figure somewhere between a Red Army soldier and a medieval knight, holding his sword aloft.

AROUND AKTOBE

AKTOBE RESERVOIR The reservoir on the Ilek River, known by the locals as the 'Aktyubinsk Sea', makes a good place to cool off in summer. To get here, take the Kandyagash road south of town. Around 9km out of town, turn left at a sign marked 'River Side'. The reservoir is 1km or so further on.

There is a pleasant hotel here, the **River Side Residence** (*8 rooms;* `987199;` **$$$$**). An orange-walled, green-roofed building right on the shore of the reservoir, it offers well-furnished air-conditioned rooms around a central restaurant, its own stretch of beach and some nicely tended gardens. If you have your own transport, this is not a bad accommodation choice in summer. The low-slung yellow-painted building next door is the **Sayahat Beach Complex** for day visitors to the reservoir (⊕ *10.00–22.00, summer only; admission adult/child T300/100*).

ESET BATYR MAUSOLEUM Continuing south along the Kandyagash road, some 27km from Aktobe you reach the village of Bestamak. Turn left onto a metalled road towards the far end of the village. You pass a sign painted with a portrait of 18th-century Kazakh military leader Eset Batyr, as the road climbs towards the mausoleum at the top of the low hill ahead. Park outside the mosque, and take a flight of concrete steps up to the mausoleum. The square-based building, with a round drum supporting a conical dome, was built in 1992. A sculpture of Eset Batyr, his right hand on his chest, is set into the façade. The heads of soldiers look out either side, as if helping to keep watch over the mausoleum.

URALSK (ORAL) *Telephone code: 7112*

The capital of West Kazakhstan Region, the city of Uralsk is one of the most historically interesting in Kazakhstan, though you do have to search hard amongst the Soviet concrete to find the remnants of this heritage. It was a centre of the Pugachev Rebellion in the 1770s, and takes pride in its status as the only city of Kazakhstan to have been visited by the Russian poet Pushkin. With some fine Tsarist architecture, it makes a good place for a short stopover.

Established by Cossacks in 1584 at the confluence of two rivers, the Ural, then called the Yaik, and the Chagan, the town of Uralsk, originally named Yaitskiy Gorodok, claims its formal year of foundation as 1613. Because of the prominent role played by the town in the Pugachev Rebellion, Empress Catherine the Great determined on the defeat of the rebellion that she would obliterate the name of Yaitskiy Gorodok from the map, and with it the memory of Pugachev. By a decree of 15 January 1775, she determined that the River Yaik would be renamed Ural, that the Yaitsk Cossack Host would henceforth be known as the Uralsk Cossack Host, and that the town would now be called Uralsk.

Under its new name, the town flourished. As it expanded northwards from its original core, smart new brick buildings appeared. It was the scene of considerable fighting during the Russian Civil War. The celebrated Red Army commander Vasily Chapaev was killed south of here, near the settlement now renamed Chapaev in his honour, while attempting to swim across the Ural River to escape White Army forces. A number of industrial enterprises, such as the Zenit weapons factory from

Leningrad, were relocated here during World War II from more vulnerable cities further to the west, further promoting the growth of the town. The discovery of a major oil and gas condensate deposit at Karachaganak near Aksai in the eastern part of the region in the late 1970s provided a further significant boost for the economic development of Uralsk and its surrounding region. Uralsk had become the administrative capital of the West Kazakhstan Region when the latter was formed in 1932. This was renamed as Uralsk Region in 1962, but reverted to its original name in 1992. While the city is officially now known by its Kazakhised name, Oral, Uralsk is still widely used.

GETTING THERE AND AROUND Uralsk's **airport** lies some 15km out of town. Air Astana flies here four times a week from both Astana and Almaty. There are two flights a week from Astana with Atyrau Airways and two more with Kokshetau Avia. Scat has a daily flight to Atyrau and on to Aktau. Some of the Scat departures also have onward connections to Baku. Transaero flies twice a week to Moscow, and there is also a weekly flight to London Gatwick on Air Astraeus, a service mainly pitched at engineers working at the Karachaganak site but which nonetheless provides a potentially useful connection for tourists wanting to make Uralsk part of their Kazakhstan itinerary.

The **railway station** (☏ 518647) sits north of the centre, at the northern end of Zhukov Street. In the square in front of the station stands an equestrian statue of General Chapaev, his sabre raised aloft, cloak billowing, left arm outstretched and a general sense of madcap action. There is a train every two days from Uralsk to Almaty, and another daily train running between Uralsk and Aktobe. Almaty to Moscow and Aktobe to Moscow trains each stop here every two days, there is a service running four times weekly between Astana and Kiev, and one a week between Kharkov and Tashkent.

The **bus station** (☏ 283109) lies east of the centre along Syrym Datov Street. The large hall within has mostly been given over to small shops. There are four departures daily to Atyrau, four to Samara, and one to Orenburg, and five a week to Aktobe. Destinations served within the region include Darinskoe, Chapaev and Aksai. Numbers to call for local **taxis** include ☏ 512323 and ☏ 211777.

TOUR OPERATORS AND AIRLINE OFFICES

✈ **Otrar Travel** 203 Dostyk Av; ☏ 515151; f 515277; e ura@otrar.kz. General Service Agent for Air Astana.

Panorama Travel Agency 165 Kurmangazy St; ☏ 505632; f 240675; e contacts@panoramatour. kz; www.panoramatour.kz. Offers tailored city tours of Uralsk as well as tours further afield in

West Kazakhstan Region, including Shalkar Lake & sites linked with the Bukei Horde. They can provide English-speaking guides.

Transavia 49 Eurasia Av; ☏/f 506100. Airline bookings, including the agent for the Transaero service to Moscow.

🏠 WHERE TO STAY

🏠 **Hotel Bayan Chagala** [304 B2] (45 rooms) 67/1 Temir Masin St; ☏ 509855; f 510459; e reservation.uralsk@chagalagroup.kz; www. chagalagroup.com. Set back from the quiet Masin St, this is a central option with reasonably, if basically, furnished AC rooms. Aimed mostly at expatriate oil workers servicing contracts linked to the Karachaganak site. **$$$$$**

🏠 **Hotel Pushkin** [304 B7] (42 rooms & 12 apts) 148B Dostyk Av; ☏ 513560; f 513566; e pushkinhotelreservation@renco.it; www. pushkinhotel.kz. This comfortable hotel, at the southern end of the town centre, & standing appropriately enough next to a statue of the Russian poet, carries the unmistakable marks of the Italian company Renco, which runs this & a

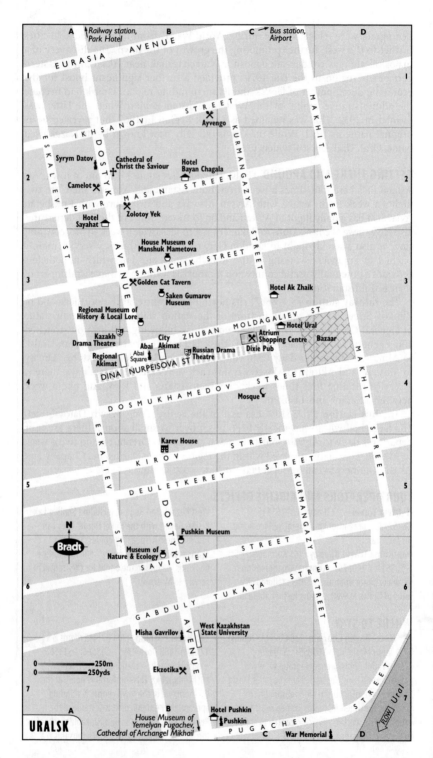

URALSK

number of other hotels across Kazakhstan: the yellow tablecloths & Italian menu in the Attila Restaurant, the gold-framed Van Gogh prints & the marble floors. The rooms are well furnished & have centrally controlled AC. In winter this is the only hotel in town with reliable heating. **$$$$$**

🏠 **Park Hotel** (46 rooms) Samal 3 Microdistrict; ↘ 530044; f 530011; e office@ parkhotel.kz; www.parkhotel.kz. In a quiet wooded spot on the bank of the Chagan River, this hotel sits north of the city in a district given over to *dachas* & to secluded residences of the local elite. The hotel comprises several cream-coloured buildings of somewhat prefabricated feel. The rooms though are well furnished, with AC & en suites. There is a capacious 2-storey restaurant block, a sauna complex & a sports room replete with climbing wall. A potentially tranquil choice, but its location is inconvenient for those without their own transport. **$$$$**

🏠 **Hotel Sayahat** [304 A2] (73 rooms) 38 Temir Masin St; ↘ 513003; f 500951. The 'Tourist' hotel is a typical Soviet-legacy concrete block. The 'luxe' rooms have been renovated, & offer springy carpet & new furniture, though no AC. Ordinary rooms are spartan. Catering is provided by a couple of small cafés. The place is conveniently located along the central Dostyk Av. **$$**

🏠 **Bus Station Hotel** (4 rooms) ↘ 283148. This place comprises a few rooms strung along a corridor above the bus station. There are dormitory beds on offer for the seriously cash-strapped, basic dbls with shared facilities, & even a reasonably furnished 'luxe' room with en suite. **$**

🏠 **Hotel Ak Zhaik** [304 C3] (12 rooms) 84 Kurmangazy St; ↘ 513021. This central, rather battered-looking, 4-storey block offers very basic dbls with shared facilities, as well as 5 rooms with en suites. The receptionist advised me that I could do better elsewhere. Unless you are on the tightest of budgets, it's sound advice. **$**

🏠 **Hotel Ural** [304 C3] (74 rooms) 80/2 Kurmangazy St; ↘ 513020, 507932. This 4-storey building has square-based columns adorning the façade & a vivid turquoise paint job. It offers basic dbls with 2 small beds & a washbasin, & shared showers & toilets. There are also 'luxe' rooms with en suite & AC. The restaurant has a large selection of cheap spirits but is sadly rather lacking in food. There is secure parking in the compound at the rear of the hotel. **$**

✕ WHERE TO EAT

✕ **Camelot** [304 A2] 195 Dostyk Av; ↘ 503901. King Arthur's castle is to be found at the base of a 5-storey block on Dostyk Av. The interior is decorated in suitable medieval style, with turreted walls around the bar, swords & furs. The food is international, but the real peculiarity of the place is a Delphic menu which gives you few clues as to what it is you are ordering. Will it be 'motley cutlets', 'passionate squaw', 'Robin-Bobin', 'small prince', 'golden balls', 'mirror of normans' or 'golden-haired poultry-maid's kindness'? **$$$$**

✕ **Zolotoy Vek** [304 B2] 44/1 Temir Masin St; ↘ 509580; e golden_100@mail.ru. This is a smartly decorated restaurant, albeit housed in an ugly modern building, with burgundy curtains & a bacchanalian mosaic on the wall. The classical theme is continued with the menu: you may, if so disposed, order a Caligula Salad. The food on offer is Eurasian, & ranges from lasagne to *beshbarmak*. There is a bar downstairs, with a cheaper menu & walls decorated in a Middle Eastern style, replete with stained-glass belly dancer. **$$$$**

✕ **Dixie Pub** [304 C4] Atrium Shopping Centre; 17 Dina Nurpeisova St; no phone. On the ground floor of a shopping centre alongside the pedestrianised Dina Nurpeisova St, the Dixie is another windowless & fairly soulless eatery, a kit pub with the atypical addition of a couple of stuffed animal heads. They serve up large portions of Western fare, including burgers, Scotch broth, pasta dishes & some good desserts. There is a bowling alley & some arcade games next door. **$$$**

✕ **Golden Cat Tavern** [304 B3] 190 Dostyk Av; ↘ 503205. This dark & somewhat airless place, its tables illuminated by candlelight, was at the time of research a meeting place of choice for the expatriate community in Uralsk. Evening drinking is accompanied by the strains of saxophone, piano & violin, the musicians watched over by a giant painted cat on the wall. The menu is a Russian-scented international mix, with the English-language version offering the intriguing 'specific cutlet'. There is a cheap set business lunch, & Shymkent beer on tap. **$$$**

✗ Ayvengo [304 B1] 46 Ikhsanov St; 507826. Housed in a modern slope-roofed building of vaguely central European ecclesiastical design, the Ayvengo's interior is a domed hall, with armour, stuffed bear & fake stone to give it a medieval feel. The menu offers a mix of Russian & European dishes, with a few specialities, such as goose stuffed with apples, available by pre-order & continuing the medieval motif. There is live music most evenings in winter. $$

✗ Café Ekzotika [304 B7] 133 Dostyk Av; 512474. A windowless eatery, the Ekzotika's décor attempts to recreate life at the bottom of the sea. The blue ceiling represents the surface of the water, & you dine amongst aquaria of fish & terrapins. The bar is decorated with wooden crabs &, ruining the theme, parrots. They do a good-value business lunch. $$

SHOPPING The central **bazaar** [304 D4] sits east of the Hotel Ural. The main entrance is on Makhit Street, which runs parallel to, and to the east of, Kurmangazy Street. There is a centrally located **supermarket** in the modern Atrium shopping centre [304 C4] (*17 Dina Nurpeisova St*) but look carefully at the prices and beware of the US$14 Viennetta.

WHAT TO SEE Most of the town's sights are found along or close to Dostyk Avenue, which runs north–south through the heart of Uralsk.

Kureni and the trail of the Pugachev Rebellion

The oldest part of town is a district known as **Kureni**, at the southern end of the town centre at the confluence of the Chagan and Ural rivers. It was here that the Cossack settlement was born. This remains a district of single-storey wooden dwellings, often with painted wooden shutters. Heading northwards through this district along Dostyk Avenue, you reach on your left, at the junction with Stremyannaya Street, the log-walled building containing the **House Museum of Yemelyan Pugachev** (*35 Dostyk Av; 264986; ⏰ 10.00–18.00 Wed–Sun; admission adult/child T100/50*). The house, one of the oldest in Uralsk, was owned by Pyotr Kuznetsov, whose daughter Ustinya became Pugachev's second wife (see box, opposite).

One room of this small museum chronicles the history of the Pugachev Rebellion. The basic weapons of Pugachev's forces, including knives, forks and clubs, are contrasted with the finer sabres, rifles and muskets of those in the Tsarist ranks. A decree of Pugachev is displayed, promising his supporters land, fishing rights and provisions. There is a stamp and coins of 'Tsar Peter III', and a curious portrait of Pugachev, painted over one of Catherine II, whose eyes are eerily still discernible. The throne Pugachev used at Yaitskiy Gorodok is on display, as is a portrait of the celebrated general, Alexander Suvorov, looking very pleased with himself, taking the captured Pugachev off to meet his fate in a small cage. A model of this highly restrictive cage is also on show. Another room looks at the life of the Yaitsk Cossacks, with photographs of net fishing across the river and of the fish bazaar. A third room, focused on a large oven, is set out as a Cossack kitchen, rich in wooden utensils. There is a living room/bedroom, with icon in the corner and a female Cossack dress and priest's robes on display. And there is a display about the visit to Uralsk of Pushkin in 1833, gathering material for his studies on the Pugachev Rebellion.

Continuing northwards along Dostyk Avenue, you soon reach on your right the pale green-walled **Cathedral of Archangel Mikhail**, completed in 1751 and one of the oldest buildings in Uralsk still standing. The main body of the church is square in plan, topped by onion domes, with a large square-based bell tower above the main entrance. The cathedral, part of the fortress area of Yaitskiy Gorodok, was at the centre of the siege during the Pugachev Rebellion. The original, more elaborate, bell tower was destroyed during the course of the siege. It was replaced initially by a wooden bell tower and then, in 1861, by the present one. The cathedral has a rich iconostasis and a largely female congregation. It served as a museum during Soviet times, and was returned to the Church in 1989.

Continue north along Dostyk Avenue, passing a road sign which still tells you that the thoroughfare is named in honour of Lenin. At the corner with Pugachev Street stands a modern statue of **Pushkin** [304 C7], looking rather dapper in a

THE PUGACHEV REBELLION

Yemelyan Pugachev, who led a major insurrection against the rule of Catherine II, was a Don Cossack, and was required to serve in the Russian army. He served in the Seven Years War and first Russo–Turkish War, but deserted during a leave of absence. He thereafter led an itinerant life, and came to formulate thoughts of rebellion against the depredations of Tsarist rule. In 1773, he proclaimed himself Tsar Peter III, who had been assassinated on Catherine's orders in 1762, exploiting a widely held peasant belief that Peter had not actually been killed. He organised revolt among the Yaitsk Cossacks, already divided into 'loyalist' and 'rebellious' factions and disturbed by a plan to organise them into Cossack regiments.

In September 1773, with a group of 300 Cossacks, he attempted to take Yaitskiy Gorodok, but was unable to secure the bridge across the River Chagan, and moved off in favour of an attack on Orenburg. The insurrection grew, Pugachev winning further recruits with his promises of liberty, land and provisions, and with threats of punishment to those who refused to support him. His supporters included many Tatars and Bashkirs as well as Cossacks, and his forces came to number more than 10,000, their organisation mimicking the Tsarist one in some respects. A detachment of Pugachev's forces moved into Yaitskiy Gorodok in December 1773, and Pugachev himself came to the town in January 1774, at one stage taking over the siege of the town's fortress, which was holding out obstinately. Its defenders included the father of the future celebrated Russian fable writer Ivan Krylov. Pugachev found time to marry a local girl, a Cossack named Ustinya Kuznetzova, although he had already married Sofia Nedyuzheva back in 1758. In April 1774, Tsarist forces under General Mansurov entered Yaitskiy Gorodok, coming to the rescue of the beleaguered fortress. Pro-Tsarist Cossacks rounded up local supporters of Pugachev, including the unfortunate Ustinya, and brought them to the fortress.

Elsewhere, Pugachev's rebellion had grown rapidly, helped by Catherine's initial failure to take the threat sufficiently seriously, and at its peak embraced much of the region between the Volga and the Urals, including the city of Kazan. But the comprehensive defeat of Pugachev's forces in August 1774 at Tsaritsyn, near Volgograd, proved a turning point, and when Pugachev made his way back to the Yaitsk Cossack region he was betrayed by a group of Cossacks and handed over to the authorities on 14 September 1774. Pugachev was placed in a small metal cage and sent to Moscow where, on 10 January 1775, in front of a large crowd, he was beheaded and quartered.

The Pugachev Rebellion seems to have encouraged Catherine towards greater conservatism. Her response was to introduce measures increasing central government control over the full territory of the empire and entrenching serfdom even more firmly.

long coat. The Pushkin Hotel is immediately beyond. Uralsk's connection with the great Russian poet rests on a short trip made by Pushkin to the town in September 1833, while carrying out his research into the Pugachev Rebellion. The results of this research would be Pushkin's *History of the Pugachev Rebellion* as well as the historical novel *The Captain's Daughter*, published in 1836. In the novel Pugachev is one of the main characters, first encountered as the mysterious guide who leads our hero, Pyotr Grinov, to the safety of an inn during a ferocious blizzard, for which act Pyotr rewards him with his hareskin jacket. Pushkin arrived in Uralsk on 21 September, together with his friend, the lexicographer Vladimir Dal. They were warmly greeted by the *ataman* of the Cossack Host, given accounts of the rebellion and visited the Kuznetsov house and the fortress.

Turning right onto Pugachev Street at this intersection, you soon encounter, on your right, a striking **war memorial** [304 D7], close to the bank of the River Ural. Two tall white-painted concrete panels stretch skywards. A frieze depicts scenes of Red Army valour and of the devastation wrought by German bombers. The faces of local Heroes of the Soviet Union, among them female machine gunner Manshuk Mametova, are depicted in relief. And there is a dauntingly long list of the names of those killed, organised by district. Behind the main monument, a simple memorial, a Red Army helmet on a rock, commemorates the 28 local people killed in the Afghanistan conflict in the 1980s.

From the university to the *akimat* Continuing further north along Dostyk Avenue from the Hotel Pushkin, you come to the main building of the **West Kazakhstan State University** [304 B6] on your right, a pastel green-painted block with protruding wings, its frontage embellished by white Corinthian half-columns. It was built in 1939 on the site of the Kazan Cathedral. Across the road is a statue of a small boy in uniform, standing next to his dying horse: it honours **Misha Gavrilov** [304 B6], a young hero of the Civil War. The impressive red-brick building with the green vaulted roof behind this is now a school. It was built in the 1870s as a private house by a wealthy merchant family named Vanyshin.

A block further north, at the corner of Dostyk Avenue and Savichev Street, is the small **Museum of Nature and Ecology** [304 B6] (*151/2 Dostyk Av;* \ *506709;* ◷ *10.00–18.00 Tue–Sun; admission adult/child T100/50*). Easily spotted by the two large roundels depicting deer on the outside walls, the museum is a branch of the West Kazakhstan History and Local Lore Museum. The first room displays mammoth tusks and the bones of other extinct species displayed against a backdrop of idealised cave paintings. There are displays too about the mineral wealth of West Kazakhstan, and of scientific works about the region. Next comes a corridor, with cases full of butterflies and assorted stuffed animals. There is a steppe diorama, featuring a pair of saiga, a marmot, jackal and steppe eagle. The final room has a woodland diorama, with a large stuffed elk amongst the trees. There is a display about the River Ural, with large sturgeon resting on panels of glass in a rather fishmonger's slab fashion. A Shalkar Lake display features heron and flamingo as well as a family of wild boar, and a display highlighting the rare species inscribed in Kazakhstan's Red Book incorporates stuffed examples of each.

This stretch of Dostyk Avenue features many fine one- and two-storey Tsarist buildings, several of them embellished with plaques recording once momentous meetings and events, such as brief stays by the Civil War commander General Frunze. Opposite the Nature Museum, the two-storey green-walled Italianate building, largely given over to a military hospital, was the Ataman House in which Pushkin stayed during his visit to Uralsk in 1833. It was the residence of Ataman

Pokatilov, who welcomed Pushkin to the town. A small part of the building now houses a **Pushkin Museum** [304 B6] (*168 Dostyk Av;* ✆ *544906;* ⏲ *10.00–18.00 Tue–Sun; admission T100*). The museum was opened during the 2006 visit to the city of President Putin of Russia. It comprises one room, smartly laid out with furniture contemporary to Pushkin's visit. There are photographs of the various places in the town visited by the Russian poet, and on a writing desk a copy of a letter written by Pushkin to his wife, Natalya Nikolaevna, describing the warm reception he had received from the local *ataman*, which had included two dinners incorporating fresh caviare. There are descriptions of other Russian literary figures to have visited Uralsk, many of whom also stayed in the Ataman House, amongst them Leo Tolstoy and the poet Vasily Zhukovsky. Also covered are the Kazakh writers, including Abai and Shakarim, who translated Pushkin's poetry into the Kazakh language.

Three blocks to the north, at the intersection of Dostyk Avenue and Kirov Street, stands a particularly grand red-brick Tsarist building, the **Karev House** [304 B5]. With three storeys, this stood proudly above the other buildings of the town on its construction in 1901. One popular local tale relating to this building is based around the rivalry between two prominent merchants, Karev and Ovchinik. The latter had built his house across the road to two-and-a-half storeys, to stand out amongst the buildings of the town. Karev therefore resolved to build his house to three stories, which would also have the effect of cutting out Ovchinik's sun. But as the third storey was nearing completion, Karev, examining progress at the site, fell from the scaffolding to his death. The building now houses the regional philharmonia and a library.

Two blocks further north, take a detour by turning right onto Dosmukhamedov Street. After four blocks, you reach on your right a fine Tsarist-era **mosque** [304 C4]. Built in 1897, this features an elegant brick minaret with arched windows up its sides, which rises up from a hexagonal entrance hall in front of the mosque proper.

Back on Dostyk Avenue, you reach, one block north of the intersection with Dosmukhamedov Street, the central **Abai Square** [304 B4]. The western side is dominated by the **regional** *akimat* building [304 B4], a fine Tsarist structure dating from 1896. The two wings of the building taper away from the main central block, which is embellished by two tall Corinthian columns rising up either side of the entrance. The park opposite features a serious modern statue of the poet **Abai** [304 B4], behind which stand the offices of the **city** *akimat* [304 B4], a dowdy block made uglier by its proximity to that of the regional *akimat*. There is a large television screen in one corner of the square, behind which stands the curved façade of the modern building housing the **Kazakh Drama Theatre** [304 A4] (✆ *507803*), built with financial support from the operators of the Karachaganak oil and gas condensate field.

The pedestrianised Dina Nurpeisova Street, still known by most locals by its former name of Teatralnaya, runs eastwards from Dostyk Avenue past the offices of the city administration. It is a popular place for evening strolling and people-watching. On the left-hand side of this pedestrian street, a little beyond the city *akimat* building, is another pleasant building of classical design, housing the **Russian Drama Theatre** [304 B4] named after A N Ostrovsky (*17 Dina Nurpeisova St;* ✆ *510871*). The theatre dates from 1859, but has occupied various buildings; its much-reconstructed current home substantially dates from 1940. White-painted Corinthian columns offset its lilac walls.

West Kazakhstan Regional Museum of History and Local Lore [304 B3]
(*184 Dostyk Av;* ✆ *506528;* ⏲ *10.00–18.00 Mon–Sat; admission adult/child T100/50*)

Opposite the Kazakh Drama Theatre on Dostyk Avenue stands a detached and elegant two-storey Tsarist-era building, topped with little octagonal minarets which give the building an Eastern feel. Built in 1879 to house a Russian–Kazakh school it now houses the West Kazakhstan Regional Museum of History and Local Lore. The displays commence with archaeology, including Stone Age implements found near Lake Shalkar and some ceramic and bronze items unearthed from the Iron Age burial mounds at Kyrkoba, some 80km east of Uralsk. A beautiful though damaged silver *rhyton*, dating from the 5th century BC and probably an import from the territory of present-day Iran, was found near the village of Dolinnoe, east of Uralsk. This curved, horn-shaped object has some intriguing decoration, including a calf's head at the tip. There is also a display of *balbals*.

The next hall covers later history, with displays on the Golden Horde and Nogai Horde, a map of the Silk Road routes and ceramic tiles unearthed from a medieval settlement close to present-day Uralsk. A display on the Kazakh khanates includes a painting of the 'crowning' of a khan by raising him aloft three times on a white felt rug. The arrival of the Cossacks is depicted by a display of household items and description of the establishment of Yaitskiy Gorodok. There is a display about Pushkin's visit to the town, as well as those of other writers, including Tolstoy. There are some interesting photographs of old Uralsk. The next room focuses on Kazakh leaders of the 18th century, including Ablai Khan and Abulkhair Khan. There is a rather violent wall painting of the Battle of Anrakay, which shows Abulkhair Khan leading the Kazakhs to victory against the Dzhungars, and a mock-up of Abulkhair Khan's golden sword. Displayed in the centre of the room is a copy of the khan's jewelled sceptre.

Next comes a room focused on the history of the Bukei Horde (see box opposite). Items on display include a copy of one of the sumptuous dresses of Fatima, wife of Zhangir Khan, and photographs of the buildings linked with the Bukei Horde still to be seen in the village of Orda. A mural depicts Zhangir Khan and Fatima, the latter wearing an elaborate embroidered costume, being shown the progress in the construction of the Orda Mosque by its architect.

The displays continue upstairs. A room focused on the early part of the 20th century and on World War II is centred on a machine gun. Then comes a room dedicated to local cultural figures, including writers and actresses, and a room devoted to musicians linked with the region, including violinist Marat Bisengaliev, who founded the West Kazakhstan Philharmonic Orchestra in 2003. The last room, covering post-independence Kazakhstan, includes photographs of President Nazarbaev visiting the region, and the white plastic helmet worn by the president during a visit to the Karachaganak field, which Nazarbaev has signed and dated.

Around the Cathedral of Christ the Saviour Continuing northwards along Dostyk Avenue, turn right two blocks north of the Regional Museum of History and Local Lore onto Saraichik Street. You reach on your left after a further two blocks an attractive single-storey brick bungalow with yellow-painted walls standing behind a metal fence. This is the **House Museum of Manshuk Mametova** [304 B3] (*51 Saraichik St;* ☎ *504693;* ⊕ *10.00–18.00 Tue–Sun; admission T100*). Through photographs and her family's personal belongings, the museum chronicles the life of machine gunner Manshuk Mametova, the first Soviet Asian woman to receive the award of Hero of the Soviet Union (see page 300).

Manshuk, who was born in Orda in the westernmost part of the region, was adopted by the childless Ahmet Mametov and his wife Amina. The Mametov family lived in this house from 1932 until 1934, before moving to Almaty where Ahmet, a doctor, fell victim to Stalinist repression and was shot in 1938. It is striking that Kazakhstan's twin revered female Heroes of the Soviet Union, Manshuk Mametova and Aliya Moldagulova, both suffered so harshly in childhood from the Soviet regime. Manshuk was studying in the medical institute in Almaty at the outbreak of war. She joined the 100th Kazakh Brigade and served as a radio operator and then nurse before becoming a machine gunner, dying valiantly in battle in Pskov Region on 15 October 1943. The museum displays a touching selection of Manshuk's personal possessions, a gift to the museum from her mother Amina. They include Manshuk's red pioneer scarf, an embroidery of the Kremlin and a children's edition of Pushkin. The first room in the museum, which focuses on Manshuk's childhood, contains a sculpture of a smiling, skittish future war hero, holding a flower. The next room has displays on the war heroes of Western Kazakhstan Region. A third is laid out as it might have looked when the family lived there in the 1930s: Manshuk's battered globe stands on a side table next to an iron bed.

Behind the house is a modern brick building, put up in the early 1990s, which contains a diorama showing Manshuk's last battle, that for the town of Nevel in October 1943, with the brave and resolute Manshuk standing firm at her machine gun while German tanks and troops advance towards her. The museum guide will at this point turn on a soundtrack of bullets flying and shells exploding, which then

THE BUKEI HORDE

Also sometimes known as the Inner Horde, the Bukei Horde has its origins in the weakened state of the Kazakhs of the Junior *Zhuz* at the end of the 18th century, riven by internal feuding and facing an increasingly assertive imperial Russia. Bukei, the younger son of Khan Nurali of the Junior *Zhuz*, requested the permission of Tsar Pavel I to occupy the lands between the Urals and the Volga. The Tsar responded with a decree of 1801 establishing the Bukei Horde. In 1812, Tsar Alexander I elevated Bukei to the rank of khan.

The most renowned of the leaders of the Bukei Horde was Zhangir Khan, who took on the role in 1824. He was well educated and westward-looking. When in 1825 the vaccination of children against smallpox commenced in the territory of the Horde, Zhangir had one of his sons vaccinated first to reassure his nervous people about the safety of the procedure. Realising that the fate of the Horde was linked to closer interaction with Russia, he opened a Russian–Kazakh School in 1841. Zhangir Khan had four wives, of whom his favourite was Fatima, an accomplished linguist and pianist, who bore him seven children. While the Bukei Horde was part of the Russian Empire and subservient to it, Zhangir Khan had considerable leeway in the administration of his own domains, including as regards revenue raising. The unsuccessful rebellion of Makhambet Utemisuly and Isatay Taymanuly in 1836–37 was directed against the excesses of Zhangir Khan as well as his close alliance with the Russians. Zhangir Khan died in 1845, at the age of 44. With his death the position of khan was abolished.

The buildings associated with Zhangir Khan's rule, including a striking mosque of a decidedly European style with columned façades, around the village of Orda in the far west of the region, make for an interesting visit but are difficult to reach, involving a long day's drive from Uralsk just to get there. Panorama Travel Agency (see page 303) can set up a three-day trip, between May and September only.

switches to patriotic music. The birch trees in the grounds of the building were brought from Nevel.

From the Manshuk Mametova Museum, return towards Dostyk Avenue, turning left at the first intersection onto Kasim Amanzholov Street. The single-storey grey-painted building on your left houses the **Museum of Saken Gumarov** [304 B3] (*120 Kasim Amanzholov St;* ⊕ *Mon–Fri 10.00–18.00; admission T100 for foreign citizens*). Its two rooms showcase the work of a local artist who died in 1995. Your guide may be Saken Gumarov's widow, Gulsara. Photographs record a bearded figure with heavy glasses and unruly hair, looking every inch the artist. Gulsara tells of a difficult life, with recognition coming very late in Saken's career, via a positive reception in the Ukraine. She recounts proudly Saken's many talents: actor and television director as well as painter, accomplished musician and pretty good dancer. She describes his paintings as 'post avant garde': they feature almost childlike drawings within irregularly shaped coloured blocks. *Seven States of Saken Gumarov* shows the artist in various poses: squatting, dancing, walking. *I Don't Want to Subdue* centres on a painted cosmonaut: Gulsara explains that the work was inspired by the tearful cries of their small son insisting that he did not wish to grow up to be a cosmonaut, 'I don't want to subdue the cosmos!' *When Gulsara was a Bird* depicts my museum guide as a feathered creature. A glass cabinet contains a collection of Saken's belongings, from a Kazakh cloak to a white Pierre Cardin shirt.

Back on Dostyk Avenue, two blocks north of the intersection with Saraichik Street sits the exuberant **Cathedral of Christ the Saviour** [304 A2]. This Russian Orthodox church has an elegant brick design, with an octagonal tower topped by a spire on which is perched a golden onion dome, and a smaller octagonal bell tower standing in front of it. The years '1591' and '1891' are carved on panels either side of the steps leading up to the church. The significance of these dates lies in the fact that the decision to build the cathedral was taken at a convention of delegates from Cossack *stanitsas* in 1886, when they agreed that its construction would provide a fine celebration of the 300th anniversary of the Cossack Host, due in 1891. But revenue raising took longer than anticipated, and the cathedral was only completed in 1907.

In the small park across from the church is an equestrian statue of **Syrym Datov** [304 A2], who led a Kazakh rebellion in the late 18th century against Tsarist Russian domination and those Kazakhs perceived to be too willing to accept Russian control. Esim Nuraliev, a grandson of Abulkhair Khan, was one of those killed by Datov's rebels. Syrym Datov is here portrayed holding out his right hand as if indicating to the invisible supporters riding behind him to slow down as they approach the busy road. The concrete bulk of the West Kazakhstan Regional *Maslikhat* stands behind the statue.

The buildings are more modern and architecturally less interesting north of here, though there are a couple of fine Soviet mosaics to be found on building walls a couple of blocks north of the Cathedral of Christ the Saviour, on the right-hand side of the road. Their subject is a homage to the Soviet construction industry: all cranes, concrete mixers and surveying equipment. The north end of Dostyk Avenue hosts a concrete square with a golden statue of **Manshuk Mametova**, holding a string of machine-gun bullets.

AROUND URALSK

DARINSKOE There is an interesting literary excursion to be made from Uralsk to the village of Darinskoe, 32km to the northeast. The attraction here is the **Mikhail Sholokhov Museum** (⊕ *10.00–18.00 Tue–Sun*). Sholokhov was a Soviet novelist, born in 1905 in the Veshenskaya *stanitsa*, heartland of the Don Cossacks, although he was not himself a Cossack. His great work, started late in 1925 and completed some 14 years later, was *The Quiet Don*, an epic novel about the lives of the Don Cossacks from around 1912 to 1920. Its main hero, Gregor Melekhov, fights on the counter-revolutionary side in the Civil War, and the novel is strikingly objective. Fortunately for Sholokhov, Stalin liked the novel, which is available in English translation in two parts: *And Quiet Flows the Don* and *The Don Flows Home to the Sea*.

Sholokhov's later literary output never approached the standard of his masterpiece, and he became a figure of the Soviet establishment. He accompanied Khrushchev on a trip to the United States in 1959 and became a member of the Central Committee of the Communist Party in 1961. He was awarded the Nobel Prize in Literature in 1965. The award rekindled old allegations that Sholokhov had not authored *The Quiet Don*, the case against him involving a combination of his youth when the epic was started, the relative weakness of the rest of his output, and his pro-regime views. Solzhenitsyn was among those to query his authorship. The Don Cossack writer Fyodor Kryukov, who had died in 1920, was identified by Sholokhov's critics as a more likely author of the work. But scientific analyses of the text, comparing this with Sholokhov's and Kryukov's confirmed outputs, have strongly supported the conclusion that Sholokhov is indeed the true author.

Sholokhov's family was evacuated here in 1942, living in Darinskoe for a little more than a year. But he returned frequently over the next 30 years for hunting trips, once commenting that he had two homelands, the quiet Don and the grey Ural. He felt himself a Cossack in the first, a Kazakh in the second. The museum was opened in 1979, in the house in which he and his family had lived. This is a modest single-storey dwelling, dwarfed by the two-storey museum extension. The family house includes many belongings linked with Sholokhov. A comfortable living room features a painting of a uniformed Sholokhov (he served as a war correspondent) surrounded by his loving family. His study centres on the desk on which Sholokhov was working on his new novel, *They Fought for the Fatherland*, a propagandist work which he never completed. His hunting rifle hangs on the wall. The next room focuses on Sholokhov's post-war hunting trips to the area. His tent and camping chair are displayed, and there are photographs of the writer showing off his vanquished ducks.

The ground floor of the adjoining museum building contains two halls of paintings, depicting local traditions such as Nauryz celebrations and a hard-fought game of *kokpar*, historical events such as the Pugachev Rebellion and Pushkin's visit in 1833, and local people. A portrait of the Logashkin family, a local farming family, is rather poignant. Grandad, his medals displayed on his chest, is seated in the centre, with younger members of his family around him. One wears a uniform, another a football shirt. None looks particularly happy. An intriguing painting in the entrance hall depicts two cattle pulling a cart on which lies an enormous beluga: the Ural River was known for its big fish, apparently.

Upstairs are a few unremarkable rooms devoted to local studies: a nature room populated by stuffed animals, an archaeology room with ceramics and knives on display, as well as some *balbals*, and an ethnography room which focuses on the range of nationalities living in the area, with costumes and household items on display from different ethnic groups. The final room, devoted to the post-independence period, includes photographs of President Nazarbaev's visit to the museum in 2005, marking the 100th anniversary of Sholokhov's birth. The armchair in which the president sat is on display. There are photographs too of Sholokhov visiting the region in later life, white haired and smiling. A copy of *The Quiet Don* presented by Sholokhov to the people of Darinskoe is also exhibited.

Not far from Darinskoe is a holiday base named **Mechta**, which sits between the oxbow Lake Tyoploe and the Ural River itself. There is accommodation here, as well as a restaurant and a range of sporting facilities, though the main attraction is the opportunity to take a boat trip on the Ural River. The Panorama Travel Agency (see page 303) can organise this. From Darinskoe, taking the road towards Uralsk, turn left after 6km, signposted for 'Mechta'. The base is another 4km on.

LAKE SHALKAR Some 75km south of Uralsk, this salty, egg-shaped lake makes for a pleasant day trip in good weather. Around 18km long by 14km wide, the lake, according to some scientists, may be a relict of an ancient sea. It is an important site for migratory birds. There are sandy beaches on the southern shore, close to the village of Saryumir.

CHAPAEV Chapaev is an agriculturally minded district capital some 125km south of Uralsk, close to the Ural River. It is of historical interest as the place of death of Vasily Chapaev, the Red Army general of the Civil War around whom a considerable cult developed in the Soviet period.

Chapaev, already a much-decorated NCO in World War I, joined the Bolshevik Party in autumn 1917, becoming the commander of the 2nd Nikolaev Division and later heading the 25th Rifle Division, which would be known as the Chapaev Division after his death. His fame was fuelled by the novel *Chapaev* by Dimitry Furmanov, who served with the general as political commissar. The novel contrasts the dedicated party loyalist Klichkov, modelled on Furmanov himself and serving, like him, as political commissar, with the brave, inspirational, but politically immature General Chapaev. A 1934 film further stoked the legend surrounding Chapaev, who also features in a huge number of Soviet jokes. These typically rely on the contrasting characters of Chapaev and Commissar Furmanov, and often include Chapaev's aide-de-camp Petka, and a female machine gunner, Anka.

Furmanov's novel describes the surprise attack on 5 September 1919 by Cossacks supporting the White forces on the headquarters of the 25th Rifle Division, which were then at the *stanitsa* of Lbishchensk. Chapaev's political commissar, Baturin (Klichkov/Furmanov having earlier being recalled to the centre, against his will), was killed, and Chapaev himself was wounded. He was helped by Petka down the steep riverbank and into the Ural. Petka stayed behind to fight off the Cossacks, eventually succumbing to them, while Chapaev attempted to swim across the river, which was being strafed by fire from the Cossack machine guns. Nearing the far bank, Chapaev was struck in the head by a bullet, and disappeared below the waters. His body was never found. Lbishchensk was renamed Chapaev in 1939, in honour of the general.

What to see Chapaev lies a kilometre or so to the east of the main road running between Uralsk and Atyrau, and makes a good place to break the journey between these two regional capitals. All the places of interest lie along Kunaev Street. In the centre of the settlement stands a large and striking **statue of Chapaev**, an angular composition which depicts the general somewhere between defiance and anguish, his legs buckling beneath him while he stretches his spindly fingers outwards towards an invisible source of support, or perhaps he is gesturing towards the enemy, or the future. Just across from here, on the corner of Abai and Kunaev streets, is a single-storey Tsarist-era **mosque**, a simple brick building, with no minaret.

A short distance to the north, along Kunaev Street, stands the two-storey Tsarist building which served during that late summer of 1919 as Chapaev's divisional headquarters. An ugly concrete extension has been tacked onto it, the whole building serving during the Soviet period as the **Chapaev Memorial Museum**. At the time of research it was closed for refurbishment, a process which is likely to involve a watering down of the museum's focus on Chapaev and on the history of the 25th Rifle Division, with more coverage on the history and ethnography of the local district, which has now been renamed Ak Zhaik, though its capital continues to bear the name of Chapaev. Museum staff promise, however, that the remodelling will not touch the rooms in the old divisional headquarters building itself, which had been reconstructed to give a sense of what the building must have looked like in 1919, including Chapaev's and Baturin's offices and, on the ground floor, a room for orderlies and duty officers, with patriotic Red Army slogans written across the large heater in the corner. Also slated to be retained is the Soviet-era diorama of Chapaev's last battle, depicting a predictably valiant general urging his troops to stay firm against the onslaught of Cossack cavalry. The red-capped Petka stands admiringly by his side. There is a bust of Chapaev outside the museum.

Kunaev Street ends at a tree-covered park, where a path fringed by plaques honouring the heroes of war ends at a tall metal **obelisk** built to resemble a bayonet. An extinguished eternal flame stands in front of it. Behind it is a wall which once recorded that here was the **place of death of General Chapaev**, but the Soviet-era inscription has now gone, replaced by a patriotic quotation from Kazakh writer Zhuban Moldagaliev, a further indication of a desire to downplay the cult of General Chapaev in post-independence Kazakhstan. Behind the wall, through a gate, is the steep bank down which Chapaev is said to have clambered towards his death. But instead of the mighty Ural below it, a change in the course of the river means that the visitor today is greeted only by a rather uninspiring side channel.

AKSAI *(Telephone code: 71133)* Some 150km east of Uralsk, the town of Aksai has little to detain the tourist, though it plays a vital role in the economic life of the region and of Kazakhstan, as well as housing a large expatriate community. Its importance is based around the presence of one of the world's largest gas condensate fields, Karachaganak, some 25km beyond the town. The origins of Aksai lie in Novogeorgievsk, an agricultural settlement established by Ukrainian immigrants in the early 20th century. With the completion in 1936 of the railway link between Uralsk and Sol-Iletsk, in present-day Russia, the settlement developed around its railway station, which bore the name Kazakhstan (and, a little confusingly, still does). In 1963 the village of Kazakhstan was made the capital of the Burlin District. It earned town status, and a further name change to Aksai, in 1967.

Aksai would have remained a quiet district capital, its economy based around wheat production and on its railway station, were it not for the discovery in 1979 of the Karachaganak field. Production began in the 1980s, under Karachaganakgazprom, which was focused on the export of gas and condensate eastwards to the gas-processing plant at Orenburg in present-day Russia. The town of Aksai developed rapidly, with new microdistricts dominated by large apartment blocks constructed of prefabricated panels emerging to the east of the lower-slung old town around the railway station. Microdistricts 4 and 5 were constructed by teams from Czechoslovakia, Microdistrict 10 by an East German team. There are still many echoes in the town of its central European builders: the main shopping centre in Aksai, for example, is named Trnava, after the city in Slovakia from which many of the construction engineers came. The main camp accommodating expatriates working at Karachaganak, situated on the western side of the town, is named the Czech Camp and is still run by a company from that country.

Following independence, and protracted negotiations, a new phase of development of Karachaganak was initiated with the conclusion of a 40-year Production Sharing Agreement, with the UK's BG Group and Italy's Eni as joint operators, and a consortium which also includes Chevron and Lukoil. The focus of the redevelopment of the field has been much more on the westward export of oil and condensate, through a new pipeline to Atyrau and thence westwards, as well as the introduction of new technologies, such as the high-pressure reinjection of sour gas. The large number of British and Italian expatriates working in Aksai have brought pubs and pizzerias, as well as an unexpectedly wide range of accommodation options.

Where to stay
Book ahead, as many of the available hotel rooms in Aksai are taken by oil companies on long-term contracts.

🏠 **Aksai Residence** (128 rooms) Building 27, Microdistrict 10; ☎ 30124, 32900; e aksairesidencemanager@renco.it. Better known in town as the 'Renco Hotel', after its Italian owners, this is a 9-storey cream-coloured building not far from the Trnava shopping centre. It is strongly focused on long-term oil company residents, but if you can get a room here you will find it well furnished, with Renco's signature Van Gogh prints on the walls & central AC. Many rooms have a kitchenette, there is a bar decked out with posters of female film stars, & a restaurant above, serving Italian food. **$$$$**

🏠 **Hotel Marko Polo** (35 rooms) Building 23, Microdistrict 2; ☎ 33975, 33974; f 32132; e marko-polokz@mail.ru. This Italian-run hotel is probably the pick of the Aksai crop: a 2-storey building decorated in soothing shades of yellow & terracotta, rooms with AC, en suites & satellite TV, & a pizzeria boasting its own pizza oven. **$$$$**

🏠 **Chagala Aksai** (125 rooms) 2/2 Druzhba Narodov St; ☎ 91170, 22459; f 22458; e reservation.aksai@chagalagroup.kz; www. chagalagroup.com. Somewhat less glamorous than the other Chagala properties, these new apartments are nonetheless clean, comfortable & well equipped for both long- & short-stay visitors. The staff are polite & helpful. **$$$**

🏠 **Hotel Bestau** (87 rooms) 7 Druzhba Narodov St; ☎ 34720, 34713; f 34717. Another slightly cheaper option, the Bestau is named after the birthplace of the wife of the 1st owner of the hotel. It nestles behind the Bestau Nightclub, which is both under separate management & shut. Its rooms, which offer both AC & en suites, are laid out on 2 floors. **$$$**

Where to eat
✕ **Arman** 2A Nauryz Boulevard; ☎ 34933. This restaurant is housed in a large bright blue-coloured complex, with plastic palm trees outside & a night club next door (⊕ Fri/Sat; admission men/women T500/300 Fri, T1,000/700 Sat). The restaurant is decorated in exaggerated opulence, with golden curtains & luxuriant chandeliers. The cuisine is European, with the English-language menu trying its best to put diners off with such descriptions as 'fungus soup' & 'motley puree from the pork'. $$$

✕ **Western Bar** 6/6A Druzhba Narodov St; ☎ 30603. This capacious building offers a look somewhere between the Wild West & rural England, with wooden beams adorning the exterior & a wagon on the roof. Wooden tables & chairs fill 2 large floors inside, there is a courtyard for outside summer dining, & even a mini golf course themed around the great buildings of the world: Taj Mahal, Big Ben & Baiterek Tower. The international menu features some Kazakh dishes & good shashlik. It is a popular place with Aksai expatriates. $$$

What to see The history of Aksai and the importance to the town of the Karachaganak field are nicely set out in the **Burlin District Local Lore Museum** (*Microdistrict 10;* ☎ *31423;* ⊕ *09.00–13.00 & 14.00–18.00 daily*), which has received support from KPO, the Karachaganak operator. It is rather unglamorously located beneath the nine-storey apartment blocks of Microdistrict 10. The first room contains cloaks and artworks belonging to President Nazarbaev which were sold at auction in 2001 to support a charitable fund led by his wife. The next room, highlighting the efforts of local people during World War II, unusually features a bust of Stalin in the corner. There is a Lenin bust next door, in a room focusing on the development of education locally. Next comes ethnogaphy, with a display based around a large section of yurt, into which have been stuffed furs, weaponry, decorated chests and musical instruments.

The next two rooms highlight the mainstays of the local economy before the discovery of the Karachaganak field, focusing respectively on the arrival of the railway and on the Virgin Lands Campaign. A balalaika on display in the Virgin Lands room, and an icon in the corner, represent the migration of Slavonic peoples into the area to support the development of the wheatfields. At the back of the foyer is a room devoted to the natural history of the area, with the usual array of stuffed animals, including a beaver gnawing through a piece of wood. Also off the foyer is a large room devoted to the development of the Karachaganak reserve. Some of the labelling here is in English, as well as Russian and Kazakh. A photograph of a tropical atoll is accompanied by a label recording that 'this is how Karachaganak looked 340 million years ago'. There is a sign from the village of Tungush, whose inhabitants were moved out, mostly to Uralsk, when the field was developed. There are models of drilling rigs, and displays highlighting the activities of companies working at the field. A large golden tap is that opened by President Nazarbaev during the ceremony to inaugurate the pipeline from Karachaganak to Atyrau, from where the liquid condensate heads by another pipeline to markets further west. A large model in the centre of the room shows the main units at Karachaganak and the pipeline running to Atyrau, though there has been no attempt made at accuracy as regards the scales or geographical relationships of the different components of the development.

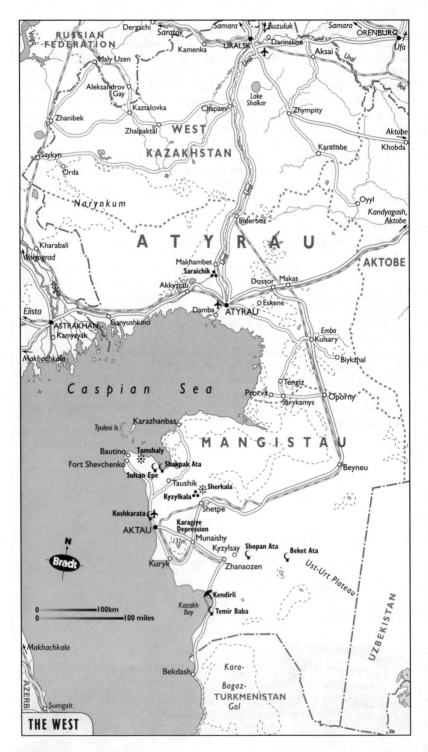

THE WEST

10

The West

Kazakhstan's two Caspian regions, Atyrau and Mangistau, are at the heart of the post-independence economic development of the country as the home to huge onshore and offshore reserves of oil. Westerners wandering the streets of the two regional capitals, Atyrau and Aktau, are far more likely to be expatriate oil workers than tourists, but the area, especially Mangistau Region, contains much of considerable interest to the visitor. The desert scenery of the Mangistau hinterland is stunning, with white limestone escarpments and isolated mountains rising up from the plains. Aktau becomes a cheerful beach resort in summer, with plans under way to turn Kendirli in the south of the region into a major resort destination. Fort Shevchenko, Mangistau's oldest town, was the place of exile of Ukrainian poet Taras Shevchenko. And the necropolises and underground mosques which dot Mangistau Region are among the most arresting of all Kazakhstan's historical monuments.

ATYRAU   *Telephone code: 7122*

Atyrau is the urban hub of Kazakhstan's important oil industry. Flanking the meandering Ural River, it has a strong boom-town feel, with ever more opulent apartment blocks rising above the muddy downtown streets, and expatriate-filled bars offering steak and kidney pies and Guinness on tap. It does however have deeper historical roots than most cities in Kazakhstan. Indeed, locals are fond of telling visitors that the foundation of their town pre-dates that of St Petersburg.

It started out in the 17th century as a fishing settlement, but soon became a part of the efforts of Tsarist Russia to strengthen its control over the area. A family of Russian traders, the Guryevs, established a wooden stockade here to help to protect the fishing catch. The settlement of Nizhny (Lower) Yaitsk was born – Upper Yaitsk was what is now Uralsk. The wooden fortress was vulnerable to attack from the local Kazakhs, who were understandably at best ambivalent about their new neighbours, and from other potential foes such as the Don Cossacks and the Khanate of Bukhara. In 1645, the Tsar granted Mikhail Guryev permission to strengthen the town, based on the model of the stone defences of Astrakhan. In the early 18th century the name of the town was changed to Guryev in honour of its founding family. The name stuck at Guryev during the Soviet period, but took the Kazakh name Atyrau in 1992, soon after independence. Mikhail Guryev's merchant family does however still live on in the three-letter airport code for the place: GUW.

The development of Guryev was given its major stimulus by the replacement of fish by oil as the major source of prosperity of the region. Crude oil, collected from shallow depressions, had long been used by the local Kazakhs for the treatment of skin diseases. Prospecting for commercially exploitable oil began in earnest towards the end of the 19th century. Crude oil found in the 1890s in the Karachungul basin was of higher quality and lighter than that around Baku in Azerbaijan, and oil extracted from this field by the Emba-Caspiisk Company marked the start of the oil industry in the area. The Nobel company opened another field, at Makat, to the northeast of Guryev, in 1913. The industry developed rapidly during the Soviet period. There are a large number of fields in production, and under exploration, many bringing together Kazakhstan's state hydrocarbons company KazMunaiGas with a range of international partners. But Atyrau's current prosperity and future development is above all pegged to the exploitation of two giant fields, the onshore Tengiz and offshore Kashagan developments.

The **Tengiz oil field** is located some 150km to the southeast of Atyrau. This huge oil deposit, around 21km long and 19km wide, was discovered in 1979. It is a challenging field, as the oil is deep, under high pressure, and contains a high concentration of noxious hydrogen sulphide. Recoverable reserves are believed to be around one billion tonnes, placing Tengiz among the ranks of the world's largest oilfields. Estimates of Kazakhstan's oil reserves promptly doubled, and commercial oil production started in 1991. The difficulties associated with the exploitation of the field led to a search for foreign partners even during the late Soviet period, culminating in the signature in 1993 by President Nazarbaev and Kenneth Derr, Chairman of Chevron, of a memorandum establishing the Tengizchevroil (TCO) joint venture. By 2002, oil production from Tengiz had reached 13 million tonnes. The considerable volumes of sulphur extracted from the hydrogen sulphide-rich oil pose major environmental challenges, and the identification of export routes or other uses for the sulphur is a vital task. Thousands of workers live at the Tengiz site itself, in accommodation blocks designed to resemble the *shanyrak* pattern at the top of a yurt, with blocks radiating out from central circular spaces. But the administrative headquarters of TCO is in Atyrau, a grey office block along Satpaev Street, and the senior management of the company is housed in a gated development of identikit beige houses not far away on the bank of the Ural River.

The **Kashagan field**, still under development, is more challenging still. The largest reserve discovered for more than a quarter of a century, the field is some 80km long and 45km wide. Like Tengiz, the field is deep, with the oil under high pressure and with a high hydrogen sulphide content. Unlike Tengiz, however, it is located beneath the waters of the northern Caspian, too shallow for many vessels, home to vulnerable species such as sturgeon and Caspian seals, and covered seasonally with ice. The field is being developed by an international consortium, with the Italian company AGIP KCO as operator during the experimental phase. A network of artificial islands is being constructed to house the offshore facilities, while an onshore processing facility is being built at Karabatan, 35km to the northeast of Atyrau, at a site renamed Bolashak ('Future') by President Nazarbaev following a visit to the place. Some 55,000 tonnes of steel has gone into the construction of the onshore processing facility alone. AGIP KCO's headquarters are also located in Atyrau, currently in the centre of town on the 'Asian' side of the river, but scheduled to be relocated to the western edge of town, on the road to the airport, where an accommodation compound is due to be built alongside it.

Beyond a couple of museums and some pleasant strolling to be had along the Ural River, there is not a huge amount of touristic interest in Atyrau. The oil boom has also resulted in some decidedly steep hotel prices, with notably slim pickings at the lower end of the scale. The city is notorious for its mud, especially in spring. The high water table, poorly developed urban drainage system, and saline soils which support a somewhat threadbare vegetation coverage are all something to do with the problem. It results in one of the more curious features of Atyrau life: the muddy water-filled troughs found outside many of the hotels, shops and restaurants in town. A brush, or a wooden stick with a bit of rag on the end of it, are to be found propped up against the troughs: implements to help you get the mud off your boots before entering. Since the muddy season is followed by the arrival of numerous mosquitoes, it can feel as though Atyrau is not the most welcoming place for tourists. More seriously, the oil boom has created resentment, as not all have reaped its rewards, and Atyrau is one of the less safe cities in Kazakhstan: walking alone after dark is not recommended. But flight connections make Atyrau the main gateway to western Kazakhstan from Europe, there is a busy nightlife, and if the expatriate bar scene is what you are seeking, this is the place.

GETTING THERE AND AROUND Atyrau **airport** is some 6km west of the town centre, along the road which starts off in town as Satpaev Street. A taxi into town costs around T750. 'Happy Way!' announces a sign on the control tower. Air Astana operates one or two flights each day to Almaty, one a day to Astana, one a day to Aktau, two a week to Almaty via Kyzylorda and Shymkent, and one a week to Uralsk. Scat has a daily flight to Aktau and to Uralsk, four a week to Aktobe and two to Shymkent. Atyrau Airways has one flight a week from Astana. Atyrau is also a direct gateway to the western regions of Kazakhstan. Air Astana has four flights a week to Amsterdam and three to Istanbul, Scat has three weekly flights to Baku, and Transaero offers two flights a week to Moscow.

The **railway station** (✆ 955549) is on the northeastern side of town, around 5km from the centre. Head north up Makhambet Utemisuly Street, turning right at the columned pastel green-painted registry office onto Baymukhanov Street. You reach the railway station on your left, towards the end of this road. There are daily connections originating in Atyrau to Aktobe, Mangyshlak (for Aktau) and Astrakhan in Russia, and two departures for Almaty, though each of these runs only every other day. Atyrau also lies on the route of trains running between Dushanbe and Moscow, Tashkent and Saratov, Khojand and Saratov, and Almaty and Simferopol (Ukraine). There is also a local train five times a week between Atyrau and Kulsary. Among the local bus routes serving the railway station is route number 14. The **bus station** is next door to the railway station. Frequent minibuses head off to Uralsk and Kulsary, with occasional departures for destinations further afield.

Getting around town is reasonably straightforward. Local buses, mostly minibuses, cost T35. **Taxis** should cost about T400 for a short journey. There are also numerous bookable taxi services, which charge a little more. These include Rhythm (✆ 252525) and Voyage (✆ 326045, *or simply 052 if calling from a landline*). If you are leaving a bar or club late at night, it is advisable to order a taxi rather than attempting to walk or hailing a cab outside.

TOUR OPERATORS AND AIRLINE OFFICES

✈ **Otrar Travel** Office 2, 3 Abai St;
✆ 355345; f 355772; e guw@otrar.kz. Also at 32 Satpaev St; ✆ 204117; f 204118. General Service Agent for Air Astana.

✈ **Transavia** Office 1, 42A Azattyk Av;
✆ 354472; f 324208; www.transavia-travel.kz. Represents Transaero in Atyrau. Also bookings on other airlines.

WHERE TO STAY
Top-range

⌂ **Hotel Atyrau** [322 D2] (94 rooms) 6 Satpaev St; ✆ 921100; f 271827; e reservation@ hotelatyrau.kz; www.hotelatyrau.kz. Housed

in the 5-storey pink-painted building directly opposite the TCO headquarters on Satpaev St, the Hotel Atyrau is a comfortable if somewhat fussily

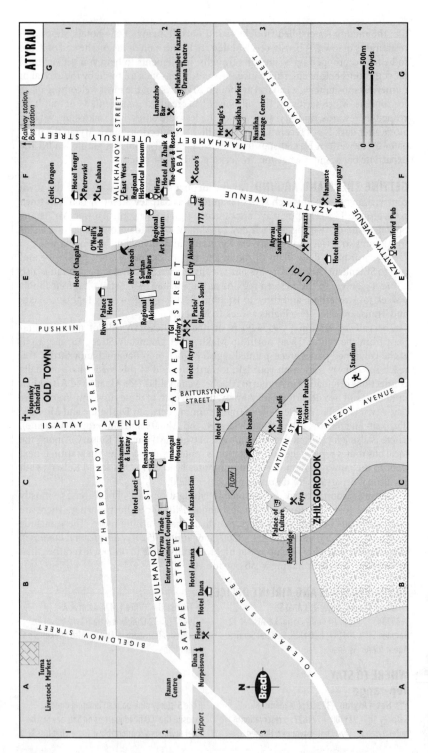

furnished 4-star option pitched, like most hotels in the city, at business travellers. Standard rooms have en-suite showers; 'deluxe' rooms have baths. Discounted rates are frequently available. **$$$$**

🏠 **Renaissance Hotel** [322 C2] (202 rooms) 15B Satpaev St; 📞 909600; 📠 909606; 📧 rhi.guwbr.dos@renaissancehotels.com; www. renaissancehotels.com. The hotel (part of the Marriott group) takes the form of 2 interlocking glass-walled pod-like structures, with colourfully furnished functional interiors & featuring nice touches like, a rarity in Kazakhstan, coffee-making facilities in the bedrooms. The one blight on customer satisfaction is the customer satisfaction surveys, left out in every corner of the rooms. Airport shuttle transfers can be arranged, for T2,800. **$$$$**

🏠 **River Palace Hotel** [322 E1] (42 rooms, 140 apts) 55 Aiteke Bi St; 📞 355241; 📠 355236; 📧 riverpalace@ducat.kz; www.hotelriverpalace. com. A concave, glass-fronted building overlooking the river, with a Modernist sculpture of uncertain nature outside the entrance, this Italian-run hotel has comfortable rooms & a decent Italian restaurant, the **Dolce Vita**, housed in the Tsarist-era brick building next door. But the b/fasts are well below the standard expected of a top-range hotel, as is the bar, squeezed unattractively into the small lobby. The apartments are mostly let out to oil companies. The rooftop swimming pool is an excellent bonus in summer. **$$$$**

Mid-range and budget
Atyrau is awash with decidedly mid-range options at rates which would get you a top-of-the-range room in many other parts of Kazakhstan. Budget rooms are scarce.

🏠 **Hotel Ak Zhaik** [322 F2] (165 rooms) Azattyk Av; 📞 327881, 327882; 📠 327866; 📧 info@ akzhaikhotel.com; www.akzhaikhotel.com. The large building overlooking the roundabout on the 'Asia' side of the main bridge is best known to Atyrau expatriates as the home of The Guns and Roses Pub (see page 326). The hotel itself is comfortable enough if unspectacular. **$$$$**

🏠 **Hotel Caspi** [322 D3] (20 rooms) 15 Satpaev St; 📞 213307; 📠 212511; 📧 hotel-caspi@ nursat.kz. Located in a central but quiet spot, down Baitursynov St (notwithstanding the Satpaev St address), the Caspi is a 3-storey pink-walled building which doesn't bother to advertise itself from the road. Given the somewhat run-down feel of the place the prices are decidedly high, though they do include VAT & b/fast. **$$$$**

🏠 **Hotel Chagala** [322 E1] (76 rooms, 235 apts) 1 Smagulov St; 📞 996096; 📠 996095; 📧 reservation.atyrau@chagalagroup.kz; www. chagalagroup.com. The 'Seagull' is something of an Atyrau institution, focused on servicing the needs of the expatriate oil industry. The group also runs O'Neill's Irish Bar, La Cabana & the Petrovski Restaurant, all located nearby. The hotel itself is a prefabricated building close to the river with simply furnished but comfortable rooms. The apartments are in a separate location,

in 3 buildings on nearby Temirzhanov St. They are furnished to a high standard, with kitchenettes in the sitting rooms, & anodyne abstract artworks on the walls. Most are however let out to oil companies. The restaurant on the ground floor of the apartments complex, **Coco's** (**$$$$**), though decorated in bland shades of beige, offers Mediterranean-tinged lunch & dinner buffets which are popular with the expatriate crowd. **$$$$**

🏠 **Hotel Dana** [322 B2] (40 rooms) 40 Tolebaev St; 📞 210863, 210901; 📠 210875; 📧 danahotel@mail.ru. It certainly doesn't offer the most inspiring location in town, hemmed in by apartment blocks, & the stuffed birds in the lobby may not be to everyone's taste, but the Dana, while no bargain, is not a bad option in this price range. Its room permutations offer all kinds of everything: ordinary or improved sgls, with or without hall, 'semi-luxe' with or without 1hr's use of the sauna. **$$$$**

🏠 **Hotel Kazakhstan** [322 C2] (70 rooms) Vladimirskaya St; 📞 202299; 📠 202298; 📧 hotel_kazakhstan@inbox.ru. This hotel squeezes into the acute angle between Satpaev & Tolebaev streets, close to the beige development of the TCO village. A vast chandelier overcrowds the lobby. Rooms have AC & en suites, & the rates include b/fast. **$$$$**

🛏 **Hotel Laeti** [322 C2] (20 rooms) 113 Kulmanov St; ☎ 201509, 201510; f 200266; e laeti@rambler.ru. This small 3-star hotel sits almost literally in the shadow of the adjacent Renaissance. It offers simple but clean rooms with en-suite showers. Airport transfers available for T1,200. **$$$$**

🛏 **Hotel Nomad** [322 E4] (14 rooms) 75B Azattyk Av; ☎ 252902; f 252901; e gilbertrego@ hotmail.com. A 3-storey pink building in a quiet location, close to the river & adjacent to the pedestrianised Kurmangazy St (which does, however, make the hotel somewhat obscure of access by car from Azattyk Av). Its restaurant offers an eclectic mix of Indian, Chinese & Mexican dishes. **$$$$**

🛏 **Hotel Tengri** [322 F1] (60 rooms) 2 Azattyk Av; ☎/f 320424, 320425; e res_tengrihotel@ mail.ru. Located close to the AGIP KCO offices, this is a comfortable but unexciting option. The apartments feature a sitting room with kitchenette. Prices include b/fast, VAT & laundry. **$$$$**

🛏 **Hotel Victoria Palace** [322 D3] (50 rooms) 17 Vatutin St; ☎/f 452760, 452770; e info@victoriapalace.kz; www.victoriapalace. kz. The main selling point of this hotel is its location in the quiet & charming, if somewhat crumbling, district of Zhilgorodok, though the hotel itself is an unattractive modern block which strikes a discordant tone in the neighbourhood. Furnishings are nothing special, but the place is comfortable enough. Rates for the suites include 1hr's use of the sauna. **$$$$**

🛏 **Atyrau Sanatorium** [322 E3] (36 rooms) 1 Alipov St; ☎ 354679, 354660; f 354660; e verbova@sanatory-atyrau.kz; www.sanatory-atyrau.kz. Located in pleasantly wooded grounds on the left bank of the Ural, this veteran sanatorium started life as a resthouse named 'Neftyannik' ('Oil Worker') & served as a hospital during World War II. 2 lower floors are still given over to those coming for week-long treatments based around the curative muds brought here from nearby Karabatan & the mineral water brought up from a depth of 360m by the 'nodding donkey' in the sanatorium grounds. But the top 2 floors have been tarted up, & serve as a more conventional hotel. The feel remains rather institutional, but the rooms have balcony, en-suite shower & AC. Standard rooms however only have a sgl bed, so couples are restricted to a pricier 'semi-luxe'. One other curiosity is the bearded bust in the grounds. I think this is of Pavlov (of 'salivating dogs' fame), though it is not labelled, but there is at least 1 other, apparently identical, statue in the town. Perhaps they bought a job lot? **$$$** sgl; **$$$$** 'semi-luxe'

🛏 **Hotel Astana** [322 B2] (8 rooms) 42A Satpaev St; ☎ 210678; f 210695. A rather peculiar-looking place, the Astana is a wooden-walled pitched-roofed structure, stuck on the end of an apartment block. Traffic thunders past along the adjacent Tolebaev St, & the cheaper rooms have en suites inconveniently across the hall. **$$$**

🛏 **Hotel Kenzhaly** Railway station; no phone. Don't let the 'hotel' tag fool you; these are just the railway station retiring rooms. Accessed from the hall on the top floor of the railway station (which is dominated by a large, & wholly out of place, chandelier) the Kenzhaly offers bed spaces, but little security, & few facilities beyond a shared toilet. A sign warns of a T500 fine for smoking; T1,000 for drinking spirits. For the desperate though, this is one of the few genuine budget options in Atyrau. **$**

✕ WHERE TO EAT
Restaurants

✕ **Fiesta** [322 B2] 5B Satpaev St; ☎ 970376; e laura_restaurant@mail.ru. Somewhat difficult to find, on the side of an apartment block set back from Satpaev St, & immediately behind a block numbered 50 Satpaev St, the Fiesta lies close to the Dina Nurpeisova Folk Music Academy. A sign outside announces that it offers the 'best of Thai, Chinese, Continental, Mexican & Indian cuisine', which is quite a claim. Pleasantly furnished in shades of orange, with waitresses in sparkly oriental outfits, the length & range of the menu appears however to defeat consistency of quality & speed of service. **$$$$$**

✕ **Il Patio/Planeta Sushi** [322 E2] 2 Satpaev St; ☎ 980063; www.rosinter.ru. The first Atyrau branch of this popular paired Russian chain is located on the 1st floor of the tall, square-based skyscraper housing the Marriott Executive Apartments. The restaurant is divided into Italian & Japanese sections; the waitresses in the Italian part sport cravats & long red aprons, those on the Japanese side are dressed as geishas. The Japanese menu lists a selection of 'the hits of 2006–07', which is odd, as the place only opened in 2008. $$$$$

✗ **La Cabana** [322 F1] Contact through Hotel Chagala – see page 323. One of a range of entertainment outlets owned by the Chagala Group, this Tex-Mex place on Azattyk Av has 2 airy floors, colourful murals of cactuses & mariachi singers, & live music on Sat evenings. The menu includes, beyond the usual Mexican fare, a list labelled 'Tex-Mex infusion cuisine' which mainly consists, curiously, of curries. The drinks menu majors on margaritas & tequila ('Lick it! Slam it! Suck it!'). The lunch menu is limited to burger & chips-type options, plus a fixed business lunch. $$$$

✗ **Namaste** [322 F4] 48A Azattyk Av; ☎ 970035. This Indian restaurant sits on the side of the tall grey metallic-tiled Premier Atyrau building, facing a grassy square centred on a statue of Kurmangazy. The interior is decorated in earth-toned shades, with waitresses in flowing south Asian-styled outfits. The menu includes Chinese & Thai options as well as Indian: dishes tend to be on the mild side, in deference to local tastes. $$$$

✗ **Paparazzi** [322 E3] 1 Alipov St; ☎ 354023. Brightly decorated in shades of yellow, red & green, with leather seats with improbably tall backs around circular tables, & a separate room decked out in relaxing wicker furniture, this Italian restaurant occupies a quiet spot amidst gardens close to the Atyrau Sanatorium. There is a full range of Italian dishes on offer. Photos of celebrities & jars of pasta line the walls, & you dine to a lounge music background. $$$$

✗ **Petrovski** [322 F1] 2 Azattyk Av; ☎ 321092; e petrovski@chagalagroup.kz; www.chagalagroup.com. Another one of the entertainment outlets owned by the Chagala Group, this place has a clean, fresh feel, with Pop Art pictures of Marilyn, Mickey Mouse & ET enlivening the walls. The menu ranges freely across the continents, with a variety of Indian dishes, pasta & pizzas, & wok-cooked meats served with jasmine-steamed rice. $$$$

✗ **Coco's** [322 F2] 2 Azattyk Av; ☎ 906096. A bland but comfortable restaurant open from b/fast onwards. The menu is predominantly European with the occasional Japanese & Korean dish. $$$

✗ **Feya** [322 C3] 1 Auezov Av; ☎ 452817. The 'Fairy' is one of the nicest places to eat in town, located at the corner of the columned arcade around the main square of the quiet Zhilgorodok neighbourhood. It is an Uzbek restaurant, whose décor is an *Arabian Nights* style evidently inspired by the Moorish touches of the nearby Palace of Culture. It offers soothing drapes, large patterned cushions, terracotta walls & embroidered tissue-box covers. The lengthy menu offers an excellent range of central Asian dishes. $$$

✗ **Lamadzho Bar** [322 C2] 3A Kantsev St; ☎ 354893. Named after a kind of pie, which is the house speciality, this is a basic but pleasingly decorated Armenian place, decked out to resemble a square in olde Yerevan, with covered booths to dine in. The proprietors also own the **Cleopatra Nightclub** next door, entered through a pyramid tacked onto the side of an apartment block, & guarded by a pair of sphinxes. The club though has a somewhat rough reputation. $$$

✗ **Aladdin Café** [322 D3] 1 Sevastopolskaya St; ☎ 452587. Enticingly located close to the summertime stretch of river beach near the Zhilgorodok District, a convenient target at the end of the riverside stroll from the main bridge, this offers a large courtyard around the café building where you can while away a summer lunchtime over beer & *shashlik*. They also do a fish *beshbarmak* if you order in advance. $$

✗ **TGI Friday's** [322 D2] 3 Satpaev St; ☎ 980064; e tgif_atyrau@rosinter.kz. Kazakhstan's first branch of this popular US chain has all the usual tat on the walls & does a good line in over-sized burgers & ribs. Tell the waiters it's your birthday & they may even sing. $$$

✗ **McMagic's** [322 F3] 116A Makhambet Utemisuly St; no phone. At the corner of the Daria shopping centre, immediately to the north of the Nasikha Bazaar, this clean fast-food place takes obvious inspiration from a well-known international chain, but alongside the burgers & chips serves good basic Turkish dishes. $$

Pubs and clubs

♀ **The Guns and Roses** [322 F2] Ak Zhaik Hotel, Azattyk Av; ☏327878; www.thegunsandroses. com. Located on the ground floor of the Ak Zhaik Hotel, this is a popular bar targeted at the expatriate oil-worker market. The walls are adorned with film posters, rock memorabilia & pictures of motorbikes, & there's a red phone box to ease homesickness for Blighty. Free Wi-Fi, & big-screen TVs showing the sport. Live music Thu–Sat evenings. They do a Sun lunch (reservations required) of roast beef with all the trimmings. $$$$

♀ **O'Neill's Irish Bar** [322 E1] 1 K Smagulov St; ☏996096. A barn-like building, located next to the entrance to the headquarters of the AGIP KCO, at the heart of the expatriate oil community in Atyrau. They have Guinness & Kilkenny on draught, a standard pub menu with good-value set-lunch options, expats watching Premiership football on the TV screens positioned at every field of view, & waitresses with emerald green aprons. The toilet signs are written in Gaelic, but if you don't know whether you are Mná or Fir they have helpfully added pictures. $$$$

♀ **Stamford Pub** [322 E4] 68 Azattyk Av; ☏252932. With football shirts on the walls & waitresses in red hockey outfits, this place attracts a mixed expatriate & local crowd. Upstairs is the cavernous & popular Mayak Nightclub (admission Tue–Thu, Sun men T1,500, women free; Fri–Sat men T2,000, women T1,000). There is also a billiard hall on the site. $$$$

♀ **East West** [322 F2] 6 Azattyk Av; ☏328540, 320800. An entertainment complex housed in a large & somewhat forbidding-looking building with red trim on Azattyk Av, this place accommodates a bar, club & restaurant. The bar, **Batyrs' Pub**, is named in honour of Kazakh warriors, its reddish décor hinting at the heat of battle, though the unappetising food offers little by way of spoils of victory. The horse-sausage sandwich is really quite peculiar. The large **East West Nightclub** is next door. Upstairs is a Russian restaurant, **Guryev**, offering Russian standards with the good range of fish dishes one would expect from a restaurant taking the name of Atyrau's founder. Batyr's Pub: $$$; Guryev: $$$$

♀ **Celtic Dragon** [322 F1] 8 Temirzhanov St; ☏355585. One of the longer-established pubs in Atyrau, whose décor is starting to look a little tired. The food is however slightly less expensive than other similar places in town, with a set lunch at just T600. Live music on Fri–Sat evenings. $$$

♀ **Miras** [322 F2] 8 Azattyk Av; ☏322352. Located in the 2-storey cream-coloured building next to the regional museum, the Miras is a fairly ordinary café with an international menu, whose selling point is the live music offered after 22.00 (except Mon) to a crowd dominated by locals rather than expats. There is a cover charge for the music (T300 Tue–Thu; T700 Fri–Sun). Expect mostly 1970s & 1980s covers. $$$

Cafés

🍽 **777 Café** [322 F2] 9 Azattyk Av; ☏329215. A central place to stop for coffee & cake, close to the roundabout on the 'Asia' side

of the main bridge, though the coffee is nothing special. There's an average restaurant, the Eurasia, in the same building. $$$

SHOPPING The **Nasikha Market** [322 F3], previously known as Rahat, is centrally located on Makhambet Utemisuly Street on the 'Asian' side of town. Come here in spring and you may find yourself walking over old wooden doors and even car bonnets, laid down between the stalls as (inadequate) protection against the mud. A market worth visiting for local colour, though industrial quantities of mud, is the **Tuma Livestock Market** [322 A1], held on the northwestern edge of town. Sheep purchased here can be despatched on site to the slaughterhouse at the back of the market.

The Ideal chain has a firm grip on the supermarket scene in Atyrau. There are branches in the **Nasikha Passage Centre** [322 F3], adjacent to the Nasikha Market, on the 'Asian' side of town, and at two locations along Satpaev Street on the 'European' one. The latter are the **Atyrau Trade and Entertainment Complex** [322

C2], just west of the Renaissance Hotel, and further west in the **Rauan Centre [322 A2],** on the corner of Satpaev and Bigeldinov streets.

Atyrau is not a great place for souvenir shopping, but there are limited and expensive selections in some of the top hotels (the shop in the Chagala has a reasonable choice) as well as in shops in the Nasikha Passage Centre and Daria Shopping Centre close to the Nasikha Market. Souvenirs based on local themes include a model of Kazakh local revolutionary heroes Makhambet and Isatay, galloping along for T25,000, and various model oil-rig tableaux, some with movable parts. The gift shop in the Chagala Hotel has an Atyrau street plan for sale, though at an alarming T2,000.

MEDICAL
✚ **International SOS Clinic** River Palace Hotel, 55 Aiteke Bi St; ☎586911; f 586211; e atu. marketing@internationalsos.com. Used mainly by expatriate corporate clients in Atyrau, this clinic is part of a major international group, but its charges are steep.

WHAT TO SEE
Ural River Snaking through the centre of the city, the Ural River, known in Kazakh as the Zhaik, is both the focus of the Atyrau cityscape and its most attractive feature. Paths have been laid out along the riverbanks: the walk from the main bridge southwards on the 'Asian' side of the river to the district of Zhilgorodok is particularly pleasant. The river changes its character radically with the seasons. In winter, the river becomes a pedestrian thoroughfare. Recreational fishermen sit huddled around holes in the ice, a tot of vodka their protection against the cold. In summer, attention shifts to the sandy **river beaches** on the 'Asian' bank, one adjacent to Zhilgorodok, the other just north of the main bridge. Beachfront cafés open for business, the smell of chips mingling with that of suncream.

At present there is only one **road bridge** in town, a fact which accounts for the considerable rush-hour congestion accumulating on either side. Further bridges, outside the centre, were under construction at the time of research. There is also a **footbridge,** but this runs somewhat inconveniently from Zhilgorodok to a residential suburb of little interest on the 'European' side, and is not much used. The road bridge, then, is the fulcrum of the city. By local convention, the river divides the two continents of Europe and Asia. This tradition is marked by the paired battered metal pavilions at either end of the bridge. Those on the western side, at the start of Satpaev Street, are marked 'Europe'. Those on the eastern side, looking down Abai Street to the tapering caramel-coloured columns of the **Kazakh Drama Theatre** named after Makhambet, are marked 'Asia'. It is to Asia that we turn first.

'Asian' side On the eastern, 'Asiatic' side of the bridge sits a roundabout overlooked by the Ak Zhaik Hotel. Azattyk Avenue heading north from here used to be a pedestrianised thoroughfare, known locally as Atyrau's 'Arbat', a miniature version of Moscow's famous pedestrian street. But the demands for more freely circulating traffic proved too great, and the avenue has now been opened up again to cars. A few metres along it and you reach two worthwhile museums, facing each other across the street.

Atyrau Regional Historical Museum [322 F2] *3 B Momyshuly St* (☎ *355305, 322912;* f *222912;* ⏰ *09.00–13.00 & 14.00–18.00 Tue–Sat; admission foreign citizens/adult/student T200/100/60)* Housed in a two-storey building with orangey-hued walls, entered from a curious glass pavilion tacked onto the side, the regional historical museum is the place to discover that there is more about Atyrau than oil. From the entrance, turn right along the central corridor to reach the room housing Atyrau's very own 'Golden Man'. A seated mannequin in the centre of the room wears the golden mail and weapons of the Sarmat chief whose remains were unearthed in 1999 in the Araltobe Barrow in Atyrau Region. A frieze decorating the wall behind this figure depicts *Sarmats before Battle*, our golden hero being dragged in an ornate cart across a remarkably muddy field (clearly, some things in Atyrau don't change) by less privileged compatriots.

The large room across the corridor, used for conferences, is dominated by a diorama of life along the Silk Road, starring a stuffed horse, wolf, saiga and camel, a painted medieval caravan, and a carved stone sheep. The room also houses a yurt, and a clump of the intricately engraved funerary standing stones known as *kulpytas* which are a characteristic feature of the graveyards of western parts of Kazakhstan. Two more decorated stone rams, a rarer type of funerary monument known as a *koshkartas*, guard the entrance to the next room: archaeology. This room focuses on the important medieval site of Saraichik (see page 331), with a relief model of the town, in a meander of the Ural River, occupying its centre. There are photographs of the site, a collection of ceramics, and a painting of happy archaeologists at work. A diorama of life in a Saraichik street features a blacksmith's forge and a pottery.

The next room is nature, centred on an illuminated globe which has not been plugged in. Stuffed animals populate dioramas illustrating various ecosystems. Caspian seals gambol around a water hole in the ice. A pelican flies out of a waterside scene. A cage of budgies adds some, albeit discordant, real birdsong to the picture. Sturgeon impress by their size.

The museum continues upstairs. The first room off the corridor is devoted to post-independence Atyrau, its walls a patriotic blue, featuring displays of the work of the main oil and gas companies active in the region, plus a display of locally produced food products, including loaves of fake bread, cans of fish and tins of caviare. Along the corridor, the room focusing on pre-Soviet history is potentially interesting, though the displays are over-cluttered and much of the labelling is in Kazakh only. There is a painting of Sultan Baybars, wistfully contemplating a glorious Caspian sunset while a sphinx hangs dreamlike in the sky. There are more ceramics from Saraichik, and a display on the founding of Guryev. Many of the displays in the room are devoted to various insurrections against Tsarist power and its allies, including the Pugachev Rebellion in the 18th century, and the campaign of Makhambet and Isatay against Zhangir Khan, ruler of the Bukei Horde, in the 19th. On display is a copy of the finery worn by Fatima, the wife of Zhangir Khan, during ceremonies to mark the coronation of Nicholas I. Fatima's refinement, intelligence and beauty were said to have bowled over the new Tsar as he waltzed with her. Another display case features Makhambet's *dombra*, along with a souvenir plate marking the 200th anniversary of his birth.

The next room is ethnography, with a collection of sheep vertebrae used for children's games (a kind of central Asian version of 'Pass the Pigs'), plus jewellery, copper and wooden utensils, saddles and clothes. There is a collection of *dombras*, including one gifted to President Nazarbaev. The final cases show off the work of modern handicraft makers, fashioning decorated wooden bowls and replica weapons. The next room, across the corridor, covers the period 1917–90 with a cluttered display of photographs, letters, medals and awards. These take you from the establishment of communist rule through the development of the oil industry, Stalinist repressions, local war heroes, and the post-war local Communist Party bosses, the last pictured in group photos of the 1950s and 1960s, sitting with their comrades beneath enormous chandeliers in the Kremlin. The last room is devoted to the leading cultural lights of the region. The room focuses on a painting of the musician Kurmangazy. His rifle is also on display. Another featured artist is the singer and *dombra* player Dina Nurpeisova. Items on show include her *dombra*, Soviet-era awards to her and a carpet bearing her face, its expression quizzical.

Regional Art Museum [322 F2] (*11 Azattyk Av;* ☎ *354803, 326453;* ⊕ *09.00–13.00 & 14.00–19.00 Mon–Fri, 10.00–13.00 & 14.00–19.00 Sat/Sun; admission foreign citizens/adult/student T200/50/30*) Across the road from the historical museum, the two-storey building with pastel green walls houses the Regional Art Museum named after Shaimardan Sariev. The displays are upstairs, in a well laid-out series of rooms benefiting from oil industry sponsorship. One room is devoted to paintings inspired by the historical art forms of western Kazakhstan: petroglyphs, underground mosques and standing stones. Another features artworks by young local artists, drawing inspiration from the Saraichik archaeological site. There is a room showcasing the work of Shaimardan Sariev, an artist born near Guryev who came to prominence in the early 1960s, the brief period of 'thaw' in the Khrushchev era, when, in the company of other young artists in Almaty, he set about the task of creating a national school of painting. But the thaw failed to last, Sariev was expelled from the Union of Artists, and he died young. The paintings in this room are mostly portraits: chisel-cheeked stern faces painted in vivid colour. There are also a couple of rooms of graphics and watercolours, some Soviet paintings praising triumphs of labour, from railway building to the construction of apartment blocks, and large canvases of Kazakh heroes, such as a purplish portrayal of Makhambet and Isatay, contemplating the view.

Zhilgorodok The pleasantest suburb of Atyrau, Zhilgorodok is a quiet, somewhat crumbling district, put up after World War II using prisoner of war labour. It lies in a meander of the Ural River, to the southwest of the main bridge. The best way to get here is along the riverside path, a walk of a couple of kilometres from the bridge. Turn inland along Sevastopolskaya Street when you reach the river beach. By road, Zhilgorodok is reached by taking Azattyk Avenue southwards. You pass a statue of the musician **Kurmangazy** [322 F4], his powerful right arm clutching his *dombra* to his chest. Turn right at the roundabout onto Auezov Avenue, passing the **Neftyannik ('oil workers') Stadium** [322 D4] on your right. You reach a silver gate topped with a red Soviet star on a stick. This marks the entrance into Zhilgorodok. Auezov Avenue is pedestrianised beyond this point.

The focus of the district is a graceful, Moorish-tinged **Palace of Culture** [322 C3], the tall arches of its façade facing a quiet square. The remaining sides of the square are fronted by arcades which give the whole place the feel of an Italian piazza. The wooden balconies and window boxes decorating buildings along the side streets, and the popularity of this district for summer-evening strolling and as a meeting point for the youth of Atyrau, all serve to reinforce Zhilgorodok's Mediterranean feel.

'European' side From the main bridge, Satpaev Street runs westwards. The long white building facing the river to the northwest of the bridge houses the **regional administration** [322 E2]. Immediately in front of this stands a tall stone statue of **Sultan Baybars** (see box, page 330) [322 E2]. On his right is a smoothed stone with petroglyphs and images recalling the engraved gravestones found across the western parts of Kazakhstan. On his left is a pyramid, replete with engraved sphinx and assorted hieroglyphics.

Walking westwards along Satpaev Street for 1km, you reach a large and somewhat windswept square, with a **statue of Makhambet and Isatay** [322 C2] at its northern side. Makhambet Utemisuly was a Kazakh poet who, with his friend Isatay Taymanuly, led an insurrection against Zhangir Khan of the Bukei Horde and his Tsarist Russian allies in 1836–37, following the imposition of restrictions on the Kazakh nomads fishing in the Ural River and pasturing their animals near rivers and settlements. Taymanuly was killed during fighting in 1838. Makhambet fled following the failure of the rebellion, and was eventually murdered in 1846. Many of Makhambet's poems are of a martial nature, and are often directed against the injustices of Zhangir Khan's rule. The statue portrays Makhambet and Isatay as heroic figures on horseback: Makhambet has his *dombra* slung over his shoulder; Isatay, wearing chain mail, is depicted as a more conventionally military-looking figure. Behind the statue, a frieze shows our two heroes directing battle. Note the rather curious figure in the bottom left corner of the frieze: a chortling sculptor, in

SULTAN BAYBARS

The presence of a large statue of a 13th-century ruler of Egypt outside the regional administration in Atyrau is explained by the belief that here, or at any rate somewhere nearby, was the place of Baybars's birth, around 1223, into a tribe of Kipchak Turks.

Captured as a boy and sold into slavery, reportedly for a rather low price as he had a bad eye, he came into the possession of the Ayyubid sultan of Egypt. Baybars was trained up as a soldier, like many of the slaves acquired by the Ayyubid ruler, who was anxious to shore up his position. This strategy was to backfire. The white slaves, known as Mamluks, established themselves as a powerful force in Egypt, and themselves took power in 1250, after having the Ayyubid heir murdered. Baybars became a successful military commander, securing a notable victory against the Mongols in 1260 at the Battle of Ayn Jalut, near Jerusalem. Welcomed back to Egypt by the new Mamluk sultan, Qutuz, Baybars promptly killed Qutuz and assumed the sultanship himself. In the following year he helped to legitimise both his own position and Mamluk rule by bringing to Cairo from Damascus a descendant of the Abbasid Caliph, and re-establishing the caliphate.

Baybars's rule was marked by considerable military success against the dual threats of the Mongols from the east and the Christian Crusaders, who had established footholds on the Middle Eastern coast. He was also a good administrator, improving the road networks across his domains, such that a letter sent from Cairo could be delivered to Damascus in four days. He closed the brothels and inns of Cairo, and at one point introduced legislation banning the wearing of men's clothing by women. But his court was also notably lavish, with its members given such duties as Slipper Holder, and he seems to have been heartily disliked by those around him. He died in 1277, apparently while attempting to murder a rival named Malik Kaher. Baybars poisoned a cup of *kumiss* but, in an episode straight out of a Danny Kaye movie, Kaher switched cups, and Baybars drank his own poison.

A somewhat more romanticised Kazakh version of the Sultan Baybars story offers a different ending, which has Baybars returning at the end of his life to the Kazakh steppes for which he had been pining during all his years in Egypt.

the process of carving a *kulpytas*, while apparently slurping on a glass of something. Evidently strong, judging by his grinning countenance.

On the western side of the square is the **Imangali Mosque** [322 C2], built in 2000 and taking its name from that of the then Akim of Atyrau, Imangali Tasmagambetov. Its blue-tiled dome stands atop a central drum. Two minarets, reaching a height of 26m, flank the building, whose exterior walls are enlivened by decorative tilework.

Head northwards along Isatay Avenue, which runs along the east side of the square. This road used to be named Taimanov Street, which was in honour of exactly the same person (Taimanov is the Russianised version of Taymanuly); the renamed version has a more populist, and certainly more Kazakh, feel. Ahead of you glimmer the gold onion domes of the **Uspensky Cathedral** [322 D1], a brick building dating from the 1880s. Its exterior walls are painted a cheerful orange. The interior features a tall, pastel-hued, iconostasis, with icons and wall paintings covering most available interior surfaces. Around the cathedral lies the somewhat ramshackle **old town**, a district of single-storey dwellings, some with log walls, most with corrugated metal roofs. There are water pumps on street corners here, and a prodigious quantity of overhead cabling. With oil-rich Atyrau developing fast, the old town is unlikely to survive much longer in its current form.

One other monument worth a glance lies further westwards along Satpaev Street. This is a statue of the musician **Dina Nurpeisova** [322 A2], which stands in front of the Folk Music Academy which also takes her name. Nurpeisova, who died in 1955, well into her nineties, is depicted in old age and in a somewhat wistful mood, cradling her *dombra* in her arms as one might hold a small baby.

AROUND ATYRAU

URAL RIVER DELTA The Ural River Delta is a wetland environment rich in waterfowl and marine fauna. The latter include the beluga and sevruga sturgeon which are the source of one of the great, though endangered, riches of the area: its caviare. The delta is one of three demonstration sites within Kazakhstan (the others being Korgalzhyn, close to Astana, and the Alakol and Sasykkol Lake System along the border of Almaty and East Kazakhstan regions) forming part of a major wetlands conservation project funded by the Global Environment Facility and implemented by the United Nations Development Programme. The intention as regards the Ural Delta is to establish a nature reserve, Akzhaik, covering 111,500ha. There are plans to develop a visitor centre and to promote the use of the delta for sustainable tourism. No tourist infrastructure had yet materialised at the time of research, but the delta is easily accessible from Atyrau and offers fine birdwatching. Among the many species found here are pelican, egret, squacco heron and glossy ibis.

To get here, head southeastwards from Atyrau on the rather pot-holed road to Damba, a village which takes its name from the earth dam constructed to keep the rising waters of the Caspian at bay. Damba lies just some 20km from Atyrau. There are some good birdwatching spots just to the south of the village. With a 4x4, you can head further into the delta, along an earth track to the scruffy hamlet of Peshnoy. This can, however, become impassable after rain. At Peshnoy you may be able to hire a motorboat from a local fisherman: he will steer through shallow channels between dense thickets of reeds, eventually taking you out to the open waters of the Caspian.

SARAICHIK One easy half-day excursion from Atyrau is to the memorial complex honouring the important medieval settlement of Saraichik. The town became prominent in the 13th century as an urban centre of the Golden Horde. It lay on the caravan route eastwards from Sarai, the capital of the Golden Horde on the Volga. Ibn Battuta, who visited in 1334, reported that the name 'Saraichik' meant 'small Sarai'. Despite muttering about the low prices secured for the horses he had to sell in Saraichik, replacing them with camels for the onward journey eastwards, Battuta seems to have been reasonably impressed with the place, and compared the pontoon bridge across the Ural River here to that at Baghdad. Saraichik was sacked by Timur's troops in 1395, but was rebuilt to serve as the capital of the Nogai Horde in the 15th and 16th centuries, before being destroyed by Cossacks in 1580. Changes in the meandering course of the Ural River have been unkind to Saraichik's archaeological legacy, and cultural layers continue to be washed away by the waters.

What to see To reach Saraichik, take Isatay Avenue out of Atyrau, which becomes the main road to Uralsk. After 47km, a large, brightly coloured concrete sign to 'Saraichik' marks the right turn to take. You reach the village of Saraichik after a further 4km. Turn right in Saraichik to reach the **Saraichik memorial complex**, which stands on the edge of the village.

The complex was built in 1999, and is centred on the 17m-high octagonal-based monument known as the **Khan Pantheon**. Built to a design of the then *akim*, Imangali Tasmagambetov, the monument takes as its inspiration the belief that seven khans of the Golden and Nogai hordes were buried in Saraichik. A piled mound of stones in the centre of the monument serves as cenotaph to the khans. From the bare branches of a tree, considered sacred, hang strips of cloth as votive offerings. Beneath the arches of the monument are engraved funerary stones to each of the khans honoured here.

The Khan Pantheon is flanked on one side by a mosque, on the other by a **museum** ((71236) 25506; ⊕ *10.00–13.00 & 14.00–18.00 Tue–Sun; admission adult/child T50/35).* A painting inside the entrance depicts Saraichik in the 14th century as a flourishing Silk Road trading centre. The main room of the museum includes a model of Saraichik at this time. There are assorted fragments of ceramics on display, including some attractively decorated items produced locally in the 14th century, terracotta money boxes and brightly coloured items of jewellery. Displays of coins minted in Saraichik in the 13th and 14th centuries are evidence of the importance of the city. On the wall, a cute painting of a girl in a golden boat feeding swans on a lake refers to a local legend. This runs roughly that Khan Zhanibek had a favourite daughter, for whom he built an artificial lake, on which she sailed in a boat of gold. The daughter died young, and the distraught Zhanibek had her buried in a golden coffin, together with her golden boat, and loads of gold jewellery for good measure. Zhanibek had all those involved in the funeral arrangements put to death, to protect the gold in the grave from looters. It is said that the golden boat still lies beneath the ground. The museum also houses seven modern *kulpytas*, symbolic gravestones of the seven khans. The displays are in Kazakh only, but you can purchase steeply priced pamphlets here in English, Russian and Kazakh about Saraichik.

The archaeological site of Saraichik itself is some 3km from here, on the bank of the Ural River, which is gradually undermining it. To get there, continue further on the road taken to reach the memorial complex. This quickly deteriorates in quality until it is just a dirt track. For the non-specialist there is not, however, much to see, and it is difficult to interpret the site from the degraded traces of former excavations.

MAKHAMBET Continuing northwards on the road towards Uralsk, you reach the district capital of Makhambet some 23km north of the Saraichik turning. The district and its capital take the name of Makhambet Utemisuly, a Kazakh poet and one of the leaders of the revolt of 1836 against Zhangir Khan of the Bukei Horde and his Tsarist allies. The main administrative buildings of the town are clustered around the large and rather empty main square, which is also flanked by a bust of Makhambet Utemisuly. In the corner of the square stands the **Makhambet District Historical and Local Lore Museum** (` (71236) 21908`; ⊕ *09.30–13.00 & 14.00–18.30 Mon–Fri; admission adult/child T70/40*). The displays downstairs run around a central circular wall, on which is painted a mural which starts out as a scene of 14th-century Saraichik but concludes as a vision of a futuristic cityscape fed by an oil pipeline, symbolising perhaps Makhambet District's role as one of the areas through which the Karachaganak pipeline passes before reaching the city of Atyrau. There are large ceramic vessels and fragments of glazed ceramic from the Saraichik site, ethnographic displays and descriptions of local literary figures and war heroes.

Climb the spiral staircase within the mural-covered wall to the second floor, which features displays on the life of Makhambet and on the 1836 uprising. These run around another mural, this one an abstract piece depicting the troubled history of the Kazakh people. The items on display include weaponry, copies of documents related to the uprising, and some decidedly romanticised paintings. One depicts an angry Makhambet pointing an accusing finger at a seated Zhangir Khan. Another shows Makhambet and fellow revolutionary Isatay Taymanuly riding their white chargers across a turquoise sky. A third focuses on Makhambet the poet and musician, portraying him playing his *dombra* to an appreciative audience. There appears to be little agreement among the various artists as to what Makhambet might have looked like.

There is a photograph of Makhambet's mausoleum in the northern part of Atyrau Region, where he was murdered in 1846. He has not been able to rest in peace. His body was originally buried minus head, this having been detached at the time of his death. His relatives were eventually able to negotiate the return of the head, and this was added to his grave. The location of the latter then lay forgotten until 1959, when one Kurak Bekturganov was able to identify it, based on oral histories. Makhambet's remains were disinterred in 1967 and taken to Almaty for study. A bust created from his study of the skull is on display, showing a slender-faced figure. Makhambet's remains were reburied in 1983.

AKTAU   *Telephone code: 7292*

The administrative capital of Mangistau Region, Aktau was a Soviet-era new town, erected on the arid banks of the Caspian, its construction linked to the processing of nearby deposits of uranium (which gave it the status of a closed city in the Soviet period) and then to the needs of the developing oil industry in the region. Its urban status dating from 1963, the centre of town is characterised by Soviet apartment blocks, hastily constructed of prefabricated panels. Modern shopfronts have been stuck on the sides of many of these. The central President of the Republic of Kazakhstan Avenue apart, the town lacks street names. Each block is known as a microdistrict, and given a number in order of the date of construction. Within each microdistrict, every apartment block also has a number, usually to be found written high up on a corner of the block, in an exercise in impersonality. The designers of the place even secured in 1976 an award named after town planner Patrick Abercrombie. The town was powered by a BN-350 nuclear reactor, which closed in 1999, and obtained its water via a desalination plant. In 1964, it was given the name Shevchenko, after the Ukrainian poet Taras Shevchenko, who was exiled nearby (see page 341). It was renamed Aktau in 1992.

Modern-day Aktau is a fast-developing place, its growth fuelled by the oil industry, as Mangistau is one of the most important oil-producing regions of Kazakhstan. Aktau port is the largest in the country. Together with the ports of Kuryk, 64km to the south, which is planned to be developed as a terminal for the export of oil by tanker to Baku, and Bautino, 145km to the north, which has emerged as a significant supply base for the offshore oil industry, Aktau is at the heart of Kazakhstan's plans both to develop its offshore hydrocarbons reserves and to develop a maritime export corridor to the west. Glitzy new office and apartment blocks have emerged, though the Soviet buildings have to date been left largely untouched. The new town is being built around, and particularly to the north of, the old. The authorities have ambitious plans for an Aktau City development north of the current city centre, involving plush new constructions, entertainment complexes, and a marina, with more than a nod to the Dubai experience. Also part of what is envisaged to be a multi-billion-dollar investment programme is the development of Kendirli, located in a secluded bay some 210km south of Aktau towards the Turkmen border, into a sophisticated modern beach resort.

GETTING THERE AND AROUND Aktau **airport** sits northeast of town. Taking the Fort Shevchenko road, turn to the right, signposted for the airport, 12km north of the city. The airport is 13km further on. Air Astana currently operates between one and three daily flights to Almaty. They also have a daily flight to Atyrau, which then flies onward to Astana, although this is run as two flights: through-passengers have to get off the plane in Atyrau and collect their onward boarding pass in that airport. Scat has a daily flight to Atyrau and then Uralsk, two a week to Almaty, with two more via Kyzylorda, six a week to Astana via Aktobe, and three a week to Shymkent. Atyrau Airways has three flights a week to Astana. International flights include three a week to Moscow on Transaero, and five a week to Baku on the Azeri carrier Air Azal. There is one flight a week to London (Gatwick), via Uralsk, run by TransGlobal Group on a Boeing 757-200 operated by Air Astraeus. Scat has a range of international services: Baku (three a week), Astrakhan (two), the Caucasian spa resort of Mineralnye Vody (three), Tbilisi (two), Rostov (two), Yerevan (two), Sharjah (two) and Mahachkala (one).

The **railway station** is out of town. Following the main road towards Zhetibay and Zhanaozen, take a signposted left turn 12km out of Aktau. The railway station, which appears to be referred to as both Mangyshlak and Mangistau station, but never Aktau, is 4km on. One train a day runs between Mangyshlak and Atyrau. There is another to Aktobe, and trains every two days to Almaty and Astana. The **bus station**, which serves destinations within Mangistau Region, is a couple of kilometres east of the centre, in Microdistrict 28. There is also a **ferry** from Aktau to Baku, departing from the port, but it does not operate to any set timetable.

TOUR OPERATORS AND AIRLINE OFFICES

Madagascar 66, Bldg 16, Microdistrict 11; ⎊312163; e info@madagascar.kz; www. madagascar.kz. Aktau-based tour company offering yacht trips & tours exploring Mangistau Region.

✈ **Otrar Travel** Bldg 39A, Microdistrict 8; ⎊300400; f 300401; e sco@otrar.kz. General Service Agent for Air Astana.

Partner Tour 5, Bldg 12, Microdistrict 2; ⎊/f 526088; e partner-tour@nursat.kz. They can put together tailor-made programmes covering most of the main sights of Mangistau Region, including day trips to Fort Shevchenko & Sherkala & 2- or 3-day packages further afield.

✈ **Transavia** 101A, Bldg 39A, Microdistrict 8; ⎊506760; f 520553; www.transavia-travel.

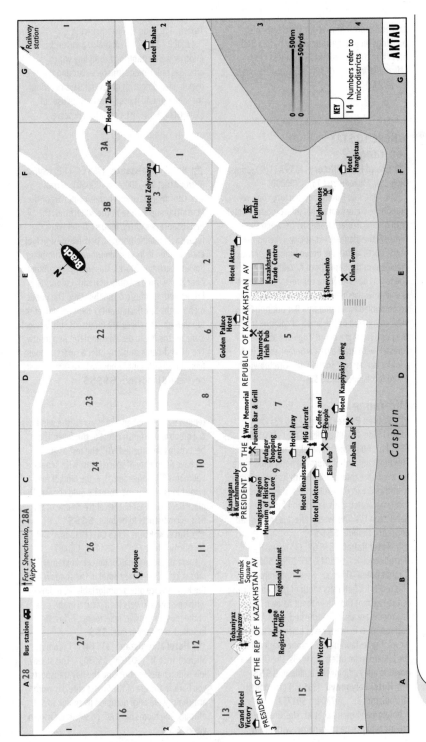

AKTAU

KEY

14 Numbers refer to microdistricts

0   500m
0   500yds

A 28   Bus station   B Fort Shevchenko, 28A   Railway station
Airport

Grand Hotel Victory
PRESIDENT OF THE REP OF KAZAKHSTAN AV

Tobaniyaz Alniyazov
Intimak Square

Mosque

Marriage Registry Office
Regional Akimat

Hotel Victory

Kashagan Kurzhimanuly
PRESIDENT OF THE
Mangistau Region Museum of History & Local Lore
War Memorial REPUBLIC OF KAZAKHSTAN AV
Fuento Bar & Grill

Ardager Shopping Centre
Hotel Aray
MiG Aircraft

Golden Palace Hotel

Shamrock Irish Pub

Hotel Renaissance
Hotel Koktem
Elis Pub
Coffee and People

Arabella Café
Hotel Kaspiyskiy Bereg

Hotel Aktau
Kazakhstan Trade Centre

Shevchenko
China Town

Lighthouse

Hotel Mangistau

Funfair

Hotel Zheruik
Hotel Zelyonaya
Hotel Rahat

Caspian

kz. Local representative for Transaero. Also bookings on other airlines. They have a 2nd branch in the Star of Aktau Business Centre (*Microdistrict 14;* \f 300090; e *sco.transavia2@ topmail.kz*).

Turist 110, Bldg 4, Microdistrict 9; \ 430000 f 310171; e pbatalov@nursat.kz. Another well-established company which arranges tailor-made itineraries around the region, including trips of several days covering the underground mosques & necropolises of Mangistau, & the Ust-Urt Nature Reserve.

WHERE TO STAY
Top-range

⌂ Grand Hotel Victory [335 A3] (90 rooms) Bldg 25A, Microdistrict 13; \ 700000; f 300050; e info@grandhotelvictory.com; www. grandhotelvictory.com. This smart modern hotel with a semicircular façade sits between the centre & the planned Aktau City development to the north, along the broad highway of the President of the Republic of Kazakhstan Av. The rooms have AC & are comfortable, & there is an impressive health centre on the top floor, accompanied by a Panorama Bar offering fine views tempered by the smell of chlorine from the pool. There is a bland 'English pub', the Old Forester, with little old or arboreal about it, & a lobby bar named 'Brown Bar', with brownish-toned furnishings. **$$$$$**

⌂ Hotel Renaissance [335 C4] (120 rooms) Microdistrict 9; \ 300600; f 300601; e rhi. scobr.dosm@renaissancehotels.com. Part of the Marriott group & close to the waterfront, the Renaissance is a glitzy, modern hotel whose futuristic, metallic-finished, pod-like design looks entirely alien in its neighbourhood of crumbling Soviet apartment blocks. The open-plan ground floor is a swirling mixture of trendy colours & fabrics, lounge music & spot lighting. The poetic menu in the Silk Restaurant is somewhat over the top though: 'the chocolate mousse is soft & sweet & makes the Aktau dream complete'. Apparently. The AC bedrooms similarly offer a smart, modern feel. The airport shuttle bus costs T6,000 & must be reserved in advance. **$$$$$**

Mid-range

⌂ Golden Palace Hotel [335 E3] (14 rooms) Bldg 40A, Microdistrict 6; \ 600170, 600171; f 600175; e gphotelaktau@mail.ru. This modern, centrally located hotel looks more brown palace than golden, with its brown-tinted windows & exterior brown tiles. The rooms are nicely decorated with dark wood furnishings & flat-screen TVs. The overall effect is somewhat antiseptic though. **$$$$**

⌂ Hotel Rahat [335 G2] (35 rooms) Microdistrict 1; \ 505013, 507205; f 505742; e rahat.hotel@aknet.kz; www.hotelrahat.kz. This red-brick hotel sits south of the centre, close to the seafront though without its own beach. The rooms are smartly furnished, with AC, large bathrooms, & in many cases balconies with sea views. The restaurant has a stone-walled décor; the billiard room offers log walls. The Olimpia bowling alley adjoins the building. **$$$$**

⌂ Hotel Zelyonaya [335 F2] (16 rooms) Microdistrict 3; \ 507304; f 501752; e hotelgreen@mail.aknet.kz. The 'Green Hotel' attempts to live up to its name, with nicely tended gardens, green blinds across the windows & a green wood-finish effect in the foyer. The best rooms are labelled 'VIP', the rest as 'luxe'. All have AC, plenty of space (most with separate bedrooms & lounge rooms), & the kind of fussy furnishings your grandmother would choose. The place lies southeast of the centre, in one of the first microdistricts to be built. **$$$$**

⌂ Hotel Koktem [335 C4] (19 rooms) Bldg 10, Microdistrict 14; \f 434479, 433487; e koktem_aktau@mail.online.kz; koktem@ nursat.kz. This 2-storey hotel in the shadow of the Renaissance offers comfortable AC rooms with en-suite showers (or a jacuzzi in the case of the most expensive 'luxe' room). B/fast is included in the room rate. **$$$**

⌂ Hotel Mangistau [335 F4] (11 rooms) Microdistrict 4; \ 503029; f 503031. This sleepy, low-slung hotel overlooking the bay transports you back to the era of the Soviet elite. Its worn armchairs were once occupied by senior Soviet officials. The rooms have AC, en suites & Caspian views. **$$$**

Budget

⌂ **Hotel Aktau** [335 E3] (40 rooms) Bldg 66, Microdistrict 2; 504707, 504750; f 502401; e laura1@pochta.ru. This shabby 10-storey Soviet building, at the southern end of the President of the Republic of Kazakhstan Av, has been given an exterior turquoise & yellow paint job in a not wholly successful attempt to brighten the place up. Only 3 floors are currently given over to the hotel. The location is however central, & the rooms offer both AC & en suites. **$$**

⌂ **Hotel Aray** [335 C3] (12 rooms) Bldg 1, Microdistrict 9; 436396, 430339. Situated in the 5-storey Soviet apartment block alongside the Hotel Renaissance, the Aray is at the other end of the Aktau accommodation scale to its neighbour. Accessed through the Bar Aray, the hotel is actually a little smarter than first impressions might suggest, offering AC rooms with en suites. A 3-room apartment is also available for US$100. **$$**

⌂ **Hotel Kaspiyskiy Bereg** [335 D4] (10 rooms) Microdistrict 7; 522628, 521643; f 506209. This airy 2-storey hotel is for those who aim to be as close to the water as possible: its rooms are within the sound of breakers hitting the beach. The furnishings are somewhat ageing, but rooms do have AC & en-suite showers. The **Kaspiyskiy Bereg Restaurant** next door is under the same management. **$$**

⌂ **Hotel Victory** [335 A4] (18 rooms) Bldg 4, Microdistrict 15; 439516, 427745; f 439501; e victoriajtel@freemail.ru. Logically enough, a less grand option than the Grand Hotel Victory, this place has a good seafront location north of the centre. You may also hear it called the Hotel Victoria. The rooms are a touch run-down, but spacious, with enclosed balconies, en suites, AC & mini-kitchenettes, with fridge & wash basin. Their publicity material puzzlingly promises 'a free-of-charge b/fast for the sum of 500 tenges'. **$$**

⌂ **Hotel Zheruik** [335 F1] (51 rooms) Bldg 15/1, Microdistrict 3A; 520702, 501158; f 520712; e jeruik@mail.ru. This 4-storey brick building with balustraded balconies lies at the southeastern edge of town. The AC rooms are clean, if dull, the cream-painted corridors have an institutional feel, & the *dizhurnaya* on each floor offers an assortment of drinks, snacks & cigarettes for sale. There is no lift. Many of the rooms are let out to companies. **$$**

✕ WHERE TO EAT

✕ **China Town** [335 E4] Nautilus, Microdistrict 4; 508116. This hangar-like Chinese restaurant, its red lanterns left dangling far above diners' heads from the high vaulted ceiling, sits above the 6-lane bowling alley of the Nautilus complex. The restaurant's Chinese dragons clash with the painted octopus guarding the bowling lanes, the toilet signs are decidedly dubious (nut for the ladies, bolt for the gents) & the restaurant offers a separate Italian menu (under the label Café Napoli) for those unenthused by Chinese food. But despite all this muddle, the food (both Chinese & Italian) is actually rather good. There is another branch of Café Napoli in the building housing the **Laguna Nightclub** close to the Kazakhstan Trade Centre. **$$$$**

✕ **Arabella Café** [335 D4] Microdistrict 7; 521717. Taking its name from Captain Blood's fictional ship, this beachfront café offers both a terrace &, for privacy, pastel-coloured circular concrete cabins. The limited menu includes *shashlik*, *manty* & *borschtt*. The bill adds a T100 daytime entrance fee; T200 in the evening. **$$$**

✕ **Elis Pub** [335 C4] Microdistrict 7; 438511. The crenellated roof & fake towers of this large complex across the road from the Renaissance Hotel, which also houses a nightclub, bowling alley & billiard hall, give the place a castle-like appearance, though inside the décor is maritime in theme. The menu ranges across pizzas, pasta & burgers: warnings on the menu that breakages must be paid for hint that the place, which attracts a mixed local & expatriate crowd, can get lively in the evenings. **$$$**

✕ **Fuento Bar and Grill** [335 C3] Microdistrict 9; 541030; e marketing@fuento. kz; www.fuento.kz. Located inside the Ardager Shopping Centre, this place attempts to exude a Spanish ambience through photographs of bullfights & honey-coloured stonework. The English menu warns: 'Spanish kitchen endless, whole will not try!' The endless Spanish kitchen includes gazpacho & paella, amidst a wide-ranging menu. The place turns into a dance venue in the later evening, & happy hour is 18.00–21.00. **$$$**

✕ Shamrock Irish Pub [335 D3] Bldg 5B, Microdistrict 5; ✆521838. This expatriate home-from-home sets its tone with the red telephone box outside & the kit-pub décor within. The eclectic menu includes burritos, pizzas & even sushi. There are a few attempts to add a more authentic Irishness, including Guinness, Kilkenny, & Irish stew, though the Cork Pizza is pushing it. $$$

⬛ Coffee and People [335 C4] Microdistrict 7; ✆530030. A popular café that serves reasonable coffee & pastries, as well as light lunches. The food is mostly European fare. $$

SHOPPING There are a couple of shopping centres along the central President of the Republic of Kazakhstan Avenue. The **Kazakhstan Trade Centre** [335 C3] in Microdistrict 4, not far from the Aktau Hotel, is the former central shopping centre of the Soviet era (⊕ *10.00–20.00*). Further north, opposite the war memorial, the **Ardager Shopping Centre** [335 C3] in Microdistrict 9 features a supermarket, cinema and eateries (⊕ *09.00–22.00*). The main **bazaar** is currently on the east side of the town centre, one block east of the war memorial, but is to be moved to a new and less congested site on the edge of town, to the east of Microdistrict 29, on the road to the airport.

WHAT TO SEE

Along the Caspian shoreline
Aktau looks out to the west across the Caspian; its waterfront is where the city breathes, especially in the blazing heat of summer. The broken glass of discarded vodka bottles on the beach, and the post-independence clifftop housing for the elite that in places cuts off access to the water, may dent the city's maritime appeal, but they do not eliminate it, and in the summer the beach gives Aktau the character of a holiday resort.

There is a pleasant walk if you follow the coast road from the southern end of the President of the Republic of Kazakhstan Avenue, where a sculpture of the sailing ship *Aktau* stands atop a large concrete wave. Take the coast road southwestwards, to the promontory at the end of Microdistrict 4, where the Hotel Mangistau lolls sleepily. The most curious sight in Aktau is found across the road from here: an 11-storey block of flats with a stumpy **lighthouse** [335 F4] stuck on the top of it. As if to humiliate this somewhat puny example of the lighthouse family, one of the neighbouring apartment blocks features a frieze of a conventional- and rather more impressive-looking lighthouse.

From the promontory, the coast road then runs northwards. At the next junction, demarcating microdistricts 4 and 5, at the seafront end of a strip of greenery, sits a statue of **Taras Shevchenko** [335 E4], picturing the Ukrainian exile looking seawards in a vaguely wistful way. A series of steps and terraces across the road in front of the statue leads down to the water. There is another flight of steps down to the Caspian at the next intersection, between microdistricts 5 and 7, behind a notably large Kazakhstani flag. One intersection further to the north of this, close to the Modernistic metallic sheen of the Renaissance Hotel, is the somewhat incongruous sight of a **MiG aircraft** [335 C4] on a concrete stick, like a life-size version of those proudly displayed plastic aircraft models. The steps here lead to a popular section of beach, lined with several cafés and the Kaspiyskiy Bereg Hotel.

Along the President of the Republic of Kazakhstan Avenue
Running a block inland from the coast, the road now bearing the name President of the Republic of Kazakhstan Avenue is Aktau's main thoroughfare and the only street in town which gets the honour of its own name. At the intersection between microdistricts 7 and 9 stands a striking **war memorial** consisting of an eternal

flame enveloped by the five white-tiled panels of a stylised concrete yurt, each panel bearing a different year of the 1941–45 war.

Mangistau Region Museum of History and Local Lore [335 C3] (*Bldg 23A, Microdistrict 9;* ✆ *426615;* ⊕ *09.00–17.00 Mon–Sat; admission T200*) A few metres northwards along the President of the Republic of Kazakhstan Avenue from the war memorial, beyond the Ardager Shopping Centre, stands the Mangistau Region Museum of History and Local Lore. Well laid out, with some interesting displays, this is one of the better regional museums, though labelling is in Kazakh and Russian only.

The displays kick off with rooms displaying a wall map of the region, and accounts of the early explorers and adventurers who visited the place, including an English merchant, Anthony Jenkinson, in the 16th century. Next come minerals, fossils (pleasingly laid out in the form of a giant ammonite) and palaeontology, with portholes offering views of prehistoric dioramas. In the next room the walls are painted blue, to highlight displays on the Caspian, with pickled fish in jars. Next comes nature on dry land, with desert, steppe and shoreline dioramas. The wild sheep of the Ust-Urt Plateau are highlighted in a mountainous tableau. A display titled 'botanic garden', featuring samples of introduced plants, is a reminder of Aktau's botanical garden, which once sat across the road from the museum, and is now giving way to residential construction, its remaining areas of greenery (not quite the right word in the context) dry and unkempt.

A circular room devoted to archaeology features a collection of Stone Age implements, identified by archaeologist Alan Medoev as part of his work to demonstrate the antiquity of settlement in the area. There is a diorama of prehistoric hunting techniques, the hunters driving animals over a cliff to their death by channelling them between specially constructed stone walls. Remnants of these stone structures have been identified in the region. There are also Bronze and Iron Age implements on display, and ceramics from the medieval settlement of Kyzylkala. The next room starts with the Kazakh khanates, and has a line of tribal signs, *tamgas*, running along the top of the display cases, including that of the Adais, the most prominent of the local Kazakh tribal groups. The arrival of the Russians is covered by photographs of migrant families: they were given 20-year rights for tax-free fishing and the collection of salt to encourage them to come. The Adai rebellion of 1870 against Tsarist taxation is illustrated with a diorama depicting the grave of a Kazakh warrior. A few steps lead down to displays covering the economy of the region during the Tsarist period, when nomads wintered in the Mangyshlak Peninsula, migrating northwards to the Aktobe Region for the hot summer. The importance of fishing is illustrated with a diorama and a striking photograph of a Turkmen fisherman straddling a huge sturgeon. A yurt houses a family of mannequins. A display of silver jewellery includes rings worn across two fingers, a symbol of the uniting of two families by marriage.

The displays continue with coverage of the Civil War and World War II. Then there is a room on the post-war period, when fishing and pastoralism remained the mainstays of the local economy. The next room covers the sacred places of Mangistau, with displays on underground mosques, mausolea and necropolises, as well as noted local musicians such as Kashagan Kurzhimanuly, whose bust is on display. There follows a room describing the construction of the town of Aktau, which displays photographs of local cultural, scientific and literary figures, and a frog from the puppet theatre. The independence room is painted a patriotic turquoise. A golden bust of President Nazarbaev stands in front of the Kazakhstani flag, and there are photographs of the president visiting the region. The next room focuses on the history of oil exploitation in the region, with photographs of the pioneers of the industry. The first wells were drilled in 1961 around the settlements of Ozen and Zhetibay. The final room is devoted to the life of the writer and politician Abish Kekilbaev. The displays here include quotations from various international figures praising his work, a carpet bearing the writer's portrait and a photograph of him in traditional Kazakh costume, flanked by the presidents of Kazakhstan and Kyrgyzstan. There is a photograph of the huge cauldron now housed in the Khodja Ahmed Yassaui Mausoleum in Turkestan, in recognition of Kekilbaev's role in securing its return from the Hermitage in St Petersburg.

Around the akimat building Walking northwards along the President of the Republic of Kazakhstan Avenue from the museum, you pass on your left a series of seven-storey apartment blocks, whose end walls are decorated with large portraits of notable Kazakhs, such as Ablai Khan and Kazybek Bi. Across the road is a rather lumpy statue of musician **Kashagan Kurzhimanuly** [335 C3], holding a *dombra*. The next intersection is centred on a roundabout, on which stands a curious piece of sculpture resembling DNA spirals. Beyond this, on the left, stand a series of public buildings, including the **regional akimat** [335 B5] and, further on, the **marriage registry office** [335 B3], the latter resembling a large concrete yurt. **Intimak Square** [335 B3] over the road, a venue for public concerts and celebrations, is flanked by a composition entitled *Intimak* ('Accord'), which features a mother holding a chubby baby who, in turn, clutches a piece of fruit. It stands between three columns, propping up a *shanyrak*.

Further north, the modern offices of the Nur Otan Party seem better suited to their previous tenants, the shipping company Kazmortransflot, as they are constructed in the form of a sleek ocean-going vessel, ploughing along the President of the Republic of Kazakhstan Avenue. Across from here stands a statue of **Tobaniyaz Alniyazov** [335 A3], who helped establish Soviet power on the Mangyshlak Peninsula, but who fell victim to Stalinist repression in 1930.

NORTH OF AKTAU

KOSHKARATA Some 20km north of Aktau, opposite the village of Akshukur on the road which runs to Fort Shevchenko, sits the necropolis of Koshkarata, the most accessible of Mangistau's remarkable 'cities of the dead' (see box). From a distance the necropolis, on the right-hand side of the road, appears to resemble a town, so elaborate and tightly packed are its mausolea. The older part of the cemetery is at its northern end, where the modern mausolea give way to *koytases* and *kulpytases*, some several hundred years old. There is a particularly fine *koshkartas*, a statue of a sheep standing on a modern plinth. This is decorated with designs of a sword, axe and gun, indicating that it marks the grave of a warrior. Other nearby graves also carry pictograms: a *koytas* embellished with a comb and a bag marks the burial place of a woman.

FORT SHEVCHENKO

Situated 140km north of Aktau, close to the natural ice-free harbour of Tyub Karagan Bay, Fort Shevchenko is the oldest town in Mangistau Region. It was established in 1846 around the fortress of Novopetrovskoye, and renamed in the late 1850s as Fort Alexandrovsky. Its main historical claim to fame rests on its role as the place of exile between 1850 and 1857 of the great Ukrainian poet Taras Shevchenko. The town was renamed Fort Shevchenko in his honour in 1939. Fort Shevchenko today is a quiet town of whitewashed bungalows, set at the foot of a rocky outcrop on which remnants of the Tsarist fort still stand. At the base of this outcrop is an elegant Tsarist chapel. The main sight of the town is a museum complex centred on a park which has its origins in the Tsarist-era Officers' Park.

ETHNOGRAPHIC MUSEUM OF MANGYSHLAK (*(72938) 22333;* ⊕ *09.00–13.00 & 14.00–18.00; admission T50)* On the left of the main entrance to the park stands the Ethnographic Museum of Mangyshlak. This is centred on a yurt-shaped hall, its outer walls decorated with some pleasant mosaics. You enter into the hall which, logically enough, is largely occupied by a yurt, 6m in diameter. The exhibits on the walls around the room include some interesting photographs of local Kazakh and Turkmen people, taken in the early years of the 20th century. There are also carpets, costumes, weapons and musical instruments. The next room features displays on the two traditional mainstays of the economy, pastoralism and fishing. The rather fearsome fishing implements on display include a spiked club and an equally menacing-looking descaler. There is a display of chunky silver jewellery in the centre of the room.

Next comes a room focused on *koytases* and *kulpytases*, with wall friezes depicting some of the items engraved on stones marking male and female graves: blacksmiths' tools on the former, a samovar, teacups and jewellery on the latter. There is also an example of one of the square-shouldered limestone human figures found on the Ust-Urt Plateau, and dated by some researchers to the Sarmat period. The figures typically have a sword and an emphasised chest, leading some to suggest that they may depict Amazon-style female warriors. The next room includes some Kazakh traditional games, such as a board for *togyzkumalak*, somewhat akin to backgammon, with nine egg-shaped indentations on each side of the board. There is also a very large stone, the centrepiece of a very basic game which involved seeing who could lift it. There are photographs of local musicians such as Muryn Zhirau, who died in 1954 and was famed by his ability to recite the entire epic cycle known as *Forty Batyrs*. The last room chronicles the arrival of Russian migrants, with their Singer sewing machines and heavy wooden furniture, and the lives of the Turkmens of the region, now few in number, with a display of Turkmen headgear, including the shaggy dandelion-like *telpek*.

TARAS SHEVCHENKO MUSEUM *(admission T50)* A path to the right-hand side of the ethnographic museum heads into the park. A plinth to the left of the path honours the senior officials of the Mangyshlak expedition involved in the march on Khiva in 1873. The statue of Tsar Alexander II which once stood on top of the plinth is now absent. A Soviet-era anti-aircraft gun stands nearby.

At the end of the path stands the elegant single-storey building, built in the 1850s, which once served as the summer residence of the commander of the fortress, and which now houses the Taras Shevchenko Museum. Shevchenko's writings are a foundation of modern Ukrainian literature, his poetry made a major contribution to the development of the Ukrainian national consciousness, and he was no mean artist either.

Born a serf in 1814, and orphaned young, Shevchenko progressed through his talent and the support of artists such as Karl Brullov, with whose help his freedom was purchased in 1838. He was arrested in 1847 for his association with the pan-Slavic Brotherhood of Saints Cyril and Methodius. The discovery by the

Scattered across the semi-desert landscapes of the Mangistau Region are numerous necropolises, containing a range of intricate stone structures, symbols of permanence and links to ancestors, constructed by nomadic peoples who left more trace of their presence in death than life. Mausolea marked the burial places of particularly revered figures, though in modern cemeteries, such as the southern part of the Koshkarata necropolis, so many wealthy Kazakhstanis have built elaborate mausolea for their deceased relatives that the graveyards start to take on the appearance of high-density housing.

In older cemeteries, other forms of funerary architecture are more important. Mangistau Region is particularly renowned for its richly decorated stone columns, rectangular in plan, a form known as *kulpytas*. The easily carved local stone and dry climate have contributed to the fashioning and preservation of beautiful forms. The upper part of the column is often more elaborately carved, frequently with a rounded top which, to some researchers, suggests the human head. Many authorities believe that the origins of the *kulpytas* lay in anthropomorphic Turkic sculptures, *balbals*, which then became stylised under pressure from Islamic doctrines. Thus, more conical designs at the top of *kulpytases* are said to suggest the helmets of warriors. Others believe that rounded forms at the top of these columns represent the sun, or cosmos. The rounded tops often surmount curving shapes. The lower part of the *kulpytas* often consists of a panel, usually decorated with geometrical or floral designs, or sometimes inscriptions such as prayers.

Another form of tombstone, which seems to have been a mark of particular respect, is a stone in the form of a sheep, known as a *koshkartas*. There are also more stylised sheep-like designs, little more than a horizontal cylinder on a pedestal, a form known as a *koytas*. Another, rarer, structure found in some necropolises of the region is a stone cenotaph in the form of a sarcophagus, a form which may have been used to honour warriors killed in distant battles. The lids of these sarcophaguses are sometimes decorated with stone models of warriors' helmets, saddles or forms in the shape of the horns of a ram.

One of the most fascinating features of the *kulpytases* and other funerary stones is the frequent appearance across their surfaces of little carved pictures, which give an insight into the lives of the deceased. The most common items on male *kulpytases* are weapons: swords, daggers, spears, axes, bows and arrows and rifles. Stones sometimes carry pictures of horses, occasionally with their rider also pictured. The gravestone of a blacksmith is decorated with pictures of his tools. Female *kulpytases* frequently picture jewellery, but all manner of household implements are occasionally observed: scissors, combs, cups, boots, even kettles. The appearance of a hand symbol perhaps suggests openness. Another common design is a *tamga*, a symbol denoting the tribe of the deceased.

There are many variations of form. Thus the necropolis of Ushkan Ata features particularly solid-looking, square-plan *kulpytases*. Some of those at the necropolis of Karagashty Aulie have a form resembling a tree. The cities of the dead of Mangistau offer a fascinating and varied insight into the lives of the people of the region.

arresting authorities of poetry critical of Tsarist rule resulted in a particularly severe punishment, and Shevchenko found himself in military exile as a private as part of the Orenburg garrison at the Orenburg and then Orsk fortresses. Despite a specific injunction from Tsar Nicholas I that he be barred from writing, drawing and painting, he managed to do all three. Indeed his artistic skills secured him a place on the military expedition sent to survey the Aral Sea in 1848–49. He was transferred to the fortress of Novopetrovskoye in 1850, and remained there until his release from military exile in 1857, two years after the death of Tsar Nicholas II. Taras Shevchenko died in 1861.

Shevchenko was able to produce many watercolours and pencil drawings during his exile in Novopetrovskoye, and these are featured heavily in the museum. Among the themes chosen are landscapes, such as a painting of fire on the steppe, the everyday lives of the Kazakh people, a series of mythical and biblical subjects, and portrayals of military life. There are portraits of the commander of the fortress, Irakty Uskov, who helped Shevchenko, and of his wife, Agata Uskova, with whom the poet seems to have been deeply enamoured. Also on display is a model of the Novopetrovskoye Fortress, and descriptions of the 1848 Aral expedition and 1851 Karatau expedition, in both of which Shevchenko's artistic skills were utilised. There is a copy of a letter to the Tsarist administration from explorer Karl Ber, petitioning for Shevchenko's release. And there is a tiny book in which Shevchenko wrote his poetry. The museum also includes various later paintings depicting Shevchenko in exile, including a 1951 canvas portraying the poet being taken by boat across the Caspian on his release from internal exile. The museum's current visitors' book starts with a message from Ukrainian President Yushchenko, who visited Fort Shevchenko in 2005.

The modern building next to the museum surrounds the simple underground room where Shevchenko apparently spent much of his time. It comprises little more than two high windows, whitewashed walls, a hard wooden bed and a writing table. Also in this building is a section of tree trunk, apparently all that remains of a tree planted by the poet, and some *kulpytases* drawn by him. Opposite the museum is a statue of a rather contemplative Shevchenko.

BAUTINO The harbour lies 4km north of Fort Shevchenko, at the village of Bautino. The road from Fort Shevchenko forks after 2km: the left-hand fork takes you to Bautino, the right-hand fork to the village of Atash, on the opposite side of the bay. Opposite the walled compound containing Bautino port is a line of attractive Tsarist-era buildings with wooden roofs and sometimes walls. The two most impressive of these were financed by a merchant named Zahar Dubskiy, who grew wealthy on the proceeds of the fish business. One of the houses was a gift for his daughter. In front of this is a bust of the moustachioed Aleksey Bautin, the first head of the village Soviet, killed in 1919 during the Civil War but immortalised by the name of the village.

The bay offers the closest good ice-free harbour to the oilfields being developed in the shallow waters of the north Caspian, and is fast developing into the centre for Kazakhstan's offshore services operation. There are several maritime support bases, lit up at night with a brightness which contrasts sharply with the dim lighting of the village. The closest, just to the north of Bautino, at the end of the promontory on which the village sits, is the base run by AGIP KCO to support the Kashagan operation. Between this base and the village is a stretch of beach.

A smart hotel has been constructed in Bautino to accommodate the expatriates working at the maritime bases. Part of the group of the same name, this is the **Chagala Hotel** (*96 rooms; 57 Fetisova St;* \ *(72938) 24634;* f *(72938) 24794;*

e *reservation.bautino@chagalagroup.kz; www.chagalagroup.kz;* **$$$$$**). This four-storeyed hotel stands immediately adjacent to the beach, with many of its comfortably furnished, air-conditioned rooms offering excellent views across the bay from their balconies. Most of your fellow guests will be oil workers staying here on four-week rotations. They warn against leaving the hotel compound after dark, as there is resentment in the village among some of those who have not enjoyed the fruits of Kazakhstan's oil boom.

EAST OF FORT SHEVCHENKO

TAMSHALY Amid the arid landscapes of the Mangyshlak Peninsula, where water is always at a premium, are a few unexpectedly verdant spots. One of the most remarkable is the canyon known as Tamshaly (the name means something like 'dripping place' in Kazakh). It lies near the coast, east of Fort Shevchenko. From the centre of Fort Shevchenko, head on the road towards Aktau, turning left after 1km, still within the urban area. Turn right after a further 4km. Since neither of these junctions is signposted, a guide is helpful. After 25km along a dusty road, the sea comes into view and the road descends sharply down an escarpment. At the base of this, take the right-hand turn where the road forks, passing the ruined walls of a long-abandoned collective farm on your left. The track bends inland up into a broad canyon, and you reach Tamshaly 5km from the fork.

A reed-fringed pool occupies the canyon floor. A path from the car park runs along the left-hand side of the pool, between the reeds and the side of the canyon. The path takes you down a short side valley to the natural theatre of rock known as Tamshaly. Water filters through porous limestone until it strikes a layer of marl. At this point it drips down from the semicircular rock face into the valley below, a permanent shower of droplets. The dripping water sustains a layer of lush green vegetation which runs around the rock face at this point, like a giant hanging basket. The valley floor is also lush, and perfumed with fragrant patches of mint. Graffiti and litter somewhat impair the beauty of the place, but it remains a remarkable spot.

SULTAN EPE To get to the interesting though mysterious site of Sultan Epe, and the nearby necropolis of Kenty Baba, take the Aktau road south of Fort Shevchenko. After 3km turn left onto the rough road which heads to the village of Taushik. Keep on this road for 55km, until you pass on your left signs for Sultan Epe and Kenty Baba. The best track to use to these sites is several hundred metres further on. The track brings you to the necropolis of **Kenty Baba** after a further 7km. Surrounded by a low metal fence, the necropolis includes a restored mausoleum of the 'tower' type, with a square base and tapering walls, rising to a circular hole in place of a roof. Around the tomb inside are piled horns of *arkhars*, brought here perhaps by hunters wishing for a benediction for successful hunting, and a fire stone, or *shiraktas*, blackened with soot, on which sheep's fat is burnt by the faithful during visits to the place. Another, again roofless, mausoleum on the site has a square base and walls of large, flat slabs, on which are incised a gallery of figures. There are horses with large phalluses, swords, camels, hands, a rifle and even a cross. The necropolis also contains many *koytases*, often decorated with an engraving of a sword.

Take the track passing behind Kenty Baba, leaving the necropolis to the right. After a few hundred metres you arrive at the necropolis of **Sultan Epe**. A large oval-shaped enclosure made by a drystone wall, enclosing a funerary structure comprising more stones, is said to mark the grave of Sultan Epe, patron of sailors, and some of his followers. The necropolis is particularly rich in examples of the sarcophagus-like *sandyktas*, often with a *koytas* resting on the top. Some of these *sandyktases* have pictures of weapons etched on the flat stones which make up their walls.

Just beyond the necropolis, on the side of a rocky canyon, is the entrance to a subterranean complex identified in a plaque as the underground mosque of Sultan Epe, dating from between the 9th and 12th centuries. The complex comprises a series of small rooms, connected by low passages. A visit here requires a great deal of stooping. The rooms are rectangular in plan, lit and aired from openings in the roof formed by concentric layers of stones. The latter are the only evidence of the presence of the complex from the surface, where they form little pink piles of stones. The ceiling is propped up by circular columns, only a couple of which are original. With none of the rooms obviously more prominent than the others, some researchers have questioned whether the complex was initially built as a mosque at all.

SHAKPAK ATA Shakpak Ata is the most architecturally impressive of the underground mosques of Mangistau Region: it is a fascinating site which deserves to be much better known. Continuing eastwards on the road running between Fort Shevchenko and Taushik, beyond the turning to Sultan Epe, you reach after a further 7km a crossroads, where a rougher track crosses the road. The track to the left is signposted to Shakpak Ata. Take this. After 3km, the striking dry-floored canyon of **Kapamsai** comes into view to the right of the road. This is a limestone canyon with dramatic overhanging walls. The track takes you down a steep descent towards the coast to the side of this canyon. At the base of this descent, another 3km on, turn right where the track forks. After a further 5km is a modern domed building. This place, built in honour of a local figure named Erzhan Haziret, celebrated for his spirituality, provides basic overnight accommodation (sleeping on the floor) for pilgrims visiting the Shakpak Ata site. There is a one-roomed museum within the building, containing items of clothing worn by Erzhan Haziret as well as, usefully, floor plans of Shakpak Ata and other underground mosques in the region.

Turn right immediately beyond this building, onto a track which runs into the broad canyon in which lies the necropolis of Shakpak Ata, a few hundred metres away. On the side of the canyon, to your left, is the **underground Mosque of Shakpak Ata**, dated according to the plaque here to sometime between the 10th and 13th centuries. The rock forming the side of the canyon has taken a honeycomb form here, a result of wind erosion. Into the rock are cut several rectangular niches, places of burial. Firestones, *shiraktases*, stand in front of these. There is a niched arched portal, covered with etchings of horses, handprints and inscriptions in Arabic. You enter the mosque through a wooden door close to the portal, then climb a few rough steps.

The plan of the mosque, strikingly, takes the form of a cross. The square central space rises to a domed ceiling with a hole in the top for light and ventilation. At each corner of the space is a column, with graceful, flat arches running between them. At the centre of this space was another *shiraktas* when I visited, though this resulted in comments from other visitors that no pilgrim would make such a fire in a mosque – its rightful place was at a graveside – and the suggestion that the *shiraktas* may have been placed there by a film company, for effect. The chamber to the south has a niched *mihrab*, with further niches around it. The chamber to the east of the central space is much longer than the others, with further niches along its walls, possibly for books. The walls of the mosque are further enlivened by small holes into which lamps would have been placed, by numerous Arabic inscriptions, and by etched drawings of horses, goats and handprints.

At the end of the longer eastern chamber is a second entrance to the mosque, a flight of steps which brings you up onto the plateau on the side of the canyon. A modern, square-based building with a metal roof has been placed above the roof over the central chamber: while a conservation measure, the structure detracts from the natural beauty of the site. Near this building, cut into the limestone plateau, are two lines of nine egg-shaped indentations: this was a board for the game *togyzkumalak*.

Beyond the necropolis, the white walls of the canyon, and tamarisk bushes in the valley floor, make for some enticing scenery. You may see flints here: *shakpak*, in Kazakh, means 'flint'.

If you are coming from Aktau, there is a shorter route to Shakpak Ata which avoids the need to come via Fort Shevchenko. An unsignposted track leads to the right off the main Aktau to Fort Shevchenko road, 71km north of the regional capital. Head towards the twin 'tower'-type mausolea, square-based stone-built structures with tapering walls, 11km away. They are part of a small necropolis named **Kusum**. After a further 9km the track reaches the crossroads formed where the Fort Shevchenko to Taushik road crosses it. Head straight on for Shakpak Ata. There are however several competing tracks, particularly on the stretch north of the Kusum necropolis, and it is easy to take the wrong turn. A guide is therefore particularly important if you take this route.

AROUND SHETPE

The village of Shetpe is an unassuming district capital located close to some striking scenery of isolated mountains amidst desert plains, lying to the northeast of Aktau. To get here, take the Fort Shevchenko road to the north of Aktau, turning right after 50km onto a road signposted to Karazhanbas and Kalamkas. Turn right on the road signposted to Shetpe at the crossroads reached after a further 48km. After a further 7km, on the left of the road, you encounter one of the fields of huge **stone spheres** found across the region. These concretions, which usually appear to be grouped in lines, may have been formed in the currents of ancient seas. Or they may be part of a game of marbles being fought out by giants. Shetpe village is another 58km on.

SHERKALA From Shetpe, take the road for Buzachi, turning left after 14km onto a road signposted to Shagir. To the right of the road is the pale escarpment of an upland known as Aktau ('White Mountain'); to the left stands the dark escarpment of Karatau ('Black Mountain'). A further 3km on, the road passes through a natural feature dubbed by local tour guides as the 'gate of fairy tales' and ahead of you the mountain of Sherkala comes into glorious view. From this angle, Sherkala looks rather like a giant yurt, with steep white walls overlaid by a layer of pink and then a conical top.

A track to the right, 4km further on, leads to the mountain. From this viewpoint Sherkala changes form, looking less like a yurt and more a lion in profile. Sherkala indeed means 'lion town'. After some 600m a faint track to the left brings you, 200m on, to the small necropolis of **Shikh Ata**. There is the small underground mosque of Temir Abdal Ata here: a niche is cut into the chalk rock face, with further small niches dug out into which books and candles would have been placed. A further chamber, cut deeper into the rock, was for prayer and meditation. Continue on for another 1km or so, circling Sherkala until you reach its northern side. The external walls of a caravanserai are just about distinguishable near the base of the mountain. Sherkala, with its steep and forbidding ascent, apparently served as a place of refuge when hostile forces threatened the settlements below. Niches are discernible on the northern escarpment wall, from where lookouts watched over the dry plains. One apocryphal local tale has it that the defenders of Sherkala were besieged for months by a hostile invading force. The invaders puzzled as to how they survived for so long without water, until a traitor informed them that a deep well ran down through the centre of the mountain. On learning this, the invaders dug a lateral tunnel through the mountain, which intercepted the well. They were able to cut the rope to the bucket, the defenders of the mountain lost their access to the water, and capitulated.

KYZYLKALA A few kilometres from Sherkala lie the remains of Kyzylkala, one of the few medieval settlements to have been discovered in Mangistau Region. This appears to have been a once important Silk Route trading settlement, which developed around the 10th century with the arrival of settlers from Khorezm. But the sacking of Khorezm by the Mongols in the 13th century prompted its decline, a decay reinforced by changes in the level of the Caspian which caused the caravans to take a new route, bypassing Kyzylkala.

To get here, take a track to the left, 3km north of the 'gate of fairy tales', a couple of hundred metres before a small copse. The track curves behind the copse, reaching the site of Kyzylkala after 1km. The walls of a fortification, square in plan, are discernible, with excavations revealing a segment of the wall. The administrative buildings, of red fired brick, lay within this. The pieces of red brick scattered around the site hint at the name given to the settlement – 'red town'. Outside the fortress lay residential and commercial districts.

Samal Canyon Another of the unexpectedly verdant spots within Mangistau's arid landscapes, not far from Sherkala, is the Samal Canyon. Heading north from the 'gate of fairy tales', take the track to your left reached after 400m. The track leads into the low hills of the Karatau range. After 4km you drive into the Samal Canyon, down which a stream and then water pipe runs. The green bushes and trees here, even willows, offer an unlikely splash of greenery between the dark rocks of the canyon walls. This hillside oasis is a delightful place, save for the empty vodka bottles scattered around.

SOUTHEAST OF AKTAU

THE KARAGIYE DEPRESSION Reaching 132m below sea level at its deepest point, the bottom of the Karagiye Depression was the lowest place in all of the former Soviet Union. It occupies a large area, with a length of some 40km. Take the road towards Zhanaozen from Aktau. After 30km the road descends into the depression, and passes across the undulating floor. Eventually rising up a steeper side ('attention! The dangerous section' warns a sign in English) there is a good viewpoint across the depression 60km from Aktau. This gives an excellent sense of the size of the feature, whose far side is often lost in the haze.

THE PILGRIMAGE ROUTE TO BEKET ATA Born in 1750, Beket Myrzagul-uly was a former military leader who became a prominent Sufi figure. Educated in Bukhara, he returned to the Mangistau Region and built several underground mosques here. He founded a *madrasa* and centre for scientific study at his underground mosque in Oglandy. He died at the age of 63, the age attained by the Prophet Muhammad, and was buried in the Oglandy Mosque. This place, in a remote location east of

Zhanaozen, on the western edge of the Ust-Urt Plateau, has become one of the most important pilgrimage destinations in Kazakhstan.

The pilgrimage route is a difficult one, along rough tracks. The pilgrims like it that way, believing that the pilgrimage should be physically challenging, and suggestions that the track be upgraded have been resisted. The route is lengthened further by the required visit to the underground mosque of Shopan Ata – a Sufi follower of Khodja Ahmed Yassaui, and reputed to have been an inspiration to Beket Ata – before actually getting to Beket Ata itself. The pilgrimage is usually made as a two-day trip, visiting Shopan Ata and Beket Ata on the first day, overnighting at the guesthouse at Beket Ata, and then returning the next morning to either Zhanaozen or Aktau. Local pilgrims make the trip in grey UAZ jeeps or minibuses. A place in one of the latter costs around T2,500 from Zhanaozen, a little more from Aktau. Tour companies in Aktau (see page 334) will organise the same trip in more comfort and at higher cost. You should bring all the food and water you need for the trip with you. Local pilgrims will bring lamb, or even sometimes a live sheep, with them for preparation at Beket Ata as a ritual meal. Foreign tourists staying the night will almost certainly be invited to share this food. Alcohol should not be brought, and visitors should dress modestly, covering their heads with a scarf or handkerchief in the underground mosques.

The guesthouse at Beket Ata is comfortable. Built in 2000, the building, which features seven mosaic-covered domes, includes a mosque, a communal eating hall with a long, low *dastarkhan* in the centre, and separate sleeping areas for men and women. You sleep on the floor, but basic bedding is provided. The guesthouse is air conditioned, though summer nights are still warm. There is no charge for sleeping here, but pilgrims are expected to leave a small donation.

Shopan Ata The pilgrimage route starts at Zhanaozen, the second city of Mangistau Region, a dusty oil town of some 100,000 people, 140km to the southeast of Aktau. From here head northeast to the village of Kyzylsay, 21km away, turning right just before you enter the village, on the road to Senek. Take the turning to the left 4km along this road. After another 4km a right turn signposted to Shopan Ata takes you onto a rough track. Do not however attempt the journey without an experienced guide as the terrain is unforgiving. After 5km you reach a cylindrical standing stone, taller than a person, surrounded by a little fence. Locals say that this was dropped by a giant named Ersary many millions of years ago and that, because the grass of that period was so tall, he never found it.

You come to Shopan Ata after another 24km. The first stopping point here is traditionally the mausoleum of Shopan Ata's son-in-law, which stands above and apart from the rest of the complex, on a plateau. The simple, roofless mausoleum is built of large flat stones, on which are carved Arabic inscriptions and pictures of camels, goats, swords and rifles, as well as the *tamga* denoting the Adai tribe, an upwardly pointing arrow.

After a prayer is recited at this mausoleum, pilgrims continue down the hill to the Shopan Ata site itself. There is a cluster of whitewashed buildings, including a mosque and guesthouse, around a soothing leafy courtyard: a modern complex built with financial support from the Kazakhstani state oil and gas company KMG. A path beyond leads past a fenced necropolis to your right. The older graves, the oldest of which apparently date back to the 10th century, lie at the far end of the necropolis. There are some fine *kulpytases*, with decorated swirls and inscriptions, as well as sarcophagus-like *sandyktases*. The path then passes through an arch guarded by a couple of stone sheep, to reach a semicircle of rock face, in which have been cut a series of chambers. Two of the entrances are closed off by wooden doors. The left-hand door leads into an underground mosque. A low carpeted hallway takes you through into a square-based room. A niched area in front of you is centred on a *mihrab*, constructed as an arched niche in the rock wall. There are further niches to each side of the room.

The right-hand wooden door leads into the rooms in which Shopan Ata and his wife lived and are buried. The first room here is a square chamber lit through a hole in the roof. Wooden poles in the centre of the room lean against this hole. After a prayer is recited, pilgrims circulate the room three times anticlockwise, touching the wooden poles at each circulation. An opening to the left leads into the room in which Shopan Ata is buried. Step across the tall threshold with your right foot first. A white sheet lies over Shopan Ata's tomb. A niched area in this room evidently was used as a hearth given the fire-blackened walls and ceiling.

At the back of the first room a passage leads to another chamber also lit from a hole in its roof. Steps lead down to a dark room where Bibi Han, the wife of Shopan Ata, is reputedly buried. To the right of the illuminated chamber a further passage leads to the grave said to be that of Darhan Bibi, Shopan Ata's daughter. Male pilgrims tend not to visit these latter graves, considered to lie in the 'female' part of the complex.

To the left of the two wooden doors, if you stand facing the semicircular rock face, are further square-based chambers cut into the rock. These contain niches, in some of which lie graves. These rooms may have been used by Shopan Ata for teaching and healing activities. From the semicircular rock face, take the path up the hill, through the oldest part of the cemetery. This takes you to a circular stone enclosure, said to mark the grave of Bayan Baba, Shopan Ata's father-in-law. Pilgrims walk three times anticlockwise around the grave. There is a *shiraktas* here in the shape of a penis: women wanting a baby light a fire at its tip.

Beket Ata Beket Ata lies 76km further on, along a rough track passing through a landscape of expanses of semi-desert punctuated by escarpments. Some 38km from Shopan Ata, the track climbs onto a ridge, offering outstanding and somewhat giddying views towards white escarpments to either side. The ridge, covered in flints, is known as Shakpaktas.

As at Shopan Ata, arrival at Beket Ata is traditionally preceded by a visit to a mausoleum on the edge of the main site. In the case of Beket Ata this is to the **Mausoleum of Oglandy Ata**, a square-based building with a conical silver dome, to the right of the track as you approach Beket Ata. An open window in the side of the mausoleum reveals Oglandy Ata's tomb. The mausoleum is linked to one of the best-known legends about Beket Ata. It is said that the class at Bukhara in which Beket Ata studied was packed with excellent students. The *pir* who taught the class was unable to decide which of his worthy students should be designated as his successor. He therefore launched his staff high into the air, telling his students that whichever of them found the staff would take over from him. Most of the students hurried towards where they perceived the staff had been thrown, but were unable to find it. Beket Ata returned to his native Mangistau. Here he came across a Turkmen shepherd named Oglandy, who had come across the staff, stuck firm in the ground. Oglandy was unable to pull it out. With an Arthurian touch, Beket Ata was able to do so with ease. A spring appeared when the staff was pulled out of the ground, and Beket Ata's status as the *pir*'s successor was confirmed. The Mausoleum of Oglandy Ata is said to be the grave of that Turkmen shepherd.

A few hundred metres further on you reach the **Beket Ata guesthouse complex**. Above the arched entrance gate to the complex is drawn the upward-pointing arrow of the Adai tribe. A family tree of the Adai tribe on a wall inside the guesthouse shows Beket Myrzagul-uly's position in the tribe. The complex also includes a kitchen block and a slaughterhouse. The complex stands on the edge of a plateau, offering great views across the desert landscape to distant limestone escarpments beyond. The complex is an efficiently organised place: there is even a helipad for VIP visitors (with another one down at the mosque site itself), and mobile phones work here.

The **Beket Ata underground mosque** is at the base of the escarpment, a walk of a couple of kilometres. You pass first through a brick gate flanked by a couple of concrete *arkhars*. A flight of steps, protected at its steepest stretches by blue-painted railings, leads down the side of the escarpment. One of the rocks passed on the way down is etched with the years 1750 and 1813, Beket Ata's birth and death. There are also brightly painted concrete statues of *arkhars* and leopards decorating the route. Towards the bottom of the escarpment is a leafy grove of rushes and tamarisk, centred on a spring. Next to this a crazy-paved mound topped with a pile of stones marks the point at which Beket Ata is reputed to have pulled his teacher's staff from the ground. The water from the spring is said to have healing properties. It is also rather salty. Troughs have been laid out nearby to attract *arkhars* to the site, but if you are not lucky enough to see any there is at least the compensation of some concrete ones amongst the tamarisk.

The path continues across a dry stream. The water from another spring just to the right of this, named Koz Bulak, is said to be good for ailments of the eyes. A flight of steps leads up from here to the entrance to the mosque. There are *kulpytases* and *koytases* to either side. Enter through a wooden door, and move to the right up into a room which, after the brightness of the walk, initially appears to be pitch black. A whitewashed chamber with rough, uneven walls, dimly illuminated from a hole high in the ceiling, can eventually be made out. A plaque in the wall marks Beket Ata's tomb. Another room, to the left of the entrance, contains a *mihrab* cut into the wall, and served both as a mosque and *madrasa*. A further windowless chamber behind this was probably a room used by Beket Ata for healing. Propped up against the wall is a polished branch: pilgrims circle three times anticlockwise beneath it, touching the branch and then their foreheads as they do so. On leaving the underground complex, the custodian told me to look up towards the escarpment I had just walked down. He pointed towards some tall natural striations on the rock face. Did they not, he asked, appear to spell out the word 'Allah', in Arabic script? They did.

Returning to Zhanaozen it is possible to use a slightly faster, more southerly, route, which passes through the village of Senek, but which bypasses Shopan Ata and is therefore not taken on the outward journey.

Further to the east is the spectacular but often overlooked **Ust-Urt Plateau**. Often described as Kazakhstan's answer to Monument Valley, this semi-desert region is scattered with vast chalk escarpments rising as much as 340m into the air. The cliffs have been shaped by seismic activity, water, wind and sand erosion, and now form giant terraces stretching hundreds of kilometres.

The plateau's status as a state nature reserve has helped protect much of its wildlife, including Indian porcupines, saiga and over half of Kazakhstan's population of dzheyran gazelle. It is also possible to see long-eared desert hedgehogs and a wide variety of birds of prey, such as Houbara bustards, Turkmen owls, Saker falcon, and short-toed and golden eagles.

The plateau is little visited by tourists as it is relatively inaccessible. The fastest way to get here is by helicopter from Aktau, or the long journey by road via Zhanaozen and Senek. It is then possible to ascend to the plateau only on foot or by 4x4, and a guide is essential. Tours and transport can be arranged via Otrar and Madagascar travel in Aktau (see page 344).

KENDIRLI BAY Some 210km south of Aktau, the secluded bay of Kendirli is today a quiet and isolated spot. But the Kazakhstan authorities have plans for a major investment programme for the development of seaside tourism here that will see the Kendirli Bay transformed into a modern resort complex, catering mainly for Kazakhstani and Russian tourists arriving by charter flights into a mooted Kendirli international airport. Protected by a 26km spit of land, the bay offers sandy beaches and warm, calm waters. The local tourism authorities boast that it is possible to swim here until October. And they promise that the water snakes don't bite.

Kendirli At the time of writing, the ambitious investment plans remain on paper and Kendirli, formerly named Fetisovo, consists of a few run-down holiday cottages and one smart gated holiday centre, run by the state oil and gas company KMG and a favoured spot for the Kazakh elite.

From Zhanaozen, take the main road south towards the Turkmen border. After 65km, where there is a left turn for the Turkmenistan road, keep straight ahead, signposted for Kendirli. The road runs down the hillside to the coast, arriving after 5km at the **Kendirli Holiday Centre** (*72934) 64885, 73163; bookings through Hotel Aruana, Zhanaozen;* (*72934) 63388; e recepshen@tnsplus.kz;* **$$$$$**). The centre offers a mix of three-bedroom 'family' cottages, 'youth' cottages divided up into four separate rooms, and 26 hotel rooms in two blocks. All the accommodation is air conditioned and well furnished. The complex was used in 2001 to host an informal meeting of five regional heads of state: if you book one of the 'family' cottages you may find yourself staying under the roof which housed the former President of Russia. Putin has been here twice: he came again for a bilateral meeting with the Kazakhstani president in 2007, and the complex is decorated with billboards to Russo–Kazakhstani friendship.

The pastel-coloured cottages surrounded by verdant lawns and rose gardens rather remind the visitor of a gated housing development. Beyond the perimeter fence, the lush greenery, supported by soil specially brought here from West Kazakhstan and constant watering, gives away abruptly to semi-desert. The place is well equipped, with sandy beaches, open-air and covered pools, water motorbikes for hire, a bowling alley and a health centre, but the overall atmosphere is somewhat Stepford-on-Sea.

Temir Baba A pilgrimage site at the southern end of Kendirli Bay, Temir Baba is worth visiting if you are staying at the holiday centre. From Kendirli, rejoin the main road to Turkmenistan, and head south, away from Zhanaozen. After 24km, take the track to the right, signposted for Temir Baba. A further 6km on, you pass between the roofless ruined houses of the abandoned coastal settlement of Aksu. This was an early base for oil exploration in the area, but lost out to Zhanaozen. Temir Baba is another 7km on, a necropolis at the base of the cliffs immediately opposite the point at which the 26km-long spit of land commences its long journey helping to protect the Kenderli Bay. The most prominent building at the site is a white-domed mosque. The necropolis sits behind this. The tomb of Temir Baba, a 13th-century figure, is a low stone-walled enclosure, which in turn sits within a smart roofless structure, financed by a local oil company. A plaque at the site reports that this was put up in 2000, under the guidance of President Nazarbaev. A well, offering waters said to have curative properties, sits in the paved area surrounded by a low fence just to the north of the mosque.

The best-known legend regarding Temir Baba involves a test of powers waged with Shopan Ata. The story runs that Shopan Ata sacrificed a sheep, took its pelt, and from that pelt was able to create a new, living sheep. Temir Baba responded by leaving the land, and starting to walk out to sea. Behind him, a spit of land formed. He had walked out 26km, and was showing no signs of tiring, when Shopan Ata conceded that Temir Baba's powers were indeed the greater of the two.

11

The South

The Syr Darya River, the Jaxartes of the Ancient Greeks, rises in the Tian Shan Mountains of Kyrgyzstan and eastern Uzbekistan and flows for more than 2,000km to the Aral Sea. The two regions of southern Kazakhstan it passes through on its journey, South Kazakhstan and Kyzylorda, are among the most touristically interesting in the country. Highlights include Turkestan, the home of Kazakhstan's most beautiful building, the mausoleum of Sufi mystic, Khodja Ahmed Yassaui; the remains of the Silk Road city of Otrar, the city whose attempts to defy Genghis Khan brought the wrath of the Mongols onto the whole of central Asia; the Aksu Zhabagly Nature Reserve, the oldest in central Asia, whose meadows are carpeted in spring by a covering of tulips; the bustling city of Shymkent, with Kazakhstan's most interesting bazaar; the Baikonur Cosmodrome, a living museum of the history of space exploration; and the Aral Sea, a manmade environmental catastrophe which is starting to fight back. The south, the most strongly ethnic Kazakh part of the country, should be an important component of any in-depth visit to Kazakhstan. Note that summers are hotter and winters milder than most of the country.

ARALSK (ARAL) _Telephone code: 72433_

Once the main port on the Kazakhstan shores of the Aral Sea, the town of Aralsk now provides a stark testament to the environmental and social disaster wrought by the diversion of the waters of the Amu Darya and Syr Darya for cotton production, and resultant desiccation of the Aral Sea (see box, page 358). Founded in 1905, with the building of the Orenburg–Tashkent railway, Aralsk became an important fishing town, its moment of glory coming in 1921, when, in response to an appeal from Lenin to provide fish for the hunger-struck people of the nascent Soviet Union the town responded with 14 railway wagons full of fish. But the drying up of the Aral Sea resulted in Aralsk losing one indispensable requirement for its life as a fishing port: its water. At one point the sea had receded some 100km from the town.

Aralsk is a poor and depressing-looking place with some 35,000 people living in single-storey whitewashed cottages. Billboards on the way into town are mostly supported by the government or NGOs declaring their various initiatives. Many householders around town have a camel or two in the yard. The completion of the Kokaral Dam in 2005, and rise in the water level of the Northern Aral Sea, has brought the water back to around 25km from the town, and the local authorities hope that, with the construction of a mooted second dam, water will once again flow into the harbour of Aralsk port. However, after years of confronting the misery of health, ecological and economic problems wrought by the loss of their sea, it will take a long time for public confidence to return.

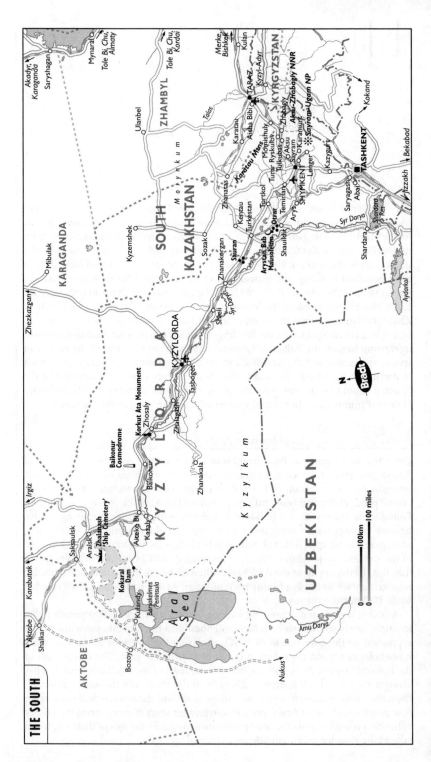

GETTING THERE AND AROUND The **railway station** is east of the centre, just off Abulkhair Khan Street. It lies on the Tashkent–Orenburg line, and there are several trains east to Almaty and west to Aktobe, as well as a train every two days to each of Atyrau, Mangyshlak and Uralsk, There are also through routes to several Russian destinations (including Moscow, Ufa and Chelyabinsk), Tashkent and Bishkek. There are two local trains daily terminating at Saksaulsk to the northwest of Aralsk. These run eastwards as far as Kyzylorda and Turkestan, respectively. **Buses** for Kyzylorda depart from outside the train station. All places of interest in Aralsk's compact centre are walkable.

TOUR OPERATOR

Aral Tenizi 10–12 Makataev St; 22256, 23691; e aralsea@mail.kz; www.aralsea.net. Not a tour operator per se but an NGO, established in 1998, which grew out of a Danish–Kazakh fishery project named 'From the Kattegat to the Aral Sea', focused on the re-establishment of a fishing industry in the Aral Sea based on introduced stocks of flounder. The project, which included efforts to educate local people, who had no tradition of eating flatfish, of the attractions of the flounder, has included the establishment of the Kambala Balyk fish-processing plant

in the town. Aral Tenizi's offices are centrally located, a couple of doors down from the Hotel Aral. They can arrange a taxi from Kyzylorda, for around T30,000, & set up tours to local places of interest connected with the desiccation of the sea, including the 'ship cemetery' at Zhalanash & the Kokaral Dam, in a UAZ 4x4, for around US$100 a day, plus petrol. They can also organise English-speaking interpreters for around US$100 a day, & offer internet access for US$3 an hour. They may also be able to arrange basic homestay accommodation in the town.

WHERE TO STAY

Hotel Aral (20 rooms) 4 Makataev St; 21479. This 4-storey building close to the port is a grim concrete block with a decrepit Soviet feel, its interior walls painted in bright yellows & greens in a failed attempt to enliven the place. The staff

are miserable & so is the atmosphere. All rooms have en suites, though many of these lack water or smell strongly of sewage; 'semi-luxe' rooms & above also offer AC but the plumbing is not improved. **$** without AC; **$$** with AC

WHERE TO EAT

Café Aral Makataev St; no phone. Attached to the hotel of the same name, the restaurant has erratic opening hours but serves beer, vodka & *shashlik*. The food & the feel of the place are underwhelming, but you wouldn't really expect otherwise. $

Karina Tokey Esetov St; no phone. This pale green building close to the museum, with no identifying sign, stands out among the limited range of places to eat in Aralsk by virtue of its roof terrace, offering a place to eat in summer which is at least open to the evening breeze, unlike the dim interiors which characterise most

of the town's eateries. The menu runs to *shashlik* & a few regional dishes. $

Unnamed Makataev St; no phone. Immediately opposite the Hotel Aral, this clean, modern café serves the usual range of *manty*, *shashlik* & salads, & vodka & beer are served from b/fast onwards, much to the relief of the clientele. The chicken *shashlik* are possibly the worst in Kazakhstan, but the other dishes are perfectly edible & the soup borders on tasty. Note that vegetarian dishes may often contain meat & that the waitresses are unconcerned by this. $

WHAT TO SEE

The harbour The place in Aralsk that provides the most vivid testimony of the consequences of the desiccation of the Aral Sea is the old harbour, just south of the Hotel Aral along Makataev Street. You are confronted with a space which is harbour-like in shape, but with dry flats and grazing livestock where the sea ought to be. Old

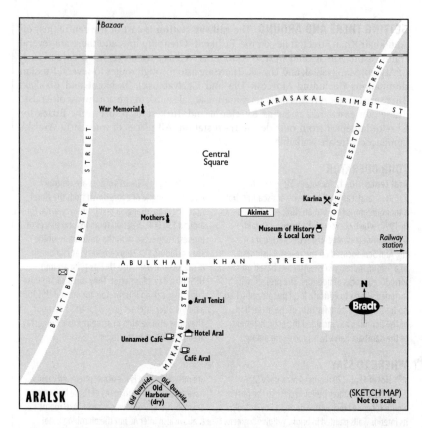

cranes stand abandoned and derelict canneries loom over the site. Along the side of the harbour abutting Makataev Street four rusting boats have been mounted onto rusting stands, as unwilling monuments to an environmental disaster. All four bear the registration of Aralribprom, the enterprise which in Soviet times ran the fish industry in the town, from boats to processing plants. Another piece of labelling added to one of the boats tells us that Alikhan and Aigerim will be together for ever. Nice for them. A log-walled house down here by the quayside, once charming and still bearing carved blue and white window frames, has been gutted, and the whole place is forlorn, with broken vodka bottles and other rubbish scattered everywhere.

Central Square Heading north from the harbour, Makataev Street hits the main thoroughfare, Abulkhair Khan Street. Immediately across this is a short pedestrian stretch, which runs into the large and rather barren central square, around which are grouped the main **administrative buildings** of the town, and several monuments. The latter include a **war memorial**, with a statue of a bereaved Kazakh woman in front of two metal pillars, preceded by an avenue dedicated to the local Heroes of the Soviet Union. There is also a monument honouring the local **mothers** who have produced heroically large numbers of offspring: it is centred on a silver statue of a woman holding out a laurel wreath in her right hand and cradling a baby in her left.

The railway station One of the sights of the town is the railway station, a single-storey whitewashed building with a tall barrel-vaulted central hall. Constructed between 1901 and 1905, the building's most notable feature is the large wall-mounted mosaic in the waiting room that commemorates the town's contribution of 14 wagonloads of fish when famine struck Mother Russia. Lenin's figure is in the top right-hand corner of the picture. Look out for the depictions of the town's railway workers, fishermen and scenes of active commerce. The contrast with the town today could not be more striking.

Aral District Museum of History and Local Lore (23077; ⊕ 09.00–12.00 & 15.00–18.00 Mon–Sat; admission T150) One block east of the central square, Tokey Esetov Street heads north off Abulkhair Khan Street. A few metres up, on the left, the single-storey building with the varnished wood exterior houses the Aral District Museum of History and Local Lore. Opened in 1988, the displays are rather tired looking, and presented in a strange sequence, but there are some interesting exhibits. The first room has a range of Kazakh ethnographic items, including one item of silver jewellery, hung down from the hair, which incorporates practical attachments for the cleaning of fingernails and the inside of the ears. A display of musical instruments includes the harp-like *adirna*, carved into the form of a saiga. Historical displays cover the Kazakh khanates and the building of the Orenburg–Tashkent railway, the latter illustrated by a mural and by segments of rail stamped with the year '1902'.

A hallway is walled with interesting pictures of Aralsk as it looked in the 1970s, including one of the Hotel Aral actually appearing rather smart. The next room features displays on the fishing industry and on regional meetings held to address the problems of the decline of the Aral Sea, including a gathering in Kyzylorda in 1993 which brought together four central Asian heads of state. The next room features the works of local artists: a collection of mainly downbeat pieces highlighting the death of the port. A cart in the centre of the room was used by Bakhyt Riskalov, local Hero of Socialist Labour, to transport fish. Local handicrafts come next, including the work of one craftsman specialised in producing fish-related souvenirs from cattle horn.

The next room looks at the Soviet period, highlighting Lenin's appeal for fish in 1921, and the positive response spearheaded by Tolegen Medetbaev, head of the Council of Deputies of Aral district. A diorama depicts an engagement of the Civil War in 1919, when Bolshevik forces seized control of this stretch of the Orenburg–Tashkent railway from the Whites, an important moment in the struggle for control of central Asia. There are a few stuffed animals, which have seen better days in every sense, and coverage of the Barsakelmes Nature Reserve, once an island in the Aral Sea providing a safe, protected haven for a range of mammals including the central Asian wild ass, known as *kulan*. The desiccation of the Aral Sea turned this island into a peninsula, raising considerable challenges for the reserve authorities.

AROUND ARALSK

ZHALANASH 'SHIP CEMETERY' The 'ship cemetery' is another sight which provides a stark illustration of the reality of the departure of the Aral Sea. To get here head out from Aralsk on the road towards the village of Zhalanash, passing soon after leaving the town on your left the old airport of Aralsk, once used to supply the Vozrozhdenie biological weapons facility. Zhalanash, whose economy is focused on the keeping of camels, is 63km from the town. In the Soviet period it was a collective farm named after the poet Zhambyl, the source of an error which has crept into several publications, including the 2004 edition of the *Reise Know-How Map of Kazakhstan*, which place the ship cemetery in the quite different settlement

11

of Zhambyl on the road from Aralsk towards Aktobe. There is also a more direct route from Aralsk to the 'ship cemetery', a 44km route travelling straight across large stretches of the former seabed. But you will need a guide to attempt this.

Take the sandy track beyond the village towards the now visible ships, beached by the side of what was once a bay. The ship cemetery is a sight which is getting smaller with every passing year, as ships are broken up for their scrap metal, exported on to China. The 11 ships that were here a few years back are now down to six. But they still make for a striking sight: large rusting vessels sitting silently in the sand. They were brought here from Aralsk when that port began to dry up. However, when the desiccation of the Aral Sea hit the bay around Zhalanash too they had nowhere else to go, and have lain here ever since. Camels wander past: the ships of the desert meeting ships in the desert. The largest of the rusting vessels here is the *Aleksey Leonov*, its fate a less than fitting tribute to the Soviet cosmonaut who was the first person to walk in space.

THE FALL, AND PARTIAL RISE, OF THE ARAL SEA

The desiccation of the Aral Sea is one of the best known of the many environmental tragedies to have afflicted central Asia. Straddling the borders of Kazakhstan and Uzbekistan, the Aral Sea was in 1960 the fourth-largest inland sea in the world, covering an area of more than $67,000km^2$. It supported a thriving fishing industry, with a rich catch of carp, sturgeon, pike-perch, bream and roach. Trading links had been established across its waters in Tsarist times, with Russian merchants in the port city of Aralsk trading with the Khanate of Khiva on its southern banks. But the Soviet authorities had long dreamt of diverting the waters of the Amu Darya and Syr Darya rivers, which nourished the Aral Sea, to irrigate the deserts of central Asia, allowing them to become a major centre for the production of cotton, their treasured 'white gold'. Irrigation canals were dug, such as the Kara Kum Canal in Turkmenistan, the longest irrigation canal in the world, which took waters of the Amu Darya westwards into the desert of the Kara Kum.

The result was that the amount of water reaching the Aral Sea fell sharply, and it began to recede. In the 1960s its water level fell on average by about 20cm a year, but this rate of shrinkage accelerated rapidly in the 1970s and 1980s. By 1990, the sea had split into two parts, the smaller Northern Aral Sea, within the territory of Kazakhstan, and the larger Southern Aral Sea, shared between Kazakhstan and Uzbekistan. By 2004, its overall surface area was little more than $17,000km^2$, only about a quarter of its original size. The Soviet planners fully expected the sea to contract: one of the great tragedies about the desiccation of the Aral Sea was that this was not the unintended consequence of the decision to focus on cotton production but one which had been predicted, its negative environmental consequences evaluated and then set aside.

The drop in the level of the water was accompanied by a sharp increase in its salinity. Freshwater fish could not survive, and in an effort to preserve some kind of fishing industry in the Aral the Soviet authorities introduced more salt-tolerant species, notably the flounder, brought in from the Sea of Azov. But the receding waters, which left the port town of Aralsk marooned far from the coast, defeated attempts to retain a fishing industry. The desiccation of the sea resulted in large salt plains, whipped up into dust storms and salt storms. Containing toxic chemicals, the result of the heavy use of fertilisers and pesticides in the cotton industry, these tormented the villagers of the region. Soils were contaminated and

KOKARAL DAM A trip to the dam which has helped reverse the fortunes of the Northern Aral Sea is a lengthy one. To get here, take the main road south from Aralsk towards Kyzylorda, taking the signposted right turn to Kambash after 80km. This puts you onto a rough road, passing Lake Kambash on your right. You reach the village of Amanotkel after 44km, and then the once coastal village of Bogen after another 25km. Some 21km further on you cross the Syr Darya by means of a rusty pontoon bridge. Thereafter the road takes you across the flat former seabed, now populated by salt-resistant plants. You head towards an area of higher ground: this is Kokaral ('Blue Island'), the peninsula which separates the northern and southern parts of the Aral Sea. The Kokaral Dam lies to the east of this, a 16km dyke running across the Berg Strait, which lies between the Kokaral Peninsula and the eastern shore of the sea.

Some 26km beyond the bridge across the Syr Darya you reach the spillway of the Kokaral Dam. The reedy Northern Aral Sea stretches north of this, fringed by

sources of drinking water polluted. Local people began to suffer a range of health problems.

Within the receding sea lay further, even more sinister, threats. A large island in the southern part of the sea, with the, under the circumstances, somewhat ironic name of Vozrozhdenie ('Renaissance'), was chosen in the Soviet period, for its remoteness and dry climate, as an open-air test site for biological weapons. Referred to only as Aralsk-7, the site was the testing ground for a range of agents, including anthrax, brucellosis, plague, smallpox and typhus, with a variety of animals used as victims. Monkeys were apparently particularly favoured. With the break-up of the Soviet Union the site was abandoned in 1991, and officially closed the following year. But by this stage the desiccation of the sea had caused the island to expand to about ten times its original size, and it has now joined the mainland, at its southern coast in Uzbekistan. US experts worked urgently with colleagues from the region to neutralise anthrax dumping grounds on the island.

The local authorities in the Aralsk area had twice attempted to redress the falling levels of the Northern Aral Sea, into which the Syr Darya flows, by the construction of sand dykes across the Berg Strait, which lies between the two sections of the sea. On each occasion some positive effects were noted before the dykes were washed away, in 1992 and 1998. A larger project was developed between the Kazakhstan Government and the World Bank, providing for the construction of the Kokaral Dam to help the Northern Aral Sea recover, coupled with renovation works along the Syr Darya River to increase water flow. Work on the Kokaral Dam was completed in August 2005, resulting in a rise in the level of the water of the Northern Aral Sea and an increase of some 13% in its surface area. Salinity levels in the Northern Aral Sea have declined sharply, and freshwater fish are starting to return. The poor saltwater-loving flounder is rather less than happy at the turn of events, but is in a minority. The World Bank argues that the dam does not deprive the Southern Aral Sea of water, since their Northern Aral Sea project is resulting in enhanced flows by means of a better-regulated Syr Darya, and excess waters in the Northern Aral Sea are sent to the southern part by spillway. But with the fate of the Southern Aral Sea strongly linked to inflows from the Amu Darya, from which take-off for irrigation purposes in Uzbekistan and Turkmenistan remains high, the future of the southern part of the sea continues to look bleak.

a white beach composed largely of pieces of sea shell. A few small boats sit on the beach. A rectangle of concrete on the beach just to the west of the spillway is the helicopter pad built for President Nazarbaev's visit to the dam in 2005. The water from the spillway forms a river which heads south towards the receding Southern Aral Sea. The pool beneath the spillway is rich in carp, evidently trapped.

BAIKONUR *Telephone code: 33622*

Baikonur, the world's largest and oldest space launch facility, is one of the most fascinating sights in Kazakhstan, the place in which many of the key achievements and dramas of the Soviet space programme unfolded. It is also one of the most difficult to visit.

The progress in the Soviet rocket programme, spearheaded by rocket engineer Sergei Korolev, required the establishment of a new test site, as the existing site at Kasputin Yar on the Volga was not suited to the large range of the intercontinental ballistic missiles (ICBMs) being developed. The site eventually selected was near the village of Tyuratam, on the Orenburg–Tashkent railway. A team of engineers under the command of Lieutenant Colonel Georgy Shubnikov arrived in 1955 to begin the construction of the complex, many coming here from work at the Semipalatinsk Test Site. The launch pad they built saw the first test launch of an ICBM, the R-7 Semyorka, in 1957. But with its large payload and range, the R-7 had potential not just as a weapon of war, but also as a space launch vehicle. Sergei Korolev himself was gripped by the dream of using rockets to reach out into space, and managed to persuade the Soviet authorities to support a programme to put a satellite into space, prodded by reports that the US were planning something similar.

On 4 October 1957, the world's first satellite, Sputnik 1, weighing only some 90kg, was successfully launched from Baikonur. Thereafter, the Soviet space programme developed with astonishing rapidity. Less than a month later, on 3 November, its timing dictated by Khrushchev's wish that it be part of the celebration of the 40th anniversary of the October Revolution, the much larger Sputnik 2 was launched, sending into space a dog named Laika. Poor Laika sadly died after a few hours in space, as there was not any provision to bring this canine cosmonaut back to earth.

Baikonur also provided the launch pad for the first manned spaceflight, that of Yuri Gagarin in Vostok 1 on 12 April 1961. The 5ft 2in-tall Gagarin (small stature was a great advantage given the cramped nature of the Vostok cockpit) was promoted to major during the flight itself, and emerged from it a major celebrity. He was killed in 1968 during an accident while retraining as a fighter pilot. Gagarin was chosen ahead of another promising young prospective cosmonaut, Gherman Titov, in part apparently because of Titov's colder personality. But Titov at least earnt the distinction later that year of being the first person to spend a full day in space, aboard Vostok 2. On 16 June 1963, Valentina Tereshkova, launched from Baikonur on Vostok 6, became the first woman in space.

Baikonur was also the launch site for the Voskhod programme, successor to Vostok, which notched up further 'firsts': Voskhod 1 in 1964 was the first space flight carrying more than one person aboard. Aleksey Leonov, aboard Voskhod 2, became in 1965 the first person to walk in space. But from the mid-1960s, while continuing to register further achievements, from the Salyut space station to the Mars 2 probe, the first to reach the surface of Mars, the Soviet space programme experienced a number of setbacks and disappointments. Korolev died in 1966 following an operation. The N-1 heavy booster rocket project ended in failure, and with it Soviet hopes of beating the Americans to a moon landing. The Baikonur Cosmodrome geared up in the 1980s to

The Kazakhstan authorities are determined to ensure that their engagement with space is more than simply the provision of territory for use as a launch pad. In a book published in 2006 entitled *The Kazakhstan Way*, President Nazarbaev devoted a whole chapter to Kazakhstan's 'way to the stars', emphasising for example that among the conditions placed on Russia as part of the rental agreement for Baikonur was helping to train up Kazakhstani experts in the field. In June 2006, Kazakhstan's first satellite, appropriately named KazSat, was launched in the presence of Nazarbaev and President Putin of Russia.

The two countries have also agreed to construct a joint rocket launch complex at Baikonur, to be named Baiterek. This will allow for launches of the Angara rocket, which will be able to carry a payload of 26 tonnes to low-earth orbit, compared with 20 tonnes with the Proton rocket. The Angara also uses a less toxic kerosene and oxygen fuel mix. This is an important issue for Kazakhstan, which has been concerned about the accidents to have befallen several Proton launches, resulting in the spillage of highly toxic heptyl fuel onto Kazakhstani territory.

Two ethnic Kazakhs are numbered among the ranks of the cosmonauts. Both are celebrities in Kazakhstan. The first Kazakh in space was Tokhtar Aubakirov, who had already established his reputation as a test pilot, including by taking off and landing a MiG-29 on a *Tbilisi*-class aircraft carrier in 1989. Aubakirov was somewhat hastily added to the Soyuz TM-13 mission launched in October 1991, joining Austrian researcher Franz Viehbock and mission commander Alexander Volkov. The motive of the Russian space authorities in including a Kazakh cosmonaut was at least in part to ensure continued access to Baikonur following the imminent break-up of the Soviet Union.

One consequence of Aubakirov's addition to the mission was to add substantially to the time in space spent by Russian cosmonaut Sergei Krikalyov, putting him on his course for the record for the person to have spent more time in space than any other human. Krikalyov was the flight engineer sent up to the Mir space station on the Soyuz TM-12 mission launched in May 1991, which included the British astronaut Helen Sharman. He was to have returned to earth in October, but Aubakirov's addition to the Soyuz TM-13 mission filled the flight engineer slot, and Aubakirov, who had not been trained for a long-duration mission, was to go back with Viehbock on the return flight eight days later, together with the returning commander of the TM-12 flight, Anatoly Artsebarsky. Krikalyov therefore agreed to stay aboard Mir for an additional tour of duty, finally returning to earth with Volkov in March 1992. He returned home to a different country than he had left, earning Krikalyov the label of 'the last Soviet citizen'. Aubakirov appears in Andrei Ujica's documentary *Out of the Present*, about Krikalyov's long spell in space. A type of potato developed in space was named the 'tokhtar' in Aubakirov's honour, ranking him alongside King Edward as one of the few people to have given their name to a variety of spud.

The second ethnic Kazakh cosmonaut, Talgat Musabaev, has notched up more than 340 days in space, first as flight engineer on the Soyuz TM-19 mission in 1994, then as commander of Soyuz TM-27 four years later. He was the commander of the 2001 mission which took the first space tourist Dennis Tito to the international space station. Tito paid US$20 million for the trip, providing much needed financial support for the Russian space agency.

a new and exciting programme: the Buran space shuttle and accompanying Energia launcher. It became operational, however, in 1988, a time of major changes in the USSR. The Buran project was deemed too expensive, and only flew on an unmanned test flight before the project was abandoned.

On the break-up of the Soviet Union, Russia inherited much of the Soviet space programme but the Baikonur launch facility lay in the territory of the newly independent state of Kazakhstan. The solution agreed in 1994 was that Russia would lease the entire Baikonur facility, including the town which supports the cosmodrome, from Kazakhstan. In 2005, Russia ratified the agreement extending the lease, for which it pays US$115 million annually, until 2050. The Russian influence in the town is very strong. Prices are denominated in roubles, and though it is permissable to pay in Kazakh tenge, expect to get change in the Russian currency. The Russian MTS mobile-phone network is dominant in the town, and cars bear Russian number plates. The town has largely become civilianised though, with the former military administration having handed over to the Russian space agency Roskosmos. But Kazakhstan has increasing aspirations of a space programme of its own (see box) and maintains its own presence in the town, including a representative of the Kazakhstan president as well as offices of the Kazakhstan National Space Agency.

The Baikonur complex covers an area of 6,717km², stretching roughly 90km in an east–west direction, 75km from north to south. There are some nine launch complexes, with a total of 15 launch pads, and two airfields. The town of Baikonur is home to 70,000 people. Its activity today includes the manned launches of the Soyuz programme, including the flights of 'space tourists', and the commercial launches of satellites using the Proton heavy booster rocket, which has been in operation since 1965.

One curiosity about the Baikonur complex is its name. Baikonur is actually a village located several hundred kilometres to the northeast of the site of the complex, in Karaganda Region. It appears to have acquired the name because the Soviet authorities, required to declare the launch site in order to register Gagarin's flight with the International Aviation Federation, had no intention of disclosing the location of the secret complex near Tyuratam. They accordingly gave its location as close to Baikonur. That name stuck and when, in 1995, the town supporting the cosmodrome, which had previously carried the name Leninsk, was formally renamed Baikonur, it actually became accurate. Strangely, in Tsarist Russia an artisan had been exiled to the village of Baikonur for seditious talk about flights to the moon.

GETTING THERE A visit to Baikonur requires official permission from the relevant Russian authorities, which for the tourist visitor can only straightforwardly be obtained through one of the travel companies experienced in bringing people here. One Baikonur-based tour operator which specialises in this business is **Tourservis** (*8–17 8th of March St;* ✆ *40275;* e *BaikonurTour@bk.ru*). They offer two- and three-night packages which, while spending a fair amount of time in museums and among the monuments of Baikonur town, also get you to some of the most interesting places on the cosmodrome itself, typically including Proton and Soyuz launch pads and at least one of the rocket assembly blocks. They ask for 40 days' notice to secure the required permission in respect of foreign citizens; 30 days for citizens of Russia and Kazakhstan. When you are in Baikonur you are required to stay with your tour guide at all times. This applies to Baikonur town as well as the cosmodrome: you may not even be allowed out of the grounds of your hotel to wander unaccompanied to the shops. Tour prices are pretty steep: at the time of research starting at around €800 per person for a two-night trip (based on a group of at least ten people, and including local travel, full board and all fees to visit the various sights). Tourservis are able to advise on the forward schedule of launches, but if you are aiming to visit to coincide with a launch, be aware that the latter are subject to postponements, for example for meteorological reasons.

Do not attempt to get here without the necessary advance permission. There are checkpoints on both the roads into town and the cosmodrome: at best you will be turned away, at worst detained for questioning.

🏠 WHERE TO STAY

🏠 **Hotel Sputnik** (120 rooms) 44 Korolev Av; 70650; f 70684; e rencobaikonur@renco.it. Built by the Italian company Renco, the Sputnik is the plushest hotel in town, consisting of 4 2-storey wings radiating from a central lobby, such that in plan the building looks satellite-like. It is on your left as you drive into town, along the main Korolev Av. Rooms have AC & satellite TV, there is a large fitness centre, & a bar next to the swimming pool. The colour scheme is the pale yellow favoured by the Renco group, with Van Gogh prints decorating the rooms. It is not however straightforward for tourists to stay at this hotel, which is geared to corporate clients. Payment is not accepted in tenge, or indeed in cash in any currency, with bank transfer the preferred payment method. **$$$$$**

🏠 **Hotel Polyot** Site No 95, Cosmodrome; 21056. There are hotels on the cosmodrome itself. One of these is the Polyot, which falls under the wing of the Russian Khrunichev Space Centre. It is located in Site No 95, on the western side of the cosmodrome, a residential area accommodating those involved in the Proton programme. A 4-storey Soviet-era building, the Polyot makes its nicer rooms available to foreign guests: these have AC but no en suites. For these, foreigners are required to pay a price several times that charged to locals, making this hotel a particularly bad deal. Most of the foreigners staying here are Western security officials responsible for guarding their firm's valuable satellites: if you have no satellite to protect you

would be much better off staying in the town. You may well find, however, that you lunch at the Polyot's canteen-like restaurant as part of an organised tour of the cosmodrome. The **Hotel Kometa** (21100), behind the Polyot, has rooms with en suites but is similarly overpriced for foreigners. **$$$$**

🏠 **Hotel Cosmonaut** (40 rooms) 71232. This balconied Soviet-era hotel at the northeastern edge of town is the most atmospheric place to stay, as it traditionally accommodates the cosmonauts themselves before their flights. It is also the hotel to which foreign tourist visitors are usually steered. Rooms are plain but comfortable, with AC & en suites. The cosmonauts mostly stay in rooms 305 & 306, whose doors bear their autographs in black marker pen. The doors have recently been replaced, presumably having run out of autograph space: among the signatures visible on the new doors is that of space tourist Anoush Ansari on that of room 305. **$$**

🏠 **Hotel Tsentralnaya** (71 rooms) 2 Lenin Sq; 42346. Living up to its name, the Tsentralnaya is centrally located along the side of the main Lenin Sq, a 5-storey balconied hotel offering basic but renovated rooms, with AC, & a *dizhurnaya* controlling each floor. **$$**

🏠 **Hotel Alkor** (14 rooms) 36 Korolev Av; 72287. Located within a 3-storey concrete office block close to the Hotel Cosmonaut, this is a basic place, though the rooms are clean enough, with AC & en suites. **$**

🍴 WHERE TO EAT

🍴 **Palermo** 14 Korolev Av; 43831. An unexpected find in Baikonur: a smart pizzeria, with wooden beams, shuttered windows, & a pleasant garden centred on a fountain. Lying at the northern end of the pedestrianised stretch of

Korolev Av known as 'Arbat', it offers pizza plus a range of Russian & international dishes. $$$

🍴 **Okhotnichny Domik** 5A Gorky St; 70154. In the centre of town, a block to the west of Lenin Sq, this is a lively place in summer, with tables spread across several terraces. There are also a couple of yurts, though placed in a less than romantic spot close to the neighbouring petrol station. The smaller of the yurts has a dining table, AC, a model of a Proton rocket, & photographs of the veteran cosmonauts Leonov & Tereshkova being entertained here on a return visit. $$

WHAT TO SEE

Baikonur town The ghosts of the Soviet Union suffuse the streets of Baikonur. Every square and major road junction seems to be marked by the statue of one of the heroes of the Soviet space programme or by a cosmic or military vehicle mounted on a plinth. The town is located to the south of the main road between Kyzylorda and Aralsk, just beyond the Kazakh village of Tyuratam.

Along Korolev Avenue The broad Korolev Avenue takes you into town from the checkpoint at its northern end. On the right side of the road, just beyond the offices housing the local administration, the rather scruffy **Mir Park** runs westwards. There is a statue here of a jubilant **Gagarin**, holding both arms aloft in triumph. At the western end of 'Peace Park' stands a weapon of war, an SS-17 ICBM, in front of which stands a bust of rocket designer **Mikhail Yangel**. The monument was installed here to commemorate the 90th anniversary of his birthday.

Back on Korolev Avenue, to the south of Mir Park, close to the side of the road, stands a monument consisting of a **Soyuz** rocket. Further south is the pleasant bench-lined Korolev Square, centred on a statue of designer **Sergei Korolev**, large of head and small of neck, gazing pensively across the town established to test his rockets. The stretch of Korolev Avenue south of here has been pedestrianised, and is known locally as '**Arbat**', aping Moscow's famous pedestrian street. This is the favoured place for Baikonur's locals to stroll on warm summer evenings. At the southern end of 'Arbat' is the town's main square, still called Lenin Square and centred on a large statue of **Lenin**, pointing towards the Tsentralnaya Hotel as if proffering directions to a group of lost tourists. This large open square was once the venue for military parades. The green-walled neo-classical building opposite the Tsentralnaya Hotel accommodates the administration of the cosmodrome.

Around Gagarin Avenue Abai Avenue, two lanes separated by a strip of green, heads westwards from Korolev Square. There is a bust of **Abai**, in front of a wall decorated with a frieze depicting Kazakh traditions. A mosaic on the back of the wall is centred on the figure of the Kazakh poet. The monument serves as a reminder in a town full of those to the Soviet space programme of Baikonur's location in Kazakhstan. Further to the west along Abai Avenue, on the right-hand side of the road, stands an old railway engine labelled 'Kosmotrans'. This stands in front of Baikonur's railway station, where commuter trains link the town with the cosmodrome to the north.

From Abai Avenue, take the next turning to the left and follow Pionerskaya Street until it intersects with Gagarin Avenue after around 600m. The four-storey concrete building at the intersection is the Baikonur branch of the Moscow Aviation Institute. Across from this, in the park, lie monuments to two tragedies to hit the launch programme at Baikonur.

A tall obelisk, behind which lies a rectangle of ground, a common grave delimited by tablets inscribed with 54 names, commemorates those who died in the accident of 24 October 1960 which has become known as the Nedelin Catastrophe. A prototype of the R-16 ICBM was being prepared for a test flight when it exploded on the launch pad. Up to 120 people are believed to have been killed, among them

Marshal Mitrofan Nedelin, the commander of the R-16 development programme. The R-16's designer, Mikhail Yangel, survived the disaster, having left the immediate area to have a quick smoke. One of those rare occasions in history when cigarettes proved good for the health. The Soviet authorities, anxious to hush up the disaster, announced that Nedelin had died in a plane crash. The next tragedy to hit Baikonur took place with grim coincidence on exactly the same day, 24 October, three years later. Another monument, depicting a rocket heading off heavenwards, lists the names of the eight people killed in a fire at Site 70 of the cosmodrome. Thereafter, no work has been done at Baikonur on 24 October: the day is instead reserved as one of commemoration for those killed during military service.

Continuing westwards along Gagarin Avenue you reach a monument still bearing the former name of the town, 'Leninsk'. Turn left at this along Barmin Street, to reach a large **An-12** transport aircraft, with its four propellers, mounted on a concrete stand. It stands in front of a group of apartment blocks constructed in the 1980s for those working on the Buran programme, which is one of the youngest parts of town.

Museum of the History of Baikonur Cosmodrome (4 *Pionerskaya St;* 50620; museum@baikonur.net; 09.00–18.00 Tue–Sat; admission 250 roubles *for foreign citizens)* From the memorials to the victims of the accidents of 1960 and 1963, continue south along Pionerskaya Street. This brings you to the Town Palace of Culture on your right; there is a mosaic frieze in the foyer celebrating the work of the builders of the cosmodrome. A stone just outside the Palace of Culture marks the place on which on 5 May 1955 the first building of the new town was constructed. Nearby stands a bust of **Georgy Shubnikov**, who was in charge of the work. On the top floor of the Palace of Culture is housed the Museum of the History of Baikonur Cosmodrome.

The first room of the museum focuses on the story of the construction of the cosmodrome, with photographs and personal items belonging to Shubnikov, and some striking photographs of the tented settlement in which the cosmodrome's builders initially lived. The town was built exclusively on the north side of the Syr Darya River so as not to waste time on the construction of bridges. The next room looks at the history of the Soviet space programme. There is a relief featuring Shubnikov, Gagarin and Korolev. A full-size model of the first Sputnik shows its simple structure and small scale – a polished metal ball from which antennae trailed. There are models of the Vostok, Soyuz and N-1 rockets, and of the Energia rocket with the Buran space shuttle on its back. There are descriptions of the work of the leading Soviet rocket designers, with models and photographs of the fruits of their work. A mannequin of a spacesuited cosmonaut lies in an uncomfortable-looking huddled position, protectively wrapped in the 'Falcon' safety harness. Also on display is a container in which space dogs would be sent up into the cosmos. A bright orange lifesuit burdened with the name 'Trout-3' is on display, together with a photograph of French astronaut Claudie Haignere, the first Frenchwoman in space, wearing it in the water while she smilingly sets off an orange flare so that she may be found. Although the fact that she is being photographed doing so rather suggests that she already has been. There are models too of some of the facilities at the cosmodrome, including one of the assembly and test blocks, where the rockets are assembled, and the Soyuz launch pad.

Displays in the corridor look at the history of the town, initially known as Zarya until it received the formal name of Leninsk village in 1958, becoming the town of Leninsk in 1966. This designation won out over an alternative proposal to name the place Zvezdograd, 'Star City'. Photographs of festivals celebrated in the town include both Russian holidays, like Maslinitsa, Russia's Pancake Day, and Kazakh ones such as the Nauryz spring holiday. The ethnographic hall, entered from the corridor, is a half-hearted affair, offering a nod to Kazakh culture with a display of items to be found in a yurt, and paintings by local artist Zhailaubay Baisalov.

Baikonur Cosmodrome The cosmodrome is located north of Baikonur town, on the other side of the Orenburg–Tashkent railway line and the main east–west road. The checkpoint marking the entrance into the cosmodrome is about 8km north of the town. The facilities are widely scattered across the open steppe; your guided tour will include only a few of the more historically interesting sites. The overall distribution of facilities across the territory of the cosmodrome tended to reflect the work of the competing design bureaux involved in moving the Soviet missile and space programmes forward. The central area of the cosmodrome was based around the processing and launch facilities of the designer Sergei Korolev. The western side, or left flank, served the ballistic missiles and space launchers developed by the design bureau of Vladimir Chelomei, including the facilities for the Proton rocket. The eastern side, or right flank, was devoted to facilities supporting Mikhail Yangel's bureau.

The 'Gagarin Pad' All the facilities on the cosmodrome are allocated a number, and a logical enough place to start a visit is the launch pad bearing the title of Site No 1. This place provided the purpose of the original facility: it was the launch pad for the R-7 ICBM, first launched from here in 1957. This was also the pad used for the Vostok rockets, and Site No 1 is now informally known as the 'Gagarin Pad', because it was from here in 1961 that Yuri Gagarin was launched into space and into history. It is still in use today, as the launch pad for the manned Soyuz programme. It is located in the central area of the cosmodrome, some 25km from the checkpoint, just beyond the collection of buildings known as Site No 2. The latter were originally constructed as residential and assembly buildings for the R-7 programme. Expect to have your permit and documents checked at the entrance to this and other facilities within the cosmodrome, as well as at the main checkpoint itself.

A complex network of metal arms and latticework cradles the Soyuz rocket at the launch pad. The rocket arrives at the pad in a horizontal position, and is then lifted carefully into place. There are large floodlights at each corner of the launch pad, powerful enough to turn night into day. On the side of the structure are painted several hundred stars, each one signifying a launch. There is a clump of trees by the side of the launch pad. Descend a flight of steps to reach an obelisk topped with a model of Sputnik 1, the world's first artificial satellite, launched from this pad in October 1957. An inscription records that the audacious assault on the cosmos was begun here by Soviet genius.

Museum of the Baikonur Cosmodrome (⊕ 09.30–16.30; admission free) In the nearby Site No 2, housed in one of the first buildings constructed here, is the Museum of the Baikonur Cosmodrome. You are welcomed in past a bust of Gagarin. A room of artworks includes paintings of Gagarin and Korolev constructed with grains of rice, and portraits made with salt, the latter gifts from the salt-rich town of Aralsk. A large exhibition hall beyond features photoboards showcasing the work of the various manufacturers and other organisations active in Baikonur town and cosmodrome. There is also a model of the cosmodrome, showing the location of the launch pads for different rocket types, each illustrated by a small model of the rocket concerned.

The displays continue upstairs. There is a golden bust of Korolev, and exhibits chronicling his work and that of other leading Soviet rocket designers. In a central hall there are items on the disasters of 24 October 1960 and 1963. Items displayed in the next room include the cabin of the Cosmos 110 satellite, launched aboard a Soyuz rocket in 1966, in which the dogs Veterok and Ugolyok survived a 22-day space flight, which stands as the longest-ever space flight by dogs. There is coverage of the flights of the early cosmonauts, with items displayed including Gagarin's military uniform. The next room attempts to offer a sense of the conditions endured by the cosmonauts, with displays including the cramped chamber of the Soyuz spacecraft, a complicated-looking arrangement to allow cosmonauts to drink water through a tube and a selection of the profoundly unappetising-looking food consumed in space. There is also a display about the work of searching for returned cosmonauts across the vast expanses of the Kazakhstani steppe.

The final two rooms highlight international co-operation, with a display on the Apollo–Soyuz Test Project of 1975. This should have provided a great historical moment for the West Sussex town of Bognor Regis, as the historic space handshake was scheduled to take place over it, but delays meant that this honour went, roughly, to the French town of Metz. There is a model of the International Space Station, and displays on cosmonauts from other countries, with souvenir items related to their flights. By tradition, cosmonauts before their flight sign a large photograph of the launch of a Soyuz rocket. The museum has already filled up one photograph with signatures and is well onto the second.

Outside the museum are displayed various items of equipment, with pride of place going to a Buran space shuttle. You can climb the steps into its fuselage, though the interior has been somewhat sanitised, with photo displays about the Buran programme on the walls. A model of a Helios satellite is in place, ready to be lifted up to the cosmos. In the nose there are aeroplane-style seats for seven passengers. You can climb up a metal ladder into the cockpit and imagine yourself a cosmonaut.

Close to the museum in Site No 2 are the two small cottages with green corrugated roofs in which Korolev and Gagarin stayed. Plaques next to their front doors commemorate their illustrious residents.

Site No 254 Some 3km from the museum, Site No 254 at the cosmodrome is home to a huge, four-storey, blue and white-painted hangar, which from the outside looks like an ordinary office block when viewed from one angle, but displays its large hangar doors from another. The building is 312m x 254m in size, and was built for the Buran space shuttle programme. Since Buran's demise it now serves as the assembly and test block (known by its Russian acronym, MIK) for the Soyuz and Progress programmes. The clean and spacious hangar where the rockets are put together is an impressive sight. Cradles allow for vertical testing of individual parts of the assemblage, but the rocket leaves the hangar for the launch pad in a horizontal position, by rail. Messages are barked out in rapid-fire Russian from a tannoy. There is a large silhouette of Korolev on the wall of the hangar, accompanied by the slogan 'the road to the stars is open'.

Cosmonauts about to set off aboard Soyuz are brought to Site 254 some four hours before launch. Here they are given a final medical test, a meal, don their spacesuits and give a press conference. You can visit the room in which the press conferences take place. The cosmonauts are protected behind a glass screen from any germs which may be carried by the media. Site 254 has been used for manned space launches since 1988: there are photographs on the walls of the cosmonauts to have set off from here.

Proton rocket assembly and launch sites The Proton rocket, a product of Vladimir Chelomei's design bureau, is a long-serving unmanned launch vehicle. First launched in 1965, the Proton remains in use, although it is slated for replacement by the Angara rocket, which can carry a heavier payload and uses a less toxic fuel mix. Baikonur is the only location used for the launch of Proton rockets, which are built at the Khrunichev plant in Moscow. Its name derives from the Proton scientific satellites which were among the rocket's first payloads.

The Proton facilities are located on the western side of the cosmodrome. From Site No 254, head back southwards in the direction of Baikonur town. Turn right after 8km. Some 32km on, a signposted right turn brings you to **Site No 200**, one of two Proton launch complexes at Baikonur, consisting of two launch pads each. Launch Pad 39, which came into operation in 1980, is still in use. As with the Soyuz rockets, the Protons are brought to the launch pad by rail in a horizontal position, and then raised to the vertical, supported by a metal cradle. A reinforced concrete bunker houses the staff at the launch site. Launch Pad 40, opposite, is no longer in operation. This is the site which has been earmarked to house the joint Kazakh–Russian **Baiterek** complex, for launches of the Angara rocket. A plaque at the site commemorates the visit of presidents Putin and Nazarbaev on 2 June 2005 to inaugurate the complex, though at the time of research construction work had not yet begun.

A few kilometres away, at **Site No 92A-50**, the payloads for the Proton rockets are assembled. This assembly and test block (MIK) of the Khrunichev plant houses in its entrance a display of photographs from the joint visit to the site of presidents Putin and Nazarbaev on 2 June 2005, marking the 50th anniversary of the cosmodrome. Foreign companies whose satellites are being taken up into space by a Proton rocket carefully prepare their valuable property in a specially guarded area of the facility. A constant year-round temperature is maintained in the assembly halls, and their staff boast of standards of cleanliness as good as any hospital surgery.

KORKUT ATA MONUMENT

Some 57km east of the turning to Baikonur along the main road between Kyzylorda and Aralsk, 16km west of the village of Zhosaly, stands an intriguing modern monument complex in honour of a figure named Korkut Ata, whose name is known throughout the Turkic world, but who in Kazakhstan is most closely associated with the musical instrument known as the *kobyz* and with the shamans who favoured it. Korkut Ata may possibly have been a real historical figure, living around the 8th or 9th century, but it is difficult now to extract historical fact from the legends and epic tales surrounding him. One of the most popular local legends is that as a young man he dreamt that he would live only to the age of 40. He therefore saddled up his beloved camel Zhelmaya, and went off in search of immortality. But wherever he went he found only groups of people digging his grave. He returned to the banks of the Syr Darya, where he sacrificed poor Zhelmaya, who clearly wasn't destined for immortality, using her skin in the making of a new musical instrument, the *kobyz*. He started to play, and while he did so, death, kept away by the beauty of the music, could not touch him. But exhaustion finally caused him to fall asleep, and at that moment death took the form of a snake, biting him.

The monument complex sits on the south side of the road, clearly visible from it. A paved road brings you to it. The whole complex, built in 1997, is shaped in plan in the form of a *kobyz*. You enter beneath a gate, with the director's office to your left, and to your right a small **museum** (⊕ *09.00–19.00*).The entrance to the latter also takes the shape of a *kobyz*, which clearly became something of an object of obsession for the designers of the place. The sound of the *kobyz* echoes through the museum, whose displays include one dimly lit somewhat cave-like room, with a golden *kobyz* illuminated in the centre. The displays offer information on the life of Korkut Ata, placing his birth at Zhankent, southwest of the town of Kazaly in the western part of Kyzylorda Region, and the place of his death just 2km from the complex, along the Syr Darya. There are of course plenty of *kobyzes* on display, including a mirrored version favoured by shamans.

There are copies on display in the museum of *The Book of Dede Korkut*, also known as *The Book of Korkut Ata*, the epic story of the Oguz Turks, revered across the Turkic world as a core text of the ethnic identity of the Turkic people, which was passed through the generations in oral form, before eventually being put to paper. Two 16th-century manuscripts are known, one from the Royal Library of Dresden, the other from the Vatican Library. The Soviet scholar V V Barthold identified the text as closest to the Azeri language, and believed that the book originated in the Caucasus. The version of Korkut Ata which appears from the book is that of a white-bearded elder, a sage bard, whose character links together the various tales in the book. In 2000, UNESCO supported celebrations commemorating the 1,300th anniversary of the book.

Back at the entrance, walk up the steps, proceeding, in effect, down the neck of the giant *kobyz* making up the complex. This brings you to a circular space, centred on a mosaic statue of a sheep. The edge of the circle is decorated with a greenish mosaic design which represents the snake which did for Korkut Ata. Further down, you pass under an arch, representing the bow being passed across the strings. You reach a platform, the main body of the instrument, with an amphitheatre in the middle, the venue for Korkut Ata-related events. Another snake-like mosaic surrounds it.

In the far left corner of the platform is a fine monument, an earlier (1980) construction which has been incorporated into the larger complex. This white-coloured concrete sculpture has four sides, each taking the form of a stylised, yes, *kobyz*, placed upside down. There is a hole in the centre of the chamber of each of the concrete *kobyzes*, leading to an arrangement of metal tubes which produces a *kobyz*-like sound when the wind is blowing with the right velocity. On the opposite far corner of the platform is a four-sided white concrete pyramid, known as the Pyramid of Wishes. Walk down a flight of steps to its base, circle it three times, and then pop inside to make a wish.

A track runs round the left-hand side of the modern complex. This leads to a reconstructed brick mausoleum on the top of a low hill 1km away. It is said to be the burial place of Aksakys, one of 40 girls attracted here by the enchanting *kobyz*-playing of Korkut Ata. The other 39 are supposed to have died of thirst in the desert, but Aksakys was sustained by milk from her goat, and managed to reach the spot where Korkut Ata played. The track continues beyond this mausoleum for a further few hundred metres, before giving way to a path. Follow the latter over the railway track towards the banks of the Syr Darya. You walk through a riparian graveyard. At the bank of the river is a gravestone, decorated with an image of a *kobyz*. Votive strips of cloth are tied to the bushes around this spot, which marks the approximate place where Korkut Ata is said to be buried. There was once a mausoleum, but this was destroyed by flooding of the Syr Darya.

KYZYLORDA   *Telephone code: 7242*

The capital of Kyzylorda Region, Kyzylorda is a low-slung, utterly charmless city spread out on the right bank of the Syr Darya, the most strongly ethnically Kazakh of any regional capital in Kazakhstan. It was founded in 1818 as a fortress of the Khanate of Kokand. Its name, Ak Mechet, referred to a white mosque on the site.

Yaqub Beg, the Uzbek military leader who was to become the ruler of Kashgaria, became commander of the fortress in the late 1840s until its capture by Russian troops under General Vasily Perovsky in 1853. The defeated Yaqub Beg fled to Bukhara, and was later to rise to become commander-in-chief of the army of Kokand. He captured Kashgar from the Chinese, and made himself the ruler of Kashgaria. Ak Mechet meanwhile was renamed Fort Perovsky in honour of its conqueror, a name later shortened to Perovsk. It became the administrative capital of a province, or *uyezd*, in the Tsarist period, and its fortunes were further boosted by the arrival of the Tashkent–Orenburg railway in 1905.

Following the arrival of Soviet rule, the city's name was briefly restored to Ak Mechet in 1922, before being changed again in 1925 to the more secular-sounding Kyzylorda. The next four years represented Kyzylorda's moment of glory, when it served as the capital of Soviet Kazakhstan, attracting a Kazakh intellectual elite including Saken Seifullin and Ilyas Zhansugurov. But with the arrival of the railway in Almaty, the capital was moved to that city. Kyzylorda settled down to life as a regional administrative centre, capital of a rice-growing *oblast* on the Syr Darya. The character of the region changed again with the exploitation of major reserves of oil in the deserts to the north of the city, and the region accounted in 2004 for some 24% of Kazakhstan's crude oil production. Today, the city plays host to the regional offices of several oil companies and oversized roads that sever it into seemingly unconnected sectors. There has been particularly strong Chinese investment in the region, especially following the acquisition of Petrokazakhstan, with its major Kumkol field, by the Chinese company CNPC in 2005.

With few museums and monuments of interest in their own right, and nowhere to get a decent meal, Kyzylorda serves only as a good starting point for visits to the western part of the region, including the Baikonur Cosmodrome and sites connected with the desiccation of the Aral Sea.

GETTING THERE AND AROUND The **airport** (⟨ 261693) is some 21km outside the centre of town. Air Astana has one or two flights daily from Almaty, and a daily flight to Astana, on Fokker-50 aircraft. Scat operates two flights a week from Almaty and to Aktau on an An-24.

The **railway station** (⟨ 292451), at the end of Auelbekov Street on the northern edge of the town centre, is one of the most impressive buildings in town. It is an elegant Tsarist design, with a central exterior staircase leading to a tall central hall, its exterior as well as the square out in front decorated with large concrete vases. The Tsarist-era building makes the boxy Soviet extension by its side look even clumsier, though the latter is at least enlivened with a frieze of Soviet man and woman busy developing the agriculture, industry and technology of the region. Its location on the Orenburg–Tashkent railway still finds an echo in the trains which stop here on their route from Moscow to Tashkent, Almaty or Bishkek. A daily train originating in Kyzylorda runs to Petropavl, and the station is also a stop for the daily trains between Almaty and Aktobe, as well as trains running every two days between Almaty and each of Uralsk, Mangyshlak and Atyrau. Other services stopping here include those between Tashkent and Ufa, Chelyabinsk and Kharkov, and between Almaty and Simferopol.

The **bus station** (*64A Bukeikhan St;* ⟨ 235208) is a run-down Soviet building in a suburban location some 3.5km outside the centre of town. This serves destinations to the east of Kyzylorda, including several departures daily to Turkestan and Shymkent, three a day to Almaty, and one each to Zhezkazgan and Tashkent. There are also minibuses and taxis here serving a similar range of destinations. Buses for destinations west of Kyzylorda, such as Aralsk, depart from outside the railway station.

Numbers to call for local **taxis** include 📞 230550, 📞 230555, 📞 262380 and 📞 273444.

TOUR OPERATORS AND AIRLINE OFFICES

✈ **Otrar Travel** Office 4, 30 Korkut Ata St; 📞 276668, 276789; f 270392; e kzo@otrar.kz. General Service Agent for Air Astana.

Rusak Travel 4/33 Zheltoksan St; 📞 275324; e RUSAK_1980@mail.ru. Can put together tailor-made itineraries to the main sights of the region, including the Korkut Ata Monument, & sites associated with the desiccation of the Aral Sea.

⌂ WHERE TO STAY

⌂ **Hotel Altyn Orda** (15 rooms) Bukeikhan St; 📞/f 238000, 238001. It may be called the 'Golden Horde', but the favoured colour is blue. There are blue walls, blue curtains & blue bedspreads, the last covering back-stiffeningly hard beds. The AC rooms are spacious, but the suburban location is convenient only for the bus station across the road. **$$$$**

⌂ **Hotel Kyzylorda** (69 rooms) 19 Tokmagambetov St; 📞 261121; f 261623; e hotel_kyzylorda@mail.ru. This centrally located 4-storey building dates from 1968, but was fully renovated in 2006, & its rooms now offer AC, satellite TV & modern furnishings. **$$$$**

⌂ **Hotel Samal** (35 rooms) 53 Abai Av; 📞 235617; f 235623; e hotelsamal@asdc.kz. This airy hotel, a single-storey building with the rooms strung along 2 wings, was built by the oil company KazAmlon Munai, some of whose senior staff live in cottages around the back. All rooms have AC, & the place is smartly furnished, though

the out-of-centre location along Abai Av is not ideal. **$$$$**

⌂ **Hotel Asetan** (20 rooms) 28 Aiteke Bi St; 📞 261466, 277959; f 272902; e asetan@mail.ru; www.asetan.kz. This is a modernised place sitting above a branch of the ATF Bank, in a good central location. All rooms are described as 'semi-luxe', & all offer AC, sumptuous-looking wallpaper, & en suites with over-complex multi-functional showers. The lift still judders, though. **$$$**

⌂ **Hotel Mirage** (19 rooms) 27A Aiteke Bi St; 📞 270234; f 273691. This mirage offers a vision of a 3-storey building faced with metallic-look tiles behind the Agzhan Market. The entrance is on Userbaev St, which runs between Aiteke Bi & Tokmagambetov. All rooms in this unremarkable hotel have AC & en suites. **$$$**

⌂ **Hotel Samruk** (12 rooms) 24 Auelbekov St; 📞 262440, f 262425. This 2-storey white-walled blue-glass building sits opposite the war memorial, not far from the railway station. Rooms are uninspiring, but have AC. **$$**

✕ WHERE TO EAT

✕ **Britannica** 21 Korkut Ata St; 📞 276852. One of the smartest places to eat in town, the Britannica is decorated in shades of cream & brown. The waiters wear bow ties & the eclectic international menu offers such dishes as 'Breton-style soup'. There is an outdoor terrace with diners shielded by a curtain of water, & a billiard hall decorated with photographs of London at the turn of the 20th century. $$$

✕ **Kyz Zhibek Retro Restaurant** 27A Aiteke Bi St; 📞 261588. Sitting in the courtyard of the

Mirage Hotel, this restaurant offers a columned interior of the sort pitched at wedding parties, & live music with a 1980s theme. The menu offers *shashlik*, & Kazakh & international dishes. There is an outdoor terrace in summer. $$$

✕ **Arlekino** 20 Aiteke Bi St; 📞 262667. This functional-looking central place has 2 halls, 1 dispensing beer & pizza, the other coffee & cakes. The wide-ranging menu includes some good Korean-style salads. $$

WHAT TO SEE

Central Square The large, green central square is surrounded by many of the key administrative buildings of the town, including the blue-domed city *akimat*, the court, Korkut Ata University and drama theatre. There is a curious monument in the centre of the square: a metal ball on a plinth, with six metal legs radiating out in a manner that gives the sculpture a vaguely extraterrestrial appearance.

Kyzylorda Regional Museum of History and Local Lore (20 Auezov St; 276152, 276274; f 276152; ⊕ 09.00–13.00 & 15.00–19.00 daily; admission T160)

Head west from the central square along tree-lined Aiteke Bi Street, passing across a narrow canal which scythes through the city centre, offering shaded benches beside its concrete banks. Golden lions guard this waterway wherever it is crossed by roads. After a couple of blocks turn right onto Auezov Street, bringing you to a junction with Tokmagambetov Street. Here, on your right, is a two-storey 1950s building, its main entrance behind a curving row of Corinthian columns. This houses the Kyzylorda Regional Museum of History and Local Lore. The museum was founded in 1939, and housed initially in a Russian Orthodox church. It was moved to its present site, which initially housed a hotel, in 1985.

The displays start with exhibits about the geography of the region, including a striking comparison of the Aral Sea as it used to be, with photographs of the fishing fleet, with the Aral Sea today, illustrated by a diorama depicting a beached boat, and a lonely hedgehog wandering across the sand. The next room features natural history, with the usual array of stuffed animal-filled dioramas and pickled snakes. A room devoted to archaeology includes ceramics from some of the important Silk Road settlements of the region, including the site of Syganak, 20km from the present-day village of Zhanakorgan in the eastern part of the region. Syganak was a major trading centre of the Silk Road until it was sacked by the Mongols. But it rose again to become the capital of the White Horde. It gradually declined, and was finally abandoned in the 19th century. There are photographs of the remnants of city walls to be seen at Syganak and at Sauran (see page 380).

The next room covers the development of the region from the 15th century. Items on display include a Dzhungar helmet, splendidly decorated with golden dragons. The displays also cover the development of the town from its origins as Ak Mechet. There are samovars, ceramics and other traded items on display, and exhibits related to the construction of the Orenburg–Tashkent railway at the beginning of the 20th century. In the next room are books and manuscripts, including the works of prominent Kazakh writers, printed here in the 1920s during Kyzylorda's brief spell as capital of Soviet Kazakhstan. The desk of writer Askar Tokmagambetov is also on display.

On the second floor the displays start with a room focused on the early Soviet period. There is a bust of Mustafa Chokai, leader of the 'Provisional Government of Autonomous Turkestan', with its capital at Kokand, crushed by the Bolsheviks in 1918. Chokai fled to Europe, where he continued his campaigning on behalf of the Turkestan nationalist movement, based around the goal of self-government for central Asia. He was associated with the establishment of the Turkestan Legion, comprising Muslim exiles and captured Soviet prisoners of war who fought on the German side during World War II, and died in Berlin, in circumstances which are still unclear, in 1941. Cast in wholly negative terms during the Soviet period, Chokai has undergone something of a rehabilitation in Kazakhstan, and a two-part film entitled *Mustafa Shokai* was released in 2008, directed by Satybaldy Narymbetov, and with Karina Abdullina, vocalist with the Kazakhstani pop duo Musicola, playing Chokai's opera singer wife Maria. The next room focuses on the talented Hodjikov brothers, each a prominent artist in a different field. A room focusing on World War II is followed by one covering the post-independence period, with photographs of visits to the region by President Nazarbaev, coverage of the main industrial enterprises of the region and a model of the Korkut Ata Monument.

There are canvases by Abylkhan Kasteyev in the corridor, and a room focused on Kazakh ethnography, with a display of items to be found in a yurt. The next room highlights the best-known musicians and writers from the region, including the singer Roza Baglanova, the 'nightingale of Kazakhstan', who donated a sparkly dress to the museum. Next comes education and sport, with photographs of Ilia Ilin, the local weightlifter who, at 17, won the 2005 World Championships in the 85kg weight category. He took gold again the next year, this time in the 94kg category, and won gold in the same category at the 2008 Olympic Games in Beijing. A room about the region's agriculture features a bust of rice farmer and two-time Hero of Socialist Labour Ibray Zhakaev, a diorama of the cultivation of watermelons and a display case with an arrangement featuring rice, cotton, fruits and vegetables. There is a room about the Soviet-era industrial development of the region, displaying the products of several local factories which did not survive long into the post-independence period. The quality of the goods on display offers a clue as to why they folded.

Along Auelbekov Street From the regional museum, head east along Tokmagambetov Street, reaching after one block the Agzhan Bazaar on your right. In front of the training centre opposite are a couple of charming statues of cosmonauts, almost entirely hidden by trees. There is a large frieze on the outside wall of the building, glorifying the Soviet-era youth movement, the Pioneers, which once occupied it. Behind this building, in a run-down park, is a statue of **Lenin**, now partially obscured by bushes. Cut through to the western entrance of the park, on Auezov Street, and turn right, then left onto Konisbek Kabantaev Street, and then right again, onto Auelbekov Street, which runs northwards to the railway station.

A couple of blocks on, at the corner with Tolibekov Street, stands a **war memorial**, a tall five-legged obelisk with a now extinguished eternal flame at its base. A couple of artillery pieces guard it against frontal attack. Two blocks further north along Auelbekov Street brings you to the square in front of the railway station. There is a resolute-looking statue in the square of the young Komsomol leader **Gani Muratbaev**.

Nearby stands a single-storey Tsarist-era building, surrounded by metal railings decorated with *shanyrak* designs. This houses the **Ak Mechet Museum** (*8 Auelbekov St;* \ *293597;* ☉ *09.00–13.00 & 15.00–19.00 daily; admission T250 for foreign citizens*). This is devoted to the history of the town from its foundation to its time as capital of the Kazakhstan Soviet Socialist Republic. The labelling is in Kazakh only, which makes the decision to charge foreigners double the entrance fee paid by locals look rather cheeky. There is a model of the moated Ak Mechet Fortress in the centre of the first room, which through photographs and displays of household utensils offers a chronology of the town's development to 1925. The next room covers Kyzylorda's four years as capital, with displays of books printed in the town by Kazakh intellectuals such as Seifullin and Zhansugurov, few of whom were to survive Stalin's purges in the following decade. In the next room is a mock-up of an office of the Central Executive Committee of Kazakhstan, with Lenin's portrait on the wall and his bust on the desk. Then come souvenir items and photographs from the 2005 celebrations marking the 80th anniversary of Kyzylorda's selection as Kazakhstan's capital. Another room is laid out as a period guest room, heavy with dark furniture.

Around the bazaar If you head west along Tokmagambetov Street from the regional museum you reach at the end of the street a bust of local writer **Askar Tokmagambetov**, clutching what appears to be a tulip to his breast, in front of the green-painted neo-classical theatre named in his honour. Turn right here along busy Kazibek Bi Street. After a couple of blocks you reach, on the right-hand side of the road, a modern monument featuring a series of heroic Kazakh figures standing in a ring. Behind this, a path leads into the town's main **park**. There is a small children's park to your right, featuring some remarkably odd compositions for tots to play on. A giant spider clambers up a climbing frame. A bull is about to charge, somewhat encumbered by the carriage he is pulling. In the centre of the park is a square adorned with a range of colourful, if somewhat weather-beaten, structures which serve as the backdrop for local photographers: two large foam doves and a pair of kissing dolphins.

Continuing along Kazibek Bi Street, cross over the roundabout and then turn left. You reach on your left the attractive, restored **Russian Orthodox church**, dating from 1878. Its octagonal tower supports a blue cupola. A smaller octagonal bell tower above the main entrance offers arches of fine decorated brickwork. In the colourful interior all available space is covered by icons and wall paintings of religious scenes. Signs at the entrance warn sternly that women in trousers, short skirts, without headwear and wearing lipstick are not admitted. The rules regarding lipstick-wearing men are unclear. Across the road, beside a small park, is a five-sided monument honouring the local Bolshevik fighters killed in the Civil War. Nearby is a single-storey Tsarist-era brick building constructed in 1878, its long façade bookended by two small brick buttresses. Once a school, it now houses a supermarket.

The road on which the church stands takes you to the heart of Kyzylorda's busy **bazaar**. From the bazaar, a road surmounted by a broad arch runs south to the **Korkut Ata Monument**, built on the bank of the Syr Darya River to commemorate the 1,300th anniversary of the Book of Korkut Ata. Paths either side of the road also take you to the monument, through metal arches and past flower beds whose blooms are fighting a tough battle against sun and vodka bottles. The monument itself is a cleverly designed structure comprising three tiled panels, the space between them taking the form of a *kobyz*. That space is occupied by Korkut Ata, riding a camel. A footpath runs alongside the river.

A block east from this monument, at the corner of Kazibek Bi Street and Korkut Ata Street, stands the blue-domed **Aitbaya Mosque**. Built in 1878, it has been heavily restored, with a new minaret. The latter has an attractive design of alternating octagonal and cylindrical segments, rising to what looks like a fine paintbrush dipped in a pastel blue. The mosque has a façade of slim columns, with patterned tiles around the arched entrance. The interior features stucco decoration around the *mihrab* and at the base of the dome. In the corner is what appears to be a well: according to the imam this runs to a secret passage through which the faithful were able to come to the mosque during the Soviet period. Light filters into the dark interior from arched windows around the dome. Across the road from the mosque is the local head office of the oil company Petrokazakhstan, housed in a building with a distinctive 'corrugated' façade.

TURKESTAN *Telephone code: 72533*

Lying between Kyzylorda and Shymkent, the Silk Road town of Turkestan (Turkistan in Kazakh) contains Kazakhstan's most impressive monument and most important pilgrimage site, the Timurid Mausoleum of Khodja Ahmed Yassaui. The town, now home to some 70,000 people, celebrated somewhat arbitrarily in 2001 its 1,500th anniversary. Its origins lie in the settlement of Shavgar, which flourished in the 9th and 10th centuries as a centre for trade and handicraft production. Shavgar appears to have declined in the 12th century, in favour of Yassi, which was probably initially

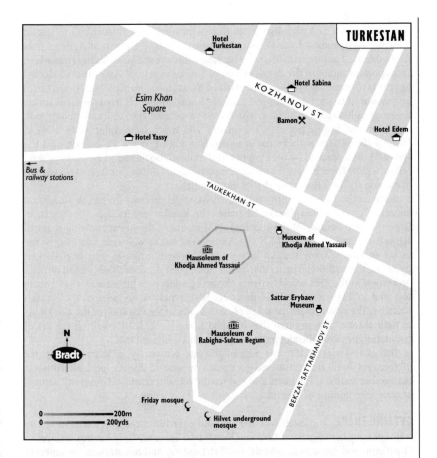

Esim Khan Square

Hotel Turkestan

Hotel Sabina

KOZHANOV ST

Bamon ✗

Hotel Edem

Hotel Yassy

Bus & railway stations

TAUKEKHAN ST

Museum of Khodja Ahmed Yassaui

Mausoleum of Khodja Ahmed Yassaui

Sattar Erybaev Museum

BEKZAT SATTARHANOV ST

Mausoleum of Rabigha-Sultan Begum

N

Bradt

Friday mosque

Hilvet underground mosque

0 ——— 200m
0 ——— 200yds

a suburb or satellite town. Yassi's fortunes in turn were linked to the presence here of a revered Sufi mystic, Khodja Ahmed Yassaui, and became a place of pilgrimage on his death.

The town grew further in importance following a visit to Yassaui's decaying grave by Timur, known in the West as Tamerlane, in 1397. Timur ordered the construction of a magnificent new monument befitting a saint of Yassaui's stature: a multi-functional building which would incorporate a vast and ornate mausoleum. His motivation was probably in part philanthropic, but in part also to help promote his rule in the area. Detailed designs were drawn up, and arrangements were also put in place for the funding, through voluntary donations, of a staff comprising a preacher, two Koran readers, a property manager, water carrier, gardener and, mysteriously, a scavenger. Construction began in 1399, but the building was left unfinished on Timur's death in 1405. The main portal and some of the interiors remain today in an incomplete state, but the building still attains a great beauty through its size, turquoise domes and stunning decorated tilework.

Details of the life of the man on whom Turkestan's importance is based are relatively sketchy. Khodja Ahmed Yassaui was born in Sayram, at that time known as Ispijab, probably around 1103. His father, Sheikh Ibragim, was a well-known local figure, but Ahmed was orphaned at the age of seven, and he moved to Yassi with his elder sister, his only remaining close relative. His teacher was the venerable Arystan

Bab, also known as Arslan Bab (both names meaning 'lion'), according to legend a former companion of the Prophet Muhammad. On the death of Arystan Bab, Ahmed moved to Bukhara, where he became a disciple of Sheikh Yusup Hamadani, an important figure in the development of Sufism in central Asia. Ahmed elected to return to Yassi, taking the name Ahmed Yassaui, becoming a highly successful propagator of Islam, based around a mystic Sufi tradition. He used the local Turkic language in his religious poetry, which made it accessible to ordinary people and, and it proved hugely popular. The poetry was much later collected in a book, *Divan-i Hikmet*, the authenticity of which is doubtful. When Yassaui attained the age of 63, that reached by the Prophet Muhammad, he retired to an underground cell, where he lived in prayer and contemplation, explaining that he had no wish to live a worldly life longer than that of the Prophet.

Between the 16th and 18th centuries Yassi, which became known as Turkestan, became a capital of the Kazakh Khanate. The Kazakh leaders chose Turkestan in large measure because of the spiritual significance of the town; allowing them to claim the Islamic heritage of Khodja Ahmed Yassaui, as well as at least part of the legacy of Timur. Many Kazakh khans and other senior figures were buried here, reflecting the traditional belief that burial close to the grave of a saint would provide protection in the next world. Among the first burials here linked with the khanate was that in 1519 of Amanbike, daughter of Janybek, co-founder of the Kazakh Khanate. The city was also the scene of ceremonies of the elevation of Kazakh khans to their throne, among them that of Ablai Khan in 1771. By tradition the act of coronation involved lifting up the new khan on a white felt mat.

Turkestan today is a major Sufi pilgrimage centre. By local tradition, three pilgrimages here are considered to equate to one to Mecca, and pilgrims far outnumber tourists. The town also houses the Kazakh–Turkish University named, of course, in honour of Yassaui.

GETTING THERE Turkestan is on the Orenburg–Tashkent **railway**, and is served by trains passing between Shymkent and Kyzylorda. There are frequent **bus** services to Shymkent, and some to Kyzylorda. Both the railway and bus stations are however inconveniently located outside the town centre. Shymkent-based travel agencies (see page 384) can put together day or overnight trips to Turkestan, also taking in the Mausoleum of Arystan Bab and Otrar. Buses and minibuses bringing pilgrims from Shymkent by respectful tradition also make a stop at the Mausoleum of Arystan Bab, Yassaui's mentor, before coming to Turkestan.

TOUR OPERATOR
Yassi-Sauran Baiburt St; ⱴf 33142. Can put together tailor-made trips to sites outside town, including Sauran & the Mausoleum of Arystan Bab.

WHERE TO STAY
⌂ **Hotel Edem** (7 rooms) 6A Kozhanov St; ⱴf 31697; e edem_kz@mail.ru. Fronted by a 2-storey bay window, this offers plain AC rooms with en-suite showers. There's a disco in the basement, with 'welcome to the hell' somewhat unpromisingly written at the entrance. The interior is decked out in suitably infernal fashion. **$$**

⌂ **Hotel Turkistan** (22 rooms) Kozhanov St; ☏ 42197; f 41426. On the side of the central Esim Khan Sq, this 2-storey building has a rather grand appearance, with a columned entrance & a circular foyer beneath a blue dome. The hotel tends to be almost empty out of season so haggle hard for a discount & expect to wait whilst the receptionist hunts around for some sheets & a towel. There is central AC but the rooms are nothing special. **$$**

⌂ Hotel Yassi (53 rooms) Taukekhan St; ⌕ 40183; ✆ 40185. The best hotel in town, though this isn't really saying very much. Owned by the Kazakh–Turkish University, it offers clean but rather spartan rooms, with AC & en suites. Ask for one of the rooms offering a (great) view across to the mausoleum. **$$**

⌂ Hotel Sabina (6 rooms) 16 Kozhanov St; ⌕ 31405. Turkestan's cheapest option is centrally located & quiet. The twin rooms are (fairly) clean, & the large display of pot plants in the foyer make up in part for the unreliable water supply. Expect to wash & flush with a helpfully provided Coke bottle. The staff are pleasant & will thoughtfully advise you on the safety of your possessions with entertaining charades. **$**

✘ WHERE TO EAT Turkestan is not a place to find inspiring cuisine. There are a few unremarkable cafés along the pedestrianised street in front of the mausoleum complex, mostly catering to lunching pilgrims. Avoid the cabbage pizzas. A couple of slightly better options are found along Kozhanov Street, a block east of the Hotel Turkistan. The **Bamon** ($) offers central Asian fare and *shashlik*, and a courtyard round the back where you can listen to loud pop music played on the stereo while watching strings of fairy lights flash on and off. The supermarkets are also reliable (and cheap) sources of picnic food, which may be your best option.

WHAT TO SEE The heart of the modern town is the pedestrian **Esim Khan Square** with its towering modern sculpture; the *akimat* is here, and the square plays host to public concerts. A pedestrianised stretch of Taukekhan Street heads east from the square along the northern edge of the mausoleum complex.

Khodja Ahmed Yassaui Museum (✆ 32754; ⏲ 09.00–18.00 daily; admission T200) If you have time, a good first port of call, before visiting the mausoleum complex itself, is the single-storey Tsarist building housing a museum, which sits in the parkland between the complex and Taukekhan Street. The first room has items found at local Bronze and Iron Age sites, as well as medieval items, including coins and decorated ceramics, uncovered from the Kultobe Hill just to the south of the mausoleum complex. The second room covers the Turkic period, with items on display including a 7th-century stone *balbal* from the Karatau Mountains: in this case a moustachioed gentleman taking a drink. There are also items excavated from a site known as Shoytobe, which is believed to be that of Shavgar, the town which represents Yassi's antecedent. There is some fine glazed earthenware of the 11th and 12th centuries, found in the upper cultural layer of the Shoytobe site.

A third room, back across the foyer, is centred on a model of the Khodja Ahmed Yassaui Mausoleum. There are exhibits related to Yassaui's life, including early 20th-century copies of the *Divan-i Hikmet*, printed in Tashkent and Kazan. There is a model of the Hilvet underground mosque, the work of one A L Schmidt in 1942. The room also includes exhibits focusing on the town as a spiritual centre of the Turkic people, with Korans and scientific works on display. The last room covers the history of Turkestan since the 15th century. A model of the interior of a Kazakh dwelling of perhaps two centuries ago features the children on a felt rug playing a game with sheep bones while Dad lolls lazily and Mum prepares the *kumiss*. The displays cover the city's period as capital of the Kazakh Khanate. A large painting at the end of the room depicts the coronation of Ablai Khan, being carried up by four bearers on a large white felt rug in front of the portal of the mausoleum. Ceramics on display include a candleholder in the form of a sheep, dated between the 16th and 18th centuries.

Khodja Ahmed Yassaui Mausoleum complex Undoubtedly the finest building in Kazakhstan, this complex makes for a stunning sight from every angle. Some 46m by 65m in plan, the building reaches a maximum height of 41m. The towering portal, dominated by the tall central arched niche, faces southeast. Its decoration was never completed and wooden timbers still protrude from square holes in the walls. A plaque on the façade records that the mausoleum has been included on the list of UNESCO World Heritage Sites. The decoration of the rest of the exterior is considerably more splendid. The northeastern and southwestern walls are decorated with blue and turquoise tiles, forming geometric designs, with a line of Arabic inscriptions above. The central dome, which stands above the main hall, the *kazanlyk*, is the largest in central Asia, its exterior glowing a warm turquoise behind the portal. It is placed on an octagonal drum, decorated with tiled Arabic inscriptions. A visit here is traditionally preceded by a visit to Arystan Bab Mausoleum (see page 382); Arystan Bab was Khodja Ahmed Yassaui's mentor.

The real star of the show though is the view from the northwest. Above the room housing Khodja Ahmed Yassaui's mausoleum is a ribbed turquoise dome, decorated with geometrical designs, standing above a tall circular drum covered in Arabic inscriptions and more delightful decorated tilework. The centre of the wall below features an arched niche covered in more elegant tilework. A further dome, smaller and considerably less ornate than the other two, sits close to the western corner of the building, above the mosque. The building was restored in the 1990s with support from the Turkish Government.

Tickets to enter the building (admission T280) are purchased from the brick ticket office near the rose garden in front of the main portal. The building was designed as a multi-purpose structure, known as a *khanaka*, comprising in total more than 30 rooms. Women without headgear should take one of the white headscarves offered at the entrance.

From the entrance you arrive first into the large central hall, or *jamaatkhana*. This square-based room impresses for its loftiness, rising up to the huge central dome, which has an internal diameter of more than 18m. It has a 'scalloped' decoration. The focus of the hall is a huge metal **cauldron** (*kazan*), cast in 1399 apparently to specifications from Timur himself. It weighs two tonnes and has a diameter of more than 2m. It is said to comprise seven metals, and is considered a symbol of unity. Among the inscriptions on the cauldron is one identifying the craftsman who built it as Abdulgaziz ibn Sharafutdin. It has a capacity of some 3,000 litres. The *kazan* was exhibited in the Hermitage in St Petersburg from 1935, but was brought back to Turkestan in 1989. Because of its presence, this room is usually known as the *kazanlyk*. The original 14th-century carved wooden doors are preserved on trestle tables at the side of the hall.

At the back of the hall is a recessed space with an arched roof. The carved wooden doors at the back of it lead to the chamber housing Khodja Ahmed Yassaui's tomb, but are usually kept locked. Due to the proximity of the tomb this space is used for prayers. To see Yassaui's tomb, enter the doorway to the right of this space. It takes you into a tomb-lined corridor. Note on your left the modern tombstone of **Ablai Khan**, a black marble tomb topped with a grey marble design shaped like a warrior's helmet, surmounted by a crescent moon. Pilgrims kiss the top of this tombstone as they pass it. Just beyond Ablai Khan's tomb is a grated opening, through which you can see the tomb of **Khodja Ahmed Yassaui** in its domed chamber. The gravestone, which bears no inscription, is a three-stepped structure, faced with serpentine.

The next doorway to the right off the central hall takes you to two further rooms, one containing many tombs, as does the corridor. Some of the tombs are fascinating pieces of sculpture. A comb and mirror are for example inscribed on the tomb of Dana Bibi, rather hinting at a lady who took pride in her appearance. The doorway off the central hall to the left of the recessed space takes you into a corridor leading to, on the right, a domed **mosque**. The dome is beautifully scalloped, and has 16 small grilled windows running around its base. There is a delightful *mihrab* of glazed tilework covering an arched niche in the wall. To the left of this corridor is a vaulted library, looking bare without books. The doorway off the central hall further to the left, the one closest to the main entrance to the building, leads to a vaulted canteen, with a large brick oven.

Around the mausoleum complex Standing in front of the mausoleum complex, close to the southern corner of the building, is a heavily restored brick structure, square in plan. This is the mausoleum of the Kazakh leader **Esim Khan**. Beyond this, near the ticket office, is the **Mausoleum of Rabi'i Sultan Begum**, which dates from the late 15th century. This is a brick mausoleum with a tiled turquoise dome atop a round drum with tiles forming Arabic inscriptions and bearing geometric designs. Rabi'i Sultan Begum was the daughter of the Timurid ruler and scholar Ulugbek, and the fourth wife of the Uzbek leader Abulkhair Khan (not to be confused with the 18th-century Kazakh leader of the Junior *Zhuz* of the same name).

A stepped path leads to an area of higher ground to the south of the mausoleum. There are a couple of brick-walled buildings here. One of these is the **Friday Mosque**, built in 1878. The interior contains a few 19th-century religious items in glass display cases and a fine wooden *minbar*. The guides will tell you that an elegant carved wooden column in the corner of the mosque and the well in the courtyard outside both date from Yassaui's time. Next to this is a low-slung modern-looking brick building with a green cupola, which contains the **Hilvet Underground Mosque**, its oldest part dating from the 12th century. Descend two flights of steps to a large hall, its wooden roof supported by a forest of wooden columns. The place is lit from windows lying close to the roof. There is a somewhat disparate collection of items on display, including books about Yassaui, a mannequin dressed as a dervish, and the worn green 14th-century coverlet of Yassaui's tomb. The place is still a functioning mosque, with prayers taking place on the mats in the centre of the room while tourists gaze at the exhibits around the walls. In the corner of a windowless square brick side room is what appears to be a well. It is actually the entrance to the tiny chamber below where Yassaui is said to have spent the final years of his life in solitude, following his attainment of the age of 63.

A path from this low hill runs down towards the well-kept rose garden in front of the mausoleum complex. On the way you pass a heavily restored brick **bath house**, with five low domes, dating from the second half of the 16th century, and in use until 1975. The central chamber of this is octagonal in plan, standing beneath a brick dome. There is a tiled octagonal platform in the centre of the room, and niches around the walls for ablutions. Several rooms run off the central chamber (a massage room, a cold water room, a hot water room), each supporting a brick dome. Various metal items, mainly jugs, buckets and bowls for splashing water about, are on display.

A few hundred metres to the south is another low hill, **Kultobe**, at which excavations have recovered items from the early medieval period. Camels graze in this area, allowing travellers in search of cliché the chance to take a photograph of them against the backdrop of the Yassaui Mausoleum.

Sattar Erybaev Museum (*72 Bekzat Sattarhanov St;* ⊕ *09.00–18.00 Mon–Sat*) In front of the rose garden running up to the mausoleum complex is a pedestrian square, with cafés and souvenir shops on its eastern side. A pedestrianised street, flanked with more shops and cafés, runs north from here, passing a modern mosque on the right. At the next junction, with Bekzat Sattarhanov Street, stands a bust of **Sattar Erybaev**, a young writer who died of tuberculosis in 1937, at the age of just 23. The single-storey Tsarist-era building behind the statue houses the Sattar Erybaev Museum. If you are interested in seeing the museum, you may have to hunt around for someone to open it up, notwithstanding its claimed opening hours. The displays chronicle the life of Erybaev and other 20th-century literary luminaries of Turkestan. One room contains a range of items which apparently belonged to Erybaev, including a *dombra* and samovar, together with piles of miscellaneous carpets and utensils, giving the place the air of a rustic antique shop.

AROUND TURKESTAN

SAURAN Some 48km northwest of Turkestan, just off the main road to Kyzylorda, stand the atmospheric ruins of the Silk Road city of Sauran. Described by early travellers as a city surrounded by seven walls, it was taken by the Mongols without a fight (its authorities would have been aware, from events at Otrar, of the likely consequences of resistance). It became a capital of the White Horde, and is the place of burial of the White Horde ruler Sasibuqa. The city appears to have physically shifted its location in around the second half of the 14th century, to a site approximately 4km north of the original centre. It later came under the control of the Shaybanids. At its peak Sauran was the largest city in the territory of modern-day Kazakhstan, and a major centre of trade and ceramics production. It boasted a sophisticated water supply system based around an underground gallery, known as a *kyariz*. But Sauran gradually declined in importance, losing ground to Turkestan, and by the 18th century it was virtually abandoned.

To get here, head out of Turkestan on the main road to Kyzylorda. Sauran is not difficult to find, provided you ignore the various signposts to 'Sauran', which direct you towards a modern village of the same name. A few hundred metres after a police checkpoint you will see, on the right-hand side of the road, a curious statue of an ear of wheat inside a large golden ring. Immediately beyond this, on the opposite side of the road, is the turning to Sauran, signposted to the fortress, whose walls are visible from the road. A bumpy track takes you under the railway, to reach the ruins of the city a few hundred metres on.

The site impresses for its ring of walls, reaching a height of up to 8m and enclosing an area of more than 40ha. An entrance gate on the northern side of the fortress is reasonably well preserved, but most of the walls have regressed into an almost natural-looking form, as if they are slowly being reclaimed by the earth. Recently excavated areas within the walls reveal square brick floors and walls of fired bricks. A trench cut through the walls provides a good sense of their massive bulk. The remains of various outlying buildings are visible from the fortress.

Taxi drivers in Turkestan will agree to bring you here and back for around T4,000, but you may need to direct them to the site.

OTRAR The city whose name is closely linked with the folly which precipitated the bloody arrival of Genghis Khan's Mongols into central Asia lies in the Otrar Oasis, a fertile agricultural area at the confluence of the Syr Darya and Arys rivers. Settlements emerged here some 2,000 years ago, at the time of the Kangui alliance. The mounds which can be seen today across the territory of the oasis, sites such as Kok-Mardan and Altyntobe, represent former towns. But the largest and most important settlement was Otrar itself, its site marked by the mound of Otrartobe. The oasis lay at the junction of important caravan routes: west to Khorezm and the Volga, south along the Syr Darya towards cities such as Merv and Nishapur, and east along the Arys to Taraz and beyond. Otrar flourished. It was also known as Farab (some scholars suggest that Otrar and Farab may initially have been separate settlements, whose names merged), and many authorities believe that the great philosopher and scientist of the Islamic world, Al-Farabi, was born here around AD872. The medieval historian Ibn Khallekan for example refers to Al-Farabi as having been born to Turkic parents in the village of Wasij, near Farab, but there is not full academic agreement about Al-Farabi's origins. Those scholars who believe his roots were Persian, not Turkic, tend to place his birth either in Faryab in Khorasan or in the region of Faryab in present-day Afghanistan.

Otrar's prosperous existence was shattered in the early years of the 13th century. At that time the oasis fell under the rule of the Khorezmshahs, whose then leader, Mohammed II, saw himself as a latter-day Alexander the Great. Mohammed II's great error was to thoroughly both mishandle and underestimate Genghis Khan. When the Mongol leader likened Mohammed II to one of his sons, the Khorezmshah raged that this suggested a relationship of subordination. When a caravan sent by Genghis Khan arrived at Otrar in 1217 its governor, Inalchuk, had the merchants arrested on spying charges. Mohammed II ordered them to be put to death and their goods seized. Genghis Khan's response was the conquest of the lands of the Khorezmshahs. He paid particular attention to Otrar, which the Mongols reached in 1219. They took the city after a five-month siege. Inalchuk was executed, and the city razed to the ground.

It recovered sufficiently to be grand enough to welcome Timur in 1405: he may have done better to stay away as he died of fever in the town. At its height the city comprised a hilltop central fortress and *shakhristan*, with an area of some 20ha, surrounded by a fortified suburban area, or *rabad*, where the ordinary dwellings and craft industries of the town were located, which covered a further 170ha. The decline of the Silk Road routes and the predations of the Dzhungars, however, led eventually to the collapse of the irrigation system on which Otrar and the other towns of the oasis depended. By the end of the 18th century Otrar had been all but abandoned.

Otrar Museum (*(72544) 21722; ⊕ 09.00–18.00 daily; admission T100 for foreign citizens*) A good first port of call before visiting the archaeological site of Otrartobe itself is the Otrar Museum. It is located in the village of Shauildir, 11km to the south of the site. If you are coming here from Shymkent, take the main road towards Turkestan, turning left after 92km at a signposted junction just to the north of the village of Tortkol. Shauildir is 45km on: the museum is at the end of the village. Coming from Turkestan, it lies south of the town, in the same direction as the Arystan Bab Mausoleum.

There is a bust of Al-Farabi out in front of the museum. The first room displays finds from excavations at several sites in the oasis, including Otrartobe, Altyntobe and Kok-Mardan. A ceramic vase from Altyntobe has a capacity of 250 litres. A frieze around the back of the room depicts old Otrar as a city of traders and intellectuals. A room to the right has further items found at Otrar, including 13th-century coins minted in the city, a clay figure of a ram, and some strange blackened lumps which are apparently bits of medieval bread. There is a room devoted to Al-Farabi, and then one about the Mongol siege, including a grisly diorama in which many of the arrows seem to be finding their mark. Upstairs is ethnography, with mock-ups of yurt interiors, a scrawny-looking stuffed falcon used to illustrate a display about hunting techniques, and something described by the English-language labelling as 'scissors for a hairstyle of pets'.

Otrartobe (*admission to the site T40*) Heading north from Shauildir, turn right after 7km at a turning signposted for the village of Talapti. The village is another 4km on, with the large low hill of Otrartobe on your right as you reach it. Only a small portion of the site has been excavated. One of the most interesting areas lies on the southwestern side of the hill, where the excavations have revealed a mosque, possibly dating from the 16th century. This part of the site is identifiable by the restored square column-bases. Two round column-bases on the northern side of the mosque mark its main entrance. Between the mosque and an excavated area of living accommodation is a square on which stands a 15th-century well, made of fired brick and which is more than 12m deep. Also interesting is an excavated area of the walls, covered with protecting scaffolding. This clearly shows the way that the earthen walls taper from base to top.

Arystan Bab Mausoleum (*admission T40*) Arystan Bab was a mentor of Khodja Ahmed Yassaui, and by tradition a pilgrimage to Yassaui's great mausoleum in Turkestan should be preceded by a visit to the mausoleum of his teacher. It lies south of Turkestan, not far from Otrartobe. To get here, take the same road north from Shauildir as for Otrartobe, but stay on the road rather than taking the right turn for Talapti. From this junction, the Arystan Bab Mausoleum is another 5km, close to the village of Kogam.

The mausoleum lies on the left-hand side of the road. It is an impressive building, originating as a 14th-century structure around Arystan Bab's 12th-century tomb, though most of what you see today dates from the early part of the 20th century. The mausoleum has a broad façade, framed by domed minarets at either end. There is a central arched space, flanked by two buttresses, and two brick domes over the left-hand side of the building. A room to the right-hand side of the arched space is a mosque, featuring nicely carved wooden pillars. There is also a small museum room. The first domed chamber to the left-hand side of the arched space contains the cloth-covered tombs of three students of Arystan Bab, whose tall tomb lies in the next chamber, beyond a metal grille. Arystan Bab is by tradition said to be a companion of the Prophet Muhammad who lived to an immense age. One popular legend states that the Prophet entrusted his beads, or a sacred persimmon stone (versions vary), to Arystan Bab for safekeeping. When Arystan Bab was journeying through the town of Sayram, a small boy asked for his beads (or persimmon stone). That boy was the future Khodja Ahmed Yassaui. With this request he became Arystan Bab's pupil.

Across the road from the mausoleum is the **Arystan Bab Hotel** (\ *(72544) 26602;* **$**). This offers very cheap accommodation sleeping on the floor either indoors or in one of three yurts, or, if you are looking for rather more creature comforts, in basic but air-conditioned bedrooms. Either way, the toilets are outside.

SHYMKENT   *Telephone code: 7252*

The capital of South Kazakhstan Region and the largest city in the south, with a population well above half a million, Shymkent is considered by urban Kazakhstanis in Astana or Almaty as a wild and lawless place. The pavements are uneven, and the driving is manic. It often hits the Kazakhstani headlines for the wrong reasons, as for example with a health scandal emerging in 2006, involving the HIV infection of

SHYMKENT

Airport →

↑ Kasiret Memorial

Kazakhstan Cinema ↑

✗ Karavella

ZHELTOKSAN ST

ZHELTOKSAN STREET

TOREKULOV STREET

STREET

Hotel Baı'myrza Sapar 🏨
Sapar Guest House 🏨

ILYAEV STREET

DULATI STREET

STREET

Ken Baba Ethnopark

Madien ✗ Coffee House
Karavan ✗

DIVAEV STREET

GOGOL STREET

ADYRBEKOV STREET

TASHENOV AVENUE

Hotel Dostyk 🏨

Upper Bazaar

Bazaar

KAZYBEK BI STREET

Shymkent Settlement Ethnopark, Railway station

Ordabasy Square

KUNAEV BOULEVARD

GANI ILYAEV BOULEVARD

KHAN TAUKE STREET

Central Park

✗ Maharaja

Regional Historical Museum 🏛

Philharmonia 🎭

Hotel Ordabasy 🏨

TURYSOV STREET

South Kazakhstan State University

Istanbul ✗

Mega Centre Shymkent

Regional Akimat

BAITURSYNOV STREET

TURKESTANSKAYA STREET

N

Bradt

✗ Vatslav

500m
500yds

0

0

MOMISHULY STREET

GANI ILYAEV AVENUE

Baterek Sapar Motel

Hotel Klara 🏨
Tsentr Sapar

AVENUE

BEIBITSHILIK STREET

Elis Café ✗
✗ Al-Farabi

AL-FARABI STREET

✗ Solishko
Fantasy World

Hotel Shymkent 🏨

RESPUBLIKA AVENUE

Pontos ✗

Al-Farabi Square

Russian Drama Theatre 🎭

many local children during blood transfusions. But Shymkent is also a vibrant and lively city, with the most colourful bazaar in Kazakhstan, and it offers a good range of accommodation and eating options. The city's parks throng with people until late into the evening in summer.

It was established around the 12th century, as a caravanserai on the Silk Route, and developed as a trading centre. In the 18th and 19th centuries it became the object of fighting between the khanates of Bukhara and Kokand. The latter won out, but the city was then taken for Tsar Alexander II in 1864 by the Russian general Mikhail Chernyaev. During the Tsarist period, one industry established here was a plant for the manufacture of santonin, a drug used for the expulsion of parasitic worms from the body. The santonin is derived from the flower heads of a variety of sea wormwood, or Levant wormwood, found in the surrounding area. Shymkent's links with this vermifuge are expressed on the city's emblem, which contains a picture of the plant. The city was renamed Chernyaev in 1914, to commemorate 50 years of its incorporation into the Russian Empire, but it reverted to Chimkent in the early 1920s.

A lead-processing plant was established in the town in the 1930s, at one stage producing around 70% of the lead manufactured in the USSR, at considerable cost to the urban environment. More factories were evacuated here during World War II. During the later Soviet period the city developed as a petrochemicals centre, with the construction of an oil pipeline to bring Siberian crude south from Omsk, and the establishment of an oil refinery, now run by Petrokazakhstan. You may be able to smell the chemicals in the air, but the haze of pollution makes for some glorious orange sunsets. Phosphorous and cement factories were added, as well as an industry based around the production of pelts from karakol lambs. Shymkent beer is one of the best-known brands in the country. Chimkent, which derives from the Russian spelling of the name of the town, was redesignated as the more Kazakh-sounding Shymkent in 1993. It is twinned, *inter alia*, with the British town of Stevenage.

GETTING THERE AND AROUND Shymkent's **airport** (535295, 945386) is some 10km out of the centre. Leave town on the Temirlan road, taking the signposted left turn for the airport after 9km. Bus route 12 will bring you here. Air Astana offers one or two flights daily from Almaty, and two a week to Atyrau via Kyzylorda. The local airline, Scat, has a daily flight to Astana, two a week to Almaty, two a week to Atyrau, and three a week to Aktau (the last with onward connections to Baku, Yerevan, Tbilisi, Rostov and Mineralnye Vody). It also flies twice a week to Sharjah and once to Moscow. Transaero flies twice weekly to Moscow.

The **railway station** (952120) sits south of the centre, at the southern end of Kabanbai Batyr Avenue. There are several services eastwards to Almaty, as well as a train which runs daily to Petropavl and another every other day to Astana. Westwards there are services to Aktobe, and every other day to each of Atyrau, Mangyshlak and Uralsk, as well as Russian destinations, including Moscow. Southbound there are services to Saryagash and one a week to Nukus in Uzbekistan. The taxi drivers outside the station are very persistent.

The situation as regards **bus** stations was in flux at the time of research, with the old bus station on Aiteke Bi Street on the western side of the bazaar largely closed. Departures are now from several points around the city depending on your destination. For Turkestan, buses use the Samal bus station, for Almaty and Taraz you need Aina, for Saryagash and Tashkent the Saule bus station is the place to ask for, and for Lenger and Sayram the Koktem bus station. Numbers to call for local **taxis** include 088 and 058.

TOUR OPERATORS AND AIRLINE OFFICES

Altex 119 Kazybek Bi St; ☎322008; f 621942. This agency offers tailor-made trips to the main sights of the region, including Otrar & Turkestan, but their main focus is the mountains of the Aksu Zhabagly State Reserve & Sayram-Ugam National Park. They run a basic camping site (**$**) in the attractive gorge of Sayram Su, in the mountains beyond the village of Kaskasu.

✈**Otrar Travel** 2 Al Farabi Sq; ☎408542; f 408540; e cit@otrar.kz. General Service Agent for Air Astana.

Shymkentturist 43 Respublika Av; ☎560226; f 560224. Organises tailor-made itineraries to the main sights of the region, including options covering some of the less well known of the many mausolea & other sacred places in South Kazakhstan.

✈**Transavia** 30 Tauke Khan Av; ☎535254; f 300100; www.transavia-travel.kz. Local representative for Transaero. Also bookings on other airlines.

⌂ WHERE TO STAY

⌂ **Hotel Shymkent** (102 rooms) 6A Respublika Av; ☎567195; f 567194. This renovated Soviet-era hotel occupies an 8-storey building centrally located across from the Fantasy World amusement park. The 2nd floor combines the b/fast room & a strip club. The staff are deceptive, rude & unhelpful &, though comfortable enough, the hotel is rather over-priced. **$$$$**

⌂ **Hotel Baimyrza Sapar** (25 rooms) 17 Kunaev Bd; ☎535001; f 535370; e baimyrza@ saparhotels.com; www.saparhotels.com. One of a number of hotels & entertainment facilities making up the Sapar Group, run by local entrepreneur Kairat Saparbaev, this 3-storeyed building stands next to the Sapar Guest House (see below) in the territory of the former Bamzik children's park. The fantasy gatehouse & outdoor pool remain from the Bamzik days, but this is otherwise an unexciting option, though the AC rooms are reasonably priced. Like other hotels in the group, the price is higher if you pay by credit card. **$$$**

⌂ **Hotel Klara Tsentr Sapar** (70 rooms) 4 Respublika Av; ☎232333; f 233023; e reservations@saparhotels.com; www. saparhotels.com. Part of the Sapar Group, this central hotel offers comfortable & reasonably priced rooms, though is somewhat inelegantly located in a trading centre. The room rate, priced as for the Hotel Baimyrza Sapar, includes b/fast & use of the sauna for 1hr. **$$$**

⌂ **Sapar Guest House** (18 apts) 17 Kunaev Bd; ☎f 535131; e sapar@saparhotels.com; www.saparhotels.com. This rather ugly but centrally located 12-storey tower is yet another member of the Sapar Group. It offers 2- & 3-room

apartments. The 2-room apartments feature a bedroom, en suite, & a lounge with dining area & kitchenette. The 3-room apartments have a 2nd bedroom. They are also available on a monthly rental basis. **$$$**

⌂ **Hotel Dostyk** (72 rooms) Adyrbekov St; ☎548498, 539973; f 545992; e info@ hoteldostyk.kz. This renovated hotel just east of the city centre has simply furnished but clean rooms, with reasonable en suites, AC & balconies. The sgls are small but the staff are polite & helpful, & b/fast is served with a smile. A good option in this price range. **$$**

⌂ **Hotel Ordabasy** (70 rooms) 1 Kazybek Bi St; ☎536421; f 535682. A Soviet-era hotel close to the bazaar, its *dizhurnayas* keeping watch over each floor. The unrenovated rooms have wooden cot-like beds, elderly furniture & grim en suites. Hot water is not always available. Renovation is gradually improving the quality of the rooms & pushing up the prices, with AC in the most expensive rooms. Adjacent to the busy roundabout known as Ordabasy Sq, this is potentially a noisy option. **$$**

⌂ **Baiterek Sapar Motel** (45 rooms) 4 Respublika Av; ☎337555; f 233023; e saparhotels@mail.ru. In the same trading centre, the Klara Tsentr Sapar, as the hotel of that name, the Baiterek Sapar Motel offers the kind of clean, central, budget accommodation that is all too rare in Kazakhstan. The reception is just next to the 'Eastern Bazaar' supermarket, & the rooms are upstairs. The 'deluxe' rooms are small & windowless, cooled by a fan. The better 'luxe' rooms are larger, & have AC. Showers & toilets are shared, but clean. **$**

✖ WHERE TO EAT

✖ **Pontos** 4 Al Farabi Sq; 550807. With murals of the Acropolis on its walls, this is a Greek-ish restaurant, though its menu varies widely, with a Japanese alter ego responsible for a range of sushi. There is a large covered outdoor area in summer & it is a popular location for families. $$$

✖ **Maharaja** Kunaev Bd; 535291. This modern building just west of Central Park, a riot of neon at night, houses a range of entertainment options. The **restaurant** is 1 floor up, with its golden mosaic work, wicker chairs, mural of the Taj Mahal & coffee tables with elephant-trunk designs for legs announcing its Indian credentials. The Indian names on the limited menu often conceal more generic dishes though: 'Shiva' turns out to be a green salad. The place is often given over to noisy wedding parties. The rooftop **summer café**, with more wicker furniture, may be a pleasanter spot. They offer pizzas & a selection of international main dishes. There is a **nightclub** on the ground floor (⊙ from 22.00 Mon–Sat; admission men/women T1,200/700 Mon–Fri, T2,500/1,500 Sat), as well as 8 lanes of **ten-pin bowling.** The Indian theme is submerged beneath a style which might better be described as 'new Kazakh entertainment complex', down to the heavies guarding the entrance. Summer café $$; restaurant $$$$

✖ **Istanbul** 11 Tauke Khan Av; 211923. This is a clean & central wooden-floored Turkish place, lying somewhere between fast-food joint & restaurant in character. The enthusiastic Turkish proprietor will try to coax you in from about 50m away. $$

✖ **Karavan** Ken Baba Ethnopark; 545283. Follow the train of stone camels into this restaurant within the 'ethnopark'. Uzbek-style *tapchans* are set out in the garden, & the food includes Uzbek & Kazakh dishes as well as 9 varieties of *shashlik*. Model sheep ignore the 'keep off the grass' signs. $$

✖ **Karavella** 22 Zheltoksan St; 212952. A maritime-themed restaurant which, appropriately, does a good fish soup. The menu also includes *shashlik* & a large selection of salads. A flautist performs here on some evenings. $$

✖ **Vatslav** 3 Turkestanskaya St; no phone. A Czech restaurant, whose spacious interior features oil paintings of gluttonous scenes. Externally, the building offers chaotically pitched roofs, with a frieze on the end wall of the neighbouring apartment block continuing the somewhat skew central European roofscape. Be warned: karaoke is the preferred evening entertainment to accompany your goulash. $$

✖ **Solishko** Fantasy World amusement park; no phone. This open-air café, with plastic tables beneath large umbrellas, is one of a number of similar basic places across the city which can offer an entertaining evening in summer, as your fellow diners start to dance on any vacant scrap of concrete to the Kazakh music introduced by the house DJ. The *shashlik* & central Asian fare is nothing special, but is cheap, & washed down with Shymkent beer on tap. The 2-storey **Elis Café** in the same park, serving up Western pop at high volume, is much less fun. $

Cafés

⌨ **Madlen Coffee House** Ken Baba Ethnopark; 532793. A good central choice for coffee, the Madlen also offers an extensive selection of desserts & non-alcoholic cocktails, served up in an airy hangar-like building decorated with models of characters from children's fairy tales. In the centre of the café is a huge tea cup, from which the head of a cheery mouse munching on a piece of cake pops up every few minutes.

SHOPPING Shymkent's expansive **bazaar** gives a clear sense that the trading routes of the Silk Road are still alive and well, even if the goods being traded are now more likely to include Chinese plastic toys and synthetic tracksuits than rare silk. The bazaar runs up the hill on the south side of the town centre. The part on the hill itself is, logically enough, known as the Upper Bazaar, while the sections of the bazaar on the lower land immediately to its north have a variety of names. The local authorities are however clearing some of these in their efforts to smarten up the city: the Ozero Bazaar was one of the victims of this process in 2007.

The Upper Bazaar is the most interesting area. A place to aim for is a row of fortune tellers. One is shown a photo, and proceeds to wave a horse whip rhythmically over it. Another rattles a percussion stick. A third is explaining to her worried-looking client that the unpropitious-looking card she has just drawn has its positive side. Another area of the bazaar sells embroidered Kazakh cloaks and hats. Several stalls appear to sell nothing but nurses' uniforms. Men scratching a living through simple shoe-repair operations are everywhere. A guy walks past with a live goat in a sack over his shoulder.

For more conventional shopping, the **Mega Centre Shymkent** (🕐 *10.00–20.00 daily*), at the corner of Kunaev Boulevard and Tauke Khan Avenue, stands in the forbidding concrete building which housed the TsUM department store in the Soviet period.

WHAT TO SEE
South Kazakhstan Regional Historical Museum (13 *Kazybek Bi St;* ⤡ *530222;* 🕐 *09.00–18.00 Tue–Sun; admission adult/student T100/50*) A good place to start your sightseeing in Shymkent is just south of the Central Park at the South Kazakhstan Regional Historical Museum. It is well laid out, with labelling in Kazakh, some Russian and occasionally English. A display on nature features the stuffed animal-filled dioramas beloved by this kind of museum. Then archaeology, with items on display from the Palaeolithic to the medieval periods. There are patterned ceramics from the Otrar Oasis and Sayram, and tilework from medieval Turkestan. Ethnography follows, with displays of jewellery, costumes and the packed contents of half a yurt. A short English-language description of the local crafts includes the intriguing 'weaving of mates'. Now that would be a good skill to have. There are displays of the utensils used by both pastoralists and crop farmers, reflecting the region's location at the interface between traditionally nomadic and traditionally settled agricultural communities. There are displays too on the Kazakh khanates.

The exhibits continue upstairs, with items relating to life in Shymkent under the control of the Khanate of Kokand in the 19th century. It was evidently not an altogether happy experience, as there were local uprisings against the demands of the Kokand khan in 1821 and again in the 1850s. The arrival of the Russians in 1864 put an end to that page of history, and Shymkent became an *uyezd* administrative capital three years later. There is a mock-up of the comfy office of the *uyezd* administrator, and one of a living room of Russian immigrants to the area in the late 19th century, with an icon in the corner of the room and a samovar on the table. Items related to the 1916 uprising against the Tsarist rulers include a photograph of the round-spectacled Turar Ryskulov, one of the rebellion's local leaders.

Coverage of the early Soviet period includes a mock-up of a 'red yurt', a scheme to bring ideologically tinged education to nomadic communities, its contents including a blackboard, arithmetic textbooks and a golden bust of Lenin. Coverage of World War II includes a list of the local Heroes of the Soviet Union inside a large red star. Photographs of the Shymkent lead factory show it geared up to wartime production. Items related to local wartime heroes include a French newspaper article, recounting the exploits with the partisan resistance of Akhmet Bektaev, an escaped prisoner of war. There is a bust of wrestler Hajimukan Munaytpasov, who gives his name to Shymkent's 37,000-capacity stadium, the home of local football team FC Ordabasy.

The displays cover some of the grimmer episodes of the late Soviet period: the bloody conclusion to the 1986 demonstrations in Almaty, the Chernobyl disaster and the war in Afghanistan. An eerie frieze depicts *balbals* with machine guns and

Red Army helmets. There are photographs of artistic and sporting stars from the region, of whom the best known internationally is the gymnast Nellie Kim, who was trained by Vladimir Baiden at the Spartak Sports Society School in the city. In the Montreal Olympics in 1976, Kim became the first women's gymnast in Olympic history to receive perfect 10 scores on both the vault and floor exercises, securing these scores with the first ever performance in the Olympics women's events of a Tsukahara with full twist on the vault, and double back *salto* on the floor. But she had to settle for silver in the all-around, beaten overall by her arch rival, Nadia Comaneci of Romania. The Portuguese-Canadian singer Nelly Furtado (full name Nelly Kim Furtado) was named after her.

Coverage of the post-independence period includes photographs of President Nazarbaev's visits to the region. There is an embroidered cloak presented to the president, and a fur-collared version given to his wife. Displays highlighting the output of local factories include packets of pasta and Shymkent beer.

South of the Regional Museum
Heading south along Kazybek Bi Street from the museum, you pass on your right the **philharmonia**, named in honour of composer **Shamshi Kaldayakov**, whose bust stands in front of the building, together with a plaque bearing the first few bars of his best-known work, the patriotic song 'My Kazakhstan'. Kaldayakov composed the music to this in 1956, with Zhumeken Nazhimedenov providing the words. Originally a celebration of the Virgin Lands programme, an adapted version of the song, with new lyrics by President Nazarbaev, was adopted as the national anthem of Kazakhstan in January 2006.

Kazybek Bi Street runs into the busy roundabout known as Ordabasy Square. Soviet and post-independence Kazakhstan collide here. A MiG plane on a metal stand seems to be taking off from the south side of the square, while the eastern side is illuminated by the golden dome of a new mosque.

Taking the road running up the hill to the right of the mosque, at the junction with Kabanbai Batyr Avenue you reach the **Shymkent settlement ethnopark**, celebrating the original settlement with various pieces of historically themed modern statuary. There is a large statue of **Kabanbai Batyr**, a warrior involved in battles against the Dzhungars, including in the defence of Turkestan in 1724. A plaque in Kazakh and Russian tells us that he spent 63 of his 78 years in the saddle, and was victorious in 103 individual combats against enemy warriors. A path leads into the park through a gate comprising carved obelisks. Pieces of stone statuary in the park are inspired by the forms of *balbals* and *koytases*.

City-centre parks
The name 'Shymkent' is believed to have meant 'turf city', and there are appropriately several parks in the centre, though they serve more as places of amusement than as green lungs for the city. The parks listed below are busy on warm summer evenings, providing food and drink and a range of entertainment: you can dance, play Russian billiards or even croon your favourite karaoke number in the open air, in each case with a throng of locals walking past you on the way to their favoured entertainment option.

From the regional historical museum, head north along Kazybek Bi Street, turning right at the junction with Tauke Khan Avenue, the east–west thoroughfare which runs through the heart of the city. On your left is the entrance to the **Ken Baba Ethnopark**, a historically minded park focused on eating and amusements, privately run by the Sapar Group (of 'lots of hotels with Sapar in the title' fame). A statue at the entrance involves three hands rising up from a base bearing the 'Sapar' logo. The hands hold up a globe, on which the territory of Kazakhstan is highlighted. On the globe dance three boys, dressed in outfits hinting at Africa, Europe and, more definitely, Kazakhstan.

Within the park itself is a series of golden sculptures of monuments standing on plinths. Described as 'Kazakhstan in miniature' the selection takes a strong bias towards the monuments of South Kazakhstan, including the Mausolea of Khodja Ahmed Yassaui and Arystan Bab, the latter having mysteriously acquired blue domes, and the Karashash Ana and Ibragim Ata mausolea in Sayram, their labels having been mixed up such that the mausoleum of Yassaui's mother advertises that of his father. If the mistake has been rectified by the time you read this, as you were. The only intruder from outside South Kazakhstan is the Golden Man, in this interpretation with his hands on his hips and ready for action. Other attractions in Ken Baba include open-air table tennis and Russian billiards, plenty of places to eat and drink, and a pond with swans, a waterfall in which cherubs frolic and a statue of a naked woman holding a jug.

Head back west along Tauke Khan Avenue. Beyond the junction with Kazybek Bi Street, on your left, is the entrance to Shymkent's **Central Park**. This offers several cafés serving up beer and *shashlik*; open-air karaoke, with customers crooning in front of a television set; assorted fairground attractions; a few odd pieces of statuary, such as a family of bears at play; and a plaque recording that the Russian singer-songwriter Vladimir Vysotsky performed in the park in 1970.

Several blocks further to the west, Tauke Khan Avenue turns into Respublika Avenue, and switches its direction to a southward one. At the start of this southward descent, opposite the Shymkent Hotel, stands another amusement park, **Fantasy World**. A statue of a rather subdued-looking **Al-Farabi** welcomes you in. Perhaps he's discomfited by the pop music. The 'Karaoke Club' here is at least surrounded by a glass wall, though your Elvis impersonation is still audible to passers-by. You can be photographed with a stuffed yellow elephant or a real live python. Or test your strength at one of the inexplicably popular automated punchbag machines.

Behind Fantasy World is the functional building housing the **South Kazakhstan Region Russian Drama Theatre** (✆ *530392*). It sits on **Al-Farabi Square**. At the time of writing the 53,000m² Shymkent Plaza development was under construction opposite.

Kasiret Memorial

This moving monument to the victims of Stalinist repression lies at the northern edge of the city. Take Kunaev Boulevard north out of the centre. At the edge of town you see the arcaded entrance to Shymkent's arboretum on your left. The Kasiret Memorial lies on the right of the road at this point. Take a flight of steps up to a conifer-lined pathway, at the end of which is a statue of a young mother holding her child. A flight of steps leads down to your left into the grassy hollow, a one-time quarry which served as the place of burial for victims of repression. The Kasiret Memorial stands here: broken marble blocks inside two metal cages. A rose-lined path leads back towards the road.

Shymkent zoo, not recommended, is further out, beyond the arboretum on your left.

AROUND SHYMKENT

TEMIRLAN Some 42km northwest of Shymkent, on the main road towards Turkestan, the small town of Temirlan, close to the Arys River, makes an interesting place to stop when making the journey between the two cities. The attraction here is a museum dedicated to the life of a local strongman (in the literal sense), the

Hajimukan Regional Sports Museum (\ *(72530) 21598;* ◔ *09.00–19.00 daily; admission T30).* Housed in a yurt-shaped building decorated with Corinthian columns, the museum tells the story of Hajimukan Munaytpasov, the champion wrestler, who died near here in 1948. A statue of the bare-chested Hajimukan stands in the centre of the museum. Behind this is a pink-hued frieze, with the wrestler painted in the centre with images of Kazakhstan around him: *kobyz* playing, *kumiss* drinking, Turkestan. The frieze also portrays places he visited during his foreign travels, such as the Eiffel Tower, and shows him lifting a camel on his back. It was his feats of strength as much as his conventional wrestling matches which built his fame in Kazakhstan. On display is a huge block, apparently weighing 350kg, which he was reportedly still able to lift at the age of 75. He had a chest size of 146cm at that age. Also displayed is a large metal bar, which he bent around his shoulders and a stone, which would be placed on his stomach while someone smashed a hammer against it. There are photographs of these feats being performed in front of large crowds, and posters advertising his appearances at wrestling bouts in circuses. The museum also has displays on other sporting personalities of the region.

One intriguing souvenir item on offer for T200 is a little model of that 350kg weight. Outside the museum stands a statue of the wrestler, showing him in action bending a bar around his back. There is also a model of the biplane *Amangeldy Imanov*, named after the leader of the 1916 rebellion against Tsarist rule, purchased by Hajimukan to help with the war effort.

SAYRAM Some 15km east of Shymkent, Sayram today is a small agricultural town of about 40,000 people, with low-slung buildings and a somewhat chaotic road system. The population of the town is dominated by ethnic Uzbeks, and Sayram is indeed often known locally as 'Little Uzbekistan'. You are more likely to hear Uzbek rather than Kazakh spoken here, and are unlikely to overhear any Russian at all. It is also one of the oldest settlements in Kazakhstan, having celebrated its 3,000th anniversary, somewhat arbitrarily, in 1999. It receives a mention in the Avesta, the holy book of Zoroastrianism. The people of Sayram were converted to Islam in the 8th century by a preacher named Iskak-bab, whose supporters defeated the existing Christian Nestorian community in combat. Local historians believe that the mosque built in Sayram by the victorious Iskak-bab, which has not survived, was probably the first constructed in the territory of modern-day Kazakhstan.

Sayram's status today as a place of pilgrimage largely rests on its associations with the Sufi mystic Khodja Ahmed Yassaui, who was born here around 1103, at a time when the town was named Ispijab. The mausolea of Yassaui's mother and father lie in the town, and are visited by pilgrims as part of a route which also takes in the Mausoleum of Arystan Bab (see page 382), and culminates in a visit to Yassaui's mausoleum in Turkestan (see page 377). Like other settlements of the area, Sayram changed hands many times: ruled by the Mongols, Timurids, Uzbeks of Abulkhair Khan and the Khanates of Kokand and Bukhara, and then coming under Russian rule in the 1860s. A relative decline in the town's importance in recent centuries has given it a distinctive feel, a small rural town packed with mausolea, minarets and other reminders of its distinguished past.

Sayram is easy to visit from Shymkent: frequent *marshrutka* minibuses make the trip, and you can also travel here in more comfort by hiring a taxi in Shymkent or booking through one of the Shymkent-based travel agencies.

What to see The centre of town is a crossroads, with the bazaar spread out on its southern side. Just to the west of this crossroads is the small **Mausoleum of**

Karashash Ana, Yassaui's mother. Square in plan, this brick building rises to a central brick dome. The façades on its southern and western sides rise higher than the others. The tomb inside the building is covered in a green cloth. A sign at the front dates the mausoleum to the 13th or 14th century, but a plaque put up in Soviet times describes it as a 17th-century building, and it has clearly been reworked through the centuries.

Continuing on this road away from the crossroads, you pass on your right a turquoise-domed modern mosque. A sign points down a side road to your right to **Botbay Ata**, a newly built square-based mausoleum with a bright turquoise dome on top of an octagonal drum. The mausoleum was funded by Botbay Ata's descendants, and constructed on the site of his grave. Retrace your steps back to the turning beyond the mosque, immediately beyond which is the **Mausoleum of Mirali Bobo**, an Islamic preacher, dating from the 10th century. Usually kept locked, it is a square-based brick building, with metal sheeting covering the dome and an arched façade. Like most of the main mausolea in Sayram it lies in a graveyard, as burial close to the grave of a revered holy person is considered auspicious. A shaded path brings you to the mausoleum from the road.

Back at the main crossroads, if you head in the opposite direction, away from the Karashash Ana Mausoleum, you pass on your left the Yusuf Sayrami School. Around the back of this is an attractive if rather stubby brick **Hisr Paygambar minaret**, with arched openings beneath its domed roof. The excavated remains of a mosque stand next to it. You can climb the tight spiral staircase of the minaret, though there is no great view at the top.

Heading north from the main crossroads, away from the bazaar, you reach on your left the **Mausoleum of Abd al Aziz Baba**, who accompanied Iskak-bab in his mission to convert local people to Islam. The mausoleum dates from the 15th century, with an 18th-century reconstruction. Take a path climbing through the surrounding graveyard to the mausoleum, which is a brick building with three metal-covered domes. There are cloth-covered tombs beneath the first and third domes, and an area for prayer beneath the central one. Continuing further, you reach another crossroads. Turn left here to reach, on your right, after a few metres an imposing columned building housing the town **museum** ((72531) 42066; 09.00–18.00 Mon–Sat; admission adult/child T100/50). The **Nauryz Park** stands opposite, with a pleasant willow-fringed lake and a big wheel. Heading in the other direction from this second crossroads, after a dusty walk of 1km or so you reach on your right, at the edge of town, the **Mausoleum of Ibragim Ata**, Yassaui's father. This is a square-based building topped with a metal-covered dome, dating from the 16th or 17th century. The mausoleum itself is often locked: the tomb is in a niche in the wall. The mausoleum lies on the side of a hill, on top of which a small graveyard spreads out.

Leaving Sayram by the road heading eastwards towards Karamurt, you reach on your left after 3km the site of the fortress of **Mertobe**. There is a car park here. Take the metal footbridge guarded by two stone gryphons across the watercourse to reach the small hill marking the site of the fortress. A flight of steps leads up it, where a plaque in Kazakh explains that Mertobe is a symbol of Kazakh unity, as the place where Tauke Khan gathered together the three judges representing the Kazakh *zhuzes*: Tole Bi, Kazybek Bi and Aiteke Bi, and all agreed to unite.

Karamurt A further 12km on, you reach the large village of Karamurt. One sight worth taking in here is the modern **Mausoleum of Zhanis Baba**. Signs in the village direct you to it. The mausoleum, in a fenced compound, takes the form of a tower with an octagonal golden spire. The mausoleum is entered via a flight of balustraded steps guarded by two stone lions. Zhanis Baba's tomb is in the basement, at the centre of an octagonal chamber, covered by a turquoise cloth. In the chamber above is a cenotaph, and tablets on the walls list the names of the sons of Zhanis Baba, who is considered the founding figure of a group of Kazakh tribes. The mausoleum was financed by their members.

TULIPS FROM KAZAKHSTAN

Max Bygraves may have sung about tulips from Amsterdam, but the origins of the plant so closely associated with Holland lie several thousand kilometres to the east. The tulip probably arrived in the Low Countries in the 16th century, when Ogier Ghiselin de Busbecq, Ambassador of Ferdinand I of Austria to the Ottoman Empire, then ruled by Suleiman the Magnificent, sent some tulip bulbs back from Constantinople to his friend, Flemish botanist Charles de l'Ecluse. The latter established them at the botanical gardens at Leiden University from where, abetted by a theft of bulbs,they helped to fuel the tulip mania in early 17th-century Holland, when members of the Dutch elite, in competition for the showiest examples, bid up the prices to astonishing levels. But Constantinople was not the place of origin of the tulip either. The largest number of the 100 or so species of the tulip genus is found in central Asia, and botanists believe that the genus appeared here around the end of the Miocene era.

Kazakhstan has a particularly rich collection – some 34 wild tulip species are found here – and thus the suggestion that Kazakhstan may be the place of origin of the tulip is a reasonable one, though there are other contenders within the region. The process of identification and classification of the wild tulips of Kazakhstan was carried out by the botanists of Tsarist Russia. Peter Pallas, a German botanist working in Russia, where he was a professor at the St Petersburg Academy of Sciences, led an expedition to central Russia and west Siberia between 1768 and 1774, covering the Altai Mountains and parts of present-day northern Kazakhstan. Among the numerous natural history specimens collected were tulips, and Pallas provided the first scientific description of a tulip from Kazakhstan (*Tulipa biflora*). These collecting expeditions were arduous and dangerous. One collector, Alexander Lehmann, became sick and died at the age of 28 on the return leg of a collecting expedition on behalf of the St Petersburg Botanical Garden in 1842. *Tulipa lehmanniana*, found in the Kyzylkum Desert, is named in his honour.

Three species found in Kazakhstan have played a particularly important role in the establishment of cultivated tulips. Two of these are found in the Aksu Zhabagly Reserve, and adjacent areas of the western Tian Shan and Karatau mountains. Greig's tulip (*Tulipa greigii*) was named after Samuel Greig, a president of the Russian Society of Horticulturalists. Kaufmann's tulip (*Tulipa kaufmanniana*) is named after a governor general of Turkestan. It is sometimes known as the water lily tulip as its flowers open out horizontally in full bloom, giving it a water lily-like appearance. The third, Schrenk's tulip (*Tulipa schrenkii*), is found across northern and central Kazakhstan to the Caspian. There are important populations in the Naurzym and Korgalzhyn reserves. It is named after Alexander Schrenk, a researcher of the St Petersburg Botanical Garden, who explored the area. The Schrenk's tulip was probably a progenitor of those sent back from Constantinople by Ghiselin de Busbecq. So, more a case of tulips to Amsterdam.

SAYRAM-UGAM NATIONAL PARK This young national park, set up only at the start of 2006, covers the slopes of the Kazakhstan side of the Ugam range of the western Tian Shan Mountains, running along the border with Uzbekistan. The park lies immediately to the southwest of the better-known and longer-established Aksu Zhabagly National Nature Reserve, and the interesting range of flora and fauna on offer in the park is broadly similar to that at Aksu Zhabagly (see below).

A good way to see the park is through the NGO **Ugam** (*22 Yubileinaya St, Lenger;* `(72547) 62055`). It is run by a somewhat larger-than-life former bomber pilot named Alikhan Abdeshev, who once flew Yak-28s out of Orenburg and who has set up a community-based tourism operation affiliated to the Ecotourism Information Resource Centre in Almaty. Ugam's head office, and the gateway to the park, is the former coal-mining town of Lenger, some 40km southeast of Shymkent. Ugam offers guesthouse accommodation (**$**) run by local families in Lenger itself, and in the villages of Kaskasu and Dikhankol, closer to the park in the Kaskasu Valley. Dikhankol is 35km from Lenger, Kaskasu is 60km. Full board is provided, with host families encouraged to serve traditional Kazakh dishes. While the accommodation in Lenger is slightly smarter, with inside toilets, Lenger itself is perhaps a little too urban an experience and too far from the mountains, and the other villages make better bases for trips into the park. A stay in a traditional Kazakh yurt can also be arranged in both Kaskasu and Lenger.

Ugam can set up a range of hiking and horseriding trips into the national park from your accommodation, including arranging guides and tents. Possible excursions include day trips to the Kaskasu and Sayram Su canyons, a longer one to the seasonal Susungen Lake, which will involve at least one overnight camp, and a hike of several days to Zhabagly village (see page 395). There is a T200 fee to enter the national park.

Accommodation here can be booked through the Ecotourism Information Resource Centre (see page 123), who can arrange pick-ups from Shymkent railway station. There are also reasonably frequent *marshrutka* minibuses between Shymkent and Lenger. If you are travelling to Lenger under your own steam, Alikhan Abdeshev will probably arrange for you to be met at the Kara Kiya Café, which accommodates the somewhat grandly titled Ugam Ecotourism Information Centre. Another worthwhile accommodation option is the campsite in the Sayram Su Canyon run by the Shymkent-based agency Altex (see page 384).

AKSU ZHABAGLY NATIONAL NATURE RESERVE

Established in 1926, the Aksu Zhabagly National Nature Reserve is the oldest in central Asia. It protects part of the Talasky Alatau range of the western Tian Shan Mountains. The territory of the reserve ranges in height from 1,100m to Peak Sayram at more than 4,200m, the latter resting at the boundary between the Aksu Zhabagly Reserve and Sayram-Ugam National Park. It offers a range of environments from steppe to upland meadows, juniper forest and snow-capped mountaintops fringed by large glaciers.

The reserve gets its name from the two main rivers flowing through its territory. The River Aksu means 'white water', the colour derived from its passage through the limestone mountains. The River Zhabagly is named from the Kazakh word meaning 'one-year-old horse'. A legend surrounding this name tells of how the first settler of this picturesque valley, arriving here with his family, was forced to leave to join his tribesfolk in a war. In his absence, the family members he had left in the valley were kidnapped by bandits, his livestock slaughtered and his yurt razed to the ground.

When our hero returned from the war he found only scorched ground where his yurt had stood. In total despair, the horse he had left as a foal suddenly ran towards him, having miraculously survived both the bandits and the subsequent winter. Our hero saw the horse's appearance as a sign that he should not give up, and persevered with the establishment of a settlement on the banks of the river he named in his horse's honour. And the horse tasted good, too. (OK, I revised the ending slightly.)

The reserve is home to many rare species of plants and animals. In late April and early May, the focus of all those who come to the reserve is the bright-red Greig's tulip: one sight, known as Red Hill because of the colour the tulips turn it in spring, boasts densities in places of more than 60 wild tulips per square metre. Kaufmann's tulip is another important species of the western Tian Shan, often found at rather higher elevations. The local tourism authorities bill these mountains as the possible birthplace of the wild tulip (see box). Among the mammal species found in the reserve, the snow leopard is one that visiting tourists are unlikely to encounter. Numbers in the reserve are low; it is confined to remote spots and hunts mainly at night. The reserve also provides a home to the white-clawed Tian Shan bear, a relative of the brown bear, the Siberian ibex and Eurasian lynx. The Menzbier's marmot, smallest of all the marmots, is endemic to the western Tian Shan. It has dark, almost black, fur on the upper parts of its body; pale yellow underneath. One further mammal rumoured by some locals to live in the remote mountains of the reserve is a yeti, a wild snowman. An expedition in the Soviet period even tried to find him.

The largest of the birds found in the reserve is the lammergeyer. You may also see the golden eagle, often found circling above the Aksu Canyon, the Himalayan griffon vulture and the Eurasian eagle owl. Another rare species found here is the blue whistling thrush: hearing its whistle is considered good luck.

WHAT TO SEE One of the most popular and worthwhile excursions is to the **Aksu Canyon**, some 30km long and between 300m and 500m deep. It is a hugely impressive sight, with the milky waters of the Aksu River racing at its base. Unlike Charyn Canyon in Almaty Region, the Aksu Canyon is verdantly wooded, with juniper and apple trees. These grow most abundantly on the north-facing side of the canyon. A 4x4 is necessary to get here. To make the trip, take the main road westwards out of Zhabagly, turning south after 8km at the village of Eltai. This takes you onto a rough track running into the hills. A barrier marks the entrance into the reserve. Passing through the hamlet of Irsu ('snake river' – I hope the name indicates that it is windy rather than that it is full of snakes) and then across a grassy plateau, you reach the edge of the canyon, 17km from Eltai. There is a ranger hut here, where your permit will be scrutinised. A path leads down into the canyon from this point: a walk of about 45 minutes down, twice that back up.

Some 8km from the ranger hut, heading eastwards along a track running beside the top of the canyon, you reach an attractive spot named Tayak Saldy. There is a roofless gazebo here, overlooking the canyon, built in the mid-1990s for a proposed visit by the presidents of Kazakhstan, Kyrgyzstan and Uzbekistan. This summer house was in the event never used by the heads of state, as it was deemed to be too difficult to access. It is still known locally as the presidents' summer house.

Another good trip involves a hike or ride into the hills just beyond the Asel Tourist Base up to the **Kshi Kaindy Waterfalls**, which have a drop of 28m. Longer trips, involving one or more overnights in the reserve, take you beyond this point up into the Ulken Kaindy Gorge, and then further up to the slopes of the glacier-covered Kaskabulak Peak, where at around 3,000m are some 2,000 Bronze Age and Iron Age petroglyphs, depicting wild animals and huntsmen on horseback.

Sights outside the reserve The **Karatau Mountains**, whose southern reaches commence a few kilometres north of Zhabagly, offer a different flora and fauna from that of the western Tian Shan. The paradise flycatcher, one of the most colourful birds found in Kazakhstan, is a particularly prized sighting. The mountains run for several hundred kilometres in a northwesterly direction, but one excursion offered by Wild Nature is an easy half-day trip from Zhabagly village. This is to what is billed as the **stalactite cave**. From Zhabagly, drive back to the main Taraz–Shymkent road, turning left onto it towards Shymkent. At the village of Ak Beyik, 12km from Zhabagly, turn right onto a track which leads you up towards the hills. Fork right at the base of the hills after a couple of kilometres, taking the track heading into the hills after a few hundred metres more. You reach on your left, a short distance on, the entrance to a mine shaft, cut in the 1930s by Soviet geologists in search of iron.

You should not enter the cave without an experienced guide, and equipped with torches and hard hats. The mine shaft runs 300m into the cave. The main stalactite in the centre is known as 'angel', because it looks like one, sort of, with a couple of white wings. A stalagmite in the corner of the cave is considered by locals to offer a remedy against male impotence; just touch it and this should do the trick. Given the nature of its purported efficacy, the stalagmite concerned is worryingly dumpy in shape.

Both Wild Nature and Zhenia and Lyuda's Boarding House (see below) can set up an excursion in the spring and autumn for keen birdwatchers to the **Shakpak Ornithological Station**, 17km from Zhabagly in the Shakpak Pass, which lies between the western Tian Shan and the Karatau mountains and is an important route for migratory birds. Birds are caught here in large nets and ringed. The number of birds caught per day can run into the thousands.

Another worthwhile sight is the **Mashat Canyon**, west of the reserve. From Zhabagly head back to the main Taraz–Shymkent road, turning west towards Shymkent. Some 44km from Zhabagly village, turn left on a road signposted for 'Kershetas', turning right at the T-junction after a further 1km. The road runs along the base of the Mashat Canyon, which has forbidding dry walls but a pleasant tree-covered floor, nourished by the Mashat River. This is filled with numerous former Soviet summer camps, several still functioning as children's holiday camps. The Samal camp at the end of the road, 13km from the T-junction, was for example formerly the Veterok, a summer camp owned by the Shymkent phosphate factory. The Mashat Canyon is being billed as a rock-climbing venue.

ZHABAGLY

Zhabagly – a farming village of around 2,000 people – lies just north of the reserve, at an altitude of around 1,100m, and serves as a base for exploration. The reserve headquarters are in the village, which is also one of the best-developed centres for community-based tourism in Kazakhstan.

GETTING THERE To get to Zhabagly, from the main Taraz to Shymkent road take the left turn, signposted for the village, about 5km west of Shakpakbaba. You pass first through the village of Abail, whose name, curiously, means roughly 'be careful'; perhaps a warning to look both ways when you negotiate the railway level crossing here. Zhabagly is the next village on. There are a couple of *marshrutkas* each day to Shymkent. Both Wild Nature, and Zhenia and Lyuda's Boarding House can arrange for a taxi to meet you if you are arriving by train or bus. From Almaty, an overnight train pitches up at Tulkubas railway station, the closest station to the reserve, at around 06.30. An overnight bus from Almaty will drop you at the district capital, Turar Ryskulov, at around 08.00.

🏠 **WHERE TO STAY AND EAT** Six homestays are offered in the village by the NGO **Wild Nature** (*Hse 14, Taldybulak St, Zhabagly;* \ *(72538) 55686;* e *baskakova2008@mail.ru; www.wildnature-kz.narod.ru*). Wild Nature is one of the organisations working with the Ecotourism Information Resource Centre in Almaty, and the accommodation may be booked through the latter or direct. Rooms are basic but clean, with small single beds, and indoor toilets in three of the six properties. Full board is provided by the host family (**$**). Wild Nature can organise English-speaking guides, horseriding, the hire of tents and binoculars, and a range of excursions into the reserve and beyond. If you book in advance, they can also set up cultural activities for groups, including a concert of *dombra* music and a participatory session to prepare *kumiss*, from horse to bowl. The director of Wild Nature, Svetlana Baskakova, is a knowledgeable and engaging English-speaking naturalist.

Another good option in the village is **Zhenia and Lyuda's Boarding House** (*12 rooms; 36 Abai St, Zhabagly;* \ *(72538) 55696;* e *innaksu@mail.kz;* **$$**). They offer pleasant accommodation and friendly service in two adjacent houses along Abai Street and a cottage round the back (ask for the latter). Each of the rooms has twin beds and an en-suite shower. The room rate, which includes full board, is a little higher than Wild Nature though still good value. Zhenia was at one time director of the nature reserve, is able to put together a good range of excursions, and can arrange guides and horses. He can also arrange overnight accommodation at Ulken Kaindy within the reserve itself, a base used by scientists which even boasts two showers. Zhenia and Lyuda work with UK travel firms specialising in ornithological and botany tours, and are able to set up longer trips, such as birdwatching around the steppe lakes of South Kazakhstan.

A different type of accommodation is offered at the **Asel Tourist Base** (\ *(7252) 500505;* **$$$**). This lies about 6km east of Zhabagly village. Take the main road through and out of the village: the tourist base is at the end of the road. Standing at 1,300m, the complex is a former pioneer camp, which has been modernised and upgraded. Most of the accommodation consists of two-bedroom cottages, with two small beds in each room, plus a shared lounge, shower room and toilet. There is also a yurt decorated in traditional style, a sauna block and a fish pond where you can catch your own supper. The accommodation is provided on a full-board basis: you eat in a wooden restaurant building, watched over by a stuffed golden eagle. The complex is run by a Shymkent-based tour operator: Asel ('Honey') is apparently the name of the granddaughter of the boss.

WHAT TO SEE Zhabagly is a farming village of around 2,000 people. The head office of the nature reserve lies on Abai Street, the main thoroughfare running through the village. A good place to start your visit to the reserve is in this building: the **Zhabagly National Nature Reserve Museum** (⊕ *09.00–13.00 & 15.00–19.00; admission T700 for foreign citizens*). The museum is often kept locked and you may need to hunt around the building to find someone to open it up. The admission charge for foreigners, seven times the rate charged to Kazakhstani citizens, is also somewhat cheeky. But the museum is professionally laid out, thanks to funding support from the World Bank, and offers a good overview of the flora and fauna of the reserve. A bust of Turar Ryskulov, the Kazakh communist politician who supported the establishment of the reserve, but who was killed during the Stalinist repression of 1938, gazes at you eagerly through large round spectacles as you enter the museum. There is a relief map of the reserve, with little models of bear, deer and snow leopard walking across it. Fossilised fish are on display from Aulie and Karabastau, two locations in the Karatau Mountains, which commence a few kilometres to the north of the western Tian Shan, separated from that range by the Shakpak Pass, and head in a northwesterly direction. Aulie and Karabastau have been included into the Aksu Zhabagly Reserve, as sites of considerable palaeontological importance, although they are several tens of kilometres from the main body of it.

The next room features displays on some of the vulnerable species found in the reserve, represented in Kazakhstan's Red Book. A wall map of Kazakhstan displays the country's national parks and nature reserves: press the buttons to light them up. The next room, the hall of nature, features a range of stuffed animal-filled dioramas illustrating the various ecosystems in the reserve including juniper forest, high mountains and the wildlife of the Aksu Canyon. In the centre of the room real juniper branches project from an artificial tree trunk, giving the whole place a smell of juniper. Bird noise is also provided by a taped recording, making a tour of this room altogether an atmospheric one. Not all of the artistic touches used here were quite so successful. The use of sugar to imitate snow in the high-mountain diorama apparently resulted in an invasion of mice, which then scurried around the scene watched by a frustrated stuffed wildcat.

In Zhabagly village, the return of the cows and sheep from their pasture as dusk approaches makes for fine early evening entertainment. The cows peel off from the herd, each turning into the gate of their own home, to be welcomed in by the lady of the house who then shuts the gate. The behaviour of the cows seems remarkably like that of commuters returning from a hard day at the office.

PRACTICALITIES For all trips into the nature reserve itself you are required to pay a reserve entry fee of T1,050 per person (again a much inflated rate for foreign citizens: locals pay just T150), plus a fee of T1,300–1,500 per group to be accompanied by a reserve ranger (this is compulsory). Adding in the cost of vehicle hire, for which you should expect to pay at least T6,000 for destinations requiring a 4x4, and that for the services of an English-speaking guide (at the time of research Wild Nature charged T4,500 a day), it is clear that the cost of visiting the main sights in the reserve soon mounts up. Against this, the scenery is stunning.

TURAR RYSKULOV

The capital of Tulkubas District, Turar Ryskulov, formerly known as Vannovka, is a quiet agricultural town, with willows lining the main street. The cattle market on the edge of town makes a worthwhile visit on a Sunday morning. The town takes its new name from that of one of the leading ethnic Kazakh politicians of the early years of communist power.

Ryskulov's rise and fall has much to do with the changing strategies of the Soviet leadership towards securing the control of the majority Muslim lands of central Asia. Born into a wealthy nomadic family, Ryskulov joined the Communist Party in 1917. Lenin was aware of the risk that the Bolshevik Revolution might be perceived in central Asia as constituting the replacement of one form of European colonial rule with another, and offered opportunities to central Asian intellectuals within the communist camp such as Ryskulov, who by 1919 had been promoted to be President of the Council of Commissars of the People of Turkestan. Ryskulov also became one of the leaders of the Muslim Bureau of the Turkestan Regional Party

Committee. But Ryskulov and his colleagues were rapidly perceived by the Soviet leadership as too supportive of Turkestan nationalist ideas. Ryskulov called for example for economic reforms to promote the industrial development of the region by transferring factories out of Moscow to central Asia, and suggested Moscow stop interfering in the internal affairs of Turkestan.

Lenin's response was to appoint a Turkestan Commission in 1920, headed by Frunze and Kuibishev, which contained no Muslims and whose task was to consolidate Bolshevik power in central Asia. The central Asian communists were accused of being in thrall to nationalism and pan-Islamism, and the Muslim Bureau was dissolved. While central Asians were still drafted into local power structures, members of the intellectual elite were largely avoided. Although Ryskulov initially kept a job within the Party, he was rapidly marginalised, finding himself by 1925 as Comintern representative in Mongolia. He fell victim to Stalin's repression, and was executed in 1938.

There is a statue in front of the building housing the municipal administration. Ryskulov's connection to the place is that his father was born in the district. On the main street also sits the **Turar Ryskulov Museum** (*(72538) 53175; ⊕ 09.00– 18.00 Mon–Sat; admission T50*). Opened in 1994 as part of the commemorations surrounding the 100th anniversary of Ryskulov's birth, the museum offers photographs and documents chronicling his life. There is also a mock-up of his office, with a painting of Lenin behind his desk and a gramophone poised to play a recording of a speech by Kalinin. There are some stuffed animals and archaeological items in the foyer, the genesis of displays that the museum plans to develop on a second floor. Outside the museum are some downbeat statues. A grindstone covered with snakes is a memorial to the famine of 1932–33. A wall of blocks, each portraying a distressed face, honours the victims of political repression. And a monument to the victims of the war in Afghanistan features seven stone tulips, one for each of the local people killed there.

A little more than 0.5km west of the western edge of town, along the road towards Shymkent, is a place called **Turikbasi**. The 'Turk's Head' turns out not to be a pub, but a spring. There is a car park, even a public lavatory, on the north side of the road. Walk through the brick gateway, to a flight of stone steps leading up the rather bleak hillside. Your destination is a modern open-sided crenellated tower. A few steps within this lead down to a spring. The legend surrounding it is linked to one Iftikhar, an Arab who helped convert the people of the area to Islam and, it is said, a relative of Yassaui. Iftikhar had left instructions that he be buried at this place. He was killed in battle by those opposing the Islamisation of the region – some accounts have it that his head was separated from his body. As he had requested, his supporters buried him at this spot and as they did so a spring gushed forth, whose waters are believed by locals to have the power to respond to wishes. Bend down to the spring, scoop up some water in the tin cup provided, and make a wish. Not falling into the spring may be a good one.

Appendix 1

LANGUAGE

Kazakh is the official language of Kazakhstan. As noted on page 20, Russian, the 'language of interethnic communication', remains important as a lingua franca, and you may find a Russian-language phrasebook useful. Information about the Kazakh language is much harder to come by, and this appendix therefore offers a short digest of some useful words and phrases. You will find that the use of even just a word or two of Kazakh will be greatly appreciated by those you meet on your travels.

THE ALPHABET The alphabet in current use is a form of the Cyrillic alphabet, introduced in 1940. It consists of 42 letters: 33 taken from the Russian alphabet, and nine extra letters.

Kazakh Cyrillic alphabet	Latinised equivalent	Approx pronunciation (where unclear from Latinised equivalent)
А а	A	As in <u>aa</u>rdvark
Ә ә	Ä	As in <u>a</u>tom
Б б	B	
В в	V	
Г г	G	
Ғ ғ	Ğ	<u>Gh</u> (from the throat)
Д д	D	
Е е	E	As in <u>y</u>esterday
Ё ё	Yo	
Ж ж	J	As in plea<u>su</u>re
З з	Z	
И и	Ï	As in <u>e</u>ve
Й й	Y	
К к	K	
Қ қ	Q	<u>Kh</u> (from the throat)
Л л	L	
М м	M	
Н н	N	
Ң ң	Ñ	As in thi<u>ng</u>
О о	O	
Ө ө	Ö	Forced, as in <u>wor</u>se
П п	P	
Р р	R	
С с	S	

Т т	T	
У у	W	As in cool
Ұ ұ	U	As in slow
Ү ү	Ü	As in murder
Ф ф	F	
Х х	X	As in loch
һ һ	H	
Ц ц	C	As in splits
Ч ч	Ç	As in chamber
Ш ш	Ø	As in shape
Щ щ	Øø	As above, but longer
Ъ ъ	"	Not pronounced
Ы ы	I	As in purpose
I i	I.	As in tin
Ь ь	'	Not pronounced
Э э	Ee	As in event
Ю ю	Yu	As in you
Я я	Ya	As in yard

BASIC GRAMMAR Like other Turkic languages, Kazakh is an agglutinative language, involving the addition of suffixes to fixed stems. The stringing together of suffixes can result in some notably long words. Another feature Kazakh shares with other Turkic languages is the importance of vowel harmony. Vowels must harmonise, including in respect of suffixes added to the stems, as regards front versus back and rounded versus unrounded vowels. There are seven cases, marked by suffixes. There is no definite article or grammatical gender. Words are usually (though not invariably) stressed on the final syllable.

Verbs agree with their subject in terms of case and number: suffixes perform these functions. Suffixes and auxiliary verbs are used to express tense, aspect and mood. Evidentiality (whether the evidence exists for a given statement) plays an important role. A subject–object–verb word order is usually followed, though other word orders are possible in some circumstances.

ESSENTIALS The Cyrillic version of each word or phrase is followed by its Latinised equivalent, as a guide to pronunciation (see above).

Good morning	Қайырлы таң	*Qayırlı tañ*
Good evening	Қайырлы кеш	*Qayırlı keş*
Hello	Саламатсыз ба	*Salamatsız ba*
Goodbye	Сау болыңыз	*Saw bolıñız*
My name is...	Менің атым...	*Meniñ atım...*
What is your name?	Сіздің атыңыз кім?	*Sizdiñ atıñız kim?*
I am from ... Britain/ America/ Australia	Мен ... Британияданмын/ Америкаданмын/ Австралияданмын	*Men ... Britaniyadanmın/ Amerikadanmın/ Avstraliyadanmın*
How are you?	Қалыңыз қалай?	*Qalıñız qalay?*
Pleased to meet you	Танысқаныма қуаныштымын	*Tanısqanıma qwanıştımın*
Thank you	Рахмет	*Rahmet*
Don't mention it	Оқасы жоқ	*Oqası joq*
Cheers!	Аман-сау болайық!	*Aman-saw bolayıq!*
Yes	Иә	*Iä*

No	Жоқ	*Joq*
I don't understand	Мен түсінбеймін	*Men tüsinbeimin*
Please would you speak more slowly	Баяу сөйлеңізші	*Bayaw söyleñızşi*
Do you understand?	Түсінесіз бе?	*Tüsinesiz be?*

Questions

how?	қалай?	*qalay?*
what?	не?	*ne?*
where?	қайда?	*qayda?*
what is it?	бұл не?	*bul ne?*
which?	қайсы?	*qaysı?*
when?	қашан?	*qaşan?*
why?	неге?	*nege?*
who?	кім?	*kim?*
how much?	қанша?	*qanşa?*

Numbers

1	бір	*bir*
2	екі	*eki*
3	үш	*üş*
4	төрт	*tört*
5	бес	*bes*
6	алты	*altı*
7	жеті	*jeti*
8	сегіз	*segiz*
9	тоғыз	*toğız*
10	он	*on*
11	он бір	*on bir*
12	он екі	*on eki*
13	он үш	*on üş*
14	он төрт	*on tört*
15	он бес	*on bes*
16	он алты	*on altı*
17	он жеті	*on jeti*
18	он сегіз	*on segiz*
19	он тоғыз	*on toğız*
20	жиырма	*jyırma*
21	жиырма бір	*jyırma bir*
30	отыз	*otız*
40	қырық	*qırıq*
50	елу	*elw*
60	алпыс	*alpıs*
70	жетпіс	*jetpis*
80	сексен	*seksen*
90	тоқсан	*toqsan*
100	жүз	*jüz*
1,000	мың	*mıñ*

Time

What time is it?	Уақыт қанша?	*Waqıt qanşa?*
It's … o'clock	Уақыт … саға	*Waqıt … sağat*
today	бүгін	*bügin*
tonight	бүгін кешке	*bügin keşke*
tomorrow	ертең	*erteñ*
yesterday	кеше	*keşe*
morning	таңертең	*tañerteñ*
evening	кеш	*keş*

Days

Monday	дүйсенбі	*düisenbi*
Tuesday	сейсенбі	*seisenbi*
Wednesday	сәрсенбі	*särsenbi*
Thursday	бейсенбі	*beisenbi*
Friday	жұма	*juma*
Saturday	сенбі	*senbi*
Sunday	жексенбі	*jeksenbi*

Months

January	қаңтар	*qañtar*
February	ақпан	*aqpan*
March	наурыз	*nawrız*
April	сәуір	*säwir*
May	мамыр	*mamır*
June	маусым	*mawsım*
July	шілде	*şilde*
August	тамыз	*tamız*
September	қыркүйек	*qırküyek*
October	қазан	*qazan*
November	қараша	*qaraşa*
December	желтоқсан	*jeltoqsan*

Getting around
Public transport

I'd like…	Маған … беріңі	*Mağan … beriñiz*
…a one-way ticket	…бір бағыттағы билет…	*…bir bağıttağı bilet…*
…a return ticket	…қайтар билет…	*…qaytar blet…*
I want to go to…	Мен … барғым келеді	*Men … barğım keledi*
How much is it?	қанша тұрады?	*Qanşa turadı?*
What time does it leave?	Сағат қаншада жүреді?	*Sağat qanşada jüredi?*
The train has been…	Поезд…	*Poezd…*
…delayed	…кешігіп келеді	*…keşigip keledi*
…cancelled	…келмейді	*…kelmeydi*
first class	бірінші дәрежелі	*birinşi därejeli*
second class	екінші дәрежелі	*ekinşi därejeli*
sleeper	ұйықтайтын вагон	*uyıqtaytın vagon*
platform	платформа	*platforma*
ticket office	касса	*kassa*
timetable	тізбе	*tizbe*
bus station	автобус аялдамасы	*avtobws ayaldaması*

railway station	вокзал	*vokzal*
airport	әуежай	*äwejay*
port	порт	*port*
bus	автобус	*avtobws*
train	поезд	*poezd*
plane	ұшақ	*uşaq*
boat	қайық	*qayıq*
ferry	паром	*parom*
car	көлік	*kölik*
taxi	такси	*taksï*
minibus	миниавтобус	*mïnïavtobws*
motorbike/moped	мотоцикл	*motocïkl*
bicycle	велосипед	*velosïped*
arrival	келу	*kelw*
departure	ұшу	*uşw*
here	осында	*osında*
there	анда	*anda*
bon voyage!	жол болсын!	*jol bolsın!*

Private transport

Is this the road to…?	Бұл жол … апарады ма?	*Bül jol … aparadı ma?*
Where is the service station?	Қызмет орталығы қайда орналасқан?	*Qızmet ortalığı qayda ornalasqan?*
Please fill it up	Толтырыңыз	*Toltırıñız*
I'd like … litres	Маған ... лит	*Mağan … lïtr*
diesel	дизель	*dïzel*
leaded petrol	этилді бензин	*eetïldi benzïn*
unleaded petrol	этилсіз бензин	*eetïlsiz benzïn*
I have broken down	Мен сынып қалдым	*Men sınıp qaldım*

Road signs

give way	жол бер	*jol ber*
danger	қауіп	*qawip*
detour	айналып өту	*ainalıp ötw*
one way	бір жақты	*bir jaqtı*
no entry	кіріс жоқ	*kiris joq*
keep clear	тазалау	*tazalaw*

Directions

Where is it?	Қайда?	*Qayda?*
Go straight ahead	Тура жүріңіз	*Twra jüriñiz*
Turn left	Солға бұрыңыз	*Solğa burıñız*
Turn right	Оңға бұрыңыз	*Oñğa burıñız*
…at the traffic lights	…бағдаршамда	*…bağdarşamda*
…at the roundabout	…көлік түйінінде	*…kölik tüininde*
north	солтүстік	*soltüstik*
south	оңтүстік	*oñtüstik*
east	шығыс	*şığıs*
west	батыс	*batıs*
behind	артқа	*artqa*
in front of	алдында	*aldında*

| near | жақын | *jaqın* |
| opposite | қарама қарсы | *qarama qarsı* |

Street signs

entrance	кіру	kirw
exit	шығу	şığw
open	ашық	aşıq
closed	жабық	jabıq
toilets – men/women	дәретхана – ер кісі/әйел	*därethana – er kisi/äyel*
information	ақпарат	aqparat

Accommodation

Where is a cheap/good hotel?	Арзан/жақсы қонақ үй қайда орналасқан?	*Arzan/jaqsı qonaq üy qayda ornalasqan?*
Could you please write the address?	Адресті жазып бере аласыз ба?	*Adresti jazıp bere alasız ba?*
I'd like...	Маған...	*Mağan...*
...a single room	...бір бөлме	*...bir bölme*
...a double room	...қос бөлме	*...qos bölme*
...a room with two beds	...екі кереуітті бөлме	*...eki kerewitti bölme*
...a room with a bathroom	...ваннасы бар бөлме	*...vannası bar bölme*
...to share a dormitory	...жатақхана бөлмесін бөлісу	*...jataqhana bölmesin bölisw*
How much is it per night/person?	Бір түнге/адамға қанша тұрады?	*Bir tünge/adamğa qanşa turadı?*
Where is the toilet?	Дәретхана кайда орналасқан?	*Därethana qayda ornalasqan?*
Where is the bathroom?	Ванна қайда орналасқан?	*Vanna qayda ornalasqan?*
Is there hot water?	Ыстық су бар ма?	*Istıq sw bar ma?*
Is there electricity?	Электр қуаты бар ма?	*Eelektr qwatı bar ma?*
Is breakfast included?	Таңертеңгі ас беріле ме?	*Tañerteñgi as berile me?*
I am leaving today	Мен бүгін кетемін	*Men bügin ketemin*

Food

Do you have a table for ... people?	Сіздерде ... адамға үстел бар ма?	*Sizderde ... adamğa üstel bar ma?*
...a children's menu	...балалар менюі	*...balalar menyui*
I am a vegetarian	Мен вегетарианмын	*Men vegetarïanmın*
Do you have any vegetarian dishes?	Сіздерде вегетариандық тағамдар бар ма?	*Sizderde vegetarïandıq tağamdar bar ma?*
Please bring me...	Маған ... әкелесіз бе	*Mağan ... äkelesiz be*
...a fork/knife/spoon	...шанышқы/пышақ/ қасық	*...şanışqı/pışaq/qasıq*
Please may I have the bill?	Маған шот әкелесіз бе?	*Mağan şot äkelesiz be?*

Basics

bread	нан	*nan*
butter	май	*may*
cheese	ірімшік	*irimşik*
oil	шемішкі май	*şemişki may*

pepper	бұрыш	*burış*
salt	тұз	*tuz*
sugar	қант	*qant*

Fruit

apple(s)	алма(лар)	*alma(lar)*
banana(s)	банан(дар)	*banan(dar)*
grapes	жүзім	*jüzim*
orange(s)	апельсин(дер)	*apelsïn(der)*
pear(s)	алмұрт(тар)	*almurt(tar)*

Vegetables

broccoli	брокколи	*brokkolï*
cabbage	қырыққабат	*qırıqqabat*
carrot(s)	сәбіз	*säbiz*
garlic	сарымсақ	*sarımsak*
onion	жуа	*jwa*
pepper(s)	бұрыш	*burış*
potato	картоп	*kartop*

Fish

carp	тұқы	*tuqı*
pike-perch	көксерке	*kökserke*
salmon	ақсерке	*aqserke*
shrimps	асшаян	*asşayan*
sturgeon	бекіре еті	*bekire eti*
trout	бақтақ	*baqtaq*
tuna	туна еті	*twna eti*

Meat

beef	сиыр еті	*sïır eti*
chicken	тауық еті	*tawıq eti*
goat	ешкі еті	*eşki eti*
horse	жылқы еті	*jılqı eti*
mutton	қой еті	*qoy eti*
pork	шошқа еті	*şoşqa eti*
sausage	шұжық	*şujıq*

Drinks

beer	сыра	*sıra*
coffee	кофе	*kofe*
fruit juice	жеміс шырыны	*jemis şırını*
milk	сүт	*süt*
tea	шай	*şay*
vodka	арақ	*araq*
water	су	*sw*
wine	шарап	*şarap*

Shopping

I'd like to buy…	Мен … сатып алғым келеді	*Men … satıp alğım keledi*

Help!	Көмек!	*Kömek!*
Call a doctor!	Дәрігерге телефон шалыңыз!	*Därigerge telefon şalıñız!*
There's been an accident	Көлік апаты орын алды	*Kölik apatı orın aldı*
I'm lost	Мен адасып қалдым	*Men adasıp qaldım*
Go away!	Кет!	*Ket!*
police	милиция	*mïlïcïya*
fire	от	*ot*
ambulance	жедел жәрдем	*jedel järdem*
thief	ұрлықшы	*urlıqşı*
hospital	аурухана	*awrwhana*
I am ill	Мен ауырып қалдым	*Men awırıp qaldım*

How much is it?	Бұл қанша тұрады?	*Bul qanşa turadı?*
I don't like it	Маған бұл ұнамайды	*Mağan bul unamaydı*
I'm just looking	Мен жай қарап тұрмын	*Men jay qarap turmın*
It's too expensive	Бұл тым қымбат	*Bul tım qimbat*
I'll take it	Мен бұны сатып алғым келеді	*Men bunı satıp alğım keledi*
Please may I have...	Маған ... бересіз бе	*Mağan ... beresiz be*
Do you accept...?	Сіз ... қабылдайсыз ба?	*Siz ... qabıldaisız ba?*
credit cards	несие карточкасы	*nesïe kartoçkası*
travellers' cheques	жолаушының чекін	*jolawşınıñ çekin*
more	көбірек	*köbirek*
less	аздау	*azdaw*
smaller	кішірек	*kişirek*
bigger	үлкендеу	*ülkendew*

Communications

I am looking for...	Мен ... іздеп жүрмін	*Men ... izdep jürmin*
bank	банк	*bank*
post office	пошта	*poşta*
church	шіркеу	*şirkew*
embassy	елшілік	*elşilik*
exchange office	ақша алмастыру	*aqşa almastırgw*
telephone centre	телефон орталығы	*telefon ortalığı*
tourist office	туристік орталығы	*turïstik ortalığı*

Health

diarrhoea	іш кету	*iş ketw*
nausea	құсу	*qusw*
doctor	дәрігер	*däriger*
prescription	рецепт	*recept*
pharmacy	дәріхана	*därihana*
paracetamol	парацетамол	*paracetamol*
antibiotics	антибиотиктер	*antïbïotïkter*
antiseptic	антисептиктер	*antïseptïkter*
tampons	тампондар	*tampondar*

condoms	ұрыққаптар	*urıqqaptar*
contraceptive	контрацептивтер	*kontraceptïvter*
sun block	күннен қорғау	*künnen qorğaw*
I am…	Мен…	*Men…*
…asthmatic	…астматикпін	*…astmatïkpin*
…epileptic	…эпилептикпін	*…eepleptïkpin*
…diabetic	…диабетикпін	*…dïabetïkpin*
I'm allergic to…	Менің … аллергиям бар	*Meniñ … allergïyam bar*
…penicillin	…пеницилинге	*…penïcïlïnge*
…nuts	…жаңғаққа	*…jañğaqqa*
…bees	…араға	*…arağa*

Travel with children

Is there a… ?	…бар ма?	*…bar ma?*
…baby changing room	…Балаларға арналған бөлме	*…Balalarğa arnalğan bölme*
…children's menu	…Балалар менюі	*…Balalar menuyi*
Do you have… ?	Сіздерде … бар ма?	*Sizderde … bar ma?*
…infant milk formula	…нәрестеге арналған сүт қоспасы	*…närestege arnalğan süt qospası*
…nappies	…жөргектер	*…jörgekter*
…potty	…горшок	*…gorşok*
…babysitter	…бала күтуші	*…bala kütwşi*
…high chair	…балаларға арналған орындық	*…balalarğa arnalğan orındıq*
Are children allowed?	Балаларға бола ма?	*Balalarğa bola ma?*

Other

my/mine/ours/yours	менің/менікі/біздікі/сіздікі	*meniñ/meniki/bizdiki/sizdiki*
and/some/but	және/шамалы/бірақ	*jäne/şamalı/biraq*
this/that	мынау/анау	*mınaw/anaw*
expensive/cheap	қымбат/арзан	*qımbat/arzan*
beautiful/ugly	әдемі/қорқынышты	*ädemi/qorqınıştı*
old/new	көне/жаңа	*köne/jaña*
good/bad	жақсы/жаман	*jaksı/jaman*
early/late	ерте/кеш	*erte/keş*
hot/cold	ыстық/суық	*ıstıq/swıq*
difficult/easy	қиын/оңай	*qın/oñai*
boring/interesting	жалықтыратын/қызық	*jalıqtıratın/qızıq*

Appendix 2

KAZAKH, RUSSIAN AND OTHER FOREIGN TERMS USED IN THE TEXT

Adirna	Harp-like musical instrument.
Aitys	Musical contest between *akyns*.
Ak nan	Bread flavoured with onion.
Akim	Governor of a region or district, or mayor of a city.
Akimat	Local administration, headed by an *akim*.
Akyn	Improvising poet/musician.
Alaman baiga	Endurance horse race.
Altybakan	Swing associated with Nauryz celebrations.
Aport	Large red-skinned apple.
Arkhar	Wild sheep, or urial.
Aryk	Water channel running alongside a street.
Astau	Large wooden tray.
Asyk	Children's game.
Ataman	Cossack leader.
Baiterek	Tree of life of Kazakh legend.
Balbal	Anthropomorphic Turkic sculpture.
Banya	Russian steam bath.
Batyr	Kazakh warrior.
Baursaki	Spherical fried doughnuts.
Beshbarmak	Kazakh dish: lumps of horse or mutton over layers of pasta.
Betashar	Ceremony of revealing the bride's face at Kazakh weddings.
Bi	Arbiter in traditional Kazakh society.
Blini	Pancakes.
Chapan	Embroidered cloak.
Dastarkhan	Low table used for meals.
Dizhurnaya	Duty attendant on the floors of more 'Soviet-style' hotels.
Dombra	Two-stringed guitar.
Elektrichka	Local train.
Epos	Epic poem.
Esik	Door of a yurt.
Estrada	Middle-of-the-road popular music.
Irimshik	Dish made from boiled and dried sour milk.
Jieran	Goitered gazelle.
Kalym	Dowry.
Kamchy	Horse whip.
Kanat	Section of the wooden frame of a yurt.

Karta	Type of horsemeat sausage.
Kazan	Cauldron.
Kazy	Type of horsemeat sausage.
Khoja	Descendant of Arabian missionaries.
Kobyz	Musical instrument played with a bow.
Kokpar	Sport on horseback, with a goat's carcass as the 'ball'.
Koshkartas	Sheep-shaped tombstone.
Koy bas	Boiled sheep's head.
Koytas	Tombstone in the form of a stylised sheep.
Kui	Piece of music.
Kuirdak	Kazakh dish made from an animal's internal organs.
Kuishy	Performer of traditional instrumental music.
Kulan	Central Asian wild ass.
Kulpytas	Decorated stone tombstone.
Kumiss	Drink made from fermented mare's milk.
Kupe	Locking railway compartment containing four bunks.
Kurgan	Burial mound, typically of the Iron Age.
Kurt	Salty dried curd balls.
Kvass	Fermented mildly alcoholic drink made from rye bread.
Kyariz	Underground gallery used for water supply.
Kyz kuu	'Catch the girl': chase on horseback.
Majilis	Lower chamber of Kazakhstan's parliament.
Mangal	Stand used for cooking *shashlik*.
Manty	Meat-filled steamed dumplings.
Maral	Large deer of the Altai Mountains.
Marshrutka	Form of transport by minivan along fixed routes.
Matryoshka	Nesting wooden dolls.
Minbar	Pulpit in a mosque.
Nauryz	Spring festival.
Oblast	Administrative region.
Olivye	Russian salad.
Oralman	Ethnic Kazakh immigrant to Kazakhstan.
Parilka	Steam room in a Russian bath.
Pelmeni	Ravioli-like Russian dish.
Piala	Handleless tea cup.
Platzkart	Economy-class train travel, featuring bunks in open compartments.
Plov	Rice-based dish with meat and carrot.
Ru	Clan. Sub-unit of a *taipa*.
Samsa	Meat-filled pastry.
Sandyktas	Sarcophagus-shaped funerary monument.
Shan kobyz	Metal musical instrument, placed between the teeth.
Shanyrak	Latticed round frame at the top of a yurt.
Shashlik	Skewered lumps of meat cooked over coals.
Shashu	Showering a wedding couple with sweets and coins.
Shiraktas	Fire stone: used for prayers at sacred places.
Shubat	Drink made from fermented camel's milk.
Shuzhuk	Type of horsemeat sausage.
Shym shi	Ornamented reed mat encircling the frame of a yurt.
Sorpa	Broth from mutton or horsemeat: accompanies *beshbarmak*.
Stanitsa	Cossack village: the core unit of the Cossack Host.
Sunduk	Box or chest.

Sybyzgy	Long flute.
Sykyrlauyk	'Squeaky': name sometimes used for the door of a yurt.
Syrnai	Clay whistle, or ocarina.
Taipa	Tribe. Sub-unit of a *zhuz*.
Tamga	Tribal symbol.
Tapchan	Raised wooden platform for dining and resting outdoors.
Togyzkumalak	Traditional Kazakh board game.
Tolengit	Descendant of Dzhungar captives.
Tor	Space for guests in a yurt, opposite the entrance.
Tore	Descendant of Genghis Khan.
Torsuk	Leather vessel for carrying *kumiss*.
Toshala	Traditional Kazakh larder.
Tubiteika	Embroidered skullcap.
Tuyuktas	Percussion instrument using two horse's hooves.
Uskuch	Fish of Lake Markakol: a variety of the Siberian *lenok*.
Uyezd	Tsarist-era administrative district.
Uyk	Dome pole in a yurt.
Yurt	Wooden-framed felt-covered dwelling of nomadic Kazakhs.
Zapovednik	Protected nature reserve.
Zhar-zhar	Song performed at Kazakh weddings.
Zhent	Powdery Kazakh sweet.
Zhetigen	Seven-stringed musical instrument.
Zhirau	Reciter of epic stories and often adviser to a khan.
Zhirshy	Performer of epic works.
Zhuz	Territory-based tribal grouping.

Appendix 3

BOOKS

History and archaeology

Hiro, Dilip *Inside Central Asia: A Political and Cultural History of Uzbekistan, Turkmenistan, Kazakhstan, Kyrgyzstan, Tajikistan, Turkey, and Iran* Gerald Duckworth & Co Ltd, 2009. A straightforward introduction to the former Soviet Republics of central Asia and their immediate neighbours.

Sala, Renato and Deom, Jean-Marc *Petroglyphs of South Kazakhstan* Laboratory of Geoarchaeology, Almaty, 2005. Lavishly photographed guide to some of the main petroglyph sites of Almaty Region and the Karatau Mountains. Can be difficult to find.

Shayakhmetov, Mukhamet *The Silent Steppe: The Story of a Kazakh Nomad under Stalin* Stacey International, 2006. Personal account of the experience of collectivisation and famine in Stalinist Kazakhstan and of the tribulations of World War II. Brings home in a moving way the extent of the miseries faced by the people of Kazakhstan during this period. Recommended.

Soucek, Svat *A History of Inner Asia* Cambridge University Press, 2000. A scholarly account of the history of a complex region.

Van der Leeuw, Charles *Kazakhstan: A Quest for Statehood* Caspian Publishing House, 2006. A history of Kazakhstan from prehistoric times to the present day, published in Almaty and available in Kazakhstan.

Post-independence Kazakhstan

Aitken, Jonathan *Nazarbayev and the Making of Kazakhstan: From Communism to Capitalism* Continuum Publishing Corporation, 2009. A portrait of Kazakstan's president, and an analysis of the emergence of both the man and the country onto the world stage.

Cummings, Sally *Kazakhstan: Power and the Elite* I B Tauris, 2005. Looks at the role and influence of the political elite in Kazakhstan.

Dave, Bhavna *Kazakhstan: Ethnicity, Language and Power* Routledge, 2007. Academic work, looking at the development of a national identity and nation statehood in Kazakhstan.

Fergus, Michael and Jandosova, Janar *Kazakhstan: Coming of Age* Stacey International, 2003. Lavishly illustrated and markedly upbeat account of Kazakhstan at the dawn of the new millennium. Available in the bookstores of upmarket hotels in Almaty and Astana, this makes for a good souvenir of a visit.

Olcott, Martha Brill *Kazakhstan: Unfulfilled Promise* Carnegie Endowment for International Peace, 2002. With a title which sounds like a rejoinder to the Fergus and Jandosova volume, this is a critical, scholarly account of post-independence Kazakhstan. By the same author, *The Kazakhs* (Stanford: Hoover University Press, second edition 1995) is sadly now out of print.

Schatz, Edward *Modern Clan Politics and Beyond: The Power of 'Blood' in Kazakhstan* University of Washington Press, 2005. Academic analysis of the relevance of clan-based ties in modern Kazakhstan.

Weller, R Charles *Rethinking Kazakh and Central Asian Nationhood* Xlibris Corporation, 2006. A critical rejoinder to those academics who argue that Kazakh and other central Asian ethnic identities and the nation states associated with them are largely artificial constructs of Tsarist and Soviet policies.

Central Asian geopolitics and the politics of oil and gas

Kleveman, Lutz *The New Great Game: Blood and Oil in Central Asia* Atlantic Books, 2003. Pacy account of the politics of oil and gas in the region.

LeVine, Steve *The Oil and the Glory* Random House, 2007. A provocative study of hydrocarbons politics in the region. LeVine, a former central Asia correspondent for the *New York Times* and then the *Wall Street Journal*, also maintains an interesting blog, at www.oilandglory.com.

Mullerson, Rein *Central Asia: A Chessboard and Player in the New Great Game* Kegan Paul, 2007. Looks at the geopolitics of the region, with the central Asian republics themselves as players (as against the 19th-century works about the 'Great Game' which tended to regard the region as merely the chessboard across which the 'game' was played out by the great powers).

Travellers' accounts

McGregor, Ewan and Boorman, Charley *Long Way Round: Chasing Shadows Across the World* Time Warner Books, 2004. Two actors ride motorbikes from London to New York the long way round. Their trip takes them the length of Kazakhstan, which they enjoy despite getting far more formal hospitality and media attention than they were looking for. The book of the DVD of the TV series.

Metcalfe, Daniel *Out of Steppe* Arrow, 2009. Adventurous traveller Metcalfe traverses central Asia in pursuit of distinct ethnic communities who are disappearing as modernity impinges on their way of life. A finely written and often moving account.

Omrani, Bijan *Asia Overland: Tales of Travel on the Trans-Siberian and Silk Road* Odyssey Guides, 2010. Beautifully written and heavily illustrated historical travelogue drawing on accounts from Fa Xian, Anton Chekhov, Marco Polo and Francis Younghusband to name but a few. Full of humour, it is an entertaining and informative read that will appeal to both armchair travellers and modern-day explorers.

Robbins, Christopher *In Search of Kazakhstan: The Land That Disappeared* Profile Books, 2007. His curiosity about Kazakhstan sparked by a conversation on a plane with a US factory worker off to meet his Kazakhstani internet girlfriend, the author has combined travelogue, tales of Kazakhstan's history and conversations with the president into a lively account.

Rosten, Keith *Once in Kazakhstan: The Snow Leopard Emerges* iUniverse.com, 2005. The author went to Kazakhstan in 1993 as a Fulbright lecturer in law, and offers an interesting account of his experiences of a turbulent period in Kazakhstan's recent history.

Thubron, Colin *The Lost Heart of Asia* Heinemann, 1994. The author travels through central Asia soon after the emergence of the independent republics. One of a spate of accounts of travels through the region written during this turbulent period. Elegantly written, though Uzbekistan grabs far more of the author's attention than does Kazakhstan. Also worth checking out if you can find it is *Goodnight, Mister Lenin* by Italian journalist Tiziano Terzani (Picador, 1993).

Culture, traditions and language

Harvey, Janet *Traditional Textiles of Central Asia* Thames and Hudson, 1997. Good introduction to the textiles of the region.

Ibrahim, Ablahat *Beginning Kazakh* University of Arizona Press, 2000. A CD-ROM-based introductory course in the Kazakh language.

Kenzheakhmetuly, Seyit *Kazakh Traditions and Customs* Almatykitap, 2006. Written in the three languages of Kazakh, Russian and English, this is an officially endorsed digest of Kazakh cultural traditions, with support from the Ministry of Education and Science, but contains much of interest. Available in Kazakhstan.

Kubaeva, Iraida *Kazakh Language Made Easy* Atamura, 2003. One of the few books available in English to help you learn the Kazakh language, though not all of the explanations are particularly clear. Or perhaps it was just me. Available at larger bookshops in Kazakhstan.

Literature

Abai *Book of Words* Abai International Club, English-language edition 2003. English-language text of the maxims, or 'words', of the most important figure in Kazakh literature, together with English translations of some of his poetry.

Esenberlin, Ilyas *The Nomads* The Ilyas Esenberlin Foundation, (English edition) 2000. English-language translation of Esenberlin's monumental three-volume retelling of the history of the Kazakh khanates. It's a complex tale involving a huge cast of characters. Available in major bookstores and some souvenir shops in Kazakhstan.

MAGAZINES

Steppe A glossy twice-yearly magazine covering the wider central Asian region, with notably strong photography. It is available at the bookstores in upmarket hotels in Almaty and Astana. Further information is available at www.steppemagazine.com.

MAPS

International Travel Maps (*530 West Broadway, Vancouver, BC V5Z 1E9, Canada;* +1 604 879 3621; +1 604 879 4521; *www.itmb.com*) publish a good 1:2,300,000 map of Kazakhstan, which has been used to produce some of the maps in this guide. The German company Reise Know-How (*79 Osnabrucker Strasse, 33649 Bielefeld;* +49 521 946490; +49 521 441047; *www.reise-know-how.de*) does a 1:2,000,000 Kazakhstan map. Bookshops in the larger cities in Kazakhstan usually have some maps available, including city plans, road maps of their regions and occasionally trekking maps. An English-language town plan of Almaty, with some historical information and useful telephone numbers on the back, is published by the Kazakhstan Agency on Land Resources Management.

The colour country map and regionals produced in this book were based on source material supplied by ITMB Publishing (*www.itmb.com*).

WEBSITES
Kazakhstan government sites All of the following have English-language pages.

www.akorda.kz Website of the president.
www.government.kz Kazakhstan government site.
www.mfa.kz Website of the Ministry of Foreign Affairs. Contains visa information.

Travel advice
www.britishembassy.kz Website of the British Embassy in Kazakhstan.
www.fco.gov.uk/travel Foreign and Commonwealth Office travel advice.
www.travel.state.gov US State Department travel advice.

News and political analysis

www.eurasianet.org News and analysis covering the central Asian region on a site run by the Open Society Institute.

www.gazeta.kz An online news agency site, with good coverage in English.

www.inform.kz The website of the National Information Agency.

www.roberts-report.com Analysis of central Asian stories put together by US academic Sean Roberts, an expert on Kazakhstan.

Information for expatriates

www.expat.kz Focused on expatriates coming to live in Almaty, this site offers plenty of information, though not all of the advice is kept fully up to date.

Culture

www.asylmura.kz The website of a project involving the archives of the Ministry of Culture and Information and the Khabar Agency, to restore, digitally clean and make available lost gems of Kazakh traditional music.

Telephone directories

www.infokz.com Online version of the Almaty business directory, also available as an annually updated English-language paper directory, the *A-Business Directory*.

www.yellow-pages.kz A hard copy of the *Yellow Pages* directory is also issued annually.

WIN A FREE BRADT GUIDE

READER QUESTIONNAIRE

Send in your completed questionnaire and enter our monthly draw for the chance to win a Bradt guide of your choice.

To take up our special reader offer of 40% off, please visit our website at www.bradtguides.com/freeguide or answer the questions below and return to us with the order form overleaf.

(Forms may be posted or faxed to us.)

Have you used any other Bradt guides? If so, which titles? . . . .
. . . .

What other publishers' travel guides do you use regularly? . . . .
. . . .

Where did you buy this guidebook? . . . .

What was the main purpose of your trip to Kazakhstan (or for what other reason did you read our guide)? eg: holiday/business/charity . . . .
. . . .

How long did you travel for? (circle one)

weekend/long weekend   1–2 weeks   3–4 weeks   4 weeks plus

Which countries did you visit in connection with this trip? . . . .
. . . .

Did you travel with a tour operator?' If so, which one? . . . .
. . . .

What other destinations would you like to see covered by a Bradt guide?
. . . .

If you could make one improvement to this guide, what would it be?
. . . .

Age (circle relevant category) 16–25   26–45   46–60   60+

Male/Female (delete as appropriate)

Home country . . . .

Please send us any comments about this guide (or others on our list).
. . . .
. . . .
. . . .

Bradt Travel Guides

IDC House, The Vale, Chalfont St Peter, Bucks SL9 9RZ, UK
☎ +44 (0)1753 893444 f +44 (0)1753 892333
e info@bradtguides.com
www.bradtguides.com

TAKE 40% OFF YOUR NEXT BRADT GUIDE!

Order Form

To take advantage of this special offer visit www.bradtguides.com/freeguide
and enter our monthly giveaway, or fill in the order form below, complete the
questionnaire overleaf and send it to Bradt Travel Guides by post or fax.

Please send me one copy of the following guide at 40% off the UK retail price

No	Title	Retail price	40% price
1	....	....	....

Please send the following additional guides at full UK retail price

No	Title	Retail price	Total
...	....	....	....
...	....	....	....
...	....	....	....

Sub total ....

Post & packing ....

(Free shipping UK, £1 per book Europe, £3 per book rest of world)

Total ....

Name ....

Address ....

Tel ....   Email ....

☐ I enclose a cheque for £........ made payable to Bradt Travel Guides Ltd

☐ I would like to pay by credit card. Number: ....

   Expiry date: ... / .... 3-digit security code (on reverse of card) .....

   Issue no (debit cards only) .....

☐ Please sign me up to Bradt's monthly enewsletter, Bradtpackers' News.

☐ I would be happy for you to use my name and comments in Bradt
   marketing material.

Send your order on this form, with the completed questionnaire, to:

Bradt Travel Guides
IDC House, The Vale, Chalfont St Peter, Bucks SL9 9RZ, UK
☎ +44 (0)1753 893444   f +44 (0)1753 892333
e info@bradtguides.com   www.bradtguides.com

Bradt Travel Guides

www.bradtguides.com

Africa

Access Africa: Safaris for People with Limited Mobility	£16.99
Africa Overland	£16.99
Algeria	£15.99
Angola	£17.99
Botswana	£16.99
Burkina Faso	£17.99
Cameroon	£15.99
Cape Verde	£15.99
Congo	£15.99
Eritrea	£15.99
Ethiopia	£16.99
Ghana	£15.99
Kenya Highlights	£15.99
Madagascar	£16.99
Malawi	£15.99
Mali	£14.99
Mauritius, Rodrigues & Réunion	£15.99
Mozambique	£15.99
Namibia	£15.99
Niger	£14.99
Nigeria	£17.99
North Africa: Roman Coast	£15.99
Rwanda	£15.99
São Tomé & Príncipe	£14.99
Seychelles	£14.99
Sierra Leone	£16.99
South Africa Highlights	£15.99
Sudan	£15.99
Tanzania, Northern	£14.99
Tanzania	£17.99
Uganda	£16.99
Zambia	£18.99
Zanzibar	£14.99
Zimbabwe	£15.99

The Americas and the Caribbean

Alaska	£15.99
Amazon Highlights	£15.99
Argentina	£16.99
Bahia	£14.99
Cayman Islands	£14.99
Colombia	£17.99
Dominica	£15.99
Grenada, Carriacou & Petite Martinique	£14.99
Guyana	£15.99
Nova Scotia	£14.99
Panama	£14.99
Paraguay	£15.99
Turks & Caicos Islands	£14.99
Uruguay	£15.99
USA by Rail	£14.99
Venezuela	£16.99
Yukon	£14.99

British Isles

Britain from the Rails	£14.99
Bus-Pass Britain	£15.99
Eccentric Britain	£15.99
Eccentric Cambrige	£9.99
Eccentric London	£13.99
Eccentric Oxford	£9.99
Sacred Britain	£16.99
Slow: Cotswolds	£14.99
Slow: Devon & Exmoor	£14.99
Slow: Norfolk & Suffolk	£14.99
Slow: North Yorkshire	£14.99
Slow: Sussex & South Downs National Park	£14.99

Europe

Abruzzo	£14.99
Albania	£15.99
Azores	£14.99
Baltic Cities	£14.99
Belarus	£15.99
Bosnia & Herzegovina	£14.99
Bratislava	£9.99
Budapest	£9.99
Cork	£6.99
Croatia	£13.99
Cross-Channel France: Nord-Pas de Calais	£13.99
Cyprus see North Cyprus	
Dresden	£7.99
Estonia	£14.99
Faroe Islands	£15.99
Georgia	£15.99
Greece: The Peloponnese	£14.99
Helsinki	£7.99
Hungary	£15.99
Iceland	£15.99
Kosovo	£15.99
Lapland	£15.99
Latvia	£13.99
Lille	£9.99
Lithuania	£14.99
Luxembourg	£13.99
Macedonia	£15.99
Malta & Gozo	£12.99
Montenegro	£14.99
North Cyprus	£13.99
Riga	£6.99
Serbia	£15.99
Slovakia	£14.99
Slovenia	£13.99
Spitsbergen	£16.99
Switzerland Without a Car	£14.99
Transylvania	£14.99
Ukraine	£15.99
Zagreb	£6.99

Middle East, Asia and Australasia

Armenia	£15.99
Bangladesh	£15.99
Borneo	£17.99
Eastern Turkey	£16.99
Georgia	£15.99
Iran	£15.99
Iraq: Then & Now	£15.99
Israel	£15.99
Kazakhstan	£16.99
Kyrgyzstan	£16.99
Lake Baikal	£15.99
Lebanon	£15.99
Maldives	£15.99
Mongolia	£16.99
North Korea	£14.99
Oman	£15.99
Palestine	£15.99
Shangri-La: A Travel Guide to the Himalayan Dream	£14.99
Sri Lanka	£15.99
Syria	£15.99
Taiwan	£16.99
Tibet	£13.99
Yemen	£14.99

Wildlife

Antarctica: Guide to the Wildlife	£15.99
Arctic: Guide to Coastal Wildlife	£15.99
Australian Wildlife	£14.99
Central & Eastern European Wildlife	£15.99
Chinese Wildlife	£16.99
East African Wildlife	£19.99
Galápagos Wildlife	£16.99
Madagascar Wildlife	£16.99
New Zealand Wildlife	£14.99
North Atlantic Wildlife	£16.99
Pantanal Wildlife	£16.99
Peruvian Wildlife	£15.99
Southern African Wildlife	£19.99
Sri Lankan Wildlife	£15.99

Pictorials and other guides

100 Alien Invaders	£16.99
100 Animals to See Before They Die	£16.99
100 Bizarre Animals	£16.99
Eccentric Australia	£12.99
Northern Lights	£6.99
Tips on Tipping	£6.99
Wildlife and Conservation Volunteering: The Complete Guide	£13.99

READERS' TRAVEL AWARDS 2011
TOP GUIDEBOOK SERIES

Index

Page numbers in **bold** indicate major entries; those in *italics* indicate maps.